UNITED STATES ECONOMIC HISTORY

by

Daniel E. Diamond

Professor of Economics
 New York University

and

John D. Guilfoil

Associate Professor of Economics
Director of Undergraduate Studies
 New York University

GENERAL LEARNING PRESS
250 JAMES STREET
MORRISTOWN, N.J. 07960

1784370

For Esther and Peggy

contents

tables

figures

preface

This book, unlike any other in the field, combines text and readings into one integrated volume. The challenge by quantitative economic historians (cliometricians) to many long accepted beliefs has greatly enlivened economic history. Utilizing econometric techniques and the computer these "new economic historians" have reopened many questions which heretofore had been considered satisfactorily answered. In turn, the more traditional economic historians have questioned the techniques and conclusions of their newer colleagues. Moreover, there are many other areas where the definitive answers have yet to be found either by quantitative or nonquantitative methods.

While a text can summarize the evidence pro and con on a particular issue it cannot expose the reader to the full richness of the controversy. This can best be achieved by referring an individual to appropriate books and/or journal articles which deal exclusively with the question at hand. Indeed, most instructors assign their students readings as well as a standard text.

The advantage of this volume is that the text and the readings are integrated. For each chapter one or more readings have been selected which expands one of the chapter's main themes. In many cases this is accomplished by highlighting a controversial question raised in the chapter such as: When Did United States Economic Growth Accelerate? Were the South and West Economically Interdependent Prior to the Development of Improved East-West Transportation Facilities? Was Slavery Profitable? Did the Civil War Retard or Spur American Manufacturing Development? What Role did the Railroads Play in Spurring U.S. Economic Growth? Can Economic Growth Occur During a Period of Declining Prices? What is the Principal Goal of Big Business? Does Gross National Product Adequately Measure the Costs of Pollution and Resource Use? Have Unions Raised Wages? and What is the Proper Role of Monetary Policy in Promoting Full Employment and Economic Growth?

In other chapters the readings expand on materials which are better suited to a reading rather than to textual treatment such as: Differing Views on the "New" Economic History; and The Significance of U.S. Investment Involvement in Europe.

This book is designed for the standard undergraduate course in Economic History. It is assumed that the student has had a one semester course in economic principles. However, since the theoretical material is presented in an elementary manner, some instructors may find this book useful in a first course in economics. In most cases the readings harmonize with the level of sophistication in the text. Exceptions were made where suitable readings could not be found at the undergraduate level. In these instances we preferred a relevant sophisticated item rather than a more elementary but less appropriate reading. The instructor can either assist the students with these few sophisticated readings by discussing them in class or, if he prefers, not assigning them.

We wish to express our appreciation to our colleagues at New York University for their helpful suggestions and criticisms. Also we wish to thank Linda Kaufthal for her accurate typing of the manuscript.

part **I**
economic history
and economic growth

chapter 1

economic history
and economics

THE EVOLUTION OF ECONOMIC HISTORY

The saga of man has been the story of his unending effort to conquer his environment. Faced with the harsh reality of limited resources, he has had to work to satisfy his many wants. And no matter how great his success, he appears never to be fully satisfied. This conflict between limited resources and unlimited wants is the basic economic problem. In less developed societies it is reflected in efforts to procure the necessities of life. Advanced economies strive for more consumer durables, better housing, improved educational facilities, more leisure, and the like. No matter what the state of economic development, there is a continuing effort to narrow the gap between scarcity and abundance. The story of this quest is the major subject area of economic history.

THE HISTORICAL SCHOOL

There are conflicting claims as to the origins of economic history. Some believe it was first developed by historians in the eighteenth century. Others trace its origins to a group of economists known as the Historical School, in the mid-nineteenth century. Economists

3

have always been students of history. Adam Smith, the father of modern economics, published *An Inquiry into the Nature and Causes of the Wealth of Nations* in 1776. In this book, popularly called *The Wealth of Nations,* Smith deals with the experience of previous periods. And Thomas Malthus' population thesis — that population growth tends to outstrip the means of subsistence — presented some twenty-five years later, depends in large measure on historical inquiry. For the most part, however, the English classical economists concentrated on developing abstract theories. The theoretical system which evolved was deductive in nature and was regarded as being applicable to all economies, without reference to time. It therefore tended to be static in nature. By the mid-1800's, the classical school was under attack on a number of fronts. Social reformers both inside and outside of England objected strenuously to the uncontrolled operation of pessimistic economic laws which bore down so heavily on the working class. A group of economists known as the Historical School sought to replace classical theories with historical generalizations drawn from empirical study. It was this group that developed and popularized the study of economic history. The Historical School, led by Roscher and Schmoller in Germany and by Leslie and Ashley in England, questioned the validity of deductive economic theories. Nationalist minded, they rejected undue reliance on abstract reasoning and its application without reference to time or place. To them, economies constantly undergo change, and depending upon the prevailing stage of economic development, certain generalizations may or may not be applicable. For example, the German Historical School rejected classical free trade theory as not applicable for the prevailing stage of German development. The discovery of "true" economic theory could only be accomplished inductively through historical investigations. One must first observe and record the facts of history and then seek to develop generalizations. The study of history thus becomes the key to unlock the secrets of the economic universe.

For about half a century (until 1900) the Historical School sought its goal of historical generalizations, and despite many excellent historical monographs, it failed. Recognition of this failure did not, however, lead to the disappearance of economic history. Scholars from many lands under the influence of the Historical School established the subject in their own countries. In the United States, economic history was championed by a large group of young economists who had studied at German universities. Less dogmatic than their teachers, they disclaimed any desire to displace abstract economics. They wished only to be left alone to continue their studies of the evolution of economic societies. In time, the statistical and historical methods of economic history found increasing favor with many economists. At the same time, a significant number of economic historians effectively utilized conventional economic theory. Groups such as the National Bureau of Economic Research demonstrated the effectiveness of combining historical inquiry with theoretical tools. Nevertheless, economic history functioned alongside rather than as a part of the study of economics.

THE "NEW" ECONOMIC HISTORY

Since World War II the movement to reunify economic history with economics has greatly accelerated. Two fundamental changes account for this phenomenon: first, the development of more sophisticated tools of economic analysis and second, the emergence of macro-economic theory, particularly the theory of economic development. The availability of more refined and powerful quantitative tools opened up many new areas of historical inquiry. Model building, improved statistical and mathematical techniques, and the use of computers have enabled investigators to organize and process data which heretofore was unmanageable. Simultaneously, the Keynesian revolution brought forth a generally dynamic body of theory. This new theory, which deals with forces influencing aggregate economic activity, now stands side by side with the traditional static theory. For the first time, the economic historian has a theory of economic development to satisfy the dynamic character of his subject matter. As a consequence, large numbers of economists have been attracted to what has been described as cliometrics, or the "new" economic history. Although more traditional economic historians question some of the techniques and the emphasis of cliometricians, it has unquestionably heightened interest in the subject and brought it closer to the study of economics. Hopefully, it is now recognized that economics, like any other discipline, has both an empirical and theoretical basis, and that neither historical investigations nor abstract determinations can stand alone. The readings at the end of this chapter by Fogel and Redlich present differing views of the "new" economic history.

THE TASKS AND LIMITATIONS OF ECONOMIC HISTORY

ECONOMIC GROWTH AND ECONOMIC INSTITUTIONS

A review of the evolution of economic history indicates clearly that economic growth has always been one of its central concerns. The inception of the Historical School was prompted by the desire to learn more about the forces that determine economic progress. The spread of economic history to other nations was prompted in significant measure by nationalistic inquisitiveness about economic development. In more recent decades, heightened interest in the subject can be traced to concern about economic growth. The shock waves of World War II sparked an explosion of economic expectations in both developing and developed economies. New nations emerging from colonial domination and older ones no longer content with economic stagnation were impatient for higher standards of living. They looked to developed nations not only for technical and material assistance but also for some possible guidelines for growth. Moreover, the problems of poverty and decaying urban centers, despite the wealth of the United States, have centered attention on economic growth. High growth rates not only enable a nation to maintain full employment of its labor force, but help it provide the needed production to eradicate poverty. Accordingly, significant attention is paid to the elements of economic growth in the chapters that follow.

No matter how critical one may consider the question of economic growth, the domain of economic history is too rich and varied to restrict it to this one topic. Next to economic growth, the development of economic institutions is the principle concern of economic historians. Indeed, economic history has often viewed economic progress or decline in terms of changes in the institutional environment. In the view of the more traditionally minded, the study of economic institutions deserves equal billing with economic growth. Economic institutions not only reveal the process of change but also the interrelationships between the economic and noneconomic environment. The development of the corporation, labor unions, government and other major institutions of American economic life are meaningful and interesting chapters in the nation's economic development.

THE COMPLEXITIES OF ECONOMIC LIFE AND PROBLEM SOLVING

Another task of economic history is to instruct us in the full complexities of the economic process. Economic history forces us to look at the total economy; to examine economic phenomena in their geographical, social, cultural and political settings. In addition, it affords an opportunity to utilize analytical tools. The results are, hopefully, not only a sharpening of skills but a new perspective on the value and limitations of theoretical tools.

Finally, economic history has a role to play in solving current problems. Most economic problems are rooted in the past. Before solutions can be considered, the problems must be properly formulated.

This requires knowledge of how the problems evolved. The historical record may also reveal the types of solutions attempted in the past, and the extent to which they succeeded or failed. At the very least it broadens an individual's perspective, and it may even prevent him from repeating many kinds of errors.

LIMITATIONS

Economics is not an exact science, nor is economic history its most precise branch. New theoretical and quantitative tools have helped but they have their limitations. Economic models must of necessity make simplifying assumptions about the real world. Data available in the historical record may be incomplete or of questionable authenticity, or both. A researcher may be forced to rely on indirect measures, or to construct his own statistical series. Moreover, there are vast areas of economic history which have not been treated adequately, either by the old or new methods of economic history. Consequently, conjectures may be made about important problems which are inadequately supported by "hard" evidence.

There is also the problem of objective reporting. Each generation rewrites history in terms of its own values. The economic historian is faced with the problem of whether to interpret events in terms of the standards of his own time, or in terms of the criteria at the time of the occurrence.

SELECTED REFERENCES

1. Joseph Dorfman. "The Role of the German Historical School in American Economic Thought." *American Economic Review,* Vol. XLV No. 2 (May, 1954), pp. 17-28.
2. Carter Goodrich. "Economic History: One Field or Two?" *The Journal of Economic History,* Vol. XX No. 4 (December, 1960), pp. 531-38.
3. N. S. B. Gras. "Economic History in the United States." *Encyclopaedia of the Social Sciences,* Vol. 1 Supplement (December, 1941), pp. 107-9; Vol. 5, pp. 325-27. New York: Macmillan & Co., 1935.
4. Douglass C. North. "The State of Economic History." *American Economic Review,* Vol. LV No. 2 (May, 1965), pp. 86-91.

readings

differing views on
the "new" economic history

ONE VIEW: *robert w. fogel*

In the brief time allotted to me I want to outline two provisional propositions concerning the new economic history.

The first proposition is that one can observe in the work of the new generation of economic historians a departure from the past sufficient to justify a title like new economic history.

The departure is not to be found in the realm of subject matter. The new generation has not turned away from the traditional theme of its discipline. The central interest of the new economic historians is still the description and explanation of economic growth. This continuity with the past holds in the small as well as in the large. The specific research projects of the new generation focus on such familiar issues as the developmental impact of railroads and canals [14] [17] [22] [36], the effect of changes in supply and demand on the growth of the iron industry [40] [12], the profitability of slavery [6] [13] [39] [44], the factors affecting the growth of productivity in agriculture [35], the effect of federal land policy on the distribution of income [3] [16], the influence of foreign trade on the creation of a market economy [33], the sources of the capital required for industrialization [9] [43], the explanation of urbanization [8] [38], and the causes of economic fluctuations [43].

Source: reprinted with permission from "The Reunification of Economic History with Economic Theory" by Robert W. Fogel, in *American Economic Review*, LV (May 1965), 92-98.

The novel element in the work of the new economic historians is their approach to measurement and theory. Economic history has always had a quantitative orientation. But much of the past work on economic data was limited to the location and the simple classification of the numerical information contained in government and business records. While continuing this pursuit, the new economic history places its primary emphasis on reconstructing measurements which might have existed in the past but are no longer extant, on the recombination of primary data in a manner which enables them to obtain measurements that were never before made, and on finding methods of measuring economic phenomena that cannot be measured directly.

In performing these tasks, the new economic historians draw on virtually the whole gamut of the theoretical and statistical models of economics. William Whitney uses input-output analysis in his attempt to measure the effect of tariffs on the rise of manufacturing during the post-Civil War period [42]. Eugene Smolensky and D. Ratajczak employ location theory to explain the growth of San Diego [38]. Paul David relies on a constant elasticity of substitution function to infer the growth of the capital stock in Chicago during the nineteenth century [7]. James K. Kindahl applied an extension of the hypergeometric distribution to estimate the number of nonnational banks in existence after the Civil War [29]. The theory of rent has proved to be relevant to the analysis of problems as diverse as the economic viability of slavery [44] and the estimation of the social saving of canals [36]. Even so rarefied a construct as the Von Neuman-Morgenstern utility index proved to be of practical value in quantifying the effect of risk on the financial enervation of the Union Pacific Railroad [19].[1]

The measurements obtained through the application of economic theory and statistics have yielded considerably more precise information than has hitherto been available. For example, Paul MacAvoy, combining regression analysis with a theory of cartel stability, has been able to date the onset and duration of the rate wars among the trunk-line railroads, to identify the initiators of these wars, to measure the intensity of the conflict and to estimate certain of the gains and losses of the participants [32]. Stanley Engerman, applying regression analysis to a body of cross-sectional data on the iron industry that has lain fallow for more than a century, has been able to produce remarkably detailed time series on the growth of the capacity of blast furnaces by state and type for the years from 1800 through 1856 [12].

Such improved information has frequently resulted in dramatic revaluations of the economic impact of past events and institutions. Thus capital theory has been used by Alfred Conrad and John Meyer, Yasukichi Yasuba, Robert Evans, Jr., and Richard Sutch to show that slavery was a profitable system [6] [44] [13] [39]. Richard Easterlin's construction of estimates of the regional distribution of income combined with Robert Gallman's new series on gross national product imply that between 1840 and 1860 per capita income in the slave South grew at approximately the same rate as the long-term average for the United States as a whole [11] [20].[2] The last finding is a startling contradiction to the traditional view that the antebellum South was economically stagnant. Other traditional views that have been upset or at least seriously challenged by the new economic history include the hypothesis that railroads were built ahead of demand [14], the view that the lag of wages behind prices during the Civil War led to unusually great prosperity for northern manufacturing interests [5] [26], and the proposition that the development of the Bessemer process was of transcending significance for the rapid emergence of a modern iron and steel industry in the United States [18] [40].[3]

My second proposition is that the new economic history represents a reunification of economic history with economic theory and thus brings to an end the century-old split between these two branches of economics.

Economic history emerged as a distinct discipline during the course of the mid- and late-nineteenth-century revolt against the deductive theories of classical economics. Led by Roscher, Knies, Hildebrand and Schmoller in Germany and by Leslie, Ingram, and Ashley in England, the original aim of the historical school (or schools) was to replace what they believed to be the unrealistic theories of deductive economics by theories developed inductively through the study of history. Yet despite a half century of programmatic proclamations and despite the many fine historical monographs produced by the school(s), no alternative theory emerged.

In a 1901 review of the accomplishments of the historical school(s), Thorstein Veblen called their effort to supplant classical theory a "failure." "There seems," he continued, "no reason to regard this failure as less than definitive" [41, p. 71]. Veblen's judgment was reaffirmed three decades later by J. H. Clapham who wrote, "Most scholars are now agreed that such an attempt failed even in the hands of Schmoller" [4, p. 329].

Recognition of this failure led neither to the disappearance of economic history nor to its reunification with economics proper. When Ashley ascended to the first chair of economic history at Harvard shortly before the turn of the century, he called for a truce between the warring factions. He disclaimed any desire to compete with deductive economics in the formulation of rival theories of value and distribution, asking only that economic history "be let alone."[4] Ashley believed that conflict was avoidable because in his view economics proper and economic history focused on different problems: the former on the static properties of modern economies; the latter on the evolution of economic societies or — as we now call it — economic growth [2]. To J. N. Keynes's contention that "familiarity with economic theory is essential to the interpretation of industrial phenomena such as it falls within the province of the historian to give" [27, p. 271], Ashley replied: economic theory revealed little about the connections of economic phenomena that could not be understood through the application of "plain common sense" [2, p. 127].

The truce for which Ashley called lasted for more than half a century. During this time intellectual enmity abated. Within economic history, scholars such as Callender, Heckscher, Cole, Hamilton, and Rostow effectively applied economic theory and statistics to the study of history. Within economics proper, empirically- and historically-oriented analysis developed far more extensively than Ashley foresaw. One of the centers of such work, although not the only one, was the National Bureau of Economic Research where Wesley Mitchell, Simon Kuznets, and others applied theory and statistics in massive empirical studies of the development of the American economy.

Still, as late as 1941, the relationship between economic history and economics proper was essentially one of truce. In that year Edwin F. Gay, on the occasion of his election as the first president of the Economic History Association, both gave recognition to the breach that remained and called for its elimination. "Full cooperation," he said, "is not yet easy or intimate and one of the first tasks of the economic historian today is to open the way to a more complete connection of the two disciplines" [21, p. 412].

In the years following World War II, the movement toward the reunification of economic history with economic theory accelerated. Among the factors that led to the quickened pace, two may be singled out. One was the substantial increase in the range and subtlety of the models encompassed by economic theory. The other was the widespread experimentation, in many fields of economics, with the adaptation of general models to specific (historical) situations — an experimentation stimulated by the upsurge in econometrics and other forms of applied mathematics.[5] With such developments Heckscher's isolated plea of the 1920's for a greater use of theory in the study of economic history [24] became a relative commonplace in the 1950's. Post-World War II texts announced their reliance on the "framework of economic analysis to elucidate the historical narrative" and treated their "emphasis on economic principles" as a mark of distinction [37, p. xi].[6]

However, the reunification of economic history with economic theory could not have been brought about merely by the interjections of theory in textbooks. Reunification required the utilization of economic theory as an integral tool in the basic research on which the discipline of economic history rests. This condition has been met, as I tried to illustrate in the first part of my comments, by an outpouring of studies published or initiated during the past half-dozen or so years.

The effort to improve the precision of measurement in economic history has been a powerful catalyst in transforming desire into reality. For as Simon Kuznets (whose work, perhaps more than that of any other scholar, inspired the new economic history) has frequently pointed out, there is an intimate connection between economic measurement and economic theory [30] [31]. Hence the emphasis placed on theory in the work of the new economic historians is neither an irrelevant, popular affectation nor a stilted superimposition. Rather it is the logical consequence of their desire to quantify the contribution of various changes in economic institutions, in factor supplies, and in technology to the rate and direction of economic growth.[7]

It is probably too soon to attempt a generalized evaluation of the quality of the output of the new economic history and of its contribution to our knowledge of the economic past. Much of this output is still in the prepublication stage or has only recently been published. And many of the debates it has touched off are in full flush.

Yet I cannot resist making one observation. N. S. B. Gras concluded his 1930 survey of the status of economic history in the United States on a gloomy note. "The universities," he wrote, "have generally neglected the study of economic history, apparently regarding it as a very special subject. There has been a lack of controversy, even of intellectual resilience, in the field" [23, p. 327].

The situation today is quite different. Controversy abounds; and the level of the debate is, in my opinion, quite high. Imaginative applications of theory and statistics have brought to the fore evidence which until recently was considered unobtainable. Moreover, the hiatus in recruitment into the field appears to have come to an end. Meetings of the Economic History Association which just a few years ago were peopled almost exclusively by scholars who received their training before or during World War II are now marked by the attendance of a large corps of young people who entered economic history during the last half-dozen years or so. And the rate of entry seems to be rising. At the same time several leading departments of economics have for the first time appointed teachers in economic history, while other departments have expanded or are in the process of expanding their appointments in this area. Vibrant is the word that best describes the present atmosphere in economic history.

REFERENCES

1. Ralph Andreano, *New Perspectives on American Economic Development* (forthcoming, Schenkman Pub. Co., 1965).
2. W. J. Ashley, "On the Study of Economic History," *Q.J.E.,* Jan., 1893.
3. Allan and Margaret B. Bogue, "'Profits' and the Frontier Land Speculator," *J. of Econ. Hist.,* Mar., 1957.
4. J. H. Clapham, "Economic History as a Discipline," *Encyclopaedia of the Social Sciences,* Vol. V (Macmillan, 1930).
5. Thomas C. Cochran, "Did the Civil War Retard Industrialization?" *Miss. Valley Hist. Rev.,* Sept., 1961.
6. Alfred H. Conrad and John R. Meyer, "The Economics of Slavery in the Ante-Bellum South," *J.P.E.,* Apr., 1958.
7. Paul David, "Economic History Through the Looking Glass" (paper presented to the Econometric Society, Dec. 27, 1963; an abstract is published in *Econometrica,* Oct., 1964).
8. _____, "Factories at the Prairies' Edge: A Study of Industrialization in Chicago, 1848-1893" (dissertation for Harvard Univ.).
9. Lance Davis, "New England Textile Mills and the Capital Market: A Study of Industrial Borrowing 1840-1860," *J. of Econ. Hist.,* Mar., 1960.
10. Lance E. Davis, Jonathan R. T. Hughes and Duncan M. McDougall, *American Economic History* (Richard D. Irwin, 1961).
11. Richard A. Easterlin, "Regional Income Trends, 1840-1950," *American Economic History,* Seymour E. Harris, ed. (McGraw-Hill, 1961).
12. Stanley L. Engerman and Robert W. Fogel, *The Growth of the American Iron Industry, 1800-1860: A Statistical Reconstruction* (in progress).
13. Robert Evans, Jr., "The Economics of American Negro Slavery," *Aspects of Labor Economics,* H. Gregg Lewis ed., Conference of Universities—National Bureau Committee for Economic Research (Princeton Univ. Press, 1962).
14. Albert Fishlow, *Railroads and the Transformation of the Ante-Bellum Economy* (forthcoming, Harvard Univ. Press, fall, 1965).
15. Robert W. Fogel, "Reappraisals in American Economic History—Discussion," *A.E.R.,* May, 1964.
16. _____, *The Developmental Consequence of Federal Land Policy, 1830-1890* (in progress).
17. _____, *Railroads and American Economic Growth: Essays in Econometric History* (Johns Hopkins Press, 1964).
18. _____, "Railroads as an Analogy to the Space Effort: Some Economic Aspects" (paper prepared for the Committee on Space, American Academy of Arts and Sciences, Aug., 1964).
19. _____, *The Union Pacific Railroad: A Case in Premature Enterprise* (Johns Hopkins Press, 1960).
20. Robert Gallman, "Gross National Product in the United States" (paper presented to the Conference on Income and Wealth, Sept. 4-5, 1963).
21. Edwin F. Gay, "The Tasks of Economic History," reprinted in Frederic C. Lane, ed., *Enterprise and Secular Change* (Richard D. Irwin, 1953).
22. Carter Goodrich and others, *Canals and American Economic Growth* (Columbia Univ. Press, 1960).
23. N. S. B. Gras, "Economic History in the United States," *Encyclopaedia of the Social Sciences,* Vol. V (Macmillan, 1930).
24. Eli F. Heckscher, "A Plea for Theory in Economic History," reprinted in Frederick C. Lane, ed., *Enterprise and Secular Change* (Richard D. Irwin, 1953).

25. Donald L. Kemmerer and C. Clyde Jones, *American Economic History* (McGraw-Hill, 1959).
26. Reuben A. Kessel and Armen A. Alchian, "Real Wages in the North During the Civil War: Mitchell's Data Reinterpreted," *J. of Law and Econ.,* Oct., 1959.
27. John Neville Keynes, *The Scope and Method of Political Economy* (Macmillan, 1891).
28. Herman E. Krooss, *American Economic Development* (Prentice-Hall, 1955).
29. James Keith Kindahl, "The Economics of Resumption: The United States, 1865-1879 (unpublished doctoral dissertation, Univ. of Chicago, 1958); published without statistical appendices as "Economic Factors in Specie Resumption: The United States 1865-79," *J.P.E.,* Feb., 1961.
30. Simon Kuznets, "The Interrelation of Theory and Economic History — Summary of Discussion and Postscript," *J. of Econ. Hist.,* Dec. 1957.
31. ————, "Statistics and Economic History," *J. of Econ. Hist.,* May, 1941.
32. Paul W. MacAvoy, *The Economic Effects of Regulation: The Trunkline Railroad Cartels and the Interstate Commerce Commission Before 1900* (forthcoming M.I.T. Press, 1965).
33. Douglass C. North, *The Economic Growth of the United States, 1790-1860* (Prentice-Hall, 1961).
34. ————, "Quantitative Research in American Economic History," *A.E.R.,* Mar., 1963.
35. William N. Parker, "Productivity Change in Small Grains" (paper presented to the Conference on Income and Wealth, Sept. 4-5, 1963).
36. Roger Leslie Ransom, "Government Investment in Canals: A Study of the Ohio Canal 1825-1860" (unpublished doctoral dissertation, Univ. of Washington, 1963).
37. Ross M. Robertson, *History of the American Economy* (Harcourt, Brace and Co., 1955).
38. Eugene Smolensky and D. Ratajczak, "The Conception of Cities," *Explorations in Entrepreneurial History,* Winter, 1965.
39. Richard Sutch, "The Profitability of Ante-Bellum Slavery — Revisited," *S. Econ. J.* (forthcoming, Apr., 1965).
40. Peter Temin, *Iron and Steel in Nineteenth-Century America: An Economic Inquiry* (M.I.T. Press, 1964).
41. Thorstein Veblen, "Gustav Schmoller's Economics," *Q.J.E.,* Nov., 1901.
42. William G. Whitney, "The Structure of the American Economy in the Late Nineteenth Century" (dissertation in progress for Harvard Univ.).
43. Jeffrey G. Williamson, *American Growth and the Balance of Payment, 1820-1913* (Univ. of North Carolina Press, 1964).
44. Yasukichi Yasuba, "The Profitability and Viability of Plantation Slavery in the United States," *Econ. Studies Quar.,* Sept., 1961.

NOTES

1. For other statements on the redirection in measurement characteristic of the new economic history and the role which theory plays in this redirection, see [1, Part I] [15] [34].

2. If slaves are included in southern society, the average annual rate of growth of southern per capita income is 1.3 percent per annum. If slaves are treated as inputs in the production of final products rather than as consumers of final products, the rate of growth of per capita income rises to a little over 1.4 percent per annum (cf. [11, pp. 530, 546]). The average rate of growth of per capita income for the U.S. as a whole between 1834-43 and 1844-53 was 1.5 percent per annum [20].

3. Because of the limitation of time and because the topic assigned to me specified the field of American economic history, this brief survey omits important contributions by scholars in the United States and abroad whose field of research is the economic history of other nations.
4. Cf. with [21, p. 412].
5. An experimentation, it might be pointed out, that has increased awareness, not only of the usefulness, but also of the limitations of existing models in the explanation of economic growth.
6. See also the prefaces to [10] [25] [28].
7. In this connection mention should be made of the Purdue Seminar on Quantitative Methods in Economic History. Convened for the first time in December, 1960, the Seminar has met annually since that date. It brings together twenty to thirty scholars for three days of intensive discussion on problems encountered in the adaptation of theory and statistics to the requirements of historical analysis.

AN ALTERNATIVE VIEW: *fritz redlich*

The purpose of this paper is to analyze the various new or current approaches to economic history. In so doing I reluctantly use the now widely accepted terms "new" economic, or "econometric," history considered by some authors as synonymous. In fact, however, there is both a broader and a narrower application of the phrase "new economic history." In the broader sense, the term embraces the work of the various authors who have in common as their aim theoretically underpinned quantitative economic history; in the narrower, it refers only to what I shall call the "model builders." Moreover the terminology seems to be in process of change.[1]

*   *   *

Two elements are constitutive for the new approaches to economic history: one is the overruling interest in quantification, the other is the use of economic theory manifested by the reliance on hypotheses and figments, as will call for our attention later. The first element, quantification, is by no means new. Fogel pointed out in his Boston address of 1963 that the effort "to discover and present numerical information relating to historical processes" is not new; and Hughes's brilliant bibliographical article in the JOURNAL OF ECONOMIC HISTORY bears out that contention.[2] Yet between December 1963 and December

Source: reprinted with permission from "New and Traditional Approaches to Economic History and Their Interdependence" by Fritz Redlich, in *Journal of Economic History,* XXV (December 1965), 480-495.

1964 Fogel changed his emphasis: now "the novel element in the work of the new economic historians is their *approach* [italics mine] to measurement and theory." Formerly, so Fogel goes on, one simply located and classified numerical information; now, however, the emphasis is on "reconstructing measurements . . . no longer extant," on combining primary data with measurements never made before, and on indirect measuring where direct measuring is impossible. It does not appear to me that these aims are held in common by the exponents of all the various new approaches.[3]

It is agreed that the quantitative approach to economic history is not new; it has been pointed out that Fogel's *specific approach* is not shared by all pertinent members of the young generation; finally, reliance on economic theory, where it was sufficiently developed to be useful, characterizes also the work of older analytical economic historians, for example in price, monetary, and banking histories and some other fields. Yet actually there is something new in what goes under the name of "new economic history" in the term's broader connotation, so that one must look for those elements which really distinguish between the traditional and the new approaches. In so doing I again disagree with Fogel.

*   *   *

The matter is rather complicated, as we will see, but one difference between the traditional and the new approaches can be characterized as follows: the old approach deals essentially with institutions, and with processes only to the extent that the latter took place within institutions. (Incidentally, the introduction of the *process* into economic history, or into historical economics if you prefer, was the work of Gustav Schmoller.) The new approach, in contrast, often goes directly at macroeconomic processes, thus disregarding institutions. If one wanted to put it pointedly, though by oversimplifying the problem, he could say: Traditional economic history deals primarily with the development of economic institutions and secondarily with processes taking place therein. The new approaches tend to deal primarily and directly with economic processes while more or less neglecting economic institutions.

This switch in approach became possible only in about the last twenty years when a genuinely dynamic theory, that is, a theory of economic development, rose beside the traditional static theory, largely useless for the economic historian, whose subject matter is dynamic. Now, in consequence of new theoretical goals essentially akin to historical ones, more economists than before are taking an interest in economic history. Now, through that increased interest, quantification and reliance on theory are growing in this field; now, these scholars are gaining a greater influence on its development. Thus, the trend toward quantification with the help of refined mathematical and analytical methods is not due only to the prevailing *Weltanschauung* and to the bias of a younger group of coevals. To the extent that its exponents started in economics it is largely due to their training; for economics, according to Milton Friedman, presumably speaking for many of his colleagues, is "a disguised branch of mathematics."[4] The economists devoting themselves to historical topics apply what they have learned. The trouble is only that the mathematical and the historical bents, except for a few extraordinary men like Schumpeter, do usually not go together, a difficulty which can only be partly overcome by appropriate training; and this means more than being steeped in economics and then taking a few courses in history for a year or so. Anyway, the key to the new development in economic history is, besides the evolution of refined economic analysis, the emergence of a new economic theory, the theory of economic development.

*   *   *

The quantitative approach to economic history has been recognized as nothing essentially new, and the application of refined mathematical and analytical economic methods would have come automatically with progress in these fields. Yet the genuinely new elements in the recent movement should not be underestimated. Beside the component already pointed out before, the younger researchers' neglect of institutions, there is another equally important one. The "new" economic historians actually *specialize,* that is on the "purely 'economic' problems of economic history," to quote from a letter of J. R. T. Hughes. Finally the introduction of modern methods of economic analysis into the quantitative approach to economic history has brought in its wake another fresh element, never used before in this area, namely, statistical inference. That is, "quantitative evidence may be used to verify a qualitative historical hypothesis." Conrad and Meyer, whose book containing the quotation will be analyzed in more detail later, refer as an example to an article by Michael C. Lovell. He infers from certain time series that the Bank of England became a lender of last resort in the crises of the eighteenth century. The qualitative hypothesis that the Bank of England came to stand for a central bank as early as that century was tested by statistical means against the actual numerical data and thus verified.[5]

The last statement has already brought us to another characteristic feature of the new approaches to economic history, but one which is only partly new — namely the use of hypotheses and figments. Test hypotheses have been used extensively by traditional analytical historians; but historians in general have shied away from the use of figments as leading to conjectural history which is generally held in disrepute. But we shall need to change our opinion to some extent, since the application of figments may provide useful tools for analytical economic history.

Hypotheses and figments are in fact two very different things, but it is a common error to confound them. Hypotheses are based on assumptions which are held to have a counterpart in reality, while figments are assumptions having no such counterparts or at least known to be irrealistic. While hypotheses reflect and are derived from reality, figments are mere "as if" constructs, without parallels in reality. A hypothesis cries for verification or, if one prefers the more modern way of thinking, for falsification. Figments as mental constructs are neither verifiable nor falsifiable. They demand justification by their usefulness. With the help of hypotheses we gain knowledge, with that of a figment we obtain a tool for the acquisition of knowledge. Scholarly work based on figments is comparable with industrial roundabout production since, as we shall see later, it leads to models.[6] To be sure, what in line with the German philosophical (that is, the Herbarth-Lotze-Vaihinger) tradition I have called "figment," has recently appeared in America under the name of "counterfactual or subjunctive conditional."[7]

If we make the use or nonuse of hypotheses or figments, respectively, the criterion, we are able to distinguish between economic historians and the builders of historical models, and we can point to essential characteristics of the various new approaches which, on the other hand, are held together by a common aim: the extensive use of modern economic analysis, concentration on the purely economic aspects of economic history, and quantification along with refined mathematics.

If with such ends in mind the researcher works with the help of a hypothesis, the outcome tends toward analytical quantitative economic history, and Douglass North's achievement is representative of the approach. On the first page of his much-discussed book, *The Economic Growth of the United States, 1790-1860,*[8] he has been articulate about the hypotheses underlying his presentation: "The gist of the argument is that the timing and pace of an economy's development has been determined by (1) the success of its export sector, and (2) the characteristics of the export industry and the disposition of the income received from the export sector." This is clearly hypothetical as opposed to fictitious, nothing is postulated that is unrealistic. North assumes what he considers correct. Using the established method of the analytical economic historian or for that matter any social scientist, he proceeds to prove his hypotheses on the basis of available material, yet emphasizing quantification. What is new in the book is neither the method nor the far-going quantification, but the subject matter. As he himself states, he emphasizes economic growth as a total phenomenon whereas it has been traditional "to provide separate treatments of the various sectors in the economy...with only superficial linkages between them." It should be understood that I do not analyze or criticize the content of the book but deal with the *method* he uses. It is essentially related to the historical quantitative tradition. The result is history beyond any doubt.

Yet regardless of the fact that North starts from hypotheses and not from a figment, there is a fictitious element implied in his work, as in that of all scholars who identify economic development with some set of figures, whatever their character. He states in the preface of his book[9] that due to the preoccupation with description and institutional change, there is "no comprehensive, integrated analysis of United States development." Economic historians have, according to North, "only incidentally discussed the process of economic growth." The content of this statement is granted to be correct, in fact entirely correct. But if North thinks that he has filled the gap, I should have to object as a matter of principle. His integrated discussion of American economic development was made possible by his bringing every phenomenon on a quantitative level; and while he gained integration thereby, he lost touch with reality. Figures are not identical with any process whatsoever. Figures are quantitative symbols which stand for something, in this case for the *result* of a process. By lining those symbols up in the form of a time series, we incorrectly create the impression that they actually represent a process, whereas they merely act as yardsticks, measuring a process. Or to express it differently, they represent a process only by the introduction of a figment, an as-if construct, and so furnish a good example of how useful figments can be in research and why their use is a widely accepted scholarly convention.

We now turn to those scholars who *base* their research on figments and begin with Fogel's work.[10] Here the fictitious character of the assumptions is beyond any doubt. Fogel investigates what would have happened to American economic development if there had not been any railroads. Now, as every schoolchild knows, there were railroads. That is, Fogel investigates what would have happened in the event that something else had happened which could not have happened. I emphasize now the phrase, which *could not* have happened. Technological development follows its own logic. Once the atmospheric engine had been developed into an efficient steam engine and the steam engine had successfully been put into boats, making steamers out of them, it was only a question of when the steam engine would be put on wheels, particularly as the railroad minus locomotive had existed for a long time. Having started from a figment, Fogel did not produce history, he produced what my friend Arthur Johnson has called quasi history, which in professional terms must be characterized as a historical model. Based on a figment it does not cry for verification — which is, of course, impossible — but for justification. Now some young friends of mine, who are by no means "new" economic historians, tell me how useful as an eye-opener Fogel's book is in teaching when used, of course, beside the standard presentations on railroad history by Chandler, the Hidys, Jenks, Overton, and others. So it is actually justified, but this does not make Fogel's product history.

Previously I have described Fogel's program of "reconstructing measurements no longer extant," of constructing yardsticks, and of measuring indirectly what cannot be measured directly. This program implies figments all the way through, because for the execution one must rely on the dependence of some figures on others, dependences which econometric theory establishes. This by necessity must be done in disregard of the historical situation in which a theoretically established interdependence of magnitudes may not come into play, because other causal factors impinge. What in theory is entirely correct becomes fictitious in the application, the result being a model rather than something related to reality. But we are not yet at the end.

There are additional elements which characterize Fogel's presentation as an as-if construct, a historical model. He himself states that he has omitted "many conspicuous aspects" because they were "too important" and "too complex" to be treated in this context. He himself knows that the validity of his findings is "not absolute" and nevertheless thinks that he has corrected unwarranted assumptions. This claim is epistemologically untenable, since one *cannot correct anything* by using a figment. As a matter of fact, one can thus only point to tendencies, a term introduced into economics by John Stuart Mill, if I am correctly informed.[11]

But I am afraid that I must criticize Fogel also for not having asked the most fruitful question. Everyone who knows French economic history in the eighteenth and English in eighteenth and early nineteenth centuries knows that then there was economic development under way without the railroad. The fruitful question, if one wished to work in this area with figments, seems to be: At what point would economic development, under way by 1800, have become an arrested development for lack of adequate transportation? The stop would have come rather late in England, because there ore and coal were available in close proximity and because of the easy access to the sea, providing a kind of unpaid-for road or canals system, if you please. The United States development would have come to a halt much earlier, or several national economies might have developed.

So much for Fogel's work. The most representative model builders besides Fogel are Alfred H. Conrad and John R. Meyer, and they are less extreme. These coauthors have made it easy for the analyst, in that they have published an elaborate methodological introduction to their collection of papers, its title being "Economic Theory, Statistical Inference, and Economic History."[12] They have elucidated the difficult subject with unusual clarity, and, while I would have used other language and while I have objections to a good many details, I can accompany them almost all the way through.[13] Specifically, I agree with them that there can be generalization in historiography to a point and that hypotheses can be tested by historical research. As to the former, if generalization is the goal, I prefer comparative history as a means toward it rather than working with hypotheses. And as to the latter, the authors themselves have indicated the difficulties involved (pp. 24 ff.), while I myself think of qualitative testing as standing on the same level as quantitative.

Now let us see how the methodological prescriptions are applied in actual research and take as representative the paper "The Economics of Slavery in the Antebellum South," first published in the *Journal of Political Economy,* Vol. LXVI (1958). We begin by comparing the basis of the article with those of the books by North and Fogel. The former, as we remember, begins with hypotheses, the latter with a figment. Conrad and Meyer (p. 45) start from a hypothesis; according to them, American Negro slavery was characterized by two production functions — namely, that of southern staples ("inputs of Negro slaves and the materials required to maintain them to the production of the southern staple crops, particularly cotton") and that of slave labor. This is what they "postulate." Analyzing the execution of this program, one finds that parts II and III of the paper use different methods. In Part II about a dozen additional assumptions are heaped on the basic one. As a matter of fact, the authors were forced to do this. Their primary quantitative material was not only shaky but also was not collected for their specific purposes. They had to make it suitable and this could only be done by introducing more assumptions. Tables 10 and 11 are each based on three of these; and as to Table 9, their number is "untold."[14] If one looks at the assumptions as such, one finds that some are hypothetical, others fictitious, such as the life expectancy of slaves and the fertility of field wenches. These are mere guesses. Under these circumstances, that is, because of the large number of assumptions and the mixture of hypothetical and fictitious ones, I must contend that the whole Part II of the paper is fictitious even though the basic assumption is hypothetical. Things look different in Part III; the figures are much better, the assumptions (estimates) very few and not basic. This part looks much more like history than Part II, and is in fact historically interesting and useful.

Nevertheless I am reluctant to consider the paper as a whole a work of history. In the original discussion over it, one speaker blamed the authors for disregarding the interrelations of economic and other social factors. The authors agreed, but the objection is in fact crucial from our point of view. Both the isolating theorist and the narrative historian (who on principle refuses to ask and answer the question, Why? and, as a true empiricist, asks only: What has happened and when?) are in one boat. They can — to be sure, for different reasons — legitimately present one side of a development only. The analytical historian cannot afford to do so; for then his presentation becomes a one-sided exaggeration — that is, a model.

Yet during the discussion the authors made another important statement: namely, that the purpose of their paper was to test "hypotheses about the profitability [from the economist's point of view] of slavery and the efficiency of the slave labor market." This program poses another question: Is this actually a historical question? An economic question, as this undoubtedly is, does not become *ipso facto* a historical one simply because the problem investigated is of yesterday or before yesterday. An economic problem becomes one of economic history only when a specifically historical element is added. As history is essentially change over time, the economic problem must be seen as changing in order to be a subject for the historian. Otherwise, if the test is unspoiled by figments, it may stand at best on the level of a historical case study.

At the time when Conrad and Meyer were working on their paper, they were aware that they were constructing a model. On page 67 they speak of "our model," on page 73 of the "validity of the model"; on page 82 we read "our model of the antebellum southern economy"; and when they first presented their paper, one discussant accepted their own characterization of the work and cited it (*ibid.,* 93). If they had stuck to that perfectly sound description, I would have had no fault to find. Historical models have been used earlier; we have been articulate about them ever since the days of Max Weber, and their refinement by mathematical means or otherwise deserves praise. But at some point, the authors changed their minds and they are now trying to sell their work as "history." And this and this alone is the reason for my protest. A model is never a piece of history, because it is conjectural or subjunctive or, in Max Weber's language used for all ideal types, a distortion of reality. This position I can not abandon even if a qualifying adjective, be it "new" or "econometric," is added. If we were to accept it as history, the piece would be bad history. It is based entirely on secondary sources without any source criticism whatsoever. In their methodological paper (p. 18), they stress the necessity of hunting for quantitative material which they consider "likely to be found." In fact, as experts in southern history have told and even shown me, it can be found in their case. If the authors wanted to write "history" they were by professional standards obliged to search for primary material; if they wanted to build a model, they were free from that obligation. As "history," most professional historians, in contrast to economists with an interest in history, will reject the piece. As a historical model it might be very useful, as only those can decide who work with the tool, for a tool it is and not a consumers' good.

I have tried to show that the result of the scholarly endeavors of both Conrad and Meyer and of Fogel is not history but quasi history. One can express this also in other terms, as has been done. These men do not write history but produce historical models. Now when one distinguishes between models by reduction and models by construction, the latter also called nonempirical models, one recognizes that there is a difference between Conrad and Meyer's Part II and Fogel's book, on the one hand, and the formers' Part III, on the other. The first named are models by construction, the last named one by reduction in that it abstracts only from the noneconomic determining factors. But models they are, so that we are cautioned against reifying them, against misplacing concreteness of them, to use the expressions of Morris Cohen and T. N. Whitehead. I am afraid the architects of the models in question and their admirers are not free from these errors. As far as I can see, the applause comes from economists rather than historians, from men never exposed to methodology and often not even to history.

The so-called new approach to economic history has revealed itself as consisting of different movements. One, as represented for example by the data-processing jobs of Davis and Hughes or by Fishlow's paper, "The Trustee Savings Banks 1817-1861,"[15] is close to the tradition of quantitative economic history but uses much more refined mathematical tools. The second, exemplified by North, is based both on quantification and on clearly defined hypotheses which are tested. The product is economic history. The third, typified by Fogel as well as Conrad and Meyer, again emphasizes quantification but is simultaneously based on figments. The result is quasi-economic history, or as-if economic history, if you please, or more exactly a historical model.

A final question remains to be asked and answered: namely, What is the relationship of the traditional economic history to the new approaches? What makes it a little difficult to answer is the fact that, like the "new" economic history in the wider sense of the term, the traditional economic history is by no means uniform. Some is microeconomic history; some corresponds to macroeconomics. One branch emphasizes figures, another institutions. Some is empiricistic, some analytical. Or, focusing on the method applied, we can distinguish between a branch using the positivistic from another using the hermeneutic, that is, the interpretative "understanding" method.

Under these circumstances it is quite impossible to confront the two approaches and characterize them with a few concise words. Yet it is not far from the truth to say that the best traditional-yet-modern economic history, beside emphasizing the study of institutions, is well aware of the role of noneconomic factors and of imponderables which the "new" economic historians specializing in the purely economic aspect of the field disregard. To the extent that traditional economic history stresses institutions, noneconomic factors, and imponderables, it might draw for theoretical support on sociology and anthropology rather than on economics; whereas the "new" economic historians rely exclusively on the latter. T. C. Cochran's interest in the cultural element in economic development, or mine in the personal element therein, simply does not interest the exponents of the new approaches.

But I am sure nothing is further from their thought than a scientific ostrich policy. Their *interests* lie in a different direction.

Once new approaches have come into existence and are here to stay, the traditional and the "new" economic history become interdependent, but interdependent in different ways since they are not uniform phenomena. To the degree that the new approach simply implies quantification with refined mathematical methods, it will probably be the successor of the traditional quantitative approach to economic history. To the extent that the "new" approach is quantitative and analytical, as in the case of North's work, the old-line empiricists will take the result and the old-line analytical economic historian will take it also, once he becomes convinced that the underlying hypothesis is tenable and the analysis correct. More interesting is the question how the traditional analytical economic history will be related to the "new" analytical economic history as practiced by Conrad and Meyer or Fogel.

NOTES

1. Papers and Proceedings of the Seventy-seventh Annual Meeting of the American Economic Association, Chicago, December 1964. The *American Economic Review,* LV (1965), 90, 91, 98.
2. Robert William Fogel, "A Provisional View of the New Economic History,'" in *American Economic Review,* LIV (1964), 377; J. R. T. Hughes, "Measuring British Economic Growth," in *Journal of Economic History,* XXIV (1964), 60 ff.
3. *American Economic Review,* LV (1965), 92.
4. *Essays in Positive Economics* (Chicago: University of Chicago Press, 1953), p. 12.
5. As to the book of Conrad and Meyer, see p. 488 and, for the citation, footnote 14. The article by Lovell, "The Role of the Bank of England as Lender of Last Resort in the Crises of the Eighteenth Century," is in *Explorations in Entrepreneurial History,* X (1957/58), 8 ff.
6. My thinking is based on the famous book by Hans Vaihinger, *Die Philosophie des Als Ob.* I have used the third edition (Leipzig: F. Meiner, 1918). An English translation by C. K. Ogden appeared under the title, *The Philosophy of 'As-if'* (London: K. Paul, Trench, Trubner & Co., 1924). See especially the Introduction, ch. iii, and Part IA, ch. ii. The English author translates the German word *Fiktion* as fiction. I prefer the term figment.
7. Stuart Hampshire, "Subjunctive Conditionals" in [Oxford] *Analysis,* IX (Oct. 1948), 9 ff. Thence Conrad and Meyer have taken the term into their book already mentioned and to be cited in note 12.
8. *The Economic Growth of the United States, 1790-1860* (Englewood Cliffs, N.J.: Prentice-Hall, Inc., 1961), p. vi.
9. *Ibid.,* p. vi.

10. Robert William Fogel, *Railroads and American Economic Growth: Essays in Econometric History* (Baltimore: Johns Hopkins Press, 1964).
11. Introduction, pp. vii, viii.
12. *The Economics of Slavery and Other Studies in Econometric History* (Chicago: Aldine, 1964).
13. I wish to register my objection to one minor point only: namely, their juxtaposition of the view that everything in history is unique, with extreme determinism. They are not sufficiently familiar with European history teaching and writing to know that since the turn of the last century outstanding historians have taken a stand which represents the middle ground. These are Jacob Burkhard in Basel, Otto Hintze in Berlin (whose student the author was), and the now-living Theodor Schieder of Cologne. One could also point to Karl Lamprecht in Leipzig, who had an approach of his own.
14. "Various hypothesized conditions"; p. 61.
15. *Journal of Economic History*, XXI (1961), 26 ff.

chapter 2

elements of

economic growth

THE WESTERN EUROPEAN HERITAGE

Economic growth flourishes in societies receptive to change. It is not a coincidence that the western world experienced sustained economic growth only after progressive forces weakened its traditional society. These changes were slow and tortuous, covering several centuries. A society which can avoid this time-consuming preconditioning process has a head start on economic growth. This was the case of the United States.

THE RENAISSANCE AND REFORMATION

The society which colonized the United States had undergone considerable cultural change. The Renaissance, a transitional period between medieval and modern times lasting roughly from the fourteenth to the seventeenth century, challenged the validity of virtually all accepted truths. A spirit of inquiry prevailed in all fields of human endeavor. The Renaissance man wanted to learn for himself about himself and his world. He read, thought, discussed, experimented, wrote, philosophized, painted, sculpted, and in the process discovered a new world. It was a world offering hope and challenge in contrast to the resignation of the Middle Ages. Reason rather than traditional authority was the proper guide for human action. Armed with knowledge, man could adapt his environment to meet his needs.

The new spirit of inquiry was accompanied by fundamental cultural changes. The isolated, self-sufficient feudal manor was superceded by flourishing commercial towns. Here the middle-class merchant and trader replaced the landed nobility, and industry, trade, and a monied economy took root. The increasing importance of secular life weakened the church and freed national governments from ecclesiastical control.

The Renaissance man's search for enlightenment militated against the power of the Catholic Church, whose dogma and teaching had dominated medieval life. Protesting church corruption, sale of indulgences, and adoration of images, many sought a new path to salvation. Monastic codes, nunneries, and the priesthood did not harmonize with the promise of improved material benefits. Priestly vocation, Luther taught, was only for the few, set apart from the many by ordination. Salvation was possible by faith alone. Each individual was responsible for his own religious life without the need of priestly intermediaries or of prescribed ritualistic "works." The Bible was a sufficient guide. This doctrine attacked the being of the church itself, and led to the freeing of secular affairs from religious control.

Every man baptized into the Christian community had a responsibility to support that community. However, as with salvation, the manner of one's calling, according to Calvin, was an individual affair. Each man should decide for himself the line of work for which he is best suited. Farmers, artisans, teachers, and businessmen, all are necessary and justified by their faith in Christ. Thus, the medieval prejudices against business activity were denied their religious support. In fact, success in business was interpreted as a sign of religious virtue. Each individual at birth was predestined for heaven or hell. No one knew what his fate would be. Nevertheless, there were signs which might reveal those who were among the elect, and economic success might be such a sign. Thus, it was worthwhile to work hard at one's calling, for the diligent, frugal man was held virtuous, the poor man lazy, and the spendthrift sinful. The more substantial one's accumulation of worldly goods, the more likely one was to enter paradise.

The Reformation, to a very large degree, recruited its adherents from the emerging middle class. Emphasis on individual salvation appealed to a class eager to shed the shackles of the past. Interpreting every man's vocation as sacred paved the way for unrestricted business activities. Finally, confiscation of church properties by the state released productive resources for the market economy. Some observers, most notably Max Weber and R.H. Tawney, have ascribed to the Reformation an indispensable role in the evolution of capitalism. They regarded the spirit of capitalism as derived from Protestantism as an essential prerequisite to the development of modern industrial society. Some scholars today feel that they overstated their case, since there is too much evidence of industrial growth in non-Protestant environments. The reading by Sigmund Diamond at the end of this chapter argues that it was labor scarcity, rather than the Protestant Ethic, which was the prime force in laying the foundation for U.S. industrial growth.

LIBERALISM AND REACTION IN ENGLAND

The dynamic forces that sparked the Renaissance and the Reformation fostered further cultural change in the eighteenth and nineteenth centuries. Emphasizing the supreme value of individual freedom and reason, liberalism sought to free mankind from all artificial restraints. All men, the liberalists held, are born with the right to life, liberty and property. These natural rights must be guaranteed — this is the raison d'être of government. Any interference with these rights in personal or business affairs is harmful to society.

It has already been noted that the void of authority resulting from the loss of church power was filled by national governments. These governments, operating on the principle of political absolutism, sought to consolidate and extend their power by a plethora of regulations over economic life. To those in the rising middle class who were not the beneficiaries of monopoly grants, these government regulations were as burdensome as the clerical restrictions they had replaced. In the name of liberalism, they sought relief from these artificial restraints which they regarded as harmful to both individual and national welfare. They demanded that all regulations prohibiting or restricting trade, domestic or foreign, be eliminated; private property and its owner's right of disposal be guaranteed; the right to contract be unrestricted; and the freedom to practice one's trade or profession in any location be assured. The government's role was to protect these rights, not to restrict them. Individual self-interest competing for economic gain was held to yield society the greatest possible wealth.

In England, which provided the principal roots of the American heritage, the middle class had been growing steadily ever since the Rennaissance. Expanding commerce, the opportunity to exploit new colonies, the Industrial Revolution, and the shift of economic activity from the countryside to the town acted to increase the wealth of the middle class. This new-found purchasing power enabled them to buy land and, thus, a voice in Parliament. A more broadly based Parliament became increasingly impatient with the whims and caprices of royal absolutism. The naturalistic philosophy of John Locke was eminently more reasonable than the divine right of kings. Royal prerogative was replaced by cabinet rule responsible to Parliament, whose control over the purse prevented any meaningful attempts by the crown to restore its power.

In England, as elsewhere, Protestantism encouraged pluralism. The middle class found its aspirations most faithfully represented in the Protestant faith. One sect, Puritanism, sought to purify the Reformation. Rejecting hierarchical church authority, it emphasized the importance of individual expression of faith. This expression could be achieved best by living a righteous and industrious life. The individual should follow his chosen Christian way free from secular and religious restraints. Although the Puritan movement passed into extreme forms of independence, and was captured by sectarian radicals, it had a lasting influence on English society. It contributed in large measure to the downfall of mercantilism and to the establishment of constitutional government.

THE UNITED STATES CULTURE

INDIVIDUALISM AND SOCIAL MOBILITY

Those who colonized the United States came in the hope of a new life. They were in the vanguard of the transitional process going on in Europe, and consequently left behind much of the rigidity that still clung to the old world. They brought with them the Protestant ethic of the sanctity of a diligent, hard-working life. The rugged virgin continent that confronted them offered an unparalleled opportunity to fulfill their material and idealistic dream. Every individual had to contribute to the taming of the physical frontier. The work was hard but the rewards great. The most successful were those who were willing to take full advantage of the almost unlimited possibilities of their economic environment. Idleness found little favor, even among those who accumulated or inherited wealth. The successful businessman and his progeny continued their active role in economic affairs. With the exception of the ante-bellum South, European aristocratic taboos on upper-class participation in work were rejected. Succeeding generations, unwilling to rest on the laurels of their forebears, searched for new horizons to conquer. Each generation regarded the one preceding as old-fashioned and, in turn, every father expected his son to surpass him and took pride in it. A youthful Frenchman, Michael Chevalier, observed on a visit to the United States in the 1830's:

> The American is educated with the idea that he will have some particular occupation, that he is to be a farmer, artisan, manufacturer,

merchant, speculator, lawyer, physician, or minister, perhaps all in succession, and that, if he is active and intelligent, he will make his fortune. He has no conception of living without a profession, even when his family is rich, for he sees nobody about him not engaged in business. The man of leisure is a variety of the human species of which the Yankee does not suspect the existence, and he knows that if rich today, his father may be ruined tomorrow. Besides the father himself is engaged in business according to custom, and does not think of dispossessing himself of his fortune; if the son wishes to have one at present let him make it himself.[1]

The second paragraph of the Declaration of Independence states: "We hold these truths to be self-evident, that all men are created equal, that they are endowed by their creator with certain unalienable rights, that among these are life, liberty, and the pursuit of happiness." This expression of the natural rights of man was the United States' interpretation of European liberalism. It was a statement of what ought to be, not what existed at the time. The United States was not born a democracy. A privileged class, whose estates spanned the Atlantic seaboard from New England to the Carolinas, dominated colonial society. Its political importance, social graces, and clothing distinguished its members from the masses. The average citizen had little voice in his government, nor was he accorded unrestricted freedom of worship. Slaves and indentured servants were in general use. Yet these American aristocrats had no permanent status. There was no secular or religious nobility. Any one discontent with his lot could move to the frontier and secure land for himself. Moreover, liberalism had taken firm roots in the new world. In every colony dissenters were calling for reform and, in one sense, the Revolution was a conflict between the common man and the privileged class. The fact that it was only a partial victory was not as important as the principles it established. For despite the forces of reaction, democratic principles expressed themselves time and time again, each time narrowing the gap between the promise and the reality of freedom. Alexis de Tocqueville, another youthful French visitor to the United States, observed in the 1830's:

In America, the aristocratic element has always been feeble from its birth; and if at the present day it is not actually destroyed, it is at any rate so completely disabled, that we can scarcely assign to it any degree of influence on the course of affairs.

The democratic principle, on the contrary, has gained so much strength by time, by events, and by legislation, as to have become not only predominant, but all-powerful. There is no family or corporate authority, and it is rare to find even the influence of individual character enjoy any durability.

America, then, exhibits in her social state an extraordinary phenomenon. Men are there seen on a greater equality in point of fortune and intellect, or, in other words, more equal in their strength, than in any other country of the world, or in any age of which history has preserved the remembrance.[2]

Despite persistent controversy about the degree of social mobility, American society has been essentially an open-class system. Rejection of the European system of nobility prevented the establishment of well-defined class lines. The availability of cheap land created a broadly based property owning class, and successive waves of immigration acted to elevate the lower classes. Moreover, sufficient evidence of mobility was present to encourage individuals to make the effort. Finally, our rapid rate of growth raised the levels of living for all classes.

The major exception to an open-class system existed in the ante-bellum South. A rigid class structure, with plantation owners at its apex and slaves at its base, allowed little vertical or horizontal mobility. The Southern gentleman was of aristocratic bearing, of distinctive dress, and well-schooled in the social graces. He often received his schooling abroad while the masses of Southern society, white and Negro, received little or no education. The average Southerner received considerably less education than his counterparts in the North and West. The Southern aristocrat spent much of his time developing political and military skills and although he was responsible for business affairs, he refused to permit the business of making a living to interfere with the art of making a life. The fact that most Southern aristocrats acquired their fortunes during their own lifetimes did not encourage them to offer the same opportunity to others. Their sensitivity on the question of slavery made them suspicious of any change. Despite the moral burden of slavery, and its irreconcilibility with the American creed, they refused to compromise their position. While the spirit of Jeffersonian Democracy prevailed, it was possible that the South might gradually eliminate slavery. However, by the 1820's, as Parrington observes:

> The humanitarian spirit that marked the thought of the preceding generation was dying out, to be replaced by a frank recognition of local economic interests. Expectation that slavery was on the way to natural extinction was yielding to the conviction that the system was too profitable to the South to permit its extinction, and this in turn bred an imperious desire to spread it westward to the Pacific. With this significant shift from apology to imperialism, it became clear to ardent pro-slavery men that lukewarm Virginians of the old tradition were not the spokesmen to entrust with the fortunes of the South, and the leadership passed to the South Carolina school. In that momentous shift much was implied. It was more than a shift from Jefferson to Calhoun; from humanitarian idealism to economic realism. It marked the complete ascendancy of a small minority of gentlemen planters

over the inarticulate mass of southern yeomanry, and the assertion
of the aristocratic ideal as the goal of southern society. It denied the
principle of democracy as the principle was understood in the North
and West, and it rejected the new humanitarian spirit of western
civilization.[3]

In contrast to the aristocratic gentlemen of the ante-bellum South,
the typical American hero of the 1800's was the self-made businessman.
Ideally he came from a poor family with little opportunity for formal
education. He began his career at the lowest level of work and by persistence, diligence, and native ability, he rose to be president of the
company, or to start a firm of his own. He was a rugged individualist,
proud of his meager background and his lack of formal training. A college
education was regarded as a handicap to a successful business career. It
allegedly dulled the rugged qualities necessary for success and wasted
some of the most productive years of a man's life. A study by Reinhard
Bendix of over 1,000 prominent business leaders of the nineteenth and
twentieth centuries, classified by career type and date of birth, reveals
that as our economy grew:

1. The proportion of heirs (individuals who acquired control by direct
   legacy or purchase) and bureaucrats (administrative workers)
   increased at the expense of entrepreneurs (individuals who started a
   business at some point in their business career).
2. The level of education of heirs and bureaucrats rose sharply while
   that of the entrepreneur remained the same.
3. An increasing proportion of business leaders began their careers in
   a management position.[4]

THE ROLE OF GOVERNMENT

The United States has always faced the basic philosoph-
ical question of how much government influence should be operative in the
economy. The doctrine of mercantilism, inherited from England, holds
that only with government planning and controls can the best economic
interests of a nation be achieved. A lack of such planning necessarily
results in a nation falling short of its economic potential. In contrast, a
laissez-faire doctrine, also a legacy from England, holds that economic
health flourishes in an environment of limited governmental activity. This
doctrine stems from the writings of the French physiocrats and was
adopted by Adam Smith in his *Wealth of Nations*. To Smith, the unregulated
pursuit of self-interest on the part of consumers, entrepreneurs, and
resource suppliers would maximize the utility derived from production
and consumption. Consumption utility would be maximized because the

consumer knew better than government what pattern of expenditures would provide him with the greatest satisfaction. Entrepreneurs, seeking to maximize profits, would willingly cater to the desires of consumers. Similarly, resource suppliers would be attracted to industries producing consumer-preferred goods, since these industries could afford to offer higher wages, interest, and rent. Thus, all would gain from a system of unrestricted consumer sovereignty. Since it was colonial mercantilist doctrine against which Americans revolted in the Revolution, it is not surprising that laissez-faire is the central theme of the Declaration of Independence. By safe-guarding national sovereignty, maintaining law and order, and protecting the rights of individuals and their property, government ensures the operation of nature's laws. Beyond this the state has no role in society. That government is best that governs least. Free and equal individuals, if left alone, can best solve their own problems.

Mercantilism, however, did not disappear with independence from Britain. Indeed, much of U.S. economic history can be written in terms of the ideological conflicts between these competing viewpoints. Foremost among the proponents of a strong central government active in economic affairs were Alexander Hamilton and the Federalist party. To Hamilton, the future greatness of America lay in the development of manufacturing. A factory system, to Hamilton, would promote immigration to the United States, contribute to capital formation, create urban centers in which farmers could market their produce, and permit division of labor. To encourage manufacturing and protect infant industries, Hamilton proposed a series of federal acts, including a protective tariff and national bank. In opposition to Alexander Hamilton was Thomas Jefferson. To Jefferson, agriculture and the small independent farmer, rather than manufacturing and the industrial laborer, were the principal sources of economic and political strength. Accordingly, he favored a limited role for government, rapid settlement of the West, and opposed protective tariffs and a national bank. Andrew Jackson, heir to the Jeffersonian tradition, was an ardent proponent of laissez-faire and rugged individualism. Thus, he strenuously opposed a central bank, and was unsympathetic to state efforts to secure federal financing of roads and other internal improvements. The crippling of Southern laissez-faire political influence following the Civil War enabled mercantilism to re-emerge as a more active force in the nation's political and economic life. Government intervention in the economy manifested itself in substantial aid to the railroads, higher tariffs, and the establishment of a national banking system. The philosophy of many Americans, however, was still laissez-faire as epitomized by Herbert Spencer's doctrine of Social Darwinism. Spencer believed that the struggle for survival existed among human beings as well as lower creatures. If human society was to be preserved, benefits had to be distributed in proportion to merit. To force superior beings to assume the burden of the inferior would adversely affect the welfare of the entire species. Competition by which one company eliminates another is the natural process by which society purifies itself. Competition and destruction of rivals is the natural order of things. A trend toward economic concentration is an evolutionary process necessitating no government intervention. This doctrine remained tenable as long as society remained simple and largely self-sufficient. However, as economic growth brought specialization, expanding markets and economic interdependence, the individual became less able to care for his needs. The opportunity of self-employment narrowed, and family income became largely dependent on giant impersonal corporations and the vagaries of the business cycle. Captains of industry arose to control vast empires, often with little concern for the welfare of the community. Monopoly rather than competition became the natural order, and contrasts between wealth and poverty became more apparent. Federal and State authorities increasingly were requested to mitigate undesirable effects of industrialization. The Englishman, James Bryce, observed this transitional process near the end of the 1800's: **1784370**

> New causes are at work in the world tending not only to lengthen the arms of government, but to make its touch quicker and firmer.
> Modern civilization, in becoming more complex and refined, has become more exacting. It discerns more benefits which the organized power of government can secure, and grows more anxious to attain them. Men live fast, and are impatient of the slow-working of natural laws. The triumphs of physical science have enlarged their desires for comfort, and shown them how many things may be accomplished by the application of collective skill and large funds which are beyond the reach of individual effort and philanthropic sympathy. There are benefits which the laws of demand and supply do not procure. Unlimited competition seems to press too hard on the weak. The power of groups of men organized by incorporation as joint-stock companies, or of small knots of rich men acting in combination, has developed with unexpected strength in unexpected ways, overshadowing individuals and even communities, and showing that the very freedom of association which men sought to secure by law when they were threatened by the violence of potentates may under the shelter of the law, ripen into a new form of tyranny.[5]

The realization that the power of concentrated business enterprises needed to be restrained found expression in the Progressive Era of the early twentieth century. For the first time, the Federal Government assumed effective regulatory authority over the practices of giant business firms. In addition, the Government initiated regulatory responsibilities in the areas of food and drug manufacturing and the use of the remaining public domain. The Great Depression of the 1930's and the subsequent realization that only the Federal Government could effectively control the business cycle, substantially augmented the Government's role in the nation's economic life. A by-product of the Government's efforts to solve the depression has been substantial involvement in efforts to secure for all Americans minimum standards of income, housing, and health care.

NOTES

1. Quoted by William E. Rappard, *The Secret of American Prosperity.* New York: Greenberg, Publisher, 1955, p. 55.
2. Alexis de Tocqueville. *Democracy in America.* Boston: John Allyn, 1873, pp. 66-67.
3. Vernon Louis Parrington. *Main Currents in American Thought,* Vol. 2, Book 2. New York: Harcourt, Brace and Company, 1930, p. 61.
4. Reinhard Bendix. *Work and Authority in Industry.* New York: John Wiley & Sons, Inc., 1956.
5. James Bryce. *American Commonwealth,* Vol. II. New York: Macmillan & Co., 1905, pp. 539-40.

SELECTED REFERENCES

1. Charles A. Beard and Mary R. Beard. *The Rise of American Civilization,* Vols. I-II, New York: The Macmillan Co., 1929.
2. Joseph Dorfman, *The Economic Mind in American Civilization,* Vols. I-V. New York: The Viking Press, 1946-59.
3. Bert F. Hoselitz. *Sociological Aspects of Economic Growth.* New York: Free Press, 1960.
4. Seymour Lipsit and Reinhard Bendix. *Social Mobility in Industrial Society.* Berkeley and Los Angeles: University of California Press, 1959.
5. Max Weber. *The Protestant Ethic and the Spirit of Capitalism.* New York: Scribner, 1958.

reading

what was the major non-economic factor which laid the foundation for u.s. industrial growth?

sigmund diamond

The story is told that Dean Donham of the Harvard Business School once asked Professor Schumpeter, after a lecture on the entrepreneur — Schumpeter's plumed knight of economic development — what was the most important single factor in accounting for the success of the businessman. Quick as a shot came the answer: "Good health." For purposes of this inquiry into certain aspects of American social structure and American values which seem to have been of decisive importance in contributing to American economic growth, certain variables — like the health of the businessman and the endowment of the country with respect to natural resources — will not be considered.

Irrespective of the offbeat on which this inquiry may end, it shall begin on a note of impeccable orthodoxy. In a section entitled "Causes of the Prosperity of New Countries," Adam Smith writes: "The colony of a civilized nation which takes possession, either of a waste country, or one so thinly inhabited, that the natives easily give place to the new settlers, advances more rapidly to wealth and greatness than any other human society." This is so, Smith argues, because the settlers bring with them superior economic institutions, "a knowledge of agriculture and the other useful arts," and the habits of disciplined, orderly work and government, and also because they use their more productive techniques in areas in which the ratio of population to resources is especially favorable.[1]

Source: reprinted with permission from "Values as an Obstacle to Economic Growth: The American Colonies" by Sigmund Diamond, in *Journal of Economic History*, XXVII (December 1967), 561-575.

Writing early in the nineteenth century, Herman Merivale, in his remarkable *Lectures on Colonization and Colonies,* took up Adam Smith's theme and offered an explanation to account for the propensity of colonial societies to be so materialistic. Speaking of colonies whose populations are made up through migration from the mother country, Merivale writes:

> In such a community the mere wants of life are abundantly supplied, but not supplied without labour. There is none of that depressing poverty which elsewhere weighs down the energies of large masses of mankind; or of that almost equally depressing dread of poverty which perpetually harasses the minds of a class somewhat higher in circumstances, which produces in some an abjectness of disposition, in others an irritable and discontented temperament; and if it sometimes sharpens the intellectual powers, often does so only to the detriment of the moral character. On the other hand, everything which adorns human life, everything which stimulates the more artificial appetites of men, be they sensual or spiritual, is either difficult of acquisition or unattainable. The colonist has little temptation to long for the enjoyment of such superfluities, for the stimulus of envy is wanting: he does not see them heightening the pleasures of others, and therefore thinks little of them. During the first period of his conflict with the genius of the wilderness, his thoughts are necessarily intent on his immediate occupation; afterwards, his daily labour for ordinary comforts, though not engrossing like the toil of men in full employment in old and industrious societies, is sufficient to occupy the common faculties of mind and body. He is in danger, therefore of sinking into a state of listless and inglorious indolence, — a state in which whole communities may vegetate on an extensive surface, raising little surplus wealth, and each generation contenting itself with the habits and the enjoyments of that which preceded it.
>
> To counteract this tendency, he has only what may almost be termed the abstract desire of accumulation; I mean the desire of amassing wealth, unconnected with the passion for its enjoyment. If there are any to whom the strong influence of this motive, unreasonable as philosophy may hold it, appears strange and unaccountable, they must recollect that the mind, in an ordinary state of vigour, requires an excitement: it must have objects, hopes, occupations, apprehensions. Political institutions may so utterly deaden it as to extinguish them: there have been examples of whole societies thus arrested in the career of material civilization. But when these are good or tolerable, the love of accumulation must, in all communities, be among the most important sources of national activity, — in new communities, it is the only one. Money-making becomes the popular passion. The acquisition of wealth confers the only substantial title to public regard. As all talent seeks one and the same channel to exert itself, he who has best succeeded in this engrossing pursuit enjoys the double honour of being at once the most powerful and the cleverest citizen of the commonwealth.[2]

"The acquisition of wealth confers the only substantial title to public regard" — in one form, the thought is a tiresome, even if true, cliché of the contemners of American society; in another, it is an aspect of American society, derived from its colonial origins, that is offered in explanation of its rapid economic growth.

In the early summer of 1853 the yacht *North Star,* bearing on board the most renowned American businessman of the day, Commodore Cornelius Vanderbilt, steamed into the port of London in the course of a world cruise. The occasion provided the London *Daily News* an opportunity to explain why men of his type had greater prestige in the United States than in England:

> America . . . is the great arena in which the individual energies of man, uncramped by oppressive social institutions, or absurd social traditions, have full play, and arrive at gigantic development. . . .
>
> It is the tendency of American institutions to foster the general welfare, and to permit the unchecked powers of the highly gifted to occupy a place in the general framework of society which they can obtain nowhere else. The great feature to be noted in America is that all its citizens have full permission to run the race in which Mr. Vanderbilt has gained such immense prizes. In other countries, on the contrary, they are trammelled by a thousand restrictions. . . .
>
> Your men of rank here — your makers of millions for themselves and tens of millions for the country — too often spend their time, their intellect, their labor, in order that they may be able to take rank among a class of men who occupy their present position in virtue of what was done for them by some broadshouldered adventurer, who, fortunately for them, lived eight hundred years ago in Normandy . . . Here is the great difference between the two countries. In England a man is too apt to be ashamed of having made his own fortune, unless he has done so in one of the few roads which the aristocracy condescend to travel — the bar, the church, or the army.
>
> It is time that the *millionaire* should cease to be ashamed of having made his own fortune. It is time the *parvenu* should be looked on as a word of honor. It is time that the middle classes should take the place which is their own, in the world which they have made. The middle classes have made the modern world. The Montmorencis, the Howards, the Percys, made the past world — and they had their reward. Let them give place to better men.[3]

If the London *Daily News* is to be believed, the businessman was remaking the world, he was remaking it faster in the United States than elsewhere, and he was more rewarded for his efforts in the United States than in England. How do these facts of social behavior and social belief relate to the colonial condition singled out by both Adam Smith and Herman Merivale as decisive in explaining American economic growth?

The fact is that a broad spectrum of feudal and other restraints and restrictions, the absence of which, according to both Merivale and the London *Daily News*, was responsible for the rapid economic growth of the United States, was present at the start of our history.

Let a few illustrations serve for the many that could be cited.

Consider the words of the Fundamental Constitution of the Carolinas, written by John Locke:

> Each signiory, barony, and colony, shall consist of 12,000 acres; the eight signiories being the share of the eight proprietors, and the eight baronies of the nobility; both which shares being of them one fifth part of the whole, are to be perpetually annexed, the one to the proprietors, the other to the hereditary nobility. . . .[4]

Or consider the instructions given to Sir Thomas Gates by the Virginia Company on the eve of his departure to Jamestown in May 1609:

> You must devide yor people into tennes twenties & so upwards, to every necessary worke a competent nomber, over every one of w^{c}h you must appointe some man of Care & still in that worke to oversee them and to take dayly accounte of theire labours, and you must ordayne y^t every overseer of such a nomber of workemen Deliver once a weeke and accounte of the wholle comitted to his Charge . . . you shall doe best to lett them eate together at reasonable howers in some publique place beinge messed by six or five to a messe, in w^{c}h you must see there bee equality and sufficient that so they may come and retourne to their worke without any delay and have no cause to complain of measure or to excuse their idleness upon ye dressinge or want of diet. You may well allowe them three howers in a somers day and two in the winter, and shall call them together by Ringinge of a Bell and by the same warne them againe to worke.[5]

Each member of the society was allotted a fixed position; his behavior was expected to conform to the prescription for behavior, often written out, appropriate to that position; and the whole was to be held together by a rigid, sometimes even a military discipline.

Or, finally, consider the words of the patent relating to Canada issued by the King of France to the Sieur de la Roche in 1589: ". . . to grant lands in full propriety to all those to whom he may concede them; that is to say, to gentlemen and to those whom he may consider persons of merit, in the form of fiefs, chatellenies, earldoms, viscounties, baronies, and other dignities, to be holden to us in such manner as he shall consider due to the services performed by the respective parties, on the condition that they shall aid in the support and defence of the territories; and to other persons of inferior ranks, on such dues and annual rentals as he may deem just."[6]

What needs to be explained is why the forms of social organization implied by such statements — forms of social organization which imposed severe, even harsh, discipline to fix people permanently in the positions allotted them — changed so drastically and in so relatively short a time, and in ways calculated to release enormous quantities of human energy.

The keynote of all North American colonial societies in their initial stages was labor discipline, and the essential purpose of their institutions was to guarantee order and stability through the attachment of each person to the position allowed him by the provision of incentives to assure docility and sanctions to punish disobedience. Unlike the Spaniards, who established their New World societies in areas where there was already a large and, to a degree, tractable labor force, the English and French colonizers had to recruit their labor force. The concessions they offered to recruit and motivate a labor force that was adequate both quantitatively and qualitatively made it impossible here to reproduce the rigidity of social structure characteristic of contemporary Europe or to maintain for any considerable time the harshness and rigor characteristic of their initial efforts at society building. To discipline a labor force — that is to say, a society — was one thing; to recruit and motivate it, quite another. The solution that was adopted for the second problem made it impossible to solve the first problem in the anticipated way, and the result was a veritable social revolution in the early seventeenth-century colonies.

What the concessions were that were counted on to recruit and motivate a labor force varied considerably from time to time and from place to place: the importation of women to be distributed as wives (which converted a labor camp or barracks into a community); the granting of certain legal and political rights ("No man will go from hence to have less liberty there than here");[7] and the conscious distribution of land. It was above all easier access to land and, in some cases, to trade, that created in the minds of those who now possessed it for the first time a sense of the greater opportunities to be had by misbehavior rather than obedience, and made them reluctant to accept even the looser discipline that remained after the concessions had been offered.

Writing about the upstart behavior of Virginians, once landless, now landowners, Secretary of State John Pory wrote to Sir Dudley Carleton:

> Our cowekeeper here of James Citty on Sundays goes accowtered all in freshe flamminge silke; and a wife of one that in England had professed the black arte, not of a scholler, but of a collier of Croydon, wears her rough bever hatt with a faire perl hat band.[8]

And all this despite the fact that the Virginia Company, through enactment of sumptuary legislation, sought to give visible symbols indicative of the social status to which it attempted to attach each person. The signal that the rigorous discipline the Virginia Company sought to impose could not survive the granting of the concessions offered to recruit a labor force came when those sworn to uphold that discipline — the very leaders of the Company — subverted it. "The servants you allow them," Captain John Smith informed the Company concerning its officials in Virginia, "they plant on their private lands, not upon that belongeth to their office, which crop alwaies exceeds yours, besides those which are your tenants to halfes, are forced to row them up and downe, whereby both you and they lose more then halfe."[9]

In New England, the discipline that had been counted on at the start to hold the society together had been somewhat different from the constraints imposed in Virginia. It was less external, more a matter of the voluntary acceptance of certain moral and religious standards, but the fact is that whatever its character and however it was imposed, it, too, could not withstand the corrosive effects of the concessions offered to raise the level of motivation of the labor force. The same body of Puritan religious precepts that had systematized the virtues making for economic success had attempted to check their free play in behalf of what was felt to be "the good of the community" and the need to avoid the sins of self-indulgence and sensuality. But the opportunities for the economic exploitation of the New World magnified the first aspect of Puritan doctrine and stunted the other, encouraged behavior that derived from the first and discouraged behavior that followed from the other, and resulted eventually in the destruction of what the Puritans had intended to be a disciplined Bible commonwealth.

How corrosive were the mechanisms counted upon to raise the level of motivation can be illustrated by reference to only two documents.

In 1653, Captain Robert Keayne, one of the richest Boston merchants of his period, wrote a 158-page will in which he attempted to justify the behavior that, years before, had resulted in his being censured for having been drunk and for having sold his goods at too high a price. Too much, perhaps, may be read into Keayne's concern with quantitative considerations even in a discussion of normative judgments. In his request that his executors petition the General Court for a reversal of the judgment against him over-charging, he says:

> And were it possible for me to know it [the reversal of judgment] certainly before I die (though it be not for the love of the money, nor for addition to my estate by it, though it was a considerable sum about 80 pounds as I remember) it would much ease and refresh my spirit in respect to the equity of it.

But it would be difficult to read too much into his resolution of the dilemma in which he found himself as a result of the discrepancy between the £4,000 of property that he disposed of in his will and the £1,000 of property that he declared himself as owning for tax purposes. One need not declare one's whole estate to be taxed, he wrote, "if he can honestly prevent it."

It is significant that Keayne ultimately justified himself in terms of the behavior that was most destructive of the social restraints characteristic of Puritan society, ceaseless energy and constant striving in economic matters: "My account books will testify to the world on my behalf that I have not lived an idle, lazy, or dronish life nor spent my time wantonly, fruitlessly or in company-keeping as some have been too ready to asperse me or that I have had in my own time . . . many spare hours to spend unprofitably away or to refresh myself with recreations . . . but have rather studied and endeavored to redeem my time as a thing most dear and precious to me and have often denied myself in such refreshings that otherwise I might lawfully have made use of."[10]

In 1653, the same year in which Keayne wrote his will, William Bradford was reading over the history he had written of Plymouth Plantation. When he came to what he had written for the year 1617, he read that the Pilgrims had pledged themselves to continue as they were, "knite togeather as a body in a most stricte and sacred bond and covenante of the Lord . . . straitly tied to all care of each other's good, and of the whole by every one and so mutually." When he reached that passage he turned the page and wrote on the back: "But (alass) that subtill serpent hath slylie wound in himselfe under faire pretences of necessitie and the like, to untwiste these sacred bonds and tyes, and as it were insensibly by degrees to dissolve, or in a great measure to weaken, the same."[11]

What Bradford did not realize was that the "subtill serpent" which he felt was responsible for the destruction of Pilgrim character and Pilgrim society had, in the first instance, been invited into the community to help that society get established. At the outset, when fields had been tilled in common and the produce equally shared, Bradford tells us, the harvests were poor; the young refused to work for the old, some wives objected that their husbands were, in fact, working for other women. "The experience that was had in this common course and condition, tried sundrie years, and that amongst godly and sober men," Bradford writes, "may well evince the vanitie of that conceite of Plato's and other ancients, applauded by some of later times; — that the taking away of propertie, and bringing in community into a commonwealth, would make them happy and flourishing. . . . For this communitie . . . was found to breed much confusion and discontent, and retard much imployment that would have been to their benefite and comfort."[12] To raise the level of labor productivity, the land was divided and given out in individual plots. And now Bradford learned, to his dismay, that the dissolving effects of economic opportunity could not be restricted solely to the realm of the economy, that the moral discipline of Puritanism could not withstand corrosion.

The same process by which a rigid social structure was exploded can be seen perhaps even more dramatically in the case of French Canada in the seventeenth century. Feudalism in French Canada was not a replica of French feudalism nor was it ever intended to be. Whatever we choose to call it, however, the fact is that those who created that society made every effort to fix people firmly into particular positions, defined the behavior appropriate to those positions, and used every device of religious and secular authority to compel obedience. What the French government wanted to create was an agricultural society the major characteristic of which, the seignorial system, was designed in such a way as to attach people firmly to the land by providing incentives for docility. What it got was something quite different. Faced with the necessity of offering concessions to induce a labor force to migrate, the authorities reduced the privileges of the seigniors, for fear that to reproduce them in Canada would discourage the peasants from migrating, and increased the privileges of the peasants, especially the right of access to land, in the hope thereby of providing incentives for immigration and hard work. What happened was that the seigniors, deprived of the opportunity to profit from the system they were sworn to uphold, began to behave not as their roles prescribed but as conditions seemed to require. Instead of confining themselves to agricultural activities, they used the land for speculation or deserted it in increasing numbers to go to the forest where they became trappers and fur traders. For the peasants, easier access to land and the same opportunities to make a quick killing in the fur trade meant an improvement in their position, compared with what it had been in France, but these added opportunities were no less destructive of the society of status and order that the authorities had established.

In 1712 Gédéon de Catalogne, a military engineer, made a survey of the more than ninety seigniories that then existed in Canada. Excluding those granted to religious orders (which were held in perpetuity), it is possible by comparing the owners of the seigniories in 1712 with those to whom they were originally granted to arrive at some estimate of the degree to which the barriers of privilege and aristocracy were melting away. Of the 76 secular grants for which it is possible to find the names both of the original grantees and the owners in 1712, only 45 were in the hands of the same family. Of all grants issued between 1620 and 1670, only 52 per cent were in the hands of the same family; of those issued between 1670 and 1710, 62 per cent were in the hands of the original family. In a sense, therefore, time was on the side of social mobility. Equally significant, it is possible to determine from Catalogne's report that of the 76 secular seigniories in 1712, at least 22 were in the hands of families that were bourgeois or lower in origin.[13] Under these circumstances it was impossible to retain the censitaire in the same subordinate position that had characterized his situation in France or even in the higher — though still subordinate — situation it had been the intention of the authorities of the new society to give him. Indeed, he rejected the very term "censitaire" because of its connotations of servility, and succeeded in having himself referred to even in official documents simply as "habitant."[14] The circle was complete when what had once been regarded as deviance came to be regarded as the norm. "I believe," wrote Intendant Denonville to Colbert, "that Mons. should not determine to cease giving letters of nobility, but it would be well to give them only to those who will enter whatever commerce makes a noble in this country."[15] In 1685, the Canadian noblesse, which had been created as the apex of a system of landed ranks and orders, was permitted without derogation of rank to engage in any form of trade.

To summarize the argument thus far: (1) The earliest societies established in North America were intended to have a degree of rigidity quite comparable, if not identical, to that characteristic of contemporary Europe. (2) Under such conditions of social rigidity it was impossible to recruit a voluntary labor force or motivate it to work with the desired will. (3) The concessions voluntarily granted by the leaders of the new societies — concessions that considerably loosened the restraints characteristic of European society — instead of having the effect they were intended to have (enlisting the allegiance of the labor force) weakened the feudal and corporate restraints of the first social order. (4) Position in the new society became primarily a function of direct economic activity, not of birth or privilege, and the greatest honors were offered to those whose activity had destroyed the old order.[16]

Put in a slightly different way, and in language that Herman Merivale would have understood, the possibility of social mobility — acquiring the wealth and status that gave claim to public regard — was a structural consequence of the colonial origins of American society, or, more precisely, of the peopling of that society through devices necessary to recruit a voluntary labor force.

The ideology that developed in connection with these changes in social structure — and ideology in which both social esteem and self-respect were largely dependent upon occupational success, in which ceaseless striving to transform the physical environment from an object of contemplation to an object for use was most highly rewarded — is an old story that needs no retelling, except perhaps to point out that its appearance in the most incongruous contexts is testimony to its persistence and strength. "The man lived in Philadelphia." wrote Mark Twain in his short story, "Poor Little Stephen Girard,"

> .... who, when young and poor, entered a bank, and says he: "Please, sir, don't you want a boy?" And the stately personage said: "No, little boy, I don't want a little boy." The little boy, whose heart was too full for utterance, chewing a piece of licorice stick he had bought with a cent stolen from his good and pious aunt, with sobs plainly audible, and with great globules of water rolling down his cheeks, glided silently down the marble steps of the bank. Bending his noble form, the bank man dodged behind a door, for he thought the little boy was going to shy a stone at him. But the little boy picked up something, and stuck it in his poor but ragged jacket. "Come here, little boy," and the little boy did come here; and the bank man said: "Lo, what pickest thou up?" And he answered and replied: "A pin." And the bank man said: "Little boy, are you good?" and he said he was. And the bank man said: "How do you vote? – excuse me, do you go to Sunday school?" and he said he did. Then the bank man took down a pen made of pure gold, and flowing with pure ink, and he wrote on a piece of paper, "St. Peter;" and he asked the little boy what it stood for, and he said "Salt Peter." Then the bank man said it meant "Saint Peter." The little boy said: "Oh!"
>
> Then the bank man took the little boy to his bosom, and the little boy said, "Oh!" again, for he squeezed him. Then the bank man took the little boy into partnership, and gave him half of the profits and all the capital, and he married the bank man's daughter, and now all he has is all his, and all his own too.
>
> My uncle told me this story, and I spent six weeks in picking up pins in front of a bank. I expected the bank man would call me in and say: "Little boy, are you good?" and I was going to say "Yes," and when he asked me what "St. John" stood for, I was going to say "Salt John." But the bank man wasn't anxious to have a partner; and I guess the daughter was a son, for one day says he to me: "Little boy, what's that you're picking up?" Says I, awful meekly, "Pins." Says he: "Let's see 'em." And he took 'em, and I took off my cap, all ready to go in the bank, and become a partner, and marry his daughter. But I didn't get an invitation. He said: "Those pins belong to the bank, and if I catch you hanging around here any more I'll set the dog on you!" Then I left, and the mean old fellow kept the pins. Such is life as I find it.[17]

Such was life as acidulous Mark Twain found it, but countless thousands found American social reality more accurately summed up in the biography, prepared by his friends, of one Antonio Lombardo, an immigrant who made good in the Promised Land:

> Mr. Lombardo came to America twenty-one years ago. He was one of hundreds who cheered joyously when, from the deck of the steamer, they saw the Statue of Liberty and the skyline of New York, their first

sight of the fabled land, America. . . . In his heart was a great hope and a great ambition.

After he had landed he paid his railroad fare to Chicago and came here with just $12 as his initial capital. Mr. Lombardo, however, accepted the hardships as part of the game, and with confidence in his own ability and assurance of unlimited opportunities began his career. He became an importer and exporter. His political influence is due largely to his interest in civic affairs and improving standards of living. . . . Like most successful men he has received much but has given more to the community in which he lives. It is to such men that America owes her greatness.[18]

The cream of the jest — and the grip of the ideology — become clear when we realize that Mr. Lombardo was no ordinary businessman, but one of the leaders of the Chicago Mafia.

Even if it were conceded that American social structure has been characterized by a high degree of fluidity for the reasons suggested here and that American values place great stress on the importance of mobility and economic success, it would still be necessary to show the mechanisms by means of which these facts of structure and ideology influence behavior. Much of the research in economic development and modernization in recent years has been devoted precisely to discovering the linkages between the data of social structure and values, on the one hand, and those of behavior, on the other. Let me here mention briefly only two aspects of American society and history that, as it were, institutionalized and powerfully reinforced the value system we have been speaking of.

The law, as we know, is an institutional factor that exercises an immediate and direct influence on the course of economic development, positively, by permitting, even encouraging, certain forms of activity, negatively, by imposing sanctions against other kinds. If then, we can find that during the nineteenth century the law as an institution was directly influenced by those aspects of American society we have been discussing — fluidity of social structure and high prestige accorded business success — we shall have located one of the important intervening variables with which we are concerned, for we shall then have discovered one of the forms through which facts of social structure and value bore directly on the making of economic decisions.

Thanks largely to the work of Professor James Willard Hurst, it is possible to say — and in more than a gross way — that nineteenth-century American law ratified social structure and social values, so to speak, and, having institutionalized them materially affected the rate of economic development.[19] The way in which the law expressed a decided preference for property as an institution for growth rather than security, the way in which law was deliberately created so as to establish a system of priorities among competing uses of scarce working capital, the way in which the law threw its weight on the side of rapid change rather than on the side of a slow rate of growth in which consideration was given to the effects on future generations of the behavior of the present generation — all of this had a profound effect in providing a salubrious climate for economic growth. The lengths to which the law went in contributing to this climate of security gave rise to the reaction with which we are all familiar. "The Fourteenth Amendment," Justice Holmes said, "does not enact Mr. Herbert Spencer's Social Statics . . . . a constitution is not intended to embody a particular economic theory. . . ." To which dissenting view the imperturbable majority might have replied in former Justice John A. Campbell's words, encapsulating a value, indeed even a version of history, in the law: "What did the colonists and their posterity seek for and obtain by their settlement of this continent; their long contest with physical evils that attended their colonial condition; their long and wasting struggle for independence . . .? Freedom. Free action, free enterprise — free competition."[20]

The oft-repeated event of American history which, as I have implied, confirmed this system of values is, of course, immigration. The effect of immigration on the establishment of certain trades and industries, what immigration meant by way of providing necessary skills and capital, its relation to the business cycle and to the introduction of machinery — much of this is now known. What I should like to do is to speculate very briefly about the consequences of immigration for the creation of labor discipline.

One aspect of that relationship — the way in which advantage could be taken of competing nationalities in order to squeeze more production out of them — is epitomized in the statement of the superintendent of Carnegie's Braddock mill in 1875: "We must steer clear as far as we can of Englishmen, who are great sticklers for high wages, small production and strikes. My experience has shown that Germans and Irish, Swedes and what I denominate 'Buckwheats' — young American country boys, judiciously mixed, make the most effective and tractable force you can find."[21] I have been told by men who worked in the automobile industry in the 1920's and 1930's that there was then practiced what they called the Balkanization of the assembly line — placing a foreman of one nationality over workmen of another so that ethnic loyalty would not interfere with the main task of production.

But this aspect of the relationship was, I am sure, less important than another — the way in which, under conditions of constant immigration, the method of proving one's American nationality came to be acceptance of the social structure and values in which American economic development had taken place. How to prove one's Americanness has never been an easy problem, but it has been especially difficult for the labor movement. Has the labor movement of any other country had to prove, in quite the same way, that it was English or French or Italian, as American workers have had to prove that they are American? With the passage of time, the criterion of American nationality shifted from what it seemed to be at the start of our national history — immigration indicated a willingness to cut all the ties that bound the immigrant to an older set of loyalties — to a more active test — a demonstration of willingness to accept the system of values within which American enterprise has developed was expected. As one magazine editor put it with crystal clarity, "You cannot be against the capitalistic system and still for America; you cannot apologize for that system or feel ashamed of it and still be a good American. You cannot indeed be a good American in the sense of being loyal to American traditions, unless you are proud of the capitalistic system."[22] If to believe this was the prerequisite for being an American, it would be difficult to conceive of any more subtle — or powerful — means of converting an immigrant population into a disciplined labor force.

In an inconspicuous footnote in *Middletown in Transition*, the Lynds quote the following passage from Spengler's *Decline of the West*: "He [the French peasant] has sat on his glebe from primeval times, or has fastened his clutch in it, to adhere to it with his blood. He is rooted in it as the descendant of his forbears and as the forbear of future descendants. *His* house, *his* property, means, here, not the temporary connexion of person and thing for a brief span of years, but an enduring and inward union of *eternal* land and *eternal* blood." To which the Lynds add, matter-of-factly, "The farmers in the Middletown's county may feel a weak dilution of this sentiment, but to most Middletown people the French farmer's devotion to the glebe of his ancestors would seem a fine, loyal sentiment but rather unenterprising."[23]

All things change with time, but some change more than others.

NOTES

1. Adam Smith, *An Inquiry into the Nature and Cause of the Wealth of Nations*, James E. Thorold, ed. (2nd. ed.; Oxford: Clarendon Press, 1880), pp. 144-45.
2. Herman Merivale, *Lectures on Colonization and Colonies* (London: Oxford University Press, 1928), pp. 612-13.
3. London *Daily News*, June 4, 1853, quoted in John Overton Choules, *The Cruise of the Steam Yacht North Star* (Boston: Gould & Lincoln, 1854), pp. 58-61.
4. Old South Leaflets No. 172, p. 2.
5. Susan Myra Kingsbury, ed., *Records of the Virginia Company* (Washington: U.S. Government Printing Office, 1906-35), III, 21.
6. William B. Munro, *Documents Relating to the Seigniorial Tenure in Canada, 1548-1854*. Publications of the Champlain Society, III (Toronto: The Champlain Society, 1908), pp. 1-3.

7. Quoted in Perry Miller, "Religion and Society in the Early Literature: The Religious Impulse in the Founding of Virginia," *William and Mary Quarterly*, 3d. ser., vol. VI (1949), p. 37.
8. Lyon Gardiner Tyler, ed., *Narratives of Early Virginia* (New York: C. Scribner's Sons, 1907), p. 285.
9. John Smith, *The Generale Historie of Virginia*, in Tyler, *Narratives*, p. 356.
10. The quotations from the will are to be found in Bernard Bailyn, ed., *The Apologia of Robert Keayne* (New York: Harper Torchbook, 1965), pp. 51, 83, 73-74.
11. *Bradford's "Of Plimoth Plantation"* (Boston: Wright & Potter, 1928), p. 42.
12. *Ibid.*, p. 163.
13. The figures are computed from Catalogne's report, in Munro, *Documents*, pp. 94-150.
14. A. L. Burt, "The Frontier in the History of New France," *Annual Report of the Canadian Historical Association for 1940* (Toronto: University of Toronto Press, 1940), p. 96; Paul-Emile Renaud, *Les Origines économiques du Canada* (Mamers: Enault, 1928), p. 370.
15. Quoted in S. D. Clark, *The Social Development of Canada* (Toronto: University of Toronto Press, 1932), p. 72.
16. The argument advanced here has been developed at greater length in Sigmund Diamond, "From Organization to Society: Virginia in the Seventeenth Century," *The American Journal of Sociology*, LXIII (March 1958), 457-75; Diamond, "An Experiment in 'Feudalism': French Canada in the Seventeenth Century," *The William and Mary Quarterly*, 3d. ser., vol. XVIII (Jan. 1961), pp. 3-34; Diamond, "Le Canada Francaise au xvii siècle: Une société prefabriquée," *Annales*, XVI (March-April 1961), 317-54.
17. Anna Randall-Diehl, ed., *Carleton's Popular Readings* (New York: G. W. Carleton Co., 1879), pp. 183-84.
18. Quoted in Fred D. Pasley, *Al Capone: The Biography of a Self-Made Man* (Garden City, N.Y.: Garden City Publishing Co., 1930), pp. 226-27.
19. See especially James Willard Hurst, *Law and the Conditions of Freedom in the Nineteenth-Century United States* (Madison: University of Wisconsin Press, 1956) and *Law and Economic Growth: The Legal History of the Lumber Industry in Wisconsin, 1836-1915* (Cambridge: Harvard University Press, 1964).
20. The quotations may be found in Benjamin Twiss, *Lawyers and the Constitution* (Princeton: Princeton University Press, 1942), pp. 54, 137.
21. James H. Bridge, *The Inside Story of the Carnegie Steel Company* (New York: The Aldine Book Company, 1903), p. 81.
22. Quoted in *The New Republic*, XXI (Dec. 24, 1919), p. 120.
23. Robert S. Lynd and Helen M. Lynd, *Middletown in Transition: A Study in Cultural Conflict* (New York: Harcourt, Brace & Co., 1937), p. 189.

chapter **3**

elements of economic growth (continued)

ECONOMIC THEORY AND ECONOMIC GROWTH

THE SOURCES OF GROWTH

Economic growth is a function of the quantity and quality of resources possessed by a nation, and the efficiency with which these resources are used. Assuming full employment, a nation experiences real gains in output by increasing the quantity of land, labor, capital, and entrepreneurial resources, *i.e.*, factor inputs, or increasing the productive efficiency of these resources, *i.e.*, productivity, or both. In U.S. economic history, land acquisitions and the westward movement of the frontier increased the quantity of land, high rates of population growth added to the labor supply and entrepreneurial inputs, and savings by individuals and businesses increased the quantity of capital. Productivity gains resulted from technological change, increases in the scale of output, and improvements in the quality of factor inputs, especially labor. Technological change made possible the utilization of submarginal lands, enabled farmers to produce higher yields from a given quantity of land, created new and improved capital equipment to assist in production, made feasible the construction of efficient systems of transportation and communication, and modernized the organization and direction of the production process. Increases in the scale of output enabled producers to practice specialization and division of labor, to spread their overhead cost and to utilize by-products more effectively. The quality of labor was enhanced by increased and improved education, training, nutrition and health care.

A simplified example illustrates the role of increased resources and productivity in economic growth. Assume: (1) an economy which produces only one type of output and utilizes only two inputs, labor and capital; (2) the inputs are fairly good substitutes for one another; (3) the economy exhibits constant return to scale, i.e., a given percentage of increase in labor and capital causes output to increase by exactly the same percentage; (4) the economy is perfectly competitive; and (5) for the moment, there are no technological innovations or other changes that can cause productivity increases. Thus, any increase in real output depends on increases in labor and capital; and the rate of economic growth y depends on the rate of increase in labor l and capital k. To determine the influence of l and k on y, their relative importance to real output must be ascertained. If labor's share of output a is 0.67 and capital's share b is 0.33, then the basic equation is

$$y = a \cdot l + b \cdot k.$$

This equation states that the economy's rate of growth is the weighted sum of the growth rates of labor and capital. Assume that l increases by one per cent per year and k by four per cent, then:

$$y = 0.67 \,(0.01) + 0.33 \,(0.04)$$
$$= 0.67 + 1.32$$
$$= 1.99.$$

Thus the annual rate of economic growth is 1.99 or roughly two per cent. If the assumption that there is no productivity change is dropped and it is ascertained that annual productivity gains enable y to increase by an additional 2.1 per cent per year, then:

$$y = 0.67 + 1.32 + 2.1$$
$$= 4.0.$$

Thus the economy's annual rate of growth is four per cent.

Kendrick[1] estimates that from 1889 to 1957 the U.S. economy grew at an annual rate of 3.5 per cent. During this period both factor inputs and total productivity increased by about 1.7 per cent per year. Thus about half the growth in real gross product was contributed by increases in real labor and capital inputs and half by increases in productivity. Up to 1919, however, productivity contributed only one-third of the output gains, whereas after 1919 the situation was reversed with productivity accounting for two-thirds of economic growth. The increased importance of productivity is attributable to a slowdown in the growth of inputs and an increase in the rate of productivity advance. As is discussed later, there was a marked decrease in the rate of population growth following World War I, which slowed the growth of labor; and the depression decade of the 1930's together with World War II sharply reduced the rate of capital formation.

PRODUCTIVITY

Because of the relative ease of measuring labor time — hours of work — productivity in terms of output per man-hour is the most common productivity measure. The numerator, physical output, includes the output from all sources and reflects not only labor time, skill, morale, training and resourcefulness, but also changes in the quantity and quality of capital, entrepreneurial skills, technology, and the like. The denominator is labor time, measured in unweighted man-hours. And although it is only a partial productivity measure, it should be noted that labor is the most important production factor, accounting in the U.S. economy for about three-fourths of total input costs. Kendrick estimates that physical output per unweighted man-hour for the private economy increased at an annual rate of 2.4 per cent from 1889 to 1957; or about twenty-five per cent per decade. (See Table 3.1.) As noted above, the data indicate that productivity did not gain at an even rate. A distinct increase in the productivity rate occurred after World War I. Evidence is also available that there has been a further acceleration of productivity since the end of World War II. The Bureau of Labor Statistics index of output per (unweighted) man-hour for the 1947-1970 period indicates an average annual increase of approximately 3.2 per cent. It should be noted, however, that any attempt to characterize this changed growth rate as a new trend is fraught with danger. Productivity gains from year to year and from period to period have been far from uniform. Trend rates derived from one period differ, sometimes considerably, from those derived from a shorter or longer period. Moreover, our past history indicates that periods of high trend often alternated with periods of low trend.

To obtain a more valid relationship between factor inputs and output, an hour of work of a skilled person should be counted more heavily than an unskilled man-hour. This allows for changes in the composition and quality of labor due to differences in levels of educa-

TABLE 3.1. *Average Rates of Increase in Productivity for the Private Domestic Economy 1889–1957*

| | Average Annual Percentage Rate of Change | | |
	1889–1957	*1889–1919*	*1919–1957*
Physical output per unweighted man-hour	2.4	2.0	2.6
Physical output per weighted man-hour	2.0	1.6	2.3
Physical output per weighted unit of tangible capital	1.0	0.5	1.3
Physical output per weighted unit of labor and capital combined	1.7	1.3	2.1

SOURCE: John W. Kendrick. *Productivity Trends in the United States.* New York: National Bureau of Economic Research, 1961.

tion, training, and experience. On this basis the productivity advance from 1889 to 1957 was somewhat slower, averaging 2.0 per cent per year. If a weighted unit of tangible capital is combined with a weighted

FIGURE 3.1. *Total Factor Productivity 1875 – 1957*

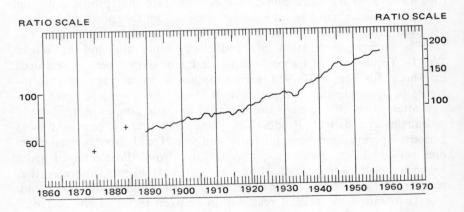

SOURCE: U.S. Bureau of the Census, *Long Term Economic Growth, 1860 – 1965.* (Washington: U.S. Government Printing Office, 1966).

man-hour, an additional refinement is achieved. This provides a so-called total productivity index since it allows for factor substitution which may account for some of the rise in output per man-hour. On this basis the productivity increase is further reduced to an annual average of 1.7 per cent. (See Table 3.1 and Figure 3.1.)

CLASSICAL GROWTH THEORY

Economic growth has always been a central concern of economic inquiry. Yet there is no universally accepted theory of economic growth. The state of the economic art, differences among nations as to their level of economic development, and the great variety of prevailing political, social, and cultural systems have thus far prevented the evolution of an eclectic theory of economic growth. The Classical School of economics, which was formally launched by Adam Smith, has a supply-oriented growth theory. The school prospered during the late 1700's and early 1800's when the Industrial Revolution had not yet provided sufficient goods and services to satisfy the basic needs of people in even the most developed economies. By today's standards, when so much of what we consume is discretionary, the "rich" nations of that period were goods-starved economies. Small wonder that so much attention was given to the need to produce more goods and services.

To the Classicists, the presence of scarcity precluded the existence of idle resources except in the most unusual of circumstances. Full employment of labor and capital was regarded as the natural state of affairs. Unemployment, if it did occur, was a temporary phenomenon generally owing to a momentary lack of confidence generated by some shock externally imposed on the economy. This viewpoint was formalized in 1803 by the French popularizer of Adam Smith, Jean Baptiste Say, in his famous law of markets. Simply stated, the law holds that the act of producing a good generates just enough income to permit the purchase of that good. Since the economy was held to be nothing more than the sum of its parts, national output would be matched by national demand. Thus, supply creates its own demand.

The Smithian prescription for economic growth was a healthy dosage of free enterprise, specialization, division of labor, and free trade. In particular, Smith stressed the need to replace the blundering hand of mercantilist governments with the invisible hand of self-interest and the competitive spirit. His writings were significantly expanded by Thomas Malthus and David Ricardo. Indeed, classical growth theory is largely grounded on the Malthusian theory of population and the Ricardian law of diminishing returns. The former holds that there is a natural tendency for population growth to outstrip the growth of agricultural output. The latter observes that as more labor is applied to a given area of land the additional increments to output first rise, but ultimately diminish. In the Classicist view the interaction of these two forces leads a nation in time to a state of maturity when further economic growth is no longer possible. Assuming an underdeveloped economy where population and the quantity of capital are small relative to the amount of land under cultivation, high wages, high profits and low rent prevail. High profits lure entrepreneurs to high levels of capital formation, which in turn promote demand for labor and keep wage payments rising. In the face of high wages, laborers are induced to procreate, population grows, more land is taken under cultivation for food supply, and lands currently being tilled are more intensively cultivated. But owing to the law of diminishing returns and the inferior fertility of additional land brought under cultivation, the productivity of land declines. To maintain the same output from an acre of land more input must be expended. This means increased costs of production and higher food prices. Higher food prices require higher wages which, coupled with growing capital accumulation, generate falling profits. Capital accumulation ceases when profits fall to such low levels that businessmen are no longer attracted to investment ventures. The labor force continues to expand as long as wages remain above subsistence levels. This fact, however, causes the labor force to grow at a faster rate than the demand for it, which in turn causes wages to fall. Once the latter reaches subsistence, no further growth occurs in population. In such a state both population growth and net capital accumulation cease. Economic growth is no longer possible and in Classicist terminology the economy has reached a stationary state.

MARXIAN GROWTH THEORY

Marxian growth theory, which builds on classical theory, takes a far more pessimistic view of the long-term outlook for capitalist society. To Marx, it was inevitable that an economy pass through a number of stages on its road to maturity. Out of feudalism there emerges capitalism, socialism, and finally, communism. It is internal stress within feudalism and capitalism that, in Marx's view, leads to their downfall. Under feudalism the stress centers on the conflict between serfs and lords of the manor. As serfs acquire their freedom they gravitate to budding towns, where they become laborers and entrepreneurs. Their hostility to manorial lords, and their desire for a strong central government which will promote the best interests of business, leads them to support the establishment of an all-powerful monarchy. With law, order, and central government established, the raison d'être and power of manorial lords declines. As these decline, enclosure movements displace serfs from the land and drive them to the cities, where they supply the labor force needed for developing industry.

In the early stages of capitalism, heavy investment occurs, triggered by the reward of high profits. As the process proceeds, competitive pressures arise which cause the profits of businessmen to fall. In an attempt to maintain profits, businessmen are induced to introduce labor-saving machines, thus creating unemployment. The situation worsens as many businessmen are driven to bankruptcy by an inability to compete. The remaining firms accumulate more and more capital in their pursuit of mechanization, the ranks of the unemployed swell, and the size of existing businesses grows. Those workers fortunate enough to be working are increasingly at the mercy of fewer and larger companies who pay their employees only subsistence wages. Business crises, part of the process of capitalist development, grow increasingly severe as the system produces an increasing quantity of goods that cannot be bought owing to inadequate wage incomes and massive unemployment. Economic misery grows until open revolution results. At this point the state assumes the operation of the few giant business enterprises that remain, and the third stage of economic development, socialism, commences. In time there occurs a gradual "withering away of the state," which is replaced by a worker controlled utopian state, communism.

THE SCHUMPETERIAN CONCEPT OF DEVELOPMENT

To the twentieth century economist Joseph Schumpeter, socialism was also an inevitable outgrowth of capitalism. This is not, however, because capitalism would generate increasing class misery. On the contrary, it is due to the very success of the system in producing a relatively affluent and democratic society. The individual most responsible for this progress is the innovator. He is the business genius who is responsible for the creation of new products, the improvement of existing products, and the development of new markets. Economic growth is the direct result of such innovations and the rate at which they occur. The giant business firms which are the hallmark of twentieth century capitalism are the products of these innovators who create them for financial exploitation of their innovations. In time, these firms outlive their founders and continue to grow under the guidance of salaried executives, who actively engage in research and product planning. The result is a growing abundance of goods and services.

As the average worker experiences the fruits of increased output, he seeks to guarantee and extend his gains through demands for a welfare state. Forgetting the source of his material comfort, he attacks the captains of industry as men of unbridled greed whose actions are motivated by the pursuit of personal profit rather than the best interests of society. In his attack the worker is aided by the intellectual. Regulation of business enterprise is demanded. The salaried executive, himself only a highly-paid employee of the company he directs, offers only feeble opposition. Left without any adequate defenders, the bastion of capitalism is taken, though the capture is effected through erosion rather than revolution. Step by step the state encroaches on economic activity until the day of the rugged individualists becomes a mere memory.

ROSTOW'S STAGES OF ECONOMIC DEVELOPMENT

Not all theories of development based on a stages concept of history view the downfall of capitalism as an inevitable or even a likely occurrence. Rostow's view of growth, for example, does not rely on any one type of ideology or economic system for its logic. The Rostovian scheme encompasses five stages. The first stage, the Traditional Society, has as its hallmark low productivity. The society has a fatalistic view of life which accepts things as they are. When this attitude changes, progress becomes possible, and the second stage, Precondition for Takeoff, is achieved. In the third stage, Takeoff, requirements for sustained growth such as transportation and power networks are constructed, and technological breakthroughs make their appearance. The United States is viewed as having been in this phase from about 1840 to 1860. During the takeoff level a savings rate equal to at least ten per cent of national income is generated. This is necessary for the financing of capital accumulation. The attitude of society is clearly pro-business. In the fourth stage, lasting from about 1860 to 1915 in the United States, there occurs a Drive to Maturity. Sustained progress occurs, primarily as a result of a significant percentage of national income — ten to twenty per cent — being plowed back into the economy for investment purposes. Output outstrips population growth. Finally, the Age of Mass Consumption is achieved. In this stage, high levels of discretionary income are generated, and consumption becomes increasingly directed towards durable goods and services.

KEYNESIAN AND POST-KEYNESIAN GROWTH THEORY

Keynesian theory provides the basis for most modern growth theory. Keynes, the most influential economist of the twentieth century, published his pathbreaking book, *The General Theory of Employment, Interest, and Money,* in 1936.

Prior to Keynes, the neoclassicists, inheritors of the classical economic tradition, believed that flexible prices and wages prevented sustained periods of excess capacity and unemployment. Assuming a perfectly competitive economy, a decline in the demand for goods and services causes the demand for labor to fall, resulting in unemployment and excess capacity. Wage rates fall and the costs of producing goods and services decline. Lower production costs permit lower product prices, thus stimulating consumer demand. Businessmen respond by increasing output and their demand for labor. Full employment is restored. This analysis failed to recognize the growing concentration of economic power in business, and the resulting inflexibility in prices and wages that characterized the twentieth century. Large business firms, in response to declines in demand for their output, continued the same price for their product and let output fall. The result was unemployment and underutilization of plant capacity. These fundamental changes in the economy required an equally fundamental revision of economic theory. Keynes filled the void. He postulated that the level of aggregate demand determines national output and employment. Aggregate demand (total spending) is composed of consumption C, which is a function of income Y, and investment I, which in turn is a function of the cost of acquiring funds and the expected rate of return. Y may be broken down into its component parts. It is either spent for consumption purposes C, or saved S. S, like C, is a function of income, rising and falling as income changes. Under equilibrium conditions, total spending equals total income, or $C + I = C + S$. Thus, at equilibrium, saving equals investment, or $S = I$. Assuming a propensity to consume eighty per cent of income ($C = 0.8Y$), and a level of investment of 200 billion dollars ($I = 200$), total income (Y) may be computed as follows:

$$C + I = Y$$
$$0.8Y + 200 = Y$$
$$0.2Y = 200$$
$$Y = 1,000.$$

If the propensity to consume equals 0.8, the propensity to save must equal 0.2. This means that the level of savings is equal to 200 billion dollars, or an amount identical to the level of investment. The economy at any one moment of time is in equilibrium. As equilibrium changes, so does the level of output and employment.

To Keynes, changes in investment spending, rather than price changes, were the principal force causing changes in equilibrium. An increase in investment generates income by some multiple of itself, the magnitude of the multiplier being determined by the marginal propensity to consume (the percentage of additional income used for consumption purposes). As income rises, both consumption and savings increase, until savings is once again equal to investment. Conversely, if investment falls, so does income, output, and employment, until savings equal investment. The economy always comes to equilibrium where planned S equals planned I. This may be at a position of full employment, but as Keynes observed, this need not be so. To achieve full employment, it may be necessary for government to influence the level of total spending through the use of monetary and fiscal policy. Assuming less than full employment, monetary policy involves increases in the quantity of money so that interest rates fall, thereby stimulating borrowing for consumption and investment purposes. There is no guarantee, however, that increasing the money supply will increase spending. Fiscal policy is more direct, since it involves increased government spending and tax decreases which stimulate consumption and investment.

Keynes' analysis is largely static in nature since it is concerned with the forces determining economic equilibrium at a moment in time. One of the most significant modern dynamic theories of growth was developed by Sir Roy Harrod of England and Evsey Domar of the United States. Both scholars, working independently, constructed similar growth models which rely heavily on Keynesian economics. Harrod and Domar observe that if the economy is to develop in an orderly manner, with planned savings equal to planned investment, growth must occur at a constant percentage rate mathematically equal to the propensity to save (the percentage of income saved) divided by the accelerator (the rate of change in investment spending generated by an increase in income). If growth exceeds this rate, proposed investment based on the accelerator outstrips the supply of savings and the economy moves explosively upward. If growth falls short of this rate, savings outstrip proposed investment and the economy moves downward. Assuming a propensity to save twenty per cent of last year's income, and a propensity to invest four times the change in income from last year to this year, we obtain an equilibrium rate of growth of five per cent, computed by dividing the propensity to save of 0.2 by the accelerator of 4. Table 3.2 shows that at a growth rate of five per cent, planned investment and planned savings remain equal. It is unlikely, however, that the economy would grow at a constant percentage. Government involvement in the economy could theoretically achieve a balanced rate of growth, but this assumes a knowledge of existing output, its past, current, and future growth, the propensity to save, and the accelerator, no small accomplishment.

TABLE 3.2. *Hypothetical National Income Growth*

Period	National Income	Change in National Income	Planned Investment	Planned Savings
1	$1000 billion	—	—	—
2	1050	$50 billion	$200 billion	$200 billion
3	1102.50	52.50	210	210
4	1157.60	55.10	220	220
5	1215.55	57.90	231.50	231.50

THE RECORD OF GROWTH

MEASUREMENT

Several aggregate statistical series exist for the measurement of economic growth. Modern attempts to develop these measures were pioneered in the 1920's and the 1930's. At the same time, researchers attempted to construct historical series of U.S. economic growth. The national income accounts constitute the most important measure of economic growth. The accounts consist of five specific measures. Gross national product (GNP) measures the total output of all goods and services in terms of their market prices. It is gross only in the sense that no allowances are made for durable goods (plant and equipment) consumed in the course of production. If capital consumption allowances, depreciation, obsolescence, and charges for accidental damage of fixed business capital are deducted from GNP, net national product is derived. When indirect business taxes (sales and excise levies) are deducted from net national product, national income is derived, which is the income — wages, profits, interest, and rent — earned by the factors of production. Personal income is the income accruing to all individuals in the economy. It is obtained by subtracting corporate income taxes, corporate savings and social security taxes from national income, and adding government transfer payments — social security benefits and interest on the national debt. From personal income, disposable personal income is computed by subtracting personal income taxes. Disposable personal income is either spent for consumption or saved. Historically, about 92-95 per cent of disposable personal income has been spent for consumption, with five to eight per cent having been saved.

Numerous problems confront the researcher who uses national income accounts as a measure of a nation's standard of living. In many developing economies the rate of population growth is so high that it may equal or exceed gains in GNP. Thus, some economists argue that population growth must be considered before a meaningful statement can be made about economic progress. Even if we divide GNP or national income by population, it provides only a rough measure of living standards since no account is taken of how income is distributed. Furthermore, national income statistics measure output in terms of market values in the year of production. Since the level of prices changes through time owing to inflation and deflation, a historical series measured in such terms may be distorted. To obtain a truer measure of output growth, the value of money should be kept constant. Dividing national income data by an appropriately weighted price index recomputes the data in real terms. The resultant constant dollar estimate, although it suffers from the inherent limitation of all index numbers, provides a more accurate picture of the real performance of the economy. Another problem is that national income statistics only measure market transactions. Goods and services produced for home consumption are not fully recorded. Thus, the statistics tend to understate true output, particularly in less developed economies where organized markets have not yet come into being. Then, too, national income estimates do not adequately reveal all costs of production. Changes in hours worked per week and other conditions of employment are not reflected. Similarly, exhaustion of national resources, restricted access to free goods (fresh air and clean water), and pressures on urban facilities are not recorded. Moreover, national income does not fully register changes in the quality or composition of national output. For example, improvements in the quality of medical care or the added utility of a new wonder drug are not adequately reflected. Finally, it is difficult to accurately estimate capital consumption allowances. Estimates are derived with little or no modification from private business accounts which are dubious on both theoretical and practical grounds. Generally, the value of a capital good is determined by the future service it is expected to render, discounted at an approximate rate of interest. Therefore, an estimate of capital's present value involves an approximation of the future. Such projections may easily prove false. Even if we ignore theoretical problems, price level and tax law changes may render even the most careful accounting estimates questionable. It also may be argued that since we deduct capital consumption allowances from GNP, we should deduct the value of all natural resources used up in production.

LONG-TERM U.S. ECONOMIC GROWTH

Unfortunately, only crude approximations of pre-Civil War national income are available. Their value lies in providing a rough guide to the early progress of American economic growth. They are presented in Table 3.3 along with population statistics in

TABLE 3.3. *National Income 1790–1860**

Year (1)	National Income (Current Prices) (Millions) (2)	National Income (Constant Prices) (Millions) (3)	Population (Millions) (4)	Per Capita Income (rounded) 2 ÷ 4 (5)	Real Per Capita Income (rounded) 3 ÷ 4 (6)
1790	$ 400	–	3.9	100	–
1800	600	$ 900	5.3	110	$170
1810	800	1,300	7.2	110	180
1820	875	1,700	9.6	90	180
1840	1,000	2,300	12.9	80	180
1850	2,500	6,000	23.3	110	260
1860	4,000	9,000	31.5	120	290

*The figures from column two fall approximately within mid-range of the conflicting statistics presently existing on pre-Civil War national income. (These conflicting statistics may be found in the source.) Column three was approximated from the general price level index used in Robert F. Martin, *National Income in the United States, 1799–1938* (New York: National Industrial Conference Board, 1939), p. 6. For a discussion of the controversy on pre-Civil War national income statistics see William N. Parker and Franklee Whartenby, "The Growth of Output Before 1840," in the source.

SOURCE: Paul B. Trescott. "The United States Government and National Income, 1790–1860." National Bureau of Economic Research Conference on Research in Income and Wealth, *Trends in the American Economy in the Nineteenth Century.* Princeton: Princeton University Press, 1960, p. 360.

order to permit a rough estimate of per capita income growth. The figures indicate that while national income in current prices grew steadily through the period, it was outpaced in the 1810's and 1820's by population growth, and that not until 1840 was the per capita income attained in 1800 once again achieved. Some economic historians challenge the accuracy of these estimates. They prefer the more optimistic conclusion evidenced by the real per capita income statistics which indicate a roughly constant living standard from 1800 to 1840. After 1840, both per capita and real per capita income show considerable growth. Fortunately, the figures after the Civil War are more reliable. They indicate a continuous secular growth in both real per capita GNP and per capita income. The former more than doubled in the period from 1869-1873 to 1907-1911, and then increased almost fourfold by 1970. The latter, which is available only from the turn of the twentieth century, increased more than threefold by the 1917-1921 period and then increased more than sixfold by 1970. (See Tables 3.4 and 3.5, and Figures 3.2, 3.3, 3.4 and 3.5.)

TABLE 3.4. *National Income 1869-1970*

| | Gross National Product | | National Income | | | |
Year (1)	Current $ (billions) (2)	Constant $ (1929 $) (billions) (3)	Current $ (billions) (4)	Population (millions) (5)	Real GNP Per Capita (rounded) (6)	Per Capita Income (rounded) (7)
1869–1873	6.7	9.1	–	39.9[1]	288.1	–
1877–1881	9.2	16.1	–	50.3[2]	320.0	–
1889–1893	13.5	27.3	–	63.1[3]	432.6	–
1897–1901	17.3	37.1	14.6	6.1[4]	487.5	191.9
1907–1922	31.6	55.0	27.2	92.4[5]	595.2	294.4
1917–1921	75.6	71.9	66.9	6.5[6]	675.1	628.2
1930	91.1	95.1	75.7	3.1	772.5	614.9
1940	100.6	121.0	81.6	132.0	916.7	618.2
1950	284.6	187.1	241.9	151.2	1237.4	1599.9
1960	502.6	239.9	414.5	180.0	1632.8	2302.8
1970	976.8	436.5	801.0	205.4	2124.9	3899.7

[1] 1870 population; [2] 1880 population; [3] 1890 population; [4] 1900 population; [5] 1910 population; [6] 1920 population.

SOURCE: (1) U.S. Bureau of the Census. *The Historical Statistics of the United States Colonial Times to 1957, Continuation to 1962 and Revisions.* Washington, D.C.: U.S. Government Printing Office, 1965, pp. 7, 139. (2) *1971 Economic Report of the President.* Washington, D.C.: U.S. Government Printing Office, 1971.

TABLE 3.5. *National Income and Product 1929-1970*

| Year | Real Gross National Product Billions of 1958 Dollars | Billions of Current Dollars | | | |
		Gross National Product	Net National Product	National Income	Disposable Income
1929	203.6	103.1	95.2	86.8	83.3
1931	169.3	75.8	68.0	59.7	64.0
1933	141.5	55.6	48.6	40.3	45.5
1935	169.5	72.7	65.4	57.2	58.5
1937	203.2	90.4	83.3	73.7	71.2
1938	192.9	84.7	77.4	67.4	65.5
1939	209.4	90.5	83.2	72.6	73.0
1940	227.2	99.7	92.2	81.1	75.7
1941	263.7	124.5	116.3	104.2	92.7
1942	297.8	157.9	148.1	137.1	116.9
1943	337.1	191.6	181.3	170.3	133.5
1944	361.3	210.1	199.1	182.6	146.3
1945	355.2	212.0	200.7	181.5	152.0
1946	312.6	208.5	198.6	181.9	160.0
1947	309.9	231.3	219.1	199.0	169.8
1948	323.7	257.6	243.0	224.2	189.1
1949	324.1	256.5	239.9	217.5	188.6
1950	355.3	284.8	266.4	241.1	206.9
1951	383.4	328.4	309.2	278.0	226.6
1952	395.1	345.5	322.3	291.4	238.3
1953	412.8	364.6	338.9	304.7	252.6
1954	407.0	364.8	336.8	303.1	257.4
1955	438.0	398.0	366.5	331.0	275.3
1956	446.1	419.2	385.2	350.8	293.2
1957	452.5	441.1	404.0	366.1	308.5
1958	447.3	447.3	408.4	367.8	318.8
1959	475.9	483.7	442.3	400.0	337.3
1960	487.7	503.8	460.3	414.5	350.0
1961	497.2	520.1	474.9	427.3	364.4
1962	529.8	560.3	510.4	457.7	385.3

TABLE 3.5. (continued)

Year	Real Gross National Product Billions of 1958 Dollars	Billions of Current Dollars			
		Gross National Product	Net National Product	National Income	Disposable Income
1963	551.0	590.5	537.9	481.9	404.6
1964	581.1	632.4	576.3	518.1	438.1
1965	617.8	684.9	625.1	564.3	473.2
1966	658.1	749.9	685.9	620.6	511.9
1967	675.2	793.9	725.0	653.6	546.3
1968	707.2	865.0	791.9	712.7	591.2
1969	727.1	931.4	852.5	769.5	631.6
1970	724.3	976.8	892.4	801.0	684.7

SOURCE: *1971 Economic Report of the President.* Washington: U.S. Government Printing Office, 1971.

FIGURE 3.2. *Real Gross National Product 1875 – 1970*

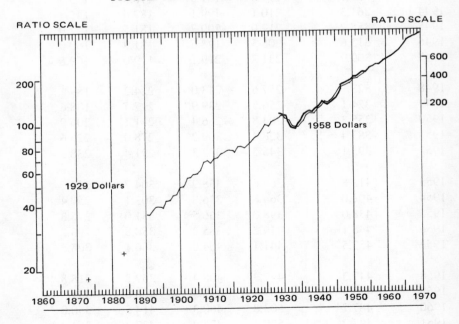

SOURCE: U.S. Bureau of the Census, *Long Term Economic Growth, 1860 – 1965* (Washington: U.S. Government Printing Office, 1966); *1971 Economic Report of the President* (Washington: U.S. Government Printing Office, 1971)

FIGURE 3.3. *Real Per Capita GNP 1875 — 1970*

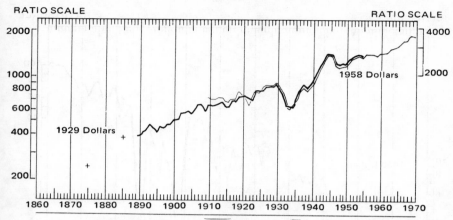

SOURCE: U.S. Bureau of the Census, *Long Term Economic Growth,*
1860 — 1965 (Washington: U.S. Government Printing Office, 1966);
1971 Economic Report of the President (Washington: U.S. Government
Printing Office, 1971)

FIGURE 3.4. *Personal Consumption Expenditures 1875 —*
1970

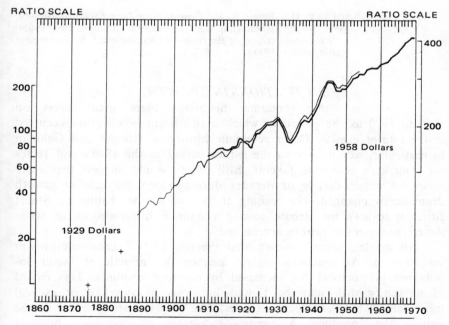

SOURCE: U.S. Bureau of the Census, *Long Term Economic Growth,*
1860 — 1965 (Washington: U.S. Government Printing Office, 1966);
1971 Economic Report of the President (Washington: U.S. Government
Printing Office, 1971)

FIGURE 3.5. *Gross Private Domestic Investment 1875 – 1970*

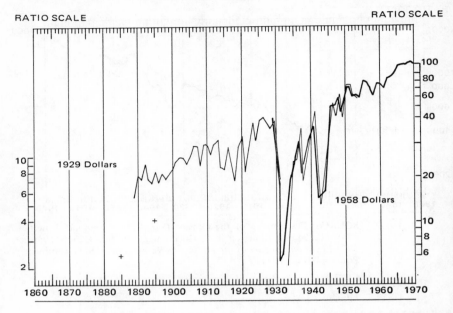

SOURCE: U.S. Bureau of the Census, *Long Term Economic Growth,*
1860 – 1965 (Washington: U.S. Government Printing Office, 1966);
1971 Economic Report of the President (Washington: U.S. Government
Printing Office, 1971)

FLUCTUATIONS IN GROWTH

Some economic historians place great stress on
1865 to 1900 as the period in which a significant acceleration occurred
in the rate of growth. Other economic historians, Rostow and Gallman
in particular, would look to the earlier period of the 1840's and 1850's
for America's economic takeoff. Still others would suggest that there
exists no magic decade or decades during which the rate of growth
dramatically changed. The reading at the end of the chapter by Stuart
Bruchey reviews the debate among economic historians as to when
American economic growth accelerated.

All scholars agree however, that the rate of U.S. economic growth
was uneven. As indicated earlier, neither the growth of factor inputs nor productivity has increased by constant amounts. This record
of uneven growth may be viewed in terms of wavelike or cyclical
movements — business cycles. Cycles, like growth, are uneven in the
pattern they produce. A composite average of twenty-six business
cycles in the U.S. from 1854-1961 reveals that an average upswing
lasts thirty months with downswings averaging nineteen months. (See
Table 3.6.) But the ten cycles from 1919-1961 have had an average

TABLE 3.6. *Business Cycles in American Economic History*

| Trough | Peak | Duration in Months | |
		Contraction	Expansion
Dec., 1854	June, 1857		30
Dec., 1858	Oct., 1860	18	22
June, 1861	Apr., 1865	8	46
Dec., 1867	June, 1869	32	18
Dec., 1870	Oct., 1873	18	34
Mar., 1879	Mar., 1882	65	36
May, 1885	Mar., 1887	38	22
Apr., 1888	July, 1890	13	27
May, 1891	Jan., 1893	10	20
June, 1894	Dec., 1895	17	18
June, 1897	June, 1899	18	24
Dec., 1900	Sept., 1902	18	21
Aug., 1904	May, 1907	23	33
June, 1908	Jan., 1910	13	19
Jan., 1912	Jan., 1913	24	12
Dec., 1914	Aug., 1918	23	44
Mar., 1919	Jan., 1920	7	10
July, 1921	May, 1923	18	22
July, 1924	Oct., 1926	14	27
Nov., 1927	Aug., 1929	13	21
Mar., 1933	May, 1937	43	50
June, 1938	Feb., 1945	13	80
Oct., 1945	Nov., 1948	8	37
Oct., 1949	July, 1953	11	45
Aug., 1954	July, 1957	13	35
Apr., 1958	May, 1960	9	25
Feb., 1961	Nov., 1969	9	106
Nov., 1970	—	12	

Average, All Cycles:

1854 – 1961		19	30
1919 – 1961		15	35
1945 – 1961		10	36
1945 – 1970		10	55

SOURCE: National Bureau of Economic Research.

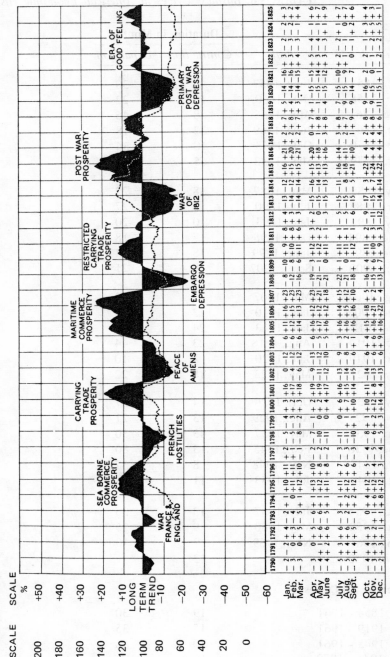

FIGURE 3.6. American Business Activity Since 1790

SOURCE: The Cleveland Trust Company

FIGURE 3.6. (Cont.)

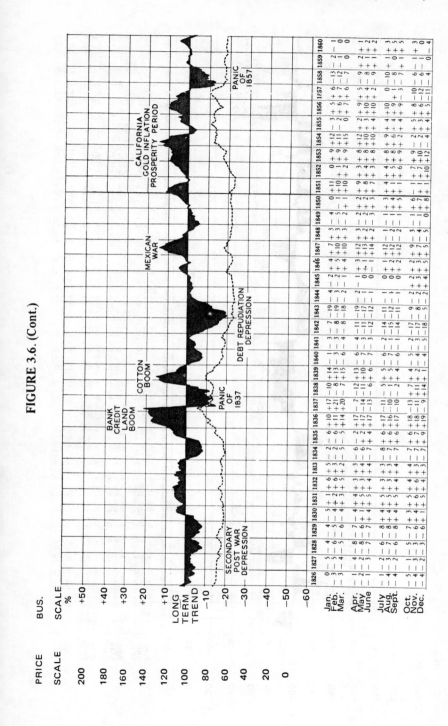

FIGURE 3.6. (Cont.)

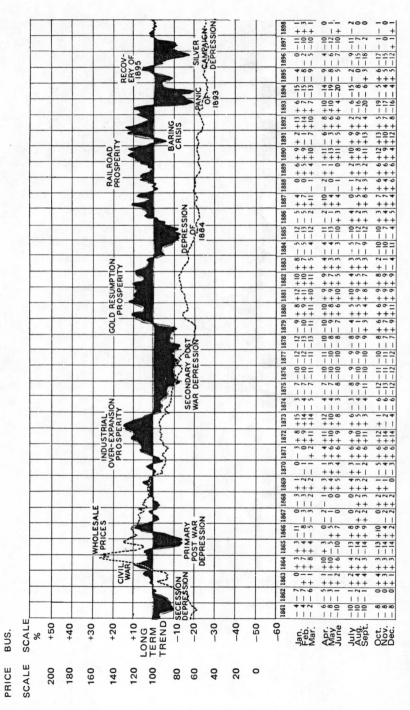

FIGURE 3.6. (Cont.)

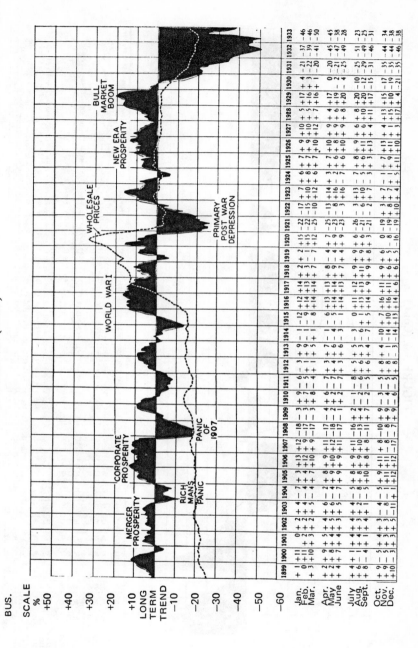

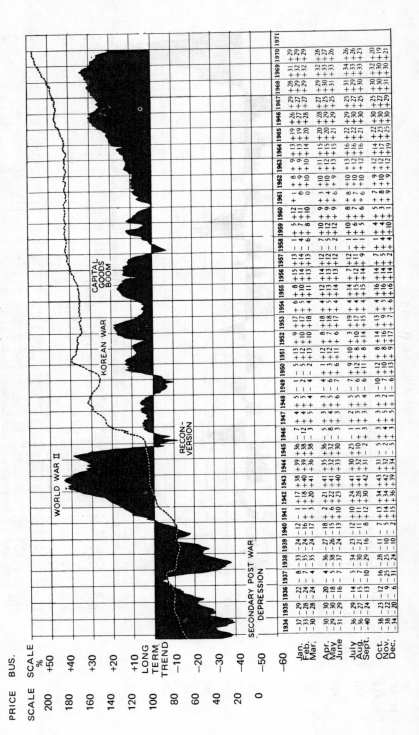

FIGURE 3.6. (Cont.)

expansion period of 35 months and a contraction period of only 15 months. And since 1945, the length of upswings has lengthened yet further, increasing to 55 months for the five cycles up to 1970. During the most recent period of expansion, from February 1961 to November 1969, the economy advanced for 106 months, the longest upswing in the nation's history. (See Figure 3.6.) At the same time the length of the downswings from 1945 to 1970 have shortened, dropping to 10.3 months. These data suggest that U.S. business cycles have become less severe in recent decades. The relatively favorable business cycle experience since World War II is due to many factors. First, and perhaps most important, has been active government leadership in promoting full employment. The Employment Act of 1946 committed the nation to a policy of maximum employment and production. Second, monetary policy and more recently fiscal policy have been used effectively to mitigate the forces of contraction and inflation. Third, the introduction of automatic stabilizers, such as unemployment insurance, "pay as you go" personal and corporate income taxes, and the farm price support program have stimulated the economy in times of recession and restrained it in periods of inflation. Fourth, institutional factors, such as the presence of strong labor unions and the farm price support program, have placed a floor on prices, thus preventing the severe deflation which characterized most major downturns before World War II. (See Figure 3.7.) Fifth, the strengthening of the Federal Reserve System and the introduction of Federal Deposit Insurance have eliminated the possibility of massive bank failures.

FIGURE 3.7. *Wholesale Price Index All Commodities 1860–1970 (1957-59 = 100)*

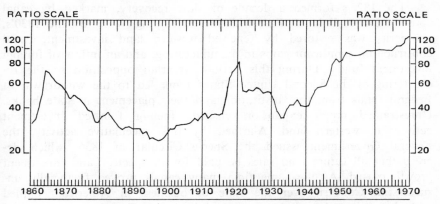

SOURCE: U.S. Bureau of the Census, *Long Term Economic Growth, 1860 – 1965* (Washington: U.S. Government Printing Office, 1966); *1971 Economic Report of the President* (Washington: U.S. Government Printing Office, 1971)

1790-1815. American economic fluctuations in the eighteenth and nineteenth centuries were closely tied to world economic developments. Adoption of a federal constitution, establishment of the national credit, and the creation of a central bank were institutional measures conducive to business prosperity in the late eighteenth and early nineteenth centuries. The Napoleonic Wars in Europe during this period provided the stimulus for prosperity. Both shipbuilding and foreign trade prospered. In 1807, war developments shut off America's trade with Europe. Savings were diverted from mercantile profits into manufacturing where, in the absence of European competition, high prices and high profits existed. Deficit government spending to finance war with Britain in 1812, coupled with the end of central bank control over the money supply one year earlier, contributed to inflationary pressures in the economy.

1815-1843. World peace, beginning in 1815, brought a decline in economic activity. With European goods once again entering U.S. markets, infant American industries faced severe competition from their older and more established foreign counterparts. At the same time, an upsurge in foreign demand for American agricultural produce and easy money conditions encouraged western migration and speculative investment activity in western land. A shift by the Second United States Bank, created in 1816, to a policy of credit restraint, severely curtailed western land investment by 1819. In the same year foreign demand for farm produce fell. Farm prices dropped, mortgages went into default, and a general scramble for liquidity ensued. A severe downturn resulted.

The 1820's formed a decade of slow recovery, marked by canal construction to link the East with the developing West. By the 1830's, prosperity was restored by renewed western land investment, canal construction, significant gains in manufacturing, and an inflow of foreign investment funds. During this period, agrarian opposition to the rechartering of the Second United States Bank led to the withdrawal of Federal funds from that institution and their placement in state banks. Unrestrained credit expansion ensued, fueling frenzied investment activity in western land. Alarmed by this speculative activity, the Federal Government issued the Specie Circular of 1836, which decreed that all future land sales be paid for in specie. Land investment growth ceased. At the same time many canals proved financially unsuccessful. Concern over the state of business in America, coupled with depression abroad, led to a withdrawal of European investments. In 1837 severe depression commenced.

1843-1860. By 1843 the depression had run its course. Easy money conditions created by unregulated state banks, war with Mexico in 1846, a flight of capital from revolution-torn Europe in 1848, the discovery of gold in California, and heavy investment in railroads provided the stimuli for expansion. By 1856 a shortage of credit acted to curtail continued investment growth. The bankruptcy of a leading New York financial institution and the withdrawal of funds from the U.S. by concerned European investors triggered the panic of 1857. The depression that ensued was short-lived, bottoming out by the end of 1858.

1860-1879. While business was initially disrupted by the onset of the Civil War, heavy government spending, financed primarily through borrowing and the printing of paper money, generated prosperity and sharply rising prices. The Federal Government, anxious to provide a market for its bonds and a uniform national currency, inaugurated the National Banking System in 1863. National banks were chartered with the power to issue paper money in amounts equal to ninety per cent of the value of their U.S. bond holdings. State bank notes were taxed out of existence. The National Banking System aggravated rather than relieved subsequent business cycles by encouraging the pyramiding of reserves in major money markets. Country and small city banks kept their legally required reserves in correspondent banks located in larger cities. This resulted in the pyramiding of most reserves in New York City, where they were lent out for investment purposes in newly evolving capital markets such as the New York Stock Exchange. At certain times of the year, most notably at planting and harvest time, an increased demand for money in rural areas would lead to a withdrawal of reserve funds from correspondent banks. New York banks were forced to call in their loans, triggering the heavy sale of securities by those to whom loans had been made. Severe stock market declines resulted. As capital markets developed, this problem grew in intensity. The close of the Civil War caused a brief downturn as the economy returned to peacetime pursuits. The prosperity that ensued was due principally to heavy investment in transcontinental railroad construction. This investment had two unfortunate effects: first, it outpaced the growth of consumer demand by western settlers, and second, it was frequently interwoven with substantial financial chicanery on the part of railroad developers. The bankruptcy of Jay Cooke and Company, a highly important banking house that had overextended itself in construction of the Northern Pacific Railroad, precipitated a money panic in 1873. Widespread bankruptcies occurred among banks, railroads and manufacturing concerns. The severity of the downturn was aggravated by a decline in construction that had commenced in the early 1870's.

1879-1908. By the end of the 1870's, crop failures in Europe had brought a boost in U.S. agricultural exports and initiated recovery throughout the economy. In the 1880's investment in railroads and newly developing manufacturing corporations provided a renewed upward economic thrust. In 1890 the Sherman Silver Purchase Act, passed under pressure from Western silver mining interests, required the Federal Government to buy a sizeable quantity of silver each month with newly issued paper currency redeemable in gold. At the same time, the failure of an eminent British banking house led to foreign gold withdrawals from the United States. The decline in the nation's stock of gold, coupled with the increasing supply of redeemable paper currency, weakened public confidence in the government's ability to maintain gold convertibility. Prosperity was further undermined by a decline in construction which commenced in 1891. In 1893 rumors abounded that the U.S. would be forced to suspend redemption. A money panic ensued which left bankruptcies and depression in its wake. During the height of the panic the Sherman Silver Purchase Act was repealed and the aid of J. P. Morgan enlisted to obtain foreign gold to shore up dwindling treasury gold stocks. The issue of silver figured prominently in the Presidential election of 1890 and ended in defeat for the pro-silver candidate, William Jennings Bryan. Economic recovery commenced soon after the election. Prosperity, except for a brief hiatus in 1903, continued to 1907. In 1907 a monetary crisis occurred, due principally to the inherent weaknesses of the nation's monetary and banking structure. In that year a normal withdrawal of funds by country banks forced the liquidation of securities by debtors at a time when stock prices were already indicating weakness. Copper stocks, in particular, declined sharply following an abortive attempt by a small group of financial speculators to boost their price. Since a number of these speculators owned stock in large city banks, their financial misfortune led to alarm on the part of depositors. Bank runs ensued. Country banks also hastened to withdraw whatever reserves they held. City banks, in a scramble for liquidity, demanded payment on all call loans, which forced further security liquidation, and fed the downward spiral of stock prices. Bank failures spread, and the nation's economy entered a brief, but severe, downturn.

1908-1921. Recovery commenced in 1908. The period that followed was characterized by brief downturns in 1910 and 1913. In the latter year, after an extensive inquiry into the sources of monetary instability, Congress established the Federal Reserve System. With the outbreak of European war in 1914, U.S. business firms became major suppliers of arms, equipment, and food to all belligerents. War-induced prosperity was stimulated further by U.S. entrance into the conflict in 1917. Except for a brief recession caused by peacetime conversion, prosperity continued after the war. A backlog of consumer demand and foreign reconstruction needs were the principal stimuli. Prices, which had been rising throughout the war, continued to climb. By 1920 the picture had changed. The Federal Reserve tightened credit, the Federal budget shifted from deficit to surplus, and bank excess reserves were depleted. A shortage of mortgage credit and high building costs caused a decline in construction. Consumer resistance to high prices and a decline in foreign demand led to high inventory levels. A severe, yet brief, recession followed during which industrial production fell roughly a third. Farm prices declined precipitously and agriculture entered an economic decline from which it did not recover until World War II.

1921-1933. Balance in the economy was restored by 1921. Except for brief inventory recessions in 1923-24 and 1926-27 the economy, sparked by an investment boom in automobiles, public utilities, and electrical equipment, continued to be strong until the summer of 1929. A stock market crash in the fall of 1929 ushered in the Great Depression. The causes of the depression were many. First, construction was in the midst of a major downswing which had commenced in 1925. Second, for almost a decade, agriculture had been a depressed sector of the economy. Third, an unhealthy international situation existed. Not only was there a heavy residue of debt owed the United States from World War I, but a persistently favorable U.S. trade balance prevented Europeans from earning the export dollars essential to repayment. During the early and mid-1920's a flow of investment funds from the U.S. masked this fact, but by the late 1920's funds increasingly were diverted to Wall Street. With the onset of depression, the situation became critical. Americans began withdrawing their foreign investments and Europeans, in the face of higher U.S. tariffs, were unable to service their debts. European defaults and currency devaluations to increase exports and decrease imports resulted. These, in turn, caused the complete breakdown of world trade. Fourth, the productivity gains of the 1920's were not fully shared by workers to permit sufficient growth of consumption. Instead they were retained as profits which largely were not reinvested for growth, but instead were loaned out to finance stock market speculation. Fifth, many of the nation's business leaders had engaged in unhealthy cor-

porate practices for personal profit. Sixth, the market for automobiles was showing signs of saturation. Seventh, the Federal Reserve
possessed insufficient powers over the nation's monetary system and
lacked effective leadership. Eighth, there existed inadequate knowledge
of fiscal policy. Finally, a general philosophy of laissez-faire by the
Federal Government created a leadership void which contributed to
sagging confidence.

The depression, which spanned forty-three months, was the most
severe in the nation's history. Industrial production, wholesale prices
and GNP all fell approximately fifty per cent below their levels in
1929. Unemployment, which stood at 3.2 per cent just prior to the
downturn, increased to a point where almost one out of every four
workers in the labor force was unable to find a job. Asset liquidation,
which became increasingly severe as the contraction proceeded, dealt
a mortal blow to the banking system. Despite the presence of the
Federal Reserve System more than five thousand banks failed. And by
early March of 1933 almost all the commercial banks in the country
had been forced temporarily to close their doors. This proved to be
the trough of the depression.

1933-1945. The New Deal, led by Franklin Roose-
velt, took office with the economy at its low point. The critical state
of the nation's economic health and effective political leadership enabled the New Deal to engage in a number of experimental and path-
breaking activities. These included abandonment of the gold standard
and devaluation of the dollar, artificial increases in the price of
silver, establishment of the National Recovery Administration (NRA),
which in essence temporarily suspended antitrust laws, enactment of
a comprehensive farm price support program, strengthening of the
Federal Reserve System, extensive regulation of the banking and
securities industries and the establishment of a social security
system. Despite these and other efforts the economy experienced a
slow recovery which lasted until 1937. In that year GNP was still
only ninety per cent of its 1929 level and unemployment remained
high. Moreover, the sharp recession which occurred in 1937-1938
eliminated much of the gains of the previous four years. The contraction was due primarily to the reduction of excess inventories which
had accumulated since 1936, excessive credit restraint by the Federal
Reserve, and a reduction in Federal deficit spending. The paring of
inventories, the easing of monetary policy, and an increase in the
Federal deficit reversed the downturn. World War II then intervened
to create massive Federal deficits which restored the economy to full
prosperity. During the war years, unusually high public and private

spending strained the productive capacity of the nation. The resulting pressure on prices was restrained by direct government price controls.

1945-1970. The end of World War II witnessed a brief reconversion recession similar to that which occurred in 1919. An economic advance followed which lasted until late 1948. Prices advanced significantly throughout the upswing owing to the removal of direct government price controls, pent-up consumer and producer demand, and large amounts of liquid assets. The Federal Reserve, instead of combating the inflation by tightening credit, cooperated with the Treasury in its refunding operations by keeping credit readily available. The 1948-49 recession was principally due to inventory liquidation. It was mild in nature and the economy, stimulated by the onset of the Korean War, soon returned to full prosperity. Initial inflation, caused by heavy consumer stockpiling and military expenditures, was checked by direct controls, increases in taxes, and the exercise of restrictive monetary policy. In 1953-54 another brief and mild recession occurred. The downturn was due to inventory liquidation, and a sizeable reduction in the Federal deficit following the end of the Korean conflict. The prosperity which followed was interrupted in 1957-58 by another inventory recession which, though the briefest of the postwar period, proved the most severe. It was characterized by a drop in the purchase of consumer durables for the first time since 1946. Residential construction, which peaked in 1955 and declined thereafter, contributed to the recession. Unemployment reached its highest level since the end of the war, 7.5 per cent. Some observers interpreted these events as evidence that the postwar prosperity had come to an end and that the economy was on the verge of a major downturn. This, however, was not the case. Personal consumption expenditures proved buoyant, and following inventory liquidation the economy turned up. The recovery that followed, however, proved weak. A most disturbing aspect of it was the unemployment rate, which failed to return to the full employment level. The expansion proved to be the shortest since the war and in the first half of 1960 the economy lapsed into recession.

The focus of economic and political discussion now turned to the issue of U.S. economic growth. The Kennedy-Johnson Administration, which took office in 1961, pursued a policy of aggressive economic expansion. In 1964, an eleven billion dollar tax cut was legislated to quicken the pace of economic activity. This and other measures returned the economy to full employment by 1966. In 1967 and 1968 substantial Federal deficits, occasioned by the Vietnam War, taxed the economy's industrial capacity and unleashed serious inflationary pressures. Prices advanced sharply, and monetary and fiscal restraint followed. In the Fall of 1969 the economy ended the longest expansion in its history. The recession which followed proved to be mild, with industrial production falling less than six per cent. Stimulative monetary and fiscal policy together with the first peace-time wage and price controls in the nation's history contributed to the recovery which ensued.

INCOME AND WEALTH DISTRIBUTION

Individual well-being is a function of both the size of the national income and wealth, and its distribution. A nation may be quite rich as measured by per capita income. However, if the bulk of the goods and services produced are controlled by a small minority of the population, as is the case in some Arab oil sheikdoms the average tribution of national income and wealth. In the eighteenth century, income was apparently more equally distributed among the colonists and colonies than was the case once industrialization commenced. The industrial revolution brought in its wake a legacy of income inequality, both between people and regions of the country. During the nineteenth century wealth was more unequally distributed in urban areas and the plantation South than in the rest of the country. Population shifts to urban areas as the nineteenth century progressed tended to enhance the inequality of wealth distribution. So, too, did the freeing of the slaves, by adding a significant population to the poorer classes. In 1810, the wealthiest one per cent of all families possessed twenty-one per cent of total wealth and the top ten per cent owned sixty-nine per cent. In 1860 the former share had increased to twenty-four per cent and the latter to seventy-two per cent. By the turn of the century, the respective shares had risen to thirty-one per cent and seventy-four per cent. When interpreted within the Keynesian framework, this unequal distribution of income and wealth had two significant economic implications. First, it provided a large supply of savings from upper income brackets to finance investment. The dividends from these investments made for further income inequality, but also provided the source of more savings for additional investment. Second, the fact that the great bulk of people received such a small share of national income meant that consumption was lower than would have been the case with more income equality.

The Great Depression of the 1930's marked a turning point in the trend of income distribution. In 1929, the top five per cent of all families received thirty per cent of personal income. By the mid-1930's their share had dropped below twenty-seven per cent and by 1946 to under twenty-two per cent. This movement towards equality was due primarily to New Deal policies and the unusually low rates of unemployment during World War II. Social security, farm price supports, pro-labor legislation and progressive income taxes benefited principally low- and middle-income groups. The wartime prosperity of World War II enabled millions of Americans who had been unemployed or employed only part time to secure attractive jobs. Between 1946 and 1962 little change was evidenced in income distribution. Since 1962 there appears to be a renewed impetus toward greater income equality. (See Table 3.7.) This has been associated with the longest prosperity in the nation's history and a major effort by the Federal Government to ease the plight of the poor.

TABLE 3.7. *Family Income Distribution 1929–1968*

	1929	1935–6	1946	1950	1956	1962	1968
Lowest Fifth	12.5*	4.1	5.0	4.8	4.8	4.6	5.7
Second Fifth		9.2	11.1	10.9	11.3	10.9	12.4
Third Fifth	13.8	14.1	16.0	16.1	16.3	16.3	17.7
Fourth Fifth	19.3	20.9	21.8	22.1	22.3	22.7	23.7
Highest Fifth	54.4	51.7	46.1	46.1	45.3	45.5	40.0
Top 5 Per Cent	30.0	26.5	21.5	21.4	20.2	19.6	14.0

*Combined figure for the lowest and second fifth.

SOURCE: U.S. Bureau of the Census. *Historical Statistics of the United States Colonial Times to 1956: Continuation to 1962 and Revisions.* U.S. Government Printing Office, Washington, D.C., 1965, 1969, p. 166; p. 24, *Statistical Abstract of the United States,* 1970, p. 323.

NOTES

1. John W. Kendrick. *Productivity Trends in the United States.* New York: National Bureau of Economic Research, 1961.

SELECTED REFERENCES

1. Bert F. Hoselitz, *et al. Theories of Economic Growth.* Glencoe: The Free Press of Glencoe, 1960.
2. John W. Kendrick. *Productivity Trends in the United States.* New York: National Bureau of Economic Research, 1961.

3. Simon Kuznets. "Long Term Changes in the National Income of the United States of America Since 1870," *Income and Wealth of the United States: Trends and Structure*, International Association for Research in Income and Wealth. Cambridge: Bowes and Bowes, 1952.
4. Wesley C. Mitchell. *Business Cycles and Their Causes*. Berkeley: University of California Press, 1959.
5. National Bureau of Economic Research. *Trends in the American Economy in the Nineteenth Century*. Princeton: Princeton University Press, 1960.
6. Walt W. Rostow. *The Stages of Economic Growth*. Cambridge: Cambridge University Press, 1960.
7. Joseph Schumpeter. *Capitalism, Socialism, and Democracy*. New York: Harper, 1947.

reading

when did economic growth accelerate?

stuart bruchey

Precisely when the economy began to grow at a *more rapid rate* is a question on which scholars disagree. The only continuous estimates of pre-1869 national income in constant prices are those compiled in the 1930's by Robert F. Martin. According to Martin, "very little actual economic advance per capita appeared in the first half of the 19th century," a failure which he attributed to "general pioneering turmoil, punctuated by controversies, first with European countries, culminating in the War of 1812 with the British, and then the series of Black Hawk, Seminole and other Indians Wars." His figures for real income per capita show a steady decline each decade from $216 in 1799 to $164 in 1829, a loss of 24 per cent. Not until 1849 did income rise to the level of 1799, and then the gain amounted only to 11 per cent over a period of fifty years. The decade 1849-59 yielded the most substantial increase of the entire period, with income rising from $235 to $296. Perhaps most surprisingly, in tracing this 1849-59 rise in income to the various sectors of the economy responsible for producing it, a calculation made in terms of current rather than constant prices, Martin depicts percentile *declines* from the previous decade in manufacturing, construction, transportation and communication, service, and "miscellaneous" (including finance), as well as agriculture. While mining and quarrying registered a small increase from 0.7 per cent to 1.1 per cent, trade

Source: reprinted with permission from *The Roots of American Economic Growth 1607-1861, An Essay in Social Causation* by Stuart Bruchey. New York: Harper and Row, 1965, pp. 76-91.

leaped from 8.4 per cent to 12.1 per cent. Implicit in Martin's figures, in short, is the thesis that economic growth was primarily the consequence of a substantial increase in trade in the 1850's.

In recent years Martin's early work has been subjected to vigorous criticism, first by Simon Kuznets and then by William N. Parker and Franklee Whartenby. Focusing both on Martin's sources and statistical methods, this criticism is too technical for review here. Believing Martin's national and per capita income figures to be too low, especially for the years 1800-40, Kuznets suggests they be revised on the basis of two main considerations. The first of these is the increase in "nonagricultural industrial employment" that occurred between 1800 and 1840. Assuming that real income per worker is greater in such employment than in agriculture, Kuznets uses urbanization statistics as an index of movement from the one to the other. Secondly, he makes an upward revision in the estimated ratio of gainfully employed to total population. All other things being equal, an increase in this ratio is assumed to result in an increase in real product per capita. Adding together the results of his re-estimates, Kuznets reaches the conclusion that instead of undergoing the decline suggested by Martin, real product per capita actually rose by 19 per cent during the period 1800-40. This conclusion rests, however, on the assumption that no change took place in the productivity of agriculture or any other pursuit during the period. To Parker and Whartenby the assumption is questionable. It must, they believe, be subjected to the "painful techniques of historical research," and in this undertaking Parker is presently engaged.

Meanwhile, Robert E. Gallman's recent estimates for the period 1839-99 of value added by commodity output in agriculture, mining, manufacturing, and construction — four sectors of the economy that accounted for between 60 and 70 per cent of the national product in the post-Civil War era — supply a firmer basis than do Martin's figures for an impression concerning both the direction of movement and some of the main sources of national income in the last two decades before the Civil War. Gallman finds that between 1839 and 1859 output grew at an average decade rate of 57 per cent. In addition to value added, by which Gallman means "the value of output, at producers' prices, less the value of materials and fuels directly consumed in production at delivered prices," Table VIII displays estimates of the value of output of fixed reproducible capital. This Gallman defines as producer's manufactured durables, construction, and the improvements to farm land. Since a high ratio of capital to output is associated with the process of industrialization, it is noteworthy that the share of fixed capital in commodity output increased from less than 23 per cent in 1839 to about 27 per cent in 1859.

TABLE VIII. *Value Added by Selected Industries, and Value of Output of Fixed Capital, in 1879 Prices: 1839–1859 (in billions of dollars)*

	Total	Agri-culture	Mining	Manu-facturing	Con-struction	Value of Output of Fixed Capital
1859	2.69	1.49	.03	.86	.30	.73
1854	2.32	1.32	.03	.68	.30	—
1849	1.66	.99	.02	.49	.16	.39
1844	1.37	.94	.01	.29	.13	—
1839	1.09	.79	.01	.19	.11	.25

SOURCE: *Historical Statistics of the United States, Colonial Times to 1957* (Washington, D.C., 1960), p. 139.

Table IX gives evidence of an acceleration in the rate of change in output per capita during the two decades, and Table X shows the shares of each of the four sectors in commodity output. Most notable in the latter table is the changing division of output between agriculture and nonagriculture, especially manufacturing. The share of manufacturing in commodity output, less than 20 per cent in 1839, rose to 33 per cent by 1859. On the other hand, despite the fact that the period saw substantial gains in real income per head, the real value added by agriculture (about 47 per cent) was not much larger than the rate of increase in population (45 per cent). In part, the explanation of the shift, as Gallman notes, is the differing income elasticities of demand for agricultural and nonagricultural products. "As income per capita rises, per capita consumption of agricultural products tends, after a time, to rise relatively little. Thus the share of income devoted to agricultural products is reduced, while that devoted to non-agricultural products is increased." This situation not being alleviated by an export surplus of agricultural products, factors of production were shifted to nonagricultural sectors to meet the requirements of the changing pattern of demand.

It remains to note Gallman's view that during the sixty-year period 1839-99 "the number of gainful workers in commodity production increased at about the same rate as population." This is a significant point. For if Gallman is right in his belief that about 64 per cent of the rise in commodity output over this period is attributable to the increasing number of workers, it is apparent how important

TABLE IX. *Commodity Output, Population, and Gainful Workers in Commodity Production, Quinquennial, 1839–1859*

Year	Output (millions of $)	Population (thousands)	Output per Capita	Gainful Workers (thousands)	Output per worker
				Absolute Figures	
1839	1,094	17,120	$64	4,484	$244
1844	1,374	20,182	68	–	–
1849	1,657	23,261	71	6,190	268
1854	2,317	27,386	85	–	–
1859	2,686	31,513	85	8,140	330
		Decennial Rates of Change (per cent)			
1849	52	36	11	38	10
1854	69	36	24	–	–
1859	62	36	20	32	23
1869	23	27	-4	19	2

SOURCE: Robert E. Gallman, "Commodity Output, 1839–1899," in William N. Parker, ed., *Trends in the American Economy in the Nineteenth Century* (Princeton, N.J., 1960), p. 16.

TABLE X. *Sector Shares in Commodity Output, Quinquennial, 1839–1859 (per cent)*

Year	Agri-culture	Mining	Manu-facturing	Construction Variant A	Variant B
1839	72	1	17	10	8
1844	69	1	21	9	8
1849	60	1	30	10	9
1854	57	1	29	13	11
1859	56	1	32	11	10

SOURCE: Robert E. Gallman, "Commodity Output, 1839–1899," in William N. Parker, ed., *Trends in the American Economy in the Nineteenth Century* (Princeton, N.J., 1960), p. 26.

was the part played by population growth in the expansion of national output. Productivity gains appear to account for the remainder of the rise, and Gallman sees these increases in output per worker as deriving in part from shifts of workers from less productive to more productive sectors of the economy, and in part to such changes *within* particular sectors as "increased supplies of other factors, improved technology, a better disposition of workers within each sector, improved workers, etc." "In 1839 income per worker in mining and manufacturing [taken together] was much higher than income per worker in the other sectors," and in consequence workers shifted relatively rapidly from agriculture to these more remunerative sectors.

Whereas Martin had emphasized the importance of trade in the 1850's, Gallman places the beginnings of an accelerated rate of economic growth "in or before" the 1840's and associates it with "the early stages of industrialization or slightly before." He expresses surprise that high rates of growth in product per head should appear so soon: the records of other countries (Great Britain is a much-debated exception) usually suggest that rapid increases *follow* rather than accompany early industrialization. But his surprise arises from his acceptance of the view of some scholars that the late 1840's marked "the beginning of U.S. industrialization." There might well be less room for surprise if it were possible to extend into the period before 1839 the kind of investigation carried out by Gallman for the years following 1839. And if the investigation revealed significant beginnings of industrialization before that year, certainly part of the explanation would be at hand for his conclusion that "U.S. product per capita must have been high from the beginning" (i.e., from 1839). Probably the favorable land-man ratio and an expanding foreign and domestic commerce also contributed to this high early product per capita.

A statistical assessment of the sources of national income before 1839 would be extremely difficult to make, however, because of the fragmentary nature of surviving data. Although federal censuses began in 1790, only in 1810, 1820, and 1840 was any attempt made to include in them either agriculture or manufactures. Census data before 1840, concludes Douglass C. North, are "so poor that they are almost worthless." Raymond W. Goldsmith agrees that our "usable" statistical record does not reach beyond that date. Although the contemporary testimony of Ezra Seaman, George Tucker, and others has yet to be evaluated in the light of modern concepts, the strong possibility is that Samuel Reznick will prove justified in his doubt "whether there is ever likely to be enough material available for any

more reliable measure" than what we now have. Shall, then, the beginnings of accelerated growth be equated with the availability of
data on national output per capita that may be statistically measured
or inferred?

Gallman has made a substantial contribution to our knowledge
of the 1840's and 1850's, but the element of uncertainty that remains
about even these decades cannot be overlooked. For one thing, he has
omitted trade, transport, finance, and other industries from his estimates. For another, while census data after 1840 are fuller than for
earlier decades, they are inadequate, and this has sometimes compelled Gallman to resort to assumptions and extrapolations rather
than historical evidence. As Neal Potter has pointed out, only 52 per
cent of Gallman's estimate of manufacturing output in 1839 are from
census data on value of products: *and this 52 per cent is itself an
estimate* that is derived from the 1840 census figures on value of
product multiplied by the 1850 census ratios of value added to value
of products. Gallman's reply to Potter is a reasonable one, but the
possibility remains that the use of similar techniques on the sparser
data before 1840 would produce results even more questionable. While,
therefore, we may reasonably conclude that growth was accelerating
in the forties and fifties, it is at least doubtful that the techniques
which give us some idea of the dimensions of that growth would be
equally successful if applied to earlier data. So long as measurable
national output (income) is employed as the criterion of growth, the
possibility must be faced that the years before 1840 will form a medieval period in American economic history.

For many historians this would be an intolerable situation. While
the kinds of evidence that historians have traditionally used support
the notion that the inter-Panic period 1843-57 indeed witnessed an
acceleration in the rate of industrialization and economic growth,
there exist good reasons for believing both processes were under
way before then. The difficult problem is estimating their significance
in relation to the later period. Some approaches to the available evidence tend to minimize the earlier years; others suggest it may be
wrong to do so. In the first category is a recent essay by Alfred
Conrad, who uses data on real wages as an index to national income.
Finding only relatively minor wage gains before 1843, Conrad suggests
that these years of a "surprisingly low rate of per capita income
growth" were ones of industrial preparation, with high proportions of
disposable income presumably being channeled into investment.
Douglass C. North arrives at a different conclusion. After unusual
statistical labors devoted to numerous aspects of American economic
change but not to the measurement of aggregate output or income,

North concludes: "If one were to date the beginning of acceleration in the economy's growth and the years when industrialization began, it would be during this period" from 1823 to 1843. Within this time span he places special emphasis upon the "accelerated growth of manufacturing throughout the Northeast" during the decade of the 1830's.

Robert W. Fogel, on the other hand, assembles a striking array of evidence in support of the thesis that the 1820's witnessed a rapid rise in the manufacturing share of commodity output.[1] The purpose of the assemblage, it is proper to observe, is to counter Walt W. Rostow's overly dramatic view that during the years following 1843 the American economy "took-off" upon a self-sustained course of accelerated growth. The first piece of evidence is Rolla M. Tryon's conclusion that while household manufacturing apparently reached a peak about 1815, "the transfer from home- to shop- and factory-made goods was rather generally completed before the close of the third decade of the nineteenth century." The decade of the 1820's was also one of rapid urbanization, with the rate of increase of city population doubling that of population as a whole. Fogel also points to the rapid growth of a number of leading manufacturing industries during the twenties, most of which "grew at decade rates which exceeded by far the 35 percent increase in population." Cotton textiles was one of the most important. In 1807 the fifteen or twenty mills in existence employed a total of approximately eight thousand spindles. By 1811, according to Albert Gallatin's report to Congress of the preceeding year, an estimated eighty-seven firms were expected to have ten times this number of spindles in operation. By 1820, the spindle total had risen from 80,000 to 191,000. These increases pale before those of the 1820's: in 1831 spindles in use numbered nearly a million and a quarter, and cotton textiles had become "a very substantial industry."

As in cotton textiles, so also in iron making and in the production of woolen goods, carpets, paper, flint glass, lead, sugar and molasses, salt, and steam engines. Arthur H. Cole estimates that factory consumption of wool rose from four hundred thousand pounds in 1810 to fifteen million in 1830, with "fully half" of the increase falling between 1816 and 1830. Carpet production grew from an output of 9,984 yards in 1810 to 1,147,500 in 1834, with most of the increase taking place during a four- or five-year period beginning in 1827. While the steam engine was not produced commercially in the United States until 1805, production was stimulated, especially after 1815, by the development of steamboats. During the 1820's 359 engines were required for this purpose alone. In 1830 Pittsburgh alone produced one hundred engines, and Cincinnati one hundred fifty.

We may summarize this brief survey of scholarly viewpoints concerning industrialization and economic growth in the pre-Civil War period by pointing out that Martin would emphasize the 1850's, Gallman the 1840's, North the 1830's, and Fogel the 1820's! But why stop here? It is true, as North points out, that census returns reveal a "drastic decline" in manufacturing output in every state of the Northeast between 1810 and 1820. But this decline, as North notes, is "much magnified by the incomplete nature of the returns for 1820 and the inclusion of household manufactures in the 1810 figure." The importance of manufactures at the earlier date is emphasized by Secretary of the Treasury Albert Gallatin's 1810 Report on Manufactures: "It may, with certainty, be inferred that...annual production exceeds one hundred and twenty millions of dollars. And it is not improbable that the raw materials used, and the provisions and other articles consumed by the manufacturers, create a home market for agricultural products not very inferior to that which arises from foreign demand." Historians have long noted the stimulus given manufacturers by the embargo and nonimportation laws following 1807. They had received an even earlier stimulus during the Revolution period from an interruption to imports and other circumstances to be discussed in the next chapter. In 1789 George Washington observed that more "substantial improvements to manufactures" had recently been made "than were ever before known in America." As we shall see, manufactures were of sufficient importance by that year to induce interests in several cities to petition Congress in their favor, and among the stated objectives of the Tariff Act of 1789 was "the encouragement and protection of manufactures."

Still the question will not down: why stop here? Why 1820? Why 1789? Why 1776? We have only to examine the first volume of Victor S. Clark's *History of Manufactures in the United States*[2] to see that ironmaking, shipbuilding, and the manufacture of clothing, nails, utensils, furniture, and numerous other products is to be found almost throughout the colonial period of American history. Would the colonial historian be justified in arguing that manufacturing and economic growth have been constants in our history from some time near its beginnings, and that the notion of acceleration is a myth? Does there exist a parallel between this notion and an earlier and better-known version of the doctrine that economic change may come with unexpected suddenness?

Lecturing at Oxford in 1880-81 on "The Industrial Revolution of the Eighteenth Century," the English historian Arnold Toynbee popularized a concept of sudden change that soon became imbedded in historical literature. Toynbee depicted an England which, prior to 1760, had been a quiet and contented world of "scarcely perceptible movement." Upon this green and joyous landscape had burst a series of inventions in spinning and weaving and in the production of power, and within a span of about twenty years machinery and steam had overrun industry, ushered in the factory system, dislocated population, blackened the air, and blighted the lives of exploited women and children. Eric E. Lampard has compiled an instructive account of the subsequent history of Toynbee's drama. By the early twentieth century it had begun to be critically examined. A. P. Usher's researches in technology revealed an almost unbroken continuity of mechanical change since the late Middle Ages. Alongside Toynbee's half-dozen or so inventors now appeared numerous skilled craftsmen, nameless and unsung, authors of small but indispensable improvements, men whose presence crowded the stage on which the drama of invention was enacted, converting it from a record of individual achievement to a social process. In Toynbee's day, however, as Herbert Heaton reminds us, little was known of sixteenth-century economic life and little of any eighteenth-century industry except textiles. Now we know, thanks to the researches of John U. Nef, that England had undergone an "industrial revolution" between 1540 and 1640 and that Holland, Sweden, and France also contributed to technical progress. Now we know, too, the fundamental relevance to that progress of early modern science. As T. S. Ashton emphasizes, this "stream of English scientific thought, issuing from the teaching of Francis Bacon, and enlarged by the genius of Boyle and Newton, was one of the main tributaries of the industrial revolution." Lengthened perspectives thus enable us to see the wisdom of Thomas C. Cochran's observation that "massive changes in physical environment such as those accompanying the rise of trade at the close of the Middle Ages or the gradual growth of industrialization from the seventeenth century on do not lend themselves to exact or brief periodization."

But Clio, it has often been observed is a fickle Muse. In recent years scholars have in varying degrees reaffirmed Toynbee's central idea of suddenly rapid economic change. As early as 1937 Usher suggested that "important aspects of the economic history of England...seem to warrant the qualified use of the term 'revolution.'" He thought the pace of technological change in particular to have been "unprecedented if not revolutionary." In 1948 Ashton, the leading authority on English economic history of the eighteenth century, entitled his masterful study *The Industrial Revolution, 1760-1830.*[3] Two years later, J. H. Plumb boldly returned to the classical point of view: "...compared with the centuries which had gone before, the changes...of the second half of the eighteenth century were both violent and revolutionary." In 1955 Heaton concluded that the "industrial revolution still stands provided you will scrap 1760 as D day and 1832 as VE day, give greater emphasis to the heavy industries, wring some of the emotion and melodrama out of the story, and develop a sense of . . . proportion."

The moral of the story seems clear. Although manufacturing had been a familiar element in the economic history of Europe for centuries, although England itself had passed through an earlier period of accelerated development between 1540 and 1640, the rapidity of technological change in the later eighteenth and early nineteenth centuries was unprecedented. Much the same point concerning the rapidity of technological change seems applicable to American experience. Manufactures occupy a familiar place in colonial economic history, but for the most part market and transport limitations dictated that they be what Clark called "neighborhood manufactures," widely dispersed rather than geographically concentrated, local manufactures protected by high transport costs from the competition of distant producers. They were "homespun industries," utilizing the tools belonging to age-old handicraft traditions rather than machinery, and in general they were small in scale. Furthermore, they were technologically "backward." Water power was employed in the mill and furnace industries, but most of the wheels were undershot and utilized only a fraction of the water power applied to them. Power transmission was "so little understood that a separate wheel was generally necessary for each article of machinery." These characteristics endured until shortly before the Revolution, when "considerable improvements were made in the application of power to milling machinery and processes." Even in England, of course, the great inventions that gave that nation her industrial eminence "were not successfully applied to manufactures until about the time of the American Revolution." Clark believed that about 1790 "manufacturing everywhere broke away from ancient technical precedents, [and that] processes of production were revolutionized."

It is clear that the availability of improved techniques formed one of the necessary conditions to a more rapid pace of growth than was possible in the colonial period. But without an expansion in the size of the domestic market in conjunction, as we shall see, with scarcity in the supply of labor, there would have been no incentive to adopt these techniques. The size of the domestic market increased throughout the nineteenth century to a far greater extent than was possible under the conditions of the eighteenth, and this consideration justifies the conclusion that American industrialization and economic growth characterize the nineteenth century far more than they do the earlier years. If, therefore, contemporary and recent scholars have called attention to developments in each of the pre-Civil War decades from the 1820's on, their emphases only italicize the significance of each of the decades.

Manufactures might have been begun to expand somewhat earlier and more largely had it not been for the high profits to be won in foreign commerce following the outbreak of the Anglo-French wars in 1793. In a day when the entire country boasted fewer than a half-dozen millionaires, the trading firm of Robert Oliver & Brothers of Baltimore made in the course of eighteen months during 1806-07 a *net* profit of $775,000. As Adam Seybert observed shortly after the end of the wars "...our catalogue of merchants was swelled much beyond what it was entitled to be from the state of our population. Many persons, who had secured moderate capitals, from mechanical pursuits, soon became the most adventurous...The brilliant prospects held out by commerce, caused our citizens to neglect the mechanical and manufacturing branches of industry." This relative neglect came to an end with the period of embargo, nonintercourse, and war, and after industrial beginnings thereby substantially enlarged had recovered in the 1820's from the setbacks sustained from renewed British competition following the War of 1812, the more rapid although not uninterrupted growth of manufactures proceeded apace.

Increasingly after about the middle of that decade and fully by the end of the following one (that is, by 1840) it is possible to speak of a domestic market truly national in its dimensions. The national market, as we shall see, made possible a territorial specialization which, as Douglass C. North has observed, raised the productivity of the economy as a whole. Its importance for American economic growth was very great. In the ninetenth century the American common market was to the United States what the European Common Market is to twentieth-century Europe. But neither market could have arisen out of economic change alone. Both were in part products of deliberate political action requiring the creation of a larger sovereignty. For this and many other reasons it would be difficult to overemphasize the importance of government to economic growth.

NOTES

1. I am much indebted to Professor Fogel and to the Johns Hopkins Press for their kind permission to make use of data from Fogel's forthcoming publication. "Railroads in American Economic Growth: Essays in Econometric History."
2. New York, 1949.
3. London, 1948.

part **II**

the colonial period

through the war of 1812

chapter 4

foreign trade and early american development

MERCANTILISM AND THE COLONIAL ECONOMY

COMMERCE, COLONIES, AND MERCANTILIST THOUGHT

The Renaissance caused fundamental political and economic changes in Western Europe. National states emerged and commerce was expanded. Nations, eager to increase their wealth and influence, sponsored explorations to find new trade routes and markets. For the five-hundred-year period 1000-1500, it was the Italian city-states of Venice, Genoa, and Pisa which dominated western trade with the East. The city of Florence played a major supportive role as a key banking and manufacturing center. From Europe wool, tin, copper, lead, arsenic, and antimony were shipped to the East in partial payment for imports of spices, drugs, sugar, dye, glass, cutlery, porcelain, rugs, and tapestries. Bullion flows to the East were necessary to offset Europe's adverse trade balance. Imports arriving in Italy were shipped to Central Europe by German merchants who traveled via Constance, Basel, Strasbourg and other ports

99

along the Rhine, or through the Brenner Pass to Munich, Nuremberg, and Frankfurt. Dutch and Flemish merchants from Antwerp, Bruges, and Ghent shipped goods to Northern Europe. Toward the end of the fifteenth century national states such as Spain, Portugal, France, and England sent out expeditions to seek sea routes to the East, thereby obviating the need to depend on Italian cities, foreign merchants, and overland routes. Most of these expeditions were neaded by Italian explorers, such as Cristoforo Colombo and Giovanni Caboto in the 1490's for Spain and England, respectively, and Giovanni da Verrazano in the 1520's for France. Spain dominated ocean commerce with the New World for most of the sixteenth century. In addition to establishing the first Caribbean colonies, she conquered Central America and large parts of South America, and explored much of the area that stretches today from the Carolinas to California. From the New World came gold, silver, sugar, hides, dyes, and drugs, while from Spain there came cloth, wines, figs, olives, iron, and luxury goods. When in 1580 Philip II of Spain assumed the throne of Portugal, Spanish influence grew more significant. Portugal had sponsored explorations, including the voyage of Vasco da Gama around Africa to India in 1498. Decline, however, set in with remarkable swiftness for Spanish trade before the century had ended. The immediate causes of Spain's decline were debilitating wars with England and the Low Countries, and the depletion of high-quality gold and silver mines in the New World. A deeper, more long-term cause of Spain's loss of power was her failure to colonize effectively the regions with which she traded and over which she exercised control. This failure to colonize was chiefly due to a desire to exploit regions for what they could yield in their existing state of development. To accomplish this, a caste system was introduced in Spanish colonies, with the Spanish acting the role of exploitive lords of the native population.

Spain's position of eminence in world trade was assumed by Holland in the seventeenth century. Like Spain, Holland was to yield its position of dominance before another century had passed due to an inadequate resource base upon which to support colonization. Holland's rise to commercial power was initiated by the Dutch merchants who had distributed eastern goods brought to Europe by Italian merchants. In 1602 the Dutch East India Company was founded. A large and highly successful enterprise, it quickly came to dominate trade with the Spice Islands. Dutch interest in the New World dates from the explorations of Henry Hudson in 1609. Five years later, the trading post of New Amsterdam was founded by Dutch merchants. In 1621 the Dutch West India Company was organized and given a monopoly of American trade. Colonies were soon established in Albany,

Long Island, and along the Hudson Valley, the Mohawk Valley, and the Delaware Bay. The fur trade provided initial impetus to Dutch activity in America, although before long shipbuilding and commercial tobacco production on large manorial estates occupied increasing attention. Beginning in 1640, the Dutch made an attempt to colonize their American possessions. Small farms of two hundred acres awaited any man who brought five laborers with him from Holland. Unfortunately, a sufficient number of colonists were not attracted. Although at mid-century Holland was the leading commercial and financial nation of Europe, the English experienced little difficulty in capturing the New Netherlands in 1664. Thereafter, Dutch influence paled before the rise of English and French power.

English colonial claims to the New World dated from the 1497 voyage of Giovanni Caboto, a venture financed by merchants located in London and Bristol. The organizers, sponsors, and explorers of this voyage were granted a monopoly of any trade originating from the expedition, with twenty per cent of all profits going to the Crown. Nothing, however, emerged in the way of trade. In 1578 Sir Humphrey Gilbert was granted the exclusive right to explore and possess "all remote and heathen lands not in the possession of any Christian Prince," with the Crown receiving twenty per cent of all the profits that resulted. While a colony was briefly established in Newfoundland in 1583, Gilbert's death brought the venture to a quick close. One year later Gilbert's half-brother, Sir Walter Raleigh, was bequeathed colonization rights. In 1587 a colony was established off the North Carolina coast, only to suffer the same fate as the earlier one in Newfoundland. In 1606 the Plymouth Company and London Company received charters for colonization. The Plymouth Company proceeded to plant an unsuccessful colony in Maine in 1607, while the London Company planted the first permanent English settlement in the New World at Jamestown in the same year. The company operating this colony was a joint-stock enterprise, and the property of the colony was held in common for all stockholders. Emigrants to the colony received one share of stock or more in the company, depending on their skill. The company was given rights to all of the region's natural resources, with twenty per cent of all gold and silver mined going to the Crown. Revenues from the area's natural resources proved inadequate to pay back the sponsors of the enterprise, and in 1624 the company entered bankruptcy. One year later it was placed under the jurisdiction of the Crown.

Four years prior to the London Company's bankruptcy, London merchants financed a group of religious dissenters in Plymouth in their attempt to establish a colony in the New World. Each emigrant received one share of the joint-stock company financing the expedition, and the right to buy additional shares. The profits of the company were to be divided after seven years. Plymouth Plantation, as the colony was called, soon proved to be as financially unsuccessful as the colony at Jamestown. In 1629 it was absorbed by another organization, the Massachusetts Bay Company, a commercial enterprise founded by a group of Puritan businessmen. The colony grew by 20,000 people during the 1630's owing to religious persecution of the Puritans by Charles I. During the same decade emigrants from Massachusetts established other settlements in Connecticut (1635), New Hampshire (1635), and Rhode Island (1636). Six other colonies were established by the English crown in the area that is now the United States. These were Maryland in 1632, New Jersey in 1664, New York in 1664, North Carolina in 1670, Pennsylvania in 1681, and South Carolina in 1719. Each one of these colonies resulted from grants by the crown to wealthy proprietors. Georgia was founded in 1733 as a buffer region against Spanish territory in Florida.

French colonial claims in the New World were based on Verrazano's explorations in the 1520's. The colony of Quebec was established in 1608. By the end of the century numerous trading posts had been established from Nova Scotia west to Lake Superior and south to New Orleans. It was the desire to convert the native populace to Christianity, and the hope to garner profits from the fur trade that led to the establishment of these sites. Extensive colonization of these areas by French farmers seems not to have been a serious goal of France. Because of this, French colonies were sparsely populated, a fact that contributed to British supremacy in North America during the eighteenth century.

England's interests and those of her West European neighbors in international trade and colonization were encouraged by the writings of the mercantilists. The school of political economy known as Mercantilism produced a body of economic thought designed to promote the unification of a nation and enhance its economic and political power. The roots of mercantilism are to be found in bullionism, the tenets of which appeared in Western Europe in the fourteenth century. In an age when precious metals served as a nation's money supply and as the only internationally accepted medium of exchange, bullionism placed great stress on stores of precious metals as the key to economic progress. Not illogically, it was believed that growing supplies of bullion went hand in hand with growing economic activity. Sovereigns also looked upon a growing supply of precious metals with favor, since this augmented the sources of tax revenues to raise and support armies and navies. The latter were important not only to suppress any recalcitrant baron's threat to national unification and centralization of power, but also to provide safety along established trade routes, and facilitate the opening of new avenues of world commerce. If a nation lacked gold and silver mines, its bullion earnings could only come from favorable trade balances (selling more goods to foreigners than were being bought), or through the acquisition of colonies endowed with gold and silver mines. Bullionism differed from its more sophisticated successor of the seventeenth and eighteenth centuries, mercantilism, in three essential ways. First, it was more concerned with maintaining the existing stock of bullion in a nation than in augmenting that stock. Second, it stressed the need for a favorable trade balance in every foreign transaction rather than in overall transactions. Third, it advocated legislation controlling individual foreign transactions, rather than general trade regulations. Thus, in England as early as 1139 a law was passed requiring wool merchants to import a certain quantity of precious metal for every sack of wool exported. And in the Navigation Act of 1381, Richard II expressly forbade any export of gold and silver.

Mercantilist writers were essentially English merchants who, building on the theory of bullionism, held that what was good for business was good for the nation. The most noted mercantilist of all, Thomas Mun (*England's Treasure by Forraign Trade*, 1664), was a director of the British East India Company. Another mercantilist, Edward Misselden (*Free Trade or The Meanes to Make Trade Flourish*, 1662) was a prominent member of the Merchant Adventurers. One early writer, Gerald Malynes (*St. George for England Allegorically Described*, 1601), subscribed to bullionist legislation which prohibited the export of any gold or silver to pay for imports. Thomas Mun attacked this view on behalf of the East India Company in 1621. Anxious to preserve the right of the company to export 30,000 pounds of bullion with every voyage of its ships, Mun argued that the export of gold and silver in the short term could bring greater long term bullion inflows, particularly if the gold and silver being exported were to be used to pay for goods that would subsequently be re-exported at higher prices.

Insofar as manufacturing was the basis of exports, mercantilists looked upon industry as being of first importance to a nation's economic progress. To enhance the quantity and quality of goods which merchants could sell abroad, manufacturing was encouraged. To promote production, laws were passed establishing bounties, protective tariffs, and restrictions on competitive colonial manufacturing and exports to England. Such legislation, by encouraging manufacturing self-sufficiency, also acted to prevent gold outflows for manufacturing imports. To encourage the development of manufacturing, it was desirable that an abundant source of cheap labor and capital exist. To keep English wage costs down, thereby keeping export prices low, a 1563 Statute of Artificers established apprenticeship regulations. In addition, writers such as Josiah Child (*A New Discourse of Trade,* 1694) and Sir Thomas Culpepper (*Tract Against Usurie,* 1621), advocated legislation fixing interest rates at low levels. Josiah Child argued that colonies might be harmful since they tended to drain a mother country of its population. Colonies should be discouraged, wrote Child, unless they existed to supply needed raw materials and buy finished goods from the mother country. They should exist solely for the benefit and enrichment of the mother country and should not be allowed to develop independently, particularly along lines which might compete with the mother country. Accordingly, extensive regulation of commerce and industry was necessary to keep the colonial economy in its proper place. It was the onerous weight of these restrictions which provided the economic basis for the American Revolution.

Another aspect of mercantilist doctrine was its advocacy of Navigation Acts. These required the use of British shipping and British middlemen in international trade. Their purpose was to deny shipping profits to foreign merchants, thereby augmenting gold earnings, and to provide peacetime employment for sailors who could staff the navy in time of war. Finally, to prevent dependence on foreign countries for food supplies and eliminate the need for gold outflows to finance such purchases, Corn Laws were passed to encourage domestic food production. These laws provided bounties for domestic agricultural production and levied tariffs against foreign food imports. Only in years of poor domestic harvest was the cheap or free entry of foreign food supplies permitted. In advocating such legislation, the mercantilists failed to realize that the importation of cheaper foreign food would contribute to lower real wages and a greater ability on the part of manufacturers to sell their wares in world markets. Mercantilist theory also erred in analyzing the effect of continued additions of gold and silver to the money supply. It was correctly observed by men such as Malynes and Child that, all else remaining equal, a growing money supply resulted in rising prices, or a fall in money's value. But this was viewed as a cause of growing employment. Now while it is true that inflation and full employment often occur together, it is not true that the former results in the latter. Indeed, the effect of inflation would be to raise export prices, thereby discouraging exports and creating unemployment in export industries. As unemployment developed in export industries it might spread to the other industries engaged in selling goods to the workers and owners of export industries. Thus, rising prices could be the ultimate creation of trade depression.

Since the mercantilists, like present day economists, were not in complete agreement on their economic theorizing, there were some writers who had misgivings about accepted mercantilist tenets. Sir William Petty (*Quantulumque Concerning Money*, 1695), for example, who in certain respects serves as a link between mercantilist and classical economic theorists, questioned whether the level of interest rates could be fixed by legislative decree, or whether it was not determined by market forces alone. Petty also questioned the value of permanently favorable trade balances which always added to the bullion stocks of a nation. He felt that it was possible for a nation to have too much money in circulation. Gold was just one commodity among many, held Petty, and should be exported for other commodities if these were in scarcer supply. Sir Dudley North (*Discourses Upon Trade*, 1691), took the argument a step further. All trade was profitable, he asserted, else it wouldn't be engaged in. For that reason, any restraint on trade was undesirable. It was left to David Hume (*Political Discourses*, 1752) to take North's reasoning even further along, and pursue a line of theorizing that would be accepted by the mainstream of classical economic thought. Hume observed that no nation could permanently maintain either a favorable or unfavorable trade balance. This was owing to the effect of gold flows on prices. As a nation continued to experience favorable trade balances, considerable increases in its gold stock would result in rising export prices. This would act to encourage the importation of cheaper foreign goods and discourage exports. Conversely, as a nation was experiencing gold outflows due to adverse trade balances, this would result in declines in the stock of money, and consequent declines in export price levels. This would encourage exports and discourage imports of higher priced foreign goods. The free market, in combination with an international specie standard, therefore, was an automatic balancer of international trade positions.

COLONIAL TRADE PATTERNS, PRODUCTS, AND FINANCE

At first the thirteen original colonies seemed suited to a complementary role in the British Empire, for their comparative advantage of production lay in supplying raw materials such as furs and lumber to England. In return they purchased needed manufactured goods. It was only with gradual economic development that an irresistible competitiveness, rather than complementarity, began to develop. Unfortunately for both concerned, the Northern colonies (New England and the Middle Atlantic region) and England were too much alike in terms of climate and production to fit effectively into a mercantilist scheme. To protect its domestic producers, England shut out the fish, grain, and flour of these colonies. The lumber, ships, naval stores, and furs which they produced were welcomed, however, because they complemented British needs. Due to a comparative advantage of production, wooden ships were thirty per cent cheaper to build in the colonies than in England. Because of this both the American and British merchant marines were heavily staffed by colonial ships. Indeed, seventy-five per cent of colonial trade was carried in these ships. It was not in lumber, naval stores, and ship construction alone, however, that the North demonstrated its economic efficiency during these times. It was also in the creation of merchant capitalists, such as Thomas Hancock. Certain colonies, of course, remained permanently suited to a complementary role down to the Revolution. These were located in the South, a region which because of climate produced goods that England needed yet could not produce herself. Because of this, the South was the principal colonial sector involved in foreign commerce with England, supplying most of the commodities of the English trade, while the North furnished the ships and the entrepreneurs which promoted that trade. (See Figures 4.1 and 4.2.)

The most important item in British colonial commerce during the seventeenth and eighteenth centuries was sugar. This was not a direct export of the American colonies. New England's principal exports were ships, lumber, naval stores, furs, whale oil, fish and meat. Unable to find a market for its agricultural products in England (to whom it shipped only one-quarter of its total exports), two-thirds of New England's exports went to the West Indies, where they were exchanged for sugar, molasses, and specie. The latter was shipped to England in payment for manufactured goods, while the molasses and sugar were either shipped to England or returned to New England to be made into rum. This rum was then sent to the African Gold Coast in exchange for slaves and specie. The specie was used to buy British manufactures, while the slaves were shipped to the West Indies in return for more molasses, sugar and specie. During colonial times, New England experienced a chronically adverse trade balance with England, purchasing twice as much from the mother country as it sold, and using its earnings in other markets to finance its trade deficits. The middle Atlantic states of New York, Pennsylvania, and New Jersey also experienced adverse trade balances with England, which worsened with the passage of time. Like New England, the Middle Colonies also shipped goods to the West Indies,

FIGURE 4.1. *Value of Colonial Imports From England 1697 – 1776*

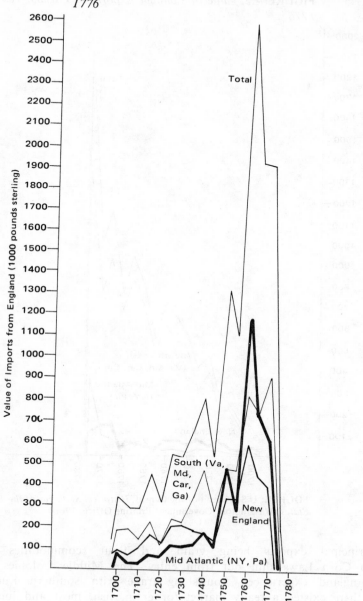

SOURCE: U.S. Bureau of the Census, *Historical Statistics of the United States.* (Washington: Government Printing Office, 1960)

FIGURE 4.2. *Value of Colonial Exports to England 1697 – 1776*

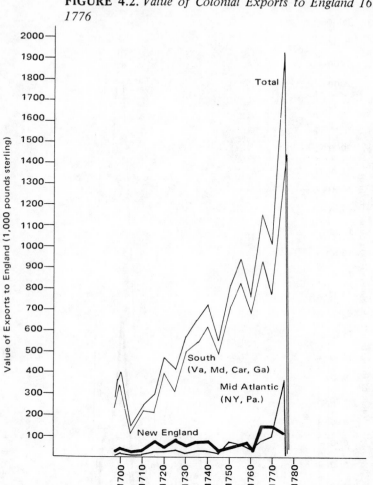

SOURCE: U.S. Bureau of the Census, *Historical Statistics of the United States* (Washington: Government Printing Office, 1960)

the principal exports being grain and flour, commodities that English Corn Laws shut out from entry. The Middle Colonies and New England experienced flourishing trade with southern Europe, where there existed a ready market for grain, fish, meat and lumber. These commodities were exchanged for wine and fruit, which were sent to England in payment for manufactured goods. Largely because of its grain and flour trade, Philadelphia surpassed Boston during colonial times as the most important colonial port. By the time of the American Revolution, Charleston, South Carolina had also passed Boston in commercial importance. The rise of this commercial center and other Southern ports was due to the importance of Southern colonial trade with England. Indeed, in 1700 more than seventy-five per cent of all colonial exports to England originated in the South. The principal export of both Virginia and Maryland during colonial times was tobacco, the cultivation of which began in 1613. With the passage of time, South Carolina's trade with England grew in relative importance due to the introduction of rice cultivation in 1695 and indigo cultivation in 1741. South Carolina was also a heavy exporter of rice to southern European ports, half of the colony's output going directly to that area. The cultivation of indigo dye was encouraged by British bounty. By the time of the American Revolution, this commodity had replaced rice as South Carolina's major export.

From 1700 to the American Revolution there occurred a five-fold expansion in the combined value of imports and exports between England and the American colonies. On the eve of the Revolution more than twenty-five per cent went to the West Indies, and about twenty per cent to southern Europe. Sixty per cent of colonial imports came from England, slightly less than forty per cent from the West Indies, and the remainder from Africa and other areas. English manufacturing imports were roughly divided between the Northern and Southern colonies. However, Southern exports to England in 1700 were four times those of New England, New York and Pennsylvania combined. This situation continued down to the Revolution, and resulted in particularly severe adverse trade balances for the Northern colonies. True to mercantilist aims, the American colonies on balance experienced a persistently adverse trade balance with England. For the period 1697 to 1776 colonial imports from England exceeded exports by 21 million dollars. This caused a continual drain of specie out of the colonies, and made the financing of international trade a serious problem.

With English coins being exported from the colonies to England, it was Spanish pieces of eight, or dollars as they were called, and French coins that provided the principal specie in circulation. These coins were acquired through favorable trade balances with the West Indies and southern Europe. They, together with the earnings of American shipping, financed trade deficits with England. Trade with Spanish and French colonies was, of course, illegal under mercantilism. When in the third quarter of the eighteenth century stricter enforcement of English mercantilist laws began, specie acquisitions from those sources declined. Specie shortages forced the colonies to rely on the issuance of bills of credit, or paper currency, to serve as a medium of exchange. Like any debtor, the colonists gained through an overissue of such currency because of the inflation which it produced. Such overissues were opposed by creditor merchants in England, and in 1751 the New England colonies, and in 1764 all the colonies, were forbidden from further issues of paper money.

MERCANTILIST REGULATIONS

England's restrictive regulations over her American colonies did not take on serious proportions until the 1760's. It took at least that much time for competitive American manufacturing to make an appearance. Moreover, it was not until then that England began effective enforcement of its mercantilist policies. Before the 1760's English domestic matters and conflict with France in the New World had occupied center stage. Mercantilist restrictions over the colonies had existed for at least a hundred years earlier, dating from the end of the English Civil War. In 1651, some four decades following the founding of Jamestown, a Navigation Act was passed in an attempt to destroy Dutch trade supremacy. This Act required that all goods shipped to Asia, Africa, and America be carried in British ships, manned for the most part by sailors of British citizenry. Goods imported from other parts of the world had to be carried either in British ships or in ships of the nation from which the goods originated. The aim of this legislation was to stimulate the British merchant marine, enhance the profits of British merchants, and eliminate the profit of Dutch merchants. A Navigation Act of 1660 required that the ship's captain and three-quarters of the ship's crew be British subjects. It also required that sugar, tobacco, cotton, indigo, ginger and dyewoods be shipped to England from British colonies. This Act sought to increase the size and employment of the British navy and enhance the profits of English merchants. This proved disadvantageous to colonial merchants who in the absence of the Act would have shipped these articles to whatever area would yield the greatest profits for the middleman. In 1704 rice and molasses were added to the list of enumerated articles. In 1705 naval stores were added, in 1721 the list was expanded to include furs and copper, and in 1764 iron, lumber, pearl ash, and hides. The major nonenumerated articles, fish, grain, and rum, were unrestricted as to shipment until 1766, when they were forbidden entry by British decree into the non-English ports of northern Europe. Intent on protecting domestic woolen and iron industries at all costs, England forbade the colonies in 1699 and 1750, respectively, to export woolen and iron products, even from one colony to another.

Restrictions on colonial imports date from the Staple Act of 1663. Designed to enhance English customs revenues, this Act required that colonial imports be shipped through English ports. Exceptions were permitted in the case of Spanish salt, wine from Madeira and the Azores, and provisions from Ireland and Scotland. The result of this legislation was to increase the prices the colonists had to pay for imported goods. In 1733 a Molasses Act was passed to benefit British West Indies sugar planters in Jamaica and Barbados at the expense of Spanish, Dutch, and French West Indian planters. The French Islands of Martinique, Guadaloupe, and Santo Domingo were particularly competitive owing to superior management and more fertile soil. This Act imposed a duty on colonial purchases from non-British plantations. It was, however, widely evaded.

Britain's mercantilist stance toward the American colonies took a decided turn following the defeat of France in 1763 in the French and Indian War. Britain decided that the colonies should contribute a larger share of the outlays for their defense and administration, and that mercantilist restrictions should be more effectively enforced. This change in attitude was due to a number of reasons. First, the French and Indian War had greatly increased British military spending. Second, the colonists had not assisted in financing the war. Third, the colonists during the war had actively traded with the French in the West Indies and Canada. Finally, with the threat of French rivalry in the New World ended, British supremacy was secure. This new era in British mercantile enforcement began with the Sugar Act of 1764. This Act, while lowering the duties on molasses by fifty per cent, was to be more stringently enforced than the earlier law. The Act expanded the list of enumerated articles, and imposed duties on foreign textiles imported into the colonies. It resulted in widespread colonial dissatisfaction. In 1767 colonial resentment was fired again with passage of the Townshend Acts which imposed duties on tea, glass, paper, lead, and paint colors, established admiralty courts to expedite smuggling cases, and affirmed the legality of general search warrants to ensure compliance with mercantilist regulations. The colonists immediately reacted by pursuing a trade policy of non-intercourse with England. In the face of this, the Act was repealed in 1770. In its wake, however, it left behind a legacy of colonial antagonism which was nurtured by subsequent acts. One of these acts triggered the Boston Tea Party. This affair centered about the British East India Company, a firm in which leading Englishmen had heavy investments. Owing to mismanagement, the company was experiencing severe financial problems. Sizeable stocks of unsold tea resided in its warehouses. In an attempt to ameliorate the company's problems, it was given the exclusive right to sell tea directly to the colonists, thus eliminating the middleman profits of English and colonial merchants, and lowering the price consumers had to pay. Colonial merchants, such as Thomas Hancock, were quick to oppose the law. They perceived it as the forerunner of monopoly grants to British companies that would before long destroy colonial business. At their instigation the first shipment of such tea was unceremoniously hijacked in Boston Harbor and dumped into the sea. Great Britain was quick to rebuke such a challenge to her authority. In the Intolerable Acts of 1774 the Port of Boston was closed pending restitution, and troops were quartered at colonial expense in the city. That was in the summer of 1774. By the spring of 1775 the American Revolution had begun.

MERCANTILIST REGULATIONS AND COLONIAL WELFARE

British mercantilist regulations were politically onerous to the colonies, but what were their effects on colonial economic well-being? Unfortunately, as is the case with many historical economic questions, those who have researched the question have arrived at diverse conclusions. Some scholars report that British policies were injurious and placed a heavy burden on the colonies, while others conclude that the impact was inconsequential. Robert Thomas's research, in particular, is worthy of examination, not because it is necessarily the definitive study, but rather because it both illuminates the question and illustrates the application of the "new" economic history.[1] Thomas's technique is to employ the fundamental economic tool of alternative or opportunity cost. To the economist, every positive decision invariably involves a number of negative decisions. For example, if an individual with a given amount of income decides to allocate a significant portion of it to purchase an automobile, he automatically gives up many alternative uses of his funds. These alternatives include other goods and services, and savings. Similarly, a nation's decision to employ comprehensive trade regulations negates the possibility of free trade and many combinations of freedom and restraint that exist in between. To determine which alternative is best, that is, which one maximizes gains one must estimate the benefits and costs associated with each possible choice. Prior to the Treaty of Paris in February 1763, which terminated the French and Indian War, the colonies had no realistic hope of achieving independence. The only question was which European power would dominate them, England, France or Spain. In Thomas's view, the colonies after 1763 had only two choices: to remain within the British Empire, subject to mercantilist regulations, or to be a free nation in a mercantilist world. Thomas confines his study to the principal instrument of British imperial policy, the Navigation Acts. Within this parameter he estimates the costs and benefits that did occur, versus those which might have occurred had the colonies been an independent nation. To do this, he studies in detail the critical aspects of colonial international trade, including exports of colonial products, imports into the colonies, and colonial shipping earnings. In addition, he assesses the compensatory benefits of membership in the British Empire. Primarily, these resulted from protection by British naval and armed forces to colonial shipping and territories, which reduced the cost of colonial maritime insurance and negated the need for a colonial military establishment. Wherever possible, he develops two separate sets of estimates: (1) an annual average for the period 1763-1772, and (2) the year 1770. Thomas's preliminary findings show that colonial membership in the British Empire resulted in net annual per capita colonial losses of 42¢ for 1770 and 26¢ for the 1763-1772 decade. Since it is presumed that per capita colonial income hovered about $100 in this period, the loss is negligible. Even allowing for a significant error factor, Thomas concludes that the largest likely loss was no more than one per cent of the national income. In contrast to Thomas, Curtis Nettels, in the reading at the end of this chapter, argues that British mercantilist policies were injurious to colonial welfare.

THE ENGLISH CLASSICIST REACTION TO MERCANTILISM

At the same time that the American colonies were engaging in political and military revolt against the oppressive regulations of mercantilism, an intellectual revolt against mercantilism was in process in England under the leadership of Adam Smith. Smith's *Wealth of Nations* attacked mercantilism on three grounds. First, it protected and fostered monopoly in production, trade, and agriculture through myriad rules and regulations that precluded the free entry of domestic and foreign firms into existing industries. Second, it resulted in English consumers being forced to pay higher prices than would have been the case given greater competition amongst businessmen. Third, it required Englishmen to bear the tax burden involved in providing for colonial defense. The history of the American colonies, wrote Smith, demonstrated that while they economically benefited a small monopoly group in England, for the nation as a whole they were a financial burden. For this reason, and in the interests of natural liberty, the colonies should be cut free from English domination. Under a system of laissez-faire, there would be complete freedom of entry into all business pursuits, entrepreneurs being directed to those areas where consumer demand was strongest and profits greatest. Freedom of entry would result in competition among entrepreneurs to produce better and lower priced goods, a situation which would benefit the English consumer far more than did the monopoly of mercantilism. The thirteen colonies, if free, could continue supplying England with needed goods, without England having to bear the burden of their defense. The goods supplied would be those which the colonists could produce more cheaply than their English counterparts. Thus, once again, the English consumer would gain. Smith recognized that production costs for the same goods varied between nations because of differences in climate, geography, and the amounts and proportions of resources. Some nations, such as colonial America, were heavily endowed with fertile land, but lacked labor, capital, and entrepreneurial talent. The opposite was true of England. Because of this fact, colonial America was more efficient in the production of agricultural goods than England. The latter, on the other hand, was superior at producing manufactured goods. It is easy to understand why these two nations gained by international trade. The Law of Absolute Advantage, as this principle came to be called, states that each nation should concentrate in those areas of production where it is most efficient, and trade for other needed goods. Adam Smith's views on international trade provided the foundation for additional analysis by Robert Torrens (*The Economists Refuted,* 1808) and the great classical economist David Ricardo (*The Principles of Political Economy and Taxation,* 1817). Both Torrens and Ricardo recognized that even if one nation produced all commodities more cheaply than all other nations, it would still gain by trade through the economic Law of Comparative Advantage. For example, consider the case of the best lawyer in town who is also the best typist. In economic terms he possesses an absolute advantage in both law and typing. To maximize production and earnings he obviously should not spend half his time typing and the other half practicing law, but rather should direct all of his efforts to law, and hire someone else to do his typing. The typist is at an absolute disadvantage in both law and typing, but comparatively speaking, the disadvantage is least in typing. Put in a national context, a nation should concentrate on the production of those goods and services where it possesses a comparative advantage. When this rule is practiced, world output and the output and consumption of every trading nation is enhanced. This analysis by Torrens and Ricardo remains in the mainstream of international trade theory to the present day.

Because all nations gain from world trade, any trade restrictions are injurious to economic well-being. Tariff barriers, according to classical economic theory, have historically been erected at the instigation of special interest groups. The average uninformed person is led to believe that tariffs are necessary to the maintenance of high wages and full employment, else foreign goods produced by low-priced labor flood the market and create massive unemployment in domestic industries. In actual fact, tariffs contribute to lower real wages. It is true that they protect inefficient industries from competitive extinction, but they do this at the expense of efficient industry growth. Tariffs force consumers to pay a higher price for the goods they buy. If the goods are imported, consumer prices are increased by the amount of the tariff, thereby enabling inefficient domestic producers to compete. The more inefficient an industry relative to its foreign rivals, the greater is the tariff protection needed, and the higher is the price paid by consumers. Because foreigners are prevented from exporting their goods, their foreign trade earnings are reduced. This limits their ability to buy from the efficient industries of other nations. Lacking these sales, efficient industries employ less workers than they would otherwise. Consequently, labor remains locked into inefficient industries protected by tariff barriers. Since wages are determined by efficiency, labor's income is less than would be the case if no tariffs existed.

Another fallacious mercantilist thesis holds that a nation should have a favorable trade balance in order to stimulate production and employment. While it is true that short-term favorable trade balances result in income creation, a perpetually favorable trade balance also results in reduced living standards. In real terms it means that a nation is shipping its goods to foreigners for them to enjoy, while in return it is receiving gold for burial in national vaults. If subsequently that gold is used to finance advance trade balances, there is a compensating increase in living standards. But if the gold is perpetually stored, its value is nil.

As already indicated, tariffs can promote a favorable trade balance by shutting out imports. This, in turn, results in enhanced production and income by stimulating aggregate demand in the exporting country. Yet for this analysis to hold, foreigners have to be ignorant of its operation. Actually, they are very aware of it, and will retaliate in kind. It is often said, in consequence, that tariffs are necessary to self-protection in a world where other nations have them. Yet this argument fails to recognize that a tariff not only harms foreigners but also the levying nation since, as already stated, it promotes the existence of inefficient industries to the detriment of efficient firms, raises consumer prices, and lowers real wages.

Economists recognize the validity of three arguments in support of tariff protection. First, in the interest of national welfare it may be necessary to provide tariff protection to industries which are vital to a nation's defence. Second, to permit infant industries to reach maturity, temporary insulation from already established foreign competitors may be necessary. Third, if a nation is only efficient in a few industries, it may be desirable to offer protection to certain inefficient industries to promote a more diversified economy which would offer greater stability of national income.

THE LEGACY OF MERCANTILISM AND THE EMERGENCE OF LAISSEZ-FAIRE

Economic theory notwithstanding, mercantilist doctrine left an imprint on western civilization that remains to the present day. Though objecting to British imposed regulations, the American colonists themselves adopted mercantilist restrictions. Such restrictions were specifically aimed at maintaining high quality in exports. Thus, in the Middle Colonies regulations provided for the inspection, grading, and packing of meat and indigo. In Massachusetts and Connecticut, laws existed which imposed regulations with respect to ship construction. In addition, to provide revenue, encourage self-sufficient production, and promote favorable trade balances, import duties were levied on a wide variety of agricultural goods and raw materials.

The advent of independence did not eliminate the influence of mercantilist doctrine in America. Charles Beard looks upon the Constitution as an instrument designed to protect existing property interests, the same charge which Adam Smith levied against mercantilist legislation.[2] Of the fifty-five members of the Constitutional Convention, Beard observed that forty owned public securities, twenty-four were private creditors, fourteen owned Western lands, and eleven had business interests in shipping and manufacturing enterprises. The Constitution, in mercantilist tradition, established a strong central government with powers to raise and support armies, regulate interstate commerce (to include the free passage of goods between states), levy import duties, dispose of Western territories, raise revenues, and issue a uniform national currency. Since those attending the Constitutional Convention stood to lose by inflationary issues of paper currency and debtor repudiation of contracts, the states were forbidden by the Constitution from issuing paper currency and impairing the obligation of contracts. The career of Alexander Hamilton, America's first Secretary of the Treasury, reinforces the Beard thesis. Hamilton, in the mercantilist tradition of aiding business interests, championed government policies which encouraged manufacturing. These included the establishment of a central bank and assumption at par of all outstanding federal and state obligations. Mercantilist legislation over private enterprise exists down to the present day in the form of pure food and drug legislation, public regulation of banking, transportation and public utilities, tax concessions to certain industries (oil depletion allowances), subsidies to others (agricultural price supports and shipping subsidies), and tariff protection to others.

U.S. FOREIGN COMMERCE: FROM INDEPENDENCE THROUGH THE WAR OF 1812

POST-REVOLUTIONARY TRADE

With the outbreak of the American Revolution in 1775 Great Britain passed a Prohibitory Act forbidding all vessels from trading with the American colonies upon threat of seizure. Anxious to weaken Great Britain's world power and to replace her as the major trading partner of the American colonies, France signed a treaty of commerce and alliance with the rebellious colonies in 1778. Under this treaty each signatory agreed to extend favored status to the other in regard to tariffs and the protection of vessels. A similar treaty was signed with the Netherlands in 1782. During the American Revolution loans and gifts of about ten million dollars were extended by France, the Netherlands, and Spain to finance the purchase of arms and ammunition by the colonies.

The return of peace destroyed the hopes of Great Britain's rivals that they would replace her as the major trading partner of the United States. Shortly after the end of the Revolution imports from Great Britain of cloth, clothing, china, glass, utensils, and hardware quickly revived under the stimulus of easy credit extensions by British merchants to their American counterparts. American exports to Great Britain, however, showed no corresponding increase. In fact, export earnings of tobacco, rice, naval stores, indigo, ships, whale oil, and pig iron, major contributors to colonial export earnings, declined significantly. The principal reason for the decline was that America was now outside of the British mercantilist system. British import duties were imposed on both tobacco and rice. To aggravate matters, tobacco prices were falling. The elimination of British bounties on naval stores and indigo caused a drop in the sales of these items. Shipbuilding suffered as the United States no longer benefited from Great Britain's navigation system. British law prohibited Englishmen from purchasing American built ships. Whale oil was subjected to severe duties. These reductions in American exports to Britain were aggravated by export declines to other areas of the world. The United States was denied access to British West Indian markets. Moreover, American flour and wheat were denied entrance into the French West Indies, while fish was subject to a heavy duty. Spain refused to let U.S. goods enter their American colonies unless, in true mercantilist fashion, they first passed through Spanish ports. Owing to the pirates of Tripoli, Tunis and Algeria, trade with southern Europe declined. So, too, did the heavy slave trade as a result of growing moral and legal condemnation of this practice.

This adverse balance of trade caused a substantial outflow of specie, and resulted in a money shortage within the United States. Numerous British firms, unable to collect from American importers, entered bankruptcy. In a desperate effort to improve America's balance of trade, John Adams, America's first minister to Great Britain, sought to negotiate a treaty eliminating trade barriers. Permission was sought from Spain to permit direct U.S. trade with Spanish-American colonies, and tribute payments were made to pirates. Unfortunately, these measures were unsuccessful. Beginning in 1785 several states imposed mercantilist restrictions on imports. New York, Massachusetts, Pennsylvania, Rhode Island, and New Hampshire levied duties on such luxuries as silverware and silk. To promote home manufactures, import levies were imposed on such commodities as hardware and alcoholic beverages. In retaliation to Great Britain's navigation laws, states such as New Hampshire, Massachusetts, and Rhode Island either subjected imports carried in British ships to special taxation or forbade British ships from loading products in American ports. Most of these measures not only failed to accomplish their goal but worked against the states imposing them, since to evade import taxes British ships sought out state ports where no such regulations existed. Moreover, tariff measures by individual states hampered the development of American manufacturing and commerce between the states.

The need for a uniform national commercial policy was evident. The Constitution, which replaced the Articles of Confederation, prohibited the states from imposing import and export duties. The Tariff Act of 1789 marked the beginning of a Federal mercantilist policy. This Act sought to provide the Federal Government with operating revenues and to encourage the development of infant industries. It levied a five per cent *ad valorem* duty on all imports with the exception of some sixty-five articles for which special imposts were assigned. These imposts varied up to a fifteen per cent levy on coaches and carriages. Paints, gunpowder, dishware, and glass were subjected to a tariff of ten per cent, while a rate of seven and a half per cent was imposed on tin and pewter manufactures, clothing, brushes, saddles, hats, paper, cabinetwork, and slit, rolled and cast iron. To protect and promote American agriculture specific levies were also placed on beer, ale, cider, cheese, malt, leather goods, soap, candles, cordage, and twine. To encourage American shipping, goods imported from the Orient in foreign ships were subjected to heavy duties, whereas a ten per cent discount was offered on all goods carried in American built and owned vessels. To promote a monopoly of the coastal trade by American shipping a Tonnage Act was passed in 1789. This subjected ships built and owned abroad to a duty of 50 cents a ton upon every entry into a United States port. American built vessels owned by foreigners were subjected to a tonnage duty of thirty cents. In advocating the passage of this legislation, James Madison asserted that it would promote the development of an American navy. In general the South opposed both the Tariff and Tonnage Acts of 1789. In their view the principal gainers from this legislation were Northern manufacturers, shipbuilders, and shipowners. In this opinion, Adam Smith would have concurred.

After 1790 there occurred a fundamental change in the composition of U.S. exports. The four major exports of 1791 were breadstuffs (7.6 million dollars), tobacco (4.3 million dollars), rice (1.8 million dollars) and lumber (1.3 million dollars). These items accounted for three-quarters of total exports. During the 1790's tobacco exports steadily declined and were replaced in importance by cotton. Cotton exports to England rose from half a million pounds to almost 16 million pounds in 1800 and to 48 million pounds by 1807. By the latter date more than half of the cotton flowing into British textile mills came from the American South. Great Britain was far and away the United States' best customer at the end of the eighteenth century, taking almost half of U.S. exports in the form of cotton, potash, bar iron, naval stores, lumber, indigo, and flax seeds. English Corn Law prohibitions still forbade the import of rice, fish, meat and grain into Great Britain. England was to be the major source of U.S. imports, accounting by the end of the eighteenth century for more than three-quarters of the total. A principal reason why Great Britain continued as the United States' most important trading partner was the fact that American citizens had a more intimate knowledge of Great Britain than they did of other European nations. A common language acted to strengthen trade ties. So, too, did the ready extension of credit by British merchant houses. Finally, as a nation of shopkeepers, Great Britain was in a position to supply American merchants with a wide variety of merchandise. France was the second best customer of the U.S., accounting for about a quarter of U.S. exports in the form of grain, flour, rice and tobacco. Spain and Portugal followed, accounting for about fifteen per cent of the total. French exports to the United States were negligible compared to those of Great Britain.

THE NAPOLEONIC WARS

The unfavorable U.S. trade balance with Britain was primarily financed by shipping profits of the American merchant fleet, and less importantly from trade earnings from France, Spain, Portugal, the Netherlands, Denmark and, after 1785, French and Spanish West Indian ports. In 1790 American ships carried sixty per cent of the goods shipped in U.S. foreign trade. From then until 1807 the United States entered a golden age of shipping and shipbuilding. (See Table 4.1 and Figure 4.3.) The total tonnage of the U.S. merchant fleet grew

TABLE 4.1. *U.S. Balance of Payments (Millions of Dollars)*

Period	Merchandise Trade Balance	Specie Balance	Service and Current Items	Dividends and Interest	Annual Net Balance	Capital Accounts	Aggregate Indebtedness
1790–1794	- 7.3	1.9	8.4	−4.1	−1.1	−0.1	70.0
1791–1795	−11.2	1.4	10.6	−4.2	−3.4	−0.2	73.2
1792–1796	−12.1	0.8	13.3	−4.4	−2.3	−0.3	75.9
1793–1797	−13.8	0.4	14.9	−4.6	−3.0	−0.3	79.3
1794–1798	−14.3	−0.2	15.6	−4.8	−3.7	−0.3	83.3
1795–1799	−14.2	−0.5	17.1	−5.0	−2.6	−0.2	86.2
1796–1800	−14.0	0.2	18.5	−5.2	−0.5	−0.1	86.8
1797–1801	−14.7	0.2	20.2	−5.2	0.5		84.3
1798–1802	−11.8	0.6	20.5	−5.2	4.2		82.1
1799–1803	−12.1	1.2	22.0	−4.9	6.1	−2.2	78.2
1800–1804	−13.5	1.4	22.5	−4.7	5.7	−2.2	74.8
1801–1805	−15.0	0.6	23.0	−4.5	4.1	−2.2	73.0
1802–1806	−18.2	1.2	23.5	−4.4	2.1	−2.2	73.1
1803–1807	−24.3	0.6	27.8	−4.4	−0.3	−2.2	75.7
1804–1808	−29.3	0.8	27.6	−4.5	−5.4		81.0
1805–1809	−29.2	0.8	27.7	−4.8	−5.5		86.6
1806–1810	−27.7	0.8	29.9	−5.2	−2.2		88.8
1807–1811	−20.0	−0.2	31.9	−5.3	6.4		82.4
1808–1812	−20.7	−0.8	29.8	−4.9	3.3		79.1
1809–1813	−12.5	−1.2	28.1	−4.7	9.6		69.5
1810–1814	−11.9	−2.2	23.8	−4.2	5.4		64.1
1811–1815	−14.0	−1.4	20.3	−3.8	1.0		63.0

SOURCE: Douglass C. North, *The Economic Growth of the United States, 1790–1860.* Englewood Cliffs: Prentice-Hall, Inc., 1961.

FIGURE 4.3. *United States Shipping Activity Index 1796 –*
1800 = 100

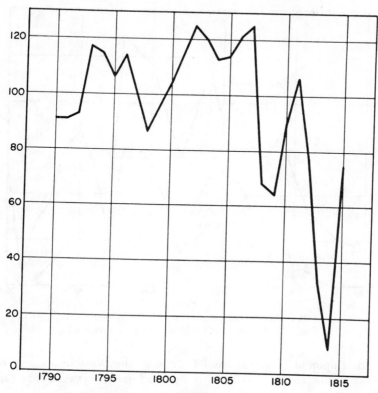

SOURCE: Douglass C. North, *The Economic Growth of the United*
States, 1790 – 1860 (Englewood Cliffs: Prentice-Hall, 1961)

from 35,000 tons in 1790 to one million tons by 1807. There were three
underlying causes for the shipping boom. First, the United States could
build and operate ships more cheaply than other nations, owing to a
ready availability of lumber and naval stores and an aggressive attitude on the part of American merchants. Second, the Napoleonic Wars
which commenced in 1793 provided an important stimulus to the
American merchant marine. With the ships of the principal belligerents, England and France, involved in war and subject to attack, neutral
U.S. merchantmen became the world's principal carriers of goods.
This is reflected in the growth of the U.S. re-export trade. (See
Figure 4.4.) Between 1790 and 1807 the value of re-exports rose from
0.3 million to 59.6 million dollars. This re-export trade centered

FIGURE 4.4. *Value of Exports and Re-exports from the U.S. 1790 – 1815*

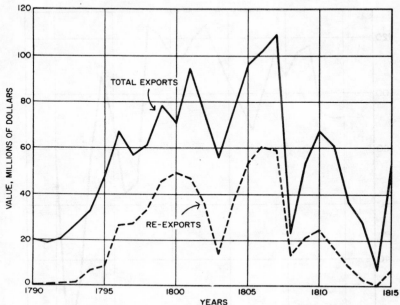

SOURCE: Douglass C. North, *The Economic Growth of the United States, 1790 – 1860* (Englewood Cliffs: Prentice-Hall, 1961)

about the shipment of goods from Europe to the West Indies and from the West Indies to Europe. It also involved trade between the Orient and Europe.

American ships, however, were not immune from capture. In the first decade of the nineteenth century about 1,750 U.S. merchantmen were seized by the British and French. British and French seizure of American shipping did not go unprotested. American feelings ran particularly high against Great Britain. As early as the 1790's there was demand for a renewed war with Great Britain. The Treaty of 1795, negotiated by John Jay, temporarily allayed these feelings. Under this treaty, Great Britain agreed to withdraw from those military posts which it still occupied in the U.S. and granted permission for the U.S. to trade with the British West Indies. A commission was established to investigate American claims rising out of shipping seizures. France's retaliation against this treaty took the form of increased shipping seizures. While the quasi-war atmosphere with France was ended by a treaty in 1800, safety from French and British seizures of

U.S. shipping proved temporary. After the destruction of the French fleet in 1805, the British navy posed the greatest threat to U.S. shipping. In 1806 England declared a blockade of the European coast. Napoleon retaliated with the Berlin Decree, under which all ships coming from England or its possessions were forbidden from entering the ports of France, Spain, Holland and Italy. The British reacted to this decree with passage in 1807 of the Orders in Council, which asserted England's rights to stop neutral ships on the high seas and deny them entry into European ports. The Orders in Council resulted in further French retaliation. Napoleon's 1807 Milan Decree ordered seizure of any neutral shipping consenting to British search. In an attempt to force both the British and French to cease the seizure of American ships, the United States passed an Embargo Act in December 1807 which prohibited U.S. ships from engaging in foreign trade. This Act, unfortunately, injured American business more than it did the British or French. The value of exports dropped from 108 million dollars in 1807 to 22 million dollars in 1808, while the value of imports fell from 139 million to 57 million. With American merchants unable to sell their goods abroad, the prices of these products dropped significantly. Large-scale unemployment and general depression ensued. This resulted in the abandonment of the embargo in 1809 and its replacement by the Nonintercourse Act. This Act permitted trade with all countries except France and England and empowered the President to reopen trade with whichever belligerent first ended its restrictive laws against neutral shipping. This law was revised in 1810 with passage of the Macon Bill, under which trade was reopened with both France and England. Under this Act, however, the United States pledged to shut off trade with one belligerent if the other belligerent repealed its restrictive legislation. This Napoleon proceeded to do in the Cadore Letter, and in 1811 a U.S. policy of nonintercourse was applied only to Great Britain. England responded by continuing to search and seize American shipping and to impress American sailors for service in the Royal Navy.

The United States declared war on Great Britain in 1812. To finance the war Congress doubled tariffs in that year. Due to a falloff in trade, however, custom revenues dwindled. Duties continued to be raised in an attempt to narrow this deficit, being levied principally on carriages, refined sugar, salt and alcoholic beverages. Trade, however, continued to worsen. The combined value of imports and exports, 245 million dollars in 1807, sank to 115 million dollars by 1812, 50 million by 1813, and 20 million by 1814. This decline in trade was due largely to a British blockade of the American coast beginning in 1813. Not until the end of hostilities in 1815 did foreign trade revive.

In that year the combined value of imports and exports equaled 165 million dollars, a figure still below the peak achieved in 1807.

NOTES

1. Robert P. Thomas. "A Quantitative Approach to the Study of the Effects of British Imperial Policy Upon Colonial Welfare: Some Preliminary Findings." *Journal of Economic History,* XXV (December, 1965), p. 637.
2. Charles Beard. *An Economic Interpretation of the Constitution.* New York: The Free Press of Glencoe, 1965. This interpretation has been criticized by a number of scholars. See, in particular, Robert E. Brown, *Charles Beard and the Constitution,* Princeton: Princeton University Press, 1956); and Forrest McDonald, *We the People,* Chicago: University of Chicago Press, 1958.

SELECTED REFERENCES

1. Charles Beard. *An Economic Interpretation of the Constitution of the United States.* New York: The Free Press of Glencoe, 1965.
2. G. L. Beer. *Commercial Policy of England Toward the American Colonies.* New York: Columbia University Press, 1893.
3. Robert E. Brown. *Charles Beard and the Constitution, A Critical Analysis of "An Economic Interpretation of the Constitution."* Princeton: Princeton University Press, 1956.
4. Joseph Dorfman. *The Economic Mind in American Civilization,* Vol. 1, Books I and II. New York: Viking Press, 1946.
5. Eli F. Hecksher. *Mercantilism.* 2 Vols. New York: The Macmillan Co., 1955.
6. Douglass C. North. *The Economic Growth of the United States, 1790-1860.* Englewood Cliffs: Prentice-Hall, Inc., 1961.

reading

did british mercantilist regulations
injure colonial welfare?

curtis nettels

Mercantilism is defined for this discussion as a policy of government that expressed in the economic sphere the spirit of nationalism that animated the growth of the national state in early modern times. The policy aimed to gain for the nation a high degree of security or self-sufficiency, especially as regards food supply, raw materials needed for essential industries, and the sinews of war. This end was to be achieved in large measure by means of an effective control over the external activities and resources upon which the nation was dependent. In turn, that urge impelled the mercantilists to prefer colonial dependencies to independent foreign countries in seeking sources of supply. If the state could not free itself completely from trade with foreign nations, it sought to control that trade in its own interest as much as possible. To realize such objectives, mercantilism embraced three subordinate and related policies. The Corn Laws fostered the nation's agriculture and aimed to realize the ideal of self-sufficiency as regards food supply. State aids to manufacturing industries, such as the protective tariff, sought to provide essential finished goods, including the sinews of war. The Navigation Acts were intended to assure that foreign trade would be carried on in such a way as to yield the maximum advantage to the state concerned.

Since the mercantilist states of Europe lacked the resources for complete self-sufficiency, they could not free themselves from de-

Reprinted with permission from "British Mercantilism and the Economic Development of the Thirteen Colonies" by Curtis Nettels, in *Journal of Economic History*, XII (Spring 1952), 105-114.

pendence on foreign supplies. Economic growth therefore increased the importance of external trade, and the preference for colonies over foreign countries intensified the struggle for dependent possessions. The importance in mercantilism of a favorable balance of trade and of a large supply of the precious metals is a familiar theme. We need only to remind ourselves that the mercantilist considered it the duty of government to obtain and to retain for the nation both a favorable trade balance and an adequate stock of gold and silver. To this end the state should help to build up a national merchant marine and should foster domestic manufacturing industries. The chief means of procuring raw materials, a favorable trade balance, and an ample supply of the precious metals was that of exporting high-priced manufactured goods and shipping services.

Despite its emphasis on government action, mercantilism was not socialism. In England, the system invoked the initiative and enterprise of private citizens. It encouraged the merchants, shippers, and manufacturers by conferring benefits upon them and by identifying their private interests with the highest needs of the state. So close was this identification that one may properly regard the theory of mercantilism as a rationalization of the special interests of dominant groups of the time. The mercantilist policy was an expression of an accord between landowners and merchant-capitalists in alliance with the Crown.

Is it possible to measure the influence of government on the economic development of an area? Whether such influence be large or small, it must necessarily be only one factor at work in the process of economic change. The range of influence of even the most powerful government is limited, whereas economic activity is world-wide in its scope and ramifications. Thus far no scheme of statecraft has succeeded in bending all the members of the perverse human family to its designs. To many students of economic affairs it may seem futile to attempt to isolate and to measure the effect of only one factor in the immensely intricate, varied, and shifting activities that are involved in the development of a large area, such as the thirteen colonies. But perhaps such an effort may serve a purpose. It at least stimulates thought, which is essential to intellectual growth, and growth — not final answers or ultimate solutions — is all that one can expect to attain in this world of perpetual change.

To begin with, we note that the thirteen colonies experienced a phenomenal development during the 150 years in which they were subject to the regulating policies of English mercantilism. Adam Smith said in 1776:

A nation may import to a greater value than it exports for half a century, perhaps together; the gold and silver which comes into it during all this time may be all immediately sent out of it; its circulating coin may gradually decay, different sorts of paper money being substituted in its place, and even the debts, too, which it contracts with the principal nations with whom it deals, may be gradually increasing; and yet its real wealth, the exchangeable value of the annual produce of its lands and labor, may, during the same period, have been increasing in a much greater proportion. The state of our North American colonies, and of the trade which they carried on with Great Britain, before the commencement of the present disturbances, may serve as a proof that this is by no means an impossible supposition.

To what extent did English mercantilism contribute to this "real wealth"—this "exchangeable value of the annual produce of ... lands and labor?" Lands and labor. Two of the most fundamental factors in the growth of the thirteen colonies were the character of the people and the nature of the land and resources to which they applied their labor. The connecting link between the two that gave the thirteen colonies their unique character was the system of small individual holdings that came into being, usually at the start of settlement. It provided a strong incentive to labor and was therefore a major factor in their development. Crevecoeur spoke of "that restless industry which is the principal characteristic of these colonies," and observed: "Here the rewards of...[the farmer's] industry follow with equal steps the progress of his labor; his labor is founded on the basis of mature, self-interest, can it want a stronger allurement...? As farmers they will be careful and anxious to get as much as they can, because what they get is their own."

Although the land system of the thirteen colonies has not usually been considered an element of mercantilism, yet it was not divorced from it. Why did the English Government grant to its colonies a benefit that was not commonly bestowed on settlers by the other colonizing powers? Small holdings inspired the colonists to work; their labor expanded production; and increased production enlarged English commerce. The resulting trade was more susceptible to control by the state than a comparable trade with foreign countries would have been. For this reason, the colonial land system may be regarded as an expression of mercantilist policy. Viewed in this light, mercantilism contributed directly to the growth of the settlements.

Such also was the effect of the policy of England with reference to the peopling of its part of America. The government opened the doors to immigrants of many nationalities and creeds. Its liberality in this respect was unique. It harmonized with the mercantilist doctrine. The Crown admitted dissenters and foreigners in order to expand colonial production and trade. Such immigrants were, to a large extent industrious, progressive, and energetic. Their productivity was stimulated by the climate of freedom in which they lived — a climate that was made possible in good measure by the indulgence of the government. The resulting growth of English trade served the needs of the state as they were viewed by the mercantilists.

We shall next consider the effects of specific mercantilist laws and government actions on the economic development of the thirteen colonies. It appears at once that such laws and actions did not create or sustain any inportant industry or trade in Colonial America. The major economic pursuits of the colonies grew out of, and were shaped by the nature of the resources of the land, the needs of the settlers, and the general state of world trade in the seventeenth century. No important colonial activity owed its birth or existence to English law. The statutes and policies of mercantilism, with an exception or two, sought to control, to regulate, to restrain, to stimulate, or to protect. In the great majority of instances it was not the role of the government to initiate, to originate, to create. All the important mercantilist laws were adopted in response to a development that had occurred. They undertook to encourage, or to regulate, or to suppress some industry, practice, or trade that had been initiated by private citizens and which they had proved to be profitable. When the origins of enterprise in America are considered, it appears that every important industry got its start by reason of the natural resources of an area, by virtue of the demand for a product, or because of such factors of trade as transportation or location. Ordinarily, the government did not subject a colonial activity to regulation by law until it had proved itself to be profitable. In Virginia, for instance, the government did not initiate the tobacco industry or attempt to stimulate its early development. Rather, the Crown sought to discourage it. After it had taken root under the influence of general economic conditions, the government stepped in to regulate it. The major Navigation Act was passed in response to the success of the Dutch in world commerce. The English Government did not legislate against certain industries in the colonies until they had grown of their own accord to the extent that they menaced their English counterparts. The currency policy which England applied to its colonies was worked out not in a vacuum but in answer to practices in which the colonists were engaging.

The effects of mercantilist laws naturally depended upon their enforcement. Since they almost invariably sought to prevent something that the colonists had found to be profitable, the task of enforcement was difficult. It required the exercise of force and vigilance.

In a general way, the government attained a reasonable success in its efforts to enforce the policies that bore directly on the southern mainland colonies, whereas the principal acts which were designed for the Middle Colonies and New England could not be made effective.

The program for the plantation area embraced several policies. The Navigation Act of 1661 excluded from its trade all foreign merchants and foreign vessels. By the terms of the Staple Act of 1663 the planters must buy most of their manufactured goods from England. Slaves must be bought from English slave traders. The area must depend upon English sources for capital and credit, and the planters could not avail themselves of legal devices in order to ease their burdens of debt.

The government made a strenuous effort to enforce these policies. The decisive action centered in the three Dutch wars between 1652 and 1675. The defeat of the Dutch drove them from the southern trade and enabled the English merchants to hold it as in a vise. After 1665 the development of the plantation colonies proceeded in conformity with the tenets of mercantilism. The effect was to retard that development, since the planters were subjected to a virtual English monopoly and were denied the benefits of competitive bidding for their crops and the privilege of buying foreign goods and shipping services in the cheapest market.

Certain conditions of the period 1675 to 1775 favored the English mercantilists in their efforts to enforce the southern policy. The geography of the Chesapeake country made it easy to exclude foreign vessels, since the English navy had to control only the narrow entrance to the bay in order to keep foreign vessels from reaching the plantations. That the tobacco ships had to move slowly along the rivers made concealment impossible for interlopers. Secondly, there was the factor of debt. Once a planter had become indebted to an English merchant, he was obliged to market his crops through his creditor in order to obtain new supplies. Hence he lost the advantage of competitive bidding for his export produce. And finally, the four wars with France, 1689-1763, served to rivet the plantation area to Britain, as mercantilism intended. The British navy provided convoys for the tobacco ships, and the expenditures of the Crown in America for military purposes provided the planters with additional buying power for English goods, thereby increasing their dependence on British merchants, vessels, and supplies.

By reason of the acts of government, the economic development of the southern colonies exhibited after 1665 about as clear an example of effective political control of economic activity as one can find. The trade of the southern colonies was centered in Britain. They were obliged to employ British shipping, to depend on British merchants, and to look only to British sources for capital and credit. They were not permitted to interfere with the British slave trade. British investments enjoyed a sheltered market in that the Crown excluded the foreign investor from the area and prohibited the colonists from taking any legal steps that would impair the claims of British creditors. The resulting dependence of the plantation country gave it a strongly British character, retarded its development, fostered discontent, and goaded the planters to resistance and revolt.

The initial enforcement of the Navigation Acts in the 1660's reduced the profits of the tobacco planters and forced them to cut the costs of production. Slavery was the answer. Appropriately at this time the English Government undertook to furnish its colonies with an ample supply of slaves. The planters were obliged to buy them on credit — a main factor in reducing them to a state of commercial bondage. The English Government forbade the planters to curtail the nefarious traffic. American slavery was thus one of the outstanding legacies of English mercantilism. That resolute foe of English mercantilist policy, George Washington, subscribed to the following resolve in 1774: "We take this opportunity of declaring our most earnest wishes to see an entire stop forever put to such a wicked, cruel, and unnatural trade."

In another sense the Navigation Act of 1661 had a discernible effect on American development. It stimulated the shipbuilding and shipping industries in New England and the Middle Colonies. It did not, however, create those industries. But the English Government drove the Dutch from the trade of English America before English shipping could meet the full needs of the colonies. The Navigation Act gave to English colonial shipbuilders and shipowners the same privileges that were given to English shipbuilders and shipowners. Undoubtedly this favored treatment spurred on the shipping industries of New England. Shipbuilding flourished there, since the colonial builders were permitted to sell their product to English merchants, and New England shipowners could employ their American-built vessels in the trade of the whole empire. New England benefited directly from the expulsion of the Dutch from the trade of English America. After New England's shipbuilding industry had become fully established (and had proved itself more efficient than its English rival) the British Government refused to heed the pleas of British shipowners who wished to subject it to crippling restraints.

English policy for the plantation area was essentially negative. It did not originate enterprises. With one exception it did not attempt to direct economic development into new channels. The exception appears in the bounty granted for indigo — a form of aid that made the production of that commodity profitable and sustained it in the lower

South until the time of the Revolution, when the industry expired with the cessation of the bounty.

The policies that affected the Middle Colonies and New England differed materially in character and effect from the policies that were applied to the South. The northern area received the privilege of exporting its chief surplus products — fish, meats, cereals, livestock, lumber — directly to foreign markets. As already noted, the northern maritime industries flourished under the benefits conferred upon them by the Navigation Acts. Freedom to export the staples of the area in company with vigorous shipbuilding and shipping industries induced the northerners to engage in a varied foreign trade. This outcome, however, was in part a result of certain restrictive measures of the English Government. It prohibited the importation into England of American meats and cereals, thereby forcing the colonists to seek foreign markets for their surplus.

The resulting trade of the northern area — with southern Europe, the Wine Islands, Africa, and the foreign West Indies — did not prove satisfactory to the English mercantilists. It built up in the colonies a mercantile interest that threatened to compete successfully with English traders and shipowners. It carried with it the danger that the northerners might nullify those features of the Navigation Acts which aimed to center most of the trade of English America in England. Nor did their reliance on foreign trade prove to be entirely satisfactory to the colonists. In time of war, their vessels were exposed to the depredations of the French. The English navy could not protect the diverse northern trades with convoys, as it protected the simpler, more concentrated commerce of the plantation area. The wartime disruption of the northern trade deprived the area of the foreign money and products that in peacetime its merchants carried to England for the purpose of buying English goods for the colonial market. The resulting decline of the exportation of English merchandise was thus deplored by the English mercantilists. Unable to procure finished goods in England, the northerners were driven to manufacture for themselves. Thence arose what the mercantilists regarded as a fatal danger — the prospect that the colonies would manufacture for themselves, decrease their purchases in England, and produce a surplus of finished goods that would compete with English wares in the markets of the world.

To avoid this danger, the English mercantilists devised their major experiment in state planning of the early eighteenth century. They undertook to foster the production of naval stores in the Middle Colonies and New England. Such products would be sent directly to England as a means of paying for English goods. They would divert the colonists from domestic manufacturing and free them from their dependence on diverse foreign trades. They would transform the commerce of the northern area in such a way that it would resemble that of the plantation area — a simple, direct exchange of American raw products for English finished goods.

The naval-stores program was constructive in intent. The government sought to shape the development of the northern area, thereby solving a serious problem. But the policy failed. It did not stimulate the production of naval stores in the northern area sufficiently to provide it with adequate payments for English goods, or to divert the northerners from their foreign trades, or to halt the trend toward home manufacturing.

This failure led the mercantilists to embrace a purely negative policy. As the trade of the northern area with the foreign West Indies increased the English Government undertook to stop it altogether. Such was its intent in imposing upon the colonies the Molasses Act of 1733. But that effort did not succeed. Again, a mercantilist policy failed to bear its expected fruit.

The early policies of mercantilism had a marked effect on the growth of the northern area. But the result turned out to be unpleasing to the English authorities. Their endeavors to give a new direction to the development of the area failed completely after 1700. A problem had arisen for which English mercantilism never found a solution.

The main element in this problem was the trend in the northern area toward domestic manufacturing. Since that trend menaced all the essentials of mercantilism, The English Government did its best to thwart it. Thus there was no more important ingredient in English policy than the determined effort to retard or prevent the growth in America of industries that would produce the sort of goods that England could export at the greatest profit. Such, chiefly, were cloth, ironware, hats, and leather goods. The effectiveness of the laws and orders against colonial manufacturing is a subject of dispute. It is difficult to prove why something did not happen. If the colonies were slow in developing manufacturing industries, was it the result of English policy or of other factors? The writer believes that English policies had a strong retarding influence. The barriers erected were extensive and formidable. British statutes restrained the American woolen, iron, and hat industries. The colonies could not impose protective tariffs on imports from England. They could not operate mints, create manufacturing corporations, or establish commercial banks — institutions that are essential to the progress of manufacturing.

It was easier to enforce a policy against American fabricating industries than a policy that aimed to regulate maritime trade. A vessel could slip in and out of the northern ports. A manufacturing plant and its operations could not be concealed, unless, as in later times, it was engaged in mountain moonshining. The exposure of factories to the gaze of officials undoubtedly deterred investors from building them in defiance of the law.

New industries in an economically backward country commonly needed the positive encouragement and protection of government. It was the rule of mercantilism that handicaps to home manufacuring should be overcome by tariffs, bounties, and other forms of state aid. Such stimuli were denied to the colonies while they were subject to English mercantilism. Not only was the imperial government hostile; equally important, the colonial governments were not allowed to extend assistance to American promoters who wished to establish industries on the basis of efficient, large-scale operations.

An important aspect of the influence of state policy is its effect on the attitude of the people who are subjected to its benefits and restraints. The colonists as a whole were not seriously antagonized by the British imperium prior to 1763. Its most detrimental policy — that of the Molasses Act — was not enforced. In time of war (which meant thirty-five years of the period from 1689 to 1763) the military expenditures of the Crown in America helped to solve the most crucial problem of the colonies by supplying them with funds with which they could pay their debts and buy needed supplies in England. The shipbuilders and shipowners of the northern area shared in the national monopoly of imperial trade. Underlying all policy and legislation was the extremely liberal action of the English Government in making land available to settlers on easy terms and of admitting into the colonies immigrants of diverse nationalities and varied religious faiths.

After 1763 the story is different. The colonies no longer received the sort of easy money that they had obtained from military expenditures during the wars. Instead, they were called upon to support through British taxes the defense establishment that was to be maintained in America after the war. Britain now abandoned its old liberal practice regarding land and immigration and replaced it with restrictive measures suggestive of the colonial policies of France and Spain. The Crown proceeded to enforce with vigor all the restraints it had previously imposed on colonial enterprise. Most of the features of the imperial rule that had placated the colonists were to be done away with. Not only were the old restraints to be more strictly enforced, they were to be accompanied by a host of new ones. The policies of Britain after 1763 merely intensified the central difficulty of the trade of the colonies. How might they find the means of paying for the manufactured goods that they must buy from England? If they could not get adequate returns, they would have to manufacture for themselves.

In its total effect, British policy as it affected the colonies after 1763 was restrictive, injurious, negative. It offered no solutions of problems. In the meantime, the colonists, having lived so long under the rule of mercantilism, had become imbued with mercantilist ideas. If the British imperium would not allow them to grow and expand, if it would not provide a solution of the central problem of the American economy, the colonists would have to take to themselves the right and the power to guide their economic development. They would find it necessary to create a new authority that would foster American shipping and commerce, make possible the continued growth of settlement, and above all stimulate the growth of domestic manufacturing industries. Thus another result of English mercantilism was the American Revolution and the creation thereafter of a new mercantilist state on this side of the Atlantic.

chapter 5

geographic expansion, agriculture, and extractive industries

GEOGRAPHIC EXPANSION

THE PROCESS OF SETTLEMENT

Several overlapping stages of westward advance have characterized the history of U.S. geographic expansion. As European settlers gained a foothold along the Atlantic Coast, the first stage in westward movement commenced. This stage involved the westward trek of hunters, Indian traders and missionaries who followed the trails blazed by wildlife and Indians. Exemplified by such men as Daniel Boone and Father Marquette, this stage moved west either to exploit new territories economically, or to minister to the spiritual needs of the Indians. It was followed by the pioneer farmer who cleared a small portion of land and cultivated it, largely for his own needs. At a later point in American economic development the pioneer farmer was preceded by the rancher, who exploited the natural resources which abounded in new areas. In time, pioneer farming was replaced by commercial agriculture. The final stage in development involved the growth of population on the land and the emergence of urban life.

135

Sometimes, as in the case of New England, westward settlement was carefully planned, while at other times, as was true of Southern colonies, it was haphazard. Unsettled western areas of New England were surveyed prior to settlement. As early as 1636 it was necessary for settlers to obtain permission of the Massachusetts General Court before emigration. Generous terms were provided to encourage emigration owing to the belief that frontier towns acted as buffer regions between hostile Indians and older settlements. The importance of such protection is evidenced by a 1694 Massachusetts statute which forbade settlers to abandon frontier towns on pain of imprisonment and confiscation of their landholdings. In Southern colonies it was not unusual for settlers to push west and survey and stake claims on their own. In penetrating westward, settlers relied heavily on navigable streams. Since the New World east of the Appalachians was blessed with numerous rivers, such as the Connecticut, Hudson, Delaware, Susquehanna, Potomac, James, Roanoke, and Savannah, penetration into the interior up to the Appalachians did not prove unduly severe. The Appalachians presented a physical barrier to the westward thrust of settlement, but even in crossing them in the late eighteenth century major rivers or valleys were employed. The four major routes used were the Appalachian Valley to the Cumberland Gap or Tennessee Valley, the Hudson and Mohawk Rivers to the Great Lakes, the Mohawk River to the upper Allegheny, and across southern Pennsylvania to the Monongahela and Ohio Rivers.

BARRIERS TO SETTLEMENT

German-Swiss settlers, emigrating to North America because of religious and political persecution at home, filled out the Mohawk Valley of New York. The Scotch-Irish, fleeing from British religious persecution and British mercantilist restrictions which forebade them to export wool from Northern Ireland, settled Vermont and New Hampshire. Famed as Indian fighters, they also pushed into Pennsylvania and Virginia as far as the foothills of the Appalachians, as did German immigrants. Besides geographic difficulties, the Indians, French, British, and Spanish posed significant obstacles. The Indians were the first hostile element, and as early as 1643 the New England colonies joined together for mutual protection against them. In a decisive 1675 battle, King Philip's War, the Indian threat to the original settlements was destroyed. After 1700 they remained a threat only to those settlers who sought to penetrate the foothills of the Appalachians. The French, who often allied themselves with the Indians against the westward movement of British colonists, represented a second obstacle. Between 1689 and 1815, a period that encompasses the Second Hundred Years War, France engaged in seven separate wars with England, six of which were fought in the New World as well as Europe. Major military strategy for both combatants centered about control of key North American rivers: the St. Lawrence, the Ohio, and the Mississippi. With a scattered population of only 80,000 Frenchmen in these areas, compared to a fairly concentrated English population of 1.3 million, it was inevitable that the British would prevail. Under the Treaty of Paris, which ended the French and Indian War of 1754-1763, England obtained sovereignty over all land east of the Mississippi, as well as all of Canada. Despite colonial hopes, British acquisition of this territory did not guarantee access to it by settlers. In an attempt to placate the Indians, who feared the subjugation of English settlement, England restrained settlers from moving further west than the headwaters of rivers flowing into the Atlantic. This Proclamation of 1763, which forbade colonists from pushing west of the Appalachians, was motivated by reasons other than that of quieting Indian unrest. It was designed to concentrate the colonies geographically, thereby easing the problems of British mercantilist administration and control. In addition, its purpose was to reserve areas west of the Appalachians for the exclusive use of Britain. Opposition to the Proclamation of 1763 was intense on the part of both colonial land speculators and settlers. Viewed as another in a series of oppressive mercantilist restrictions, it was one more link in the chain leading to Revolution.

Following independence from Great Britain, American settlers pushed over the Appalachians. In 1792 Kentucky was admitted as a state, followed by Tennessee in 1796. Once again the westward thrust of Americans encountered opposition from the native population and foreign powers. England continued to occupy forts along the Great Lakes despite an agreement to abandon them following the Revolution. In the Jay Treaty of 1795, Britain again agreed to withdraw and once again she failed to do so. Land hungry speculators and settlers demanded U.S. retaliation. Largely owing to such demands by these "War Hawks," war was declared in 1812. Not until the end of the war in 1815 did England finally abandon the forts in question. Spanish colonies represented the fourth barrier to the westward advance of American settlers. These were both numerous and widely scattered. They included settlements in Florida dating from 1565, New Mexico from 1598, Texas from 1716, Arizona from 1700, and California from 1769. Major American cities of today such as Santa Fe (1609), San Antonio (1716), San Diego (1769), San Francisco (1776), and Los Angeles (1779) were original centers within these settlements. In the Treaty of Paris of 1763 France ceded the Louisiana Territory to Spain. A conflict soon ensued with Spain involving American use of the Mississippi River and the port of New Orleans, and Spanish incitement of the Indians to attack and contain western settlers. Bargaining from military and political weakness, Spain agreed in the 1795 Treaty of San

Lorenzo to evacuate all posts which she held east of the Mississippi, to permit the United States free access to the Mississippi River and the port of New Orleans, and to cease her intrigues with the Indians. In 1800 Napoleon's France reacquired the Louisiana Territory from Spain. Fortunately for the United States Napoleon's need for money and his inability to send significant numbers of French troops to the New World led to an abandonment of his colonial schemes. In 1803 the United States was able to purchase the Louisiana Territory from France for fifteen million dollars. This vast region included an area which covers thirteen of the present continental United States: Louisiana, Arkansas, Oklahoma, Kansas, Missouri, Nebraska, Iowa, South Dakota, North Dakota, Minnesota, Colorado, Wyoming and Montana. Between 1804 and 1806 an expedition headed by Meriwether Lewis and William Clark explored part of this vast region via the Columbia River as far west as the Pacific Ocean. Napoleon's defeat at Waterloo in 1815 firmly established U.S. sovereignty over this territory. (See Table 5.1 and Figures 5.1 and 5.2)

Federal Administration

The possession of newly acquired western land posed administrative and settlement problems for the United States. The issue to be decided was as old as the nation itself. Immediately following the Revolution the states of Virginia, North Carolina, South Carolina, and Georgia laid claim to land west of the Mississippi. In addition, Virginia, Connecticut, Massachusetts, and New York asserted conflicting claims to the Old Northwest, or what is today the Midwest. Maryland, Pennsylvania, Delaware, New Jersey, New Hampshire, and Rhode Island had no claims. Fearful that the acquisition of large blocks of western land by other states would diminish their influence, they demanded that the Federal Government be charged with the disposition of territories beyond the Appalachians. This position prevailed, and in 1802 the last state to hold western land claims relinquished them.

Three immediate problems required solution by the Federal Government. First, should the method of settling new lands in the West follow the rectangular, orderly survey procedure practiced by New England colonies, or should it be permitted to proceed along the haphazard lines practiced in Southern colonies. Second, the issue of the price, if any, to be charged had to be solved. The higher the price of western land, the greater might be Federal revenues, but the slower would be the pace of actual settlement. The Federalist Party of Alexander Hamilton supported a high-price land policy, arguing that it would yield significant revenues and limit the need for taxes. Moreover, a slow rate of settlement, it was argued, would prevent labor shortages from developing that would inhibit eastern factory

TABLE 5.1. *Territorial Expansion of the United States 1790-1891*

Accession	Date	Gross Area (land and water, square miles)
Territory in 1790*		888,811
Louisiana Purchase	1803	827,192
By treaty with Spain:		
Florida	1819	58,560
Other areas	1819	13,443
Texas	1845	390,144
Oregon	1846	285,580
Mexican Cession	1848	592,017
Gadsden Purchase	1853	29,640
Alaska	1867	586,400
Hawaii	1898†	6,423
Total		3,615,210

*Includes that part of drainage basis of Red River of the North, South of the 49th parallel, sometimes considered part of the Louisiana Purchase.

†Other territory acquired in 1898 includes Puerto Rico, Guam and the Philippines.

SOURCE: U.S. Bureau of the Census. *Historical Statistics of the United States, Colonial Times to 1957.* Washington, D.C.: U.S. Government Printing Office, 1960, Series J1-2, p. 236.

development. Then, too, a limited settlement pace would act to maintain the value of eastern lands. Jeffersonian Democrats, on the other hand, favored a liberal land policy on the ground that abundant, cheap land would promote an agrarian and democratic society. The Land Ordinance of 1785 provided a framework for solution of these two issues. The Ordinance established four important principles which were largely followed throughout the settlement of the public domain: (1) a mathematically designed plan of settlement; (2) survey before settlement; (3) the creation of a standard land unit of uniform shape and area with boundaries physically marked on

FIGURE 5.1. *Expansion of Settlement 1790 – 1820*

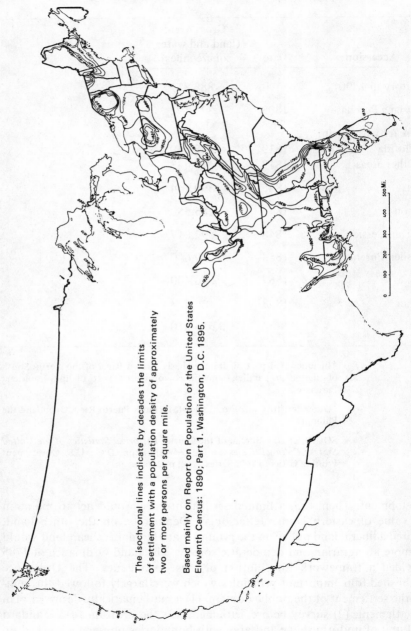

The isochronal lines indicate by decades the limits of settlement with a population density of approximately two or more persons per square mile.

Based mainly on Report on Population of the United States Eleventh Census: 1890; Part 1. Washington, D.C. 1895.

SOURCE: U.S. Department of Agriculture

FIGURE 5.2. *Territorial Expansion of the United States*

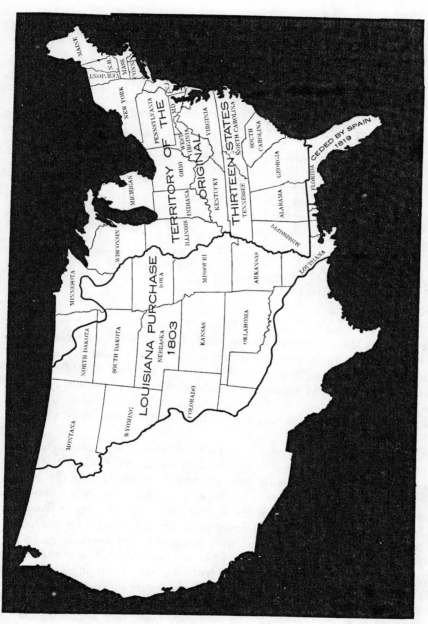

SOURCE: U.S. Bureau of the Census

FIGURE 5.3. *Locating and Dividing the Public Domain*

Section 9. Township 3 North, Range 2 West of the Principal Meridian

Township 3 North, Range 2 West of the Principal Meridian

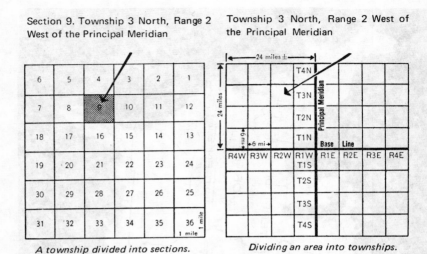

A township divided into sections.

Dividing an area into townships.

SOURCE: U.S. Department of Agriculture

the ground; and (4) the sale of land at public auction with a stated minimum price. Land was to be sold at auction in minimum lots of 640 acres, or one square mile, at a price of not less than $1 per acre payable in cash. Before any bids would be accepted each section was to be surveyed and divided into townships of thirty-six square miles comprising thirty-six 640-acre lots. (See Figure 5.3.) Every other township was to be sold as a whole.

The third major issue was how territories should be administered, and under what procedure they should be admitted as states. The Northwest Ordinance of 1787 dealt with these matters. It provided that the Northwest Territory be divided into no fewer than three nor more than five states. Until the population of the territory reached 5,000 males it was to be governed by Congressional appointees. Once the population reached 5,000 it was to be permitted its own legislature, the lower house being elected by free males owning fifty acres or more of land, and the upper house being appointed by Congress from a slate of nominees presented by the lower house. To be elected to the lower house a man needed to own a minimum of 200 acres. To be appointed to the upper house required the ownership of at least 500 acres. To be named Governor, a man needed to possess a minimum of 1,000 acres. Once a territory obtained a population of 60,000 it was to be admitted to the union as a state and granted the right of self-governance. Slavery was prohibited in the Northwest Territory and religious liberty guaranteed.

LAND COSTS

Immigration to the Old Northwest following passage of the Ordinances of 1785 and 1787 proceeded at an exceedingly slow pace. The high price of land, the need to buy a minimum of 640 acres, and Indian troubles acted to restrict immigration. No farmer working with only his family to assist him could hope to bring 640 acres into immediate cultivation, and few could afford a cash outlay of $640. In the face of disappointing land sales and the immediate need for funds by the Federal Government, Congress began to sell large land tracts to private land companies which were to play the role of middlemen in selling land to settlers. One such organization was the Ohio Company, headed by Reverend Manasseh Cutler, and composed largely of Revolutionary War Veterans. In 1787 Congress granted Cutler and his associates five million acres on liberal terms. Although the contract stipulated a minimum price of $1 per acre, payment was permitted in depreciated government securities, and price allowances were made for poor quality lands. As a consequence, the effective price paid was only between eight and nine cents an acre. A year later Congress granted a tract of one million acres lying along the Ohio River between the Great Miami and Little Miami Rivers on similar terms to a company led by John Cleves Symmes. Unfortunately, both Cutler and Symmes suffered financial reverses, which prompted Congress in 1792 to curtail further large grants. The principal positive results of both schemes were the successful settlements begun at Marietta and Cincinnati, Ohio.

After this abortive attempt to sell land in wholesale lots, Congress turned its attention to liberalizing individual land sales. In 1796 the minimum acreage which a settler could buy was reduced to 320 acres. While the price per acre was raised to $2, half of the purchase price was deferrable for one year. In 1800 the minimum acreage was reduced to 320 acres, with only fifty per cent of the purchase price payable in cash. Of the balance, one half was due in two years and the residual in four years. In 1824 a settler could buy a minimum of 160 acres and pay for it over a period of five years. Such liberal land policies resulted in substantial immigration to Ohio, Indiana and Illinois before 1815, with settlers often reaching the region by traveling from Philadelphia to Pittsburgh and then following the Ohio River north. In 1803, Ohio was admitted as a state. Shortly after, farmers in this region were generating sufficient surpluses to sell in domestic and foreign markets. The Ohio and Mississippi Rivers served as a principal means for transporting these surpluses to market. The port of New Orleans, because of its location at the mouth of the Mississippi, served as a distribution center. In part as a consequence of this enlarged economic activity, and the resulting population immigration, Louisiana became a state in 1812.

TRANSPORTATION

In the absence of navigable water routes, the packhorse was the dominant means of overland transportation in the interior region of the United States in the eighteenth century. Due to the high cost and time consuming nature of packhorse transportation, the only commodities which could be shipped were those with high value and low perishability. The chief commodities fulfilling such requirements were fur and, to a lesser degree, whiskey and guns. Packhorse companies occasionally operated on a significant scale, utilizing as many as one hundred to two hundred horses. However, the development of a more efficient transport vehicle, the wagon, dictated their demise, an event that rapidly took place as trails were widened sufficiently to permit the accommodation of wagons. The Conestoga Wagon, with a capacity of six tons, became the principal vehicle of overland transport in the 1790's. Its great advantage lay in its cargo capacity, which reduced freight costs to between fifteen and thirty-five cents a ton-mile. Precise costs depended on road conditions and the terrain.

With independence and the adoption of a federal constitution there began a drive for the construction of surfaced roads. In 1792 a turnpike era was inaugurated with construction by a private company of a macadamized road which linked Philadelphia and Lancaster, Pennsylvania. The road, sixty-six miles long, cost about seven thousand dollars a mile to construct. Tolls of two to four cents a mile were charged depending on the commodity transported. These were collected at various points where wooden pikes lay across the road, blocking passage until turned aside by the gatekeeper. The success of the Lancaster Pike encouraged private construction of turnpikes. State governments, seeking to stimulate these activities, granted companies liberal charters and often invested heavily in these ventures. By 1811 New York State had chartered one hundred and thirty-five companies to construct fifteen hundred miles of highway, and the New England States had charters with one hundred and eight companies. The general result of such activities was overinvestment in relation to the demand for transportation services. Turnpikes did cut transportation costs significantly, lowering them to ten to fifteen cents a ton-mile, but their costs of construction were extremely high. Moreover, they were still too expensive for the shipment of bulky commodities such as grain and flour. Many shippers found turnpike tolls prohibitive. To make matters worse, widespread evasion of tolls was practiced by those using the pikes. As a consequence, new construction ceased during the 1820's.

AGRICULTURE

OBSTACLES TO AGRICULTURAL GROWTH

It is exceedingly difficult to divorce one sector of an economy from others and analyze its contribution to economic growth. This is because the development of a particular industry is dependent on other sectors. To illustrate, agriculture is crucial to economic development because it must supply sufficient food and fiber to feed and clothe the population before other output goals can be achieved. Any significant commitment of resources to manufacturing must be preceded by a substantial increase in agricultural productivity. Yet, while agricultural development is a prerequisite for a sound manufacturing takeoff, agriculture's long-term growth rate is determined by developments in manufacturing. After a certain point manufacturing growth accelerates agricultural growth. In turn, the latter through a release of resources permits manufacturing to grow yet faster. For example, nineteenth-century American manufacturing required capital and labor. Agricultural earnings from the export of surplus tobacco, cotton, grains, and meat provided capital funds for manufacturing. In turn, the growth of manufacturing fostered the development of capital equipment, which was of immeasurable aid to the farmer in increasing productivity. This permitted an accelerated movement of labor into manufacturing.

Agriculture is the economic backbone of practically all undeveloped countries. Due to a lack of markets, transportation facilities, and other capital equipment, the farming practiced is generally of a self-sufficient rather than commercial nature. An American colonial farm during the seventeenth and eighteenth centuries was part of an infant industry struggling for survival. With inadequate inputs of labor and capital to apply to a large quantity of land, inefficiencies were high and output low.

Self-sufficient, family-operated farms characterized United States agriculture as late as the early nineteenth century. In 1800 over ninety per cent of the population was still living on small, self-sufficient farms. This was not owing to the expensiveness of land. On the contrary, land was relatively cheap. Rather, it was due to the scarcity and relative dearness of labor to cultivate the land. This distinguishes early America from many underdeveloped countries of today, where overpopulation relative to other resources is a deterrent to economic growth. In addition to farm size, other important consequences stemmed from the land-labor ratio prevalent in early American farming. First, extensive rather than intensive cultivation of land was practiced, very little attention being paid to soil care and conservation. Great Britain, on the other hand, because of the size of population relative to land area, was forced to improve soil productivity and make every use of available land areas. It is not surprising, therefore, that eighteenth century scientific advances in the field of agriculture took place in England and were not readily adopted by colonial farmers. Second, only those products requiring relatively little attention, such as corn and hogs, were raised. Another significant characteristic of self-sufficient farming is the lack of product specialization. In the absence of urban markets it is not feasible to concentrate production on one or two crops. Without these markets from which to derive sales revenue the farmer is without any source of money income, and consequently he must produce most of what he needs to survive. Thus, he diversifies his operations. Only as markets expand does farming become a business enterprise. Once this happens geographic regions begin to specialize in those crops for which they possess comparative cost advantages. Often the availability of transportation dictates the type of commodities sold in emerging markets. Some commodities are so bulky and of so little unit value that their shipment entails prohibitive transportation costs. Corn was such a commodity around 1800. What the farmer was forced to do was to convert it into whiskey or feed it to hogs, which could then be driven overland to market. In this way, substantial transportation economies were acheived.

THE NORTHERN FARMER

From an early date the cultivation of corn was adopted from the Indians. Corn had many uses. It was consumed directly, used to make corn whiskey, or, if a surplus existed, fed to livestock. The first explorers had been quite impressed by the large tracts of corn under cultivation by most Indian tribes. These fields were cared for communally by the women and children of the village, joined by men at planting and harvest times. The implements of the Indians were quite crude, being limited to such items as sticks, stones, and animal bones. While corn was the main staple of the Indians, they also produced pumpkin, squash, beans, sweet potatoes, and tobacco. The first three items were generally produced in the same fields and interspersed with corn. This method of cultivation was copied by early colonists. Northern farmers also took under cultivation wild crops indigenous to the New World such as cranberries, huckleberries, blackberries, raspberries, cherries, plums, honey, and maple syrup.

In addition he also raised a wide variety of crops and livestock which he brought with him from Europe, including peas, turnips, parsnip, carrots, wheat, rye, buckwheat, barley, oats, flax, apples, cattle, horses, hogs, poultry and sheep. Flax and wool provided the raw materials for homespun clothing manufacture. The livestock population was, of course, quite limited. The animals were not only scrawny by today's standards, but little or no care was paid to their feeding. In the early days of colonization, in fact, it was forbidden to feed the scarce corn supplies of the colonies to animals. Due to a lack of feed in winter, a large part of the livestock was customarily slaughtered in late fall and the meat salted down for future consumption. Only after some time were farmers to follow the lead of Britain in using turnips as winter food for the animals, and in breeding livestock to increase their size.

In colonial days the New England town formed the nucleus of the agricultural system. These towns were laid out along manorial lines that characterized European agriculture in the Middle Ages. In addition to private plots of from fifty to two hundred acres located at varying distances around the town, each community had meadows, fields and wasteland used in common by all farmers. Farmers typically lived in or near the town, where political life centered about the meeting house, and religious and social life about the church. Besides cooperating in the use of a common swine and cow herder, the farmers assisted one another in house building, plowing, and fence construction. As population grew and pressed upon coastal areas, groups of people petitioned for the right to establish other towns further inland. In this manner farmers pushed into New Hampshire, Vermont, and southern Maine. Farmers in New England did not fare as well as their counterparts in New York, New Jersey, and Pennsylvania. Economically, they were at a cost disadvantage because of the region's rocky and hilly land, bad soil, and relatively severe winters. Because of these conditions New England was least able of any section of the nation to make a successful transition from self-sufficient to commercial farming. Not only was the bulk of New England's agricultural produce shut out from English markets due to restrictive mercantilist practices, but domestic markets as well, because of higher production costs compared to other colonial regions. Moreover, the profitability of the carrying trade, shipbuilding, fishing, and by the early nineteenth century, factory production, added to the unattractiveness of agriculture. As resources increasingly were diverted to these other pursuits, New England imported grain from the agriculturally more efficient Middle Atlantic states. During the late colonial period and the early decades of independence, an increasing number of New England farmers turned their attention to dairy and vegetable production. The perishability of these items necessitated their cultivation close to the point of their consumption. The growth of urban areas such as Boston stimulated the output of these crops.

Not only did Dutch and German farmers of the Middle Atlantic colonies possess superior soil, but they also brought farming skills and techniques from Europe which were superior to those of most New England colonists. Wheat was the major crop of the area. It found a ready market as early as the 1650's in the West Indies, a region which specialized in sugar cane production. The Hudson Valley was dominated by large landed estates begun by the Dutch and continued by the British. These farms, each of which stretched for as much as fifteen to twenty miles along the Hudson River, were originally granted to patroons who agreed to finance the emigration of at least fifty persons. These manoral lords had the right to establish towns and appoint town officials. Such a medieval approach to settlement soon proved unpopular, and the system was modified in 1640 to permit farms of 200 acres, owned by settlers who financed the emigration of five men. Ten years later small farms were further encouraged through a system of land grants and loans payable over six years. The major factor militating against large-scale farming was labor shortage. Such shortages, which resulted in high wage costs, were intensified by the alternative employment opportunities available on virgin lands and in emerging urban industry. Slavery was not a satisfactory solution to this problem. Slave labor was not economically feasible owing to cold and lengthy winter periods during which nothing could be cultivated.

Early Midwestern farming was also of a self-sufficient kind. The problem of clearing the land, a limited labor supply, the virtual absence of capital, and the inaccessibility of markets restricted production. Around the turn of the nineteenth century a typical Midwestern farmer's capital stock seldom exceeded $150, and his landholding rarely exceeded 200 acres. The process of bringing a Midwestern farm into cultivation was time consuming and laborious. Migrating from Southern and Middle Atlantic areas, the farmer and his family arrived with livestock (a few pigs, a cow, and a horse or two), crude farm implements, a rifle and ammunition, and a stock of flour in order to subsist during the first year. The farmer's first task was clearing his property of trees and underbrush. Girdling was the method used. It involved removing the bark from tree and cutting a ring around the trunk to prevent the flow of sap. Once the tree was dead, it was either burned in place or cut down for the use of its lumber in constructing a cabin. On the average it required about a year to clear two acres of land. Thus, after a decade the farmer would only have cleared approximately twenty acres. As with the first settlers, the Midwestern farmer placed heavy initial reliance on corn. Besides furnishing him with food and liquor, the stalks of the plant were used as fodder for the livestock. Wheat was a more difficult crop to grow, and was only raised after the land was well cleared and plowable. On the other hand, hogs were easier to raise, being fed corn residuals, nuts and roots from the trees, as well as being permitted to roam the surrounding acreage for fodder. High transportation costs required that only goods with a high value relative to their weight be shipped East. However, the Ohio and Mississippi rivers provided a cheap vehicle permitting Midwestern farmers to ship surplus corn, pork, flour, and whiskey to Southern markets.

THE SOUTHERN FARMER

In the South weather conditions were too warm to permit the satisfactory cultivation of wheat. Initially, the South's principal cash crop was tobacco. It was first introduced from the West Indies in 1613 and inaugurated American farming as a commercial enterprise. Unlike the crops of the New England and Middle Atlantic regions, Southern crops were complementary rather than competitive with those of England, the largest potentially tappable market open to the colonies. Before tobacco was cultivated in the colonies, the English had been forced to rely on high-priced Spanish imports. The high price prevailing for tobacco in the 1610's acted as a strong inducement for farmers to turn all their attention to this crop. Indeed, to promote self-sufficiency in food supply, a law was passed in Virginia as early as 1616 requiring farmers to raise a minimum amount of corn before tobacco could be cultivated. Other colonies prohibited corn imports. These laws had two aims: one was the simple goal of preventing famine, and the second was the mercantilist inspired desire to promote self-sufficiency in food output. Corn cultivation was also encouraged by the fact that its price, unlike the prices of other commodities which were fixed by law, was permitted freely to find its own market level.

The expansion of colonial tobacco cultivation acted to depress world prices. By 1630, it fetched less than one-eighth the price it had brought in 1620. Cooperative efforts among the farmers to raise prices resulted in the destruction of large quantities of surplus stocks. For the most part, however, such acts did not succeed. The farmer, instead of producing less in response to falling prices, produced more in order to maintain his previous profit level, a traditional reaction of farmers which runs counter to the positively sloped supply curve of the typical economics textbook. This acted to depress prices further. Despite occasional interruptions in the downward secular price drift, many small farmers were forced out of business. Large plantations which were able to utilize low-priced slave labor fared somewhat better. Low tobacco prices encouraged a move to virgin soil in order to lower production costs. In the Old South not only were land prices higher, but previous tobacco production had exercised a destructive effect on the soil. Rather than enriching the soil, it was cheaper simply to shift cultivation to new land. By the turn of the nineteenth century tobacco production had spearheaded the westward movement of Southern farmers to Kentucky, Tennessee and southern Ohio. Following 1800 tobacco cultivation experienced an economic decline. A number of factors contributed to the decline. First, competition from East and West Indian producers and high European duties against American tobacco sharply reduced foreign demand. Second, the soil depleting impact of many decades of tobacco culture in the Old South raised production costs. Third, and perhaps most important, a more attractive alternative crop arose — cotton.

Besides tobacco, rice and indigo were major Southern commercial crops prior to 1800. Rice cultivation began in the swampy land around Charleston, South Carolina. The heavy use of slave labor to construct irrigation systems spread its cultivation into North Carolina and Georgia during the eighteenth century. Since only lowland areas accessible to irrigation were suitable, farmers raising this crop were forced to adopt scientific farming techniques. Indigo dye which grew on highland as opposed to the lowland of rice was often grown in conjunction with rice. It required attention at times when rice cultivation did not. Indigo cultivation required considerable skill, however, which contributed to high production costs and the need for British subsidization. The end of such bounties following American independence necessitated the abandonment of indigo culture.

After 1800 cotton cultivation experienced considerable growth. It found a ready and growing market in the textile factories of England, where heavy reliance had been on supplies from India and the Caribbean. The early Spanish explorers found cotton being grown, and there is evidence that from the earliest colonial times there was limited cotton cultivation in the South. The cultivation of long staple sea-island cotton was introduced to the United States in 1786. While the seeds in the fiber were easier to remove than those of the short staple variety, it still required considerable hand labor. Moreover, it was not suitable for inland production. The cotton gin, invented in 1793 by Eli Whitney, drastically reduced labor costs. Before this invention, a skilled field hand could clean but five pounds a day. With the cotton gin a laborer could clean fifty pounds of cotton a day, enabling the U.S. to supply the burgeoning factories of England with large quantities of relatively cheap fiber. A vast expansion of cotton culture followed, which brought in its wake an increasing need for slaves to work in the fields.

Slavery was first introduced in Virginia in 1619, and by 1630 was present in all the colonies. By 1750 there were about 250,000 slaves in the colonies, a figure that grew to 700,000 by 1790, and about 1.5 million by 1815. The importance of slavery to the Southern economy is exemplified by South Carolina where slaves numbered twice the free population. In contrast, abhorence of slavery, together with its economic unprofitableness in Northern farming led to its prohibition in New England and the Middle Atlantic states by 1800. Slavery was also morally repugnant to a minority of prominent Southerners. Both George Washington and Thomas Jefferson urged the abolition of the system and provided in their wills for the freeing of their slaves. However, the opportunities for substantial economic profit in cotton, and the need for slave labor to provide for that cultivation, acted effectively to block abolition in the South. Despite Southern opposition, Congress, under pressure from Northern states, prohibited further slave importations in 1807. In 1800 the leading cotton producing states were South Carolina and Georgia. From these states cultivation spread north into North Carolina and Virginia, and west to Tennessee.

THE POLITICAL ECONOMY OF AGRICULTURE

The early farmer struggled to clear his land and produce food surpluses. His land was heavily mortgaged. Whatever cash revenues he could accumulate were needed to buy rudimentary supplies and to pay interest and taxes. The farmer, in short, was a debtor, and always striving to earn enough to pay his debts. As a debtor, he observed that his economic well-being was directly related to the amount of money in circulation. On the one hand, significant increments in the money supply caused rising prices, which in turn increased farm revenue and eased debt payments. On the other hand, a reduction in the money supply initiated price declines, which cut farm incomes and increased the real burden of debt. For these reasons the farmer actively supported the issuance of paper money by colonial and state legislatures. Creditors, on the other hand, opposed such measures. In England, they succeeded in pressuring Parliament in 1764 to forbid colonies from issuing paper currency. It should be noted that despite the many problems facing the farmer in the late colonial period, he generally prospered. The reading by Sachs at the end of this chapter discusses the economic conditions of the Northern farmer in the period between the French and Indian War and the beginning of the Revolution. After the Revolution the struggle between creditors and debtors continued, reaching a climax in Shays' Rebellion in 1786. The leader of the revolt was Captain Daniel Shays, a Revolutionary War officer and alleged signatory to a document that urged treason against the state of Massachusetts. The rebellion took place in Massachusetts, a state that after 1780 imposed higher taxes, refused to issue additional paper money, and stringently enforced foreclosure proceedings against defaulting debtors. The farmers reacted with force by breaking up foreclosure proceedings, physically closing courts, and storming jails. In response, the

Governor of the state imposed order by the use of troops. Shays' Rebellion is of historical and economic importance in that it hastened the call for a Constitutional Convention and dramatized the economic bias of the farmer in money matters.

The farmer's interest included not only money matters, but also taxes, particularly those which he felt were discriminatory. It has been already pointed out that whiskey was a major cash crop. A packhorse could carry only four bushels of rye, but if converted into whiskey an equivalent of twenty-four bushels could be carried. Viewing this commodity as an excellent source of tax revenue, Alexander Hamilton convinced Congress that it should levy an excise tax on whiskey beginning in 1791. Domestically produced whiskey was taxed at from nine to twenty-five cents a gallon depending on alcoholic content, and imported spirits at from eleven to thirty cents a gallon. The farmers of western Pennsylvania reacted to this legislation in the so-called Whiskey Rebellion of 1794. Federal troops were called to enforce the tax, a fact which resulted in collection costs equaling sixteen per cent of the resulting revenues. Farm opposition eventually forced repeal of the tax.

EXTRACTIVE INDUSTRIES

FORESTS
The land was not only a source of farm produce, but also a supplier of many materials that were the basis of early industry. Wood was the major source of both fuel and building materials. It also provided potash and pearl ash, two ingredients used in soap and glass manufacture. Oak trees provided timber for the shipping industry and pine trees supplied masts and such naval stores as pitch, tar, and resin. The latter items were used to caulk boat seams and to waterproof ship timbers.

Wild animals were sources of furs and hides. In the North and West furs from the beaver, fox, muskrat, raccoon, marten, and mink were actively sought, while in the South deerskin provided the major animal hide. Indians did much of the trapping, exchanging their catch for such products as blankets, guns, gunpowder, knives, pots, and trinkets. In the original thirteen states trapping declined as population expanded, and the search for animals pushed progressively west. Prior to the Louisiana Purchase, the control of extensive western territories by France, England, and Spain, together with Indian hostility, restricted American access to fur regions. The Louisiana Purchase, by placing western land areas under the control of the United States, enabled America to become a major factor in the fur trade. The principal American fur entrepreneur was John Jacob Astor. He emigrated from Waldorf, Germany following the

American Revolution and began engaging in the Canadian fur trade, initially for export to Europe, and after 1800 also for export to China. In 1808 Astor obtained a charter from New York State establishing the American Fur Company, an enterprise that he hoped would take over the then British dominated fur trade between the Mississippi and Missouri Valleys. In addition, Astor established the Pacific Fur Company to construct a trading post on the Columbia River at what is now Astoria, Oregon, from which furs would be shipped to China. However, the threat of British seizure of this site during the War of 1812 led Astor to sell his enterprise to a British company and concentrate his activities east of the Rockies.

METALS

Iron ore deposits were the major raw materials for the early metals industries. Essential for such diverse objects as tools, nails, horseshoes, anchors, stoves, pots, and firearms, iron deposits were both abundant and widespread in the colonies, being located in Vermont, Massachusetts, New York, New Jersey, Pennsylvania, Maryland, Virginia, and the Carolinas. With the westward movement of settlers additional deposits were found in Kentucky and Tennessee. On the eve of the American Revolution the colonies had more forges and furnaces than England and Wales combined, and accounted for fifteen per cent of world production. This relatively important position owed to the abundance of timber to supply charcoal, the major fuel in the smelting of iron. Lead was another useful metal. During colonial days it was found in Virginia and Massachusetts, and used in the production of pewter, bullets, printing type, paint, and glass. The demand for lead exceeded available domestic supplies until discovery of rich deposits within the Louisiana Territory, particularly around St. Louis, Missouri. Copper was a third metal of considerable importance. However, until the opening of the Midwest and Far West domestic supplies were inadequate to fill demand.

FISHING

The coastal character of colonial America made fishing an important industry. The principal centers of the fishing industry were Boston and Marblehead, Massachusetts, and the principal crop was codfish. The best codfish was either consumed at home or cured for shipment to Catholic France and Spain. Lesser grades were sent to the West Indies as food for slaves. Other fish, such as mackeral, herring and haddock were also farmed. The New England fishing industry was severely curtailed by the Revolution, but revived substantially following the initiation of bounty payments by the Federal Government in 1789. The industry reached a peak in the year 1807 when it employed about 2,000 ships. The smaller but almost as important whaling industry centered about Nantucket, and provided such products as sperm oil for candle manufacture, whale oil for illumination, whale bone for corsets, and ambergris for the preparation of perfumes. The industry reached its peak shortly before the American Revolution. At that time it numbered about two hundred ships, which roamed the Atlantic as far south as Brazil. All but destroyed by the American Revolution, the industry slowly recovered following independence. The size of the fleet remained under one hundred ships from the Revolution to 1815, but the size of each ship increased about fourfold.

SELECTED REFERENCES

1. T.P. Abernethy, *Western Lands and the American Revolution.* New York: Appleton-Century-Crofts, 1937.
2. Percy W. Bidwell and John I. Falconer. *History of Agriculture in the Northern United States, 1620-1860.* Washington, D.C.: Carnegie Institution of Washington, 1925.
3. Lewis C. Gray. *History of Agriculture in the Southern United States to 1860.* 2 volumes. Washington, D.C.: Carnegie Institution of Washington, 1933.
4. R. McFarland. *A History of the New England Fisheries.* Philadelphia: University of Pennsylvania Press, 1911.
5. P.J. Treat. *The National Land System, 1785-1820.* New York: Treat, 1910.

reading

was the pre-revolutionary northern farmer prosperous?

william s. sachs

Many writers treating the late colonial period have touched upon the subject of economic fluctuations, but no agreement is found as to the duration, intensity, and amplitude of these alterations of good and bad times. Nor has any investigation as yet assembled all the available data necessary to an understanding of this phenomenon. Since agriculture constituted an important aspect of the colonial economy, some light may be shed upon these economic vicissitudes by an examination of Northern agricultural conditions in the two decades preceding the Revolution.[1]

Although contemporaries depicted the period of the French and Indian War as one of great prosperity, the benefits that farmers derived from the war were not strikingly impressive. From 1755 to 1759 inclusive, prices of agricultural products remained almost stationary, while prices of almost all other commodities climbed steadily.[2] Meanwhile, as provincial governments commenced to raise and outfit regiments, taxes began to mount. Thus, while farmers' outlays were unmistakably increasing, the evidence of price data indicates a lag in farm income.[3] Admittedly, an exact computation of agricultural income for this period is impossible, since we do not know how much farmers produced. Nevertheless, price data together with other available information can provide a rough approximation of how the agricultural classes fared.

In 1759 and 1760, prices of agricultural products exhibited a significant upward movement for the first time since the beginning of the war.

Reprinted with permission from "Agricultural Conditions in the Northern Colonies Before the Revolution" by William S. Sachs, in *Journal of Economic History*, XIII (Summer 1953), 274-290.

CHART 1 *Monthly Relative Wholesale Prices at Philadelphia (Base: 1741 − 45 = 100)*

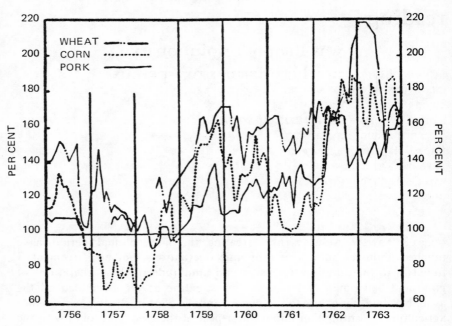

SOURCE: Computed from monthly average prices in Bezanson, *Prices in Colonial Pennsylvania,* pp. 381-85, 396-403.

This relatively short period of farm prosperity came to an abrupt end in 1761 when a severe drought laid waste the crops. Governor Bernard of Massachusetts proclaimed a day of public prayer to the end that God "would visit us with refreshing showers, as may still preserve the remaining fruits of the earth, and bring forward the withered grass, that there may be fruit for man and beast,"[4] The supplications went unanswered, no rains came to moisten the parched earth, and crops withered before they were ripe.

The next year the colonists again suffered from unrelenting droughts and serious crop failures. Complaints of distress were heard from every quarter — from the lower classes in the cities who found wages out of line with famine prices and from farmers who saw their income shrinking while debts mounted.[5] Frontier communities, especially hard hit, flooded legislatures with petitions for relief.[6] Pontiac's Revolt in 1763 added further hardships to frontier counties, particularly in Pennsylvania. However one may impute material gains made from war, certain it is that farmers, for whom the war years were not years of exceptional prosperity, emerged from the war in serious economic plight.

At about the same time that poor harvests brought economic hardship to the farm population, merchants also were complaining of depressed trade and financial stringency. The agricultural depression contributed directly to this business slump.[7] At a time when English merchants were pressing their American debtors for settlement of balances outstanding, payments from rural areas to urban merchants were not forthcoming; exports of farm products to foreign ports, an important source of remittance for American merchants, were drastically curtailed; and rural buying shrank when other markets also were contracting.[8] On the other hand, the postwar business depression, although aggravating the situation, did not produce any striking effect upon the economic fortunes of agriculture. Following a lively speculation in real estate, land values seem to have been generally depressed by 1763.[9] For most farmers, however, what was derived from the land and what possible improvements could be made upon it were matters of greater significance than the money ratings imputed to land. With the first abundant harvest, prices of farm products dropped from their famine peaks. The fundamental question in relation to prices is, however, how severe was the decline?

TABLE 1. *Average Prices of the Fourth Quarter of the Year at Philadelphia*

Product	Unit	1756	1757	1758	1759	1760	1763
Wheat	S–bu.	3.36	3.44	4.10	5.42	5.16	5.42
Flour	S–cwt.	11.33	11.11	12.67	16.31	15.16	14.42
Corn	S–bu.	2.11	1.70	2.13	3.41	3.06	3.69
Beef	S–bbl.	50.00	44.50	47.50	50.00	51.93	68.73
Pork	S–bbl.	60.50	61.63	59.17	69.53	71.17	93.33

By referring to Table 1 (and also to Chart 1), we can compare prices of agricultural commodities in 1763 with those that farmers obtained during the war years. Philadelphia has been selected because it was the most important colonial market for provisions, because price data for that port are most adequate, and because Pennsylvania currency, in which prices are measured, was relatively stable. Since the heaviest trading in farm products took place during the fall months, the last quarter of each year has been selected for comparison.

Excluding the famine years of 1761 and 1762, a period when farm income was much reduced,[10] quarterly averages in 1763 were even slightly above those of the prosperous years of 1759 and 1760, except for flour.

In comparison with the remainder of the war years, prices of all important agricultural commodities were substantially higher in 1763.[11]

By the end of 1763, prices of farm produce still hovered at relatively high levels, while shortages, particularly of animal products, made themselves felt. Unable to procure provisions on the Continent for the army garrison at Nova Scotia, John Hancock was forced to turn to Ireland for supplies.[12] Similarly, John Watts ordered a shipment of pork from Ireland, as that commodity was "excessively dear" at New York.[13] In December of 1763 John Van Cortlandt instructed his various agents to remit in wheat to New York as the demand for that article was brisk.[14] On January 14, 1764, John Watts informed his correspondent at Madeira that he would try to ship wheat from Philadelphia, for "here [New York] it is not to be had without an advanc'd price and scarcely then."[15] At Philadelphia, however, the produce market was no more favorable to such operations than at New York. "Corn @ 5/ not 300 Bushels to be got — flour @ 19 to 20/ — pork 5 pounds. Few barrels to be had, bought up months past," wrote Thomas Riche of Philadelphia in response to an order for provisions from the West Indies.[16] The new army contractors of the Pittsburgh district, finding themselves unable to secure sufficient provisions for fulfilling the terms of their contracts, effective as of April 13, 1764, requested that the army administration sell them the surplus food supplies obtained from the previous contractors.[17]

Yet in 1764 American merchants complained persistently of poor markets abroad.[18] Why then should prices of provisions in home markets remain at moderate levels when exports constituted the main outlet for farm surpluses? The answer is to be found in trade statistics. With the cessation of privateering, production of large crops, and a fall in freight and insurance rates after the war, the volume of overseas commerce expanded rapidly.[19] American importers found it decidedly more profitable to send out their ships full-freighted than empty while vessels bringing goods to America sought return freight. In turn, the augmented volume of trade created a strong demand for agricultural products.

Farmers' difficulties immediately following the termination of war were the result of financial liabilities incurred when crop failures had reduced their income. Debts, both public and private, weighed heavily upon them, while in every province postwar taxes were taking a larger chunk out of farm income than they had before the war.

In New England particularly, postwar taxes were extremely heavy, while public creditors further aggravated the situation by adding their weight to a policy of rapid currency contraction.[20] It is little wonder that in an area of relatively low agricultural productivity, yet experiencing the heaviest taxation and most marked currency appreciation north of the

Potomac, debts constituted the one great complaint of farmers.[21] Shortly after the end of the war, however, Connecticut and New Hampshire eased tax burdens considerably by using the Parliamentary grant to liquidate their liabilities, and with the appearance of good harvests both of these colonies realized improved economic conditions more rapidly than else-where in New England.[22]

Although rural taxes in New York were higher after 1763 than before the war, it can hardly be said that they were burdensome.[23] In Pennsylvania, taxes on rural real estate were relatively light in the postwar years. Of a total annual assessment of £34,855, about one-half came from Philadelphia and Chester Counties and the city of Philadelphia.[24] Although times were hard immediately after the war, farmers of the middle colonies did not seem to have been heavily involved in debt litigation, foreclosures, or in other types of legal action indicating financial disabil-ities. Quite in contrast with New England, complaints of such a nature were conspicuously absent from newspaper columns, legislative journals, reports of government officials, and other media of public expression. In these colonies, where taxes were relatively low, agricultural productivity high, and currency contraction slow, it did not take farmers long to emerge from hard times once large crop yields succeeded those of the drought years. German farmers, enjoying flourishing conditions, took no part in the agrarian disturbances that occurred in Pennsylvania in 1764. More significant still, the economic grievances of the disaffected western sector pertained mainly to Indian affairs, land speculation, and disburse-ments of public funds — they did not include complaints of economic distress or demands for debtor relief.[25] Similarly, the tenants' revolt in New York in 1765-1766 was not connected with depressed agricultural conditions; it was essentially an attempt of farmers to extricate themselves from a landholding system that denied them secure tenure.[26] It would be strange indeed that men who so copiously poured forth their economic complaints, real or imagined, and who were ready to secure their demands by force of arms should be so negligent as to omit any reference to hard times if they were suffering from an economic depression.

Not only were crop yields large in the years after 1763, but prices which farmers received were excellent. Students of price history have pointed out the divergence in the movement of imported- and domestic-commodity prices at New York.[27] A similar divergence seems to have taken place at Philadelphia; while domestic-commodity prices moved rather upward, prices of imported commodities seemed to oscillate around a horizontal trend.

With prospects of an abundant harvest, agricultural prices at Phila-delphia declined somewhat in 1764. From the last quarter of that year, however, prices of farm products began a steady and uninterrupted rise

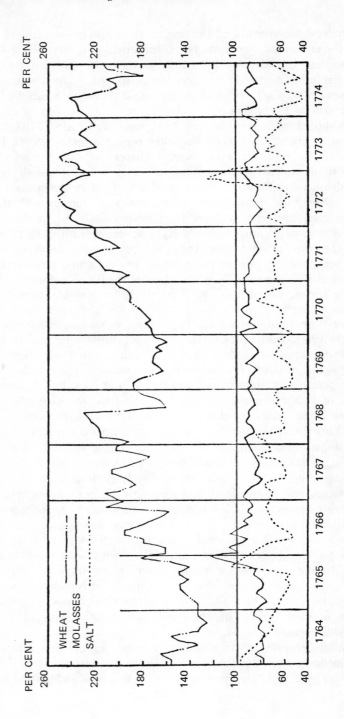

CHART 2 *Monthly Relative Wholesale Prices at Philadelphia*
(Base 1741 – 1745 = 100)

SOURCE: Computed from monthly average prices in Bezanson *et al.*
Prices in Colonial Pennsylvania, pp. 404-14.

which was not arrested until the middle of 1768. The price of wheat, Pennsylvania's major crop, rose from a monthly relative of 125 to 230 (1741-1745 = 100), surpassing the famine peak of 1763! In 1769 the price of wheat turned definitely downward but still stood substantially above the price levels of 1764. The average price of the lowest quarter of 1769 was still above the highest quarterly average of 1764, and 28 per cent over the lowest quarterly average. The price movement of flour strongly paralleled that of wheat, while prices of corn, beef, and pork displayed a similar tendency.[28]

On the other hand, prices of salt, rum, and molasses, like those of agricultural commodities, dropped drastically after the war. But unlike farm-commodity prices, prices of this group of products fell well below the base or prewar period and, except for the brief period of nonimportation in 1765-1766, failed to rise much above the depressed price levels of 1764. The lowest quarterly average price of New England rum in 1769 was but 9 per cent above that of 1764,[29] molasses only 8 per cent higher, while salt dipped to 11 percent below. From evidence of scattered prices — mainly those of osnaburgs, a representative coarse linen fabric — Anne Bezanson and her associates have indicated the course of prices of British imported textiles as falling after the Peace of Paris and fluctuating around a horizontal trend from about 1764 to 1775.[30] Although prices of farm implements and finished metal products are nonexistent for this period, the available evidence affords reasonable ground for belief that this group of products fell in price during the 1760's.[31] For what amounts or in what proportions farmers exchanged their surpluses of salt, molasses, rum, iron products, and dry goods we do not know, since consumption statistics are unavailable. However, since these commodities constituted rather important single items of farmers' budgets in the eighteenth century,[32] the conclusion is almost inescapable that farmers' per unit expenditures decreased in relation to farm revenue per unit of output.

After 1769 merchants once again began to enjoy a period of political calm and generally improved business conditions, at least until the latter part of 1772 or early 1773. Farmers, too, shared in the general prosperity. Prices of agricultural products again began to climb, reaching even higher peaks than before, and not until the eve of the Revolution did any significant decline occur from the new high levels. Meanwhile, prices of salt, molasses, and rum remained fairly constant at the levels of the preceding decade.

The prevailing high prices of agricultural produce from 1764 to 1775 were mainly the result of an expansion in demand from abroad. Beginning in 1764, a series of poor crops converted England from a grain exporting to a grain importing nation.[33] European ports formerly supplied with

English grain immediately turned to the British colonies in America to supply the deficit.[34] On February 19, 1766, the British Parliament modified its corn laws to allow the importation of American grain duty free.[35] British merchants sought American foodstuffs not only for their home markets but also to fulfill their contracts with foreign mercantile houses.[36] Poor crops in scattered parts of Europe in 1766 and more serious crop failures beyond the Atlantic the next year further augmented the demand for American provisions.

Table 2 represents tonnage cleared annually from the three major ports of the Northern colonies to the two most important foreign markets for American agricultural staples. This record, while it does not show particular commodities shipped, provides a rough, over-all indication of quantity change and of the direction of trade to specific areas. The strong demand for American foodstuffs is especially noticeable in the tonnage statistics of Philadelphia, the largest colonial mart for provisions. From 1765 to 1769 tonnage clearing to the West Indies declined absolutely, but that to southern Europe increased almost threefold, surpassing exports to the West Indies for the first time in colonial history. Improved markets in the West Indies after 1769 further augmented the demand for Pennsylvania grain and flour but reversed the movement of exports. For the entire period, however, the major increase in Philadelphia's export trade, as measured by tonnage, was with southern Europe.[37] Exports of New York, ranking next to Philadelphia as a grain-exporting port, followed a some-what similar course to that of the Quaker City. Boston, however, lacking a highly productive hinterland and a prominent staple having a strong demand abroad, witnessed its foreign-export trade develop in a different direction from that of its sister ports to the south. From 1765 to 1769, tonnage cleared from Boston to southern Europe remained almost station-ary, while a 15 per cent increase took place in tonnage cleared to the West Indies. By 1772 exports to the West Indies, on the basis of tonnage, had grown by an additional 19 per cent. But while these markets offered Boston traders strong allurements, exports to southern Europe dwindled to insignificant proportions.[38]

An analysis of the consensus of contemporary opinion reinforces the conclusions drawn from the preceding data. Unfortunately, farmers left no letters, carefully kept diaries, or other written records from which the historian might form some judgment about what they thought their eco-nomic position to be. Thus, our conclusions must be based on different types of evidence coming from people who were not tillers of the soil and whose interests were at times diametrically opposed to those of farmers.

During the early political controversies with Great Britain, colonial agitators advanced the argument of the "poverty of the people" and

TABLE 2. *Tonnage Cleared from Philadelphia, New York, and Boston*

Year	Philadelphia West Indies	Philadelphia Southern Europe	New York West Indies	New York Southern Europe	Boston West Indies	Boston Southern Europe
1764	–	–	7,340	1,882	–	–
1765	13,494	4,455	8,385	3,190	7,806	1,075
1768	12,019	7,255	6,981	2,360	10,095	1,333
1769	11,114	12,040	5,466	3,278	8,995	1,081
1770	13,842	10,940	7,005	2,920	8,248	813
1771	13,449	7,110	7,708	2,029	9,171	1,113
1772	15,674	8,415	8,076	2,449	10,703	555

SOURCE: Harrington, *The New York Merchant*, pp. 356-68.

predicted the most dire results for the rural population as a consequence of British legislation. Some even insisted that these grim forebodings were actually taking place.[39] Such contentions had as their purpose the creation of a favorable opinion in order to secure modification of specific Parliamentary legislation regarded by the colonists as inimical to their interests.

After the Sugar Act was modified and the Stamp Act repealed, all utterance on agricultural distress practically ceased. In fact, the complaints came only from urban quarters and were concerned not with farm distress but with soaring prices, food shortages, and rising costs of living. As early as the Stamp Act controversy, "Colbert" argued that a policy of conducting no business without stamps would hurt Britain because large orders of grain were "bought up or shipped by orders from home, and if it should remain here now it will be sold at a cheaper rate to our increasing manufacturers."[40]

With the continuing high prices of food, complaints emanating from the cities mounted. One writer depicted farmers as literally rolling in wealth and urged that more people take up farming in order to increase the supply of wheat and to reduce its price.[41] Another New Yorker accused farmers of getting rich at the expense of city people. "In Consequence of the Scarcity and Dearness of Provisions in Europe . . . upwards of Twenty sail of European ships arrived last Week in different Ports of America, in order to purchase Wheat," he wrote. "This must of Consequence raise the Price of Wheat and other Provisions upon us, already too high for the Poor of this City . . . If those Ships get their Loads of Wheat, it will benefit Farmers that have it to sell, but it must impoverish the Citizens, in advancing the Price of Provisions."[42]

By 1766 a persistent agitation developed in New York City to prohibit the exportation of provisions until prices should fall to "reasonable levels." "Flour has risen to the enormous price of twenty four shillings per [cwt], which . . . is higher than it rose in the last war, and considering the prodigious scarcity of money . . . how can we afford to pay for bread even to the price which it is now risen?" When prices have risen to a point at which people cannot possibly pay, the author argued, "it must demonstrate the strongest reason" to embargo exportation of food supplies.[43] "The price of wheat and provisions are . . . already too high for the poor of this city," claimed another, while advocating similar measures.[44] Colonial legislatures, however, took no effective steps to halt the rising prices of food, and protests from city dwellers continued.[45]

By no means were such protests against high food prices motivated by humanitarianism, or by a purely philanthropic desire to ease the burdens of the "deserving poor." The mercantilist mind, regarding low costs of production as beneficial and wages as directly related to the cost of living or the level of subsistence, naturally viewed with hostility a rise in the price of indispensable necessities. Taxpayers did not relish a rise in poor rates which mounting prices might occasion. Merchants generally looked upon high prices of commodities earmarked for exportation with disfavor, and some exporters were not slow in accusing farmers of cupidity and outright profiteering. Benjamin Fuller, a Philadelphia merchant, informed his correspondent that "wheat is now at 5/6, but its a kind of nominal price — the farmers are Rich and are loth to part with it at that."[46] ". . . tho' the last Crop is said to be a tollerable good one yet the Farmers having been used a long time to great prices the most of them are become wealthy, and therefore will keep back their supply unless they can obtain what they call a good price," another Philadelphia merchant reflected in 1773.[47] Nevertheless, artisans and mechanics, small shopkeepers, and common laborers, finding it ever more difficult to make ends meet, fully supported the publicists who urged legislative action to beat down climbing prices of food. John Woolman's "Conversation between a thrifty Landholder, and a Labouring man" posed the problem confronting the lower urban classes as follows:

> Labouring Man: I observe of late years that when I buy a bushel of grain for my family, I must do more work to pay for it than I used to do twenty years past. What is the reason of this change?
>
> Landholder: Towns and villages have a gradual increase in these provinces, and the people now employed in husbandry bear, I believe, a less proportion to the whole inhabitants . . . but the main cause is that of Sending So much grain & flower abroad.[48]

Massachusetts offered bounties for the production of wheat and flour, among other reasons, to free itself of outside dependence for food supplies for its maritime towns.[49] However, it was the city governments which, possessing a large degree of control over local consumption and more amenable to the pressure of a grumbling and resentful citizenry, attempted in many ways to alleviate the disabilities of their consumers. New York City, frustrated in 1763 from assizing provisions in its public markets at rates lower than those current, turned to other stringent regulatory practices aimed at depressing retail prices.[50] Boston followed closely in the footsteps of New York in strengthening its code regulating public markets.[51] Nevertheless, the continuation of a seller's market provided incentives to speculation and temptations for traders to buy up supplies before they ever reached the markets, frequently causing serious food shortages. By 1769 the situation at Boston had become so serious that a town meeting appointed a committee "to investigate and propose methods for the General Court to prevent forestalling of the markets."[52] A petition to the Pennsylvania Assembly in 1772 from the inhabitants of Germantown, made up largely of artisans, claimed that butter and middling flour were being bought up before reaching the public market and requested legislation to prevent "engrossing and forestalling."[53] It is not at all strange that mercantilist regulations regarding prime necessities were strengthened by city administrations at the same time all other types of mercantilist enactments were disintegrating.[54]

The validity of the claims and denials, charges and countercharges, accusations and vindications of those who partook of the heated arguments over food prices, trading practices, and government regulation is of no concern here. What is relative to this study is the fact that complaints of hard times emanated almost wholly from urban groups and did not picture farmers as victims of depressed economic conditions. When it is considered that over 90 per cent of the population made their living directly from agriculture, the years from the Peace of Paris down to the Revolution may be viewed as fairly prosperous for the major body of income receivers.

NOTES

1. This paper is part of a much broader study on business fluctuations now in progress.
2. At Philadelphia the average price of salt for the last quarter of 1758 stood 32 per cent above that of the first quarter of 1756, while molasses rose 40 per cent and domestically distilled rum advanced by 57 per cent. For New York, the price rise of salt was 65 per cent, molasses 38 per cent, and rum 9 per cent. Over the same period the quarterly average price of salt at Boston advanced by 20 per cent, molasses by 31 per cent, and rum by 17 per cent. Price statistics are based on the average monthly wholesale prices as quoted in Anne Bezanson, Robert D. Gray, and Miriam Hussey, *Prices in*

Colonial Pennsylvania (Philadelphia: University of Pennsylvania Press, 1935), pp 395 ff., and Arthur H. Cole, *Wholesale Commodity Prices in the United States, 1700-1861* (Cambridge: Harvard University Press, 1938), Statistical Supplement, pp. 37 ff. Unless otherwise stated, all further references to prices will be based on those sources.

3. As the army moved into the interior, many farmers in those areas probably increased their income through supplementary occupations, such as carting supplies to army posts or engaging in construction work during the slack season. To Jacob Wendell, September 17, 1775, and to John Osborne, September 29, 1755, Robert Sanders, Letter Book of Robert Sanders at Albany, 1752-58. MS. in New-York Historical Society (hereafter referred to as N.-Y.H.S.). Accounts of firewood delivered at an army post at Schenectady, New York, include over eighty names per year, with amounts delivered varying from one to 1,231 loads per person. The majority of persons listed in those accounts delivered under one hundred loads. Berent Sanders, Account Book, 1746-59. MS. in N.-Y.H.S.

   The movement of provisions from interior points to the major seaports was partly diverted as the army moved inland. Thus, inland farmers might have obtained higher prices than the price indexes indicate. For example, the price of flour at Albany, usually based on the New York price current minus transportation charges, owing to army demand, was at times quoted at higher rates than prices at New York. To Osborne, November 7, 1755, May 15, 1756, B. Sanders, Letter Book. Or, inland farmers might have sold their products to army purchasing agents at prices below those current at the major shipping points and actually made greater gains by reducing or eliminating transportation and handling charges. See Gage to Whately, August 10, 1764, C. E. Carter, ed., *The Correspondence of General Thomas Gage with the Secretaries of State, 1763-1775* (New Haven: Yale University Press, 1931-33), II, 238.

4. *Boston Gazette and Country Journal,* August 24, 1761. *Boston News-Letter,* August 27, 1761.

5. For evidence of farm distress, *cf.* Fitch to Egremont, April 15, 1762, *Fitch Papers* (Connecticut Historical Society, *Collections,* XVII-XVIII), II, 200. Ward to Sherwood, G. S. Kimball, ed., *Correspondence of the Colonial Governors of Rhode Island, 1723-1775* (Boston and New York: Houghton Mifflin Co., 1902-3), II, 336. To Collinson, December 7, 1762, A. H. Smythe, ed., *The Writings of Benjamin Franklin* (New York: The Macmillan Co., 1905-7), IV, 182 f. To Scott, Pringle, Cheap and Company, June 20, 1762, *The Letter Book of John Watts* (N.-Y.H.S., *Collections,* LXI), p. 62. Smith to H. Lloyd, May 21, 1762, *Papers of the Lloyd Family* (N.-Y.H.S., *Collections,* LIX-LX), II, 628. To Bradshaw and Alexander, August 9, 1762, Gerard Beekman, Letter Book. MS. in N.-Y.H.S. For urban complaints, *cf.* New York City, Common Council, *Minutes of the Common Council of the City of New York, 1675-1776* (hereafter referred to as N.Y.C., *M.C.C.*) (New York, 1905), VI, 336. For details of the Common Council's attempt to depress food prices, see Richard B. Morris, *Government and Labor in Early America* (New York: Columbia University Press, 1946), pp. 160-61.

6. *Acts and Resolves of the Province of Massachusetts Bay* (Boston, 1869-1910), IV, 632-33 n., 695-96 n., 783-86 n., J. R. Barlett, ed., *Records of the Colony of Rhode Island and Providence Plantations in New England* (Providence, 1856-65), VI, 347 f.

7. There is no agreement on dating among scholars who have dealt with the subject. For example, Arthur M. Schlesinger has dated the beginning of the business depression in 1763. *The Colonial Merchants and the American Revolution* (New York: Columbia University, 1918), pp. 56 ff. Charles M. Andrews has dated the business depression as beginning in 1762. "The Boston Merchants and the Non-Importation Movement," Colonial Society of Massachusetts, *Publications,* XIX, 181. Harry D. Berg has presented evidence of the existence of a business depression in Philadelphia as early as the fall of 1760.

"Economic Consequences of the French and Indian War for the Philadelphia Merchants," *Pennsylvania History*, XIII (July 1946), 187-88. Since classification of periods of "prosperity" and "depression" is based mainly upon statements made by merchants or found in newspapers, a subjective element is introduced. Deciding when the transition from one phase to another occurred is rendered still more difficult by the fact that the order of events of business fluctuations in the eighteenth century did not necessarily follow the same sequence of those usually associated with business cycles in the modern sense. Virginia D. Harrington, for example, although dating the depression from 1763, has characterized "wartime prosperity" as "gradually disappearing in New York since 1760." *The New York Merchant on the Eve of the Revolution (New York:* Columbia University Press, 1935), p. 316.

8. William T. Baxter, *The House of Hancock: Business in Boston, 1724-1776* (Cambridge: Harvard University Press, 1938), pp. 142-43, 162-66. Watts, *Letter Book*, pp. 20, 45, 178. To Nicholson, March 16, 1762, Daniel Clark, Letter Book, 1760-63. MS. in Historical Society of Pennsylvania (hereafter referred to as H.S.P.). S. Mifflin to S. Galloway, June 16, 1761, Samuel Galloway, Correspondence. MS. in New York Public Library (hereafter referred to as N.Y. Pub. Lib.). To Southwick and Clark, August 26, 1762, G. G. Beekman, Letter Book.

9. Fred A. Shannon, *America's Economic Growth* (New York: The Macmillan Co., 1951), p. 53. James T. Adams, *Revolutionary New England, 1691-1776* (Boston: The Atlantic Monthly Press, 1923), pp. 262-63. Lawrence H. Gipson, *Jared Ingersoll: A Study of American Loyalism in Relation to British Colonial Government* (New Haven: Yale University Press, 1920), p. 261.

10. Theoretically, it is possible for farm income to increase as a result of a poor crop, if over a given range of output demand is less than unity. In view of the complaints of farm distress and the widespread practice of subsistence agriculture, that such was the result for a substantial majority of farmers is highly improbable.

11. Price movements at New York paralleled those of Philadelphia. However, last quarterly averages in 1763 were somewhat below those of 1759 and 1760, about equal to quarterly averages of 1758 but above fourth quarterly averages of 1756 and 1757. Boston price data are more meager than that of the other two ports. Prices of wheat, however, indicate a similar trend. Fourth quarterly averages of wheat, in shillings per bushel, were as follows: 1756—3.36; 1757—4.50; 1758—5.00; 1759—6.17; 1760—5.16; 1763—5.58.

12. Abram E. Brown, *John Hancock, His Book* (Boston: Lee & Shepard, 1898), pp. 29-30, 35, 38.

13. To P. and J. Benson, January 28, 1764, Watts, *Letter Book*, p. 222. Also see to Erving, September 26, 1763, to Franks, January 28, 1764, *ibid.*, pp. 187, 223.

14. To Maer, to Hilton, December 15, 1763. Also, see to Younghusband, November 20, 1763, John Van Cortlandt, Letter Book, 1762-69. MS. in N.Y.Pub.Lib.

15. To Scott, Pringle, Cheap and Company, Watts, *Letter Book*, pp. 214 f.

16. To Scott, July 29, 1763. Riche finally loaded the ship with lumber. To Scott, August 3, 1763. Riche also informed his other correspondents in a similar vein. To Cornell, November 31, 1763, to Searle, December 29, 1763. As late as April 5, 1764, he wrote to Parr and Buckley, ". . . our wheat is high and not readily to be had." Riche, Letter Book. MS. in H.S.P. The firm of James and Drinker of Philadelphia was looking toward Ireland for supplies of pork. To Parvin and James, November 30, 1763, to Clitherall, December 1, 1763, James and Drinker, Letter Book. MS. in H.S.P.

17. For details of the affair, see Gage, *Correspondence*, II, 23, 237-43, 245-49, 251, 254, 279, 307-8, 310, 381. Note that Gage, although vigorously opposing the demands of the contractors when the issue was brought before the Secretary of War, admitted the claims of the contractors that provisions were not readily obtainable.

18. C. Biddle to S. Galloway, June 13, 1764, Galloway, Correspondence. To D. Lux, May 23, 1764, to Lux and Potts, June 13, 1764, William Lux, Letter Book, 1763-69. MS. in N.-Y.H.S. To Maer, March 19, 1764, Van Cortlandt, Letter Book. To J. Riche, April 16, 1764, to Cornell, August 18, 1764, Riche, Letter Book. *Newport Mercury,* October 22, 1764. *Pennsylvania Gazette* (hereafter referred to as *Pa.Gaz.*), March 21, 1765.

19. Harrington, *New York Merchant,* pp. 316-17. Emory R. Johnson *et al., History of Foreign and Domestic Commerce of the United States* (Washington, D.C.: Carnegie Institute of Washington, 1915), I, 120 f.

20. The land tax in rural districts of Massachusetts rose to about 20 per cent of income so that the tax was more than triple the normal rate. Adams, *Revolutionary New England,* p. 251. Concerning postwar taxation in Rhode Island, Samuel G. Arnold wrote, "Paper was fast disappearing by means of heavy taxation imposed for the purpose of its redemption . . . . Since the revolution there has been no taxation in this state, comparable in severity to that which the colonists thus placed on themselves to preserve their credit." *History of the State of Rhode Island and Providence Plantations 1636-1790* (New York: D. Appleton & Co., 1859-60), II, 254. In Connecticut, over one half of the £192,000 provincial debt was extinguished by taxation by 1764. Lawrence H. Gipson, "Connecticut Taxation and Parliamentary Aid Preceding the Revolutionary War," *American Historical Review,* XXXVI (July 1931), 721-35.

21. Arnold, *History of Rhode Island,* II, 251. *Rhode Island Colonial Records,* VI, 406. Oscar Zeichner, *Connecticut's Years of Controversy, 1750-1776* (Chapel Hill: University of North Carolina Press, 1949), pp. 46 ff. Gipson, *Jared Ingersoll,* pp. 252-53. Unlike the agricultural disturbances that took place in New York in 1765-66, the riots that occurred in the agricultural counties in Connecticut were intimately bound up with anti-creditor sentiment. Irving Mark, *Agrarian Conflicts in the Colony of New York, 1711-1776* (New York: Columbia University Press, 1940), p. 41. *Newport Mercury,* June 30, 1766.

22. "O.Z." in *ibid.,* August 27, 1764. William H. Fry, *New Hampshire as a Royal Province* (New York: Columbia University, 1908), pp. 409-20. Gipson, "Connecticut Taxation," pp. 735-38 and *Jared Ingersoll,* pp. 261-62. However, cf. Zeichner, *Connecticut's Years of Controversy,* pp. 46 ff., 81 ff.

23. The annual amount raised by taxation was £40,700. Chalmers Papers, New York, IV, 65. MS. in N.Y.Pub.Lib. Watts complained that taxes fell "near four shillings in the pound on houses in the city." To Monckton, April 14, 1764, Watts, *Letter Book,* p. 243. Taxes on rural real estate, however, were much lighter. Harrington, *New York Merchant,* p. 39. Moreover, one half of all taxes due for 1765-67 was canceled by applying £59,250 of the Parliamentary grant to sink the colony's bills of credit. *The Colonial Laws of New York from the Year 1664 to the Revolution* (Albany, 1894), IV, 801-4.

24. *Votes and Proceedings of the House of Representatives of the Province of Pennsylvania* (Philadelphia, 1752-76), V, 120. Lands of the western counties of Northhampton, Berks, Lancaster, and York were rated far below what the assessed value should have been. Charles H. Lincoln, *The Revolutionary Movement in Pennsylvania* (Philadelphia: University of Pennsylvania Publications, 1901), p. 49. The apportionment of taxes made in 1760 was adhered to until the Revolution. Yet throughout the 1760's the value of farm produce in the western counties increased far more rapidly than elsewhere in the colony. See Stevenson W. Fletcher, *Pennsylvania Agriculture and Country Life, 1640-1840* (Harrisburg: Pennsylvania Historical and Museum Commission, 1950), pp. 124-26, 251.

25. For grievances of the western sector, see Lincoln, *Revolutionary Movement in Pennsylvania,* pp. 98-113.

26. For grievances of the tenant farmers of New York, see Mark, *Agrarian Conflicts*, pp. 131-63.

27. Herman M. Stocker, "Wholesale Prices at New York City, 1720 to 1800," *Wholesale Prices for 213 Years* (Ithaca: Cornell University, Agricultural Experiment Station, Memoir 142, 1939), p. 203. Cole, *Wholesale Commodity Prices*, pp. 13-16, esp. Chart 6.

28. The movement in the price of corn differed from that of wheat in timing. The price of corn began to rise earlier, reached its peak in 1766, moved downward until 1768, and began to rise again in 1769 while the price of wheat was falling. The price movement of animal products, however, lagged behind that of wheat in timing of its swings.

29. Because rum prices so closely paralleled those of molasses it was felt that to include rum in Chart 2 would have complicated the graph unnecessarily.

30. Bezanson *et al.*, *Prices in Colonial Pennsylvania*, pp. 291-92.

31. Prices of pig and bar iron declined steadily in the 1760's. However, some types of lumber products rose between 1764 and 1770, but the price of pine boards declined. Although indexes of wages are not available for this period, it is doubtful if wages rose during the postwar decade. Cf. Morris, *Government and Labor*, pp. 47, 142 n., 190-92, 196.

32. The relative importance of specific articles, of course, cannot be determined, since consumption statistics are not available. However, these are the commodities most frequently discussed in relation to farm expenditures, although there is less agreement on the extent of importance of each particular product or group of products. For example, cf. Stevenson W. Fletcher, "The Subsistence Farming Period in Pennsylvania Agriculture," *Pennsylvania History*, XIV (July 1947), 186-87, Margaret E. Martin, *Merchants and Trade of the Connecticut River Valley, 1750-1820* (Northampton: Department of History of Smith College, 1939), p. 5. Percy W. Bidwell and John I. Falconer, *History of Agriculture in the Northern United States, 1620-1860* (Washington, D.C.: The Carnegie Institution of Washington, 1925), pp. 127-30.

33. *Ibid.*, p. 133.

34. "Wheat 5/10 . . . and believe will rise to 6/ in a few days occasioned by a demand abroad," wrote Van Cortlandt to Stevenson and Company as early as April 24, 1765. For similar comments, see to Adams, to Hilton, December 9, 1765, Letter Book. "Encouraged by your Favours of the 26th Jany & 16th Feby that our produce would be in great demand," Daniel Roberdeau of Philadelphia wrote to Fernandez and Company of Maderia, April 27, 1765, Letter Book, 1764-71. MS. in H.S.P. William Allen asked for thirty Mediterranean passes, explaining that Philadelphia merchants had large orders "to ship up the streights, where they are advised corn will be in demand." To Barclay and Sons, October 14, 1765, L. B. Walker, ed., *Extracts from Chief Justice William Allen's Letter Book* (Pottsville: Standard Publishing Co., 1897), pp. 67 f. For such advices from European grain importers, see Searle to S. Galloway and Steward, March 14, April 26, July 8, 1765, Galloway, Correspondence. Lamar, Hill and Bisset to T. Wharton, April 20, 1765, Wharton Papers. MS. in H.S.P. For other data in regard to the large European demand by 1765, see to Gurly and Stephens, June 28, 1764, Riche, Letter Book. To Sanders, June 27, 1764, to Welch and Company, April 1, 1765, to Meredith, April 6, 1765, to Kells and Sons, April 11, 1765, Lux, Letter Book, and *passim*. G. Champlin to C. Champlin, November 12, 1765, *Commerce of Rhode Island* (7 Massachusetts Historical Society, *Collections*, IX-X), I, 132. "Extracts from the Letter Book of Benjamin Marshall," *Pennsylvania Magazine of History and Biography*, XX, 210.

35. 6 Geo. Ill, c. 4, c. 5.

36. *Newport Mercury*, December 1, 1766. *Pa.Gaz.*, December 25, 1766, May 4, October 1, 1767. William Lux of Baltimore, who acted as a wheat purchasing agent for British merchants, had much to say regarding British purchases of American grain at Baltimore

and Philadelphia. Lux, Letter Book, *passim*, especially to Tucker, December 1, 1766, to Sanders, March 30, 1767, to Loyall, May 22, 1767. To A. Orr, March 18, 1768, Orr, Dunlope and Glenholme, Letter Book, 1767-69. MS. in H.S.P. To Habersham, November 14, 1766, to Turnbull, to Chalwell, Novermber 25, 1766, Roberdeau, Letter Book. Also, see Mary A. Hanna, *Trade of the Delaware District Before the Revolution* (Northampton: Department of History of Smith College, 1917), pp. 264, 296-97, 318-19.

37. Trade statistics of valuation of exports and of exports of specific commodities for scattered years indicate a tendency similar to that indicated by tonnage statistics. In 1769 the official value of Philadelphia's exports to southern Europe amounted to £203,752 while that to the West Indies totaled £178,331. The same year, almost 4,000 tons of wheat and about fifteen and a half tons of bread and flour were exported to southern Europe. The proportion of the value of exports represented by these commodities is uncertain. According to Lord Sheffield's estimate for 1765, wheat, bread, and flour accounted for about 65 per cent of Philadelphia's aggregate value of exports. By 1771 exports to southern Europe fell to almost one ton of wheat and 8,832 tons of bread and flour, while 12,253 tons of bread and flour were exported to the West Indies.

Trade statistics also indicated that as Philadelphia's exports to southern Europe became permanent, flour assumed greater importance in relation to wheat. From April 1765 to April 1766 Philadelphia's aggregate exports amounted to 367,522 bushels of wheat and 168,426 barrels of bread and flour. The West Indies usually imported a relatively small amount of wheat. By 1772 aggregate exports of Philadelphia showed only 92,012 bushels of wheat but 284,872 barrels of flour. Statistics are based on the following sources: Johnson *et al.*, *History of Commerce*, p. 92; Edward Channing, *A History of the United States* (New York: The Macmillan Co., 1905-27), III, 116-17 *n.*; Lord (John Baker Halroyd) Sheffield, *Observations on the Commerce of the American States* (London, 1784), Apps. IX, X, XI; Chalmers Papers, Philadelphia, II, 83.

38. Samuel E. Morison has explained the decline of Boston's trade with southern Europe as the result of the British discriminatory duty on direct importation of wine. "The Commerce of Boston on the Eve of the Revolution," American Antiquarian Society. *Proceedings*, N.S. XXXII, 36-38. However, Harold A. Innis presented convincing evidence that after 1763 New England was unable to compete successfully with the more advantageously located Newfoundland fishery in supplying the markets of Europe with codfish. *The Cod Fisheries; the History of an International Economy* (New Haven: Yale University Press, 1940), pp. 187-201.

39. See *Pa.Gaz.*, March 21, 1765. Dickinson to Pitt, December, 1765, quoted in Hanna, *Trade of the Delaware District*, pp. 307-9. Isaac N. P. Stokes, *Iconography of Manhattan Island, 1498-1909* (New York: R. H. Dodd, 1915-28), IV, 759.

40. *Pa.Gaz.*, January 9, 1766.

41. *Ibid.*, December 25, 1766. *New York Gazette or Weekly Post-Boy* (hereafter referred to as *N.Y.Gaz.*), December 18, 1766.

42. *Pa.Gaz.*, November 13, 1766. Also quoted in *South Carolina Gazette and Country Journal*, December 16, 1766.

43. Article from New York, dated November 24, 1766, in *Newport Mercury*, December 1, 1766.

44. Article from New York, dated November 17, 1766, in *ibid.*, November 24, 1766. "Tho' Provisions rise here," complained another writer, "yet it is said there is little Doubt but they [English ships] will get their Loads." (Weyman's) *N.Y.Gaz.*, February 16, 1767.

45. "Never was a Country so embarrassed as this . . . the difficulty to live here is inconceivable, the markets as high as ever." Maunsell to Gates, May 15, 1767, quoted in Stokes, *Iconography*, IV, 775. A Philadelphian depicted the difficulties of the poor as follows: ". . . the miseries of the poor are disregarded and yet some of the lower rank

of the people undergo more real hardship in one day, than those of a more exalted station suffer in their whole lives." *Pa.Gaz.*, February 12, 1767. A "Tradesman" in New York asked, "Are our circumstances altered? Is money grown more plenty? Have our tradesmen full employment? Is grain cheaper?" *New York Journal*, December 17, 1767.

46. To Scott, Jr., September 5, 1770, Benjamin Fuller, Letter Book. MS. in H.S.P.
47. Stocker and Wharton to C. Champlin, August 6, 1773, *Commerce of Rhode Island*, I, 448. "The Country growing rich from the exorbitant prices that the produce of all kinds have been for some years past," wrote Fuller to Scott on December 26, 1772, Letter Book. For similar comments, see *Commerce of Rhode Island*, I, 171. To Tucker, to Loyall, January 19, 1767. Lux, Letter Book.
48. Amelia M. Gummere, ed., *The Journal and Essays of John Woolman* (New York: The Macmillan Co., 1922), p. 466.
49. Massachusetts, *Acts and Resolves*, IV, 527. All these attempts ended in failure. The primary purpose of the bounties seems to have been the desire to develop native staples for exportation.
50. During a period of rising prices, the incentive for "engrossing and forestalling" were rendered attractive. The measures aimed at preventing traders from buying up farmers' produce before it reached the public markets. Thus, by bringing farmers and consumers together under governmental supervision, and by eliminating the profits of middlemen, it was hoped that retail prices would tend to fall. N.Y.C., *M.C.C.*, VI, 338 ff. The assize of butter, however, was kept below market price from 1763 to 1769. Farmers refused to bring butter into the market until the assize was repealed. *Ibid.*, VII, 181.
51. Boston, Registry Department, "Boston Town Records," *Records Relating to the Early History of Boston* (Boston, 1881-1909), XVI, 29 ff.
52. *Ibid.*, XVI, 302.
53. Pennsylvania, *Votes and Proceedings*, VI, 426-27.
54. Morris, *Government and Labor*, pp. 77-78, 148, 150-51. E. A. J. Johnson, "Some Evidence of Mercantilism in Massachusetts-Bay," *New England Quarterly*, I (July 1928), 395.

chapter 6

labor, capital and
entrepreneurship

POPULATION AND LABOR

POPULATION GROWTH AND DISTRIBUTION
The population of the colonies in 1700 numbered approximately one-quarter of a million. Virginia and Massachusetts were the most populous colonies, accounting for over forty-five per cent of the total. Of the three major regions, New England, Middle Atlantic, and South, the latter was most populous. By the eve of the American Revolution population had grown to roughly two and a half million. (See Table 6.1.) At the time of the first census in 1790, it had expanded to almost four million, and was equally divided between the North (including the Middle Atlantic States) and South. While Philadelphia, New York, Boston, Charleston, and Baltimore were thriving cities, only 200,000 lived in urban areas containing 2,500 people or more. Ninety-five per cent of the population lived in rural areas contained within the boundaries of the thirteen original states. Only 200,000 people lived west of the Appalachians. One person in every five or six was a slave. By 1800 population stood at slightly over five

172

million, and by 1815 it had expanded to over eight million, about the population of New York City in 1970. Forty-eight per cent of these people lived in the Middle Atlantic and New England states, thirty-seven per cent lived in the South, and fifteen per cent lived in the West. More than ninety per cent continued to reside in rural rather than urban areas. Most of the population was American by birth, indicating that the high rate of population growth for the period was due to a high birth rate rather than immigration. From 1800 to 1820 a quarter of a million immigrants entered the United States, a figure about equal to the population of the nation in 1700. This influx of people might have been greater except for British restrictions on emigration.

TABLE 6.1. *Population of the American Colonies and the United States 1610-1820*

Year	Population	Year	Population
1610	350	1720	466,200
1620	2,300	1730	629,400
1630	4,600	1740	905,600
1640	26,600	1750	1,170,800
1650	50,400	1760	1,593,600
1660	75,100	1770	2,148,100
1670	111,900	1780	2,780,400
1680	151,500	1790	3,929,000
1690	210,400	1800	5,297,000
1700	250,900	1810	7,224,000
1710	331,700	1815	8,419,000

SOURCE: *Historical Statistics of the United States. Colonial Times to 1957.* Washington, D.C.: U.S. Government Printing Office, 1960.

LABOR SCARCITY

Substantial labor shortages characterized the nation from early colonial days to 1815. A scarcity of labor forced the early colonists to cooperate with one another in building houses and fences and in clearing and plowing the land. Heavy reliance was placed on the use of indentured servants and slaves. Indentured servants were of two types, voluntary and involuntary. Passage to the colonies cost an English laborer about three years of income. He often sold himself to a shipmaster or emigration broker for a period of three to five years to pay for his transportation and upkeep. The length of servitude was a function of his passage cost and the extent of his productivity, as determined by skill and training. Involuntary servants were generally debtors and vagrants who were considered an undesirable burden on the mother country. Criminals and, on occasion, kidnapped individuals were also transported, although these formed a small minority of the total number shipped. Involuntary servants were indentured for periods ranging from seven to ten years. Both voluntary and involuntary indentured servants were quite common in the colonies. Indeed, fully half of all colonial immigrants arrived in an indentured status. While Great Britain had no regret about shipping vagrants to the colonies, she entertained other thoughts in connection with skilled workers. The latter were viewed as a scarce and valuable resource, and their emigration to the colonies was forbidden by Parliamentary decree.

Indentured servants and slaves ameliorated but did not eliminate labor shortages. As a consequence, wages were some forty per cent higher in America than in Great Britain. This situation existed, as Adam Smith observed, despite higher living costs in England. Wage floors in the United States, as elsewhere, were established by the alternative employment opportunities available to existing workers. Since farming was the major area of employment, early American manufacturers were faced with the problem of attracting labor resources out of agriculture. The bulk of the nation's labor force for most of the colonial period was required to produce the food and fiber needed for the necessities of life. Moreover, the availability of cheap land made it possible for individuals to engage in entrepreneurial agricultural pursuits. From the beginning, farmers used their spare time to manufacture a number of goods for home consumption or sale. Early manufacturing tapped this labor supply through the Putting-Out System. Under this method of production, sometimes called the Domestic, or Cottage System, manufacturers left raw materials at the farm where the farmer, his wife, and children worked to produce a finished good, such as cloth or shoes. As agricultural output expanded, it was possible to attract labor resources from the farm to staff the emerging factory system around 1800. Under the Waltham System, which prevailed in most of New England, factories were staffed by the daughters of farm families. Attracted to factory work by the opportunity to meet new people and earn money for a dowry or other purposes, they were housed in dormitories and strictly supervised in both their working and nonworking hours. This parietal responsibility was undertaken to allay the fears of parents concerning their daughters' physical and spiritual safety. In factories in and around Providence, the so-called Rhode Island system prevailed. It involved staffing factories with entire families who were housed in company dwellings.

Hours of work in the early days of the nation were quite lengthy. The typical workweek in 1815 was seventy-two hours, consisting of a twelve hour workday and a six day workweek. Earnings varied depending on the type of labor employed and the sex and age of the workers. In 1815 unskilled males averaged six dollars a week, females three dollars a week, and children a dollar and a half a week. Wages under the Cottage System were lower. This was because the worker could stay within the comfort of his home and produce at his leisure without being subject to constant employer supervision.

LABOR UNIONS

The trade union movement in the United States dates from the post-colonial period. Its source is to be found in the tradition of mercantilist guilds where craftsmen, who performed entrepreneurial as well as labor functions, banded together to fix prices, wages, hours, working conditions, and apprenticeship rules. As early as the 1790's such skilled craftsmen as shoemakers, printers, carpenters, tailors, hatters, and masons founded embryonic labor unions. One of the oldest, the Philadelphia Cordwainers, was founded in 1794. This association of shoemakers was the first American union to use collective bargaining in employer negotiations and a closed shop, under which all workers had to be unionized. It had the distinction of having the longest continuous life of any labor union before 1815. It expired in 1806 as the result of a landmark legal decision which held that labor unions were, *per se,* in violation of the common law principle of conspiracy. Under this principle it was illegal for either businessmen or laborers to organize for the purposes of fixing prices or wages, since this represented a conspiratorial restraint of trade detrimental to the public welfare. In the wake of this case numerous other suits were brought against existing unions seeking to have them labeled conspiracies in restraint of trade. During this period of litigation unions gained the sympathy of Jeffersonian Democrats, while the business community received the support of most Federalists.

CAPITAL

SOURCES OF CAPITAL

Capital, like labor, was a very scarce resource in both colonial America and the early United States. Its limited availability acted as a drag on economic development. Early capital needs were supplied by four sources. First, and most important, were domestic savings. They principally took the form of personal savings on the part of settlers who produced more than they consumed. Typically, they invested the surplus in home construction and land improvement. A second source was earnings from the domestic and foreign sale of goods and services, particularly farm goods and shipping. A third source was foreign loans and investments, principally from British merchants who subscribed to colonizing ventures such as the Plymouth, Virginia, and Massachusetts companies. A fourth possible source was the money and banking system. To understand this latter source fully, one must know the practices which prevailed in the colonial and post-revolutionary periods.

THE MONEY AND BANKING SYSTEM

From an economic point of view, capital encompasses tangible goods, such as building and machinery, or loanable funds (money). It is necessary that loanable funds, or liquid capital, be turned into tangible capital before economic growth can occur. As with most nations of the world, the preferred form of colonial money for both domestic and international trade were the precious metals, gold and silver. Because the colonies had an unfavorable trade balance with England, they experienced a continued specie outflow which caused a constant specie shortage. Specie in the form of French coins and Spanish pieces of eight, or dollars as the latter were called, was earned through favorable trade balances with the French and Spanish West Indies, but these coins, like other specie, mostly flowed to England. As a consequence, the colonists were forced to use barter in their trading transactions. Early colonial governments accepted such commodities as furs, corn, tobacco, and animals in payment of taxes, and in turn paid government officials in such goods. Tobacco was a valuable commodity in the early southern colonies. Too bulky to be exchanged from hand to hand, warehouse receipts for tobacco served as a medium of exchange. From the exchange of warehouse receipts convertible into tobacco, to the exchange of paper money convertible into specie, land, or other goods was but a brief step, and all colonies before long used this means of augmenting the money supply. In 1690 Massachusetts issued the first colonial paper currency. It took the form of bills of credit payable to soldiers who took part in a war against the Indians. The bills, which by colonial decree were acceptable at a premium over specie in the payment of taxes, were a promise to pay the bearer a specified amount of specie at a future date. Having begun the issuance of paper currency, colonial governments found it all too easy to resort to the printing press for additional supplies whenever they found themselves in need of funds. During the first half of the eighteenth century Rhode Island, Massachusetts, Connecticut, and Virginia issued paper currency out of all proportion to the amount of

TABLE 6.2. Nominal and Real Values of Colonial Paper Money Issues (Pounds Per 1000 Population)

Year	Pennsylvania		New York		Virginia		Massachusetts		Rhode Island	
	A*	B	A	B	A	B	A	B	A	B
1715									5000	143
1720			1200	750			2520	53	3400	71
1725	945	706					3420	57	2540	42
1730	1330	877					2730	34	5800	71
1735	1000	615					2340	22	11900	94
1740	935	570	1255	785			1355	12	18300	166
1745	780	443	2700	1385			3210	23	22000	158
1750	707	413	2000	1115			9660	47	14900	73
1755	702	316	1850	1031	212	163	4230	21	19500	52
1760	2660	1660	3500	1900	1800	1262	25000	121	31500	59
1765	1440	830			1000	618	168000	82	14200	23
1770	855	553	502	280	39	8	153000	75	1300	2
1774	804	482	1030	575			109000	53	3650	5

*Columns A: Nominal paper money issues. Columns B: Nominal amounts converted to pounds sterling at current exchange rates.

SOURCE: Roger W. Weiss, "The Issue of Paper Money in the American Colonies, 1720–1774," *Journal of Economic History*, Vol. XXX, No. 4, December 1970, p. 779.

specie available for conversion. As was to be expected, the currency declined in market value below the par value stated on its face, a fact which annoyed English creditors who received such funds in settlement of outstanding accounts. (See Table 6.2.)

Another form of paper currency was issued by colonial banks. These banks were both publicly and privately owned, and often established with a capitalization of land rather than specie. Based upon the land's capital value, banks issued notes which were lent to borrowers. These notes, like the paper currency of colonial governments, tended to be overissued in terms of their tangible capital backing. This was particularly true of notes issued by New England banks. The overissue of paper currency was aggravated by devaluation schemes of many of the colonies. Colonial governments, to attract Spanish pieces of eight, overvalued them in terms of shillings. This served to lower the value of shillings, thereby reducing the real shilling debt owed English creditors. In 1751, at the insistence of English businessmen, Great Britain intervened in colonial monetary affairs. The Currency Act of that year fixed the price of the Spanish dollar in terms of shillings and forbade New England from issuing further paper currency or chartering additional land banks. The Currency Act of 1764 extended these restrictions to all the colonies. Once again colonial resentment was fueled and another link forged in the chain of grievances leading to revolution. Economic historians do not agree as to whether colonial paper money issues impeded or aided colonial economic growth. Those who take the negative view point out that excessive money issues inevitably depreciated in value, thereby discouraging savings, the basis of capital accumulation. In addition, they encouraged speculative excesses which generated a boom and bust economy. Those who take the positive view assert that given the absence of adequate specie, paper money issues were essential to provide the investment funds necessary to business expansion and economic growth. Moreover, they point out that not all paper money issued depreciated in value. The readings at the end of this chapter by Bullock and Ferguson illustrate these conflicting viewpoints.

The American Revolution itself was financed largely by paper currency issued by the states and the Continental Congress. The latter, which did not possess the power to tax and, therefore, the ability to honor its promissory notes, soon witnessed a marked decline in the value of its paper issues. As a result, prices soared. By 1780 a Continental dollar was worth only two cents, and a pair of shoes was selling for $100 in Continental currency. To assist in the financing of the war, Robert Morris founded the Bank of Pennsylvania in 1781. This bank, which paid Washington's army and purchased provisions for them, was succeeded in

1784 by the nationally chartered Bank of North America. Half of the Bank's capitalization of $300,000 was contributed by the Continental Congress. During the same period two other banking institutions were founded, the Bank of New York and the Massachusetts Bank. All three banks were of a specie type, that is their capitalization was in the form of gold or silver. Based on this specie they made loans in the form of bank notes. To avoid tying up bank assets, loans were made for a maximum of thirty days.

Following adoption of the Constitution in 1789, the Federal Government assumed all debts of both state governments and the Continental Congress at par. It did so at the urging of Alexander Hamilton, who argued that such a measure would enhance the credit rating of the United States, inspire business confidence, and augment the money supply of the nation. The total debt at the time was 77 million dollars, of which 40 million was Federal domestic debt, 25 million was state domestic debt, and 12 million was foreign debt owed principally to France, Spain, and Holland. Hamilton also advocated the creation of a central bank. Such an institution, he argued, would provide the nation with a sound paper currency, lend to government and business, and act as a fiscal agent for the Federal Government. Once again, Congress heeded Hamilton's advice. The First Bank of the United States was created by Congress in 1791 and granted a twenty-year charter. Its capitalization was set at ten million dollars, four-fifths of which was to be privately subscribed. Twenty-five per cent of all private subscriptions had to be in specie, the remainder was payable in U.S. bonds. The Federal Government paid for its twenty per cent share with the proceeds of a loan made by the Bank itself. As fiscal agent of the Federal Government, it kept all government deposits, shifted these deposits from branch to branch depending on where they were needed, supplied specie to the mint, paid interest on the Federal debt, assisted in the collection of taxes, and engaged in foreign exchange transactions on behalf of the Treasury. Branches of the Bank were located in all major cities of the nation, including Philadelphia (the main office), New York, Boston, Baltimore, Charleston, Washington, Savannah, and New Orleans. In addition, the Bank exercised a measure of control over the activities of state chartered banks, whose number had grown to twenty-eight by 1800. Not only did the U.S. Bank lend to state banks when they needed funds, but it also restrained any possible overissue of bank notes by collecting and returning state bank notes for convertibility into specie.

Despite the effective operation of the First United States Bank, specie continued in very short supply. A Mint Act had been passed in 1786 which, based on recommendations of Thomas Jefferson, tried to create a coinage system grounded on the Spanish dollar. It decreed that the silver content of the American dollar should equal that of the Spanish dollar, and that fifteen ounces of silver would be accepted at the U.S. Mint in payment for one ounce of gold. The Act provided for the minting of a ten dollar gold piece, a one dollar silver piece, a ten cent silver piece, a copper penny, and a copper half penny. Except for the latter two coins, however, no coins were struck under the authority of this Act. The Coinage Act of 1792, based on a study of U.S. coinage problems by Alexander Hamilton, incorporated all of the measures contained within the Mint Act of 1786 except those relating to the types of coins to be minted. It provided for the coinage of three gold pieces in the amount of $10, $5, and $2.50, five silver pieces in the amount of $1, $.50, $.25, $.10, and $.05, and two copper pieces in the amount of $.01 and $.005. The free and unlimited coinage of silver at a ratio of fifteen to one was provided, with no seigniorage charges being exacted from suppliers of specie for the costs of converting raw metal into coin. Unfortunately, while the world price ratio of silver to gold was 15 to 1 in 1792, it soon drifted to 15.5 to 1. With a prevailing mint ratio of 15 to 1, this meant that the Federal Government was overvaluing silver, a fact which brought into operation a monetary law of economics named for the man who first observed its operation, Sir Thomas Gresham, financial adviser to Queen Elizabeth I of England. Gresham's law states that "bad" (overvalued) money drives "good" (undervalued) money out of circulation. In the case at issue, 15 ounces of silver were presented to the U.S. mint for one ounce of gold. The latter was then shipped abroad where it could be exchanged for 15.5 ounces of silver. Fifteen of these 15.5 ounces would then be exchanged for an ounce of gold. To aggravate matters, the world price ratio of silver to gold moved to 16 to 1 by 1808. With gold being drained from the U.S. Treasury for shipment abroad, no gold coins circulated in the United States. Nor, as it turned out, did silver coins. This was because Spanish pieces of eight contained a slightly higher silver content than the U.S. dollar. Both coins, however, were accepted in the West Indies at par primarily because of the newness of the U.S. coins. Speculators began, therefore, to melt down Spanish coins, present the resulting silver to the U.S. mint for coinage into American dollars, and ship the latter to the West Indies where they were exchanged for pieces of eight. To end such speculation Jefferson ordered the termination of all silver coinage in 1806. With both American gold and silver coins out of circulation, the United States relied for specie on Spanish and French coins earned in favorable trade balances with these nations and their colonies. This situation continued until the 1830's.

In 1811, the charter of the First Bank of the United States expired and was not renewed. The demise of the bank resulted principally from the opposition of Jeffersonian Democrats who argued that (1) seventy per cent of the bank's stock was foreign owned, (2) the bank aided Northern interests much more than Southern, (3) it possessed undue monopoly power, and (4) it was an unconstitutional creation of Congress. State banks who sought to take over the business of the First Bank of the United States joined the Jeffersonians in their attack. When the conflict reached the Senate, that body found itself divided 17 to 17 on the issue of charter renewal. The tie was broken by Vice-President George Clinton, who voted against renewal largely on the basis of personal animosity toward Albert Gallatin, then Secretary of the Treasury and an ardent supporter of charter renewal. The liquidation of the First Bank of the United States encouraged the growth of state banks. This growth, from 88 in 1811 to 250 by 1815, was partially the result of state bank absorption of the business of the First U.S. Bank. It was also due, however, to deficit spending by the Federal Government, a war-induced prosperity, and the rise of manufacturing establishments sheltered from foreign competition. With no regulatory supervision, state banks engaged in an overissue of bank notes in relation to their specie holdings. This contributed to a run on the banking system in 1814, forcing the suspension of specie payments.

ENTREPRENEURSHIP

MERCHANT CAPITALISM

From its earliest beginnings America has been blessed by a rich supply of aggressive businessmen. Challenged by an untouched continent, and largely unfettered by social, economic, and political rigidities, they rose almost immediately to play a major role in the leadership of the nation, a position which they have never relinquished. The earliest American entrepreneurs had five distinguishing characteristics. First, for the most part, they conducted small scale operations. Second, they typically supplied much of the labor and capital requirements of their business enterprises. Third, they conducted their businesses either as sole proprietorships or as partnerships. Fourth, owing to a poor transportation network which precluded firms in other geographic areas from shipping their goods any distance, they operated in noncompetitive markets. Finally, they were regarded as leaders of the community because of their business success.

The major type of entrepreneur before 1815 was the merchant capitalist. Owing to poor domestic transportation facilities his chief concern lay in world trade. While primarily interested in wholesaling, convenience and the conditions of the time often required him to conduct a retail business as well. Indeed, many merchants began their career as retailers. Merchant entrepreneurs were diversified businessmen, dealing in a variety of commodities and engaging in a number of activities. Even if they wished to, most American merchant entrepreneurs were unable to specialize because of the inadequacies of the money system. Many were forced to rely on barter, accepting goods which otherwise they would not have stocked, as payment. The immature character of the financial community forced merchants to perform many banking and insurance functions, such as drawing up and accepting bills of exchange, converting foreign exchange, holding deposits, and providing for the sharing of risks. The absence of adequate common carriers also forced them to provide their own transportation facilities. Their ships commonly carried the goods of other merchants, as well as mail and passengers. In some cases their need for ships led to participation in shipbuilding. At any given time, however, a merchant rarely owned more than half a dozen ships, preferring to sell them after two or three voyages for a profit and build new ones. His investments were not restricted to stocks of goods and ships, but also included real estate, government bonds, and the securities of banks, insurance companies, manufacturing establishments, railroads, and public utilities.

Merchant entrepreneurs were primarily sedentary businessmen. Most of their time was spent in counting houses located in the ports of Boston, New York, Philadelphia, Baltimore, or Charleston. They did little traveling, relying instead upon agents, ship captains, and domiciled merchants in other trading centers throughout the world. In turn they often served in their own ports as an agent for other merchants. Their extensive use of agents did not prevent them from exercising a considerable measure of control over their business. Indeed, it provided more time to study, plan, and direct operations. Utilizing their encyclopedic knowledge of world commerce, they scrupulously planned each voyage in great detail. Moreover, they tried to be in constant touch with their agents in order to learn of market changes and to alter instructions if market conditions warranted it. However, the great distances involved, the irregularity of mail service, and the lack of standardized products required that their agent have important discretionary power. The agent had the responsibility for selling the cargo at the best price, and then either crediting the proceeds less his commission to the principal's account, or using it to buy a return cargo. The need for additional capital and the desire to spread risks often encouraged merchant capitalists to enter into business partnerships. Of the members of the New York Chamber of Commerce in 1775, 61 out of 104 carried on their business as partnerships. The basis and types of partnerships varied. Family ties were particularly important to some, while others originated simply through a business association. Many partnerships were on a temporary basis. A group of merchants might join together to purchase a boat, operate it for two or three voyages, and then sell the vessel and terminate the association. In this way a merchant could participate in a number of different ventures in a relatively short period of time.

THOMAS HANCOCK AND JOHN JACOB ASTOR

Of the many successful merchant entrepreneurs which America produced in this period two of the most interesting were Thomas Hancock of Boston (1703-1764), and John Jacob Astor of New York (1763-1848). Thomas Hancock, after serving seven years of apprenticeship, set himself up in 1724 with some aid from his father as an independent bookseller close to Boston Harbor. In a few years he had built a flourishing business. He realized, however, that continued specialization in bookselling was impractical, and of limited profitability. He therefore became a general merchant selling both domestic and imported goods. His orders to England for cloth, paper, tea, and cutlery soon became more numerous than those for books. As an importer of British goods the problem arose as to how he might properly pay for them. As pointed out earlier, the New England colonies produced few commodities which were saleable in England. After trying unsuccessfully to sell local commodities, such as pork, lumber, corn, and even the tracts of New England clergymen, he was forced to turn to a more circuitous route. A search for commodities which would yield him sufficient pounds sterling led to whale products — oil, fins, and whalebone — which were highly prized in Britain. Hancock exchanged local goods for whale products in nearby ports such as Nantucket, or as far north as Newfoundland. Once involved in foreign trade it was natural for Hancock to enter the shipping business. His interest in shipping, however, was not great. Hancock frequently had only a part ownership in his ships and usually his interest was sold after a year or two. In addition to foreign trade and shipowning, Hancock's other interests included real estate, banking, manufacturing, and mining. While Hancock sold both at retail and wholesale, the bulk of his business was with village merchants and captains of coastal vessels who regarded him as a wholesale supplier of European goods. A review of Hancock's accounts indicates that he seldom handled money. He was forced to rely upon a number of complex barter and credit schemes. Triangular transfers of goods, bills of exchange in kind, and triangular transfers of credit were generally used in order to overcome the inadequacies of the money system. Despite these complications, Hancock managed to operate an extremely profitable business. When he died in 1764, he left an estate of approximately half a million dollars.

John Jacob Astor, a German immigrant, began his business career in the early 1780's in New York City retailing musical instruments and furs. Although he subsequently dealt in a wide variety of commodities, these two lines constituted his principal stock in trade. An improved money system, commercial banking facilities, and a strong demand for furs in Europe enabled Astor to specialize to a much greater degree than Hancock. Until the 1790's Astor spent a good deal of his time on fur expeditions in New York State and Canada, and on trips to England and Germany. In the process he gained considerable knowledge of the fur trade and international markets. As discussed in Chapter Five, he soon became a leading fur merchant as well as an outstanding general merchant dealing in both domestic and imported goods. As Astor's activities became more sedentary, he turned his attention to the oriental trade. At first, the China trade involved one or two ships leaving for Canton each year and returning directly to New York. But after the War of 1812 it became more complex. For example, a ship might leave New York with a large cargo of furs and miscellaneous dry goods. It would then proceed to one of the Hawaiian Islands where it would deposit part of its cargo in return for sandalwood, a commodity greatly in demand in China for incense. While the sandalwood was being cut, the ship might go north to trade with the Russians for seal skins and other furs. After returning to the Hawaiian Islands for the sandalwood, the ship would then proceed to Canton to trade for spices, silk and china. It would then return to New York where part of the cargo would be auctioned off, part would be sent on to Europe, and part would be shipped to the West Indies. Following 1825 Astor withdrew from the merchant business and invested his wealth in New York real estate. It was from appreciation of the latter that the bulk of the Astor fortune was subsequently derived. When Astor died, the value of his fortune was estimated at 25 million dollars.

BUSINESS ORGANIZATION

In addition to sole proprietorships and partnerships, unincorporated joint stock enterprises and corporations existed in the colonies and in the early United States. Unincorporated joint stock enterprises were distantly related to the typical U.S. corporation of today. They were participated in by many capitalists, each of whom owned stock in the enterprise. Here all similarity with today's corporation ended, however, for unincorporated joint stock enterprises did not hold charters to operate from sovereign governments. Moreover, each stockholder in these ventures was fully responsible for all business and private debts incurred by his fellow stockholders.

The corporations of colonial days were granted charters from legislative assemblies. Such charters required a special act of the assembly, and were only conferred on organizations performing an essential service for the public. Thus, the earliest corporate charters were granted to local governments, educational and religious institutions, and charitable organizations. In the business sphere only public utilities qualified for charters. Early charters went to companies operating waterworks, wharves, turnpikes, bridges, canals, banks, and insurance houses. To encourage and protect these organizations, legislative charters conferred the privilege of limited liability upon the directors and stockholders of such corporations. During and after the struggle for independence, state governments followed the practice of predecessor colonial governments in incorporation practices. Between 1775 and 1801, 326 charters were issued, 207 of which were conferred upon bridge, turnpike and canal companies, 34 upon banks, 33 upon insurance companies, and the balance on other enterprises. In the late eighteenth and early nineteenth centuries, the privilege of incorporation was actively sought by manufacturing establishments who used mercantilist arguments in support of their quest. First, it was held that manufacturing made the country self-sufficient. Second, it was asserted that domestic manufacturing acted to prevent gold outflows to pay for manufacturing imports. Third, it was held that manufacturing stimulated exports, thereby augmenting specie flows to the United States. Such arguments appealed to state legislators, although they refused to grant immediate freedom of liability to the stockholders. Thus, when a charter was granted the Hamilton Manufacturing Society in 1797, the stockholders were held responsible for the debts of fellow participants. Still, the growth of corporate charter grants after 1800 was quite substantial. Between 1800 and 1815, over 1,500 were issued.

State governments, faced with a swelling volume of corporate petitions, could not continue the practice of granting corporate charters by special acts of the legislature. They were forced to pass general laws which prescribed certain standards of incorporation. Any applicant who met these standards was entitled to a charter. New York State pioneered in such legislation in 1811.

SELECTED REFERENCES

1. William T. Baxter. *The House of Hancock; Business in Boston, 1724-1775*. Cambridge: Harvard University Press, 1945.
2. J. R. Commons and others. *History of Labor in the United States*, Vol. I. New York: Macmillan, 1918.
3. Virginia D. Harrington. *The New York Merchant on the Eve of the Revolution*. New York: Columbia University Press, 1935.
4. John T. Holdsworth. *The First Bank of the United States*. Publications of the National Monetary Commission, Vol. IV, No. 1. Washington, D.C.: U.S. Government Printing Office, 1911.
5. C. P. Nettels. *The Money Supply of the American Colonies Before 1720*. Madison: University of Wisconsin Press, 1934.
6. Kenneth Porter. *John Jacob Astor, Business Man*. Cambridge: Harvard University Press, 1931.
7. Abbot E. Smith. *Colonists in Bondage*. Chapel Hill: University of North Carolina Press, 1947.

readings

did colonial paper money issues promote economic growth?

ONE VIEW: *charles j. bullock*

The paper money that so long cursed the American colonies was issued by acts of the several legislatures. Massachusetts had led the way, in 1690, with an issue of bills that were used to defray the expenses of a disastrous military expedition. Her example proved contagious; and, by 1712, New Hampshire, Rhode Island, Connecticut, New York, New Jersey, North Carolina, and South Carolina had issued quantities of bills of credit in order to meet the outlays occasioned by Queen Anne's War. In subsequent years bills were emitted as a regular means of defraying the current expenses of government; and, as the volume of paper accumulated, a great depreciation ensued. Sooner or later all the plantations were deeply involved in the mazes of a fluctuating currency, for the burdens attending the various wars of the eighteenth century were so great as to induce even the most conservative colonies to resort to this easy method of meeting public obligations. Virginia succumbed last, in 1755, but made large issues in the ensuing years.

A second excuse for issuing bills of credit was found at an early date. In 1712, South Carolina created a public loan bank, and issued bills that were loaned to its citizens at interest, upon real or personal security. This expedient was followed sooner or later by

Reprinted with permission from *Essays on the Monetary History of the United States* by Charles J. Bullock, New York: Macmillan, 1900, pp. 32-59.

187

nearly all of the other colonies. Rhode Island easily distanced all competitors in the readiness and facility with which she created loan banks; while Pennsylvania, New Jersey, and Delaware followed a more conservative course than most of the other plantations.

The abuses attending both forms of paper currency were usually of the most flagrant sort. Bills were issued for the payment of current expenses or extraordinary outlays, and taxes would be voted for the purpose of redemption. Then subsequent assemblies would extend the period during which the paper money should be current, or would neglect to levy sufficient taxes for its withdrawal. Thus the currency tended always to accumulate, and its depreciation increased. Sometimes a legislature would resolve that the bills in circulation should not exceed a certain sum, but such a declaration would prove utterly worthless. In almost every colony the first issues were to remain current for a short time only, and were to be redeemed speedily by taxes; but the periods were gradually lengthened to twelve, sixteen, or twenty-five years. Laws were often passed providing for the emission of new bills to replace worn or mutilated issues. Then the new money would frequently be placed in circulation without withdrawing and cancelling the old, while bills that had been withdrawn for the original purpose of destroying them would often be reissued for current expenses. In some colonies it happened that paper issued upon loan would not be repaid at the stated periods, and interest payments were commonly in arrears. When this occurred, the legislature would frequently extend the time of the loans, and sometimes a large part of both principal and interest would never be repaid. In this respect Rhode Island was probably the worst offender. Her loan banks were placed in the hands of a few favored persons, called "sharers," who happened to possess the requisite "pull." The "sharers" then proceeded to lend out the money at a rate of interest that was, for the first ten years, five per cent higher than that which they were obliged to pay to the colony. In some cases the fortunate "sharers" would sell their privileges for premiums that sometimes amounted to as much as thirty-five per cent. The results of such performances can readily be imagined.

Although the colonial bills of credit were not always made a legal tender, they were usually given a forced circulation. Most of the advocates of paper money would have agreed with the New York legislature that bills not legal tender were useless. The direst penalties — fines, imprisonment, and confiscation — were imposed upon those evil-disposed persons who should dare to discriminate in favor of specie; but such forcing laws were as ineffectual in supporting the credit of the paper money as they have proved in all other cases.

When older issues had depreciated hopelessly, "bills of a new tenor" were often emitted; and these were sometimes followed by others of a newer tenor. Thus it happened that issues of the "old tenor," "middle tenor," and "new tenor" circulated concurrently at different rates of depreciation, the legislature usually undertaking to fix the relative values of the three classes of currency. In order to prevent depreciation some of the issues bore interest, but this was a provision that was readily repealed by subsequent assemblies.

As has always been the case, the appetite for paper money increased with the issues of bills of credit. Complaints of the scarcity of money almost invariably followed each emission, and one pretext after another was found for issuing larger quantities of paper. Trade was said to be decaying, public buildings had to be constructed, fortifications were needed, and dozens of other things must be done by setting the printing presses at work. The experience of the colonies demonstrates conclusively the impossibility of satisfying the desire for "more money" by issuing a paper currency. Depreciation commenced at an early date, and tended to increase as time went on. In New England sterling exchange was 133 in 1702, a rate corresponding exactly to the rating of the dollar at 6s. In 1713, it rose to 150, and had reached 550 by the year 1740. The climax was reached in Massachusetts and Connecticut in 1749 and 1750, when exchange was quoted at 1100, indicating a depreciation of nearly 9:1. In Rhode Island, the old tenor bills finally sank to 23 for 1. In the middle colonies the depreciation never reached such figures. In Pennsylvania exchange once reached 180, while the par of exchange for specie was not higher than 166½. In Maryland exchange rose from 133 to 250. In North and South Carolina the paper currencies finally sank to one-tenth the value of sterling.

Such fluctuations in the standard of value wrought intense hardships. In 1741, Governor Shirley stated in his message to the Massachusetts legislature: "A creditor who has the misfortune of having an outstanding debt, of the value of 1000 pounds sterling, contracted anno 1730, can now receive no more in our courts of judicature... than the value of about 650 pounds sterling." Between 1741 and 1749 exchange rose from 550 to 1100, so that, as Douglass said, "Every honest man not in debt lost about one-half of his personal estate." A widow who had had an income of £3 found by 1748 that this was reduced to about one-eighth of its original value. Clergymen's salaries suffered a corresponding reduction, so that Massachusetts passed an act allowing them to receive bills of credit "only at their real value." Harvard College is said to have lost £10,000, and the Scotch Charitable Society of Boston suffered sixty-six per cent loss upon the repayment of some of its investments. Under such conditions of demoralization, it is not strange that the legislature of Massachusetts complained of "universal infectious corruption" in the conduct of public affairs, and that Hutchinson observed that "the morals of the people depreciate with the currency."

In 1749, when the currency had depreciated to nearly one-eleventh of its nominal value, Massachusetts succeeded in redeeming it at a rate of 7½ shillings of paper for one shilling of specie. This was accomplished with the aid of a grant of money which Parliament had voted in order to recompense the colony for its expenditures during King George's War. Efforts were made to secure the coöperation of the other provinces of New England, but without immediate result. Connecticut finally adopted a plan similar to that followed by Massachusetts, and decided to retire her currency at the rate of 8 5/6 for 1. Some years later, New Hampshire made a tardy provision for at least a part of her paper issues; and Rhode Island exchanged her bills for treasury notes, or allowed them to be paid for taxes at a high rate of depreciation. The opponents of resumption in Massachusetts predicted that such a policy would deprive the people of a circulating medium, and ruin all branches of trade. The result was that a specie currency was restored and industry prospered. Prior to this time, Newport had controlled the importation of West India goods into some parts of Massachusetts. This trade at once passed over to Boston and adjoining ports, and Rhode Island paid the penalty for her obstinate adherence to a fluctuating paper currency.

During this carnival of fraud and corruption, interference by an act of Parliament had often been invoked. English merchants had sometimes complained to the Board of Trade concerning the losses to which the dishonest American currencies had subjected them. The instructions of colonial governors frequently directed that consent should be refused to the passage of laws for the emission of paper money. The governors often opposed most vigorously all attempts to issue a depreciating currency, and violent contests with the legislative bodies not infrequently ensued. In Massachusetts, the governor's salary was refused when he could not be induced to consent to such measures; and in South Carolina, no acts passed the assembly for four years on account of a deadlock over the subject of paper money. Such occurrences were by no means peculiar to these two colonies, and the political party that stood for popular rights, as against the prerogative of the royal or proprietary governor, regularly included all the advocates of paper currencies. When threats or open defiance failed, the assemblies were accustomed to resort to bribes in order to accomplish their purpose. Finally, in 1751, Parliament passed an act prohibiting any of the New England colonies from emitting bills of credit and making them legal tender; but permission was given to issue treasury notes that should be redeemed at the end of brief periods from the proceeds of taxation, and should not be given a forced circulation. Such a wholesome restriction was immediately denounced as "destructive of the liberties and properties of his Majesty's subjects" in the colonies; but, in 1764, Parliament passed another act which imposed a similar regulation upon all the other plantations, and required that outstanding bills of credit should be gradually retired.

This legislation put an end to probably all further issues of legal tender bills. But "treasury notes" or "orders" or bills of still other names, receivable at the provincial treasuries, were extensively employed until the time of the Revolution. The New England colonies made a regular practice of issuing treasury notes that were redeemed by taxes within short periods, and usually bore interest. Similar issues under various names can be found elsewhere. In 1769, Maryland succeeded in emitting $318,000 of bills upon loan, and a larger issue followed in 1773. In 1771, New York created another bank of £120,000, but the bills were made legal tender only at the treasury; and finally, upon the eve of the Revolution, Pennsylvania and New Jersey attempted to reëstablish their loan offices. In 1774, therefore, there must have been a considerable amount of paper in circulation in America. Pelatiah Webster estimated the "circulating cash" of the thirteen states at $12,000,000 at this time. He thought that one-half or three-fifths of the currency of Pennsylvania was made up of paper, and believed that this proportion was not exceeded in other states.

Under the political conditions that prevailed in the colonies, it was inevitable that the question of paper money should get into politics. In Massachusetts, this occurred in 1713, when banking projects were being agitated, and eight years later Dr. Trumbull tells us that the paper money party had become identified with the "popular" or "liberal" party. This was natural, since the governors and their councils often combated vigorously all measures that tended to depreciate the currency. Sometimes the governors undoubtedly opposed a paper medium because they had a just appreciation of its evils; at other times they seem to have been concerned chiefly with the prospect that their fixed salaries would inevitably be paid in bad money; and, often enough, they received from England explicit instructions that were intended to leave them no opportunity to exercise their own discretion. In colony after colony, party lines came to be drawn upon this sole issue; and when opposition was encountered from the governors or councils, deadlocks frequently ensued. Public disturbances were often aroused by these controversies over paper money, and a factional and disorderly spirit was engendered. There can be no doubt that the debtor class, as a rule, accorded an active support to the inflationist party; and conducted a persistent agitation for a cheap currency with which existing debts could be more easily paid. Even Franklin was unable to deny, in 1764, the truth of the allegation that in some colonies, at least, paper money had been issued "with fraudulent views" through the influence of the debtor classes. Douglass wrote, in 1749: "The Parties in Massachusetts Bay at present, are not the Loyal and Jacobite, the Governor and Country, Whig and Tory, or any religious sectary denominations, but the Debtors and the Creditors. The Debtor side has had the ascendant ever since anno 1741, to the almost utter ruin of the country." He said: "Paper-money-making assemblies have been legislatures of debtors,...; and as much has been admitted by several of the historians of colonial affairs. It is probable that Thomas Paine did not overdraw the picture when he wrote: "There are a set of men who go about making purchases upon credit, and buying estates they have not wherewithal to pay for; and having done this, their next step is to fill the newspapers with paragraphs of the scarcity of money and the necessity of a paper emission, then to have a legal tender under pretence of supporting its credit, and when out, to depreciate it as fast as they can, get a deal of it for a little price, and cheat their creditors; and this is the concise history of paper money schemes."

There is evidence that, as time went on and the lessons of sad experience were learned, the leading merchants and propertied classes in the colonies began to appreciate fully the evils of the fraudulent paper currencies. As early as 1714, a town meeting in Providence protested against further issues of paper. (At about the same time in the assembly of New York, the members from New York City opposed an increase of the bills of credit.) In 1717, merchants of South Carolina protested against the policy of the inflationists in that colony. Three years later, Thomas Hutchinson and other leading citizens of Boston urged the legislature to emit no more bills upon loan, and to retire outstanding issues as soon as practicable; while, at the same time, Salem instructed her representatives to oppose further measures of inflation. In 1723, "Gentlemen and Merchants of Philadelphia" pointed out to the legislature the danger attending the use of paper money; while Franklin has written concerning the Pennsylvania issues of 1729: "The wealthy inhabitants opposed any addition, being against all paper currency, from an apprehension that it would depreciate, as it had done in New England, to the prejudice of all creditors." In 1731, merchants of Newport protested against renewed emissions of bills of credit in Rhode Island. In Massachusetts, Hutchinson tells us that, when the land bank of 1740 was under consideration, "men of estates and the principal merchants in the province abhorred the project...." At nearly the same date, Douglass said that "they who call out loudest for this Paper Medium, are not our large Traders." In 1750, leading citizens of Rhode Island sent to the King a remonstrance against the conduct of the paper-money party, stating that the landholders of the colony had mortgaged their lands as security for the loans extended by the province, and now found it to their interest to increase the volume of paper in order that they might pay their debts with worthless currency. Two years later twenty-five merchants and traders of Hartford presented to the Connecticut legislature the following interesting petition for relief: "As the medium of trade is that whereby our dealings are valued and weighed, we cannot but think it ought to be esteemed of as sacred a nature as any weights and measures whatsoever, and in order to maintain justice, must be kept as stable; for as a false weight and a false balance is an abomination to the Lord, we apprehend a false and unstable medium is equally so, as it occasions as much iniquity, and is at least as injurious." Finally, Pownall has left us the following explicit statement: "The majority of the men of business and property in the Colonies have ever heretofore wished to have the assemblies restrained by act of Parliament, from the power of giving the sanction of a legal tender to their paper money."

At this point it may prove interesting to review briefly the arguments that were advanced in the eighteenth century for and against government paper money. The first issue of bills of credit in Massachusetts called forth a pamphlet, written probably by Cotton Mather, in defence of paper money; and the controversies that ensued during the next eighty or ninety years resulted in a veritable deluge of writings dealing with the subject. Nearly thirty pamphlets appeared between 1714 and 1721; and, in 1728, government issues of paper were defended in a master's thesis at Harvard College. The flood of publications continued until the close of the century, when it was thought that the Federal Constitution had finally barred the door to further issues of bills of credit.

The advocates of paper currency always claimed that it was the only means by which a sufficient circulating medium could be secured, and many historians have accepted this plea with discreditable complacency. The opponents argued, on the other hand, that an adequate stock of specie always existed until it was displaced by a cheaper form of money; and that complaints of a scarcity of silver were never so common as they always became after repeated emissions of bills of credit. When, for instance, the inflationists in Massachusetts were endeavoring to secure larger issues of paper, in 1712, Judge Sewell answered, in his speech in the legislature: "I was at making the first bills of credit in the year 1690. They were not made for want of money; but for want of Money in the Treasury." Dr. William Douglass argued in 1740: "The more a Country grows in good Trade, the more *true Medium* of Trade it acquires." At a later date, John Witherspoon, Pelatiah Webster, and Thomas Paine voiced similar opinions. These writers always insisted, as Douglass had done in 1740, that "a trading Country must have regard to the universal commercial Medium, which is Silver; or cheat, and trade to a Disadvantage." Like Paine, they inquired: "But why, since the universal custom of the world has established money as the most convenient medium of traffic and commerce, should paper be set up in preference to gold and silver?" Frequently, the advocates of bills of credit argued that a large paper currency would stimulate trade, and thus lighten the weight of the taxes that would ultimately be levied for redeeming the bills issued. Douglass replied that inflation caused extravagance and speculation; and Paine retorted: "Paper money is like dram drinking; it relieves for a moment by deceitful sensation, but gradually diminishes the natural heat, and leaves the body worse than it found it." When the inflationists urged that magnificent public improvements could be undertaken by means of government issues, Douglass reminded them that some one must ultimately pay for all such indulgences. Again, when depreciation set in, and specie rose to a premium, the friends of paper always claimed that the bills of credit had not deteriorated, but that silver had risen in value on account of the demands of persons who desired to export bullion. To this effect Franklin wrote in 1729: "I need not say anything to convince the judicious that our bills have not yet sunk, though there is and has been some difference between them and silver; because it is evident that the difference is occasioned by the scarcity of the latter, which is now become a merchandise, rising and falling like other commodities as there is a greater or less demand for it or as it is more or less plenty." Douglass replied: "The repeated large Emissions of Paper Money are the Cause of the frequent rise of the Price of Silver and Exchange." This, he argued, was equivalent to saying that the bills had depreciated. Under such conditions, the premium on silver must follow, "the same as the Tides do the Phases or Course of the Moon." After the depreciation of the paper had gone to such lengths that it could no longer be denied, its advocates always advanced, with the greatest complacency, the suggestion that the fall in the value of the bills of credit had operated as a gradual and insensible tax upon the community; so that no great harm had been done after all. To this optimistic view it was readily replied that such a tax was the most unjust and harmful method ever devised for meeting public expenditures. It taxed only those who were so situated that they could not avoid it, and benefited sharpers, speculators, and dishonest debtors. It devoured the estates of widows and orphans, paralyzed legitimate business undertakings, and wrought untold injury to public and private morals. Yet the advocates of a depreciating currency still insisted that bills of credit were a necessity, and that government should assume its proper duty of supplying money directly to the people No better answer has ever been given than is found in the following words of William Douglass: "In all Countries excepting in Paper Money Colonies, the People support the Government: it is absurd to imagine that a Government finds Money for its People, it is the People who by their Trade and Industry, provide not only for their own Subsistence, but also for the Support of Government...."

This chapter of our monetary history presents a sufficiently dark and disgraceful picture. But certain important facts still remain to be noted before we pass from the subject of provincial paper currencies. For eighty years the people of the colonies were schooled in the belief that bills of credit furnished a proper and convenient means of defraying public expenditures, ordinary as well as extraordinary. Such issues of paper would depreciate, and could ultimately be wholly repudiated, or could be redeemed at a fraction of their face value. Under such circumstances, there inevitably developed a strong disinclination to permit taxation to be practised on any scale commensurate with the public needs. The habit of paying taxes readily and regularly is not easily acquired, while it is lost with the utmost facility. The colonists, for three generations, were trained in a bad school of public economy; and had learned lessons that were soon to bear bitter fruit. It is not at all remarkable that, in the Continental Congress of 1775, members are reported to have entertained strong objections to burdening their constituents with taxes, when it was possible to send to a printer and obtain a wagon load of money, one quire of which would pay for the entire sum needed to prosecute the struggle for independence. In opposing the attempts of Parliament to levy taxes upon them, the colonies were contending not only against "taxation without representation," but also against taxation in any form. They were quite as certain that it was impracticable to secure representation in that body, as they were that Parliament ought not to tax them without their consent. Finally, as a matter of simple historical fact, there can be little doubt that the acts of 1751 and 1764, which suppressed further issues of bills of credit, contributed not a little to the final breach with the mother country. In 1744, when Parliament was considering the advisability of prohibiting colonial issues of paper money, the New York assembly resolved that such a measure would be contrary to the constitution of Great Britain, incompatible with the rights and liberties of Englishmen, and likely to subject America to the absolute will of the Crown. The action finally taken by Great Britain aroused the most bitter feelings of resentment; and the law of 1764 was enacted at a time when the minds of Americans were excited over the Stamp Act, and the wisdom of the restrictions imposed upon the paper currencies was the less likely to be admitted. In 1766, when he was examined before the House of Commons, Franklin gave it as his deliberate opinion that one reason for the impatience and disrespect which the colonies were manifesting toward Parliamentary authority was "the prohibition of making paper money." Too little attention has been given to this fact by most American historians.

AN ALTERNATE VIEW: *e. james ferguson*

The use of fiat money was a solution to the problem created by a shortage of coin and the absence of banking institutions. The colonies mined no precious metals themselves, and the coin brought in by commerce flowed outward in purchase of British commodities. An undeveloped country, America could not produce enough to buy the goods needed for its economic development; more was always imported than American cargoes of tobacco, wheat, furs, and naval stores could procure; hence an unfavorable balance of trade existed with Britain. The gap was bridged by advances of credit from British merchants, but the flow of hard money was toward Britain rather than America. What coin existed in the colonies came mainly from trade with the Spanish and French West Indies. Its circulation was largely confined to merchants, and its stay was likely to be of short duration — it was a commodity for export rather than a medium of exchange. There were no banks or credit institutions to enlarge the money supply by employing the available specie to back a paper medium.

The colonies tried various ways of coping with the problem. Barter was common in rural areas, and staple products such as tobacco,

Reprinted with permission from *The Power of the Purse* by E. James Ferguson, Chapel Hill: University of North Carolina Press, 1961, pp. 4-9, 15 and 24.

wheat, and even deerskins, were by law declared a medium of exchange. Much business was accomplished without cash payments. Storekeepers usually gave a year's credit to farmers, accepting their crops in payment. Merchants dealt with one another on account, settling balances only at long intervals. Early in the eighteenth century, the colonies tried to attract foreign coin by giving it an artificial value, fixing such rates that hard money with a silver or gold content equivalent to £100 British sterling had a legal value of £133 to £178 in different provinces. The results were dubious. As the colonies grew in wealth and population, the money supply became increasingly inadequate to the requirements of the economy. The inhabitants felt the need of a medium of exchange which, unlike coin, would not "make unto itself wings and fly away."

The solution was fiat money. It was issued for general economic purposes through "land banks"—the primary mode of social welfare activity in which colonial governments engaged. The legislature printed "bills of credit" which were lent out at low interest, usually 5 percent. The loan was secured by mortgages taken on the borrower's property. An individual could get only a limited sum, and after an initial period of grace, when he was liable only for the annual interest, he had to repay the principal over a period of years. As he spent the proceeds of the loan in buying land, making improvements, or paying debts, the bills entered into general circulation. As he and other borrowers repaid the government, the bills were canceled and retired. Then they were reissued, or successive banks were established to keep up a continuous flow of loans. The colonies thus used their wealth in land as the basis of credit, creating a medium of exchange out of "*solid* or *real* property...melted down and made to circulate in paper money or bills of credit."

In the eighteenth century, land banks became the panacea for economic depression. When trade worsened, specie went out of circulation and the dearth of a circulating medium was keenly felt. The injection of money and credit into the economy was, from all appearances, so often beneficial as to confirm the idea that paper money was the cure for depression. A modern economist finds the tactics of colonial government analogous to those of the New Deal and in some ancestral relationship to present-day Keynesian doctrine. Except in New England, few contemporaries doubted that land banks stimulated the economic growth of the country. In the middle colonies, where they were most successful, the loans served as a substitute for taxes. Interest received by the government was sufficient to pay most of the ordinary cost of administration. Pennsylvania managed a land bank almost continuously after 1723 without mishap. For more than twenty-five years before the French and Indian War, the interest received by the government supported expenses without the necessity of direct taxes. Relative freedom from taxation probably contributed to Pennsylvania's remarkable growth.

The other middle colonies were also fortunate in their experiments. New Jersey enacted three separate loans up to 1735, and the interest enabled the government to suspend direct taxation for sixteen years prior to 1751. Delaware issued land bank notes from 1723 to 1746, with apparent benefit to the province. New York extended its land bank of 1737 until the last installment of the principal was due for repayment in 1768, when all classes demanded its renewal, and in 1771 the bank was reinstituted by virtue of a special act of Parliament. Governor Tryon's report in 1774 showed that the interest from loans comprised about half the provincial revenue — an amount which nearly matched expenses in time of peace. In Maryland the first land bank was established in 1733. Its notes fell considerably below par, but later rose to nominal value. In 1769 a new bank was begun, and it functioned without incident until the Revolution.

Land banks were less successful in New England and the South. Virginia never adopted one, but in North and South Carolina land bank loans figured in the early depreciation of paper money. Similarly, the land banks of the New England colonies, particularly Rhode Island, contributed to the decline of currency in that area and brought on the first statutory regulation of paper money by Parliament.

Land bank emissions eased the revenue problems of colonial governments in some degree because taxes were more easily collected when citizens had access to money. But the difficulties of war finance drove the colonies to another use of paper money. It is this system of "currency finance" that is most important as the background of government practice during the Revolution.

The ordinary expenses of colonial governments were small. Officials drew fees rather than salaries, and the few public services were usually handled by local government. Such provinces as Pennsylvania and New York spent no more than £5,000 a year apart from war expenses. Taxation was adjusted to these limited needs. Imposts and excise taxes afforded a maintaining fund, while direct levies on polls and property raised what other funds were needed. But revenues could not be freely expanded. Heavy duties on imports drove off trade or caused smuggling, and direct taxes, if levied in specie, struck the citizens with undisguised force and often took a long time to collect.

It was difficult or impossible for governments to borrow from their own citizens. The wealth of the country did not exist in liquid form. Private capital was tied up in lands or commodities, and no banks or business corporations had yet been formed. When war or other emergencies required large outlays, colonial governments discovered no alternative to paper money. Massachusetts first employed it in 1696, and eventually all the colonies took it up. Currency finance became the ordinary recourse in war, and it was adapted to the regular operation of government in time of peace. Although practice varied in details, the colonies developed something like a uniform system conducted on the basis of known principles. Massachusetts, the single exception, went on a sound money basis in the 1750's Elsewhere the methods can be described in general terms.

To meet war expenditures or financial emergencies, colonial legislatures printed money as needed and put it into the hands of the officials who bought supplies or paid the troops. The act which authorized the emission nearly always assigned specific taxes to its redemption. If import duties produced about £5,000 a year, the income for four years ahead might be allocated to redeem £20,000 in bills of credit. If a further emission of money was necessary, the legislature might pledge the impost for a further term or commit the general property tax. Taxes for years ahead were appropriated to the withdrawal of money emitted in a single year.

This system was merely a way of anticipating tax revenues and had somewhat the character of a forced loan; yet there was little objection on grounds of principle, and the procedure answered nicely to the general situation. Its primary virtue was its avoidance of any transactions in specie. There was no need to find hard money either to pay present expenses or future debts. Wholly by its own action, in default of moneylenders, the government obtained a credit by pledging the assets it could command.

The money issued by the government was not convertible into gold or silver, and its value was not sustained by the promise of interest, although sometimes interest was paid. It was usually, but not always, legal tender in private transactions. Regardless of any stipulation on the face of the notes, the basic security was the fund assigned to their withdrawal. Taxes and other incomes of the government had to be sufficient to create a general use for the bills and thus ensure their negotiability. Since the money was created and upheld solely by political acts, confidence in the government was essential to its value. The holder had to be confident that withdrawals would be continuous and that future governments would have both the will and the ability to collect taxes. When this confidence existed, the money passed readily in day-to-day transactions without undergoing much scrutiny. But colonial legislators had some grasp of the quantity theory of money and understood that the amount must not exceed too far the requirements of trade at existing price levels, or depreciation would occur regardless of guarantees.

Under conditions prevailing in colonial America, currency finance facilitated the retirement of public debts, and the ease with which the debt could be retired was in rough proportion to its size. If it was large, paper money was plentiful and widely distributed; the government could withdraw a large fraction of the outstanding currency every year by levying heavy taxes payable in the certificates of indebtedness themselves. As withdrawals shortened the supply of currency to the point where collections were difficult, the debt ceased to be a problem, and the remaining currency could be left in circulation to serve the needs of trade. It was gratifying to the colonists that fiscal operations did not at any point involve specie, which had to be drawn from overseas. Common opinion distinguished between debts which had to be paid in specie and those which could be extinguished by the withdrawal of a paper medium. Specie debts were regarded as privileged, onerous, hard to discharge; paper money or certificate debts were the ordinary thing, comfortably suited to the country's abilities. The means of payment lay at hand, and the people were taxed in a medium that was accessible to them.

...Older historical studies tend to exaggerate the debtor-creditor conflict over paper money in colonial times. It is evident that when currency was reasonably well handled, such conflicts did not become serious. The details of any currency emission were a public question; the existence of the practice itself was not. Ideally, men of property would have preferred coin or a currency convertible upon demand into precious metals, but most of them shared the popular belief that there was no alternative to the existing system. They were not afraid of it as long as the government was under aristocratic control. When Parliament passed the Restraining Act of 1764 forbidding the enactment of legal tender laws, protests were entered by New York, Pennsylvania, Maryland, Virginia, and South Carolina — colonies which were scarcely in the grip of leveling elements. As the legal tender status of paper money was the crux of any conflict between debtors and creditors, these protests against the Restraining Act of 1764 would have been inconceivable if propertied men had felt they had anything to fear. "Contrary to the traditions that historians have perpetuated," writes a modern student of economic thought, "a critical analysis of the contemporary literature indicates that the proponents as well as the critics were not poor debtors or agrarians, but for the most part officials, ministers, merchants, and men of substance and learning in general."

...Upon reviewing the evidence, it appears that the impression of colonial public finance conveyed by later scholars gives a misleading background for a financial history of the Revolution. The efforts of the American provinces to create a medium of exchange, provide agricultural credit, and equip government with the means of incurring and discharging responsibilities, hardly constitute a "dark and disgraceful" picture, nor, on the whole, a record of failure. Most colonies handled their currency with discretion and were successful in realizing the purposes associated with its use. Except for Massachusetts, where depreciation had given it a bad name, paper money was the "ancient system" which by the time of the Revolution had existed as long as most people could remember. Mindful of its dangers, men of property still accounted it a useful and necessary device. Perhaps their sense of security was in some degree based upon false premises — British restraints may have accounted for the conservative management of paper money in certain colonies. Governors and their appointive councils certainly repulsed many a drive for paper money legislation. But if the British connection afforded them a sheltered environment, the propertied and aristocratic classes of American society were in most provinces unaware of it. The legislatures which they dominated continued to emit paper money as a regular procedure. In time of war, all the colonies but one were unreservedly committed to currency finance as the only way of meeting the situation. Emissions might then be overlarge, as the Revolution was to prove, but the common need precluded any nice regard for the effect upon contracts.

chapter 7

early manufacturing

PRE-FACTORY PRODUCTION

There are four general types of manufacturing: home, craft, mill, and factory. The first involves members of the family working, with limited capital and skill, in their own domicile. The second, which initially begins in the home, requires the services of a skilled craftsman not found in the average home. As the market for the craftsman's output expands, he moves his operation out of the home and employs fellow craftsmen. Mill production requires more capital and employs a relatively large number of unskilled workers drawn from the surrounding area. A shortage of capital, inadequate technical knowledge, and the limited size of the market prevent mills from engaging in large scale production and/or engaging in more than one phase of the manufacturing process. Factory production combines larger amounts of capital, labor, and technical knowledge, services a larger market area, and may engage in all phases of the manufacturing process from the processing of raw materials to the fabrication of the finished good.

FARM HOUSEHOLD MANUFACTURING

Agriculture provides the economic backbone of most undeveloped economies. As economic development occurs, resources are increasingly diverted from agriculture and natural resource exploitation to manufacturing. Early American manufacturing was based on three foundations: the processing of agricultural goods, the processing of natural resources, and the manufacture of items necessary for trade (ships, naval stores, barrels, etc.). Most manufacturing was done on the farm for home consumption, although in time surpluses were produced for sale. The farmer's wife was kept busy spinning and weaving home-grown flax and wool into clothing for the family. Linen and wool were often woven together to form a durable fabric known as linsey-woolsey, while cotton, if obtainable, was combined with wool to make jeans. Almost all farms were equipped with a spinning wheel and hand loom to assist in fabric production. Corn was a raw material in the manufacture of bread and whiskey. Other grains, fruits, and vegetables were preserved or used in producing beer, ale, and cider. The meat from home-raised hogs was smoked and salted, and the fat used for the manufacture of soap and candles. In an attempt to earn some cash during the idle winter months, the average farmer often took to making casks to hold the fish, salt, tobacco, molasses, rum, and naval stores that formed the staples of commercial trading. He also spent his time making nails from iron bars that he bought from a local iron mill, and manufacturing shingles and other wood products from the abundant timber at his doorstep. While the farmer and his family could spin and weave clothing, make bread, and preserve fruits and vegetables with relative ease, tasks such as the milling of wheat, sawing of timber in large quantities, and the curing of leather for shoes and outer garments were more easily performed at central mills by specialized tradesmen. Similar conditions applied to brick, glass, pottery and utensil production. Free land was often given by colonial governments to encourage the establishment of these mills.

FOREST INDUSTRIES

The nation's forests provided the United States with many of its first industries. Due to the widespread existence of forests, lumber production was located wherever a source of water could be found to provide power for sawmills. By 1810 there were some 2,500 sawmills scattered throughout the nation, with a heavy concentration in New York and Pennsylvania. Sawmills were relatively simple affairs, consisting of little more than a shed and a crude power saw. Typically, farmers brought in timber they wanted cut and it was sawed into planks, cooperage (barrel) materials, and clapboard. Forests also provided the raw material for homes, furniture, fences, vehicles, farm implements, shipbuilding, tanning, charcoal (the major fuel), tar, pitch, resin and turpentine. The production of the latter four items was encouraged in the colonies by British bounty as early as 1705. Manufacture centered in North Carolina owing to the abundance of pine trees from which these products were drawn. American leather-making possessed a comparative cost advantage through the abundance of animal hides and tanning barks, principally oak and hemlock. Other forest products were potash and pearl ash, produced by the reduction of wood by fire, and utilized for soap and glass manufacturing.

Forests also were responsible for the rise of the American shipbuilding industry. Owing to the abundance of pine and oak stands from which masts and timbers could be fashioned, colonial ships were constructed at two-thirds the cost of British ships. Shipbuilding centers existed in Boston, where colonial ships were built as early as 1631, Newport, New York, Philadelphia, and Baltimore. By 1760, one-third of the British fleet had been constructed in the colonies. During this period output totaled 350 ships a year.

IRON PRODUCTION

The ubiquitous presence of iron ore and charcoal encouraged the widespread establishment of iron mills. The first mills were established in Lynn and Taunton, Massachusetts in 1640, and by the American Revolution mills were located in New York, New Jersey, Maryland, Vermont, the Carolinas, Kentucky and Tennessee. These mills provided the raw material for the manufacture of a wide variety of products, including iron pots, utensils, farm equipment, nails, wire, horseshoes, anvils, anchors, cannons, stoves, and parts of engines, firearms and wagons. Iron was originally made by combining iron ore with charcoal, igniting the latter, and directing a blast of air from hand or water powered bellows onto the burning charcoal. This produced carbon monoxide gas which removed oxygen from the iron ore, replacing it with carbon. The resulting alloy of carbon and iron was termed pig iron. If all carbon were removed from pig iron, wrought iron was produced. Carbon removal was accomplished by blacksmiths who heated the pig iron and beat it until all carbon was eliminated and the desired product shape obtained. Steel was manufactured from wrought iron through the addition of carbon to it, a process achieved through heating the iron with charcoal. The resulting product, called blister steel, was of uneven quality. It was made into a high quality product, called crucible steel, by breaking it up and melting it in small fire-clay crucibles using charcoal as fuel. The cost of this operation in terms of charcoal consumption was high, three tons of fuel being used to produce one of steel.

Ample timber supplies made it possible for the United States to produce iron at a relatively low cost. England's forests were not so extensive, however, and as a result she produced iron at a high cost. This encouraged

England's entrepreneurs to seek a substitute fuel. In 1709, Abraham Darby successfully utilized coke, a by-product of coal, which was in ready supply in England. Coke's one drawback was that it produced pig-iron of high carbon content because it came in contact with the ore. Hammering alone could not remove all this carbon. The problem was solved in 1783 by another Englishman, Henry Cort, through the use of puddling. This process involved the introduction of reverberatory furnaces to separate the ore from the fuel, and the use of puddlers to stir the molten iron with long rakes to permit the complete oxidation of impurities. At the same time that puddling made an appearance, grooved rolling mills came into general use in England. Hot puddled iron was poured through these mills to be rolled into whatever shape the grooving in the mills was designed to produce. Thus, the need for blacksmiths was eliminated, and considerable labor savings realized. The presence of an ample supply of charcoal discouraged American ironmakers from adopting these English innovations. Following the Revolution, therefore, it was necessary for them to seek active tariff protection against the importation of a better quality European product.

OTHER MILL PRODUCTION

Gristmills, like sawmills and ironmills, were initially located throughout the colonies. In time they became heavily concentrated in the wheat growing Middle Atlantic colonies, in particular Pennsylvania, Delaware, and New Jersey. Small-scale operations characterized the typical mill, with average output totaling a hundred bushels of flour a day. Fulling (woolen) mills were located mainly in the Northeast because most sheep were raised in that region. These mills bought homespun and woven fabric, and then cleaned, smoothed and dyed the cloth. By 1810 about 1,700 fulling mills were in operation. During the colonial period the manufacture of woolen goods was more important than cotton manufacturing due to the difficulty of deseeding cotton fiber. This situation, however, was reversed in the nineteenth century due to the invention of the cotton gin, restrictive mercantilist legislation, the scarcity of skilled labor for woolen goods production, the fact that sheep raising did not expand as quickly as cotton output, and the increasing dearness of woolen goods compared to cotton goods. Although the War of 1812 stimulated demand for woolen goods, home production rather than factory production continued to dominate the industry. As late as 1815 the major center of the woolen industry, Connecticut, had only twenty-five woolen factories engaged in spinning and weaving operations. In these factories, which employed an average of 40 to 45 workers, all weaving was performed on hand looms.

By 1815 two general types of manufacturing existed in the United States. One required the use of power driven machinery and the other utilized only hand tools. The former necessitated mill production. In addition to the products already discussed, these mills produced brass, refined sugar, paper, gunpowder, brick, glass, and alcoholic beverages. The typical mill was a small-scale affair, employing less than ten men. In contrast, the largest enterprises used as many as 150 men and represented a capital investment of $200,000. Under hand-tool manufacturing, the entrepreneur often employed no people and performed all labor functions himself. Carpenters, coopers, cabinetmakers, clockmakers, blacksmiths, coppersmiths, tinsmiths, silversmiths, jewlers, potters, shoemakers, hatters, weavers, tailors, buttonmakers, bakers, and tobacconists are examples of this type of manufacturer. Successful entrepreneurs employed fellow craftsmen as a means of increasing output. It was within these establishments that the trade union movement, organized along mercantilist guild lines, first began.

PREREQUISITES FOR FACTORY PRODUCTION

The Industrial Revolution of the United States lagged behind that of England by three or four decades. Labor shortages were an important factor contributing to this situation. A scarcity of labor prevented the development of large-scale business firms in colonial America. As was pointed out in Chapter Six, indentured servants provided only a partial solution to the problem. Moreover, because firms were small and had modest capital requirements, skilled workers, if so inclined, could easily start their own businesses. Most of the early factories were forced to rely on part-time farm labor, particularly women and children. To augment the work force, vocational schools to teach spinning to the young were established. A second prerequisite to U.S. factory development was adequate capital. Here, too, there was considerable scarcity. As was discussed in Chapter Six, the four principal sources of capital were the personal savings of individuals, the profits of American merchants in domestic and foreign commerce, foreign loans and investments, and paper money issues of governments and banks. A third prerequisite was the growth of adequate markets and the development of an efficient transportation system to reach these markets. Earlier chapters pointed out the limited nature of urban centers and transportation prior to 1815.

A fourth prerequisite was technological change, particularly involving machinery and specialization. The machines that characterized the Industrial Revolution were of two types. First, like the power loom, they were labor saving devices involved in textile manufacture, or second, like the steam engine, they were sources of power to drive other machines. Water provided the earliest source of power and dictated the location of early mills. The steam engine, invented and perfected by Thomas Newcomen in 1705 and James Watt in 1769, allowed industry to locate at other than water sites. However, due to the high cost of steam engines and ready availability of rivers and streams, water power dominated American manufacturing until late in the nineteenth century. The classic articulation of the principle of specialization is found in Adam Smith's *Wealth of Nations*. It observes that the "greatest improvement in the productive powers of labor, and the greater part of the skill, dexterity, and judgement with which it is anywhere directed, or applied, seem to have been the effects of the division of labor." Within a short time American entrepreneurs began to apply the principal of specialization to manufacturing. In 1782 Oliver Evans engaged in the first practical application of the assembly line technique. In his Delaware flour mill he devised a continuous production process that cleaned and ground wheat, and cooled, sifted and barreled flour mechanically without the use of manual labor. Six men were employed in the plant to close barrels. With this technique the Evans plant achieved a level of output three times that of other flour mills. In the early 1800's the incorporation of the assembly line into general factory production was spurred when Eli Whitney and Simeon North independently applied the concept of interchangeable parts to the manufacture of firearms. A mold was made for each of a firearm's metal parts. After each part was forged it was filed down to fit the mold within an accuracy of 1/32 of an inch. In this way, the part from any one firearm would fit any other and mass production was made possible. This not only accelerated the production process but in addition produced a more uniform product and reduced the need for skilled labor. The development of interchangeable parts was not confined to the firearms industry. Independent of Whitney and North, important breakthroughs were made in the clock industry. The reading at the end of this chapter traces the development of the clock industry from the craft to the factory stage. It is difficult to exaggerate the importance of technological breakthroughs to the future progress of American industry. Without it, U.S. manufacturing output would be but a fraction of its present magnitude.

The final prerequisite for U.S. factory development was independence from Great Britain. This was essential because mercantilist regulations hampered American manufacturing development. To cite three examples, as early as 1699 Parliament had passed a Woolen Act forbidding the colonies from exporting woolen yarn or cloth to other colonies or to foreign nations; in 1730 the exportation of hats from the colonies was forbidden and colonial manufacturers of hats were required to serve an apprenticeship of seven years before practicing their trade; and in 1750 the colonies were forbidden to manufacture most iron products. These laws were designed to support the development of British manufacturing at colonial expense. The production of pig iron was encouraged because it was a needed raw material for the British iron industry. However, the use of this pig iron by the colonists in manufacturing iron products was forbidden, because it competed with English manufacturing interests. These restrictions were another source of disquiet leading to Revolution.

THE BIRTH OF THE FACTORY SYSTEM

COTTON TEXTILE INNOVATIONS

The factory system in the United States, as in England, began with the cotton textile industry. For this reason a rather detailed review of the industry's early history is in order. Since the Industrial Revolution began in England, it is understandable that practically all major inventions in the area of textile production came at the hands of English innovators. To maintain their manufacturing superiority, England jealously guarded these innovations and forebade their exportation to other nations. The major contributions of early English textile innovators are summarized in Table 7.1. There are two major steps in the production of cloth from raw cotton. These involve the spinning of thread from combed and cleaned raw cotton, and the weaving of the thread into fabric. Kay's flying shuttle increased a weaver's ability to turn out fabric, which increased the demand for thread and inspired innovations in spinning. The inventions of Hargreaves, Arkwright, and Crompton markedly increased spinning productivity. This resulted in thread output increasing at a much faster rate than the ability of weavers to use it effectively for fabric production. In turn, this triggered the invention of the power loom, which mechanized weaving operations.

TABLE 7.1. *Major English Inventions in Cotton Textile Manufacturing 1733-1785*

Year	Innovator	Invention
1733	John Kay	Flying Shuttle
1770	James Hargreaves	Spinning Jenny
1771	Richard Arkwright	Water Frame
1779	Samuel Crompton	Mule
1785	Edmund Cartwright	Power Loom

During the 1780's considerable effort was expended in the United States on devising machinery to increase thread output. Prospective American inventors were aided in their efforts by state funds. Subsidized spinning mills were established utilizing the crude machinery being invented. Unfortunately, the machinery devised was ineffective. At about the same time U.S. manufacturers attempted to pirate English equipment. Subsidies were offered to English textile workers to immigrate to the United States and construct from memory copies of the machines they had tended abroad. The firm of Almy and Brown was among those offering such bounties. Originally a Quaker merchant house, the company had been operating inefficient spinning machines in the basements of people's homes. The thread was then woven into fabric by the women of those households. In 1789 an English workman named Samuel Slater was induced to come to Providence, Rhode Island to build and manage a spinning mill for Almy and Brown. The mill, tended by nine children, began operations in 1791 with copies of Arkwright equipment. Its success was immediate and established Almy and Brown as the only profitable spinners of machine-produced thread in the nation. Slater, who has been termed the father of American manufacturing, opened his own mill in 1799. So, too, did other workers in the employ of Almy and Brown once they learned how to construct and operate the machinery. By 1800 over twenty such mills existed. Almy and Brown themselves continued to expand, building new mills in 1806 and 1807.

MILL SIZE, OUTPUT QUALITY, AND INDUSTRY GROWTH

Despite the industry's initial growth, cotton mills remained small and the quality of their output uneven. Small mill size resulted from a number of factors, principally inadequate supplies of capital and labor, limited markets, and the state of technical knowledge. The inability of firms to do their own weaving forced them to utilize the Putting-Out System. With cloth production scattered in surrounding homes, no effective supervision over the diligence of labor or quality of cloth was possible. This resulted in a product of uneven quality and high cost, particularly in relation to that produced in Britain. The industry was also hampered by a limited supply of raw cotton. Eli Whitney's invention of the cotton gin overcame this problem in 1793. Further stimulus to the industry came from the Embargo Act of 1807 and the War of 1812, which barred British cloth from entry to American markets. The decline of foreign commerce during this period also had the effect of transferring capital resources to the textile industry. The number of cotton spindles in the United States, which totaled 4,500 in 1805, increased to 130,00 by 1815. Raw cotton consumption increased from 500 to 90,000 bales. Within the vicinity of Providence alone, 169 mills existed by 1815. In the same year the industry employed 100,000 workers and had a capitalization of 40 million dollars.

SELECTED REFERENCES

1. T. S. Ashton. *The Industrial Revolution, 1760-1830*. London: Oxford University Press, 1961.
2. A. C. Bining. *British Regulation of the Colonial Iron Industry*. Philadelphia: University of Pennsylvania Press, 1933.

3. James L. Bishop. *A History of American Manufactures from 1608-1860*, Vol. I. Philadelphia: Young, 1868.
4. Carl Bridenbaugh. *The Colonial Craftsman*. New York: New York University Press, 1950.
5. Edward Cameron. *Samuel Slater, Father of American Manufacturers*. Freeport: Wheelwright Co., 1960.
6. Victor S. Clark. *History of Manufactures in the United States, 1607-1914*, Vol. I. New York: McGraw Hill, 1929.
7. Jeannette Mirsky and Allan Nevins. *The World of Eli Whitney*. New York: The Macmillan Company, 1952.
8. Rolla M. Tryon. *Household Manufacturing in the United States, 1640-1860*. Chicago: University of Chicago Press, 1917.

reading

the transformation of american manufacturing from the craft to the factory stage: a case study.

john j. murphy

Although the aggregate growth rate of the American economy was relatively slow between the Revolution and 1840, certain sectors did expand at a rapid rate, and from these sectors originated some of the factors responsible for the later dynamic growth of the whole system. One such sector involved the making of clocks. Never large by any measure, the clock industry was, nevertheless, a leader in the introduction of the system of interchangeable parts production and in the mass marketing of a "luxury" consumer good.[1] The purpose of this article is to outline and to analyze the transformation of this activity from a craft to an industry and, in particular, to indicate the factors which influenced Eli Terry, the main entrepreneur of the transformation.

The craft of clockmaking was a natural place for the introduction of the techniques of industrialization. By the mid eighteenth century the clock was a "veritable instrument of precision"[2] and British clockmakers were so skilled that they were able to provide the basis for the development of the engineering sciences of the time.[3] These artisans relied upon a significant division of labor; they knew what tools could accomplish; and they generally knew how to make such tools. They were also virtually alone in making use of gauges and other measuring devices as a daily part of their work.[4] They did not introduce into their own activities the ideas and techniques of the emerging industrial system; but their skills, brought by numerous emigrants to the New World, were prerequisites of the innovations introduced into clockmaking in the United States.[5]

Reprinted with permission from "Entrepreneurship in the Establishment of the American Clock Industry" by John J. Murphy, in *Journal of Economic History*, XXVI (June 1966), 169-186.

211

The usual American clockmaker operated in a manner similar to his European counterpart and made clocks out of brass, iron, and steel. A group of clockmakers in a rural region of the Connecticut Colony, however, began in the eighteenth century to make clocks out of wood, and it was from this branch of the trade that the American industry evolved. These craftsmen worked oak, apple, laurel, and cherry into the necessary wheels, pinions, arbors, and plates. Only the hands, the weights, the pendulum bob, the crown wheel part of the excapement, and occasionally the face were made of metal.

Wooden-clock makers had to mark the large lenticular wheels with a square and compass, and then cut and shape them by hand; they were not forced, however, to whittle out teeth with penknives, as many nineteenth-century historians liked to infer.[6] The shop of such a clockmaker was similar to the one James Harrison operated in the early stage of his activity:

> He had only the common tools of a house joiner for preparing the wood part of the clocks. A foot lathe for turning and dividers, (commonly called a compass) a fine saw, and file were the tools by which he made the teeth or cogs of the wheels. This is said to be so, by those now living who saw him do the work.[7]

The method of wooden-clock makers was not much different from that of brass-clock makers, as shown in the very technical description of the latter's operations left by Daniel Burnap, from whom Eli Terry learned brass clockmaking.

> After your work is cast, first take your frame plates & hammer them hard (as you must all the rest of the work). After hammering they must be filed flat & then scraped 'till there is no filings to be seen. After that they are to be pinned together & filed square. After that take the wheels & find the center of them with the compasses & open a hole so that it will fit the wheel arbor. Then file them flat, & then put them upon the arbor & turn them true upon the top. Then turn a race at the bottom of the rim of the wheel. Then file out the crosses. After that cut the wheels with the engine in the following manner....[8]

Either type of clockmaker usually supplied only the works, the customer being required to have a cabinetmaker provide a case. When cased, such clocks stood well over six feet, averaged one and three-quarters feet in breadth and about nine inches in depth, and weighed over one hundred pounds. The bulk of the item was one of the factors which tended to limit the market of a clockmaker to the geographic region which could be reached in one day's journey from his shop.

The general procedure an artisan clockmaker followed was to begin to work only after a customer came to his shop, made a downpayment, and specified a preference. Some may have operated as Milo Norton claimed

Gideon Roberts of Bristol, Connecticut did: "[He] would manufacture two or three of his clocks, which would occupy weeks of his time, and packing them in his saddle bags, mount his horse, and travel off until they were disposed of."[9] Henry Terry's description of his father's activity, however, describes the more common pattern: "So limited was the demand for clocks at this time, and so inadequate his means of making them, that after finishing three or four he was obliged to go out with them on horseback, and put them up where they *had been previously engaged or sold*" (italics are mine).[10]

Wooden clock movements were of such heavy construction and rough workmanship (their wheels and pinions caused great friction) that usually they were designed to run for thirty hours instead of eight days, the norm for brass clocks. This crudity of wooden clocks confined their demand to poorer rural consumers, even though the relative ease of working with wood and the lesser degree of precision required by wooden parts made it possible to produce a wooden clock at about half the cost of a brass one (that is, between $15 and $25 per wooden movement). Prior to the nineteenth century, the combined difficulties of production and restricted demand limited the output of a wooden clockmaker to a maximum of ten clock movements per year.[11]

It was within these conditions that Eli Terry began to operate as a clockmaker. Besides his apprenticeship in Burnap's shop, Terry also served in the shop of Timothy Cheney, an outstanding wooden-clock artisan. Consequently, when Terry began to operate he was one of the few men proficient in making both brass and wooden clocks.

Terry settled in Plymouth, Connecticut, in 1793 and for the next decade, with a "hand engine for cutting the teeth or cogs of the wheels and pinions, and . . . a foot lathe for doing the turning," he made brass and wooden clock movements in the same manner as any other clock craftsman. Shortly after the turn of the century he came to realize that he could sell clocks "without being an itinerant himself," and he began to make provision for manufacturing clocks "more extensively."[12] He inaugurated this policy in a shop that he obtained from Gershom Fenn, a local tailor. During the next four years, Terry improved his equipment, constructed additional tools and machinery, and began to produce clocks in quantity.[13]

Before he obtained the Fenn property, Terry, at best, could start only three or four clocks at one time. By the time he relinquished the Fenn shop, Terry was able to commence production on about twenty-five clocks at a time. This was due to the new machinery which he began to utilize. This machinery included two pieces Terry invented himself — one for cutting the teeth of wooden clock wheels and one for cutting the leaves of the pinions.[14]

With this equipment and the new types of drills and lathes the equipment required, Terry was producing parts which were essentially interchangeable.

Terry entered the second phase of his production experiments in January 1806 when he obtained his first full-scale factory. The lease on this property gave Terry the right to erect a shop "not more than twenty feet square to be improved for turning and doing mechanical business by water," but it limited his source of nonhuman power to the water which could be conveyed "through a hole six inches square."[15] Chauncey Jerome wrote about the local townsfolk's reaction to Terry's activities, "The foolish man, they said, had begun to make two hundred clocks; one said, he never would live long enough to finish them; another remarked, that if he did he never would, nor could possibly, sell so many, and ridiculed the very idea."[16]

Before enough time had passed to prove the local townsfolk right or wrong, Terry came into contact with Edward and Levi Porter, brother "merchant capitalists" in the nearby community of Waterbury. The diverse activities of these men included a firm which fitted up and finished clock movements.[17] The Porters distributed these clocks, plus other items, through local peddlers. In the summer of 1806, the Porters and Terry entered into a contract under which Terry undertook to make four thousand wooden clock movements within three years; the Porters were to furnish the necessary stock and Terry was to receive $4.00 per movement.[18]

The property obtained in January was too small for such an operation; thus Terry had to find a new site, which he did on July 24, 1806, when he purchased seventeen acres of land with "the Mills thereon standing."[19] It took Terry at least a year to design, build, and install the machinery he needed in order to commence production. When the necessary equipment was ready, Terry began to produce five hundred clocks at a time. Evidently there were no serious production difficulties, for in 1808 Terry delivered to the Porters one quarter of the agreed order and then proceeded to fulfill his part of the contract by the end of 1809.[20]

Exactly where the Porters sold the clocks is not known, but it is likely that it was via peddlers who operated in New York State.[21] This was the beginning of the large-scale distribution of wooden clock movements through peddlers as the "more bold and enterprising ventured abroad with their one horse wagons fifty or a hundred miles from home, and sold their clocks at the amazingly low price of twenty-five or thirty dollars."[22]

That the Porters did sell Terry's output without too much difficulty is indicated by the fact that they paid Terry substantial sums in 1810.[23] Henry Terry recorded the consequences of this: "The success attending this enterprise was such as to give a new impulse to clock-manufacturing as a money-making business, and was so successfully brought to a close that the idea of retiring from business was entertained by him, although he was still a young man."[24]

In 1810 Terry did "retire" from producing in order to devote himself to solving what had emerged as a major problem in the mass marketing of clocks.[25] The clock movements Terry produced in quantity between 1807 and 1810 were the same as wooden-clock artisans made. They were very bulky and this limited any widespread market for them. Before mass production clocks could become a continuing business a more compact movement had to be developed, and it was to this task that Terry devoted his talents from 1810 to 1812.

By the end of 1812, Terry felt close enough to a solution to purchase a new site. How long it took him to equip this factory cannot be determined, but it seems reasonable to assume that he was not ready to produce until he obtained a quitclaim right which permitted him to construct a dam fourteen feet high. This was granted in February 1814.[26]

The small clocks Terry initially produced involved only minor modifications of the standard tall-clock movement and they proved to be unsatisfactory. Terry, therefore, began to experiment with a completely new movement design which resulted in the first model of what was to become the famous "Pillar and Scroll" shelf clock.[27] On June 12, 1816, Terry received the first of six patents issued to him on this movement design.

With this new design Terry accomplished a truly remarkable rearrangement of the *works*; an arrangement which permitted a case only twenty inches high. This innovation was one of the most radical developments in the early history of the industry. "Terry literally tore up and threw away the clock plans that had been the standards for nearly two centuries and made an entirely new plan."[28]

Terry once again introduced new production equipment and techniques. Though the extant data do not permit a precise listing of the equipment Terry used to produce shelf clocks in quantity, indirect evidence indicates its general nature. The most provocative item among this evidence involves six patents covering machinery for making clock parts. Not only were all of the patentees connected with the Bristol-Plymouth region of Connecticut, but they all received their patents on the same day, August 22, 1814. This was within a few months of the time that Terry was first able to manufacture small clocks in quantity. In the Bristol-Plymouth region, Terry's factory was the only entity wherein such machinery could have been utilized. Unfortunately no record of the precise nature of five of these patents exists. They are simply listed in the general records of the patent office as covering machinery for the following purposes: making time parts of wooden clocks, turning and slitting of pinions for wooden clocks, cutting and pointing the wheels of wooden clock teeth and pinions, pointing the wire used in wooden clocks, and a plate to be used in the boring of holes in wooden clock parts.[29] (The patentee listed for the first of these machines was James Harrison, who had introduced some of the first water-powered equipment into the making of wooden clocks.)

Specific information is available concerning the sixth patent. This was issued to Asa Hopkins and covered a machine for the cutting of wheels of wooden clocks. Forty years later Henry Terry described this machine with the reluctant notation that it was still in use even though he thought his father had developed a better one:

> [Hopkins'] invention or improvement was for the use and introduction of three arbors or mandrels, by means of which one row of teeth on a number of wheels were finished by one operation; a machine still in use, although superseded at the time, by the construction of an engine by Mr. Terry, with only one mandrel, which was used for many years afterwards, and has not been abandoned to this day.[30]

This improvement of a machine for cutting the wheels of wooden clocks was not Eli Terry's only production innovation. "Being a great mechanic," he developed machinery for making clock cases, and this included the first circular saw used in Plymouth.[31]

The equipment introduced into Terry's factory was driven by water-power "carried by a tin wheel on an upright iron shaft."[32] Over the course of the following decade this machinery was modified through a series of minor innovations, as Eli Terry noted in a patent suit he filed against Seth Thomas.[33] These changes did not significantly revise the general procedure, however, and the description of the factory which employed Hiram Camp at the end of the 1820's applies almost as well to the factory Terry operated at the beginning of that decade:

> In making the wood movements great care was necessary in the selection of the wood. The plates were made of oak split out and then planed up. In the first place the piece was planed level on one side, and then a gauge run around to mark with a plane which was a slow process. The wheels were made of cherry which was sawed out in strips of a width and thickness suitable for the wheels, then planed up nicely, then drilled off at sufficient distances to sweep out the wheels, the center of the sweep running in the hole which was about ⅛ of an inch, after which the teeth were cut, then the wheels were taken singly and put on the spindle of a lathe, and a fine piece of sand paper held against the wheel, after which it was creased and ornamented, then a rag with a little linseed oil held against it which made a finish. The count wheels were turned out so as to have a projection of the side in which the spaces were cut for the count. The pinions were made of laurel or what we call ivy. This is a fine grained wood that is of small growth. It is gathered from the woods thrown under cover to dry. It is a crooked bush, and was sawed into the right length of the pinions with two saws

on one mandrell, which made the faces of the ends agree, then these pieces were set under an upright lathe and drilled about an half inch deep of a size right to admit the pivot, a small piece of wire which was inserted; then this piece is reversed, and this pivot is set in a hole under the lathe, and is then drilled for the other pivot, and when driven is ready for turning. The gauges are hung on same small pivots, rest on the piece in process of turning, which when the work is brought down to the right size drops by.[34]

Another first-hand viewer described the essential features of a wooden-clock factory in far less technical, but perhaps more graphic, words:

I watched the piles of thin boards of cherry, touched by swift saws, falling as clock wheels into boxes below. Then I found that the clocks were not made by one man, but by as many sets of men and women as there were pieces; and then they were assembled.[35]

Eli Terry's activities as an innovating entrepreneur came to an end when he successfully introduced the wooden shelf clock, which very quickly "revolutionized the whole business."[36] In little more than a decade he had radically changed the method of making clocks and the arrangement of the clock mechanism. He had contributed to the introduction of a much more extensive system of distribution and, above all, he had forged one of the initial links in that chain which has come to be called "the American system."

Why did Terry innovate? This question requires an analysis of three factors. First, what motivations led Terry to exploit the opportunities open to him? Second, what conditions, primarily of an economic nature, favored the undertaking of such innovations? Finally, what particular events either reduced the uncertainty facing Terry or increased his perception of the correct solution to the problems which he had to solve?[37]

Although no personal records of Eli Terry are known to exist, secondary evidence does show that he was motivated more by a desire to perfect clocks as timekeeping instruments than by a desire simply to make money or to increase the size of his enterprise — motivations commonly ascribed to early nineteenth-century American entrepreneurs.[38] Terry's drive to improve clocks as timepieces is well shown by his record of inventions. From his first patent — which was also the first clock patent issued in the United States — in 1797 to his final patent in 1845, very few years passed when he did not design some new arrangement for clockworks or some new form of clock parts.[39] This interest in clocks *qua* clocks explains why Terry "entertained" the idea of retiring from business as early as 1810 (at the age of 34), and why he did retire permanently in the mid 1820's, even though he was only 52 years old and the head of a thriving business firm.[40]

Henry Terry's description of his father's life in the quarter of a century following his retirement also indicates Eli's preference for artisan activity. In those "years of comparative leisure," wrote Henry, Eli spent his time in making clocks by artisan methods "chiefly in reference to accuracy as timekeepers.... These things he did, to the neglect, many times, of taking suitable care of what property he had before accumulated."[41]

If Terry's interest was primarily in artisan and inventive operations, why did he embark upon innovations which produced clocks in quantity? One answer to this question is to be found in Terry's inability to support himself as a clock artisan. The limited demand which existed within the market that he could serve from his shop forced him in the decade after he settled in Plymouth to repair clocks and watches, to engrave metal, and even to keep such items as spectacles for sale.[42] Although this was not especially different from the activities of other clockmakers in the area—none of whom were noted for their wealth—Terry may have been less successful than most. Years later E. A. Fenn recalled:

> About the year 1800 there lived a sort of indolent, thriftless, unpromising young man by the name of Eli Terry. His birthplace was the same as mine, Plymouth, Connecticut. He sought the hand and heart of a Miss Warner, and was bitterly opposed by her friends on account of his inability to support her .... The Warners were solid old Puritan stock, and despised laziness, but, notwithstanding all opposition, they were married, set up housekeeping, and soon destitution and want was about all that seemed visible for future days.[43]

As this account suggests, Terry was faced with the alternatives of ceasing to make clocks or of making them in such a way that he could earn a livelihood from the business.

The relatively large investment he had in capital equipment may also have stimulated Terry to look for ways to produce and sell more clocks. His ability to produce a complete clock shows that he was in possession of tools and equipment worth over two hundred dollars, and it would not have required an exceptionally profound amount of insight on his part to recognize that a more consistent use of this capital would aid in reducing his poverty.[44]

To increase his use of this equipment by artisan methods, Terry would have had to utilize a large number of apprentices. Clockmakers in the rural regions of Connecticut, however, found it even more difficult than their counterparts in urban communities to obtain such help. In fact, at times rural clockmakers had to perform all of the necessary tasks themselves.[45] Inasmuch as one of the main functions of an apprentice was to supply power, the difficulty of obtaining apprentices certainly stimulated the search for alternative means of driving the lathes and engines.[46]

The Connecticut region also provided some distinct factor advantages. The majority of raw materials could be obtained in the surrounding forests and fields. Only select woods such as cherry and mahogany, as well as the small amount of brass and glass used, had to be procured from nonlocal sources. In addition, because every farm boy of the time had some experience working with wood, once clock manufacturing was proven successful the manufacturers were able to obtain locally the type of semiskilled laborers that they needed.[47]

For the type of production innovations Terry introduced there was a technical advantage to be found in the shape of clock parts. They were all patterned on one of the basic geometrical figures (primarily the circle and the ellipse), and thus his tooling task was much easier that than faced, for example, by Eli Whitney.[48] This advantage, however, does not downgrade Terry's technical accomplishments, for he came to produce in quantity a product which consisted of over one hundred parts and which required a significant degree of accuracy.[49]

These factors were influencing all of the clockmakers in the rural region of Connecticut where Terry operated, and it is not surprising that at the same time Terry was embarking upon his innovations others in the region were also introducing important changes.[50] The efforts of these other clockmakers made Terry's task somewhat easier, for they reduced the uncertainty that Terry faced and in some instances they may have made Terry "subjectively certain" of the outcome that he envisioned.[51]

One of the more important of these men was James Harrison of Waterbury. Prior to Terry, Harrison began to use waterpower to run three or four lathes and with this equipment he produced clock parts from 1802 until 1806.[52] Although he was an ingenious mechanic, Harrison lacked business acumen and was consistently in debt. After numerous mortgages on his establishment he finally disposed of his "Clock factory with all the appurtenances and conveniences thereto" to the Porter brothers exactly *four days after* Terry purchased a new factory on the basis of the contract that he had entered into with these same Porters.[53] What Harrison did subsequently is not definitely known, but it is likely that he joined Terry for a while and that this clever mechanic aided Terry in the construction of the new machinery which Terry introduced.[54]

Terry may also have gained information about the marketing of clocks from the experiences of Harrison. The Porters did not contract with Terry for 4,000 clocks without some definite knowledge of the capability of the market to absorb the item in such quantities. To have peddled clocks earlier, however, they must have obtained them from Harrison, for he was the only clockmaker in Waterbury.[55] This, of course, would explain what Harrison did with the output he could produce using water-powered equipment.

Another local clockmaker engaged in innovating activities was Gideon Roberts of Bristol. Roberts also started to produce clocks with the aid of waterpower in the first decade of the century and by 1810 was shipping movements to Richmond, Virginia, where he had established a shop "to make cases."[56] Thus Roberts penetrated the southern market—a market which became essential to the success of the wooden-clock industry—before Terry began to mass produce a shelf clock for sale in similar markets.

Terry was also influenced by his main master, Daniel Burnap. Although Burnap followed the normal artisan pattern, he did use the dull moments in his business to make parts which he could integrate into future clocks. Of necessity this meant that the precast parts had to be as uniform in size as the techniques of the time would permit. Thus, in Burnap's shop Terry was exposed to three essential ideas: division of labor, uniform parts production, and production in anticipation of sales.[57]

In discussing the sources of influence on Eli Terry, one immediately thinks of what relationship, if any, existed between him and Eli Whitney, who was carrying out his experiments just forty miles to the south at Mill Rock. In the 1890's, Hiram Camp wrote that Terry "invented a way of cutting the wheel teeth by machinery, which process it was said was hinted to him by Eli Whitney."[58] This, however, appears to be pure romanticism, for neither Henry Terry nor Chauncey Jerome mentions any connection and it is hard to believe that they would have passed up such an opportunity. Nor had Camp mentioned the connection in a piece written in the 1860's.[59]

Knowledge of Whitney's activities would not have been too important to Terry. For one thing, they were using different raw materials and thus required totally different machinery. For another thing, neither appears to have understood the significance of the system he was introducing and thus would not have been influenced by process innovations.[60] Finally, Terry successfully accomplished the quantity production of clocks before Whitney had proven it definitely feasible to produce guns in quantity.

Terry's production innovations would have been of little value to him had he been unable to market his increased output. But Terry was fortunate enough to be operating in the region in which had developed the Yankee peddler system, the most wide-ranging and efficient quantity-marketing mechanism available in the early nineteenth century.[61] By 1800 these itinerant merchants were taking advantage of the ever-increasing number of turnpikes to bring goods made in Connecticut to all the rural regions of the new country.[62] It was this system of walking capitalists that Terry used to reach the market that he needed.

Quantity production and transient merchandising quickly became the twin pillars upon which the clock industry was firmly established. Almost immediately the mass marketing of clocks passed from general peddlers to specialists—"yeleped clock pedlars," as Dr. Alcott called them[63]—who for over twenty years took the output of Connecticut clock manufacturers "abroad for a market, and principally to the southern and western States."[64] And as long as Eli Terry remained an active producer, the elite item in the peddlers' wagons was "Terry's Patented Clock."

In carrying out his innovations, Terry made numerous decisions for which he did not possess sufficient information to eliminate the uncertainty of the outcome. But the uncertainty had been reduced to the point where Terry was able to perceive the possibility of success. It was this perception that made Terry a classic Schumpeterian innovator.

Before Terry began his innovations, a maker of wooden clocks with the aid of one or two apprentices was able to produce a maximum of ten clock movements per year. These movements sold at the clockmaker's shop for $15 to $25, and the consumer was still without a case. With a case, the total price rose to between $25 and $40. Shortly after Terry's last major innovation, with ten men and two women he was manufacturing annually, 1,100 clocks.[65] And at his factory a peddler could buy a completely cased wooden clock for only $10.[66] It was also possible to transport these clocks economically to all sections of the then-existing United States.

Terry's innovations were quickly imitated by others, as Dr. Alcott observed:

> The public mind in a Yankee county was not content that Eli Terry should make his thousand of dollars a year, while they only got an old fashioned living at one dollar a day or so; and one after another in the contiguous towns . . . they found the way into the same business.[67]

By the Census of 1820 this imitation had resulted in three major clock factories in Plymouth (not counting Terry's) and in individual enterprises in the nearby communities of Bristol, Litchfield, Winchester, and Waterbury.[68] These establishments manufactured annually over 15,000 wooden clocks (a minority of which did contain a few brass parts). This was a large enough output produced at a low enough price to eliminate artisan clockmaking in all of the rural regions of the country.[69]

Although Terry's ideas and techniques were diffused quickly into competitive firms, they found their way only very slowly into other industrial activities. None of the histories of woodworking machinery indicate any direct connection between the advances made in Terry's shop and advances made elsewhere, even though several of Terry's workmen did migrate to other sections of the country.[70] Nor did other industries immediately emerge in the clockmaking area of Connecticut. But from Terry's innovations in making wooden clocks, there is a direct line to the innovations which resulted in the manufacturing of brass clocks, "at just the time when the brass mills were in a position to meet this demand."[71] And it was this combination of the system introduced by Terry to produce wooden clocks and the machinery and skill required to produce brass clocks which found its way out of the clock industry and into the manufacturing of locks, pins, toys, and springs.[72]

Eli Terry emerges as a decision maker who was concerned mainly with problems of an immediate nature. He was not interested in pursuing the industrial growth of the industry nor was he attempting to develop either his region or his nation, as is so often the case with modern governmental entrepreneurs. And he was not even primarily motivated by that *sine qua non* of early nineteenth-century American capitalism, the profit-maximization motive.

Neither was he a lone deviate who through his own ingenuity and foresight completely changed traditional ways. His actions were contingent upon both his environment and his own abilities. He made clocks in the midst of a society which was exerting pressures which favored economic change and with a raw material and technical equipment which were adaptable to such change. Many of his contemporaries also responded to these pressures, but Terry responded most successfully because he was both fortunate enough to have the requisite background and shrewd enough to observe and to learn from the experiences of others. In this regard the history of Eli Terry adds evidence to the argument that it is more the lack of knowledge than the lack of entrepreneurial motivation which is responsible for the slowness of the introduction of change into lesser-developed regions.

That Terry's success can be attributed in part to the specific time and place he lived in no way detracts from the individuality of his accomplishments. None of the factors which influenced his decisions afforded him significant objective knowledge to guarantee the success of his undertakings. In the final analysis he undertook his innovations because he believed in the possibilities of doing things in these different ways. This was, in part, a consequence of his acute awareness of the world he lived in. The irony of the situation is that he was not aware of what was going to result. For Eli Terry's greatest achievement was to destroy the tradition and skill which, as a master clock artisan, he valued so highly.

NOTES

1. The fact that its product was a consumer good gives the clock industry a special distinction in innovating at such an early stage in the nation's industrial development. T. S. Ashton commented upon the lack of such innovation in British development: "The varied trades that provided things for the ultimate consumer were (apart from the pottery trade)

hardly affected immediately"; *The Industrial Revolution, 1760-1830* (London: Oxford University Press, 1948), p. 92.

2. A. P. Usher, *A History of Mechanical Inventions* (rev. ed.; Cambridge, Mass.: Harvard University Press, 1954), p. 311.

3. W. Bowden, M. Karpovich, and A. P. Usher, *An Economic History of Europe since 1750* (New York: American Book Co., 1938), p. 307.

4. Robert S. Woodbury claims that interchangeable-parts production requires precision machine tools, precision instruments of measurement, accepted measurement standards, and certain techniques of mechanical drawing. By the eighteenth century British clockmakers possessed all of these factors but were still not producing interchangeable parts. They lacked two things: nonhuman power and the concept. Woodbury, "The Legend of Eli Whitney and Interchangeable Parts," *Technology and Culture*, I (1959/1960), 247.

5. The failure of the British trade to incorporate the new techniques is a classic example of Thorstein Veblen's thesis of "the penalty of taking the lead." *Imperial Germany and the Industrial Revolution* (New York: Viking Press, 1954), ch. ii.

6. E.g., A. S. Bolles, *Industrial History of the United States* (Norwich, Conn., 1879), p. 226. Henry Terry comments on the wide currency given to the "jackknife" story in *American Clock Making: Its Early History, and Present Extent of the Business* (Waterbury, Conn., 1870), p. 2.

7. *Ibid.*, p. 24.

8. Burnap goes on for eight pages describing each operation in great detail. Reprinted in Penrose Hoopes, *Shop Records of Daniel Burnap, Clockmaker* (Hartford, Conn.: Connecticut Historical Society, 1958), p. 109.

9. "Historical Sketches of the Town of Bristol," Bristol (Conn.) *Press* (Jan. 26, 1872). Chauncey Jerome claimed something similar for Eli Terry, but in this instance Jerome's remembrance may be more fancy than fact; *History of the American Clock Business for the Past Sixty Years* (New Haven, Conn., 1860), p. 36.

10. "A Review of Dr. Alcott's History of Clock-Making," Waterbury (Conn.) *American* (June 1, 1853). In the book he published in 1870 Henry phrased it this way: "Most of these when completed were to be delivered to purchasers, who had previously engaged them"; *American Clock Making*, p. 2.

11. This may be too high an estimate. Chauncey Jerome and Henry Terry place Eli Terry's output in the opening years of the nineteenth century at 6 to 10 clock movements per year. This was larger than the annual output of such a brass-clock maker as Daniel Burnap, who in twenty years "charged for fifty-one clocks and thirteen separate clock dials for which he was paid a total of £667-5-0." Hoopes, p. 37. The average Pennsylvania clockmaker made 4 or 5 clocks per year. "Had he been able to make more it is improbable that he could have disposed of them"; George Eckhardt, *Pennsylvania Clocks and Clockmakers* (New York: Devin-Adair Co., 1955), p. 31.

12. H. Terry, Waterbury *American* (June 1, 1853).

13. E. A. Fenn, "Eli Terry's Invention," *The Manufacturing Jeweler*, V (June 1889), 514.

14. H. Terry, Waterbury *American* (June 1, 1853).

15. Land Records, Plymouth, Conn., III (Jan. 23, 1806), 450.

16. Jerome, p. 17. This ridicule must have left a strong impression, for Henry Terry also mentions it in the Waterbury *American* article.

17. J. Anderson, *The Town and City of Waterbury, Connecticut, from the Aboriginal Period to the Year 1895* (New Haven, Conn., 1896), II, 259.

18. H. Terry, Waterbury *American*; Jerome, p. 36.

19. Land Records, Plymouth, Conn., III (July 21, 1806), 208.

20. H. Terry, Waterbury *American*. Henry claimed that it took his father "a considerable part of the first year" to outfit the mills purchased in the summer of 1806. Eli Terry, however, did not dispose of the shop obtained in January 1806 until the end of 1807. This

may mean that it took him that long to install the necessary equipment in the larger establishment. This sequence also fits the fact that Terry did not deliver any clocks to the Porters until 1808.

21. Jerome, p. 12. This was a major innovation in the marketing of clocks, even though the peddlers had been selling other items in such places for at least fifty years. See R. M. Keir "The Tin Peddler," *Journal of Political Economy*, XXI (March 1913), 255-58.

22. W. A. Alcott, M. D., "The History of Yankee Clocks and Clock-Making," Boston (Mass.) *Daily Evening Traveler* (April 13, 1853).

23. In the autumn of 1810 the Porters began to transfer to Terry property valued at $7,000. Terry used part of this property in transactions which transferred land to four of the most prominent men in Plymouth "in consideration of $2,332." In checking as efficiently as the Land Records permit, it does not appear that Terry made any capital gains out of these transactions and, inasmuch as he obtained the mills in the summer of 1806 for $2,000, it may be that these four men provided Terry with some of the capital that he needed at that time. These transactions are noted in detail in Murphy, ch. iv. (cited in footnote to title).

24. H. Terry, Waterbury *American*.

25. Eli Terry sold his factory to two workmen, Silas Hoadley and Seth Thomas. This was the start of the Seth Thomas Clock Co., now a division of General Time.

26. Land Records, Plymouth, Conn., V (Feb. 12, 1814), 326.

27. "Draft of Patent Suit, Eli Terry vs. Seth Thomas," New Haven, Conn. (April 28, 1827). Reprinted in B. Mussey and R. M. Canedy, *Terry Clock Chronology* (Bristol, Conn.: mimeographed, 1948), pp. 25-28.

28. L. Barr, "Eli Terry Pillar and Scroll Shelf Clocks," supplement to the *Bulletin of the National Association of Watch and Clock Collectors*, IV (Dec. 1952), 3. This clock is usually honored today for its case — which Terry did not design — and very little cognizance is given to Terry's truly remarkable accomplishment in designing the works.

29. George Eckhardt, *United States Clock and Watch Patents, 1790-1890* (New York: privately printed, 1960), pp. 29-30, 49-51. The patentees were respectively: James Harrison, Pharris Bronson and Joel Curtis, Joel Curtis and Dimon Bradley, Anson Sperry, and Joel Curtis. These patents were issued only hours before the British burned Washington and consequently they were not given newspaper coverage. The originals perished in the Patent Office fire of 1836 and duplicate copies have never been obtained.

30. Waterbury *American* (June 1, 1853).

31. Jerome, p. 41. An interesting question is raised about Eli Terry's perception of importance, in that he never obtained a patent for improvements he made in machinery even though he obtained nine patents for changes he made in clock mechanisms.

32. John Boyd, *Annals and Family Records of Winchester, Conn.* (Hartford, Conn., 1873), p. 515.

33. "Draft of Patent Suit." Terry claimed that Thomas "was unwilling to change his tools and machinery to cater upon said new manufacture."

34. Camp, *Sketch of the Clock Making Business, 1792-1892* (New Haven, Conn., 1893), pp. 2-3.

35. "Address of General Joseph R. Hawley," in J. J. Jennings, ed., *Centennial Celebration of the Incorporation of the Town of Bristol* (Hartford, Conn., 1885), p. 72.

36. Jerome, *History*, p. 39.

37. The central framework of analysis used in this paper is a combination of A. P. Usher's sequence of an "individual act of insight" and the general features of risk and uncertainty theory as developed by G. L. S. Shackle and B. S. Keirstead. See especially, Usher, *A History of Mechanical Inventions* (rev. ed.; Cambridge, Mass.: Harvard University Press, 1954); Shackle, *Time in Economics* (Amsterdam: North-Holland Publishing Co., 1957); and Keirstead, *An Essay on the Theory of Profits and Income Distribution* (Oxford: Basil Blackwell, 1953).

38. Cf. Thomas C. Cochran, "Role and Sanction in American Entrepreneurial History," in *Change and the Entrepreneur* (Cambridge, Mass.: Harvard University Press, 1949), pp. 163-64; and Tibor de Scitovsky, "On the Decline of Competition," *Social Change*, III (1941), 32.

39. The prolific inventiveness of Terry's mind is shown in the number of experimental models of his which are on exhibit in such institutions as the Bristol (Conn.) Clock Museum. Terry's first patent was for a new method of constructing an equation clock; his last for a method of suspending the balance wheels of clocks.

40. Terry's health was apparently not impaired, for fifteen years after he retired he married for the second time—a marriage which resulted in the birth of two sons, one coming when Terry was 70, the other when he was 71.

41. Waterbury *American*.

42. *Ibid.*

43. *The Manufacturing Jeweler*, V (1889), 514.

44. At the beginning of the nineteenth century the clock engine and the plating mill were valued at $30 each, while lathes ranged from $2 to $12. "Inventory of Ezra Dodge," Probate Court Records, District of New Haven, Conn., 1798; and Hoopes, pp. 97-98.

45. For example, prior to the time he commenced manufacturing clocks Eli Terry had only one apprentice, Herman Clark; H. Terry, *American Clock Making*, p. 3.

46. H. J. Habakkuk notes something similar about cotton textiles; *American and British Technology in the 19th Century* (Cambridge, Engl.: The University Press, 1962), p. 33. If clock artisans could have paid higher wages they would have obtained sufficient apprenticeship help, as is shown by the response of local labor to the wages paid by clock manufacturers: "And then, again, the price of labor on the farms around was raised because so many young men were employed in connection with the factory, or in selling them in adjacent towns when made"; Alcott, Boston *Daily Evening Traveler* (1853).

47. *Ibid.*

48. Cf. J. Mirsky and A. Nevins, *The World of Eli Whitney* (New York: Macmillan, 1952).

49. The greater accuracy required by brass parts was *the* factor which delayed the successful quantity manufacturing of brass clocks.

50. In communities close to where Terry lived, four men were making wooden clocks in the first decade of the century; they were Lemuel Harrison, Timothy Barnes, Gideon Roberts, and James Harrison.

51. On subjective certainty, objective uncertainty, see B. Keirstead, p. 20 ff.

52. On April 15, 1802, Harrison leased for seven years thirty-six rods of land "including the shop and where the logs now lie which carry the water to Harrison's works . . . ." Land Records, Waterbury, Conn., XXVII (April 15, 1802), 530. Anderson stated that the shop was seven feet by nine feet; II, 259.

53. Land Records, Waterbury, Conn., XXX (July 26, 1806), 176.

54. Harrison was one of the six men who obtained patents on the same day in 1814.

55. Cf. Anderson, II. 259.

56. C. Beals, *The Making of Bristol* (Bristol, Conn.: Bristol Public Library Association, 1954), p. 80. Candace Roberts, Gideon's daughter, was a constant visitor at the home of Eli Terry and even lived there for a period in 1806. Diary of Candace Roberts, Bristol Public Library, Bristol, Conn.

57. On the basis of two advertisements which appeared in Connecticut newspapers some writers have claimed that Burnap was utilizing a system of interchangeable parts production by 1790. Hoopes finds no evidence for this. The claims made for Burnap arise from a confusion between precast parts of uniform shape and the mass production of interchangeable parts. All clockmakers had to make parts as uniform in size as possible if they were to avoid the very technical mathematical calculations which the accurate meshing of wheels and pinions of different sizes and functions required. What was

different about Burnap is that he produced various components ahead of time and held them in stock until a clock was ordered.

58. Camp, p. 1.

59. "Hiram Camp's Scrapbook of Newspaper Clippings (1860-1890)," Connecticut State Library.

60. Mirsky and Nevins make this point in connection with Eli Whitney, p. 139. Neither Henry Terry nor Chauncey Jerome mentions the system *per se.*

61. This interpretation of the peddler system runs counter to what is generally accepted. I have developed the case for the peddlers in my "Establishment," (cited in footnote to title) ch. vi.

62. Timothy Dwight, *Travels in New England and New York* (New Haven, Conn., 1821), II, 54.

63. Alcott, Boston *Daily Evening Traveler* (1853).

64. John C. Pease and John M. Niles, *A Gazetteer of the States of Connecticut and Rhode Island* (Hartford, Conn., 1819), p. 59.

65. "Original Reports of Manufacturers," Fourth *Census of the United States* (1820).

66. Account Books of Rensselaer Upson (1822-1852), Connecticut State Library.

67. Boston *Daily Evening Traveler* (1853).

68. There were also two factories attempting to produce all-brass clocks in quantity. "Original Reports of Manufacturers," Fourth *Census.* In 1836, just prior to the demise of the wooden-clock industry, there were in Bristol alone sixteen factories making clocks and clock parts and annually producing in excess of 100,000 finished clocks.

69. Cf. Eckhardt, p. 25, and D. F. Magee, "Grandfather Clocks: Their Making and Their Makers in Lancaster County," *Historical Papers and Addresses of the Landcaster County Historical Society,* XXI, No. 4 (1927), 65.

70. E.g., Joseph V. Woodworth, *American Tool Making and Interchangeable Manufacturing* (New York: W. Henley, 1905).

71. William B. Lathrop, "The Development of the Brass Industry in Connecticut," *Tercentenary Commission of the State of Connecticut,* XLIX (New Haven: Yale University Press, 1936), p. 8. The manufacturing of brass clocks became increasingly important from 1832 on. Right after the depression of 1837 a one-day brass clock was developed, which brought an end to the manufacturing of wooden clocks. Most of the key entrepreneurs who brought about this transformation (particularly, Chauncey Jerome, Seth Thomas, and Silas Burnham Terry) received their initial training in manufacturing clocks in Eli Terry's factory.

72. In 1832 Eli Terry, Jr., entered the lock business in what was the forerunner of the Eagle Lock Co.; Francis Atwater, *History of the Town of Plymouth, Connecticut* (Meriden, Conn., 1895), pp. 240-41. Another son of Eli's, Silas Burnham Terry, developed in the 1840's a process to harden the temper coil springs. This was just one of the many advances inaugurated by the makers of clock springs. See "Manufacture of Clock Springs." *American Artisan,* XIV (January 3, 1872), 11-12. Alexander Johnston claimed that the only competent mechanics Dr. Howe could find when he began to manufacture his machine for making pins were "among the men who had been working on brass clocks"; *Connecticut, A Study of a Commonwealth Democracy* (Boston, 1890), pp. 360-61. Finally, in the 1850's, a number of clock companies in Bristol began to manufacture mechanical toys; Norton, Bristol (Conn.) *Press* (May 31, 1872).

part **III**

from 1815

through the civil war

chapter 8

geographic expansion and internal transportation

PUBLIC LAND POLICY

DISPOSAL PHILOSOPHY

From 1815 to 1865 Federal land policy continued to be liberalized. One cause of the growing liberality was the shift in Federal finance from deficit to surplus. With the exception of deficits incurred during the depressions of 1819-21 and 1837-43, and the Mexican War, the Federal Government's revenues were more than adequate for its needs. However, the most important reason for the change in Federal land policy was the attitude of the American people. Early prioneers viewed the frontier as a free economic good, available to anyone who would take the trouble to possess it. Agrarian interests which dominated American politics until the Civil War strongly favored a liberal land policy. Another spokesman for such a policy was Henry Clay of Kentucky, a leader of the Whig Party. Around 1820 Clay evolved a rationale which demonstrated the importance of rapidly developing the West. His "American System," primarily a justification for higher tariffs, sought the development of home markets for home industry, and the development of a self-sufficient mercantilist economy in which the industrial East would provide manufactured goods and the agricultural West food and raw materials. In order to promote internal self-sufficiency, Clay held that a comprehensive program of internal improvements was needed to reduce transportation costs. This could be financed through a high protective tariff, which not only would yield the necessary revenues, but also encourage home industry.

Since Clay's primary interest was in the industrial East, he was not considered a major spokesman for the West. This distinction belonged to Thomas Hart Benton of Missouri who, together with his followers, would accept nothing less than outright cession of the public domain to the Western states or to bona fide settlers. Benton's position that free land was the salvation of the nation's poor received considerable sympathy from Eastern intellectuals. Perhaps the most famous of these, Horace Greeley, served as the publicity agent for the West. His tireless lecturing and writings in the *Herald Tribune* and elsewhere had significant impact on public opinion. Equally important was the support of labor movement intellectuals. George Henry Evans and Thomas Skidmore, two influential New York union leaders in the 1820's and 1830's, believed free land was the principal means of alleviating the workers' distress. The fact that few laborers were able to or desired to take advantage of free Western land did not prevent the thesis from gaining wide workingclass support. Although Eastern industrialists were uneasy about the possibility of Western lands attracting their labor force, they were interested in developing Western markets. The fact that a liberal land policy and high tariffs seemed compatible helped to overcome their doubts. This was particularly true when it became apparent that they were losing few workers to the West.

Serious opposition to a liberal land policy came only from those who still adhered to the Federalist policy of limited disposal, and from the South, which saw its political power ebbing away as each new Western state entered the Union. Although the Federalist Party retired from the national scene shortly after the War of 1812, some members of the Whig Party, most notably President John Quincy Adams, continued to doubt that a liberal land policy was in the country's best interest. The South's negativism was more significant. As long as the West was tied economically to Southern markets the South did not seriously oppose the extension of its frontier. However, the building of a national transportation system weakened these economic ties and linked the agricultural West to the industrial East. Such an alliance meant the slow but certain dissipation of Southern influence in the national government. Moreover, the pioneer-type farmer who was attracted to the new West was not interested in cotton or slavery. In the South's view, free land and free labor eventually became synonymous. Finally, the South's strict constitutionalism opposed free land because it was not specifically authorized by the founding fathers.

Albert Fishlow's reading at the end of this chapter reviews the inter-regional trade between the South and the West prior to the Civil War. He seriously questions the conventional view here expressed that the economies of the South and West were importantly linked prior to the development of improved transportation facilities.

MAJOR LAND ACTS

The Land Acts of 1820 and 1832 evidenced the triumph of the liberal land policy forces. These acts reduced minimum acreage sales to 80 and 40 acres respectively, and the minimum price to $1.25 an acre. During the same period pressure for free land was exerted by settlers who were moving into areas not yet surveyed or open for sale. The Pre-emption Act of 1841 gave squatters the right to buy their land in 160-acre tracts at $1.25 an acre before other bids were entertained. With passage of this Act, settlers were now free legally to press the frontier forward as fast as their courage and resources would allow. Benton and other Western Congressmen had tried to couple a graduation bill with pre-emption, but had not been successful. Generally, public land was sold at the minimum price or very close to it, and as a result only better lands were sold, leaving increasing quantities of vacant land as the frontier pushed westward. For many years commissioners of the General Land Office had pointed out the irrationality of selling varying grades of land for about the same price. In 1854 the liberal land forces were able to muster enough votes to pass the Graduation Act. For the first time land could be sold below the minimum price. A tract that remained unsold for ten years was reduced to $1 an acre, after fifteen years to 75¢ an acre, twenty years to 50¢ an acre, twenty-five years to 25¢ an acre, and thirty years or more to 12½¢ an acre. The Act, which affected about 77 million acres, greatly accelerated land sales, and together with the Pre-emption Act, contributed to a great wave of land entries which reached a peak in 1855-56.

Pre-emption and graduation were only stepping stones to the ultimate goal of free land. The Homestead Act of 1862 appeared to make this a reality. Southern opposition to the rapid settlement of 160-acre farms not suitable for slavery had effectively blocked the passage of free land legislation before the Civil War. As late as 1860 a bill providing for free lands was vetoed by President Buchanan for fear that it would upset the precarious political balance between slave and nonslave forces and incite Southern secession. The Act of 1862 provided that "every person who is the head of a family or who has arrived at the age of twenty-one years, and is a citizen of the United States, or who has filed his declaration of intention to become such, as required by the naturalization laws, shall be entitled to enter one quarter section, or a less quantity, of unappropriated public

TABLE 8.1. *U.S. Land Sales 1815–1865 (Millions of Dollars)*

Year	Sales	Year	Sales
1815	1.3	1841	1.4
1816	1.7	1842	1.3
1817	2.0	1843	0.9
1818	2.6	1844	2.1
1819	3.3	1845	2.1
1820	1.6	1846	2.7
1821	1.2	1847	2.5
1822	1.8	1848	3.3
1823	0.9	1849	1.7
1824	1.0	1850	1.9
1825	1.2	1851	2.4
1826	1.4	1852	2.0
1827	1.5	1853	1.7
1828	1.0	1854	8.5
1829	1.5	1855	11.5
1830	2.3	1856	8.9
1831	3.2	1857	3.8
1832	2.6	1858	3.5
1833	4.0	1859	1.8
1834	4.9	1860	1.8
1835	14.8	1861	0.9
1836	24.9	1862	0.2
1837	6.8	1863	0.2
1838	3.1	1864	0.6
1839	7.1	1865	1.0
1840	3.3		

SOURCE: U.S. Bureau of the Census. *Historical Statistics of the United States, Colonial Times to 1957.* Washington, D.C.: U.S. Government Printing Office, 1960, p. 712.

land." However, the land was not completely free. Every homesteader had to pay a $10 filing fee plus $26 for survey costs ($34 for territory on the Pacific Coast). In addition, a settler did not receive title until he had cultivated, improved and lived on the land for five years. If he did not wish to fulfill these requirements, he could commute his entry, that is convert the homestead with a pre-emption right to pay the regular minimum price per acre any time after six months following the date of filing.

During the early years of the Act the commutation privilege was rarely used. Prior to June 30, 1880, only about four per cent of homestead entries were commuted. Following this date the practice became quite common and the Homestead Act, instead of being used by bona fide settlers, often was the vehicle for profiteering and land grabbing. It would be wrong to assume that the Homestead Act triggered a massive movement West on the part of settlers. In fact, most of the best land in the U.S. had already been taken up before the Civil War. Moreover, the frontier by this date had pushed to arid territory where a farm of 160 acres often was too small for family support. Thus, the Homestead Act was far from the boon which many have suggested.

Table 8.1 indicates that public land sales were highly cyclical. Indeed, the course of pre-Civil War business cycles can be seen from these figures. The concentration of land sales in 1835 and 1836, and their decline in the depression which followed through 1843, are particularly noteworthy.

LAND GRANTS

The environment which produced a liberal land policy for settlers was conducive to opening up the public domain for other purposes. Extensive land grants were made for several reasons, including military service, education, transportation, irrigation and drainage. The granting of land to encourage and reward military service is the oldest form of land grant. In our early history it was common to set aside specific public domain regions for this purpose. Military districts were designed to provide a buffer of trained veterans between the older settlements and hostile Indians. The failure of most recipients to exercise their warrants, and delays in locating and registering claims, however, invariably forced Congress to open these areas to general settlement. When warrants were negotiable they were sold to land speculators at nominal prices. Most veterans had no special interest in the frontier and regarded land bounties as part of their compensation for military service. Total military bounties accounted for approximately 4.2 per cent of the original public domain. (See Table 8.2.)

From an early date Congress set aside certain tracts for the support of education. The Land Ordinance of 1785 provided that lot 16 of every township should be set aside for the maintenance of public schools. Congress' intent was for the states to rent the land and use the proceeds to support common schools. The states after experimenting with several tenant schemes found the procedure unworkable, and in 1824 they successfully petitioned Congress for the right to sell the lands and invest the proceeds. In 1848 the Act organizing the Oregon Territory allocated the revenues from section 36 of each township in all states and territories

TABLE 8.2. *Disposal of Public Domain**

Nature of Disposals	Acres (Million)	Percentage of Total[†]
Sales and Grants − chiefly to private interests	658.0	45.6
Settlers	287.3	
Timber and stone, timber culture, desert land laws disposals	34.9	
Private land claims − prior to U.S. control	34.0	
Other − not classified	301.8	
Military bounties	61.0	4.2
Educational grants	98.6	6.9
Railroad grants	131.4	9.1
Wagon roads, canals, swampland and other internal improvement grants	89.6	6.2
Total	1038.6	72.0

*Data refers to years 1781–1964

[†]Original public domain, 1442.2 million acres, includes Alaska and Hawaii

SOURCE: U.S. Department of the Interior, Bureau of Land Management. *Public Land Statistics 1964.* Washington, D.C.: U.S. Government Printing Office, 1965, page 6

established after that date for the support of common schools. The common schools of the several states also benefited in part from a number of other Federal land programs. These included the Saline Grants, which donated valuable salt lands to all states admitted to the Union between 1803 and 1875, except California, Florida, Louisiana, Mississippi, and Nevada; the Swamp Land Grants, which transferred ownership of Federal swampland to the fifteen states wherein they were located; the Distribution Act of 1841, which granted 500,000 acres to each public land state for improvements; and the Five and Three Per Cent Grants, which provided the states with the appropriate percentage of the net receipts of public land sales within their respective borders. In addition to land grants to support common schools, Congress made provisions for institutions of higher learning. Beginning with the old Northwest Territory, all new states

FIGURE 8.1. *Railroad Land Grants*

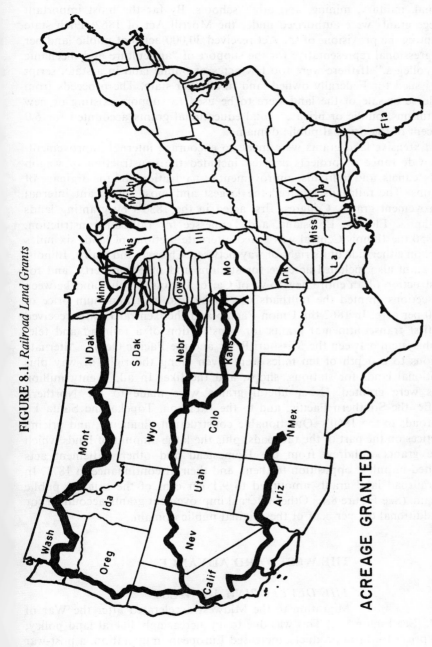

ACREAGE GRANTED

The shaded areas are in proportion to the acreage received by the railroads. They do not show the exact location of the granted lands, which in general formed a checkerboard pattern.

SOURCE: U.S. Department of Agriculture

received grants of varying amounts—usually two townships—to support a state university. After 1889 these provisions were liberalized to support normal, military, mining, and other schools. By far the most important college grants were authorized under the Morrill Act of 1862. Each state accepting the provisions of the Act received 30,000 acres of public land per Congressional representative for the support of "agriculture and mechanic arts colleges." If there were too few acres of public land in a state, script was issued for Federally owned land in another state. The proceeds from the lease or sale of the land were to be used to support existing or new institutions, public or private. Total educational grants accounted for 6.9 per cent of the original public domain.

Extensive land grants were made to encourage internal improvement. The wide range of projects assisted included the construction of wagon roads, canals, and railroads, improvement of navigation and the drainage of swamps. The railroads received the largest and most significant internal improvement grants. Congress first acted in the 1830's by granting lands in Illinois, Florida, Louisiana, and Tennessee for railroad construction. In 1850 the Illinois Central was ceded alternate sections of land, six miles wide, on either side of its right of way between Chicago and Cairo, Illinois. The grant also included acreage for stations and other property, and for construction of an entire new town of Cairo, Illinois. Public land between the sections granted the railroads was to be sold at a minimum price of $2.50 per acre. In 1862 the Union Pacific and the Central Pacific received the first transcontinental grants for construction of a railroad and telegraph system between the Missouri River and the Pacific Ocean. Alternate sections to a depth of ten miles were given along the right of way plus additional lands for stations, shops, and the like. In all, twenty million acres were granted. Other liberal grants were made to the Northern Pacific, the Southern Pacific, and to the Atchison, Topeka and Santa Fe Railroads in the 1860's. Questionable construction, financing, and pricing practices on the part of the railroads, plus the large amount of lands which these grants withdrew from the Homestead and other settlement acts resulted in public opposition to them, and their discontinuance in 1871. In all, railroad land grants amounted to 9.1 per cent of the original public domain. (See Figure 8.1.) Other internal improvement grants accounted for an additional 6.2 per cent of the original public domain.

THE WESTWARD ADVANCE

THE DEVELOPING MIDWEST

Migration to the Midwest accelerated after the War of 1812. (See Figure 8.2.) This was due to an increasingly liberal land policy, high prices for farm products, increased European immigration, a post-war Eastern business depression, the westward advance of tobacco cultivation

FIGURE 8.2. *Expansion of Settlement 1790 – 1890*

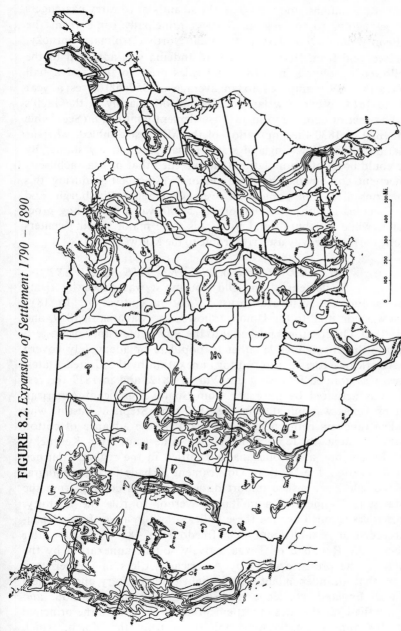

The isochronal lines indicate by decades the limits of settlement with a population density of approximately two or more persons per square mile.

Based mainly on Report on Population of the United States Eleventh Census: 1890, Part 1. Washington, D.C. 1895.

SOURCE: U.S. Department of Agriculture

(which pushed a number of small farmers ahead of it into the Ohio Valley), subjugation of the Indians, and the use of the steamboat to carry passengers and their belongings to the region. Settlers principally came from the states of Pennsylvania, New Jersey, Virginia, North Carolina, Kentucky, and Tennessee, and from Germany. In 1816 Indiana was admitted to the Union, followed by Illinois in 1818. Land sales grew to five and a half million acres in 1819, compared to an average of 350,000 acres a year from 1800 to 1814. While new land entries fell off sharply in the 1820's owing to the onset of depression in 1819, settlement continued. (See Table 8.1.) From 1820 to 1830 the population of the Midwest doubled, whereas the population of the New England states remained relatively stable. By 1830 Ohio could boast of a population that exceeded that of Massachusetts and Connecticut combined. The three major Western cities during this period, in terms of size of population, were Cincinnati, Pittsburgh, and St. Louis. Cincinnati, with a population of 25,000 was a major hog processing center, while Pittsburgh and St. Louis were major trading centers located along the most heavily used river route to the Midwest.

THE OLD SOUTHWEST AND THE FAR WEST

Settlement of the Old Southwest was paced by rising cotton prices and the westward thrust of cotton cultivation. In 1817 Mississippi was admitted to the Union, followed by Alabama in 1819, and Missouri in 1821. Other settlers pushed into the Spanish territory of western Florida. Since Spain was unable either to populate or adequately govern this area, American settlers petitioned for annexation by the United States. This request was granted following the War of 1812, and in 1819 the rest of Florida was acquired by purchase from Spain. Significant American settlement of Texas was initiated in the 1820's by Stephen Austin, who led a band of ranchers being pushed westward by the advance of cotton planters into the area. By 1830, about 20,000 Americans from Kentucky, Tennessee, Mississippi, and Louisiana had settled in the region. Alarmed by rapid colonization, the Mexican Government forbade further immigration and land sales, established import duties on goods coming from the United States, and appointed a military governor to rule the territory. American settlers rebelled against these policies, and in a war for independence succeeded in establishing their freedom in 1836. Shortly after independence, the Republic of Texas actively sought annexation by the United States. The presence of many American settlers in the territory and the fear that an independent Texas might enter military and political alliances with England, challenge the South in cotton cultivation, and compete with the United States in settlement of the West were the principal arguments for annexation. Despite opposition from the North, which feared the extension of slavery and war with Mexico, Texas was admitted to the Union in 1845.

FIGURE 8.3. *Territorial Expansion of the United States 1790 – 1917*

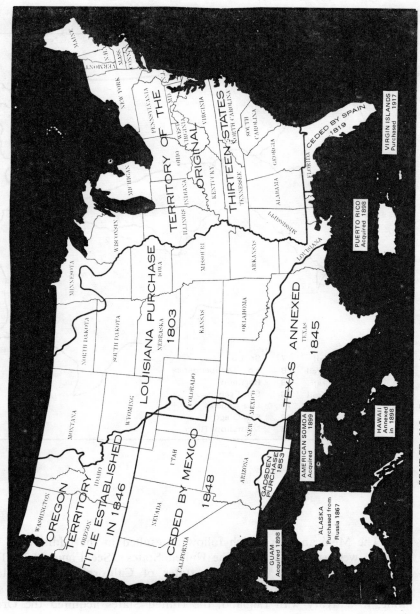

SOURCE: U.S. Bureau of the Census

FIGURE 8.4. *Overland Trails to the Far-West*

KEY

1	Oregon Trail	7	St. Louis
2	Santa Fe Trail	8	Fort Independence
3	Spanish Trail	9	Portland
4	Mormon Trail	10	San Francisco
5	California Trail	11	Los Angeles
6	New Orleans	12	San Diego
		13	Mississippi River

The Mexican War which followed resulted in the addition of substantial western territories to the United States. (See Figure 8.3.) These territories encompass the present states of California, Nevada, Utah, Arizona, and part of Colorado and New Mexico. About the same time, in a treaty with England, the United States acquired the Oregon Territory, a region which today includes the states of Washington, Oregon, and Idaho. California was the first of the new territories to become a state. By 1850, it had attracted 93,000 settlers, principally as a result of gold discoveries at Sutter's Mill, forty miles outside of Sacramento. The other territories were more difficult to populate. Unlike California, these areas were not readily accessible by ship. Most settlers were forced to take one of two overland routes (see Figure 8.4). The more northerly and shorter of the two was the Oregon Trail, stretching from Fort Independence in western Missouri, along the Platte River to Fort Laramie in what is today Wyoming. A traveler could then continue along the Oregon Trail into Oregon Territory, or take the California and Mormon trails into California. The other overland route was the Sante Fe Trail, which also began in Fort Independence, Missouri. After pushing South to Sante Fe, New Mexico, and joining with the Spanish trail, it linked up with the Mormon trail about seventy-five miles south of Salt Lake City.

To attract settlers to these regions free land was offered. In the early 1850's settlers in New Mexico were given 160 acres of land; and in Oregon they were offered 640 acres if married, and 320 if single. The large land grants were necessary due to the semi-arid conditions prevalent in the area. Free land proved a significant inducement to settlement in Oregon, if not in New Mexico. By 1860 Oregon had been admitted to the Union and could boast of seventeen acres of cropland for every person in the state. This compared to four acres of cropland per person in Kansas and three in Minnesota, where much land was being sold, but where many of the purchases were being made by large-scale speculators rather than settlers.

As the westward advance proceeded, the South, in terms of political power, was anxious to maintain the status quo between slave and nonslave states. As new states sought to enter the union, the South pressed for balanced admission. In 1819 there existed eleven free states and eleven slave states. Under the Missouri Compromise of 1820, Missouri was admitted as a slave state and Maine as a free state. These tradeoffs continued to 1850, when the pattern was changed. In the compromise of 1850, California was admitted free, with slavery being permitted in the New Mexico and Utah territories. Four years later the Kansas-Nebraska Act repealed the Missouri Compromise and provided that popular sovereignty should govern the future status of slavery in these territories. The heated reaction of the North to this Act resulted in the formation of the modern Republican Party. The triumph of this party in electing Abraham Lincoln to the Presidency in 1860 triggered secession.

SPECULATION IN WESTERN LANDS

A natural concomitant of a liberal land policy was increasing land speculation. The first major speculation occurred in the 1830's, stimulated by rising cotton and grain prices. Public land sales increased from 2.3 million acres in 1830 to 14.8 million acres in 1835, and

25 million acres by 1836. Speculation was financed by a rapidly growing banking system and private finance companies. The latter's interest charges were as high as thirty-five per cent or more. These rates were paid because settlers hoped for even greater percentage gains in the appreciation of their landholdings. At the height of the boom, land which originally cost $1.25 an acre was being sold at $30. Such speculation, coupled with overinvestment in canal construction and an overextension of loans by an unregulated banking system, generated unsustainable economic ebullience. A collapse came in 1837, triggered by a fall in cotton prices, the withdrawal of funds by English investors, and Andrew Jackson's specie circular of 1836, an executive order that required the use of specie in payment for public land purchases. Land sales dropped sharply, and did not recover fully until the 1850's.

During the 1850's the same hopes of rapid land appreciation which had gripped the nation in the 1830's led to overinvestment in Western land. Railroad construction, the immigration of German and Scandinavian farmers, and an abundance of credit from an unregulated banking system fueled the speculation. Land sales which had ranged between $900,000 and $3,300,000 a year from 1840 to 1852, soared to $11,500,000 in 1855. A good deal of this activity was of a large-scale nature. Iowa records reveal the acquisition of 2.8 million acres by 100 parties. Two million acres were acquired in Illinois by 112 parties, and one million acres in Michigan by 20 parties. Land companies capitalized at a half million or a million dollars were buying tracts ranging from 100,000 to a million acres for subsequent resale to settlers in Iowa, Illinois, Indiana and Wisconsin. Once again, a corrective downswing was inevitable. It came in 1857. During the ensuing recession land sales dropped sharply. Settlers found themselves unable to meet their mortgage payments or to secure further bank loans. To aggravate matters, President Buchanan ordered the sale of vast tracts of land in Iowa, Wisconsin, Kansas, Nebraska, and Minnesota to provide needed Federal revenues. Unable to obtain the purchase price, squatters found their farms sold out from under them. Buchanan's action, together with his veto of a homestead act providing free land, was a major factor in turning farmers away from the Democratic Party. This promoted the election of Abraham Lincoln in 1860.

THE ECONOMIC GEOGRAPHY OF A CONTINENTAL NATION

TOPOGRAPHY

By 1860 the continental land area of the United States as it exists today had been molded. It contained four major physical divisions: two lowland regions and two highland regions. The lowlands embrace a broad interior plain covering the nation's central section and a smaller area bordering the Atlantic and Gulf coasts. The elevated regions embrace the Appalachian Mountains in the East and the Rocky Mountains in the West. The Appalachians are the less extensive and the more regular of the two highland regions. The range runs from north to south paralleling the Atlantic coast. The Rockies, with more breadth and height, extend from Canada to Mexico and cover a full third of the United States. Some of its systems run parallel to the Pacific Ocean whereas others form almost right angles with the coastline.

SOIL

The United States possesses a variety of soils which differ importantly in fertility, mineral content, ability to hold moisture, and susceptibility to erosion. In the broadest terms the two major soil groups found in the United States are the pedalfers and pedocals. The former occur principally in the humid, forested regions of the East, whereas the latter occur mainly in the subhumid to arid grassland and desert regions of the West. The pedalfers have had most of their valuable minerals, expecially calcium, leeched away by heavy rainfalls and are thus acidic. However, if liberally treated with lime they may be very productive soils. The pedocals, on the other hand, are generally rich in lime and other mineral nutrients. They are easily cultivated and are highly productive if rainfall is adequate or if the land can be irrigated. Pedalferic soils are subdivided into podzolic, gray-brown, and red-yellow earths. Pedocalic soils are subdivided into chemozemic, chestnut, brown, and gray earths. There is also an intermediate subgroup, prairie soil, which possesses characteristics of both pedalfers and pedocals.

Podzolic soil predominates in New England. The soil is rocky, sandy, and poorly drained, and the climate is too cold to allow a sufficiently long growing season for most crops. Thus, the area is best suited for forests, recreation, or nonagricultural purposes. From southern New England to the Mississippi River, as well as in some sections of the Pacific Northwest, gray-brown earths dominate. A moderate and moist climate produces good soil, particularly if it is properly limed. Further south are the red-yellow earths. Although inherently inferior to the gray-brown soils, desirable climate and good physical constitution yield productive agricultural land. The prairie earths of the nation's central section lie within the relatively high rainfall region of the pedalfers, but possess many characteristics of the pedocals. The soil is only mildly acid and very rich in organic matter. The tall grasses which originally covered this area prevented the leeching effects of the climate and thus produced some of the finest crop land in the world. (See Figure 8.5.)

Chemozemic soil lies mainly west of the prairie region, running from the eastern Dakotas southward into Kansas. Generally the soil is excellent, particularly for grain production. Further west in a semiarid environment are the chestnut earths, which in most cases are best suited for

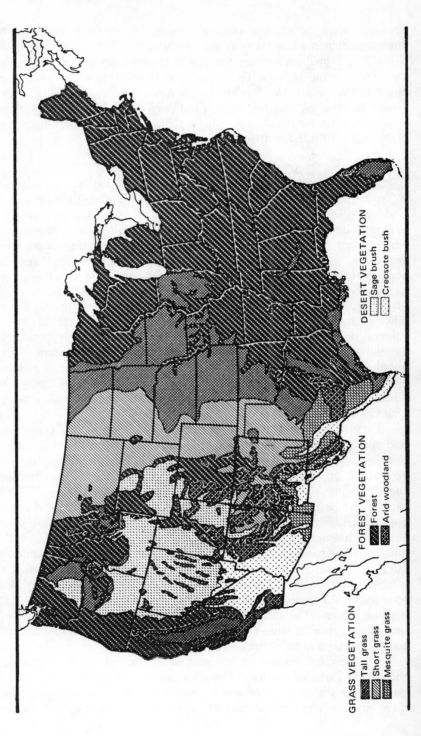

FIGURE 8.5. *Native Vegetation*

GRASS VEGETATION
Tall grass
Short grass
Mesquite grass

FOREST VEGETATION
Forest
Arid woodland

DESERT VEGETATION
Sage brush
Creosote bush

range use. As the average annual rainfall diminishes, brown earths and subsequently gray earths dominate. These are largely semidesert to desert soils whose light color is due to the absence of humus and the abundance of minerals. They permit some marginal farming and if properly irrigated may yield a variety of crops. The soils of the Far West embrace a number of subgroups. The northern Pacific Valley with its heavy rainfall is dominated by gray-brown soils. The extent of agriculture is limited, however, by the rough, mountainous terrain. The more southern coastal regions receive considerably less moisture and are best adapted to irrigated production of citrus fruits and vegetables.

WATER

The United States possesses ample water resources. The nation's mean annual rainfall is approximately thirty inches. However, there is considerable regional variation depending on topography, prevailing winds, and the proximity of large water masses. (See Figure 8.6.) Generally, average annual precipitation tends to decrease from east to west, with the 100th meridian serving as a rough dividing line between adequate and inadequate precipitation. East of the 100th meridian, average annual rainfall varies from 60 to 80 inches on the Gulf coast to 20 to 30 inches on the Great Plains. West of the 100th meridian, with the exception of the northwest Pacific Coast where the rainfall is quite heavy, average annual precipitation varies from under 10 inches in the desert regions to as much as 20 inches elsewhere.

Approximately 21.5 inches, or about 70 per cent of the 30 inches of average annual precipitation, returns to the atmosphere through evaporation or transpiration of vegetation and is not available for further use. The balance of 8.5 inches either runs off the land to feed streams or soaks into the ground. The 31 most easterly states on the average receive over 70 percent of the national water yield, whereas the 17 westernmost continental states, which contain almost 60 per cent of the United States' land area, receive the balance. Over one-half of this latter area, including nearly all of Nevada, Arizona, New Mexico, North Dakota and South Dakota, has a natural water yield of less than 1 inch annually.

When precipitation falls on highland areas, it is possible to harness the stream flow as a source of energy. The amount of power available is a function of the stream's slope and the volume of precipitation. Thus, high elevations which receive substantial precipitation possess the greatest water power potential. In the United States these conditions are found primarily in the East and Northwest. In the East, the Great Lakes drainage area, which encompasses Niagara Falls and the St. Lawrence River, is particularly well suited for power sites. The natural storage reservoir formed by the Lakes obviates the need to construct artificial reservoirs to regulate stream flow, one of the major costs of harnessing hydroelectric

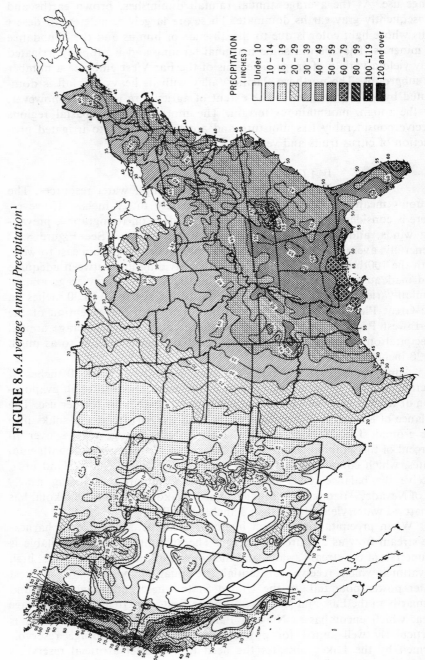

FIGURE 8.6. *Average Annual Precipitation*[1]

PRECIPITATION
(INCHES)

Under 10
10 – 14
15 – 19
20 – 29
30 – 39
40 – 49
50 – 59
60 – 79
80 – 99
100 –119
120 and over

[1] Averages derived from records of the U.S. Weather Bureau over a period of years.

power. The Connecticut, Potomac, and Tennessee river basins also are important sources of eastern water power. In the Pacific Northwest, the Columbia River and its tributaries are ideally suited for water power development. They flow over 1,200 miles and drop as much as 3,000 to 6,000 feet en route from their Rocky Mountain sources to the Pacific Ocean. The central Sacramento-San Joaquin Valley of California, and the Colorado, Missouri, and Arkansas River basins are other important western water power sources.

TIMBER

Originally forests occupied about half of the United States land surface. The principal stand occurred in the East, which was almost completely blanketed from the Atlantic Coast to the prairie lands beyond the Mississippi. In the Central and Western United States, grass, shrubs, and desert lands were only occasionally interrupted by narrow forest strips along streams or in highland areas. The Rocky Mountains contained substantial forests, particularly in its northern domain. In the far West, the more humid climate along the Pacific Coast produced forests even more magnificent than those of the East. Both eastern and western forests contain a wide variety of species, with hardwoods (deciduous species) dominating the former, and softwoods (conifers) the latter. Although the original forest and other natural vegetation have been greatly modified by clearing, cultivation, and development of the land, the basic pattern still prevails. Five forest regions exist in the Continental United States, three in the East, and two in the West. Northeastern forests, which encompass northern New England and New York and reach as far west as northeastern Minnesota and as far south as North Carolina contain principally sugar maple, birch and other hardwood species. On the lighter soils, white pines and other softwoods are found. Central hardwood forests, which cover most of the nineteen states located in the central eastern United States, contain mostly oak species. Walnut, cherry and aspen are some of the other hardwoods found in this area. Often these hardwoods mix with softwoods such as pine and hemlock. The region's good soil and ample precipitation produced virgin forests of excellent quality and great height. The southern forests, which embrace the southeastern Atlantic and Gulf coasts and extend as far west as Arkansas and southern Missouri, contain principally pines of the shortleaf, longleaf, loblolly and slash varieties. Hardwood stands of oaks, gums, and elms are found on the higher alluvial bottom lands along streams and swamps. The Rocky Mountain forests which extend from Canada to Mexico are dominated by eighty-foot pines such as lodgepole and yellow pine, hemlock, red cedar, and Douglas Fir. The most extensive growth is found in northern Idaho and western Montana. The Pacific Coast forests, which traverse

Washington, Oregon, and California, include some of the heaviest forest stands in the world. Growth is found on both the east and west slopes of the several mountain ranges — the Sierra Nevada and the Cascades to the east, and to the west the coastal ranges which rise immediately from the Pacific Ocean. In Washington and western Oregon Douglas Fir is the most common specie, while California forests include pines, cedars and firs. Also in this region are the giant sequoias and redwoods.

MINERALS

Besides forests, the United States is endowed with bountiful mineral resources. All the major minerals — coal, petroleum, natural gas, iron, copper, lead, zinc, and aluminum — except tin are present in moderate to large quantities. Only the ferroalloy or additive metals — manganese, nickel, chromium, and cobalt — important for making steel are in short supply. Coal is present in the Appalachian region extending from Pennsylvania to Alabama, Illinois, Kentucky, Iowa, Missouri, Kansas, Oklahoma, Texas, and Michigan. Oil has been found in Pennsylvania, Kansas, Oklahoma, Arkansas, Texas, Louisiana, the Gulf Coast, California, Illinois, Indiana and the Rocky Mountain region. Oil shale is located in Colorado, Wyoming, and Utah. Natural gas, commonly discovered while searching for oil, is found mainly in Texas, Louisiana, Kansas, New Mexico, and Oklahoma. Major iron deposits have been found in New York, Pennsylvania, New Jersey, Alabama, and the Lake Superior region of Michigan and Minnesota. Copper deposits are found in Michigan, Utah, Montana, New Mexico, and Nevada. Lead is found in Missouri, Idaho, Utah, Kansas, and Oklahoma. Zinc is to be found in the same regions. Aluminum's raw material source, bauxite, is found in Arkansas, Alabama and Georgia.

THE EXTRACTIVE INDUSTRIES

In the period before 1860, the major extractive industries were lumber and iron. From 1815 to 1865 lumber production increased fifteenfold. In 1860 it was second only to textiles in nonagricultural economic importance and had a gross product value of $100 million. Chicago was the lumber center of the nation owing to the output of Wisconsin, Michigan, and Minnesota. Older areas such as New York, Pennsylvania, Maine, and Connecticut continued to be major suppliers. Iron ore provided the nation with the raw material for the iron and steel industry, the fourth largest nonagricultural industry in 1860. Iron ore came principally from a number of small-scale mines located in Pennsylvania, the Lake Champlain area of New York, the Salisbury district of Connecticut, and the Morris County region of New Jersey. By the Civil War, however, the supplanting of charcoal by coal as the principal fuel in iron and steel production led to the industry's concentration in Pennsylvania. In 1860 the latter was supplying the nation with fifty per cent of total output. Other important extractive industries were coal, copper, lead, and gold. Coal experienced moderate growth in the period prior to the Civil War. Anthracite coal, mined in eastern Pennsylvania, was used primarily as a home fuel, and beginning in the 1840's for iron production. Bituminous coal, found in the Appalachian Mountains extending from Pennsylvania to Alabama, came to supplant charcoal as a fuel in iron production in the 1850's. Significant mining of copper did not commence until the early 1840's when large deposits were tapped in the upper Michigan region. This area by 1860 was supplying three-fourths of total output. After its discovery at Sutter's Mill, gold output grew steadily, and it soon became the most valuable mineral product of the nation.

INTERNAL TRANSPORTATION AND THE GROWTH OF URBAN AREAS

ECONOMIC IMPORTANCE

The development of an effective internal transportation system is an essential ingredient of economic growth. As transportation facilities improve, markets grow and significant cost savings can be passed on to consumers in the form of lower prices. There are several reasons for these economies. First, regional and national markets replace local markets. As a result, local monopoly breaks down and is replaced by market competition. Second, geographic specialization in production occurs as each region produces the goods for which it has a comparative cost advantage, trading these items for goods produced in other regions. Third, mass production results, which in turn promotes further cost savings. Fourth, easy accessibility is provided to natural resources. Fifth, labor mobility is enhanced, which produces a more efficient work force. Finally, technological innovations are spurred in response to growing markets. There would be little point in developing agricultural machinery to enhance farm productivity, if the crops couldn't be shipped to market.

Transportation costs are a major factor in plant location decisions. The larger freight costs are as a percentage of total costs, the greater their influence. Freight costs encompass the shipment of raw materials to the plant and the movement of finished products to consumer markets. The closer the plant is to the market, the lower will be market freight costs and the higher will be raw material freight costs. The nearer the plant to the raw material site, however, the lower will be raw material shipment costs and the higher will be market shipment costs. Other things being equal, the entrepreneur will find it advantageous to locate his business at that point where the sum of both costs is minimized. This is not the only choice available to the manufacturer. If economies of scale are not present in one large plant, a manufacturer may elect to build two smaller plants, one at the source of raw materials and one in the marketplace. For most of the period before the Civil War the absence of reasonably priced and reliable internal transportation facilities, particularly in the interior, forced most producers to locate their plants closer to markets rather than to raw material sources.

URBAN GROWTH

During this period the major cities located along the Eastern Seaboard and Gulf Coast experienced considerable growth. Their port facilities serviced both international and coastal trade. In 1820, seven per cent of the population lived in cities of 2,500 or more people. By 1860, twenty per cent of the population lived in these urban centers. The five major cities of 1820, New York, Philadelphia, Baltimore, Boston and New Orleans, maintained their ranking to 1860. Southern and New England cities, however, such as Charleston, Richmond, Washington, and Salem declined relative to western cities such as Cincinnati, St. Louis and Chicago.

New York City's leadership was due to its trading eminence. It was the first to establish regularly scheduled transatlantic crossings, which encouraged shippers and passengers to use its facilities. A significant percentage of coastal and international trade, including the shipment of cotton from Southern plantations to both New England and European textile mills, were arranged and financed by New York firms. A highly developed auction system for the prompt sale of goods was another inducement for businessmen to use New York facilities. Finally, the construction of the Erie Canal in the 1820's provided access to the agricultural producing regions of the Midwest.

ROAD CONSTRUCTION

By the 1820's the private turnpike era which had begun in the 1790's ground to a halt. The Federal Government failed to fill the gap left by a declining number of private companies. In 1830 Andrew Jackson issued his famous Maysville Veto, which opposed the use of Federal funds for the construction of a sixty-mile road from Maysville, Kentucky to Lexington, Kentucky. In the same decade the operation of the National Pike was transferred from Federal to state jurisdiction. By that time the Pike, begun in 1811 in Cumberland, Maryland had pushed to Columbus, Ohio, and by 1852 it reached as far west as Vandalia, Illinois, a total distance of eight hundred and thirty miles. Despite the end of the turnpike era, its accomplishments were substantial; while no paved roads existed in 1793, by 1830 the United States had 15,000 miles.

A renaissance of road building activity occurred between 1845 and 1857. This period was characterized by the building of wooden plank roads. Owing to the ready supply of timber, these plank roads were considerably cheaper to build than macadamized roads. Construction costs ranged from a thousand to twenty-five hundred dollars a mile compared to ten thousand dollars a mile for the National Pike. In addition, plank roads could support heavier loads than macadam, and unlike dirt roads were not greatly affected by heavy rainfall. Their one great disadvantage was their rapid rate of physical deterioration. Under the best of circumstances they had to be rebuilt before a decade had passed.

WATERWAYS

Waterways were the cheapest and easiest means of penetrating the interior of the United States. Most major cities are located on water sites. Thus, Boston, New York, Charleston, and Savannah are situated on the Atlantic Ocean; Los Angeles and San Francisco on the Pacific Ocean; Detroit, Cleveland, Milwaukee, and Chicago on the Great Lakes; Washington on the Potomac River; Baltimore on the Chesapeake Bay, and Philadelphia at the juncture of the Delaware and Schuykill rivers. Similarly, all four of the largest western cities of 1830 were on major water sites: Cincinnati on the Ohio, Pittsburgh at the juncture where the Allegheny and Monongahela form the Ohio, St. Louis on the Mississippi just below the mouth of the Missouri, and New Orleans at the mouth of the Mississippi. Each of the major rivers were fed by numerous tributaries which formed an internal waterway transportation system. This was particularly true in the case of the Mississippi and its major tributaries, the Ohio and Missouri rivers. Among the many rivers that link up with the Mississippi from the East are the St. Croix, Chippewa, Wisconsin, Rock, Illinois, Kaskaskia, Yazoo, and Big Black. From the West come the Minnesota, Iowa, Skunk, Des Moines, St. Francis, White, Arkansas, and Red rivers. Tributaries to the Ohio from the North are the Muskingum, Scioto, Great Miami, and Wabash, while from the South come the Kanawha, Big Sandy, Licking, Kentucky, Green, Cumberland, and Tennessee. Beginning in Montana, the Missouri also has numerous tributaries, among them the Musselshell, Milk, Yellowstone, Grand, Cheyenne, White, Niobrara, James, Big Sioux, Little Sioux, Platte, Kansas, Chariton, Osage, and Gasconade. Such a catalog of names gives a good indication of the vast reaches of territory into which the Mississippi River system penetrates, and its importance to early pioneers.

The western pioneer made abundant use of waterways in shipping his surplus produce to market. It was prohibitive to ship bulky farm goods over trails or roads. On the other hand, these products could be cheaply floated downstream. Costs of shipment were as low as five cents a ton mile. In the 1820's some three thousand boats a year would float down the

Mississippi network, each carrying about twenty-five hundred dollars worth of cargo, containing wheat, flour, whiskey, lumber, pork, apples, cider, and cheese. However, voyages were slow, the journey from Cincinnati to New Orleans and back taking six months. And ice in winter and floods in spring often made river traffic impossible. The movement of goods upstream was particularly slow and costly. Sailing ships, which were efficient carriers of commerce in international coastal trade, were not suitable for most inland waterways. High banks and trees interfered with air currents and narrow rivers made navigation almost impossible. The only alternative was the use of flat boats pulled by horses or mules, which at best could move freight against the current at two to three miles per hour. As a result, only about ten per cent of the volume of downstream traffic returned upstream. The steamboat changed this. In 1807 Robert Fulton's *Clermont* demonstrated the feasibility of stream driven vessels; and by the end of the War of 1812 approximately twenty steamboats were carrying freight regularly. From this date their numbers grew steadily until more than 750 were operating on the eve of the Civil War. In general, they carried goods upstream at about one-third of the cost of flat boats and in one-fifth the time. They were particularly significant to the commerce of the Mississippi River System.

It has been estimated that by 1860 some $300 million worth of cargo moved on the western rivers of the nation, principally the Mississippi. The Civil War severely curtailed traffic. With the return of peace, river traffic growth on the Mississippi resumed, reaching a peak around 1880. In relative terms, however, it began to decline in the 1830's as alternative means of transportation, canals and railroads, made their appearane. Nevertheless it is almost impossible to overestimate the importance of such traffic to the pre-Civil War western farmer, for not only did it lower the cost of goods which he sold, but it lowered the price of goods which he bought. His standard of living, therefore, increased considerably. The strategic position of New Orleans at the mouth of the Mississippi guaranteed its prominence in commerce as long as waterways were the principal vehicle for western commerce. (See Table 8.3.) On the eve of the Civil War, it ranked second only to New York as the largest American seaport, and because of its position in the cotton belt, was the largest export city of the nation.

One of the great disadvantages of river transportation was its geographic inflexibility. Canals, which joined major water arteries, helped overcome this difficulty. A canal era began about 1825 and lasted until the depression of 1837-43 in the eastern United States and until the Depression of 1857-59 in the West. Construction of the first United States canal dates back to 1792. However, it was the Erie Canal which inaugurated major canal construction in 1817. The Erie traversed three hundred

TABLE 8.3. *Steamboat Arrivals in New Orleans*

Year	Arrivals
1815	40
1820	198
1830	989
1840	1,573
1850	2,784
1860	3,566

SOURCE: Frank H. Dixon. *Traffic History of the Mississippi River.* Washington, D.C.: U.S. Government Printing Office, 1915, p. 15.

and sixty-four miles and cost approximately $20 thousand a mile to construct. It provided the Atlantic Coast with access to the Great Lakes and Ohio territory, and guaranteed New York's position as the nation's leading port. Through the Erie came lumber, grain and meat products to eastern markets, and textiles, leather goods and other manufactures to the West. Freight charges between New York and Buffalo were reduced from $100 a ton to $15 a ton. The success of the Erie Canal encouraged the spread of canal construction. (See Table 8.4.) Ohio and Indiana extended the Erie System, linking the Ohio River and Lake Erie. Pennsylvania, anxious to divert some commercial traffic from the Erie, linked up with the West by a system of canal and rail lines between Philadelphia and Pittsburgh. Almost four hundred miles in length, the Pennsylvania mainline cost some $10 million to build. Unfortunately, the terrain over which it ran militated against low-cost operation. Philadelphia merchants still found it cheaper to patro-

TABLE 8.4. *Cycles of Canal Construction 1815–1860*

Period	Mileage
First Cycle, 1815–34	2,200
Second Cycle, 1834–44	1,200
Third Cycle, 1844–60	900
Total For All Cycles	4,300

SOURCE: Harvey H. Segal. "Cycles of Canal Construction," in Carter Goodrich, *Canals and Economic Development.* New York: Columbia University Press, 1961, p. 172.

TABLE 8.5. *Distribution of the Commodity Trade of the Midwest 1835–1853*

	Percentage of Trade Shipped by:		
Year	*The Erie Canal*	*The Mississippi River*	*Other Routes**
1835	24	62	14
1839	38	46	16
1844	44	44	12
1849	53	38	9
1853	62	29	9

*The Pennsylvania Mainline, the Pittsburgh Turnpike, and the Cumberland Road.

SOURCE: Harvey H. Segal. "Canals and Economic Development," in Carter Goodrich, *Canals and Economic Development.* New York: Columbia University Press, 1961, p. 231.

nize the Erie Canal. Other major canal construction included the linking of Lake Michigan and the Mississippi via the Illinois River in the 1840's and the joining of Lakes Huron and Superior in the 1850's. The importance of the Erie Canal is demonstrated by the fact that between 1835 and 1853 its share of the Midwest commodity trade increased from twenty-four per cent to sixty-two per cent. (See Table 8.5.) It is noteworthy that during the same period the Mississippi's share of trade declined from sixty-two per cent to twenty-nine per cent.

Most canals were constructed with public funds. It has been estimated that between 1815 and 1860 seventy per cent of canal construction costs were provided by government. State governments in particular, spurred on by competition with one another, overinvested in canals. Between 1820 and 1840 state debts grew from a negligible amount to about two hundred million dollars, mainly because of canal construction. As revenues proved inadequate to service canal debt, many states proceeded to default on their obligations. Subsequently, practically all canals were sold to private enterprises, and many state constitutions were rewritten forbidding state governments from engaging in such construction. By the Civil War canals were in a state of relative decline. There were three principal reasons for this decline. Canals were slow, extremely expensive to build, and inoperable in freezing weather. These disadvantages might not have proven fatal, except for the appearance of the railroad, which though more expensive to construct was faster and cheaper. In 1860 the volume of railroad traffic equaled that of canals. Twenty years later almost half of the 4,500 miles of canals constructed had been abandoned.

RAILROADS

It was the railroad which unified the far-flung geography of the United States and made of it one common market. Ironically, the coming of the railroad was looked upon by many as a menace. In particular, those associated with canals and turnpikes regarded it as a threat to their economic well-being. State and local governments which had substantial investments in canals were often among the most hostile. Some farmers objected because they feared losses in grain and hay sales as horse-drawn transportation declined. Finally, the fifteen mile an hour speed of the railroad in the 1830's was regarded by some as a threat to life and limb. The first modern railroad was the Baltimore and Ohio, which was begun in 1828 to link Baltimore with the West. Its principal aim was to garner some of the freight business being enjoyed by New York's Erie Canal. The road began partial operation in 1830, a year in which less than twenty-five miles of track existed in the United States. About this time the city of Boston commenced constructing a road to connect with the Hudson River, similarly to divert business from New York. Most early roads were built in New England and the Middle Atlantic states due to high population density and the relative abundance of capital in these regions.

Initially, roads were constructed to link canals and rivers, but this limited goal was rapidly transcended. By 1840, three thousand miles of track existed, a mileage equal to that of canals. The 1840's witnessed a significant acceleration of growth, so that by the end of the decade the United States boasted more track mileage than any other country in the world, nine thousand miles. In the 1850's four major trunklines traversed the Appalachians. They were the Erie Railroad which linked New York with Dunkirk on Lake Erie in 1851, the Pennsylvania Railroad which linked Philadelphia and Pittsburgh in 1852, the New York Central which linked New York with Buffalo on Lake Erie in 1853, and the Baltimore and Ohio Railroad which linked Baltimore and Wheeling, West Virginia on the Ohio River in 1853. In the same period the South, following the North's lead, began significant construction of rail links with the West. By mid-decade a railroad-river complex had been constructed which made Atlanta the southeastern center for western grain and meat, and by 1859 New Orleans and the Gulf States also enjoyed rail connections with the West. Southern railroads, however, due to a shortage of capital, were inferior in quality to those of the North. On the eve of the Civil War thirty thousand miles of track existed in the nation and railroad investment totaled one and a quarter billion dollars. All regions east of the Mississippi were effectively united.

Most railroad capital came from state and local governments and foreign investors. Forty per cent of northern roads and fifty per cent of southern roads were financed by public funds. Loans and stock purchases were the common means by which states and municipalities supplied capital. It should be pointed out, however, that state governments for the most part made little attempt to own and operate the roads, looking upon such ventures as essentially private enterprises affected with a public interest. The Federal Government provided both indirect and direct aid. The former took the form of railroad surveys and preferential tariff treatment for the import of iron rails. Direct aid took the form of land grants. (See Table 8.2.) Foreign investment in the railroads commenced in the 1850's. By the late nineteenth century foreigners were dominant stock and bond holders in such emerging giants as the Pennsylvania and New York Central railroads.

The Civil War spurred railroad construction in the North and opened the way for a federally financed transcontinental system. The discovery of gold in California had spurred agitation for construction of such a system in the 1850's. While the nation agreed on the need for such a road, disagreement existed as to whether a northern or southern route should be pursued. Southern secession from the Union settled the issue. In 1862 Congress chartered the Union Pacific Railroad to build a road west from Omaha, Nebraska. At the same time, a previously chartered California corporation, the Central Pacific, pushed eastward from San Francisco to meet the Union Pacific.

SELECTED REFERENCES

1. F. J. Dewhurst, *et. al. America's Needs and Resources: A New Survey.* New York: Twentieth Century Fund, 1955.
2. Albert Fishlow. *American Railroads and the Transformation of the Ante-Bellum Economy.* Cambridge: Harvard University Press, 1966.
3. Carter Goodrich, Julius Rubin, and Harvey H. Segal. *Canals and American Economic Development.* New York: Columbia University Press, 1961.
4. Benjamin Hubbard. *A History of Public Land Policies.* Madison: University of Wisconsin Press, 1965.
5. George R. Taylor. *The Transportation Revolution, 1815-1860.* New York: Holt, Rinehart and Winston, 1951.

reading

were the south and west economically interdependent prior to the development of improved east-west transportation facilities?

albert fishlow

Like Gaul, the antebellum United States was divided into three regions: North, South, and West. Unlike Caesar, however, economic historians have been more concerned with the opportunities thus afforded for regional specialization than the varying warlike characteristics of the populace. From their investigations has arisen one of the abiding generalizations of the structure of the pre-Civil War economy: an industrial North, an agricultural West, and a staple South—all extensively interdependent. This view was summarized by Louis Schmidt in 1939 and has been again brought into prominence by Douglass C. North just recently.

> The rise of internal commerce after 1815 made possible a territorial division of labor between the three great sections of the Union—the West, the South, and the East. . . . The South was thereby enabled to devote itself in particular to the production of a few plantation staples constituting a large and growing surplus for the foreign markets and depending on the West for a large part of its food supply and in the East for the bulk of its manufactured goods and very largely for the conduct of its commerce and banking. . . . The West became a surplus grain- and livestock-producing kingdom, supplying the growing deficits of the South and the East.[1]

It is this position I wish to reconsider in this paper. Specifically, I shall hold that the trade between the West and South was always of limited importance to both regions: the South was neither a major market for

Reprinted with permission from "Antebellum Interregional Trade Reconsidered" by Albert Fishlow, in *American Economic Review*, LIV (May 1964), 352-364.

western produce nor in dire need of imported foodstuffs. Thus to paraphrase (and negate) the comment of Guy Callendar more than half a century ago, the commerce between different agricultural communities in America has played a less important role in our economic history than has recently been argued. Rather, the rapidly growing commerce between East and West played the significant role. In the second part of the paper, with the assistance of a set of interregional trade estimates, I shall show that there was indeed a relative expansion both in regional exports and in their domestic consumption. Interregional exchange was a prominent feature of American antebellum development, but not as a result of interdependence among all regions.

THE TRADE BETWEEN WEST AND SOUTH

For much of the period from 1815 to 1860 New Orleans was the great shipping point for the produce of the interior. The growing volume of receipts at New Orleans, far overshadowing the value of tonnage from the western states arriving at tidewater by the Erie Canal, testifies to that. Unfortunately, however, the produce finding its way to the Crescent City included much beside western exports, as many have recognized in passing. I wonder whether this limitation has been sufficiently appreciated. As early as the 1820's, receipts of cotton, tobacco, sugar and molasses amount to more than half the total value of imports; by the 1850's, these southern commodities made up some three-fourths of the total.[2] For the time when New Orleans was a depository for western products almost exclusively we must go back before the spread of the cotton culture to the western South in the latter 1810's. Thereafter, the trade between the West and the South is most certainly not "recorded in receipts at New Orleans."

This is not to deny that western products did follow the winding course of the Mississippi to New Orleans in significant amounts for much of the period. As late as 1849, it has been estimated that some 40 percent of the western exports of corn, a third of the flour, three-fourths of the salt meat, and two-thirds of the whiskey all were shipped to that southern gateway.[3] Very little was retained for consumption within the South, however. Most was shipped on to northern cities or foreign ports. Table 1 shows the extent of this re-export. Not until the very end of the period were more than half of the principal imports of foodstuffs consumed within the South, including shipments to other southern cities. By then the failure of receipts to keep pace with the rapidly growing export potential of the West meant that consumption of western imports was not notably above the levels established a decade earlier.

Although Table 1 does not go back before 1842, there is no reason to believe that the trend described by it was broken then. We would expect

Year Ending August 31	Flour (bbls.)	Corn (sacks)	Pork (bbls.)	Bacon (hhds.)	Beef (bbls.)	Lard (kegs)	Whiskey (bbls.)	Value ($000's)
1842–45*								
Receipts†	491,836	490,169	333,232	30,856	36,023	654,063	81,537	$ 8,275
Exports‡	245,542	189,573	244,115	8,012	19,835	575,974	7,274	4,823
Consumption	246,294	300,596	89,117	22,844	16,188	78,089	74,263	$ 3,452
Ratio of consumption to receipts	.50	.61	.27	.74	.45	.12	.91	.42
1846–49								
Receipts†	1,043,949	1,887,984	507,219	57,760	78,393	1,204,501	126,005	$20,824
Exports‡	726,399	1,446,457	308,492	25,303	49,417	1,064,975	15,948	13,830
Consumption	317,550	441,527	198,727	32,457	28,976	139,526	110,057	$ 6,994
Ratio of consumption to receipts	.30	.23	.39	.56	.37	.12	.87	.34
1850–53								
Receipts†	817,244	1,306,799	441,235	87,378	69,446	1,005,985	140,090	$22,211
Exports‡	304,836	496,277	234,578	30,232	49,624	910,169	8,970	10,803
Consumption	512,408	810,522	206,657	57,146	19,822	95,816	131,120	$11,408
Ratio of consumption to receipts	.63	.62	.47	.65	.29	.10	.94	.51
1854–57								
Receipts†	989,735	1,588,001	325,243	67,658	48,433	702,801	141,424	$26,300
Exports‡	529,863	820,267	139,447	16,127	28,340	724,726	7,179	13,053
Consumption	459,872	767,734	185,796	51,531	20,093	−21,925	134,245	$13,247
Ratio of consumption to receipts	.46	.48	.57	.76	.41	−.03	.95	.50
1858–61								
Receipts†	1,149,695	1,820,616	275,246	63,910	42,287	448,381	139,129	$24,984
Exports‡	425,542	410,004	39,543	4,907	15,051	405,351	4,425	6,873
Consumption	724,153	1,410,612	235,703	59,003	27,236	43,030	134,704	$18,111
Ratio of consumption to receipts	.63	.77	.86	.92	.64	.10	.97	.72

SOURCE: *Hunt's Merchants' Magazine*, 1842, pp. 391–92; 1844, pp. 419–21; 1845, pp. 370–72; 1846, pp. 406–09; 1847, pp. 413–14; 1848, pp. 511–16; 1849, pp. 554–56; 1850, pp. 536–37; 1851, pp. 602–05; 1852, pp. 489–92; 1853, pp. 624–29; 1854, pp. 475–77; 1855, pp. 601–04; 1856, p. 474 and New Orleans *Price Current*, Sept. 1, 1856; 1857, pp. 603–07; New Orleans *Price Current*, Sept. 1, 1858, 1859, and Aug. 31, 1861; *DeBow's Rev.*, 1860, p. 521.

*The year 1843 is not included.

†Calculated in homogeneous physical units by dividing total dollar receipts of product by price of physical unit.

‡Foreign exports plus coastwise shipments to Boston, New York, Philadelphia, and Baltimore. Unspecified coastwise shipments were credited to southern ports.

New Orleans to be even more important for its re-export functions the further back we go in time because there was no access to the Erie Canal from the already relatively densely settled Ohio Valley until 1833. There are indications suggesting that this was so. Information upon total receipts at New Orleans and total exports, foreign and coastwise, is available for two earlier years, 1837 and 1833. In the former the exports actually exceeded receipts, while in the latter the difference is only slightly positive. This signifies little consumption at New Orleans, and because coastwise trade with other southern cities was limited until the 1850's, affirms the same for total imports of western produce. In any event, total receipts of western produce at New Orleans were very much smaller before the early 1840's—less than half as much in 1836-40 than 1841-45; so consumption necessarily would have been limited even if all foodstuffs were retained.[4]

The significance of the Mississippi to the West therefore was only secondarily as a route to the South. Rather it was a means of reaching eastern and foreign ports, and especially the former; until the later 1850's, twice as much was re-exported to northern cities as to other nations. Laments for the decline of New Orleans as a site of western receipts did not blame declining southern appetites, but, properly, focused on the rapid construction of rail feeders that narrowed the economic hinterland of New Orleans. Nowhere was the shift more obvious than in the Ohio Valley. The proportion of flour flowing eastward or northward from Cincinnati increased from 3 percent in the early 1850's to 90 percent in 1860; similarly for pork, there was a shift from 7 percent to 42 percent.[5] Table 1 shows the combined effects of these shifting loyalties and the more rapid growth of that part of the West tributary to the Lakes: almost twice as much flour, eight times as much pork and bacon, twice as much lard, and three times as much of both corn and beef were exported from New Orleans in 1846-49 than in 1858-61.

These more refined consumption data permit us now to re-examine the trade in foodstuffs between West and South from the standpoint of its relative importance to each region. For the West this means the relative importance of the southern as opposed to the eastern and foreign markets; for the South it means a comparison of the imports of western commodities with the volume of southern production. Table 2, drawing upon the estimates of total western exports of A. L. Kohlmeier, satisfies the first requirement. It demonstrates convincingly the limited extent of the southern market. In total value, less than a fifth of western products were consumed in the South throughout. Only a rising trend of salt meat consumption kept the record as good as this, and here the border states were responsible. In 1853, Louisville contributed a fifth of the pork and bacon received at New Orleans; in 1860 its share had increased to a third.[6]

TABLE 2. The Importance of the Southern Market to the West (Percent)

Commodity	1839*	1844	1849	1853	1857	1860	1842*	1844	1849	1853	1857	1860
	Proportion of Western Exports Shipped Via New Orleans						Proportion of Receipts of Western Produce at New Orleans Consumed in the South					
Flour	53	30	31	27	34	22	42	50	30	60	41	86
Meat products	51	63	50	38	28	24	41	31	34	62	69	95
Corn	98	90	39	37	32	19	46	70	21	44	65	91
Whiskey	96	95	67	53	48	40	80	95	89	90	93	98
Total foodstuffs	49	44	40	31	27	17	37	38	29	52	52	85
	Proportion of Western Exports Consumed in the South						Proportion of Western Exports Re-exported Via New Orleans					
Flour	22	16	9	14	14	19	31	15	22	13	20	3
Meat products	21	19	17	24	19	23	30	44	33	14	9	1
Corn	45	63	8	16	21	17	53	27	31	21	11	2
Whiskey	77	90	60	48	45	39	19	5	7	5	3	1
Total foodstuffs	18	17	12	16	14	14	31	27	28	15	13	3

*Years ending circa August 31, but not exactly in the case of eastern exports. Note that the 1842 consumption proportions at New Orleans have been applied to 1839.

SOURCE: Proportion of Western Exports shipped via New Orleans: A. L. Kohlmeier, *The Old Northwest as the Keystone of the Arch of American Federal Union* (Principia Press, 1938), pp. 33, 52-53, 83-85, 116-17, 146-48, 191-93, 248-49. Meat products include livestock (estimated for 1839-53). In certain instances there are small inconsistencies between the text descriptions and the summary chart. These have been decided as best possible; they do not affect the results. Total foodstuffs include wheat, which is not shown separately. The proportion is determined from total values as obtained with western prices. See the Technical Appendix (obtainable from the author) for more detail.

Proportion of New Orleans Receipts Consumed in the South: Table 1. Meat products are the weighted sum of bacon, pork, and beef. Total foodstuffs include lard and whiskey, but exclude wheat. This slight incomparability with panel 1 does not influence the findings.

Proportion of Western Exports Consumed in the South: Panel 1 times panel 2.
Proportion of Western Exports Re-exported via New Orleans: Panel 1 minus panel 3.

If relatively unimportant to the West, the imports were truly minute compared with the production of foodstuffs within the South itself. The 1842 corn consumption of 241,049 sacks (= 2 bushels each) is far less than 1 percent of the 1839 southern crop of 225 million bushels; the corresponding ratios for the census years 1850 and 1860 increase to be sure, but reach a maximum in the latter years of only .9 percent! For wheat the situation is not greatly dissimilar. Wheat imports (principally in the form of flour reckoned as five bushels per barrel), amounted to 960,000 bushels in 1842, 2,600,000 in 1850, and 4,250,000 in 1860. Output was 25 million bushels in 1839, 20 million in 1849, and 38 million in 1859. At best, due to the poor crop of 1849, imports aggregate 13 percent of the total. Note that although imports increased rapidly between 1850 and 1860, local production increased still more rapidly; so the South was less dependent at the end of the decade than at its beginning. Despite the simultaneous boom in cotton, the share of the South in national wheat output actually increased over this interval. Not surprisingly, the relative importance of meat products is more akin to the self-sufficiency in corn. The 1850 census credits to the southern states a product of almost $49 million in slaughtered animals — an estimate that must be raised to $119 million to compensate for understatement. Imports of pork, bacon, and beef aggregated only $3.6 million in the comparable year 1850. In 1860, the ratio of imports, similarly calculated, climbed to the 5 percent mark.[7]

The independence of the South evinces itself even more clearly when contrasted to the role western imports played in satisfying eastern deficiencies. As early as 1849 the 7.5 million equivalent bushels of wheat retained in the East augmented local production by 20 percent. By 1860 the imports exceeded actual output by 20 percent; that is, imports accounted for 53 percent of consumption. In corn and meat products, the East moved from self-sufficiency in the former and imports of a little more than 7 percent in the latter to deficits of 20 percent in both products. Growing eastern demands furnished the wherewithal for western expansion; in turn, that region became dependent upon the abundance brought forth upon the lands across the Alleghenies.[8]

One possibility remains to refute these contentions: that would be a substantial flow of western produce directly to southern sites, and bypassing New Orleans. Such a circumstance is doubtful. The shipments from Cincinnati to down river ports other than New Orleans do not appear to be of any significance. During the years 1848-50, less than 1 percent of the provisions shipped from that city to New Orleans were destined to these other ports; of corn the ratio is 10 percent, but Cincinnati was not the leading southern forwarder; of flour, another growing export of St. Louis, the proportion is about 20 percent on average. At the other side of the transaction, receipts at different southern cities appear limited. Shipments up the Cumberland and Tennessee rivers "supplied a local market in Western Kentucky and were comparatively limited in quantity." The shipment of 297,119 pounds of meat from Vicksburg to Jackson in 1850 is no more than .1 percent of the receipts at New Orleans in the same year. Distribution by rail from Mississippi river points to the interior South likewise is doubtful. The Memphis and Charleston Railroad carried only 4,000 tons of all varieties eastward to the latter city in 1860—too small to count.[9]

Routes to the South other than the Mississippi and the limited channels enumerated above were virtually nonexistent before the war. There was no through connection at all between western and southern railroads and the tortuousness of many transshipments would soon cause exorbitant expense. The underlying economics also make shipment via New Orleans far more probable. Not only was that city a major distribution point, but the limited back haulage would make for low rates upstream. Logic seems to have its counterpart in fact. The *Internal Commerce Report* for 1887 remarks: "There was no trade between the Western cities and the Southern plantations, very little even with the towns; it all paid tribute to New Orleans. . . . Of these shipments upstream over 75 percent. . .were articles which had previously been sent downstream."[10] If the border states of Kentucky and Tennessee be regarded as part of the West rather than the South, some further trade undoubtedly occurred that is not reckoned in here, particularly in livestock. But it is hardly clear that such a treatment is more appropriate: in their commitment to slavery, size of farms, ethnic character of population, and, indeed, in the case of Tennessee its considerable production of cotton, these states were part of the South. Note again, therefore, that our trade figures from the West actually overstate consumption of western foodstuffs because they include the downriver shipments from Louisville.

Despite this, the clear picture that has emerged is one of tenuous linkage between the two regions. To the West, the South was a minor matter for its own demands. And as early as 1839, more western products were shipped directly eastward than re-exported via New Orleans. Table 2 records the re-export trade in its fourth panel. After 1849 it dwindles rapidly and becomes insignificant by 1860. By then New Orleans was far from the central pivot it had been in the 1810's. On the other side, the southern states were far from dependent upon the agricultural largess of the West for their needs. The greater than average per capita production of corn, peas, and beans in the South supports this observation; so, too, do the larger cattle and swine inventories. The southern social structure, with its large numbers of landowners with few slaves or none at all, also may be invoked. It is suggestive of an economic organization with both widespread self-sufficiency and local sale of foodstuffs to nearby plantations. In conclusion, one may contrast the strength of this case for little southern consumption of western produce with the virtual absence of affirmative evidence for the conventional wisdom of a close interconnection.[11]

ANTEBELLUM TRADE MORE GENERALLY

Another perspective from which to view this West-South trade is the context of the other interregional flows. I have set out some estimates of these for various years from 1839 through 1860 in Table 3. Their derivation is described fully in a technical appendix available from the author upon request. Briefly, I may indicate here the nature of these estimates. The trade flows to the West and from West to East directly are obtained by valuing Kohlmeier's shipments of specific commodities, and adjusting for undercoverage; eastern consumption of western products counts in imports via New Orleans and subtracts foreign exports. The flow from West to South is made up of all receipts at New Orleans less imports of cotton, sugar, molasses, and tobacco with consumption determined by the proportion of the selected products of Table 1 retained in the South.[12]

TABLE 3. *Interregional Merchandise Trade Flows* (Millions of Current Dollars)*

| Year | Originating Region | Receiving Region | | |
		North	West	South
1839	North	–	19.7	85.6
	West	11.8	–	14.9
		7.1	–	5.5
	South	39.7	6.3	–
		15.1	2.2	–
1844	North	–	25.2	73.2
	West	20.1	–	19.9
		14.5	–	7.6
	South	32.4	6.2	–
		11.6	3.5	–
1849	North	–	41.4	80.0
	West	36.8	–	36.1
		24.2	–	10.5

TABLE 3. (continued)

Year	Originating Region	Receiving Region		
		North	*West*	*South*
	South	32.0	8.1	—
		18.9	4.8	—
1853	North	—	94.5	147.1
	West	63.2	—	36.9
		47.9	—	19.2
	South	61.9	17.2	—
		33.0	11.9	—
1857	North	—	163.1	165.7
	West	96.9	—	49.1
		45.8	—	25.5
	South	71.1	13.2	—
		38.0	5.5	—
1860	North	—	164.3	213.8
	West	146.5	—	42.8
		107.6	—	36.4
	South	69.4	20.3	—
		44.6	13.6	—

*Uppermost figure refers to gross flow whether for consumption or re-export; bottom figure is estimated consumption. In the case of the South-North entry this is limited to northern purchases of southern cotton, sugar, and molasses.

SOURCE: See Appendix (obtainable from the author), Tables A-10, A-11.

The flow from North to South is derived by subtracting the trade from the West to the South from estimated total southern import capacity; the South-North exchange is also a residual.

One important limitation of these data should be noted. The flows for the most part exclude full distribution mark-ups since they are valued at the wholesale prices of the region of origin. This procedure has been adopted since the regional allocation of expenditures for freight, insurance, banking, and other services is largely unknown. A measure of the maximum understatement of commerce is given by the extent of inter-regional price disparity. Sample calculations for both 1839 and 1860 for the West-East trade point to a weighted average differential of 20 percent. Similar calculations for the South-West exchange show a somewhat smaller variation of perhaps 15 percent, depending upon whether southern or western prices are used to value western imports. The trade data of Table 3 are too small by the proportion of this differential accounted for by extraregional payments.

Despite this restriction and the uncertainties in the attempt—due in part to the unsatisfactory nature of some of Kohlmeier's estimates, in part to the variation in quoted prices even within the same region, and in part to the necessity of valuing "merchandise" by the ton—these figures do suggest an order of magnitude that is probably closer to the truth than the variety of other similar figures that are current.[13] Kohlmeier's estimate for western trade in 1844, as quoted from the *Congressional Globe,* is $120 million for imports and $115 million for exports. Yet in that same year the Erie Canal valuation for western shipments, which we have used in our derivations, were, respectively, $14.8 million and $15.9 million, and that artery carried something like half the exports and even more of the imports, according to Kohlmeier's own estimates. The East-West figures also go beyond the calculations contained in *Statistics of Foreign and Domestic Commerce* wherein both through and way tonnage — much of the latter consisting of local coal destined for eastern seaports — are valued at generous prices to reach what appears to be a rather high value. Similarly, these flows between North and South are an improvement over Kettell's unbounded conjectures of 1860.[14] His total imports into the South are as great as $462 million whereas the maximum value of cotton, to-bacco, rice, and naval stores exports before the Civil War was never more than $275 million, against which must be reckoned direct foreign imports of some $35 million and imports from the West of almost equiv-alent size.[15]

The data of Table 3 fix the West-South traffic as one of limited scope. Whether we use gross flows or net consumption, the trade always ranks at the lower end of the spectrum. In its meager rate of growth it stands in sharp contrast to the increasing exchange between West and North. Where consumption of western produce by North and South was at approx-imate parity in 1839, the former was absorbing three times as much by 1860. Gross flows diverge most sharply in the decade of the 1850's as the extension of direct and more efficient East-West transport routes drew the commerce that had once been transshipped from New Orleans. The reciprocal flows inward to the West show the same asymmetrical development. From the earliest, high-valued merchandise was able to bear the cost of transportation and entered from the East, leaving for the South the distribution of assorted groceries and locally produced sugar and molasses. Thus in 1839 the West already depended more heavily upon the East than the South for its imports. By 1860 the advantage had grown enormously; almost ten times as much of western purchases came from the East than upriver. However one reads the record, the tale is straight-forward: an initially narrow commerce between the West and the South that failed to keep pace with the rapid expansion in western argicultural bounty and which was supplanted by a total exchange between East and West that ranked first by 1860.

This is not to gainsay the continuing trade between North and South. Over most of the antebellum period the coastwise trade was the most important artery of interregional commerce. Certainly until the mid-fifties the southern market was the largest that faced the North. Yet it is one about which we know perhaps least. Often it is assumed that the South possessed a higher propensity to consume foreign imports, obviously blunting the impact of its demands upon domestic development of manufactures. Yet the sheer size of the market must have given it a key role in American industrialization prior to the 1850's. Philadelphia in particular among the northern cities seems to have cultivated that territory for its rapidly increasing output of machinery.

Table 3 does more than garb these specific flows with greater statistical precision. It enables us for the first time to examine in quantitative terms the role of interregional trade in antebellum development. Adherents to the tenet that it is the domestic market that counts can take heart from the results. Even if we suppose northern distribution of imported merchandise accounts for a fourth of its shipments to other regions, domestic consumption of the produce of other regions exceeds foreign exports in every year. More significant still is the obvious relative growth in the domestic market during a period of accelerated income advance. Exports to other regions increase from $109 million in 1839 to $480 million in 1860; exports to other countries from $102 million to $316 million.[16] The regional variation is of interest. The North always fared better in exports to other regions than abroad; conversely the South depended more upon old England than New England for sales of its great staple. The West moves from a southern to a northern stance: in 1839 foreign countries afford a slightly better market for its foodstuffs than the still predominantly agricultural East and plantation South; by 1860, domestic consumption exceeds exports by a substantial margin.[17]

Export base proponents also can find much to their taste. The sum of the exports to other regions and abroad increases in importance between 1839 and 1860. Relative to gross national product in the former year they are 13 percent; in the latter 19 percent. Over this period their potential influence was therefore considerably enhanced. Again, the specific regional patterns deserve mention. Southern exports increased only slightly, from 23 percent to 29 percent of income. The West's dependence upon an external market radically altered from less than 13 percent to 23 percent of its product. The northern export percentage moved intermediately from 10 to 15. The region displaying the greatest increase in income and population, the West, also had the stimulus of the most rapidly growing external market, exactly as export base theory would predict.[18]

FINAL COMMENT

Full exploration of these intriguing suggestions is beyond the scope of this paper. But before the analysis of the role of interregional trade in American antebellum development can press home, further advances in two directions will be required. Refinement and extension of the basic trade estimates is an essential step; a promising possibility is a complementary approach from the side of regional consumption requirements. Equally urgent is modification of the export base theory to render it more amenable to empirical test. At present it does not completely satisfy this criterion.

Such a restatement can draw upon some of the preliminary findings reached here. The transition of the West from reliance on a foreign to a domestic market, in contrast to continued southern dependence on overseas markets, suggests that differences in destination of exports may play a greater role than has been recognized. Exports to another region may be more stable and less subject to competition than sales on a world market; regional interdependence may also bring with it a greater reciprocal inflow of labor, capital, and institutional influences. Whatever the merit of this speculation, the approach must certainly come to grips with our central result: the small, and lessening, linkage between the West and the South. Interregional interdependence there was before the Civil War, but increasingly exclusive of the South, a circumstance not unrelated, one might add, to the decision for Confederacy by the South, and that for Union by the West.

NOTES

1. Louis B. Schmidt, *Internal Commerce and the Development of a National Economy Before 1860* (J.P.E., 1939), p. 811. Cited by Douglass C. North, *The Economic Growth of the United States, 1790 to 1860* (Prentice-Hall, 1961), p. 103.
2. For the 1850's, U.S. Treasury Department, Bureau of Statistics, *Report on Internal Commerce for 1887* (Washington, 1888), p. 209. For the earlier period I have estimated the value of cotton, tobacco, sugar, and molasses receipts and compared these with total receipts given in the *Report*, p. 191 (see Table VII-4, *Railroads*).
3. See Table 2 *infra*.

4. *Report on the Internal Commerce for 1887,* pp. 199, 215, 285 ff., 377; Thomas S. Berry, *Western Prices Before 1861* (Harvard Univ. Press, 1943), p. 581. Source difficulties aside, one reason why it is not easy to go back before 1842 is the lack of dollar values and specific prices to enable conversion of receipts and exports to homogeneous units. This means an arduous task of reconciling different scales of measurement, as well as lack of weighted annual prices.
5. Berry, *Western Prices,* p. 91; Israel Andrews, *Trade and Commerce of the British North American Colonies,* House Executive Document No. 136, 32nd Cong., 2nd Sess., p. 711.
6. Kohlmeier, *Old Northwest,* pp. 118, 202.
7. These census data for the South exclude Delaware, Maryland, and Missouri. The relationship between reported value of slaughtered meat products and actual value is taken from the ratio of the national census totals to the aggregates reported in Robert E. Gallman, "Commodity Output, 1839-1899," *Trends in the American Economy in the Nineteenth Century* (Princeton Univ. Press, 1960), p. 46. Although the comparisons here have been made in terms of single years, the reader can quickly satisfy himself from the annual averages of Table 1 that the use of a longer interval near the census dates reinforces the conclusions if it affects them at all.
8. Eastern consumption was calculated as the sum of direct exports to the East as estimated by Kohlmeier, plus re-export to northern cities from New Orleans, minus shipments abroad from eastern ports. For 1860 these last could be obtained directly from the Report on Commerce and Navigation for that year; for 1840 they were estimated as national
9. *Hunt's Merchant's Magazine,* XXIII (1850), p. 542; Kohlmeier, *The Old Northwest,* p. 202; John H. Moore, *Agriculture in Ante Bellum Mississippi* (Bookman Associates, 1958), p. 111; *American Railroad Journal,* 1860, pp 840-41 (the through receipts of the Memphis and Charleston were converted to tonnage on the assumption of a 3-4 cent ton-mile rate and a length of road of 271 miles).
10. P. 205.
11. There has never been unanimous acceptance of substantial interdependence between West and South. Among the prominent dissenters is Isaac Lippincott in his excellent, but neglected, "Internal Trade of the United States, 1700-1860," *Washington University Studies,* IV, Part II, No. 1 (1916). See too the review of North's *Growth of the United States* by Richard Easterlin in the *J. of Econ. Hist.,* 1962, p. 125. George Rogers Taylor, in *The Transportation Revolution* (Rinehart, 1951), comments on the role of New Orleans as a forwarder and the decline of the function, but does not discuss southern consumption explicitly.
12. This yields an upper bound for southern receipts from the West since residual receipts include hemp from Kentucky, etc. A comparison with the same method used for the East, and the same escalation factor for undercoverage, gives smaller imports in every year. The two estimates are quite close absolutely, however.
13. One test of the data is the apparent sense they make with regard to capital inflows to the West (for this region since both imports and exports are derived independently the comparison is meaningful). Table 3 shows the West as a capital importer in 1853 and 1857, as an exporter in 1844 and 1849, and in approximate balance in 1839 and 1860. The first set of years coincide with rapid western expansion, the 1840's with less frenetic extension onto new lands, less railroad canal construction, etc.
14. Kohlmeier, *Old Northwest,* pp. 56-57; *Statistics of Foreign and Domestic Commerce,* Senate Exec. Doc. No. 55, 38th Cong., 1st Sess., pp. 129, 181; Thomas P. Kettell, *Southern Wealth and Northern Profits* (New York, 1860), p. 75.
15. The derivation of these sums is shown in the calculations in the appendix. My imports are understated since exports are valued f.o.b. and hence exclude some of the revenues. If these additional receipts brought inports of services, my import capacity would approxi-

mate merchandise imports. These still fall far short of Kettell. I would point out in this connection that such services neither are as large nor was the South as dependent upon the North as is sometime suggested. Commission rates for cotton were low and ocean transport costs a small proportion of value. On the second point, little of the cotton crop was re-exported through northern ports (5-8 per cent in the late 1850's), many of the charges for pressing, storage, drayage, etc. were local, and there was as rapid growth of southern banking in the 1850's as nationally, measured by loans and discounts outstanding.

16. The total consumption of domestic produce of other regions is the sum of the bottom entries of Table 3 plus three-fourths the flow of eastern merchandise to other regions. Western imports of salt and iron from the East are treated as of domestic origin while coffee and sugar are treated entirely as foreign; all trade from North to South is treated as merchandise. Since the ratio of imports of manufactures to census value of eastern domestic production (minus the two important processing industries of sawing and milling) is less than .2 in 1849 and 1859, the adjustment is not likely to overstate the domestic market. For exports and imports by class, see North, *Economic Growth*, pp. 284, 288, and for detail on western imports from the East see the Appendix (obtainable from the author).

17. These comparisons consist of the sum of consumption of western products by North and South as given in Table 3 and the national exports of breadstuffs and provisions, amounting in millions of dollars as follows: 1839, $14.1; 1844, $18.0; 1849, $38.2; 1853, $33.0; 1857, $74.7; 1860, $45.3.

18. The current dollar gross national product estimates are those of Robert E. Gallman in "Gross National Product in the United States, 1834-1909," to be published in Volume 29 of *Studies in Income and Wealth*. They were converted to regional values for 1840 and 1860 by the use of Richard A. Easterlin's regional relatives for the two dates as given in Seymour Harris, ed., *American Economic History* (McGraw-Hill, 1961), p. 528. Western exports are approximated by the sum of domestic consumption in South and North plus foreign exports of breadstuffs and provisions; southern exports are made up of sales of cotton, tobacco, rice, naval stores, and molasses (see Appendix, Table A-7); northern exports to other regions are estimated as in fn. 17 to which are added national exports of manufactures and semimanufactures. For both North and West the results are not exact, but they should be close to the correct magnitudes.

chapter **9**

labor, capital, and

the entrepreneur

POPULATION AND LABOR

POPULATION GROWTH AND DISTRIBUTION

The U.S. population of 1815 was 8.4 million. Forty-eight per cent resided in the Northeast, thirty-seven per cent in the South, and fifteen per cent lived in the West. Only seven per cent of the population lived in cities. The bulk of the population consisted of people born in the United States who were descended from English, Scotch-Irish and German immigrants. About twenty per cent was black. At the close of the Civil War, the population stood at about 35 million. In terms of their shares of the total population, the Northeast and South had declined, while the Midwest had grown appreciably. By 1865, the Midwest and South each had about one-third of the total population. The Northeast had about thirty per cent, while the Far West accounted for the remainder. Twenty per cent of the population was urban. About fifteen About fifteen per cent was black.

The pre-Civil War rate of population growth averaged between 32 and 36 per cent per decade, resulting in the doubling of the population

TABLE 9.1. *U.S. Population, 1815–1865*

Year	Population (Millions)	Increase Over Preceding Decade	
		Number (Millions)	Percent
1815	8.4		
1820	9.6	2.4	33.1
1825	11.3		
1830	12.9	3.3	33.5
1835	15.0		
1840	17.1	4.2	32.7
1845	20.2		
1850	23.3	6.2	35.9
1855	27.4		
1860	31.5	8.2	35.6
1865	35.7		

SOURCE: U.S. Bureau of the Census. *Historical Statistics of the United States, Colonial Times to 1957.* Washington, D.C.: U.S. Government Printing Office, 1960, p. 7.

every twenty to twenty-five years. (See Table 9.1.) Consequently, population doubled between 1815 and 1840, and again by the end of the Civil War. This rate of growth is one of the highest ever recorded in modern times. It was well above the rate experienced by the European countries from which the American settlers had come, and it is equal to or higher than today's so-called population explosion in the underdeveloped countries. It primarily resulted from high levels of fertility. Bountiful natural resources, the sparseness of settlement, and a shortage of labor encouraged large families. Children in many rural areas were an economic necessity if a family wished to expand its cultivation of farm land, while in the cities child labor was in great demand in the emerging manufacturing sector. Marriages occurred at an early age and married couples showed little ability or desire to practice family limitation. High infant mortality rates caused many families to increase their size beyond desired limits to insure themselves against loss of children. In some instances the number of births per family approached the biological limit, and it was not atypical to find farm families with as many as 15 children. A Congressman in the early 1800's referred to the process by which a newly married couple within a generation begot a dozen or more children as the American multiplication table. Birth rates during this period averaged as high as 55 per 1,000 total population. They did fall slightly but persistently throughout the period, however, numbering about 50 per 1,000 by the Civil War. The reasons for this fall in fertility was primarily associated with urbanization and a rising level of living. Urban living with its weakening of the cohesiveness of family life, the improved status of women, and increased costs of rearing children tended to increase the marriage age and make large families burdensome. Indeed, as early as 1703 a substantially lower fertility characterized urbanized New York County at the southern tip of Manhattan Island in contrast to the remainder of New York colony. The rising living standard which accompanied urbanization further reduced birth rates by sharply curbing infant mortality, increasing the need and cost of formal education, placing a premium on job mobility, and making large families unfashionable. Whereas half of the U.S. population was under seventeen years of age in 1815, by the time of the Civil War half of the people were under twenty.

The mortality rate, like the birth rate, was high during the nation's early history. Estimates for the early 1800's place the death rate at about 35 per thousand population during normal years and at 45 to 50 during epidemic periods. The latter were relatively rare due to an ample quantity of land which kept the density of settlement low and thus minimized the incidence of epidemics. Available evidence indicates that there was very little change in mortality experience until after 1850. By the end of the Civil War, however, the death rate had declined to about 25 per 1,000.

IMMIGRATION

For most nations, birth and death rate statistics would suffice to explain the course of population growth. This is not the case for the United States. Increases in the rate of immigration from 1815 to 1865 also contributed to population growth. (See Table 9.2.) Before 1832, less than 50,000 new Americans entered the country each year. This grew to between 50,000 amd 100,000 a year from 1832 to 1844, and soared to between 100,000 and 428,000 a year from 1845 to 1854. The latter year represents the high-water mark in pre-Civil War immigration. The substantial immigration of the 1840's and early 1850's, which stood at eight per cent of the population, was a result of the Irish potato famine of 1845-46, the European political revolutions of 1848-49, and the employment opportunities available in the United States. The bulk of immigrants came from Ireland and Germany. The Irish tended to settle in the eastern cities of Boston, New York, and Philadelphia, while the Germans pushed inland, either to take up farming or to settle in developing urban centers such as Cincinnati, Milwaukee, and Chicago. Most immigrants were males under 45 years of age who were older than the median age of 19 prevailing in the United States. This fact, together with declining death rates, contributed to a slight aging of the U.S. population during this period.

TABLE 9.2. *U.S. Immigration, 1820–1865*

Year	Thousands of Immigrants	Rate of Immigration*
1820	8.4	
1825	10.2	1.2[†]
1830	23.3	
1835	45.4	3.9
1840	84.1	
1845	114.4	8.4
1850	370.0	
1855	200.9	9.3
1860	153.6	
1865	248.1	6.4

SOURCE: U.S. Bureau of the Census. *Historical Statistics of the United States, Colonial Times to 1957.* Washington, D.C.: U.S. Government Printing Office, 1960, p. 57; *Statistical Abstract of the United States: 1970.* Washington, D.C.: U.S. Government Printing Office, 1970, p. 91.

*Annual rate per 1,000 population. 10 year rate computed by dividing sum of annual U.S. population totals by sum of annual immigrant totals for same 10 years.

[†]The rate of immigration is for the following periods: 1821–30, 1831–40, 1841–50, 1851–60, 1861–70.

The impact of immigration on U.S. population growth is debatable. According to one theory, immigration has no net long-run effect on population growth unless the immigrants introduce a more efficient economic organization or a different pattern of consumption; otherwise, immigration will be balanced by a reduction in the natural increase of the native population. This theory, which was espoused by French and English writers early in the eighteenth century, was employed by Benjamin Franklin in 1753 when he argued against allowing large numbers of German settlers into the colonies. At the time he believed that the Colonial population was at a maximum relative to the means to support it. In the 1890's, Francis A. Walker, director of the United States Census Bureau, revived the theory by contending that progressive declines in native birth rates, which he stated began about 1830, were due principally to the large influx of immigrants. Natives, reacting to the competition of immigrants for jobs and resources, and shocked by their low standard of living, substantially reduced their birth rate. According to Walker, native fertility rates at the beginning of the nineteenth century would have been greater without any immigration. Walker and those who shared his views used these arguments to justify the passage of restrictive immigration legislation. Four reasons have been put forth to refute this thesis. First, the birth rate had begun to decline before large scale immigration took place. Second, European countries have experienced comparable decreases in their birth rates unaccompanied by any substantial immigration. Third, Walker ignored a number of other forces which have had a depressing effect on fertility, such as the declining supply of free land, urbanization, high levels of living and the like. Finally, for almost every decade in the nineteenth century, immigration's contribution to population growth exceeded the total due to decreases in fertility for all causes. At the same time it is probably true that the population size was not increased by the full amount of net immigration. Immigrants, by settling principally in the cities, intensified the urbanization process and the accompanying reduction in fertility. Moreover, immigrants by pushing the native labor force up the occupational ladder, contributed to geographic and occupational mobility which tends to popularize small families. Finally, immigration by supplying cheap labor hastened the industrialization process, and thus increased the rate of economic growth which also acts to curb fertility.

Of the many factors that influence immigration, economic considerations are usually the most compelling. Even in instances where noneconomic motives appear to be primary, a careful analysis indicates they are underlaid by the basic desire to enjoy a higher standard of living. For example, despite the much romanticized flight of the Pilgrims from England to the Colonies in order to achieve religious freedom, most colonists came in search of cheap land, high profits, and better wages. America, with its vast quantities of unoccupied land and its emerging industrial complex offered almost unlimited economic opportunities. In contrast, Europe, with a growing scarcity of land and increasing population pressures, offered little else but misery, particularly to its lower income class. In some countries the practice of dividing inherited land among the heirs generation after generation had decreased individual land holdings to an uneconomic size. In other nations much of the land was held in large estates with landless peasants in a state of economic serfdom. To a considerable extent knowledge of the United States was disseminated among immigrants by word of mouth. A member of a family or a neighbor would immigrate to the United States and then send back word of the favorable economic climate. When he had saved enough to pay passage for his family or friends, they would follow. In Ireland, for example, a custom developed whereby one or two sons of a family would immigrate first, and then in time as passage money was earned, the balance of the family would join them. In addition to these informal procedures, steamship lines, western and southern states, and manufacturing companies actively encouraged immigration. All of these groups conducted extensive propaganda campaigns in Europe and elsewhere describing the advantages of coming to America.

Many offered inducements to those who agreed to immigrate. Some states provided cheap land or a tax-exempt lease, while transcontinental railroads seeking settlers for their federal land grants offered reduced transportation rates, immigration reception homes, and liberal credit for the purchase of land. Shipping companies helped recruit laborers for United States employers by assisting immigrants in acquiring passage money or by offering lower fares. Some American companies imported contract labor. A contract laborer worked for an employer for a specific time period until he had paid for his passage. The bulk of Chinese and Japanese immigrants were induced to come on this basis.

The importance of economic factors is evidenced by the fact that immigration flows followed closely the path of the business cycle. Typically, short-run immigration movements reached their peaks during prosperity periods and then fell slowly as business activity contracted. This is understandable since the immigrant had to be reasonably certain that he could secure a job shortly after he arrived. He required the most optimistic assurances of his relatives and friends in the United States before he had the courage, or the passage, for such a long voyage. During periods of recession and depression the new arrival had the most difficulty in finding a job, and if he were lucky enough to be employed he was likely to be the first to be laid off if business conditions worsened.

There is some controversy as to whether push or pull factors were most important in influencing immigrant flows. The conventional view is that "pull" factors were most important. Harry Jerome writes that the "study of the international aspects of cyclical fluctuations in the current of migration, particularly of the immigration movement into the United States, reveals that this movement is on the whole dominated by conditions in the United States. The 'pull' is stronger than the 'push'."[1] Others, however, would stress "push" forces such as the Irish potato famine and the European upheavals attending the political turmoil of the 1840's. Still others believe that push and pull factors are equally important.

THE LABOR FORCE

The U.S. labor force participation rate remained fairly constant from 1815 to 1865 at about thirty-five per cent of the population. In terms of sex and age composition, women and children were a more important part of the labor force early in the period than they were by the time of the Civil War. In the 1830's up to half of all employees in U.S. textile mills were children, a figure that declined steadily thereafter. As late as 1850, twice as many women were employed in textile mills as men. However, female employment was not as prevalent in other industries.

In 1860 women comprised only one-fifth of the labor force. Farming continued throughout the period as the major occupation. By the time of the Civil War, only a million and a half people were involved in manufacturing, compared with over six million in agriculture.

Wages increased every decade with the exception of the 1850's, when they declined. The net rate of increase averaged about fifteen per cent. At the same time the workweek was being shortened. A twelve-hour day, six-day week was common in the United States following the War of 1812. In the 1830's agitation developed for a ten-hour day, a goal that was partially realized in 1840 when president Van Buren established it for federal workers. By 1860, the ten-hour day was beginning to make inroads in the private sector owing principally to pressure from trade unions.

THE TRADE UNION MOVEMENT

Trade union growth from 1815 to 1865 was closely correlated with business fluctuations. Unionism made gains during periods of economic upswing only to be largely destroyed with the onset of contraction. Most unions in existence in 1815 were decimated in the economic downturn of 1819, recovered in the late 1820's and early 1830's, grew substantially in the prosperity of the mid 1830's, disappeared in the panic and depression following 1837, and revived in the prosperity of the late 1840's and 1850's. During the pre-Civil War period labor's interest extended to reforming society as well as improving conditions of employment. Interest in the former area was particularly evident during periods of economic contraction. The Mechanics Union of Trade Associations, organized in 1827, is regarded as the first trade union federation in the United States. For the first time unions composed of skilled craftsmen in different trades joined together in a city central type of labor organization. The association grew out of a Philadelphia carpenters' strike for a ten-hour day which received the support of other building trades. The strike failed but the experience of cooperation led to a more permanent organization. All labor groups in the area were invited to join and those trades which had no unions were urged to organize. Similar city centrals were formed in other large eastern cities. In 1828 the Mechanics Association helped to establish the Workingmen's Party, the first recorded labor party in the world. Other workingmen's parties were formed in other major cities. Caught up in the spirit of Jacksonian democracy, their goals included limitations on the monopoly power of business, especially banks, abolition of convict labor, debtor prison, and the compulsory militia law, the introduction of free public education, mechanics (workers) lien laws, and the ten-hour day.

Foremost among the leaders of workingmen's parties were Robert Dale Owen, Thomas Skidmore, and George Henry Evans. Owen espoused a free educational system called "state guardianship" whereby the state would establish boarding schools where both poor and rich children would receive instruction at no cost. He hoped that this would prevent individuals from acquiring "antisocial habits" and that in time society could proceed on a cooperative rational basis. Skidmore, a self-educated New York machinist, regarded the unequal ownership of property to be the source of all social evils. He urged that all debts and property rights be cancelled and society's assets distributed equally among the people. Under this system of "agrarianism" any citizen who gave up his natural rights to property would be guaranteed a "living wage." Evans, a painter by trade, believed that technological change was the root of the workers' plight. Machines, he felt, would continue to displace human labor, with chronic unemployment and low wages as the result. The remedy lay in free grants of land from the public domain to groups of craftsmen and farmers who would form self-sufficient frontier townships. Although workingmen's parties had some success at the polls, disagreement among their leaders, public criticism of some of their radical programs, disillusionment among the workers with schemes they neither fully understood nor supported, and absorption of many of their program by the Democrats and Whig Parties led to their early dissolution. The receptiveness of the major political parties to incorporate organized labor's demands into their platforms negated the need for a separate labor party. With the demise of the workingmen's parties in the early 1830's, organized labor again turned to more immediate economic considerations. A rising price level and prosperous business conditions spurred a new wave of union activity. The period's most significant achievement was the establishment of the National Trades Union. Comprised of several city centrals, it was instrumental in the establishment of the ten-hour day for federal government employees in 1840. Its life, however, was short as both national and local unions fell victim to the financial panic of 1837 and the severe depression which followed.

The absence of union activity during the depression, coupled with severe unemployment, caused many workers to turn again to a variety of reform movements. Associationism, New Agrarianism, and producers' and consumers' cooperatives attracted the most support. Associationism sought to solve man's problems by reorganizing society into small independent national associations or phalanxes. Based on theories of the French Socialist, Charles Fourier, each phalanx was to be limited to about 1600 producing members, living a primarily agricultural life. To assure harmony and cooperation the members of each of these "socialistic communities" were supposed to have common interests. Popularized in the United States through the efforts of Albert Brisbane, who had a regular column in the *New York Tribune*, more than 40 phalanxes were established in the 1840's.

Despite some limited success, by the 1850's most had been terminated. The New Agrarianism was an extension of George Henry Evans' earlier efforts to make free land the salvation of the workingman. Evans, who had benefited from his experience with workingmen's parties, concentrated his efforts on the two major political parties and avoided links with radical schemes. At the same time, like the Associationists, he did advocate a withdrawal from the growing industrialization and interdependence of nineteenth century America. With other intellectuals he helped found the National Reform Association which sought support for homestead legislation as the price for securing the workingman's vote. Although Evans did not achieve his goal during his lifetime, he helped to popularize the free land movement. Producer cooperatives were initiated by a number of craft unions. Some shops were on a small scale, others operated in the general market. Almost all weakened rather than strengthened the sponsoring union by drawing heavily on its personnel and financial resources. Most were abandoned or converted into private businesses within a short period of time. Consumer cooperatives had somewhat more success since they served both the consumer and the social needs of the worker without the financial risks of producer cooperatives. By the early 1850's the movement had gathered considerable strength, particularly in New England. Indeed, had it not been for the disruptive effects of the Civil War, consumer cooperatives might have become a coordinate arm of the U.S. trade union movement.

Except for some minor gains, the above schemes did little to improve the worker's economic or social position. Once prosperity returned labor again emphasized short-run economic objectives. Of particular significance was the formation of a number of national unions during the 1850's and early 1860's. Improved transportation and communication facilities now made possible cooperative action by geographically dispersed local unions in a particular craft. The national union movement sought to establish a uniform wage scale in order to avoid competition between firms based on wage differences, and to limit the importation of low-wage workers into a given locality in order to replace the existing labor force. In time the national union superceded the local as the key element in the trade union movement.

Judicial hostility, as well as business depressions and misdirected union efforts militated against significant union growth in pre-Civil War years. In the tradition of the *Philadelphia Cordwainers* Case of 1806 unions were held to be conspiracies in restraint of trade. By the 1840's, however, a slight easing occurred in judicial attitudes. In 1842, in *Commonwealth v. Hunt,* Massachusetts' Chief Justice Shaw ruled that an association of workers could not be ruled a conspiracy unless it pursued unlawful goals or utilized illegal means to accomplish its aims. The union in this

TABLE 9.3. *American Securities Owned Abroad in 1853 (millions of dollars)*

	Total Outstanding	Foreign Owned	Per Cent Foreign-Owned
United States	$ 58.2	$ 27.0	46
States	190.7	111.0	58
Counties and cities	93.3	21.4	23
Railroad bonds	170.1	43.9	26
Railroad stocks	309.9	8.0	3
Banks and insurance	279.6	7.1	3
Canal and navigation	58.0	2.5	4
Miscellaneous	18.8	1.1	6
	$1,178.6	$222.0	18

SOURCE: Federal Reserve Bank of Boston. *A History of Investment Banking in New England,* (1960 Annual Report). Boston, 1961, p. 10.

case was seeking the establishment of a closed shop and the general betterment of its members, two goals which Shaw ruled to be legitimate objectives. However, this decision did not result in the immediate abandonment of the conspiracy doctrine as an impediment to union growth.

CAPITAL

SOURCES OF CAPITAL

Throughout U.S. economic history domestic savings were the principal source of capital. This period was no exception, with personal savings being most important. While net foreign savings never constituted more than ten to eleven per cent of gross capital formation, they did provide an important supplement to domestic savings, particularly in the 1830's and 1870's. Great Britain was the leading exporter of capital to the United States. Relative political stability, an economic and legal system rooted in western culture, and high rates of return made the United States attractive to British investors. Prior to the Civil War most foreign investments were in government and railroad bonds. (See Table 9.3.)

CAPITAL'S SHARE OF NATIONAL OUTPUT

Gallman estimates that capital's share of national output grew in the decades preceding the Civil War. In real terms gross national capital formation as a percentage of gross national product increased from nine per cent in the decade 1834-43 to 14 per cent by 1849-58.[2] Gross national capital formation includes investment by Americans whether carried out at home or abroad. Due to the importance of foreign investment in this period Gallman prepared a second estimate of capital formation — gross domestic capital formation — which includes all domestic investments whether financed by U.S. citizens or foreigners. On this basis capital's share rose from 10 per cent to 15 per cent during the same period. It should be noted that both estimates exclude value added by home manufacturing and the value of farm improvements made with farm construction materials. Thus, the data conform to the capital formation and product definitions which are in use today. The increasing importance of capital in the nation's economy tends to support Rostow's thesis that an accelerated rate of capital formation and economic growth go hand in hand.

During the period, the composition of capital formation changed slightly. New gross construction as a percentage of gross domestic capital formation fell from 79 per cent in 1834-43 to 77 per cent in 1849-58 while manufacturers' producer durables (plant and equipment) rose from 21 per cent to 23 per cent. Data on changes in inventories are not available. These changes reveal the trend which was to prevail for the balance of the 1800's. By the 1893-1904 decade manufacturers' producers durables had increased its share to 51 per cent and construction's share had declined to 49 per cent.

THE CREATION OF THE SECOND U.S. BANK AND BANKING REFORM

The chaotic financing of the War of 1812, widespread currency depreciation, and a desire to resume the convertibility of paper money into specie convinced U.S. political leaders in 1815 that an error had been made in not renewing the charter of the First Bank of the United States. In 1816, five years after the demise of the First U.S. Bank, the Second Bank of the United States was chartered for a twenty-year period. The Bank did not immediately assume the role of a central monetary authority. From 1816 to 1819 its leadership was marked by incompetency and fraud. Like most state commercial banks, it overextended bank note loans in relation to its specie reserves. The bankruptcy of one of its major branches led to the 1819 appointment of a new President, Langdon Cheves, who proceeded to correct these abuses. Unfortunately, Cheves' extreme conservatism prevented the central bank from fostering credit flows to facilitate business expansion. Nor did Cheves provide effective regulation over the many state banks of the period, which grew from 208 in 1815 to 307 by 1820. (See Table 9.4.)

The bulk of state banks were poorly organized, financed and managed. For example, it was not unusual for a shareholder to pay his capital sub-

TABLE 9.4. *Number of Banks in the United States 1815–1865*

Year	Number of Banks
1815	208
1820	307
1830	329
1835	704
1840	901
1845	707
1850	824
1855	1,307
1860	1,562
1865	1,643

SOURCE: U.S. Bureau of the Census. *Historical Statistics of the United States, Colonial Times to 1957*. Washington, D.C.: U.S. Government Printing Office, 1960, pp. 623–24.

scription in a series of installments. After the first installment was paid, the bank stock was often used by shareholders as collateral for a loan to finance further installment payments. In addition, many institutions ignored the general rule of thumb followed by sounder state banks that bank note issues should not exceed three times the value of a bank's capital. As a result notes were issued out of all proportion to the specie available in a bank's vaults for convertibility. To forestall specie conversion many banks delayed in converting their notes until a minimum time period had passed, issued notes in small denominations, and required borrowers to spend notes in distant localities. In an attempt to limit some of these abuses, Pennsylvania, Maryland and Virginia passed laws forbidding the issuance of notes with face values below five dollars.

The extent of a bank's soundness often hinged on the area of the country in which it was domiciled. Banks in New England and Middle Atlantic urban centers tended to have reasonable capital strength and followed sound banking principles. As a consequence, these institutions were generally able to maintain specie convertibility during economic crises when most U.S. banks were forced to suspend specie payments. Southern and western banking suffered not only from a lack of capital and mismanagement, but from an insufficient number of institutions as well. To compensate for the relative shortage of private capital and to promote the development of business enterprise, state governments often provided banking capital. In most instances the capital stock owned by state governments did not exceed fifty per cent of the total stock outstanding. The disparity in the practices between sound and speculative banks caused the latter's notes to circulate at less than their face value. This invoked Gresham's law to the disadvantage of conservative banks. People tended to hoard better quality bank notes and use overvalued country bank notes for business transactions. To stop this practice Boston banks created the Suffolk Bank System in 1819 to bring the value of country bank notes up to par. Under this System country banks were required to keep specie on deposit in Boston for redemption at their market price. If any country bank refused participation in the System, its bank notes would be accumulated and presented to it for payment at par. The Suffolk Bank System, in effect, was a clearing agency. By checking the overissue of notes by country banks, it acted to create a currency of uniform value for the region. Another measure to improve banking practices was pioneered by the State of New York with the creation of a Safety Fund System in 1829. Under its aegis, each state bank was required to deposit three per cent of its capital worth into a safety fund, out of which the debts of any failing bank would be paid. To preclude such failures from occurring, periodic examinations were required of all state banks.

THE SECOND U.S. BANK UNDER BIDDLE

Perhaps the most important development during this period was the leadership exercised by the Second United States Bank under Nicholas Biddle. In 1823 Biddle assumed the Presidency of the Bank, a post he held until its demise in 1836. He has often been called the nation's first central banker, not because of any specific powers delegated to him, but because of the powers which he assumed. An aristocrat and economist, Biddle took it upon himself to act the role of a central banker by regulating the nation's banking system. He did this by lending specie to needy banks, regularly returning bank notes to state banks for redemption in specie, expanding and contracting loans to promote orderly economic expansion, engaging in foreign exchange transactions to stabilize the international value of the dollar, and acting as fiscal agent for the Federal Government. Most of Biddle's power came from the latter function. The Second U.S. Bank served as the depository for federal funds, made loans to the Government and serviced the national debt. The Bank's success was widely recognized, and the Bank of Spain, when reorganized in 1829, was modeled along the same lines.

Unfortunately, Biddle and the Second U.S. Bank were not without enemies. Country banks resented the power and supervision exercised over them by the Bank. So did city banks, who envied the business enjoyed by the Bank. Banks in New York City were particularly anxious to see the demise of Biddle's bank, because the location of the Bank's main office in Philadelphia militated against New York's emergence as the financial center of the nation. The Bank's most formidable foe was Andrew Jackson, President of the United States from 1829 to 1837. Jackson had been opposed to banks in general and the issuance of paper currency in particular ever since his youth. In one of his early business transactions he had sold 6,000 acres of land in return for the paper of a private merchant who subsequently went bankrupt. He also resented the interest charges which he had been forced to pay during his business career. An advocate of specie money, Jackson opposed the Second Bank on the grounds that it was unsound, unconstitutional, dominated by Eastern money interests to the detriment of Western and Southern debtors, and largely owned by foreign stockholders. Biddle precipitated a showdown with Jackson by prematurely pressing for rechartering of the Bank in the Presidential election year of 1832. A rechartering bill was passed by Congress but vetoed by Jackson. Biddle's support of the unsuccessful Presidential aspirant, Henry Clay, further aggravated the Bank's position. Following Jackson's re-election, he ordered the Treasury to cease deposits of federal funds in the Second U.S. Bank and to place them instead in state banking institutions, familiarly referred to as the Pet Banks. Additional efforts at rechartering proved futile, and Biddle had no option but to commence dissolution of the Bank in 1835. Even before this date, however, state banks were expanding in anticipation of the Bank's demise. Between 1830 and 1835 they more than doubled in number, and in the latter year the overissue of paper currency accelerated. Much of this currency was being used to finance speculative investment in western lands. To halt such speculation, Jackson issued his famous Specie Circular, which required that all future payments for public land be in either gold or silver. A money panic and depression soon followed.

THE INDEPENDENT TREASURY, FREE BANKING AND THE MONEY SUPPLY

Since Jackson regarded state banks with much the same suspicion as he had the Second Bank of the United States, he and his supporters sought the complete separation of the banking system from the Treasury. Under his successor, Martin Van Buren, this was accomplished in the Independent Treasury Act of 1840. Under this legislation, all payment to the Federal Government after a specified date had to be made in specie. These payments were deposited in government owned vaults located in major centers of population. Although the Act was quickly repealed with the transfer of power from the Democrats to the Whig Party, it was re-enacted in 1846. The principal advantage of the System was that it protected the funds of the Government from potential loss during periods of widespread bank failures. Its principal disadvantage was that it retarded the economic growth of the economy. Persistent Treasury surpluses in the 1870's and 1880's resulted in drains of specie out of the private economy and into Federal vaults at a time when they were most needed to finance increases in output. To counter this deflationary influence the Treasury periodically intervened in the economy through the purchase of securities from the banking system for specie and the placement of federal funds in the banking system.

The demise of the Second U.S. Bank left regulation of the banking system to the states. A variety of approaches was adopted. A handful of states enacted banking laws that were a model of soundness and conservatism, some chose to make banking a state owned monopoly, others provided for little or no control, and the balance outlawed banks completely. New York's Free Banking System, initiated in 1838, and the Louisiana Banking Law of 1842 were examples of sound banking legislation. The former pioneered in ending the system of granting bank charters by special legislation and established general standards of incorporation under which any individual or group of individuals could enter the banking business. Under the law a prospective bank was required to deposit federal or state bonds with the state comptroller. In return he received an equal sum in state issued bank notes. Mortgages could be used as backing only if they represented property with twice the value of the loan. Even then, only half of the bank notes issued to any one institution could be so secured. Specie reserves of 12.5 per cent had to be kept by all banks for redemption purposes. Any failure to redeem bank notes resulted in the state selling a bank's bonds in order to maintain convertibility. The Louisiana Banking Law required banks to maintain specie reserves equal to one-third of the value of both their notes and deposits. The remaining two-thirds of the value of their obligations had to be backed by nonrenewable commercial paper of ninety days duration. Before this legislation it had been standard practice to require specie backing only for notes, and to permit banks to invest their depositors' funds in real estate and security loans of long-term duration. Both the New York and Louisiana systems served as models for subsequent banking legislation.

State owned banking was initiated in a number of states with mixed results. For example, the State Bank of Indiana, half of whose capital was supplied by the state, was quite conservative in both the issuance of notes and granting of loans. As a consequence, the bank, with its seventeen branches, was successful. On the other hand, Mississippi's bank, a third of whose capital was supplied by the state, heavily overinvested in inflated real estate and was forced into bankruptcy during the first downturn in economic activity. In states with little or no regulation, not only were poor quality securities utilized for bank capital and bank note backing, but outright fraud was practiced in the reporting of specie reserves. It was not unheard of for the specie of one bank to be shipped to another bank just a few steps ahead of the bank examiner, or for banks to locate themselves in remote regions inhabited only by wildcats ("wildcat banks") to encumber specie redemption. As a consequence, bankruptcies were inevitable. For example, of 900 state banks in existence in 1840, only 691 were in business three years later, and of 880 banks in 1851, only 750 remained two years later. Still, the number of institutions grew. By 1860, some 1,500 state banks were in existence. Since these institutions issued different bank notes in varying denominations, about nine thousand diverse notes were in circulation by the time of the Civil War. Under such a situation, counterfeiting was rampant and bank note values varied substantially in terms of par. A weekly journal, *Thompson's Bank Note and Commercial Reporter*, was published to list the various types of money and their true value. Under these circumstances it is not surprising that a number of states legislated outright prohibition of banks. By 1852 seven states, most of which were located in the West, had taken such action.

COINAGE AND DEMAND DEPOSITS

Supplementing bank note circulation were both gold and silver coins. In 1834 Congress established a mint ratio of silver to gold of 16 to 1. In terms of the free market ratio of 15.8 to 1, this represented a slight undervaluation of silver, a problem which was intensified with time. By 1851, the market ratio had dropped below 15.5 to 1, encouraging the melting down of silver coins to sell for gold and causing them to disappear from circulation. In an attempt to encourage the circulation of silver, Congress reduced the silver content of newly minted coins by seven per cent, which resulted in a new mint ratio of less than 15 to 1. This resulted in the undervaluation of gold, which ordinarily would have encouraged the melting down of gold coins. However, a provision in the 1853 Coinage Act empowered the Mint to accept only such silver as it needed to supply the nation's coinage needs. Before long an adequate number of silver coins were in circulation. Gold coins by the 1850's were also sufficient for the nation's needs. The output of American mines, gold shipments to the United States by foreign investors, foreign trade earnings of the American merchant marine, and the overvaluation of gold caused by the Coinage Act of 1837 all contributed to an adequate supply. Therefore, by the time of the Civil War the coin shortage which had plagued the nation in the eighteenth and early nineteenth century had abated.

Another positive development was the emergence of demand deposits as an important medium of exchange. Eastern city banks as early as the 1830's were using checking accounts to replace bank notes in the making of loans. By the 1850's checks had become the dominant form of money in this region, and in the decade following the Civil War they came into general use in the West and South.

CIVIL WAR FINANCE AND THE NATIONAL BANKING SYSTEM

The onset of the Civil War came at a time when the Federal Government was ill-prepared to finance a major conflict. The country had just experienced a major recession in economic activity during which the Government had difficulty in borrowing funds, there was no central bank from which the Government could secure funds and the Federal Government had not levied excise taxes for over a generation. The principal source of Federal revenue, customs, was inadequate to meet war costs. There are three sources of funds to finance a war — taxes, borrowing, and the issuance of paper money. Of these, only the first is noninflationary, since it does not change the total level of spending in the economy, but only reallocates resources from the private to the public sector. Both the second and third measures are inflationary since they may increase both the money supply and the level of spending at a time when the economy is operating at full employment. In financing the Civil War, the Federal Government used all three measures, but relied most heavily on borrowing and the printing of paper money. The two major taxes imposed were excises and an income tax. The latter, legislated for the first time in the nation's history, was in effect for ten years, and despite widespread evasion, produced significant revenues. Approximately one-fifth of the cost of the war was derived from tax sources. Government attempts to borrow from the state banking systems were not very successful. This was largely due to Treasury Secretary Salmon Chase's insistence that a major part of these loans be in the form of specie. This hard money philosophy forced the banking system to suspend specie payments, and weakened the confidence of the banks in the Federal Government. Consequently, the Government shifted its emphasis from bank borrowing to public borrowing. The latter was placed under the direction of Jay Cooke and Company, a leading investment banking house.

The inadequate sums derived from taxes and borrowing forced the Federal Government early in the conflict to turn to the issuance of paper money. The bulk of this paper money took the form of United States Notes or Greenbacks, so called because of the green ink used to print them. By the end of the war they had been issued in an amount almost equal to one-half of the total quantity of currency outstanding. These notes, the first paper money ever issued by the Federal Government, were made legal tender for all debts, public and private. Because of the large amount issued and their lack of convertibility into specie, they circulated at a substantial discount compared to gold dollars, the amount of discount being highly correlated with Northern victories and defeats in the battlefield. Largely due to this method of financing, the U.S. money supply increased threefold from 1860 to 1865. Since the output of goods and services increased only half as much, the value of money dropped fifty per cent. The prices of goods and services, including gold, doubled, so that by the end of the war one gold dollar was equal to two greenback dollars. To bring about convertibility at par between gold and greenbacks, Congress passed the Contraction Act of 1865 to diminish the quantity of paper money outstanding. At the end of this chapter, the economic effect of the Greenbacks on the cost of financing the Civil War is discussed in a reading by Wesley Clair Mitchell.

The difficulties which the Federal Government encountered in borrowing at reasonable interest rates led it to re-enter the area of banking regulation. Its most immediate goal was to increase the market for U.S. Bonds. A subsidiary objective was to provide a uniform national currency to replace the 9,000 different types of bank notes in circulation. The National Banking System, enacted into law in 1863, was based largely on New York's Free Banking System. The principal features of the National System were (1) the granting of national charters to groups of individuals possessing stated capital requirements, the amount of capital varying with the size of the community to be served; (2) the privilege of note issue in an amount equal to ninety per cent of the par value of U.S. Bonds deposited with the Comptroller of the Currency; (3) minimum reserve requirements against deposits and outstanding notes, the reserve against deposits varying with the size of the community served; (4) the use of national banks as depositories for federal funds other than customs duties; and (5) periodic examination of national banks by the Comptroller of the Currency. Congress's expectation that most state banks would seek national charters in order to earn double rates of interest (both on their U.S. Bond holdings and their bank notes based on such holdings) was not realized. As a result, in 1865 a ten per cent prohibitive tax was imposed on state bank notes, a measure which forced most state banks to apply for National Banking System membership. The change was dramatic. State banks, which numbered some 1,600 in 1861, declined to about 250 by 1868. On the other hand, national banks numbered about 1,600 in 1868.

THE ENTREPRENEUR

THE TRANSITION TO THE INDUSTRIAL ENTREPRENEUR

The dominance of the merchant entrepreneur in the period before 1815 rested on his ability to function profitably on his own behalf. Although merchants like Hancock and Astor served as agents for others, they were primarily principals acting in their own name. In time, however, a new type of businessman arose, the industrial entrepreneur, who was large enough to market his own products either directly or through commission agents. Relegated to a subservient role, the merchant entrepreneur lost his identity and a good deal of his profit. Now it was the manufacturer's name that was most important, and it was he who reaped the bulk of the profits.

The impact of these changes is illustrated by the career of Nathan Trotter (1787-1853), a prominent merchant entrepreneur of Philadelphia. Trotter, for many years a successful merchant specializing in metals, found his business deteriorating in the 1830's and 1840's. More and more he experienced competition from manufacturers who were selling directly to the consumer, or dealing through commission merchants acting in their behalf. Since these agents needed little capital, their numbers multiplied rapidly. Trotter, in order to keep his customers (primarily small handicraftsmen) supplied with a full line of goods, was forced to do more business than he wished on a commission basis. He found this degrading as well as not very profitable. Elva Tooker in her biography of Trotter points out:

> Trotter did not like doing business on commission, and he went so far as to conceal the fact that he did not own all the goods in which he dealt. Moreover, he did not find commission selling very profitable. Between 1835 and 1848 there were only three years in which he made more than $1,000 from his commission business. Nevertheless, his customers virtually forced him to participate in this profitless business; had he not done so, many a customer would have gone elsewhere.
>
> It is a little sad to read the Trotter correspondence toward the close of Nathan's life. The old days of the general merchant were clearly gone — the days when a merchant could enter in his books: importing cost, add 120 per cent. Nevertheless Trotter continued to think of himself as a general merchant, running his own risks, making a profit that was more dependent on thoughtful planning than on the hustle and bustle that had come to characterize business as it was practiced in his later years. He preferred the days when the initiative for a sale came from the customer and when customers came to him knowing that from him they could be sure of getting quality products. The new system was characterized by a constant drive and pressure from the manufacturer. The manufacturer took the initiative in urging a sale, and if the wholesaler was not willing to push the product the manufacturer by-passed him to the customer or found another wholesale outlet.[4]

The time had come when the key to business success lay in the development of manufacturing and domestic markets rather than the profits of foreign trade. The factory system, larger quantities of capital, and an accelerated rate of technological change made possible production on a grand scale. What was needed was a new type of business leader who would organize and harness these forces for mass markets at the lowest possible prices. Some merchant entrepreneurs perceived what was happening and turned their attention from trade to manufacturing. Most, however, were content to follow their old lines of business.

COMPETITIVE MARKETS AND THE CORPORATE FORM

Improved transportation in the 1840's and 1850's enabled businessmen to compete in markets which previously had been inaccessible. They also found themselves subject to the competition of rival firms from other geographic regions. This competition was not always looked upon with favor, particularly from firms who had once enjoyed monopoly status in their regions. As early as the 1850's business firms were complaining of competitive excesses prevalent in their industry. Often they sought to control such competition by entering into trade associations with rival firms. The Ohio salt manufacturers banded together into a trade association in 1851, followed by the American Brass Association and the American Iron Association in 1853 and 1855, respectively.

During this period partnerships and proprietorships continued to dominate the entrepreneurial scene. Despite the fact that the number of firms being incorporated doubled during the 1850's, corporations constituted a minority of companies in almost all industries. For example, as late as the Civil War, they comprised less than half the number of firms in the iron industry. Public reluctance to grant corporations privileges such as limited liability and freedom to invest outside the state in which they were incorporated restricted their growth.

State and local governments, in an effort to encourage the flow of capital and entrepreneurial talent into public utilities, granted more liberal charters to public utilities than to other corporations. Private public utilities often were given a virtual carte blanche in their activities. Unfortunately, grants of both monopoly power and independence of action often resulted in the rendering of inadequate service at unduly high prices. When state governments sought to alter their original charters to provide greater supervision, they met with judicial opposition. In 1819 the Supreme Court ruled in the *Dartmouth College Case* that states were powerless to alter or cancel the terms of contracts granted in perpetuity by previous legislatures. As a result, public authorities found themselves without an effective means to police abuses by public utilities. In attempting to solve the problem, states adopted the practice of chartering competing utilities, a practice judicially sustained in 1837 in *Charles River Bridge v. Warren Bridge*. This, however, was not a thoroughly satisfactory procedure, for it resulted either in cutthroat competition injurious to the public or in the merger of the two competing utilities. Not until post-Civil War years was effective regulatory reform initiated.

Public utility growth during the period was related to the rapid development of urban areas. Illuminating gas companies began operations in Boston in 1822 and soon spread to other major cities. Public horsedrawn urban streetcar systems were initiated in New York in the early 1830's and by 1860 forty such systems were functioning in various U.S. cities. In 1856 the Western Union Telegraph Company was founded. Within ten years it had built a line to California, laid a transatlantic cable, and eliminated all other firms in the industry by merger or competition.

NOTES

1. Harry Jerome. *Migration and Business Cycles.* New York: National Bureau of Economic Research, 1926, p. 208.
2. Robert E. Gallman. "Gross National Product in the United States, 1834-1909," *Output, Employment and Productivity in the United States after 1800.* New York: National Bureau of Economic Research, 1966, p. 11.
3. Gallman's figures include a separate set of data which include non-market capital formation. On this basis capital's share of national output shows little change in the pre-Civil war period.
4. Elva Tooker. *Nathan Trotter, Philadelphia Merchant.* Cambridge: Harvard University Press, 1955.

SELECTED REFERENCES

1. John R. Commons. *History of Labor in the United States*, Vol. I. New York: Macmillan, 1918.
2. Davis R. Dewey. *State Banking Before the Civil War.* Washington, D.C.: U.S. Government Printing Office, 1910.
3. Thomas P. Govan. *Nicholas Biddle.* Chicago: University of Chicago Press, 1959.
4. N. S. B. Gras and H. L. Larson. *Casebook in American Business History.* New York: Crofts, 1939.
5. Bray Hammond. *Banks and Politics in America From the Revolution to the Civil War.* Princeton: Princeton University Press, 1957.
6. Marcus L. Hansen. *The Atlantic Migration.* Cambridge: Harvard University Press, 1940.
7. Fritz Redlich. *The Molding of American Banking: Men and Ideas.* New York: Hafner, 1947-51.
8. Norman Ware. *The Industrial Worker, 1840-60.* Boston: Houghton Mifflin, 1924.

reading

the greenbacks and the cost of the civil war

wesley clair mitchell

THE PROBLEM AND THE METHOD OF SOLUTION

The reader who turns back to the account of the debates upon the legal-tender bills will find that most of the unfortunate consequences that followed their enactment were foretold in Congress — the decline of real wages, the injury done creditors, the uncertainty of prices that hampered legitimate business and fostered speculation. But a majority of this Congress were ready to subject the community to such ills because they believed that the relief of the treasury from its embarrassments was of more importance than the maintenance of a relatively stable monetary standard. There was little of that confusion between economic and fiscal considerations that has frequently been held responsible for the attempts of government to use its power over the currency as a financial resource. Rather, there was a conscious subordination of the interest of the community in a stable monetary standard to the interest of the government in obtaining funds to carry on the war. It is therefore incumbent upon one who would judge the policy from the standpoint of its sponsors to inquire into the financial effects which to them seemed most important as well as into the effects on the distribution of wealth....

What effect had the greenbacks upon the amount of expenditures incurred?

Wesley Clair Mitchell, *A History of the Greenbacks* (Chicago: University of Chicago Press, 1903), pp 403-419.

Few questions raised by the legal-tender acts have attracted more attention.... Even while the first legal-tender bill was being considered its critics declared that if made a law it would increase the cost of waging the war by causing an advance in the prices of articles that the government had to buy. As the war went on the soundness of this view became apparent. Simon Newcomb, writing early in 1865, estimated that by the end of 1864 the greenbacks had increased the amount of indebtedness incurred by the federal government $180,000,000 beyond the amount that would have been incurred had the specie standard been maintained. Even if the war should end in 1865, he prophesied, $300,000,000 more would be added to this needless augmentation of the debt.

When the war was over and the divers reasons that had deterred many men from criticising the financial policy of the government were removed, competent writers began to express similar views with freedom. For example, Mr. H. R. Hulburd, comptroller of the currency, said in his report for 1867: "Probably not less than 33 per cent. of the present indebtedness of the United States is owing to the high prices paid by the government while its disbursements were heaviest," Mr. C. P. Williams put the increase of debt at one-third to two-fifths; C. A. Mann, at one-fourth; S. T. Spear, at a billion dollars; L. H. Courtney, an English critic, at nearly $900,000,000. Of later discussions that of Professor H. C. Adams has attracted the most attention. He estimated that of the gross receipts from debts created between January 1, 1862, and September 30, 1865, amounting to $2,565,000,000 the gold value was but $1,695,000,000 — a difference of $870,000,000 between value received and obligations incurred.

All of these estimates seem to rest either upon guesses or upon reduction of sums borrowed in currency to specie value. The former method of arriving at the result inspires little confidence even when the guesses are made by men intimately familiar with the federal finances, and the latter method assumes that all government expenditures rose in proportion to the decline in the specie value of the greenback dollar, and that all revenues remained what they would have been on a special basis — assumptions subject to important exceptions. The problem of ascertaining the financial consequences of the greenback issues is much too complex to be solved by methods so crude. Some branches of expenditure were much affected by the depreciation of the currency, other branches but little. The effect of the paper currency on the receipts of the government is quite as important a part of the problem as the effect on expenditures, and examination shows that here as there different items were affected in very different degrees. Finally, the greenbacks were themselves a "loan without interest" though, on the other hand, they increased the volume of the interest-bearing debt by augmenting expenditures. These three topics, then — the influence of the paper-money standard on ordinary expenditures and reciepts, and on interest— must all be examined by anyone who hopes to frame an adequate estimate of the net effect of the greenbacks on the cost of the war. As will appear, however, examination of these topics is beset by serious difficulties.

GREENBACKS AND EXPENDITURES

It is a familiar remark of writers on public finance that all things required by government fall into one of two categories — commodities and services. . . . This elementary distinction regarding the objects of government expenditure is of very great importance for the present problem. For, since prices advanced in much greater ratio than wages, it is clear that the greenback issues must have increased the sums paid for commodities more than the sums paid for labor. Indeed, this difference between increase in cost of commodities and of labor seems to have been much wider in the case of the government than in the case of private persons; for, . . . the wages of federal employees were advanced on the average considerably less than the wages of other persons. Clearly, then, the first step in any estimate of the effect of the legal-tender act upon the expenditures incurred by government during the war should be a careful separation of expenditures for commodities from expenditures for services.

Accordingly, it is a very serious obstacle that one encounters in finding that such a separation cannot readily be made. A statement of the expenditures of the preceding fiscal year is published in each annual report of the secretary of the treasury. But in these statements the items are arranged rather according to the department of government through or for which the specified sums were spent, than according to the object of expenditure. For example, the first general division of expenditures is placed under the caption "Civil," and under this caption the first three items are "For Congress, including books," "For executive," "For judiciary." It is obvious that each of these items must include payments for both commodities and services; but there is no way of separating the two classes of payments.

A more detailed statement is given in the annual *Account of the Receipts and Expenditures of the United States* rendered by the register of the treasury. But even these bulky documents do not make possible such a division of expenditures as is desired. A careful examination of the register's accounts for the fiscal years 1863-65 shows that about one-third of the total expenditures each year consists of items which appear to include payments for both labor and commodities in unknown proportions. Such, for example, are expenditures upon fortifications, armories, and hospitals, repairs of ships, construction of buildings, incidental expenses of various bureaus, and the like. The best that can be done with these accounts is to divide the items into three classes: (1) expenditures for salaries and the like, most of which appear to have been little affected by the paper currency; (2) expenditures for commodities; (3) expenditures that include payments for both commodities and labor. Even with such a scheme of classification it is sometimes difficult to decide where certain items should be placed.

If this division of expenditures be accepted, the next step is to determine in what ratio the expenditures falling within each of the three classes shall be assumed to have been increased. In the first class the largest items are the pay of the regular and volunteer armies. The wages of private soldiers was increased from $13 to $16 per month after May 1, 1864. Since this increase was made with the avowed object of compensating soldiers in some measure for the decline in the purchasing power of the paper money, one must consider three-sixteenths of the pay of the army after that time as an addition to the money cost of the war. It is not improbable also that, had the specie standard been maintained, it would have been unnecessary to grant such lavish bounties to stimulate enlistments. If so, a part at least of the large sums reported as paid in bounties should be added to the increase in the cost of the war. To be on the safe side, however, this item will be neglected. As for other employees of the government besides the soldiers, it appears that in few cases were the money salaries increased beyond the scale prevailing before suspension. No doubt it was largely from motives of patriotism that so many men in humble as well as in conspicuous positions remained in the service of the government at wages they would have accepted from no private employer. Their self-sacrifice lessened the effect of the greenbacks upon the cost of the war in dollars and cents. But from any other than the narrowest fiscal point of view it was one of the most unfortunate consequences of the paper-money regime that the men who were serving the country faithfully were compelled to submit to a great decrease in their real imcomes.

With respect to the second of the above described classes of expenditures, the question of interest is whether the depreciation of the currency affected the prices paid by the government for commodities as much as it did prices paid by private purchasers at wholesale.... the statistical material gleaned from the *Aldrich Report* indicates that public contractors did not advance their prices quite as rapidly as other dealers. But it must be remembered that the two series there brought into comparison are not constructed in the same fashion — one series gives the averages of four relative prices each year; the other gives the relative average prices of twelve months in some cases and of prices for unstated dates in others. Moreover, many of the government series are based on prices of 1861 instead of for 1860, and in the former year the government seems to have been paying rather higher prices than in the latter. Still further the whole number of articles included in the government list is not great, and about half belong to a single and financially unimportant group—drugs and chemicals. Finally, it is not improbable that there were changes in the qualities of some articles accepted from contractors that account for a relatively slight increase in price. For these various reasons the divergence between the two series possesses little significance.

Much greater weight should be attached to the general conclusion... that the dominant factor in determining prices during the war was the fluctuating valuation of the currency. There is no reason why knowledge that he would be paid in greenbacks should affect in different degrees the prices that a dealer would ask from the government and from private men. Since, then, the fairly satisfactory wholesale-price data show a rather close parallelism between prices of commodities and of gold, it seems fair to infer that the sums asked of the government for identical goods also rose and fell in rough agreement with the premium. True, prices seem not to have advanced so quickly as did the gold quotation, but neither did they fall so quickly. Everything considered, then, the most trustworthy index of the increase in the sums expended by the government upon commodities is probably found in the average premium upon gold in the several fiscal years.

An even larger element of conjecture enters into the estimate of the increase in the expenditures of the third class, which includes payments for both commodities and labor. So far as commodities are concerned it is as fair here as in Class II to apply the average premium upon gold as an index of the increase. But with reference to labor a new problem arises. The salaries of most persons in the regular service of the government, aside from soldiers, were not increased at all. But the titles of the items grouped in Class III as they appear in the register's accounts seem to indicate that the great mass of the labor was not that of officials, but that of workmen employed on a strictly commercial basis. In constructing fortifications, erecting and repairing public buildings, etc., it is probable that the government or its contractors paid as much for the labor hired as a private employer would have done.... Assuming so much, we have two ratios of increase in expenditure for this class—one applicable to the prices of commodities, the other to the wages of labor. Since there is no way of distinguishing between expenditure for goods and labor it is necessary to make some purely arbitrary assumption regarding their relative amounts. The simplest assumption is that the increase in the total expenditures of Class III was midway between the average premium upon gold and the average increase in money wages. Perhaps this assumption may be accepted as well as any other, for, if no definite reason can be assigned for it, neither can any reason be assigned in favor of any rival assumption.

In accordance with the preceding plan, Table LXIV has been constructed to show the probable increase in the expenditure of the govern-

TABLE LXIV. *Estimated Increase in the Ordinary Expenditures of the Federal Government Caused by the Greenbacks (In millions of dollars)*

	Fiscal Years				
	1862 Six Months	1863	1864	1865	1866 Two Months
Expenditures:[1]					
Class I, salaries, etc.	92	242	259	408	45
Class II, commodities	82	214	258	402	43
Class III, both labor and commodities	89	238	294	405	44
Assumed ratio of increase:					
Class II[2]	3%	37%	56%	102%	43%
Class III[3]	3%	27%	44%	77%	49%
Estimated actual increase:					
Class I, increase in pay of soldiers[4]	–	–	6	62	20
Class II	2	58	93	203	13
Class III	3	51	90	176	14
Total estimated increase each year	5	109	189	441	47

[1] The figures for the fiscal years 1863–65 are obtained from the annual reports on "Receipts and Expenditures." For the second half of the fiscal year 1862 the ordinary expenditures were estimated on the basis of the "Treasurer's Accounts" (*H. R. Ex. Doc. No. 4*, 38th Cong., 1st Sess.), and these expenditures were divided among the three classes according to the proportions given by the computations for 1863. Similarly, the expenditures for the months July and August, 1865, are assumed to be two-thirds of the total for the quarter July to September and are divided among the three classes in the same ratio as the expenditures for the fiscal year 1865.

[2] Average premium upon gold as given in Appendix A below.

[3] Average of premium on gold and increase in money wages according to system of variable weights, as shown by Table XXX above. For wages in each fiscal year I have taken the index number for January of the corresponding calendar year.

[4] Three-sixteenths of pay of army (except bounties) after May 1, 1864, as the pay is reported in "Receipts and Expenditures." For the months July and August, 1865, the increase is computed on one-half the sum stated by the paymaster-general as paid to the army between June 30 and October 31. (*Ex. Doc. No. 1*, Part II, p. 898, 39th Cong., 1st Sess.)

ment caused by the issues of paper money between the date of suspension and August 31, 1865, when the public debt reached its maximum amount. The total increase for the whole period is $791,000,000. After all that has been said of the elements that enter into the problem it is hardly necessary to insist strenuously that this total is but a very rough estimate.

THE GREENBACKS AND RECEIPTS

Almost all the writers who have discussed the financial consequences of the legal-tender acts have confined their attention to the increase of expenditures. This procedure is perhaps natural for ardent critics of the paper-money policy, but a little consideration shows that it is unfair. The reports of the secretary of the treasury give the government revenue under five heads—customs, sales of public lands, direct tax, miscellaneous sources, and internal revenue. Of these receipts some were and some were not affected by the greenback issues. In accordance with the provisions of the first legal-tender act customs duties were paid in gold, and the *ad valorem* duties were assessed on the foreign specie valuation of goods. The receipts from this source therefore remained on substantially the same footing as if specie payments had been maintained. During the war receipts from the sales of public lands were an item of little importance—less than $1,000,000 per year—despite the decline in the value of the currency that might be paid by the purchaser of lands. The receipts from direct taxes were all collected under one law passed six months before suspension. This law fixed the total amount of the tax at $20,000,000 and determined the precise amount to be raised by each state. Accordingly the legal-tender acts had no effect upon this item—except that the states were enabled to pay their quotas in greenbacks instead of in gold. The revenue derived from miscellaneous sources includes a considerable number of small items. Of these, some were doubtless increased by depreciation, *e.g.*, proceeds of sales of captured and abandoned property. Other items were unaffected, *e.g.*, receipts of fees by American consuls abroad. Premiums on sales of gold coin among these miscellaneous receipts may be set down from the present point of view as clear gain.

The last of the enumerated government receipts remains, the internal-revenue duties. This system of taxation was inaugurated by an elaborate law passed July 1, 1862, which imposed certain duties, partly *ad valorem,* partly specific, upon a great variety of manufactured articles; imposed a tax upon the gross receipts of canals, railroads, theaters, etc.; taxed auction and brokers' sales; required licenses for practicing professions; levied an income and a legacy tax, and placed certain taxes upon articles of luxury, such as carriages, pianos and plate. This law was superseded two years later by another internal-revenue act which raised the rates of taxation, and increased the number of articles made to pay duties.

At the time the first law was passed the depreciation of the currency was not great, and probably the rates of taxation imposed do not differ much from what they would have been upon a specie basis. But without any modification of the terms of the law, the progressive rise of prices must have caused an increase of the revenue from *ad valorem* duties, and from taxes on gross receipts and upon incomes. Receipts from specific duties, licenses, etc., however, probably did not increase except as changes were made in the law or in its administration. While, then, the yield of this most important of the sources of federal revenue was materially affected by the legal-tender acts, it would be too much to argue, as was done with reference to expenditures for commodities, that it was increased in the ratio indicated by the premium on gold. Some arbitrary assumption, however, must be made regarding the ratio of increase if any estimate is to be had. Again, it is perhaps best to adopt the simplest expedient, and count the increase of receipts from internal taxes at the full amount indicated by the premium, but, on the other hand, take no account of the increase of receipts from miscellaneous sources. Since the latter sums are relatively small, it is probable that an estimate thus made will err rather on the side of over, than of understating the increase of revenue.

The total increase of receipts shown by this method as applied in Table LXV is $174,000,000. Again the caution is hardly necessary that the result is to be accepted subject to a wide margin of error.

TABLE LXV. *Estimated Increase in the Ordinary Receipts of the Federal Government Caused by the Greenbacks (In millions of dollars)*

	Fiscal Year 1862 (Six Months)	Fiscal Year 1863	Fiscal Year 1864	Fiscal Year 1865	Fiscal Year 1866 (Two Months)
Current receipts:					
From customs	33.5	69.1	102.3	84.9	31.3
From sales of public lands	.1	.2	.6	1.0	.1
From direct tax	1.8	1.5	.5	1.2	.0
From miscellaneous sources	.5	3.0	47.5	33.0	12.3
From internal revenue	—	37.6	109.7	209.5	64.4
	35.9	111.4	260.6	329.6	108.1
Assumed ratio of increase	3%	37%	56%	102%	43%
Estimated actual increase	0	10	39	106	19

So far the discussion of the increase both of expenditures and of revenues has proceeded as if the paper currency had exerted none but simple and direct effects. There were other financial consequences of the shift from the specie to the paper standard, however, that were not unimportant, though they were indirect and difficult to gauge. Three of the most prominent must be indicated.

1. It is probable that not a little of the lavishness with which public funds were appropriated by Congress during the war can be traced to the paper-money policy. At least such was the opinion of a man so well placed to observe the operations of the treasury as Hugh McCulloch. In his report of 1867 he said: "As long as notes could be issued and bonds could be sold at a premium or at par, for what the statute made money, there was a constant temptation to liberal, if not unnecessary, expenditures. Had the specie standard been maintained and bonds been sold at a discount for real money, there would have been an economy in all branches of the public service which unfortunately was not witnessed."

2. If the paper currency tempted the government to reckless expenditures, it also predisposed the people to submit more willingly to heavy taxation. It has been remarked several times that the advance of money wages and of money prices made most people feel wealthier, and, feeling wealthier, they were less inclined to grumble over the taxes.

3. But while the feeling of prosperity may have been instrumental in procuring a cheerful acceptance of war taxes, it is very doubtful whether the net effect of the paper-money system was favorable to revenue. It was pointed out in the last chapter that the lagging of money wages behind money prices necessarily diminished the consumption of wealth among wage-earners. In so far as this diminution affected the consumption of articles that paid either an import or an excise duty — and there were but few articles exempt from taxation by one of these methods — the fall of real wages must have lessened the tax receipts. Much the same must have been true, although in less degree, of the indirect taxes collected from the consumption of the great agricultural class, if...farmers were injured rather than benefited by the price fluctuations. On the other hand, the extravagance of the fortunate families enriched by the receipt of high profits tended to increase the revenue for the time being; but it is improbable that the increase of receipts from the enlarged consumption of this limited class offset the decrease of receipts from the enforced economies of wage-earners and farmers.

While, then, these indirect effects of the paper currency on expenditures and receipts could not by any system of bookkeeping be brought to definite quantitative statement, it is probable that their net result was unfavorable to the treasury.

THE GREENBACKS AND THE PUBLIC DEBT

It may seem that in a discussion of the financial consequences of the legal-tender acts account should be taken of the effect of the desertion of the specie standard upon the terms on which the government could borrow. The resort to a legal-tender paper currency, one may argue, is a confession of acute financial distress and as such must depress the market for bonds. Therefore, to the financial loss caused by the increase of expenditures should be added a second loss from the unfavorable terms to which the government had to submit in selling its securities.

Of course, it is true that the secretaries of the treasury in their efforts to borrow money were obliged to agree to some very hard bargains. There was little ground for exultation over the sale at par of bonds bearing interest at 5 or 6 per cent. in gold when the currency received from purchasers was worth in specie but 50 per cent. of its face value. But this loss arising from the difference in value between the paper dollars received by the treasury for bonds and the specie dollars which the treasury contracted to pay bondholders after a term of years is not a further loss in addition to the losses discussed in the preceding sections, but rather these same losses looked at from another point of view. For, the estimate of the increase of expenditures above receipts, and therefore of debt contracted, rests precisely upon the decline in the value of the paper dollar from the specie standard. One may arrive at an estimate of the loss either by computing the increase in the number of dollars that had to be borrowed in paper money to be repaid in gold, or by estimating the decline in the specie value of the paper money raised by the sale of bonds; but to make estimates by both of these methods would be to include two guesses at the same item.

It is, of course, true that, had gold bonds been sold largely at less than par for paper money, a second loss would have been incurred from the discount in addition to the loss from the smaller purchasing power of the currency received. But, as a matter of fact, the deviations from par in the subscription prices for bonds were not of great importance. The prices of government securities did not fluctuate very widely during the war, for the very good reason that these prices showed merely the value of one set of government promises to pay, viz., bonds — in terms of another set — viz., greenbacks. Most factors that affected the credit of the government would affect the specie value of all its promises in much the same manner, and therefore would not alter materially the ratio of one to another.

It remains only to say a word about the effect of the legal-tender acts upon the interest charge borne by the government. The great financial argument in favor of the greenbacks has always been that they constitute a "loan without interest." However many millions the depreciation of this currency added to the principal of the public debt, the greenbacks should be credited with whatever sum was really saved in this fashion. But against the saving of interest effected by issuing greenbacks instead of selling bonds should be put down the loss of interest on the increase of debt arising from the augmentation of expenditures. If the rate of interest be taken at 6 per cent, a simple calculation shows that the interest saved by the greenbacks up to August 31, 1865, was but $28,000,000 greater than the interest lost through the excess of increase of expenditures over the increase of receipts as shown by Tables LXIV and LXV. By the end of this period the augmentation of debt caused by the greenbacks had apparently become greater than the volume of greenbacks in circulation, so that from this time forward the annual loss of interest probably exceeded the gain.

CONCLUSION

The public debt reached its maximum amount August 31, 1865, when it stood at $2,846,000,000. Of this immense debt the preceding estimates indicate that some $589,000,000, or rather more than a fifth of the whole amount, was due to the substitution of United States notes for metallic money. Little as these estimates can pretend to accuracy, it seems safe at least to accept the conclusion that the greenbacks increased the debt incurred during the war by a sum running into the hundreds of millions. If so, it follows that, even from the narrowly financial point of view of their sponsors, the legal-tender acts had singularly unfortunate consequences.

chapter 10

agriculture

REGIONAL PATTERNS

THE NORTHERN FARMER

The shift of the New England economy from agriculture and other primary pursuits to manufacturing, which was initiated in the late eighteenth and early nineteenth centuries, was intensified during this period. The transformation was due to three major factors. New England's unfavorable terrain and climate placed it at a comparative disadvantage to other regions of the country. The continuing development of an internal transportation system enabled New England urban centers to tap the more efficient grain producing regions of the Middle Atlantic and Midwestern states. The growing opportunities for labor in the nascent manufacturing sector attracted workers from agriculture. As resources shifted from agriculture into manufacturing a concurrent change occurred in the mix of agricultural output. Increasing attention was paid to more specialized, high-priced crops such as vegetables, fruits, sheep, horses, and dairy cattle. Although the typical New England farm remained small, some consolidation did occur as farmers emigrated from the region to

303

western New York and the Midwest, and as livestock cultivation gained ground. Despite these changes, agriculture continued to be a major factor in the New England economy to the Civil War.

The principal change in Middle Atlantic agriculture during this period was the spread of cultivation to its western lands. Speculation in these newer sections of the states was quite common. In New York the price of land ranged from $2 to $4 an acre, depending on fertility and proximity to transportation facilities. Credit terms offered by land companies were quite liberal, farmers having as much as nine years in which to pay for their purchase. Payment in the form of potash, wheat, and livestock was often accepted. Tenant farming was also permitted with a share of the crop going to the landlord as rent. Gristmills were built both to make settlement more attractive and to provide land speculators with an additional source of revenue from settlers. While an acre of ground might cost a farmer about $3, an additional labor cost of $15 an acre was involved in clearing and fencing land. The construction of a small log cabin represented an additional labor input valued at about $50. Although the small-scale farmer performed practically all labor himself, he was forced to make cash outlays for farm implements and livestock. Equipment such as a hoe, plow, cart, axe, and saw represented an approximate expenditure of $50, while a pair of oxen and a couple of cows cost about $100.

The first commercial crops raised in these newer areas were potash and pearl ash, produced from the incineration of timber gathered in the process of clearing the land. Skins and furs from the animals of the area provided another source of cash earnings. After a small quantity of land had been cleared, corn cultivation was practiced. Corn was the universal crop of the United States. It could be grown on inadequately cleared land and in soil of low fertility, and yet yield a relatively high output per acre. In addition, it was a hardy crop which was resistant to disease. These characteristics, together with the minimal care required for its cultivation made it an inexpensive feed for livestock. As a foodstuff, it possessed a high caloric content. In its many forms such as pone, bread, hominy, johnnycake, mush, and fritters, it was the early staff of life for Americans. As a commercial crop, it took the form of hogs and whiskey, which unlike corn brought high market prices relative to their transport costs. Cattle were also raised, and the surplus driven overland to market. Once a sufficient quantity of land had been cleared by the farmer (the clearing of an entire farm taking as much as a generation), attention centered on wheat as the basic commercial crop. The availability of growing urban markets in centers such as Harrisburg, Philadelphia, New York and Baltimore encouraged expansion. Due to the abundance of land, extensive rather than intensive cultivation was practiced. A major exception to this rule was the agriculture practiced by the German farmers of southeastern Pennsylvania. These settlers embraced the use of scientific techniques such

TABLE 10.1. *Prices of Corn, Pork, and Wheat 1815-1860*

	Corn* (Dollars per Bushel)	Pork* (Dollars per Barrel)	Wheat† (Dollars per Bushel)
1815	$.86	$23.22	–
1820	.70	19.14	–
1825	.48	13.19	–
1830	.52	13.21	–
1835	.67	17.46	–
1840	.62	15.53	–
1845	.53	11.16	$1.08
1850	.64	13.71	1.29
1855	.73	17.79	2.46
1860	–	–	1.54

*Prices are 9 year moving averages for the Philadelphia market.

†Quoted prices at the New York market.

SOURCE: Douglass C. North. *The Economic Growth of the United States, 1790-1860.* Englewood Cliffs: Prentice-Hall, Inc., 1961, pp. 260, 263.

as crop rotation, the use of fertilizer, and the breeding of cattle, all in an attempt to increase productivity. Wheat production in New York reached a peak during the decade of the 1830's and in Pennsylvania in the 1840's. Thereafter it experienced an absolute decline owing to the destructive effect of both disease and unscientific farming practices. New York, in particular, suffered severe crop losses from a plague of the Hessian fly and Nudge. More telling was the destructive effect of careless farming practices, such as inadequate tillage and weeding and a failure to fertilize, that destroyed the value of soil for wheat cultivation. Another major grain of the North was oats. Often planted in rotation with wheat or corn, the crop was used principally as a feed for livestock. Owing to a low value in relation to its bulk, it was not profitable to ship oats any distance overland. Barley, rye, and buckwheat were other important grains for the northern farmer. These either were used as flour, made into liquor, or used as animal feed.

The hallmark of Midwestern farming was the rapid expansion of commercial agriculture. Although the great bulk of western settlers continued to practice self-sufficient pioneer farming, increasing surpluses from the region found their way to eastern and southern markets. As transportation facilities became more extensive and efficient, the process was accelerated. The principal crops of the area were wheat, corn, hogs, and cattle. Wheat and corn prices paced westward expansion. (See Table 10.1.) When the prices of these crops were high, settlers were encouraged to clear and cultivate virgin land. The increased supply of grain which resulted reduced prices until such time as demand growth began once again to pressure prices upward. The periods 1816-1818, 1832-1836, 1846-1847, and 1850-1856, were characterized by sharply advancing prices.

The period also witnessed a shift in the region's crop emphasis from corn to wheat. As in the Middle Atlantic States, the availability of more cleared land and transportation facilities made wheat the more profitable crop. As a commercial crop, wheat possessed certain distinct advantages. It was readily marketable, easily stored, and its price was sufficiently high to justify heavy transportation charges. Its commercial profitability was evidenced by the fact that western wheat farms possessed higher land values, greater quantities of farm equipment and horses, a higher ratio of improved to unimproved land, and used the services of more hired labor than did other farms. Beginning with the Erie Canal in 1825, transportation facilities were constructed which permitted the East to replace the South as the major market for Western produce. This development influenced Western allegiance in the developing sectional conflict leading to the Civil War. Whereas in the 1820's most of the Midwest's agricultural produce was shipped to Southern markets, by 1860 the bulk of it was moving to the East.

THE SOUTHERN FARMER

Unlike the New England and Middle Atlantic economies, which directed increasing attention to nonagricultural pursuits during this period, the South's principal energies continued to be tied to agriculture. Despite this fact, in Virginia, a state which led the nation in 1860 in tobacco and slave sales, the average size farm of 324 acres had a lower value than the average size New York farm of 106 acres. This was because of the Southern practice of investing in unimproved land which often remained uncultivated for an extended period of time. Thus, while sixty-eight per cent of New York farmland and sixty-one per cent of Pennsylvania farmland were improved, Virginia farms contained but thirty-six per cent of improved land and North Carolina farms had but twenty-seven per cent. The practice of keeping capital tied up in unimproved farmland had two effects. First, it tended to preclude small farmers from occupying and productively using the land. Second, like slavery, it had the effect of immobilizing capital which otherwise might have been utilized for the promotion of industry.

During this period, cotton assumed unquestioned dominance as the South's major commercial crop. Burgeoning foreign and domestic demand for cotton fiber encouraged expanding production. Rising cotton prices

FIGURE 10.1. *Public Land Sales and Cotton Prices: 1814 – 1860*

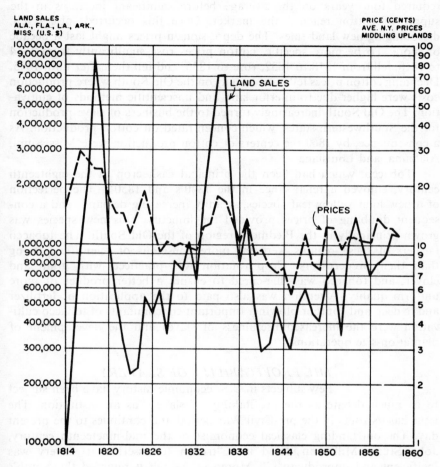

LAND SALES
ALA., FLA., LA., ARK.,
MISS. (U.S. $)

PRICE (CENTS)
AVE. N.Y. PRICES
MIDDLING UPLANDS

LAND SALES

PRICES

SOURCE: Douglass C. North, *The Economic Growth of the United States, 1790 – 1860* (Englewood Cliffs: Prentice-Hall, 1961), p. 124.

paced westward expansion. (See Figure 10.1.) As in the case of Northern wheat and corn, the movement westward occurred in a cyclical pattern, depending upon price movements. As virgin lands came under cotton cultivation, cotton output expanded greatly, resulting in a cyclical price decline which caused planters to divert cotton land to other uses, principally corn and livestock production. As demand caught up with supply and prices revived, output was again directed to cotton and it spread to new lands. The process of buying, clearing, and cultivating additional acreage required four years on the average before significant increases in the supply of cotton reached the market. Once this occurred, prices fell, discouraging new land sales. The depression in prices might last a decade or more. To be more specific, cotton prices rose significantly from 1814 to 1818, fell from 1818 to 1832, rose to 1836, and fell thereafter until 1845. Declining cotton prices fell most heavily on the Old South where production costs were higher due to inferior land and unscientific methods of cultivation. The Old South increasingly turned to the business of slave production for the Southwestern states, which concentrated on cotton production. As a consequence, by 1860 the centers of cotton production were Mississippi, Alabama, and Louisiana.

Tobacco, which had been the principal cash crop in the eighteenth century, enjoyed a renaissance in the 1840's and 1850's. The perfection of a new light yellow leaf species, steadily increasing demand, and a consequent doubling of prices provided the impetus. This new species was grown principally in the Piedmont region of the Old South. The tobacco farmers of these regions were far more conscious of scientific farming than their predecessors. Crop rotation was practiced with grain and clover, and tobacco was flue-cured to ensure a better product of more uniform quality. Attention was also paid to the application of fertilizer and to deep and contour plowing. Important concomitants of tobacco cultivation were the increased usefulness of slaves and the development of plantation-size operations.

THE PROFITABILITY OF SLAVERY

Few subjects in U.S. economic history have been subject to as much debate as the profitability of slavery as an institution. The issue has its roots in the pre-Civil War period and continues to the present day. The outstanding classical economist of the mid-nineteenth century, John Stuart Mill, considered it a "truism to assert that slavery was inefficient and unproductive."[1] Moreover, he felt it retarded the South's industrial development. Free labor, he wrote, was "so much more efficient than slave labor that the employer can pay a considerably greater value in wages than the maintenance of his slaves cost him before and yet be a gainer by the change." Mill did, however, recognize that "so long as slave countries are underpeopled in proportion to their cultivable land, the labor of slaves . . . produces much more than is sufficient for their support." It was only "as population pressed upon the land that slave labor decreased in value." At the dawn of the twentieth century, Alfred Marshall, the distinguished neoclassical economist, also spoke of the "well-known fact" that slave labor was not economical.[2] Marshall's point of view was elaborated in 1905 by the Southern historian, Ulrich B. Phillips, who held that slavery was both inefficient and an obstacle to Southern economic development. This view was based on the fact that the cost of slaves in terms of cotton increased by 1,000 per cent from 1800 to 1860 without any corresponding increase in slave productivity. In 1800 a prime field hand was worth about 1,500 pounds of cotton, in 1818 about 3,500 pounds, in 1837 about 10,000 pounds, in 1845 about 12,000 pounds, and in 1860 about 15,000 pounds. Moreover, the rate of return on slave capital, as measured by the hiring rate for slaves, failed to match the interest rates which could have been earned in other pursuits. That hiring rate, which largely was determined by the wage rate for all labor, increased from $100 a year in 1800 to only $150 by 1860. The price of a prime field hand, on the other hand, increased from $450 in 1800 to $1,800 by 1860. This "irresistable tendency to overvalue and overcapitalize slave labor," Phillips wrote, stemmed from growing competition among Southern planters in the sale of cotton and purchase of slaves, and in a "tendency to 'frenzied finance' in the cotton belt." He concludes:

> In employing free labor, wages are paid from time to time as the work is done, and the employer can count upon receiving from the products of that labor an income which will enable him to continue to pay its wages in the future, while his working capital is left free for other uses. He may invest a portion of his capital in lands and buildings, and use most of the remainder as circulating capital for special purposes, retaining only a small percentage as a reserve fund. But to secure a working force of slaves, the ante-bellum planter had to invest all the capital that he owned or could borrow in the purchase of slaves and lands; for the larger his plantation was, within certain limits, the more economies he could introduce. The temptation was very strong for him to trim down to the lowest possible limit the fund for supplies and reserve. The slaveholding system thus absorbed the planter's earnings; and for such absorption it had unlimited capacity, for the greater the profits of the planters the more slaves they wanted and the higher the slave prices mounted. Individual profits, as fast as made, went into the purchase of labor, and not into modern implements or land improvements. Circulating capital was at once converted into fixed capital; while for their annual supplies of food, implements and luxuries the planters continued to rely upon their credit with the local merchants, and the local merchants to rely upon their credit with northern merchants and bankers.
>
> Thus there was a never-ending private loss through the continual payment of interest and the enhancement of prices; and, further, there was a continuous public loss by the draining of wealth out of the cotton belt by the slave trade. With the stopping of the African slave trade, the drain of wealth from the lower South was not checked at all, but merely diverted from England and New England to the upper tier of southern states; and there it did little but demoralize industry and postpone to a later generation the agricultural revival.[3]

Phillips' position remained unchallenged until the late 1950's when a path-breaking econometric study by Alfred Conrad and John Meyer concluded that

> Slavery was apparently about as remunerative as alternative employments to which slave capital might have been put. Large or excessive returns were clearly limited to a few fortunate planters, but apparently none suffered excessively either. This general sharing in the prosperity was more or less guaranteed, moreover, if proper market mechanisms existed so that slaves could be bred and reared on the poorest of land and then be sold to those owning the best. Slavery in the immediate ante-bellum years was, therefore, an economically viable institution in virtually all areas of the South as long as slaves could be expeditiously and economically transferred from one sector to another.[4]

In addition they rejected the proposition that slaveholding absorbed plantation earnings (due to the payment of interest and the steady increase in the price of slaves), thereby causing an over-capitalization of the labor force. They point out that slave productivity (value of cotton output per field hand) rose, and that the concentration of Southern capital in cotton was primarily an entrepreneurial decision not required by the institution of slavery. (See Figure 10.2.) Slaves were capable of being trained to perform a variety of functions as evidenced by their use in Southern cotton factories, coal mines, ironworks, and the building of railroads. The fact that the majority of slaves were employed in cotton cultivation stemmed from the superior profits available in this area. The South was merely practicing the sound economic principals of specialization. In sum, Conrad and Meyer conclude that slavery was profitable and that it did not impede Southern economic growth.

Conrad's and Meyer's thesis, however, has been vigorously challenged by a number of economic historians. The essence of the criticism is that they failed to take an overview of the impact of slavery on the vitality of the Southern economy. Douglas Dowd observes that even if the slave system was profitable it dampened the spirit of entrepreneurship and hindered industrial development. This resulted primarily from the domination of the plantation economy which suppressed a significant part of the population for the financial benefit of a small ruling class. Eugene Genovese adds that slavery placed nonagricultural pursuits such as banking, industry, and commerce in a subsidiary position to agriculture, thereby enhancing the leisure and social graces of a landed aristocracy and degrading the profit-making quest of entrepreneurs. In the reading at the end of this chapter Conrad and Meyer answer their critics and, in turn, are challenged once again by Douglas Dowd and Eli Ginzberg.

FIGURE 10.2. *Cotton Prices, Slave Prices, and Slave Productivity*

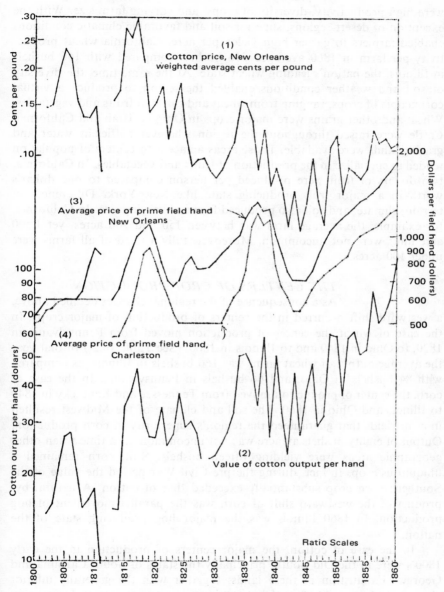

SOURCE: Alfred H. Conrad and John R. Meyer, *The Economics of Slavery* (Chicago: Aldine, 1964), p.77.

FAR WESTERN AGRICULTURE

The principal characteristics of Far Western agriculture were high productivity, diversity of crops, and varying farm size. With the exception of desert regions, superior soil and favorable climatic conditions enabled farmers to garner high yields per acre. California wheat productivity per farm in 1860 averaged 316 bushels compared with 166 bushels in Illinois, the nation's leading wheat state. At the same time, the diversity of soil and weather conditions enabled the region to produce a virtual cornucopia of crops, ranging from wheat and cattle to fruits and vegetables. Wheat and other grains were major crops in Oregon, Utah and California. Cattle were raised throughout the region wherever sufficient water and grazing lands were available. Those areas adjacent to centers of population tended to specialize in the production of fruits and vegetables. In California, two dollars of fruit were produced per person compared to one dollar's worth in a major fruit producing state like New York. Differences in terrain, climate, and soil also produced farms of varying size. In California, for example, the average farm was between 150 and 200 acres, yet 1,500 acre units were not uncommon. Moreover, fully a third of all farms were under 100 acres.

THE CENTERS OF CROP PRODUCTION

As a consequence of the regional changes detailed above, a westward shift occurred in the centers of production of major crops. In the case of wheat the center of production moved from Pennsylvania in 1820, to Ohio in 1840 and to Illinois in 1860. (See Table 10.2.) In that year the average output of wheat farms was 166 bushels in Illinois, as compared with 84 bushels in Ohio, and 66 bushels in Pennsylvania. In the case of corn, the center of production moved from Tennessee and Kentucky in 1840 to Illinois and Ohio in 1860. The soil and climate of the Midwest resulted in crop yields that guaranteed the region's superiority in corn production. Output of eighty bushels an acre was not uncommon, at a time when other geographic areas were yielding fifteen bushels. Still, corn remained a ubiquitous crop. In fact, during the pre-Civil War period the value of the Southern corn crop substantially exceeded that of cotton. A natural by-product of the westward shift of corn was the parallel movement of hog production. In 1860 Illinois was the major hog producing state of the nation.

In the case of cotton, the major centers of production in the early 1800's were in the Old South, principally the states of South Carolina and Georgia. Exhaustion of these lands, together with the generally inferior character of the soil, forced production westward to meet burgeoning demand. By 1840 the center of production was located in Alabama, and by 1860 in Mississippi. Tobacco, unlike other major crops, passed through a

TABLE 10.2. *The Leading States in Cotton, Corn and Wheat Production 1820–1860*

	Cotton	
1820	*1840*	*1860*
South Carolina	Alabama	Mississippi
Georgia	Georgia	Alabama
	Corn	
—	Tennessee	Illinois
—	Kentucky	Ohio
	Wheat	
Pennsylvania	Ohio	Illinois
New York	Pennsylvania	Indiana

SOURCE: U.S. Bureau of the Census. *Statistical Abstracts of the United States.* Washington, D.C.: U.S. Government Printing Office, various years.

complete cycle. In the eighteenth century, production was centered in the Piedmont region of Virginia, Maryland, and North Carolina. However, significant price declines owing to general overproduction and increasing competition from Cuban, Colombian, and Sumatran planters, coupled with increasing costs due to burdensome mortgage debt and exhaustion of the soil substantially reduced the profitability of tobacco cultivation. As a result, significant acreage was abandoned. For example, in 1817 as much land was abandoned in North Carolina as was under cultivation. The centers of production moved westward to lower cost virgin land, particularly in Kentucky and Tennessee. While these areas continued to flourish during the balance of the period, during the 1840's and 1850's resurgence of production occurred in the Piedmont area. This was due principally to the development of more scientific farming and a sharp increase in prices. As a result, by 1860 the centers of production were located both in the Piedmont region and Kentucky and Tennessee.

During the 1820's beef cattle raising was limited principally to small-scale production and was common to all regions. As pioneer farmers pushed west onto the prairie lands of northern Indiana, central Illinois, Missouri, Iowa, and eastern Kansas and Nebraska, they found a treeless terrain covered by grass growing upwards of six feet high. The grass was ideal for livestock feeding, a fact which encouraged the raising of beef cattle. No one farmer could afford to raise large herds, and generally began his business enterprise by raising two or more surplus animals. Since it would have been economically unprofitable to drive such a small herd of cattle to market, the occupation of cattle drover originated. The drover, who operated as far south as Texas, went from farm to farm collecting surplus stock. Once a sufficiently large supply of cattle was gathered, they were usually driven overland to urban centers such as Indianapolis and Cincinnati. As the intensive settlement of prairie areas proceeded, and farmers succeeded in enclosing and cultivating prairie land, the more enterprising of the drovers began to purchase their own ranchlands. These spreads were quite large, often totaling 20,000 acres. In 1860 the principal cattle raising state was Texas, followed by Illinois.

FARM MECHANIZATION

THE IRON PLOW

The expansion of commercial agriculture was impeded by a shortage of labor. The South, as the first region to pursue commercial farming, was the first to face this dilemma. Its solution, as already discussed, was slavery. Other regions concentrated on farm mechanization. From 1800 to 1850 output per farm worker showed practically no change. However, from 1850 to 1870, a period hailed as the first agricultural revolution, worker productivity increased twenty-three per cent. The principal technological breakthroughs were of a labor saving rather than land saving character. Innovations occurred in plows, cultivators, rakes, threshers, mowers, and reapers. In the years immediately following the War of 1812 the wooden plow continued to be the major farm implement. Typically, a large wooden plow required the use of two men and a double team of oxen. It is significant that in the first plowing match of the Massachusetts Society for Promoting Agriculture, in 1817, only wooden plows were in evidence. Two years later Jethro Wood succeeded in producing a cast iron plow with interchangeable parts. The use of this plow grew rapidly in the East, and in an 1830 Massachusetts plowing match, all plows were cast iron. However, in the Midwest, iron plows did not replace those made of wood until 1840. The labor saving impact of this innovation is evidenced by the fact that an iron plow required half the labor and animal power of a comparable wooden one. Despite the improved efficiency of the iron plow, it was not without its disadvantages. It was costly to produce, and some varieties of soil, particularly those in the Midwest, tended to stick to the iron, making plowing an extremely arduous and tedious task. The search for a better plow was rewarded in 1837 when John Deere produced one made of steel. It was an immediate success, costing approximately one-half that of an iron plow. The principal reason for the reduction in costs was the more efficient factory fabrication of steel plows versus the local manufacturing of iron plows by blacksmith shops. Factory production expanded from an annual rate of 4,000 in 1838 to 13,000 two decades later.

CULTIVATORS, REAPERS AND THRESHERS

A concomitant to the development of metal plows was the introduction of the cultivator. Light in weight and versatile, it could perform multiple functions previously requiring both a plow and hand hoe. In 1820 the one-shovel cultivator was introduced, followed by the two-shovel unit in 1850 and the straddle row cultivator of six shovels in 1860. Becuase of its multifunctional nature its productivity exceeded that of the plow. For example, in corn cultivation one cultivator's output was greater than that of three plows. The augmentation of farm output made possible by plows and cultivators dealt with the planting process. It was also necessary to improve efficiency in the harvesting of crops. Although crude versions of reapers, mowers, and threshers appeared in the 1820's and 1830's, it was not until the 1850's that they entered into widespread use. McCormick, who first invented his reaper in 1834, initiated factory production in 1847 in Chicago, close to Midwestern wheat fields. By 1851 production of 1,000 machines a year was achieved, and by the end of the decade output had reached 4,000 a year. The McCormick Reaper enabled nine men to do the work of fourteen. While most reapers were convertible into mowers, they tended in this capacity to clog in grass and tear up soil. Mowers became a practical farm implement in 1859 with the introduction of the Wood mower. It enabled one man and two horses to produce the same output as ten men. The thresher was in evidence on a small scale as early as 1815. Its principal functions were to separate the wheat from the chaff and measure and bag the resulting grain for shipment. A markedly improved version was patented in 1836 by John Pitt. The Pitt Thresher came into general use in the 1840's. Utilizing the labor of four men, it had an output of twenty to twenty-five bushels of wheat an hour. An enlarged machine, which appeared after 1850, averaged thirty or more bushels an hour.

Land-saving capital was not in general use in the United States before the Civil War. Only in older Eastern regions around centers of population where land values were high did farmers find it profitable to engage in investments such as fertilizer and the seed drill. The latter provided for more orderly planting of crops in contrast to the broadcasting of seed by hand. Introduced in the 1850's in the wheat regions of Pennsylvania and New York, it enabled farmers to utilize a given quantity of land more intensively. On the other hand, few Western farmers in the era of abundant land cared to invest in land-saving capital.

NOTES

1. John Stuart Mill. *Principles of Political Economy with Some of Their Applications to Social Philosophy.* New York: Augustus M. Kelley, 1965, p. 250.
2. Alfred Marshall. *Principles of Economics.* New York: Macmillan, 1948, p. 561.
3. Ulrich B. Phillips. "The Economic Cost of Slaveholding in the Cotton Belt," *Political Science Quarterly*, Vol. XX, 1905, pp. 257-75.
4. Alfred Conrad and John Meyer. *The Economics of Slavery.* Chicago: Aldine Publishing Company, 1964, p. 66.

SELECTED REFERENCES

1. Percy W. Bidwell and John I. Falconer. *History of Agriculture in the Northern United States, 1620-1860.* Washington, D.C.: Carnegie Institution, 1925.
2. Alfred H. Conrad and John R. Meyer. *The Economics of Slavery.* Chicago: Aldine Publishing Co., 1964.
3. Paul W. Gates. *The Farmer's Age: Agriculture 1815-1860.* New York: Holt, Rinehart and Winston, 1950.
4. Eugene D. Genovese. *The Political Economy of Slavery.* New York: Random House, 1966.
5. Lewis C. Gray. *History of Agriculture in the Southern United States to 1860.* Magnolia: Peter Smith, 1958.
6. Ulrich B. Phillips. *American Negro Slavery.* Magnolia: Peter Smith, 1959.

reading

was slavery profitable?

alfred conrad, john meyer,
douglas dowd, and eli ginzberg

ALFRED H. CONRAD (for JOHN R. MEYER and himself): Every economist must be pleased to start some hares; it can become embarrassing, however, when they begin to breed like rabbits. In the ten years since we first tried our slavery model in public, in Professor Gerschenkron's history seminar, more than thirty published arguments addressed to that model have come to our attention. We don't pretend to know whether that represents an increased output over preceding decades. Besides, in our youthful enthusiasm we gave the impression that we were disposing, once and for all, of a piece of intellectual game that was already rather high. In any event, the apparent egocentricity that turned up all those papers and articles may be explained, if not justified, by Ralph Barton Perry's dictum that every reader looks up two references in an index: sex, and his own name.

The recent discussion on the profitability of slavery in the ante-bellum South can be surveyed along three lines. First, a number of questions of fact, or evidence, have been raised. Second, the capital model that we used has been criticized as irrelevant. And third, the model, as a piece of economic analysis, has been attacked as insufficient to answer the historical questions we put to it.

As for factual or data questions, Fritz Redlich is not a man to mince words. He has characterized Part II of our paper, which is where the

Reprinted with permission from "Slavery as an Obstacle to Economic Growth in the United States: A Panel Discussion" by Alfred H. Conrad, *et al.,* in *Journal of Economic History* XXVII (December 1967), 518-540.

317

model works, as simply "fictitious." He means more by this remark than what is implied by saying that *I Promessi Sposi* is a work of fiction and not an historical account of the Counter-Reformation in the Duchy of Milan, or that John Motley could not really know the drunken indiscretions of Egmont or the midnight fears of William of Orange (though Motley may come closer to Mr. Redlich's definition of history than does Fishlow or Fogel, for example). What he *means* is that our Table 9 presents estimated returns on investments in prime field hands under a number of assumptions as to yield per hand, capital outlay, farm-gate cotton price, and slave longevity. Modal values and other measures of central tendency were used where we had distributions of estimated values, but the range over various land fertilities and capital outlays was given in full, so that the sensitivity of our results to different price and interest rates might be tested. The individual values are old-style historical facts; the modal values are statistical estimates, which is a class neither necessarily nor epistemologically equivalent to fiction. We were aware that the census data on longevity were questionable, and we considered whether the estimates were consistent with population trends. Such a comparison is presumably a form of "source criticism." But how does one estimate the rate of return on a piece of capital *without* estimating its life expectancy?

What new information, then, has emerged from the recent literature? Eugene Genovese urges that the medical costs should be at least 50 per cent higher and perhaps double our estimate. He raises the cost of over-seers from a range of $5 to $15 per hand, to $22.50. He points to our unfortunate assumption that a stock consisting largely of mules and oxen could be self-reproducing, but he doesn't really reveal how large a pro-portion of horses and donkeys would be sufficient to maintain the stock— in Mississippi cotton counties, for instance, horses accounted for one-quarter to almost half of the total work animals in 1860, depending upon the size of the farm. He would raise our food and clothing expenses, and he would have us add as costs "several dollars worth of Christmas presents per slave," the "regular and expensive vacations in watering places," and the large sums planters spent on tutors, academies, and finishing schools for their children. However secure or insecure may be the inference that the regular vacations were widespread in the South, the gross analytic error of counting trips to Saratoga as costs should make it unnecessary to pursue the question further.

A more serious factual objection was raised by Edward Saraydar. He argued in a note in the *Southern Economic Journal* that we used data from plantations that *purchased* all provisions as though they represented the costs on self-sufficient plantations. Combining such underestimates of costs with *upward*-biased average yields from specialized plantations, we would obviously have overestimated the rate of profit. Saraydar redid the average yields by returning to the 1850 Census, but at the cost of several downward biases and one arithmetic oversight. Richard Sutch, after raising a disturbing question about the relevance of our model, which we will discuss below, observed, first, that our yields did come from self-supporting plantations, and second, that yields estimated from the 1860 Census data are much closer to the ones we used than to Saraydar's estimates. Mr. Sutch then went on to calculate the rate of appreciation on slaves — an annual increase of 7.56 per cent — from population and slave price increases. To remove speculative effects, he turned more directly to cotton plantations and estimated the internal rate of return exclusive of the rising slave prices, by limiting the appreciation rate only to the 2.15 per cent slave population increase. He found that cotton farming was clearly profitable in the new South and concluded that land prices in the new areas could not rise fast enough to capture the full rent, from which one should predict the press of cotton production (as it actually occurred) into the new western lands.

Robert Evans has contributed to the evidence on slave-hiring practices — and, incidentally, on training and skills — and on the internal slave trade. Most of the interest in his two papers arises from the alternative model that he proposed for estimating rates of return, but his evidence on slave-hire-to-purchase ratios and trading differentials both lend strong support to the conclusion that the slave economy was viable. When he compares the specific slave *trade* returns to skilled wage rates, he finds some compensation in the traders' labor income, presumably to pay for the social disrepute in which the trade was held. But even admitting the difficulties of comparing occupational requirements, the evidence does not indicate that the traders were treated as pariahs.

In criticizing Evans, and later in a review of our book, Thomas Govan raised again (cf. his 1942 work) several factual questions, the most troubling of which relate to the depletion of the fertility of cotton lands. Our discussion of soil exhaustion is a "perverse belief" and a "disregard of reality." From the other side, however, Genovese claimed that we did not take sufficient account of the soil depletion pressed upon the South by the slave-and-cotton economy, and he cites further evidence on fertilizer requirements as well as contemporary discussion. At the worst, we may have been clumsy in identifying the central tendency.

We would argue with Fogel and others that the social savings Genovese computed and the rates of return we calculated could both well be *facts*. But that is not the point. There has been much use of the word "guessing" in the discussion, but very little unearthing of new, direct evidence to refute the estimates we used. Only Sutch and Evans have contributed new evidence and in both cases it buttresses the case of the profitability of slavery.

There has been novelty in the model-building department, however. Let us start by reviewing what we actually did. In order to estimate the profitability of Southern slavery we computed the rate of return on an investment in slaves by the familiar procedure of capitalizing an income stream. In order to include all the relevant income we considered two production functions, one, for the production of cotton, in which the labor of prime field hands was the major input, and a second, in which the natural increase of the marketable slave population was looked upon as the production of capital goods. It should not be necessary to repeat that we did not need to assume, and that we never did assume, the existence of specialized breeding farms, in order to make the computation meaningful. However, to answer some of the denials that have appeared in the literature, let us repeat that we found enough references to "breeding wenches" and "proven breeders" in the secondary and primary source material to suggest, at least, that some ante-bellum Southerners got the idea.

We also did not estimate the returns *as-if* there were breeding farms. Slaves, like other people, reproduced themselves, and their children were sold as capital instruments. We estimated the returns from that appreciation of the capital stock of the slave South. We made the estimates because it has been argued, repeatedly, that southern slavery had been about to disappear because it was not profitable. We asserted that the values which we derived from the market data led directly to the inference that enough individual men in the South were making a commercial profit that large-scale slavery was not likely to disappear automatically.

A number of alternative models have appeared in the last few years. We have already mentioned Robert Evans' procedure. He computed the net yearly income from the yearly hire received by owners of slaves when they were rented out to work. The advantage of this procedure is the relatively direct, as opposed to residual, nature of the income data. A major danger, of course, is that evidence from slave hires might be biased in the direction of a special class of slave stock. Evans did try to restrict his observations to unskilled labor, but we have been unable to judge his success in this regard. The rates of return on slave capital from his computation are safely above contemporary railroad bond yields and short-term money rates.

Yasukichi Yasuba introduced the problem of *economic* rent—the difference between the price of capital instruments and the net reproduction cost—in an alternative evaluation of the viability of slave system as a whole. For a given region or crop, he argues, the market price is relevant, but for the viability of the system as a whole, only the costs of reproduction of the capital—that is, the cost of rearing slaves—are relevant. He rewrote our basis postulate, therefore, as follows:

> ...If the portion of the price of slaves which represents capitalized rent was increasing, it is a sign of the increased profitability of slavery...To say that capitalized rent was positive is the same thing as to say that the rate of return based on the reproduction costs of slaves was above the market rate of interest, provided that non-economic factors did not affect the determination of the price and there was no lag nor anticipation in capitalization...

Because the supply of slaves, especially after the prohibition of further imports from Africa, was largely independent of profits, a discrepancy between prices and costs could last longer than would be the case for ordinary capital. This, he argued, is precisely what happened: the demand curve shifted to the right more rapidly than the supply curve could shift, with the result that the economic rent persisted, and indeed increased, over the ante-bellum period. Capitalized rent rose continuously from 1821 to 1855, with a decline between the prosperous late 1830's and the depressed early 1840's. On this basis, as distinguished from our findings on the marginal efficiency of slave capital, valued at market prices, Yasuba concluded that the slave system was viable.

This argument was pressed further by Richard Sutch and Douglass North. Much further, since North concluded that we failed to accomplish our objective and simply perpetuated the miserable controversy around profitability and viability. In fact, he says, "there is no possibility that slavery was economically not viable." Given the existence of rent on land and on slaves, short-run unprofitability would result in a readjustment of land rents or slave prices, sufficient to restore equilibrium. Only if the wages of free labor fell to subsistence, they argue, so that slave prices fell to zero, or at least below their cost of reproduction (in which case the rents would fall to zero), could the system become economically nonviable. If this argument simply refers to the fact that with upward sloping supply curves there will apparently always be a margin of private rent, then it must come up against Mrs. Robinson's demonstration that the rising supply curve is a necessary, but not sufficient, condition for the existence of rent in a particular industry. To be more specific, refutation of the arguments of those who said slavery was uneconomic, required proof that slave markets were viable and operative. Those who insist that there was "no possibility of slavery being unprofitable" come very close to assuming away the central question by simply assuming that viable slave markets existed. Furthermore, North is arguing as if slavery were a self-contained system. Actually, the cotton-slave-plantation system was *not* a closed system; it had to bid slave labor away from other uses. One of the results of our study was the demonstration that slave labor was highly mobile. Quasi-rents probably existed in the alternative uses and would have to be part of the plantation bid. Therefore, the presence of some rent or quasi-rent in the price of slaves and of cotton lands is not enough to make viability a foregone conclusion. Something more remains to be proved.

Sutch and North both recognize that if the slaves were less efficient than free labor, slave prices need not have fallen to zero to render the system nonviable. The lower limit would be the subsistence or reproduction cost of slaves; in the face of all the literature on the inefficiency of slave labor, this hardly seems an empty question. Slave rents or quasi-rents should have been continuously threatened by the supply of presumably more efficient free labor. Now, in order to argue that market prices will respond successfully to such erosion, one must visualize that the declining stream of rents is instantaneously reflected in falling slave prices, and that those prices will not hover above the subsistence margin set by the difference in productivity. The stream of rents yielded by slaves from the time they could cover their variable — that is, subsistence or reproduction — costs, to the time when they retired or expired, is the key variable. It is not self-evident that the capitalized sum of that stream must always equal the prices of slaves in a period of declining prices and yields. With any lag in price adjustments, the system might well become nonviable. North's closing point, that if slave prices were pegged by the requirements of conspicuous consumption, land prices must have fallen to an equilibrium solution, seems to ignore the possibility that the land would be in demand for the production of cotton or many other commodities with more efficient free labor. We may have underestimated the returns by using market price rather than the cost of reproduction, but we were certainly not tilting at windmills.

In general, an exclusive reliance upon calculation of quasi-rents to establish the economic viability of slavery *as a system* greatly oversimplifies. And it was definitely not the context in which the historical arguments were conducted. Rather, those who contended that slavery was uneconomic argued that slave markets were pathological and disequilibrated. Stress was placed upon investor irrationality and a divergent pattern in the development of cotton and slave prices. The specific contention was that in the immediate ante-bellum period a rational investor would not find it profitable to "buy into" the slave system. We demonstrated that this was certainly not obvious and almost certainly was fallacious.

Importance also attaches to differences in the pattern of economic viability of slavery by regions and particular applications, particularly since much political controversy in the pre-Civil War period centered about the issue of whether new lands should be admitted to slave culture. We demonstrated that this emphasis upon growth of slave lands was hardly quixotic. An expanding slave system was much more profitable than a stagnant system, not only for those who occupied the new lands, but for those who remained back on the older lands of the South, engaged in a combination of agriculture and slave breeding. Indeed, looking at the political controversies of the period immediately prior to the war, it is perhaps not too extravagant to claim that the war might have been avoided if southerners had been satisfied to restrict their slave system to lands on which it was already established.

In another set of papers the irrelevance of our model has been argued on very different grounds. From a variety of starting points, Douglas Dowd, Eugene Genovese, Harold Woodman, Thomas Govan, and Fritz Redlich all arrived at the conclusion that we could not settle any significant issues with a business model, or a capital model, because slavery was not *simply* a business or a capitalist enterprise. There may be a meaningful distinction to be drawn between the question of the *relevance* of a model of the slave system as a business enterprise, and the *sufficiency* of such a model for the problems of growth and development. Let us look first at the question of relevance.

Why is our economic model argued to be irrelevant by these historians? In Douglas Dowd's words:

> ...For the southerner to convert himself to beliefs and behavior which would support and comport with slavery required a concentration so intense that all else became secondary—including the process of capital accumulation...Who would be inclined to use the term "capitalist" to describe the owners of Southern wealth? Apart from a William Gregg here and there, southern capital was *planter* capital. Planters were of course interested in profits; so were medieval "businessmen" (as jarring a term as "southern capitalists"). But neither group approached the question of capitalist accumulation in the sense in which the northern manufacturers did ...

In Genovese's terms, the argument runs as follows:

> ...however brisk the slave trade, considerable sentimental pressure existed to inhibit a purely rational approach to buying and selling slaves. Any notion that slaveholders as a class could or would have abandoned their estates to invest in more remunerative pursuits...— in other words, to transform themselves into capitalists—rests on a vulgar economic determinist outlook, contradicts the actual historical experience, and ignores the essential qualities of slave-based Southern life.

. . .

The question of whether or not the slaveholders earned a return equal
to that accruing to Northern capitalists is not an especially significant
political or social question.

. . .

Economists have assumed that an affirmative answer would prove
slaveholding to have been just another business; as Schumpeter warns
us, statistics can never disprove what we have reason to know from
simpler and more direct methods.

Now, to be accused of vulgar economic determinism, which must be
related to vulgar Marxism, is a serious business, and we would like to say
something on that point. First of all, we were not attempting to prove that
slaveholding was "just another business" — that explication has nothing to
do with our thesis, and is itself untrue. We were looking for evidence on
profits, because their alleged absence has been offered as a reason why
the American Civil War was unnecessary. We believe that we did find
evidence of competitive profit rates in slavery and concluded, first, that
they were an additional and significant reason, along with any possible
Southern quixoticism and Gothic imagination, to explain the South's willingness to fight; and second that those profits could have provided the capital
for further growth.

Having read our Schumpeter, too, we are prepared to wear the Marxist
shoe, if it fits. But we reserve the right to reject the vulgar model, on
grounds of taste. Let us see if we can outline a Marxist interpretation of
history that will admit the relevance of our capital model. We shall borrow
liberally, but not slavishly, from Maurice Merleau-Ponty.[1] Discussions of
Marxism and historical determinism have often been conducted as if
causality implied that each event had to have a linear relationship with
another event, about which it could then be determined whether it was
"economic" or "ideological," or even *simply* economic or ideological.
Marxism, or economic explanation, is then thought to be vanquished when
one can point to "ideological" causes. But neither materialistic history
nor econometric history is more abstract than idealistic history or
spiritualistic history. At the heart of the Marxist interpretation is the
idea that nothing can be isolated in the total context of history, but also that
because of their greater generality economic phenomena make a greater
contribution to historical discourse. Now, to recognize that the economic
phenomena do not explain everything is not the same as to relegate the
production of material conditions to the outbuildings of history. We don't
believe that slaves were simply or merely capital, or that the southern
gentleman was simply or merely *homo faber*, but that does not make a
capital model irrelevant or a precise limitation of the opportunity costs
of the enterprise a waste of time, nor does it render the capitalization of
an income stream from slaves a figment or a fiction. History passes

through *homo faber*, and the production of material conditions, the production and transformation of laws, customs, beliefs, styles of civilization, even the content of consciousness—all these are mutually penetrating and fully reciprocal.

Let us quote from the last paragraph of our conclusion, before going on to consider the *sufficiency* of our model:

> Although profitability cannot be offered as a sufficient guarantee of the continuity of southern slavery, the converse argument that slavery must have destroyed itself can no longer rest upon allegations of unprofitability or upon assumptions about the impossibility of maintaining and allocating a slave labor force. To the extent, moveover, that profitability is a necessary condition for the continuation of a private business institution in a free-enterprise society, slavery was not untenable in the ante-bellum American South.

In this last part, now, we will be less polemical. The arguments of Genovese, Dowd, and many before them, have linked Southern slavery directly to Southern stagnation. In Genovese's words:

> Even if it could be established that plantation profit levels did stay high and that long-range prospects looked good, it would not follow that capital was being accumulated in a manner guaranteeing a politically viable economic development.

Frankly, we never had a model sufficient to deal with the question. About the best we can do on this matter is to define the problem in terms of some recent work on agrarian reform and Southern development.

There are two essential points that are frequently overlooked when the discussion settles down to Southern backwardness. To begin, the ante-bellum Southern economy was not stagnant. North, Easterlin, Williamson, and Nicholls have all demonstrated that the prosperity of the plantation economy was real, that income grew as rapidly in the prewar South as in the rest of the nation, and that cotton was the most important influence in the ante-bellum growth of the economy. Apparently, though, retardation did occur in the rate of Southern economic growth in the period between 1860 and approximately 1880. As Engerman has pointed out, it was 1890 before the South again achieved the per capita income levels enjoyed in 1860. In very large measure both the absolute and relative failure of the South to achieve standards of economic welfare comparable to the rest of the country can be attributed to the losses or the growth not achieved in the two decades of the 1860's and the 1870's. Stanley Engerman and Louis Rose have examined the devastation and capital losses due to the war and the emancipation, and William Nicholls has discussed with deep insight how in the postwar period agrarian values persisted, then rigidified, and finally corrupted the southern social structure to the point where tradition hardened in a dense barrier against further progress.

Perhaps the most important single illustration of the war's disruptive impact is to be found in the pattern of British cotton imports during the second half of the nineteenth century. Statistics on these are shown in Table 1. Quite noticeably, a sharp rise in world prices for cotton in the early 1860's elicited a rather rapid increase in the supply of cotton from areas outside the American South. In particular, an almost fourfold increase occurred in the average level of East Indian cotton exports to Britain between 1860 and 1865. By contrast, almost fifteen years were required to displace this new cotton from the British market after the war terminated; it was not until the 1880's that the South regained its absolute and relative prewar position in the British markets once more. Displacement from conventional market outlets would, of course, have retarded southern development during the 1860's and 1870's even without any war-induced physical destruction.

The timing of southern economic retardation also seems important. If most southern underdevelopment is attributable to only two decades of stagnation, difficulty resides with any insistence that it was slavery or some southern slave-induced mentality that lies at the root of southern economic problems. Such an argument is confronted with the difficulty of explaining why these problems should have been particularly pronounced or observable only during two decades. Why was Southern growth not retarded during the height of the slaveholding period or just before the Civil War? Or why did slavery-induced mental attitudes not prove such a hindrance after 1880? By contrast, hypotheses that emphasize war dislocations and destruction are completely consistent with retardation's being restricted to the war period and its immediate aftermath.

Economic considerations or (if you wish) profit-seeking are also quite sufficient to explain the South's concentration upon agricultural development. The South seemed fully capable of developing manufacturing capacity when technological or economic circumstances made such a course attractive, as in the pre-Civil War period and subsequently around the turn of the century. When steam-powered textile mills became possible or more economical than water-powered mills, the locus of the textile industry slowly but surely shifted from New England to the South, eventually resulting in the substantial post-World War II trauma of New England textile mill towns.

In short, the South was not an isolated, self-contained economy. It is a gross exaggeration to talk about the ante-bellum Southern states as a colonial and tributary economy, locked into dependence upon the North. The terms of trade with England, as well as with New England, were excellent, and the South was well represented in the national government.

TABLE 1. *Prices and Quantities of British Cotton Imports, 1850 to 1889*

Year or Decade	Imports by Origin (in thousands of bales per year)						Average Prices by Types		
	Ameri-can	Brazil-ian	Egyp-tian	Peru-vian	East Indian	Total	Ameri-can	Brazil-ian	East Indian
1850's	1,638	132	103	9	406	2,288	$5^{11}/_{16}$	$7^7/_{16}$	$4^5/_8$
1860	2,581	103	109	10	563	3,366	$6^1/_4$	$8^3/_{16}$	5
1861	1,841	100	98	10	987	3,036	$8^9/_{16}$	$9^3/_4$	$6^5/_{16}$
1862	72	134	147	20	1,072	1,445	$17^1/_4$	$18^1/_8$	$12^7/_8$
1863	132	138	248	23	1,391	1,932	$23^1/_4$	$24^1/_4$	$19^1/_4$
1864	198	212	319	60	1,798	1,587	$27^1/_2$	$28^3/_4$	$21^1/_2$
1865	462	340	414	131	1,408	2,755	19	$19^1/_4$	$14^1/_2$
1866	1,163	407	200	112	1,867	3,749	$15^1/_2$	$17^1/_8$	12
1867	1,226	437	198	129	1,511	3,501	$10^7/_8$	$11^5/_8$	$8^3/_4$
1868	1,269	637	201	101	1,452	3,660	$10^1/_2$	$11^5/_8$	$8^1/_2$
1869	1,040	514	226	106	1,496	3,382	$12^1/_8$	$12^1/_2$	$9^3/_4$
1870's	1,977	388	277	102	899	3,643	$7^7/_8$	$8^3/_8$	$5^3/_4$
1880's	2,755	246	260	57	631	3,949	$5^{15}/_{16}$	$6^1/_8$	$4^1/_8$

Note: Taken from the *Cotton Trade of the United States*, as in turn derived from the Senate Report on Cotton Production and Consumption, Fifty-third Congress, third session, Report 986.

Of course, agricultural development, whether a "prerequisite" for industrialization or not, might hold back the initial growth of the industrial sector, especially if agriculture is stuck in a traditional and static position. In that case, agrarian reform is apparently the prerequisite. Alexander Gerschenkron identifies two aspects of this reform:

> ... it is supposed to increase the productivity of agriculture so that its growing produce will allow shifts of population out of agricultural areas and will support the increasing numbers of men engaged in non-agricultural pursuits. ... It is supposed to eliminate the traditional restraints on the mobility of the agrarian population and its freedom to exercise a free choice of occupation.

Now, some increase in productivity in the ante-bellum cotton culture can be easily demonstrated, but there is a distinguished chorus to remind us that having once revived the almost moribund institution of slavery as an answer to labor shortage, the South stopped where it was, eagerly abetted in this tendency by its machines — the slaves. Abolition, then, was apparently necessary as the first item on the reform agenda, though the postwar experience must make us question whether it could lead to an essentially different system of cultivation. In the American South it is not obvious that the problem was ever one of moving from a communal to an individualistic system of production.

With regard to eliminating traditional restraints on mobility, obviously the slave population was without free choice of occupation. But, given the market conditions for cotton, and the ease with which market incentives drew production to the fertile western lands, it is not clear exactly what increased mobility might have accomplished for Southern agricultural development in the prewar period.

Indeed, let us speculate that the crucial moment for agrarian reorganization and the formation of prerequisites came not in 1860, in the United States, but in the last decade of the eighteenth century. At that point southern agriculture had recovered effectively and rapidly from the Revolutionary War. Then, in 1794, there came the gin and forty-cent cotton. Some kind of structural response was called for, especially in the face of an impending labor shortage. Two alternatives seem plausible: (1) a thoroughgoing agrarian reform to freehold, individualist cultivation, as in the northern cereal lands; or (2) the extension of slavery and the evolution of the slave market to facilitate the movement of productive resources to the West. The actual choice that was made does not seem to have been necessarily eccentric or irrational. Certainly that was not the moment at which agrarianism became stagnant, rigid, and inimical to development in the South. Instead of searching, fruitlessly, for the signs of morbidity which were supposed to lead inexorably to a "genuine" agrarian reform, we can observe that slavery was profitable, indeed viable, and that the moral conflict, instead of appearing to be an avoidable blunder, takes on real meaning. What remains is the devastation of the War years, and the failure of the thoroughgoing reform to take hold. There is still much to be explained, and it may be at this point, where the institutions are less boldly outlined, that the social history is most sorely needed.

DOUGLAS DOWD: Whether in the slavery or the new economic history controversies of the past decade, one moves to a feeling that the participants are often talking past one another, talking to themselves and to what may loosely be thought of as their respective adherents. The new economic historians, it may be said, put one in mind of rather light-hearted evangelists; while those who dissent from their innovations seem, by comparison, stuffy, oldfashioned, fearful of the new truths, perhaps of truth itself.

As is well-known, when controversies take on such characteristics, it is because procedures and conclusions, rather than assumptions and aims, form the stuff of the controversy. Only apparently are the discussions concerned, then, with the same subject matter, for the parameters are different, and they are different because — quite appropriately for both parties — the purposes are different. The slavery controversy provides a useful basis for an exploration of this question, not least because it came as the opening gun of the new economic history, a decade ago, when Messrs. Conrad and Meyer presented their twin papers on methodology and on slavery to the joint EHA-NBER meetings and I served as a critic.

Then, as still today, I puzzled over what Conrad and Meyer were trying to show. If they were attempting to demonstrate that Ulrich B. Phillips (in his *American Negro Slavery, inter alia*) was wrong, there was much more than the profitability of slavery on which to focus, for by the time they wrote Phillips had been quite thoroughly discredited on both narrow and broad questions, perhaps most completely by Kenneth Stampp (in his *Peculiar Institution*). I had thought, by then, that contemporary historians had come to view Phillips and his works more as sociological than as historical materials; documents, almost, revealing how a partisan of the Lost Cause viewed the evolution of that society. And was it not generally accepted by students of the South that writers like Phillips took the position that slavery was unprofitable because to do otherwise would muddy the more fundamental justifications for the system?

There is often something to be said for precise refutations of mistaken notions, to be sure. But what can be said that is positive diminishes to the degree that a general analysis would do. It is of course reasonably obvious that in any functioning social system, slave or otherwise, there will be incomes that are high at the top and decrease as one moves to the bottom of the social scale; and that power will be roughly proportionate to income and wealth. What is less obvious are the costs of a given system—costs in terms of alternatives foregone, as well as the social and human costs of the existent reality.

For the American South, it surely was good business sense that led planters to emphasize cotton cultivation, slaveholding, and slavebreeding; and good business sense was also good economic sense, if the short run and the interests of those in power are taken as guiding criteria. But when we speak of economic development it is not business sense or economic sense for the short run as viewed by those in power that are, or should be, taken as the appropriate referents for judgment; for then we are speaking not only of structural realities and changes in the economy, but also of far-reaching social and political structures and changes.

As I said a decade ago, one cannot evaluate the meaning of slavery as though it were merely one kind of a labor force rather than another, *ceteris paribus*. Slavery normally implies and requires, and especially in the United States implied and required, a slavery-dominated society as much as a society dominating slaves. In turn, this meant that whatever business considerations might support the continuation of the slave-cum-cotton system, these were immeasurably reinforced by the social and political imperatives—ever more on the defensive in the ante-bellum South—of maintaining a slave society. Is this not made more evident when we examine the post-Civil War development of the South?

I should have thought it would be unnecessary to raise these questions once more, except that here we are meeting again on the subject; and, more vividly, we are aware of new work tending to move in the same directions as the earlier work of Conrad and Meyer. I have been away from the United States for a year, having just returned a week ago. Consequently, I have been unable to read Stanley Engerman's latest contributions on the South, slavery, and the Civil War. But may I not assume that Robert Fogel represented Mr. Engerman accurately in his article[2] on the new economic history? There it is said:

> The retarded development of the South during the last third of the nineteenth century and the first half of the twentieth was due not to stagnation during the slave era, but to the devastation caused by the Civil War. As Stanley Engerman points out, if *ante-bellum* growth-rates had continued through the war decade, southern *per capita* income would have been twice the level that actually prevailed in 1870. So disruptive was the war that it took the South some thirty years to regain the *per capita* income of 1860 and another sixty years to reach the same relative position in national *per capita* income that it enjoyed at the close of the *ante-bellum* era. The case for the abolition

of slavery thus appears to turn on issues of morality and equity rather than on the inability of a slave system to yield a high rate of economic growth (p. 647).

In a paper delivered to this Association in 1956, in which I attempted to explain the late nineteenth- and early twentieth-century retardation of the southern economy, I did not say, nor do I recall anyone else having said, that southern stagnation was due to "stagnation during the slave era." But I do recall arguing that it was the consequence of slave society, in all its ramifications, that explains that stagnation. To reopen that argument here and now would be impossible, as well as unrewarding, just as it would be impossible to come to grips even partially with all the questions that arise from the works of Messrs. Conrad, Meyer, Fogel, Engerman, and others now cultivating the new vineyards. But perhaps our brief excursion can provide a basis for fruitful discussions in the meeting today.

Perhaps I am mistaken, but I believe I am correct in seeing the new economic history as an attempt to incorporate the methodology of neo-classical economics and the procedures of econometrics with the materials and the questions of economic history — with the added notion that economic history will thereby be strengthened, made more scientific. In its essence this entails the central use of partial equilibrium analysis. Such an approach may or may not be appropriate for the analysis of questions of narrow focus and very short time periods, where the pound of *ceteris paribus* can serve as a temporary safe haven for "other things." Can it do so when we concern ourselves with changes taking a long period, and that neither begin nor end with economic, let alone quantitative, matters?

It was of utmost significance that slavery in the United States could not be maintained without vitally affecting "all other things," whether that slavery was profitable or not. As Stanley M. Elkins has so capably shown in his *Slavery*,[3] American Negro slavery was the very "worst" the world had known, in its nature and in its consequences, whether it be compared with ancient or contemporaneous slavery (in, for example, Brazil or the Caribbean). What does "worst" signify in this context, and why should it have been so? Slaves have always and everywhere been cruelly treated (and always with exceptions), and black slaves especially. Even so, their treatment, their rights (or total lack of rights), their "family" lives, the depths to which racism sank, the manner in which the present and long-distant future of black slaves (even, as we know, their past) was distorted and doomed — in social, psychological, political, and of course economic terms — in the United States reached the lowest of depths. Why should this be so, in the land of the free and the home of the brave? Was not economic individualism adhered to in the South? It surely was, extending even to trafficking in human beings as commodities. Did not Enlightenment, did not Christianity, extend into the American South? Most assuredly, but as with economic individualism, certain exotic notions had to be grafted onto otherwise healthy plants. To achieve such exoticism took a mighty effort, an effort that became obsessive, compulsive, and sickening not just to those who lived under the system, but also to those who lived from it and with it and for it.

Which brings me to the postwar period, if a bit abruptly, with Mr. Engerman's contributions in mind. Without asking how *ante-bellum* growth rates could have continued indefinitely; without asking, that is, how the South could have maintained its power in the nation while it also maintained slavery (with or without westward expansion); without asking whether or not there was some determining relationship between the Civil War and the socioeconomic system of the South and its power struggle with the North; without asking any of these questions, let us point to some questions that relate growth to development, and war destruction to growth and development.

Keeping in mind the well-recognized distinctions between growth and development, between quantitative and qualitative change (and keeping in mind, too, their connections), let us examine the notion of "*ante-bellum* growth rates continuing through the war decade" and even more, beyond that time. By 1860, the South showed few significant signs of moving away from its dependence on slaves and cotton. The signs that such a concentration might be something less than promising had begun to appear already during the Civil War; but what were then mere whispers turned into a roar in the years after 1870. Were the falling cotton prices (among other prices) in the last quarter of the century a function largely, if at all, of the Civil War? Is there any reasonable basis to assume either (1) that slave-breeding would have maintained the supply of slaves within economically viable magnitudes, or (2) that political realities would have allowed the reopening of the external trade? Has anyone specified the maintenance of slavery (and the power of those who would so maintain it) in the United States in the late nineteenth century might be made compatible with economic development? Or how its forceful abolition (apart from the Civil War) would have been accomplished? Or its peaceful abolition, by those squarely dependent upon it? Is there any ground for believing that the kinds of structural (economic, political, social) changes that are implied by economic development would have ensued in a South whose economy could no longer "thrive" on the basis of agriculture (for the majority of either its white or its black population)? And, given that the slaves were in fact (legally) emancipated, how does one explain the persistence of all the essential qualities of *ante-bellum* southern society in *post-bellum* southern society, down to the very recent past? Civil war damage? But is it not difficult to believe that for eighty years the southern economy was retarded by war destruction, in the light of what we have seen of so many other war-damaged economies in our own lives? Can the answers to any of these questions be turned to the advantage of the relevant conclusions of the new economic history? Or to its procedures? Can we learn nothing about our own economic development from our studies of the complex interrelationships of development (or its lack) in the contemporary underdeveloped world?

Furthermore, and in a different vein: What is the point of the analyses that have occupied these studies? "The case for the abolition of slavery" *of course* "turns on issues of morality and equity rather than on the inability of a slave system to yield a high rate of economic growth." To state otherwise would be to say, one presumes, that an economically viable slave system is to be recommended to . . . whom? The underdeveloped countries? Of course not, and the sneers of the new economic historians to such a query are appropriate. But then what is the point? If students of the South had earlier believed the system was profitable, what then, besides elegance, was the point of going on? Or did we have to be told, once more, that the Civil War was terribly destructive? Are we going back to Ranke, "simply" recording the facts, with technical trimmings? Or are there more vital tasks facing social scientists today; more vital, more demanding, more promising?

Of course slavery was profitable. And of course imperialism has been profitable. And of course the status quo in today's underdeveloped countries is profitable. Profitable, in all cases, to investors, whose definitions of profit do not go beyond the balance sheet and the income statement, and whose definitions of propriety are quite identical with their definitions of property. And of course slavery damaged both whites and blacks in the long run (and most, also, in the short run). And imperialism damages most citizens of both metropolis and colony, in the long run; and similarly with underdevelopment. Nor is it difficult to show that the damage that accrues from such systems is not solely, or mostly, economic; it is social, psychological, political, cultural. As it is also true that economic development both requires and brings about social, political, psychological, and cultural changes.

We are concerned in these meetings with obstacles to economic development, a focus that requires us to look at reality. That is a considerable improvement over the earlier inclinations of economists to develop and to use abstract models that, if they had any application at all, were relevant only to highly industrialized, political stable societies, operating within basically capitalist institutions. But improvements do not constitute sufficiencies; and especially they do not if their effect is to fragmentize an area of inquiry that requires broadening, deepening, and an enhanced sense of relevance.

Because in practice the meaning of economic development extends out and down so broadly and deeply, the analysis of development, not to say its implementation, must be as broad and as deep. This is to say that "experts" in economic development must take on the staggering task of attempting to understand the functioning of *societies*, and the manner in which *social* change takes place. One of my criticisms of the new economic history, and not only in its manifestations as regards the South, is that its methods, its thrust, are in exactly the opposite direction from that so desperately needed in the field today. Market relationships (for capital, commodities, labor) are indeed central to the functioning of an economy, as the heart is to the body. But the heart functions in relationship with a nervous system, and a circulatory system, and, among other things, in an environment. If the problem is a heart murmur, perhaps—no more than perhaps—total concentration on the heart itself will do. But those who will understand a cardiac condition, and prescribe for it, require themselves to understand the body in all its essential functions and characteristics. The lack of economic development is a problem in today's world that does not fall within the purview of the man who thinks in terms of heart murmurs. And the South had a cardiac condition in the nineteenth century.

To say that slavery was profitable and yet it inhibited economic development is not to say that slavery but that slave society in the United States in the nineteenth century, during and after its existence, inhibited economic development. But this is to say something else: Both before and after emancipation, social, economic, and political power in the South was held by those who had helped to create, and fought to maintain, slavery; nor was there a lack of interested parties in the North either before or after the War. For the South to develop economically, it was essential— and it is essential—either for a social upheaval within the South to take place, and/or for steady pressures, positive and negative, to be introduced from "outside." Power—its sources and its uses—has to be changed; that is, its possessors have to be changed.

What is true for the South is true for other societies that would develop. To detail such changes, let alone to understand, advocate, and support them, on a country-by-country basis is not only to move out from partial equilibrium analysis, but to move into the swirl and turbulence that characterize the world. And that suggests the stance of the committed and concerned social scientists—distasteful though such an idea is to our profession—more than that of the cheerful and comfortable economist.

ELI GINZBERG: Let me suggest to you how someone who has been working for the last thirty years on human resources in connection with economic development thinks about the argument at hand. I am well placed to do so at the moment because I've just finished a book called *People and Progress in East Asia*. It has nothing to do with slavery. I have, however, remembered my chapter titles, and they may serve as a kind of mirror for the discussion at hand. The first point is, if you're going to have economic development, it must be tied in with the concept of nationhood with the exercise of some kind of governmental power that is effective over a region. The one thing we know about the American slave system is that it finally operated in such a way as to destroy the Union for a time. So some connection must be made between discussions of profitability and the destruction of the Union. Professor Conrad did mention that possibly slavery would have been profitable had it been contained in the original states, but we know that's just what the slave owners would not settle for. Lincoln offered them that as a compromise; they refused to accept it, from which I deduce that maybe they knew their interests best and thought they would die on the vine if they accepted the offer. That was Lincoln's estimate, and that's why he made the offer. I think, therefore, you just cannot deal with such short-run approaches without setting the question into at least the national frame.

The second point I wish to make is that economic development has something to do with the standards of living of the mass of the population. There were large numbers of slaves in the South, and in some states they were in the majority. Now I suppose you can have very rapid development with very substantial inequalities of income. I submit that probably sooner or later fundamental conflict arises here. We may have misled many developing countries by failing to understand the importance of energizing rural life and giving the people who have a contribution to make to increased output some share in a better life. This is just what slavery did not do. I have no doubt, therefore, that in the short run it was profitable for the slave owners to exploit their slaves, but I would argue that, for the long run, this was really not a profitable way to expand the economy at something like an optimum level.

Let's take the question of education in the South. We know that it was forbidden to educate a slave. Not only does this mean that few of them were educated, but that it was a crime to do so. That means that the South inhibited economic development by insisting that it would not make use of the latent potential of a large part of its labor force. One of the most important aspects of the acquisition of skills is that it depends largely on the individual having some incentive to increase his skills, so that he and his family can get some advantage from it. It is my understanding that in a system of slavery this was generally impossible. We know there were a few slaves in the cities who made a deal with their masters but they were exceptional. In the nature of the case there was no incentive for the bulk of the Negro population in the South to improve themselves. In fact, they got into very bad habits of doing as little as possible, except under maximum coercion. Once again, it is perfectly possible to argue that slavery was a profitable system. The question is: how profitable, for whom, and for how long? And on those three counts I would say history is clear. Slavery broke up the Union, it had to be expanded in order to stay profitable, and it was a poor way of using the human resources of the region.

Let's take the question of management or entrepreneurship. We know that thought control became such an essential part of the South that anybody who dissented had to leave the South. I submit again that is a bad way to run the economy. Hitler did it, but not very successfully. If one of the systems of coercion that is needed to operate an economy is the suppression of dissent, that economy is in a bad way. And we know that many able people of the South left the South, if they could possibly get away. The whole tendency of the system was antidevelopmental, except within the narrow context of "getting a few more dollars out of your slaves." That's not sufficient because economic development requires specialization and more specialization. And that's exactly what was impossible with an agricultural system like this. You could use the land for ten years, twenty years, thirty years, forty years, and then you finally had to get new land. Slaves could not be used in a factory system because factory employment and slavery did not mix. There were, of course, a few slaves in the mines and a few out on contract. On the whole, the system of social control was in fundamental conflict with long-term economic development. I think that is the critical point. I would like to remind you that the first legal case on slavery in the history of the United States that I have been able to uncover was in 1629 in Jamestown. The issue had very little to do with economics, but much to do with social control. This was a case of punishing a white man who had slept with a Negro woman. The colonists understood quite well at that point in time that is was only through very rigid social controls that they could maintain the kind of society they wanted to maintain. I remind you finally that the title of my book, *The Troublesome Presence*, comes from a quotation of Abraham Lincoln in his eulogy of Henry Clay. Lincoln said that Henry Clay sought to remove the "troublesome presence" of the *free* Negro from the backs of the slave owners. I submit that if the only way you can have economic development is to ship a labor force back to Africa, you may be in trouble.

NOTES

1. Maurice Merleau-Ponty. *Sense and Non-Sense*. Translated by H. L. and P. A. Dreyfus. Evanston, Ill.: Northwestern University Press, 1964, chs. viii, ix.
2. Robert W. Fogel. "The New Economic History: Its Findings and Methods," *Economic History Review*, *XIX* (Dec. 1966), 642-56.
3. Stanley M. Elkins. *Slavery*, New York: Grosset and Dunlap, 1963.

chapter 11

manufacturing and foreign commerce

MANUFACTURING

THE DECLINE OF HOUSEHOLD PRODUCTION

Between 1815 and the Civil War the population of the United States increased about fourfold. The volume of manufactures, however, increased twelvefold. And over the fifty-year period 1810 to 1860 the capital investment in manufacturing increased twentyfold.

Why manufacturing developed at this rapid rate before the Civil War is a question with which economic historians long have been concerned. Some writers have emphasized technological innovations. In particular, the railroad has received substantial attention. So, too, has the power loom and the application of coke to iron making. Still others emphasize demand growth as the responsible element. The growth of population, income, and urban demand, it is felt, provided the challenge to which increased manufacturing growth was the response. Yet others stress supply. To them it was raw material price reductions and cost reductions owing to growing firm size and improved economic organization which stand out as being most important. Each of these theories has been subject to review

337

and criticized as being only a partial explanation of the growth process. Reason and evidence suggest that all of the theories, and not any one, explain pre-Civil War American manufacturing growth.

The process of U.S. manufacturing expansion, once begun, fed on itself and resulted in cumulative output gains. Profits from the shipping trade provided part of the capital sums necessary to initiate factory production. Merchants supplied the necessary entrepreneurial talent and organizational ability. Their talent turned to the copying and improvement of British technological innovations. Improved transportation permitted the growth of large scale production by expanding the outer limits of the market. Increasing adoption of the corporate form pooled the savings of numerous individuals and financed large scale production. That, in turn, generated income gains that fueled growing consumer demand and provided investment funds for factory expansion.

U.S. manufacturing in 1815 was still dominated by household production. The principal types of household production were food processing, liquor distillation, weaving, clothing manufacturing, and home construction. Craft production both inside and outside the home included tasks performed by tailors, weavers, hatters, shoemakers, saddlers, blacksmiths, wagon makers, carpenters, cabinetmakers, coopers, bakers, and shipbuilders. Mills were involved in the production of yarn, iron, lumber, flour, finished woolen goods, paper, potash, bricks, and alcoholic beverages. Factory production was about to commence in the manufacture of cotton textiles. Between 1815 and 1830 household manufacturing declined in the Eastern United States, and increased in newly settled Western states. From 1830 to the Civil War, the decline in household manufacturing was universal. Between 1840 and 1860 household manufactures declined from $1.70 to $.80 per capita. Home textile output, which stood at nine yards per capita in 1825, was but one-third of a yard by 1855. The decline of household production in the United States was correlated with the growth of transportation. Its decline was most rapid in those regions accessible by turnpikes, canals, and railroads, and most delayed where these transportation networks had not penetrated.

THE TRANSITION TO FACTORY PRODUCTION

Adequate supplies of labor, raw materials, power, machinery, and technical knowledge are as essential to large-scale machine production as access to markets. As indicated earlier, the farmer's daughter and other children supplied the major source of labor to the earliest factories. Raw materials, such as lumber, tanning bark, hides for leather, and iron ore were found in relative abundance in the United States, and cotton, wheat, and wool were produced on the nation's farms. Water provided the major source of power to drive mill and factory machinery until the Civil War. In the 1840's hydraulic turbines began to replace water wheels owing to their efficiency and cheapness. Steam engines, while in heavy use in England, were not used to any significant extent in the United States because of the expense involved in building and maintaining them. Steam power in the 1840's cost five times as much as water power. By 1860, however, steam was making inroads due to a diminishing supply of available water sites, improvements in steam engine construction and maintenance, and the greater availability of coal due to more efficient transportation facilities.

Machine tools are an essential ingredient to the development of factory production. The essence of mass production is the division of the manufacturing process into its logical component parts. This division requires the use of interchangeable parts. Machine tools enable workers to produce parts of uniform size, shape, and quality. These parts can then be used for the production of either consumer goods (such as clocks and firearms) or capital goods (such as textile machinery).

The United States lagged behind Britain in the early development of machine tools. This was largely due to small, localized markets, inadequate transportation and capital facilities, and British mercantilist restrictions prior to the Revolution. As a result, English tool builders dominated the field until a decade or two before the Civil War. A number immigrated to the United States. Marc Brunel, for example, became a citizen in 1796 and was actively involved in canal construction, planning the fortifications of New York Harbor, and the building of cannon. While a guest at Alexander Hamilton's house he first became interested in the construction of block machinery. Joseph Jenks emigrated from England in 1642 and constructed the first mint machinery and iron mill machinery, as well as the first machines for drawing wire, and the first fire engine. Hugh Orr, who emigrated from Scotland in 1738 introduced edged tools and the trip hammer. At least one major invention was conceived of in connection with commercial intercourse between Great Britain and the United States. The Great Western Railway operated a steamship line between Bristol and New York. In planning for a steamboat larger and faster than any hitherto afloat, the company required construction of a heavy paddle shaft that existing machinery could not produce. The shaft's designer turned to James Nasmyth, who proceeded to invent the steam hammer to perform the task. Numerous other inventions were derived from English inventors touring the United States. Joseph Whitworth, called the foremost tool builder of the nineteenth century, visited the nation in 1853. He was profoundly impressed by the machines he found in operation there and widely circulated the knowledge he had gained upon his return to England. In a report which he published about his visit he wrote:

The labouring classes are comparatively few in number, but this is counterbalanced by, and indeed, may be regarded as one of the chief causes of, the eagerness with which they call in the aid of machinery in almost every department of industry. Wherever it can be introduced as a substitute for manual labor, it is universally and willingly resorted to . . . . It is this condition of the labour market, and this eager resort to machinery wherever it can be applied, to which, under the guidance of superior education and intelligence, the remarkable prosperity of the United States is mainly due.[1]

Early American tool builders included the Jenks and Wilkinson families. The latter were actively engaged in the construction of canal locks, and pioneered in building steamboat and textile mill machinery, as well as slide lathes. James Brown, an employee of the Wilkinsons in 1817, was responsible for the production of beveled gear cutters, boring machines, grinders, and improved Blanchard lathes. In 1851 Joseph Brown developed an inexpensive caliper which permitted measurements of a thousandth of an inch, thereby spurring the growth of standardized parts manufacture.

Concurrent with the growth of the machine tool industry, a number of other inventions appeared which created new industries and accelerated factory development. The number of inventions correlated with economic growth. During the 1820's the Federal Government granted an average of 500 patent grants a year. This number increased to 600 a year during the 1840's, and by the 1850's it had increased to 2,500 a year. Innovations of great importance occurred in the food processing industry. Handmade tin cans first appeared in the 1820's. From that decade to the Civil War the principles of food sterilization and preparation were perfected. Initially the industry was confined to seafood, but by the 1840's it had expanded to fruits and vegetables. The machine production of cans began in 1855. Gail Borden's perfection of the vacuum evaporation process in the 1850's led to the canning of milk in 1865. During the Civil War the industry was further stimulated by the need to provide processed food to the army. Elias Howe's invention of the sewing machine in 1846 was also important. It was particularly crucial to the growth of the boot and shoe and garment industries. The sewing machine was responsible for shifting the locus of boot and shoe production from the home to the factory. Factory production, by permitting division of labor and improved supervision of workers, yielded a product of lower cost and more uniform quality. Factory production in the men's clothing industry did not commence until the Civil War. During that period the large demand for uniforms could not be satisfactorily met by household production. Other inventions of note included the machine production of paper, Charles Goodyear's vulcanization of rubber, Cyrus McCormick's mechanical reaper, John Deere's steel plow, and Erastus Bigelow's power loom.

The impact of the Civil War on the food processing and men's clothing industries was mirrored in other sectors of the economy. In particular, those industries related to the war effort were stimulated. In addition to men's clothing and food processing, these included the boot and shoe, leather, woolen textile, lumber, iron, wagon, and armaments industries. Until recently, economic historians generally believed that the Civil War served to spur industrial growth. The reading at the end of this chapter, by Cochran, questions this assumption. In turn, Cochran's thesis is attacked by Salsbury.

Most mills and factories before the Civil War were single proprietorships, partnerships, or unchartered joint stock companies. Partnerships, a more sophisticated version of the simple proprietorship, were created to pool capital and entrepreneurial talent. Joint stock companies, the predecessor of the modern industrial corporation, provided an effective vehicle for combining hitherto competing partnerships or proprietorships into a single production and pricing unit. In the Northeast, particularly New England, they were a significant economic force as early as the 1820's, while in the South they were not important until the 1850's. It was in the textile industry, with its relatively large scale production and capital needs, that the stock company predominated. Often attacked as a vehicle of monopoly and private wealth, the stock company was vigorously defended by early entrepreneurs. Nathan Appleton argued that "manufactures cannot be carried on to any great extent in this country in any other manner than by joint stock companies," while Erastus Bigelow asserted that without the joint company "Massachusetts can never, as a manufacturing community, attain to a high degree of productive power." By the 1850's, as a result of expanding markets, growing capital needs, and relaxation of state incorporation laws, the public stock corporation was gaining a foothold on the industrial scene. Its dominance, however, did not come until after the Civil War.

COTTON TEXTILES

It was noted earlier that factory production in the United States began in cotton textiles. The typical textile mill of 1815 was engaged in spinning thread for distribution to surrounding cottages to be woven into fabric. It was also observed that (1) this homespun was of uneven quality; (2) British cloth was preferred; and (3) the Embargo of 1807 and the War of 1812 stimulated the American textile industry by shutting out British textiles from American markets. With the return of peace, British goods once again appeared in American markets and the demand for U.S. homespun dropped precipitously. In New England practically all spinning mills were forced to close. Only in the vicinity of Philadelphia where the hand-produced product of weavers matched that of England in quality, and the frontier, where homespun was the only reasonably priced fabric, did the market for American textile yarn survive. While tariff protection, which commenced in 1816, provided some relief, the need for a revolutionary reorganization of procedures in the industry was evident.

The pioneer in this reorganization was Francis Cabot Lowell, the father of "big business" in the United States. Lowell, a wealthy merchant, had observed the operation of power looms on a visit to England immediately before the War of 1812. Armed with the concepts of the assembly line and interchangeable parts, Lowell organized the Boston Manufacturing Company in Waltham, Massachusetts in 1813, and proceeded to build the first factory in the United States wherein all phases of textile production were conducted in one building. These operations involved four stages: the preparation of the fiber, the spinning of thread, the weaving of cloth, and the bleaching, dying and printing of the cloth. Because the cloth produced by Lowell was of high and uniform quality, the success of his venture was immediate. In 1815 the sales of the company totaled $412. By 1820 they had grown to $260,658. In ten years the dividends paid to investors equaled more than twice their original investment. Beginning in 1822 other factories were established by Lowell in Massachusetts, New Hampshire, and Maine. These were staffed predominantly by farm girls who were housed in company dormitories. By 1850 the company produced one-fifth of all U.S. cotton cloth output.

The trail blazed by Lowell was quickly followed by other astute textile firms. The alternative was obvious. Spinning mill owners either enlarged the scope of their operations through the installation of power looms, or faced decline and eventual bankruptcy. As the transition occurred, textile factories arose which handled every step in the production process. By 1820 there were about 800 power looms in the nation, and the textile industry had recovered almost to its position of 1815. The center of the industry had shifted from Rhode Island to Massachusetts, and the typical firm was growing in size. Continued tariff protection, the expansion of banking facilities, and the growth of markets all contributed to industry growth. During the 1820's a fivefold expansion in the number of spindles occurred, and a tenfold increase in the number of looms. The quality of textiles produced became finer, and as this occurred the industry's ability to compete with British goods was enhanced. Primarily as a result of this growth, manufacturing surpassed commerce in importance in New England. By 1830 calico print cloth was as important as the coarse sheeting that decades earlier had been the only item produced. In the minds of consumers, however, British goods still held a slight edge, as evidenced by the fact that domestic goods were often sold under British labels, while cheap

English cloth masqueraded as American merchandise. Still, by the 1830's the American textile industry was strong enough to weather a downward revision of protective tariff rates.

The factory system spelled the end of the cottage system and the rise of the factory town. Because of the rocky and hilly land that made the region unfit for efficient farming, it was not too difficult to lure the New England farmer and his family out of agriculture to staff cotton textile factories. In addition, the many rivers and streams in the region provided the power to operate factory machinery. Despite the migration of farm families to factory towns and the influx of significant numbers of immigrants, labor remained in short supply. Thus it was that in England, the home of the power loom, hand looms continued to be used long after they had been abandoned in the United States.

The need to adopt labor-saving machinery in the U.S. textile industry had three important effects. First, it led to American inventions in an industry which hitherto had been completely dominated by British innovations. Second, it increased U.S. labor and capital productivity, thereby lowering textile costs. Labor's increased productivity is evidenced by a fourfold expansion in spindles between 1831 and 1860 accompanied by a twofold expansion in textile labor employment. (See Table 11.1.) Not only did the ratio of capital to labor increase, but so, too, did capital's productivity. This is illustrated by the fact that cotton production increased at a faster rate than the number of spindles. Third, it reduced textile prices and enhanced America's ability to compete in world markets. Cotton sheeting that sold for 18¢ a yard in 1815 was priced at 2¢ a yard by 1860. Concurrent changes occurred in the number and size of firms. The number of firms in the industry grew until 1840, when an historic high of 1,240 was reached. Thereafter, the number of firms declined. Further increases in output were made possible by significant growth in the output of the remaining firms. Increasing firm size yielded important economies of scale, a fact which further enhanced the industry's productivity. Most of the larger companies were located in New England, where the industry remained heavily entrenched down to the Civil War. In 1860, a typical New England factory averaged 6,700 spindles compared to 2,900 in the Middle Atlantic States. There were 3.8 million spindles in New England compared to a million in the Middle Atlantic States, 300,000 in the South, and 40,000 in the West. Operations in the South and West remained primitive, one-half of the output of these regions still consisting of yarn only. The industry's increased efficiency made possible significant profits. One Rhode Island firm which began operations in 1850 with a capitalization of $250,000 had generated $680,000 in dividends and an additional $500,000 in retained earnings by 1860. It is not surprising that cotton textile manufacturing was the largest United States industry. Significant though it was in size, however, it was well behind its major rival, the British textile industry. The latter in 1860 had six times as many spindles in operation. The Civil War, by shutting off raw cotton supplies to the North, temporarily slowed the growth of the industry. However, by 1880 twice as many spindles were in operation in the industry as in 1860.

TABLE 11.1. *The U.S. Cotton Textile Industry 1815-1900*

Year	Establishments	Spindles (millions)	Employees	Cotton Used (millions of pounds)
1815	—	0.1	—	—
1820	—	0.2	—	—
1831	795	1.2	62,177	77.8
1840	1,240	2.3	72,119	113.1
1850	1,094	3.6	92,286	276.1
1860	1,091	5.2	122,028	422.7
1870	956	7.1	135,369	398.3
1880	756	10.7	174,659	750.3
1890	905	14.2	218,876	1,118.0
1900	973	19.0	297,929	1,814.0

SOURCE: Melvin Copeland. *The Cotton Manufacturing Industry of the United States.* Cambridge: Harvard University Press, 1912.

IRON

American technological breakthroughs in cotton textile production were not matched in iron manufacturing. The United States, with an abundance of charcoal fuel, was not under the same stimulus as the English to seek new fuel sources and methods of production. As a consequence, the United States lagged behind England in the inventive process, and progress in the adoption of new innovations was slow. Since charcoal and iron ore were ubiquitous in location, and markets widespread and isolated, iron mills before the 1830's were small, numerous and scattered throughout the nation. One early constraint, however, was the need for water power to operate the bellows. Thus, the bulk of iron produced came from the following river valleys: Schuykill, Hudson, Potomac, and Housatonic. Not until the 1840's were the puddling process and rolling mills in wide use in American iron making. As indicated in Chapter 7, in the puddling process the iron and the fuel are separated by a wall, permitting the use of a more impure fuel, coke, and enabling the worker to manipulate the iron without removing it from the heat. This resulted in substantially lower operating costs. Rolling mills eliminated the need for blacksmiths and permitted the mass production of iron shapes, further reducing costs. When coke began to replace charcoal, a second locational constraint emerged which restricted mills to the vicinity of coal deposits. Coal fuel, of both the anthracite and bituminous variety, came into important use in the 1840's and 1860's, respectively. The former was found in eastern Pennsylvania and the latter was mined in western Pennsylvania. Anthracite iron supplanted charcoal iron in the east in the 1840's. In the west the dominance of charcoal iron over coke iron continued well into the 1850's despite its higher price. This was because of the abundance of timber in the west and the superior quality of charcoal iron, a fact that made it more desirable for the production of nails, hardware, and agricultural equipment. Improvements in the quality of coke iron in the 1850's without increases in its price, coupled with the growth of demand for train rails and industrial equipment not requiring the highest grade of iron spurred the growth of iron produced by coke in the 1860's. By the 1870's bituminous pig iron dominated crude iron production in the United States.

TABLE 11.2. *The Ten Leading Manufacturing Industries of 1860*

Industry	Employment (thousands)	Value of Product (millions of $)	Value Added (millions of $)
Cotton Textiles	115.0	107.3	54.7
Lumber	75.6	104.9	53.6
Boots and Shoes	123.0	91.9	49.2
Flour and Meal	27.7	248.6	40.0
Men's Clothing	114.8	80.8	36.7
Iron	49.0	73.2	35.7
Machinery	41.2	52.0	32.6
Woolen Products	40.6	60.7	25.0
Carriages, Wagons, & Carts	37.1	35.6	23.7
Leather	22.7	67.3	22.8

SOURCE: Eighth Census of the United States: Manufactures.

MAJOR INDUSTRIES AND MANUFACTURING REGIONS

By the time of the Civil War, only Great Britain produced more manufactures than the United States. The major American industries, in terms of value added, were cotton textiles, lumber, boots and shoes, flour and meal, men's clothing, and iron (See Table 11.2.) Of these industries, boots and shoes provided the most employment, followed by cotton textiles and men's clothing. All these industries depended heavily on products of the land in their production processes, and all but one-third produced clothing or food items.

The Middle Atlantic states led the nation in manufacturing. (See Table 11.3.) It contained the greatest number of manufacturing firms, produced the greatest output, and provided more manufacturing employment than any other section of the nation. New England was second and the West third. The West, however, possessed a greater number of manufacturing firms than did New England. On the average, Western firms were much smaller in size than those in New England, as evidenced by New England's greater capital investment in manufacturing. The South lagged behind the nation in manufacturing development. By 1860 the value of its manufactures was less than half that produced in the West and one-fifth that produced in the Middle Atlantic states. Only in the newly opened Pacific section of the country was manufacturing output smaller than that of the South.

TABLE 11.3. *The Geographic Location of Manufacturing in 1860*

Region	Number of Firms	Capital Investment (millions of $)	Employment (thousands)	Value Added (millions of $)
Middle Atlantic	53,287	435.0	546.2	358.2
New England	20,671	257.5	391.8	223.1
West	36,785	194.2	209.9	159.0
South	20,631	96.0	110.7	69.0
Pacific	8,777	23.4	50.1	42.7

SOURCE: Eighth Census of the United States: Manufactures.

FOREIGN COMMERCE

TRADE TRENDS

Despite the significant growth of manufacturing, the United States in 1860 was still, by and large, an agricultural country. It is not surprising, therefore, that agricultural products dominated our export trade. A change in the composition of those exports was evident, however, early in the period. Exports of tobacco, fish, naval stores, fur, rice, and indigo declined relative to the exports of cotton, flour, wheat, corn and lumber. Cotton found a ready market in English textile mills, while flour, wheat, and corn found access to the European Continent. In 1820 cotton, which had replaced tobacco as the nation's major export, represented two-fifths of U.S. exports, and by 1840 almost two-thirds. (See Table 11.4.) Thereafter, it steadily declined, but remained at well over half of all exports until 1860. At that time England, anticipating eminent war between the States, stockpiled large amounts, causing it again to constitute two-thirds of total exports. During the Civil War northern blockades all but destroyed the cotton trade. Foodstuffs, principally wheat, flour, corn, and pork products, and manufactures, principally lumber products, naval stores, whale products, and skins and furs, accounted for approximately equal shares of total exports. Manufactured goods constituted between fifty and seventy-five per cent of U.S. imports. (See Table 11.5.) Major imports included iron goods and fine quality fabrics of wool, cotton, and silk. Also of importance were such nonmanufactures as coffee, tea, sugar, and fine quality liquor.

TABLE 11.4. *Percentage Breakdown of U.S. Exports 1820–1860*

Year	Cotton and Other Raw Materials	Foodstuffs	Manufactures
1820	60%	23%	17%
1830	61	20	19
1840	67	17	16
1850	61	20	19
1860	68	18	14

SOURCE: Douglass C. North. *Economic Growth of the United States 1790–1860.* Englewood Cliffs: Prentice-Hall, Inc., p. 284.

Europe was the United States' principal trading partner from 1815 to 1865. It supplied two-thirds of our imports and purchased three-quarters of our exports. As in the colonial period, England dominated American international trade, with France second in importance. Trade with the West Indies during this period was in relative decline. The United States experienced adverse trade balances from 1815 up to the Civil War. (See Figure 11.1.) The only exceptions were years of depression when, owing to declining personal income, imports fell. Simultaneously, falling prices stimulated exports. Earnings of the U.S. merchant marine and foreign investment flows to the United States financed trade deficits. By the Civil War, foreigners owned one-fifth of American manufacturing and transportation capital. The acceleration of immigration to the United States in

TABLE 11.5. *Percentage Breakdown of U.S. Imports 1821–1860*

Year	Raw Materials*	Foodstuffs	Manufactures
1821	18%	17%	65%
1830	22	13	65
1840	26	14	60
1850	17	12	71
1860	24	17	59

SOURCE: Douglass C. North. *Economic Growth of the United States 1790–1860.* Englewood Cliffs: Prentice-Hall, Inc., 1961, p. 288.

*Includes coffe, tea, fruit, and spices.

the 1830's and 1840's provided a new source of capital to finance trade imbalances. Although individual immigrant savings were small, the cumulative totals of this group were substantial. In the 1850's gold flows from California provided an additional source of funds.

TRADE FLUCTUATIONS

Following the restoration of peace in 1815, there occurred a significant revival of American foreign commerce. This revival was sparked by a substantial pent-up demand on the part of both foreigners and Americans for goods which could not be obtained during the war. From 1819 to 1830 there occurred a recession in U.S. foreign commerce. Three reasons account for the decline. First, the pent-up demand of the postwar years was satisfied. Second, the United States and Europe erected tariff walls. Third, the growth of American domestic commerce diverted entrepreneural attention away from foreign markets.

Tariff reductions commencing in 1833 stimulated a modest increase in the volume of foreign trade during the 1830's and 1840's. However, the sharp decline in product prices following the panic of 1837 resulted in a decline in total dollar value. From 1847 to the Civil War foreign commerce enjoyed a period of significant growth. Three factors accounted for this growth. First, gold discoveries throughout the world, including the United States, caused prices to rise, which in turn stimulated production and trade. Second, tariffs continued to decline. Third, poor crops in Europe created famine conditions. European countries turned to the United States for food supplies. In particular, England, which had become dependent on outside food supplies to support its growing industrial population, was forced to repeal its Corn Laws. These laws had restricted severely the importation of American grain. Happily, the growth in demand

FIGURE 11.1. *U.S. Imports and Exports 1790 – 1860*

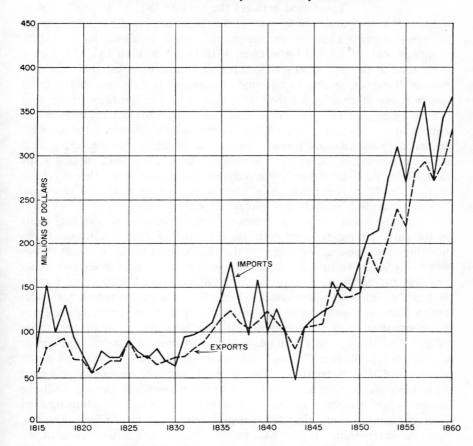

SOURCE: Douglass C. North, *Economic Growth of the United States, 1790 – 1860* (Englewood Cliffs: Prentice-Hall, 1961), p.84.

for U.S. food exports coincided with great increases in American farm output. Even though cotton still retained its position as the dominant export, foodstuffs from the late 1840's on accounted for a growing share of U.S. foreign trade. The Civil War caused a decline in both exports and imports. The former was due entirely to the cessation of cotton exports. All other exports, particularly grains, grew significantly. From 1860 to 1863 wheat exports expanded ninefold and grain replaced cotton as the leading export. English crop failures in the early 1860's helped contribute to the large demand for American grain. A Northern blockade of Southern ports, and a rise in tariff walls, accounted for import declines.

THE MERCHANT MARINE

The period between the War of 1812 and the Civil War was one of growth and then decline for American shipbuilding and shipping. In terms of gross tonnage the merchant marine increased its size from a prewar peak of 1.1 million tons in 1810 to 5.5 million by 1861. For a short time in the mid-1850's U.S. tonnage almost equalled that of Great Britain. However, relative to national income and population, shipbuilding and shipping never achieved the importance it held in the period preceding the Embargo Act of 1807. Per capita tonnage in foreign trade stood at approximately eight tons in 1855 as compared to thirteen tons in 1807. Increasingly the nation turned inward to develop manufacturing and domestic commerce. America's continued reliance on wooden sailing ships rather than iron steamships eventually led to the decline of the merchant marine. In 1826 American ships carried 93 per cent of the country's foreign trade, but by 1860 they carried only 66 per cent.

As was noted earlier, America's competitiveness on the high seas in the early 1800's stemmed from its comparative cost advantage in the building of wooden sailing ships. By the 1830's some of this cost advantage was being lost. The fine stands of American oak and pine along the coastline was rapidly being exhausted. Shipbuilders were forced to go farther and farther inland to find suitable logs. This sharply increased transportation charges, which constituted the principal item in timber costs. Even more important was the refinement of ships powered by steam and made of iron. Ironically, it was America which pioneered in the development of the steamship. Robert Fulton's *Clermont* successfully navigated up the Hudson in 1807. Thirteen years later the American built *Savannah*, equipped with both steam and sail, made the first transatlantic voyage utilizing steam. While American businessmen saw the potential of steamships for river and coastal trade, they felt it would never be a match for the sailing ship in international trade. Meanwhile, British shipbuilders, aided by generous government construction and operating subsides, pressed forward. By the early 1840's British steamships, including the ships of the newly formed Cunard Line, were making regular transatlantic crossings. Shortly thereafter, England began to replace her wooden ships with iron ones. Abundant supplies of coal and iron located close to the coast, together with superior knowledge of metallurgy, provided the British with a decided comparative cost advantage over the United States. By the early 1850's approximately one-fourth of newly constructed British tonnage was iron. These ships' larger cargo spaces further injured the position of American sailing ships. In a vain effort to recover some of their lost market, American shipbuilders turned to the clippers. More a work of art than a commerical vessel, the clipper was a long narrow ship standing high in the water. It required a heavy complement of sail and a large crew to man her. It was built for speed rather than for economy. These "greyhounds of the seas" could travel as fast as some present day ocean going vessels. They cut the run from New York to Canton, China from 150 days to 84 days. However, their small cargo capacity and high operating costs made them very expensive to operate. Except for runs to California following the 1849 gold discoveries, they proved to be unprofitable. First constructed in the mid-1840's they were, for the most part, discontinued after 1851. By the Civil War American shipping was increasingly being restricted to the profitable coastal trade, which since 1818 had been protected by Federal law. In addition, large numbers of American shipowners sought foreign registry for their vessels. This practice was accelerated sharply during the War as Confederate raiders preyed on Northern shipping.

TARIFFS
During this period tariffs continued to supply the Federal Government with its principal source of revenue. It has already been observed that American manufacturing experienced substantial growth from 1807 to 1815, and that the return of peace brought numerous bankruptcies among infant American industries who found themselves unequal to foreign competition. Northern manufacturers, seeking relief, lobbied for more substantial tariff protection. Despite the opposition of New England shipping interests, an average import duty of twenty per cent was imposed in 1816. This represented an increase of approximately five per cent over the tariff level prevailing prior to the War of 1812. This increase only whetted the appetite of protectionists. As manufacturing gained in relative importance to shipping, the conflict between merchant capitalists, who opposed all protective tariffs, and industrial capitalists, who favored high tariffs, intensified. As the former lost economic and political power, the protectionists were increasingly able to impose their will. As a result, tariffs were raised in 1818, 1819, 1824, and 1828. The Tariff of 1828, termed by its opponents the Tariff of Abominations, raised the average duty to over fifty per cent. This rate was the highest of any tariff prior to the Civil War. (See Figure 11.2.)

The West supported Northern industrialists in their demand for tariff legislation. Western states reasoned that rapid growth in Northern urban industry would stimulate demand for Western foodstuffs. Influenced by Henry Clay's "American System," the West also believed that the revenues gained from high tariffs would be used to develop transportation facilities between the manufacturing East and the agricultural West. The South continued its traditional opposition to tariffs, which it believed favored Northern manufacturers at the expense of Southern cotton growers. Their opposition stemmed from their dependence on European markets for the export of cotton and their desire to pay lower prices for manufactured

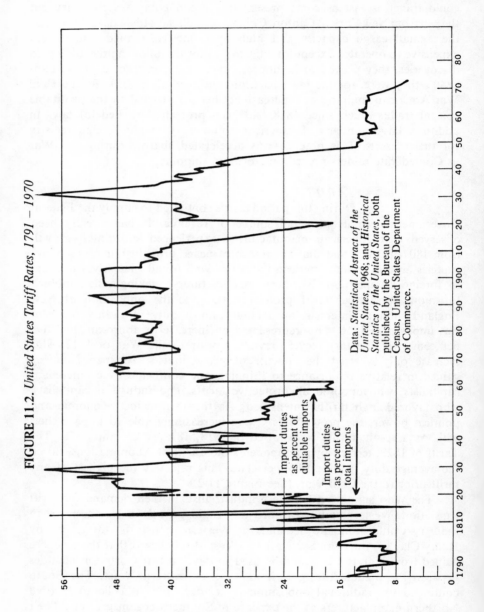

FIGURE 11.2. *United States Tariff Rates, 1791 – 1970*

Import duties as percent of dutiable imports

Import duties as percent of total imports

Data: *Statistical Abstract of the United States,* 1968; and *Historical Statistics of the United States,* both published by the Bureau of the Census, United States Department of Commerce.

SOURCE: Robert L. Young and Ingo Walter, *The Formation of United States Trade Policy* (New York: New York University Institute of Finance 1971), p. 26.

goods. In 1832 South Carolina asserted state sovereignty and declared in an Ordinance of Nullification that it had no intention of abiding by the tariffs of 1828 and 1832. The latter reduced rates to about thirty-five per cent, the average level in effect in 1824. Had a compromise tariff not been passed in 1833, the issue of state secession may well have been decided in the 1830's rather than the 1860's. In deference to the South, tariff walls were generally lowered from 1833 down to the Civil War. By the outbreak of the Civil War they were at about the same level as they had been in 1816. The need for substantial revenues to finance war expenditures and the absence of Southern representatives in the Congress resulted in substantial tariff increases during the Civil War, and the average level was raised to forty-five per cent.

NOTES

1. Joseph W. Roe. *English and American Tool Builders*. New Haven: Yale University Press, 1915, p. 104.

SELECTED REFERENCES

1. Victor S. Clark. *History of Manufactures in the United States. 1607-1914*, Vol. I. New York: McGraw Hill, 1929.
2. Melvin T. Copeland. *The Cotton Manufacturing Industry of the United States*. Cambridge: Harvard University Press, 1912.
3. Emory R. Johnson, *et al. History of Domestic and Foreign Commerce in the United States*, Vol. I. Washington, D.C.: Carnegie Institution, 1915.
4. Douglass C. North. "The United States Balance of Payments, 1790-1860," *Trends in the American Economy in the Nineteenth Century. Studies in Income and Wealth*. Princeton: Princeton University Press, 1960.
5. Frank W. Taussig. *The Tariff History of the United States*. New York: G. P. Putnam's Sons, 1964.
6. Caroline Ware. *The Early New England Cotton Manufacture*. Boston: Houghton Mifflin, 1931.

readings

did the civil war retard or spur american manufacturing development?

ONE VIEW: *thomas c. cochran*

In most textbook and interpretative histories of the United States the Civil War has been assigned a major role in bringing about the American Industrial Revolution.[1] Colorful business developments in the North—adoption of new machines, the quick spread of war contracting, the boost given to profits by inflation, and the creation of a group of war millionaires—make the war years seem not only a period of rapid economic change but also one that created important forces for future growth. The superficial qualitative evidence is so persuasive that apparently few writers have examined the available long-run statistical series before adding their endorsement to the conventional interpretation. The following quotations taken from the books of two generations of leading scholars illustrate the popular view.[2]

"The so-called Civil War," wrote Charles A. and Mary R. Beard in 1927, "...was a social war...making *vast changes* in the arrangement of classes, in the accumulation and distribution of wealth, *in the course of industrial development*."[3] Midway between 1927 and the present, Arthur M. Schlesinger, Sr., wrote: "On these tender industrial growths the Civil War *had the effect of a hothouse*. For reasons already clear . . . nearly every branch of industry grew lustily."[4] Harold U. Faulkner, whose textbook sales have ranked near or at the top, said in 1954: "In

Reprinted with permission from "Did the Civil War Retard Industrialization?" by Thomas C. Cochran, in *The Mississippi Valley Historical Review*, XLVIII (September 1961), pp. 197-210.

the economic history of the United States the Civil War was extremely important. . . . In the North *it speeded the Industrial Revolution* and the development of capitalism by the prosperity which it brought to industry."[5] The leading new text of 1957, by Richard Hofstadter, William Miller, and Daniel Aaron, showed no weakening of this interpretation: "The growing demand for farm machinery as well as for the 'sinews of war' led to American industrial expansion. . . . Of necessity, *iron, coal, and copper* production boomed during the war years."[6] A sophisticated but still essentially misleading view is presented by Gilbert C. Fite and Jim E. Reese in a text of 1959: "The Civil War proved to be a boon to Northern economic development. . . . Industry, for example, was not created by the war, but wartime demands *greatly stimulated and encouraged industrial development* which already had a good start."[7] In a reappraisal of the Civil War, in *Harper's Magazine* for April, 1960, Denis W. Brogan, a specialist in American institutions, wrote: "It may have been only a catalyst but the War *precipitated the entry* of the United States *into the modern industrial world*, made 'the take-off' (to use Professor W. W. Rostow's brilliant metaphor) come sooner."[8]

In all of these reiterations of the effect of the Civil War on industrialism, statistical series seem to have been largely neglected. None of the authors cited reinforce their interpretations by setting the war period in the context of important long-run indexes of industrial growth. Since 1949, series for the period 1840 to 1890 that would cast doubt on the conventional generalizations have been available in *Historical Statistics of the United States, 1789-1945.*[9] In 1960 a new edition of *Historical Statistics* and the report of the Conference on Research in Income and Wealth on *Trends in the American Economy in the Nineteenth Century* have provided additional material to support the argument that the Civil War retarded American industrial development.[10] These volumes give data for many growth curves for the two decades before and after the war decade — in other words, the long-run trends before and after the event in question. The pattern of these trends is a mixed one which shows no uniform type of change during the Civil War decade, but on balance for the more important series the trend is toward retardation in *rates* of growth rather than toward acceleration. This fact is evident in many series which economists would regard as basic to economic growth, but in order to keep the discussion within reasonable limits only a few can be considered here.

Robert E. Gallman has compiled new and more accurate series for both "total commodity output," including agriculture, and "value added by manufacture," the two most general measures of economic growth available for this period. He writes: "Between 1839 and 1899 total commodity output increased elevenfold, or at an average decade rate of slightly less than 50 per cent. . . . Actual rates varied fairly widely, high rates appearing during the decades ending with 1854 and 1884, and a very low rate during the decade ending with 1869."[11] From the over-all standpoint this statement indicates the immediately retarding effect of the Civil War on American economic growth, but since most of the misleading statements are made in regard to industrial growth, or particular elements in industrial growth, it is necessary to look in more detail at "value added by manufacture" and some special series. Gallman's series for value added in constant dollars of the purchasing power of 1879 shows a rise of 157 per cent from 1839 to 1849; 76 per cent from 1849 to 1859; and only 25 per cent from 1859 to 1869.[12] By the 1870's the more favorable prewar rates were resumed, with an increase of 82 per cent for 1869-1879, and 112 per cent for 1879-1889. Thus two decades of very rapid advance, the 1840's and the 1880's, are separated by thirty years of slower growth which falls to the lowest level in the decade that embraces the Civil War.

Pig-iron production in tons, perhaps the most significant commodity index of nineteenth-century American industrial growth, is available year-by-year from 1854 on. Taking total production for five-year periods, output increased 9 per cent between the block of years from 1856 to 1860 and the block from 1861 to 1865. That even this slight increase might not have been registered except for the fact that 1857 to 1860 were years of intermittent depression is indicated by an 81 per cent increase over the war years in the block of years from 1866 to 1870.[13] If annual production is taken at five-year intervals, starting in 1850, the increase is 24 per cent from 1850 to 1855; 17 per cent from 1855 to 1860; 1 per cent from 1860 to 1865; and 100 per cent from 1865 to 1870. While there is no figure available for 1845, the period from 1840 to 1850 shows 97 per cent increase in shipments, while for the period 1870 to 1880 the increase was 130 per cent. To sum up, depression and war appear to have retarded a curve of production that was tending to rise at a high rate.

Bituminous coal production may be regarded as the next most essential commodity series. After a gain of 199 per cent from 1840 to 1850 this series shows a rather steady pattern of increase at rates varying from 119 to 148 per cent each decade from 1850 to 1890. The war does not appear to have markedly affected the rate of growth.[14]

In the mid-nineteenth century copper production was not a basic series for recording American growth, but since three distinguished authors have singled it out as one of the indexes of the effect of the war on industry it is best to cite the statistics. Before 1845 production of domestic copper was negligible. By 1850 the "annual recoverable content" of copper from United States mines was 728 tons, by 1860 it was 8,064 tons, by 1865 it was 9,520 tons, and by 1870 it was 14,112 tons. In this series of very small quantities, therefore, the increase from 1850 to 1860 was just over 1,000 per cent, from 1860 to 1865 it was 18 per cent, and from 1865 to 1870 it was 48 per cent.[15]

Railroad track, particularly in the United States, was an essential for industrialization. Here both the depression and the war retarded the rate of growth. From 1851 through 1855 a total of 11,627 miles of new track was laid, from 1856 through 1860, only 8,721 miles, and from 1861 through 1865, only 4,076 miles. After the war the rate of growth of the early 1850's was resumed, with 16,174 miles constructed from 1866 through 1870. Looked at by decades, a rate of over 200 per cent increase per decade in the twenty years before the war was slowed to 70 per cent for the period from 1860 to 1870, with only a 15 per cent increase during the war years. In the next two decades the rate averaged about 75 per cent.[16]

Next to food, cotton textiles may be taken as the most representative consumer-goods industry in the nineteenth century. Interference with the flow of southern cotton had a depressing effect. The number of bales of cotton consumed in United States manufacturing rose 143 per cent from 1840 to 1850 and 47 per cent from 1850 to 1860, but *fell* by 6 per cent from 1860 to 1870. From then on consumption increased at a little higher rate than in the 1850's.[17]

While woolen textile production is not an important series in the overall picture of industrial growth, it should be noted that, helped by protection and military needs, consumption of wool for manufacturing more than doubled during the war, and then *fell* somewhat from 1865 to 1870. But Arthur H. Cole, the historian of the woolen industry, characterizes the years from 1830 to 1870 as a period of growth "not so striking as in the decades before or afterwards."[18]

Immigration to a nation essentially short of labor was unquestionably a stimulant to economic growth. Another country had paid for the immigrant's unproductive youthful years, and he came to the United States ready to contribute his labor at a low cost. The pattern of the curve for annual immigration shows the retarding effect of both depression and war. In the first five years of the 1850's an average of 349,685 immigrants a year came to the United States. From 1856 through 1860 the annual average fell to 169,958, and for the war years of 1861 to 1865 it fell further to 160,345. In the first five postwar years the average rose to 302,620, but not until the first half of the 1870's did the rate equal that of the early 1850's. Had there been a return to prosperity instead of war in 1861, it seems reasonable to suppose that several hundred thousand additional immigrants would have arrived before 1865.[19]

In the case of farm mechanization the same type of error occurs as in the annual series on copper production. "Random" statistics such as the manufacture of 90,000 reapers in 1864 are frequently cited without putting them in the proper perspective of the total number in use and the continuing trends. Reaper and mower sales started upward in the early 1850's and were large from 1856 on, in spite of the depression. William T. Hutchinson estimates that most of the 125,000 reapers and mowers in use in 1861 had been sold during the previous five years.[20] While the business, without regard to the accidental coming of the war, was obviously in a stage of very rapid growth, the war years presented many difficulties and may actually have retarded the rate of increase.[21] Total sales of reapers for the period 1861-1865 are estimated at 250,000 — a quite ordinary increase for a young industry — but the 90,000 figure for 1864, if it is correct, reinforces the evidence from the McCormick correspondence that this was the one particularly good year of the period. During these years William S. McCormick was often of the opinion that the "uncertainties of the times" made advisable a suspension of manufacturing until the close of the war.[22]

For a broader view of agricultural mechanization the series "value of farm implements and machinery" has special interest. Here the census gives a picture which, if correct, is explicable only on the basis of wartime destruction. Based on constant dollars the average value of machinery per farm *fell* nearly 25 per cent in the decade of the war and showed nearly a 90 per cent gain in the 1870's.[23] Differing from these census figures is a series prepared by Marvin W. Towne and Wayne D. Rasmussen based on the production of farm machinery. While this obviously does not take account of destruction of existing equipment or the rapid increase in the number of farms, the record of new production is hard to reconcile with the census figures. The production of implements and machinery reckoned in constant dollars is a sharply rising curve from 1850 on, with increases of 110 per cent from 1850 to 1860; 140 per cent from 1860 to 1870; and 95 per cent from 1870 to 1880.[24] Meanwhile the number of farms increased by about one third in each of the decades of the 1850's and 1860's and by one half in the 1870's.[25] Whatever interpretation is given to these figures, it does not appear that the war greatly increased the trend of agricultural mechanization. The series for gross farm product in constant dollars shows wide variations in increase from decade to decade, with the 1860's in the low group. The gains were 23 per cent, 1840 to 1850; 42 per cent, 1850 to 1860; 21 per cent, 1860 to 1870; 52 per cent, 1870 to 1880; and 20 per cent, 1880 to 1890.[26]

Much American business expansion was financed by short-term bank loans continuously renewed. Thus major increases in business activity should be mirrored in increases in bank loans, both for financing short-term transactions and for additions to plant and working capital that would, in fact, be paid off gradually. If there was a really great Civil War boom in business activity it should be indicated in the series "total loans" of all banks. But it is not. In constant dollars, bank loans fell slightly between 1840 and 1850, and rose nearly 50 per cent by 1860. It should be noted that none of these three decadal years were periods of high prosperity. During the war Confederate banking statistics were not reported by the comptroller of the currency, but by 1866 there is a comparable figure for the nation as a whole, and in constant dollars it is some 35 per cent below that of 1860. Even by 1870 the constant dollar value of all loans was more than 15 per cent lower than just before the war. If instead of examining loans one looks at total assets of all banks the decline in constant dollars from 1860 to 1870 is reduced to 10 per cent, the difference arising from a larger cash position and more investment in government bonds.[27]

Net capital formation would be a more proper index of economic growth than bank loans or assets. Unfortunately, neither the teams of the National Bureau of Economic Research nor those of the Census Bureau have been able to carry any reliable series back of 1868. From colonial times to 1960, however, the chief single form of American capital formation has undoubtedly been building construction. Farm houses, city homes, public buildings, stores, warehouses, and factories have year-by-year constituted, in monetary value, the leading type of capital growth. Gallman has drawn up series for such construction based on estimating the flow of construction materials and adding what appear to be appropriate markups.[28] Admittedly the process in inexact, but because of the importance of construction in reflecting general trends in capital formation it is interesting to see the results. The rate of change for the ten-year period ending in 1854 is about 140 per cent; for the one ending in 1859 it is 90 per cent; for 1869 it is 40 per cent; and for 1879 it is 46 per cent. Taking a long view, from 1839 to 1859 the average decennial rate of increase was about 70 per cent, and from 1869 to 1899 it was about 40 per cent.[29] The *rate* of advance in construction was declining and the war decade added a further dip to the decline.

Since the decline in rate is for the decade, the exact effect of the war years can only be estimated, but the logic of the situation, reinforced by the record of sharp cut-backs in railroad building, seems inescapable: the Civil War, like all modern wars, checked civilian construction. The first year of war was a period of depression and tight credit in the Middle West, which checked residential and farm construction in the area that grew most rapidly before and after the war. In both the East and the West the last two years of the war were a period of rapid inflation which was regarded by businessmen as a temporary wartime phenomenon. The logical result would be to postpone construction for long-term use until after the anticipated deflation. The decline in private railroad construction to a small fraction of the normal rate exemplifies the situation.

Lavish expenditure and speculation by a small group of war contractors and market operators gambling on the inflation seem to have created a legend of high prosperity during the war years. But the general series on fluctuations in the volume of business do not bear this out. Leonard P. Ayres's estimates of business activity place the average for 1861 through

1865 below normal, and Norman J. Silberling's business index is below its normal line for all years of the war.[30] Silberling also has an intermediate trend line for business, which smooths out annual fluctuations. This line falls steadily from 1860 to 1869.[31] Much of Silberling's discussion in his chapter "Business Activity, Prices, and Wars" is in answer to his question: "Why does it seem to be true that despite a temporary stimulating effect of war upon some industries, wars are generally associated with a long-term retarding of business growth . . . ?"[32] He puts the Civil War in this general category.

Collectively these statistical estimates support a conclusion that the Civil War retarded American industrial growth. Presentation of this view has been the chief purpose of this article. To try to judge the non-measurable or indirect effects of the war is extremely difficult. But since further discussion of the conventional qualitative factors may help to explain the prevailing evaluation in American texts, it seems appropriate to add some conjectural obiter dicta.

Experience with the apparently stimulating effects of twentieth-century wars on production makes the conclusion that victorious war may retard the growth of an industrial state seem paradoxical, and no doubt accounts in part for the use of detached bits of quantitative data to emphasize the Civil War's industrial importance.[33] The resolution of the paradox may be found in contemporary conditions in the United States and in the nature of the wartime demand. The essential wastefulness of war from the standpoint of economic growth was obscured by the accident that both of the great European wars of the twentieth century began when the United States had a high level of unemployment. The immediate effect of each, therefore, was to put men to work, to increase the national product, and to create an aura of prosperity. Presumably, the United States of the mid-nineteenth century tended to operate close enough to full employment in average years that any wasteful labor-consuming activities were a burden rather than a stimulant.

By modern standards the Civil War was still unmechanized. It was fought with rifles, bayonets, and sabers by men on foot or horseback. Artillery was more used than in previous wars, but was still a relatively minor consumer of iron and steel. The railroad was also brought into use, but the building of military lines offset only a small percentage of the over-all drop from the prewar level of civilian railroad construction. Had all of these things not been true, the Confederacy with its small industrial development could never have fought through four years of increasingly effective blockade.

In spite of the failure of direct quantitative evidence to show accelerating effects of the war on rates of economic growth, there could be long-run effects of a qualitative type that would gradually foster a more rapid rate of economic growth. The most obvious place to look for such indirect effects would be in the results of freeing the slaves. Marxists contended that elimination of slavery was a necessary precursor of the bourgeois industrialism which would lead to the socialist revolution. The creation of a free Negro labor force was, of course, of great long-run importance. In the twentieth century it has led to readjustment of Negro population between the deep South and the northern industrial areas, and to changes in the use of southern land.

But economically the effects of war and emancipation over the period 1840 to 1880 were negative. Richard A. Easterlin writes: "In every southern state, the 1880 level of per capita income originating in commodity production and distribution was below, or at best only slightly above that of 1840. . . . [This] attests strikingly to the impact of that war and the subsequent disruption on the southern economy."[34] In general the Negroes became sharecroppers or wage laborers, often cultivating the same land and the same crops as before the war. In qualification of the argument that free Negro labor led to more rapid industrialization it should be noted that the South did not keep up with the national pace in the growth of non-agricultural wealth until after 1900.[35]

Two indirect effects of the war aided industrial growth to degrees that cannot accurately be measured. These were, first, a more satisfactory money market, and, secondly, more security for entrepreneurial activity than in the prewar period. The sharp wartime inflation had the usual effect of transferring income from wage, salary, and interest receivers to those making profits. This meant concentration of savings in the hands of entrepreneurs who would invest in new activities; and this no doubt helps to explain the speculative booms of the last half of the 1860's and first two years of the 1870's which have been treated as the prosperity resulting from the war. Inflation also eased the burdens of those railroads which had excessive mortgage debts. But a great deal of new research would be needed to establish causal connections between the inflationary reallocation of wealth, 1863 to 1865, and the high rate of industrial progress in the late 1870's and the 1880's.

The National Banking Act, providing a more reliable currency for interstate operations, has been hailed as a great aid to business expansion although it would be hard to demonstrate, aside from a few weeks during panics, that plentiful but occasionally unsound currency had seriously interfered with earlier industrial growth.[36] The existence of two and a half billion dollars in federal bonds also provided a basis for credit that was larger than before the war. This led to broader and more active security markets as well as to easier personal borrowing. But two qualifications must be kept in mind. First, local bank lending to favored borrowers had probably tended to be too liberal before the war and was now put on a somewhat firmer basis. In other words, since 1800 a multiplication of banks had made credit relatively easy to obtain in the United States, and in the North this continued to be the situation. Second, the southern banking system was largely destroyed by the war and had to be rebuilt in the subsequent decades. It should also be remembered that by 1875 some 40 per cent of the banks were outside the national banking system.[37]

Because of a few colorful speculators like Jay Gould, Daniel Drew, and Jim Fisk, and the immortality conferred on them, initially by the literary ability of the Adams brothers, the New York stock exchange in the postwar decade appears to have mirrored a new era of predatory wealth. But one has only to study the scandals of the London and New York stock exchanges in 1854 to see that there was little growth in the sophistication or boldness of stock operators during these fifteen years.[38] In any case, the exploits of market operators were seldom related in a positive way to economic growth. Even a record of new issues of securities, which is lacking for this period, would chiefly reflect the flow of capital into railroads, banks, and public utilities rather than into manufacturing. Very few "industrial" shares were publicly marketed before the decade of the 1880's; such enterprises grew chiefly from the reinvestment of earnings.

There was strong government encouragement to entrepreneurial activity during the Civil War, but to ascribe to it unusual importance for economic growth requires both analysis of the results and comparison with other periods. Government in the United States has almost always encouraged entrepreneurs. The federal and state administration preceding the Civil War could certainly be regarded as friendly to business. They subsidized railroads by land grants, subscribed to corporate bond issues, and remitted taxes on new enterprise.[39] Tariffs were low, but railroad men and many bankers were happy with the situation. Whether or not American industrialism was significantly accelerated by the high protection that commenced with the war is a question that economists will probably never settle.

The building of a subsidized transcontinental railroad, held back by sectional controversies in the 1850's, was authorized along a northern route with the help of federal loans and land grants when the southerners excluded themselves from Congress. Putting more than a hundred million dollars into this project in the latter half of the 1860's, however, may have had an adverse effect on industrial growth. In general, the far western roads were built for speculative and strategic purposes uneconomically ahead of demand. They may for a decade, or even two, have consumed more capital than their transportation services were then worth to the economy.

To sum up this part of the obiter dictum, those who write of the war creating a national market tied together by railroads underestimate both the achievements of the two decades before the war and the ongoing trends of the economy. The nation's business in 1855 was nearly as intersectional as in 1870. Regional animosities did not interfere with trade, nor did these feelings diminish after the war. By the late 1850's the United States was a rapidly maturing industrial state with its major cities connected by rail, its major industries selling in a national market, and blessed or cursed with financiers, security flotations, stock markets, and all the other appurtenances of industrial capitalism.

But when all specific factors of change attributable to the war have been deflated, there is still the possibility that northern victory had enhanced the capitalist spirit, that as a consequence the atmosphere of government in Washington among members of both parties was more friendly to industrial enterprise and to northern-based national business operations than had formerly been the rule. It can be argued that in spite of Greenbackers and discontented farmers legislation presumably favorable to industry could be more readily enacted. The Fourteenth Amendment, for example, had as a by-product greater security for interstate business against state regulation, although it was to be almost two decades before the Supreme Court would give force to this protection. By 1876, a year of deep depression, the two major parites were trying to outdo each other in promises of stimulating economic growth. This highly generalized type of argument is difficult to evaluate, but in qualification of any theory of a sharp change in attitude we should remember that industrialism was growing rapidly from general causes and that by the 1870's it was to be expected that major-party politics would be conforming to this change in American life.

Massive changes in physical environment such as those accompanying the rise of trade at the close of the Middle Ages or the gradual growth of industrialism from the seventeenth century on do not lend themselves readily to exact or brief periodization. If factory industry and mechanized transportation be taken as the chief indexes of early industrialism, its spread in the United States was continuous and rapid during the entire nineteenth century, but in general, advance was greater during periods of prosperity than in depressions. The first long period without a major depression, after railroads, canals, and steamboats had opened a national market, was from 1843 to 1857. Many economic historians interested in quantitative calculations would regard these years as marking the appearance of an integrated industrial society. Walter W. Rostow, incidentally, starts his "take-off" period in the 1840's and calls it completed by 1860.[40] Others might prefer to avoid any narrow span of years. Few, however, would see a major stimulation to economic growth in the events of the Civil War.

Finally, one may speculate as to why this exaggerated conception of the role of the Civil War in industrialization gained so firm a place in American historiography. The idea fits, of course, into the Marxian frame of revolutionary changes, but it seems initially to have gained acceptance quite independently of Marxian influences. More concentrated study of the war years than of any other four-year span in the nineteenth century called attention to technological and business events usually overlooked. Isolated facts were seized upon without comparing them with similar data for other decades. The desire of teachers for neat periodization was probably a strong factor in quickly placing the interpretation in textbooks; thus, up to 1860 the nation was agricultural, after 1865 it was industrial. Recent study of American cultural themes suggests still another reason. From most standpoints the Civil War was a national disaster, but Americans like to see their history in terms of optimism and progress. Perhaps the war was put in a perspective suited to the culture by seeing it as good because in addition to achieving freedom for the Negro it brought about industrial progress.

NOTES

1. This article is based on a paper presented by the author at the annual meeting of the Mississippi Valley Historical Association in Louisville in April, 1960.
2. These particular authors are cited merely as examples of historical opinion, not because they are more in error than others. The reader needs only to take down other texts from his own shelf to find similar statements.
3. *The Rise of American Civilization* (2 vols., New York, 1927), II, 53. In this and the following quotations the italics are mine.
4. Homer C. Hockett and Arthur M. Schlesinger, *Land of the Free: A Short History of the American People* (New York, 1944), 355. Schlesinger wrote the section beginning with the Civil War.
5. *American Economic History* (7th ed., New York, 1954), 345. The same statement appears in a later edition (New York, 1960), 345.
6. *The United States: The History of a Republic* (Englewood Cliffs, N. J., 1957), 381.
7. *An Economic History of the United States* (Boston, 1959), 284.
8. "A Fresh Appraisal of the Civil War," *Harper's Magazine* (New York), CCXX (April, 1960), 140.
9. U. S. Bureau of the Census, *Historical Statistics of the United States, 1789-1945* (Washington, 1949).
10. U. S. Bureau of the Census, *Historical Statistics of the United States: Colonial Times to 1957* (Washington, 1960); *Trends in the American Economy in the Nineteenth Century* (Princeton, 1960), published by the National Bureau of Economic Research as Volume XXIV of its *Studies in Income and Wealth*.
11. *Trends in the American Economy*, 15.

12. *Historical Statistics* (1960 ed.), 402. "Constant" or "real" means dollars adjusted to eliminate price changes. It should be remembered that all series expressed in current dollars need to be corrected for rather violent price movements during these fifty years. Precise adjustments would vary with every series, and would involve many problems, but the movement of wholesale prices in general (Warren-Pearson Index) may be roughly summarized as follows. In 1850 prices were 12 per cent lower than in 1840, but by 1860 they were 11 per cent higher than in 1850. From 1860 to 1865 prices rose 99 per cent, but by 1870 the increase for the decade was only 46 per cent. By 1880 the decline for the decade was 26 per cent, and for the decade ending in 1890 it was 18 per cent. *Ibid.,* 115. In other words, current dollars are a very unreliable indicator, particularly as applied to wholesale prices.

13. *Ibid.,* 365-66.

14. *Ibid.,* 357.

15. *Ibid.,* 368.

16. *Ibid.,* 427-28.

17. *Historical Statistics* (1949 ed.), 187. This table is not carried back to 1840 in the 1960 edition.

18. Arthur H. Cole, *The American Wool Manufacture* (2 vols., Cambridge, 1926), I, 392.

19. *Historical Statistics* (1960 ed.), 57.

20. William T. Hutchinson, *Cyrus Hall McCormick* (2 vols., New York, 1930-1935), II, 67.

21. *Ibid.,* II, 67-95.

22. *Ibid.,* II, 88.

23. *Historical Statistics* (1960 ed.), 285. For price index see note 12, above.

24. *Trends in the American Economy,* 276.

25. The percentage increases were 41 per cent (1860 over 1850); 30 per cent (1870 over 1860); and 51 per cent (1880 over 1870). *Historical Statistics* (1960 ed.), 278.

26. *Ibid.,* 284.

27. *Ibid.,* 624. The reader is again warned that deflation of current dollar values for this early period is an inexact process.

28. *Trends in the American Economy,* 60-64.

29. *Ibid.,* 24. Gallman has two alternate series which I have averaged. For the purposes of this paper either series leads to the same conclusions.

30. Leonard P. Ayres, *Turning Points in Business Cycles* (New York, 1939), 14; Norman J. Silberling, *The Dynamics of Business* (New York, 1943), 50.

31. Silberling, *Dynamics of Business,* 61.

32. *Ibid.,* 66.

33. Ayres, Silberling, and some other students of economic activity such as Herbert Hoover, however, blame the breakdown of the 1930's on the dislocations caused by World War I. *Ibid.,* 65-66. See also *The Memoirs of Herbert Hoover: The Great Depression, 1929-1941* (New York, 1952), 105.

34. *Trends in the American Economy,* 85.

35. Simon Kuznets (ed.), *Population Redistribution and Economic Growth: United States, 1870-1950* (2 vols., Philadelphia, 1957-1960), I (*Methodological Considerations and Reference Tables*), 729-32; II (*Analysis of Economic Change*), 109.

36. See Bray Hammond, *Banks and Politics in America: From the Revolution to the Civil War* (Princeton, 1957), 663-67, 670.

37. *Historical Statistics* (1960 ed.), 628, 638.

38. See James K. Medbury, *Men and Mysteries of Wall Street* (Boston, 1870), 319 ff.; Margaret G. Myers, *The New York Money Market* (2 vols., New York, 1931), I, 140.

39. Myers, *New York Money Market,* I, 296; National Bureau of Economic Research, *Capitol Formation and Economic Growth* (Princeton, 1955), 382. See also Carter Goodrich, *Government Promotion of American Canals and Railroads, 1880-1890* (New York, 1960).
40. W. W. Rostow, *The Stages of Economic Growth* (Cambridge, Eng., 1960), 95.

AN ALTERNATE VIEW: *stephen salsbury*

Much has been written about the Civil War. Until quite recently, however, historians were concerned mainly with its cause and they largely ignored the economic effects of the War. In the nineteenth century most northerners simply blamed the War on slavery. In the same period southerners merely accused politicians of being irresponsible and claimed that fanatical abolitionists ignited the conflict. But to Charles A. Beard, writing in the 1920's, these old statements seemed unconvincing.

Beard viewed America's history as a great movement away from Jefferson's agrarian type of society to the capitalistic, industrial, mechanized, and urban society that we have now. In his view, the forces that moved people were economic ones and not idealistic concerns over states' rights or over the immorality of slavery. Beard's pre-Civil War America consisted of a northern, capitalistic, industrial economy with, opposing it, the southern agricultural system. He saw the economic interest and political power of the South, in the Electoral College, the Senate, House of Representatives, and Supreme Court, as frustrating the economic needs of the rapidly growing industrial north.

Professor Louis Hacker stated the Beard thesis in its most extreme and naked form in his book, *The Triumph of American Capitalism.* "By 1860," he summarized,

> a critical situation had arisen in American affairs. Because the southern planter capitalists were in control of the instrumentalities of the national state and, as a result, were thwarting the advance of the (too slowly) growing northern industrial capitalism, their claims to power had to be challenged. This the newly formed Republican party did. The partical success of the Republican party at the polls in 1860 drove the southern leaders—pushed on by extremists in their midst who were under heavy economic pressures—into secession. The Civil War broke out. The Union government, after the departure of the southern legislators, was now wholly possessed by the Republican party.[1]

Reprinted with permission from "The Effect of the Civil War on American Industrial Development," by Stephen Salsbury, in Ralph Andreano, *The Economic Impact of the American Civil War,* Cambridge: Schenkman Publishing Co., 1962, pp. 161-168.

In Beard's words, the Civil War was the "social cataclysm in which the capitalists, laborers, and farmers of the North and West drove from power in the national government the planting aristocracy of the South. Viewed under the light of universal history, the fighting was a fleeting incident; the social revolution was the essential portentous outcome."[2]

This explanation of the causes of the Civil War lead Beard and Hacker to the conclusion that the conflict spurred economic growth in the United States:

> The Second American Revolution (Civil War) while destroying the economic foundation of the slave-owning aristocracy, assured the triumph of business enterprise. As if to add irony to defeat, the very war which the planters precipitated in an effort to avoid their doom augmented the fortunes of the capitalist class from whose jurisdiction they had tried to escape. Through financing the federal government and furnishing supplies to its armies, norther leaders in banking and industry reaped profits far greater than they had ever yet gathered during four years of peace. When the long military struggle came to an end they had accumulated huge masses of capital and were ready to march resolutely forward to the conquest of the continent — to the exploitation of the most marvelous natural endowment ever bestowed by fortune on any nation.[3]

But Beard made no systematic use of statistical evidence in trying to analyze the War's effect.

Prior to 1860 southern planters successfully used their power in the national government to oppose measures such as the tariff, the Homestead Bill, national banking, etc., favored by the northern industrialists and western farmers. Beard, however, made no attempt truly to evaluate the importance of such measures in economic terms and merely assumed that because northern capitalists could not get their way, their plans for expansion and profits were hindered and that economic growth was thus retarded. Starting with this assumption, Beard saw the War as aiding industrialism. He argued that the transference of power from the Democratic to the Republican party (a condition which lasted, with two short exceptions, from the 1860's until 1932) enabled businessmen to shape government policies in ways that were most helpful to their plans for profit and expansion.

Beard cited the policies and legislation which, he claimed, specifically aided economic growth. He considered as most important the direct federal aid to the vast transcontinental railroad projects; it started with the subsidy and land grant to the Union Pacific and Central Pacific railroads in 1862 and included federal land grants in the following years to the Northern Pacific, Kansas Pacific, Santa Fe (Atlantic and Pacific), and Southern Pacific routes. The protective tariff was named as specifically aiding economic growth. He named also the acts designed to make easy the removal of land (whether farmland, timberland, or mineral land) from the public domain to private hands, the Immigration Act of 1864 which gave federal blessing to the importation of workingmen under contracts "analogous to the indentured servitude of colonial times," and the national banking laws and many others.[4]

But more important than any specific legislative act, according to Beard's interpretation, was the ascendancy of the Republican party in Washington; this created a climate that tolerated no interference with the private capitalists. Gone were the Jacksonian ideas that opposed the concentration of economic power in the hands of large corporations. After 1860, Leland Stanford, Collis P. Huntington, John D. Rockefeller, John M. Forbes, Jay Gould, and Mark Hanna had almost unlimited freedom to do as they pleased. And when men such as these ran into trouble with labor, their control of the government assured them that federal power would be used to smash opposition.

Charles Beard's main effort was to explain why the United States in the period between 1860 and 1910 became the world's most productive and powerful industrial nation. In giving his explanation, he made only a random use of statistics. But while he was perfectly content to make almost totally undocumented assertions, such as that which attributed the post-Civil War boom to "huge masses of capital made available by war profits far greater than...[capitalists] had ever yet gathered," Louis Hacker attempted to support this argument by statistical evidence. He used, for instance, an analysis of the census data to substantiate the thesis that "industrial capitalism (more particularly, *heavy* industry) benefited from the Civil War and it continued to make great forward strides (despite a severe depression) after the political victory was firmly secured."[5]

Lately, the role of the Civil War in positively contributing to the American Industrial Revolution has been questioned. Among the most recent and able of these questioning re-evaluations is Thomas C. Cochran's *"Did the Civil War Retard Industrialization?"*[6] In "reiterations of the effect of the Civil War on industrialism," he writes, giving examples, "statistical series seem to have been largely neglected."[7] Cochran's conclusion, after an examination of statistics (available mainly in the 1949 and 1960 editions of *Historical Statistics of the United States*[8] and in the report of the Conference of Research on Income and Wealth in *Trends in the American Economy in the Nineteenth Century*), strongly suggests that the Civil War slowed industrial growth.

Cochran observes that generally during the two decades preceding the Civil War (1840-1860) and the two decades (1870-1890) following the ten-year census period in which the war occurred, the rate of growth exceeded that of the "war decade" (1860-1870). In short, he points to rapid expansion between 1840 and 1860, then actual stagnation in some areas, and but slight increases in most others during the war period (1861-1865), which caused a slower growth rate for the decade 1860-1870, and finally a resumption of rapid growth in the decades between 1870 and 1890.

Behind Cochran's conclusion that the Civil War retarded industrial growth lies the very unstatistical and also partly unsubstantiated assumption that by 1840 all the ingredients favorable to fast industrial growth were overwhelmingly present in the American society. This implies that by the end of the Van Buren administration, the ground was laid for an almost continuous and ininterrupted expansion. This expansion, however, did not occur and the assumption is made that disruptive effects of the Civil War removed vital capital building goods and services from the economy between 1861 and 1865, making the growth after 1865 less rapid than it otherwise would have been.

Now, available statistics do indicate certain American economic reverses during the War. Cotton production almost ended, cotton textile manufacturing in the North fell sharply, and so did the construction of new railroad tracks. Yet, despite this, other segments such as bituminous coal, Pennsylvania anthracite, pig iron, and railroad rails continued to expand, although some at a slightly reduced rate. From this point of view, statistics show that the economy grew less rapidly during the five Civil War years than at other times. We might fairly conclude that war disruption was partially, at least, responsible for this.

Yet the conclusions of Beard, Hacker, and the other historians who claim that the Civil War speeded the Industrial Revolution do not stand or fall on an analysis of the short run, immediate effects which the War had upon the economy. Rather, these conclusions, which see the War as assuring the "triumph of capitalism," and as producing a long term surge of industrial production, rest on longer range analyses.

Professor Cochran's arguments may be met by comparing the post-Civil War growth rate with prewar activity. If one does this, some surprising results present themselves. Let us, for example, instead of comparing the three decades 1850-1860, 1860-1870, 1870-1880, as Cochran does, compare the decade preceding the Civil War (1850-1860), with that immediately following it (1865-1875).[9] Pig iron production in tons, which he considers as "the most significant commodity index of nineteenth century American industrial growth,"[10] increased about 50 per cent between 1850 and 1860, but more than doubled between 1865 and 1873 before it fell, due to the depression which started in 1873.[11] Bituminous coal, "the second most essential commodity series,"[12] tells a similar story: here production increased slightly less than 100 per cent during the decade of 1850-1860, while during the years 1865-1875 it increased by about 145 per cent. Railroad track construction, which he deems "essential for industrialization," tells an even more striking story: during the period 1850-1860 about 20,000 miles of track were laid down, compared to roughly 40,000 during the decade 1865-1875. Clearly then, in these three areas which Cochran considers the most important indicators of nineteenth century economic growth, the postwar decade evidences a substantial boom with growth rates much above those of the pre-Civil War era.[13]

Although this kind of analysis tends to cast doubt on the argument and could be used to support Hacker's assertion that "industrial capitalism (more particularly, heavy industry) benefited from the Civil War," such a conclusion would have the weakness which plagues any attempt to assess the economic effects of the Civil War by reference to growth rates, and industrial or agricultural output. Such statistics tell us only how much was produced, or how much the growth rate declined or increased, but they do not tell us why. This returns us to the nonstatistical explanation of Beard which conflicts dramatically with Cochran's underlying assumption that all the ingredients for rapid economic growth dominated the American society by the beginning of William Harrison's administration.

Professor Cochran recognizes that what he calls "indirect effects" may have had some influence upon post-Civil War economic development. For purposes of analysis we can put these "indirect effects" into two categories. First, there were the changes in the political and social system which the War produced; and second there were the stimulants, such as inflation and the creation of a substantial federal debt, which resulted directly from the War itself. Relative to the second category, Cochran admits that "sharp wartime inflation had the usual effect of transferring income from wage, salary, and interest receivers to those making profits, . . . (which) meant concentration of savings in the hands of entrepreneurs who would invest in new activities."[14] He also points out that inflation "eased the burdens of those railroads which had excessive mortgage debts."[15] But Cochran seems willing to dismiss these effects of the War with the casual statement that "a great deal of new research would be needed to establish casual connections between the inflationary reallocation of wealth, 1863 to 1865, and the high rate of industrial progress in the late 1870's and 1880's."[16] With this sentiment one can only agree. We add that until such attempts are made one must be careful about characterizing the Civil War as a retarder of industrialization.

Cochran's analysis is similar in his statements about the effect of expanded and superior credit resulting from the establishment of national banks and the increase of the national debt from $64,000,000 in 1860 to over $2,700,000,000 in 1866.[17] He gives no statistics which would indicate the impact of the new banking system and the enormous federal debt, but merely states that "since 1800 a multiplication of banks had made credit relatively easy to obtain in the United States, and in the North this continued to be the situation."[18] Further, he observes that the War destroyed southern banking, and that by 1875 some 40 per cent of the banks were still outside the national banking system. With these statements there can be little disagreement, yet it is difficult to see how they prove or disprove the thesis that the War retarded economic growth. In precise terms, how easy was credit to obtain before 1860? Was there ample credit for large scale ventures? Was there any change in this picture after 1865? If there was, did it result from the War? These questions still remain to be answered. And the fact that some "40 per cent of the banks" in 1875 were outside the national banking system seems almost irrelevant without a great deal of additional analysis which is not supplied.

Finally, Cochran recognizes that he must meet the argument which asserts that the Civil War changed the social structure of the nation. He agrees that there is a "possibility that the northern victory had enhanced the capitalist spirit"; but he maintains that this "highly generalized argument is difficult to evaluate." This is undoubtedly true (and the same statement could be made about most attempts to explain human behavior). But the Beard thesis is not so vague but what it is subject to some trenchant criticism. It is possible to analyze in detail the measures which the Republican Party enacted, and to determine how they affected economic growth. It has already been suggested that it may be feasible to measure the amount of investment capital made available by the creation of the national banking system, and the large national debt. There might also be a thorough quantitative study of government aid to internal improvements. While it is true that "federal and state administrations preceding the Civil War could . . . be regarded as friendly to business," it might be well to compare, as Professor Cochran suggests, federal and state aid during and after the Civil War with that in other periods. This should include an attempt to determine the precise amount in constant dollars made available to transportation enterprises by the various state and local governments and the national Congress. We do have readily available information on federal land granted for such purposes. Some idea of the new Republican attitude can be gained from the fact that, in the single year 1865, the national government granted more land for internal improvements than in all years prior to 1861.[19]

There can be no doubt that the exodus from Washington of southern congressmen speeded by ten years or more the building of our entire transcontinental railroad network. Mr. Cochran suggests that such ventures were "built for specultative purposes uneconomically ahead of demand . . ." and thus concludes without supplying any evidence that they may "for a decade or even two have consumed more capital than their transportation services were then worth to the economy."[20] Although this judgment is not necessarily wrong, it will take much research to prove it one way or the other. Certain it is that the building of our vast transcontinental railway systems, which is partially reflected in 40,000 miles of track laid down between 1865 and 1875, had enormous economic effects both from the point of view of consuming (thus stimulating) the products of heavy industry, and of opening up agricultural land in California, Kansas, Nebraska, Wyoming, Colorado, Utah, Idaho, Montana, Washington, Oregon, Arizona, Nevada, and New Mexico. Here it must be noted that since the first transcontinental road was not finished until May, 1869, the statistical impact of these roads in agriculture would not be seen until the decade 1870-1880.

Professor Cochran's assertion that the Union Pacific, during its first decade, was a drain on the economy has been sharply challenged by Robert Fogel. Fogel not only analyzes the rate of return on the Union Pacific's cash expenditures; he also presents estimates of the line's "social return," that is, the increased national income due to the railroad but not reflected in the company's earnings. In both respects Professor Fogel finds the Union Pacific a success, returning an average of 11.6 per cent on its cash expenditures for the first decade of its operation, and an average social return of 29.9 per cent for the same period.[21] While it must be conceded that the social return statistics as yet mean little since we have few comparable figures for other railroads or other kinds of investments, it is only by this type of investigation that we will finally be able, through the aid of numbers, to shed light upon the question of the economic effect of the Civil War on the railroads.

Finally, however, we must face the inherent limits of statistics. Cochran's argument that the Civil War's contribution to the "spirit of capitalism" is difficult to measure is all too correct. Such actions as those of the Republican-appointed Supreme Court, which interpreted the Fourteenth Amendment to the Constitution to insure the sanctity of corporate property and to protect it from attacks by hostile state legislatures, are not subject to statistical measurement. Yet they vitally affected industrial development, at least the industrialism which characterized nineteenth century America.

In summary, historians must not discard or avoid statistics; they can prove invaluable in drawing a clear picture of what happened. Numbers may even answer questions such as, was the Union Pacific a stimulant to economic growth? and if so how? and in what areas of the economy? Yet the broader question — did the Civil War accelerate industrialism by placing in undisputed power men of business?—is only partially susceptible to statistical analysis. We can gain insight into the impact of some measures (tariffs, aid to railroads, land distributed under the Homestead Act, etc.)

through numerical data, yet historians must never fail to integrate such information with interpretations based upon nonstatistical social, political, and psychological analysis.

NOTES

1. Louis M. Hacker, *The Triumph of American Capitalism* (New York, 1940), p. 339.
2. Charles A. Beard and Mary R. Beard, *The Rise of American Civilization* (New York, 1933), vol. II, p. 54.
3. *Ibid.*, p. 166.
4. Beard and Beard, *Rise of American Civilization*, vol. II, p. 106.
5. Hacker, *Triumph of American Capitalism*, p. 438.
6. Thomas C. Cochran, "Did the Civil War Retard Industrialization?", *Mississippi Valley Historical Review*, vol. XLVIII (Sept., 1961), p. 198.
7. *Ibid.*, p. 198.
8. Bureau of the Census, *Historical Statistics of the United States 1789-1945* (1949), and Bureau of the Census, *Historical Statistics of the United States Colonial Times to 1957* (1960).
9. Note that many of the series used by Professor Cochran, especially those in *Trends in the American Economy in the Nineteenth Century*, are not year-by-year statistics but show changes only every tenth year (usually the census year) and thus it is not possible strictly to compare the decade 1850-1860 with the decade 1865-1875.
10. Cochran, "Did the Civil War Retard Industrialization?", p. 200.
11. See Table VI-2, Part Five.
12. Cochran, "Did the Civil War Retard Industrialization?", p. 200.
13. See Table VI-2, VI-3, Part Five.
14. Cochran, "Did the Civil War Retard Industrialization?", p. 207.
15. *Ibid.*
16. *Ibid.*
17. See Table IX-1, Part Five.
18. Cochran, "Did the Civil War Retard Industrialization?", p. 207.
19. See Table VII-5, Part Five.
20. Cochran, "Did the Civil War Retard Industrialization?", p. 209.
21. Robert W. Fogel, *The Union Pacific Railroad, A Case in Premature Enterprise*, pp. 95-103.

part **IV**

**from the civil war
to world war I**

transportation and

the growth of industry

THE GROWTH OF OUTPUT

A very substantial growth in output characterized the United States economy from the close of the Civil War through 1915. Annual real rates of growth averaged about five per cent a year, a rate well above those experienced in the 1815 to 1865 period. Real per capita income by 1915 was about two and a half times its level in 1865. (See Table 3.7.) These gains occurred in a period when years of price declines outnumbered years of price increases by about three to two. From 1865 to 1896 prices more than halved, reaching a level in the latter year equal to the level of prices in 1843. (See Table 3.12.) This pattern followed fairly closely that of prices from the close of the War of 1812 down to 1843. However, in the earlier period output per capita did not register the gains that it did following the Civil War. The economy experienced a number of recessions despite this substantial growth. (See Table 3.9.) Prices began to rise in the economy after 1896 and continued moving upward for the remainder of the period. Practically all of the increase in output and income in the United States from 1865 to 1915 was domestically generated. Foreign commerce continued to decline relative to domestic commerce.

TRANSPORTATION

TRANSCONTINENTAL RAILROADS

During the Civil War construction had begun on the nation's first transcontinental railroad. In 1869 the Union Pacific building from the East, and the Central Pacific from the West, linked up at Promontory Point, Utah. Almost immediately other transcontinental routes were undertaken to link the East and West. The Southern Pacific, taking the most southerly U.S. route, joined Los Angeles with El Paso, Texas, which had rail connections with New Orleans. Also taking a southerly route, the Atchison, Topeka and Santa Fe pushed out from Chicago to Los Angeles via St. Louis and Kansas City. At the same time, the Northern Pacific Railroad of Jay Cooke and Henry Villard, pursuing a northerly route, joined Chicago with Portland, Oregon and Seattle, Washington. James J. Hill's Great Northern Railroad provided the most northerly span between East and West, joining Duluth, Minnesota with Seattle, Washington. Simultaneously the Pennsylvania Railroad in 1869, the Baltimore and Ohio in 1874, the New York Central in 1877, and the Erie Railroad in 1880 completed trunk lines connecting eastern cities and Chicago. By the 1880's and 1890's rail construction was centered in the Midwest. Consequently, by the end of the century Chicago could boast of being the nation's rail center and second largest city. Only the South lagged in the development of a comprehensive interregional rail system. The South's relatively small population in comparison with the North, paucity of industry, shortage of capital, and the availability of low-cost coastwise shipping between the Northeast, Southeast, and Southwest caused the delay. The construction of a trunk line between the Northeast and Southeast was not completed until the 1890's, and it was not until the twentieth century that rail connections between the Southwest and Southeast came close to matching those between the Midwest and East.

Capital expenditure for railroad construction, like construction expenditures in general, was cyclical in character, with cycles varying anywhere from one to two decades in length. Fluctuations in railroad investment were partially correlated with fluctuations in general business, being both influenced by and influencing prosperity. Railroad investment reached peaks in 1873, 1882, 1891, and 1911, while the economy reached peaks in 1873, 1882, 1890, and 1910. Railroad construction reached troughs in 1876, 1886, 1897, and 1920, as did the economy in 1879, 1885, 1897, and 1919.

RAILROADS AND GROWTH

Railroad expansion in this period lowered shipping costs, enabled the nation to become one common market, and spurred economic growth. Construction outlays averaged twenty per cent of gross capital formation in the 1870's, fifteen per cent in the 1880's, and close to ten per cent up to World War I. By this time the amount of track mileage reached an historic peak. (See Figure 12.1.) Railroad construction, in fact, exceeded the growth of population. In 1860 there was one mile of track to every eleven hundred people, and by 1920 one mile to every four hundred and twenty people. By World War I, ten per cent of the capital of the United States was invested in railroads, and the industry employed about four per cent of the labor force.

FIGURE 12.1. *Miles of Road Operated — Railroads 1832 — 1965*

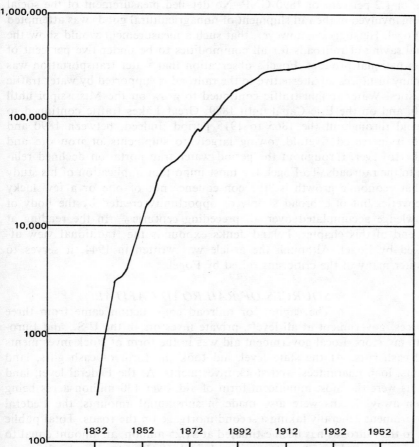

SOURCES: U.S. Bureau of the Census *The Statistical History of the United States From Colonial Times to the Present* Fairfield Publishers Stamford, Connecticut, 1965

U.S. Bureau of the Census *The Statistical Abstract of the United States 1967* Washington, D.C., 1967

There is little question as to the railroad's major significance within the broad spectrum of innovations leading to economic growth. However, econometric studies by Robert Fogel and Albert Fishlow challenge the crucial importance given railroads by some economic historians. Fogel calculated the 1890 interregional cost of shipping agricultural products by rail and water.[1] Owing largely to the slowness of water transportation, Fogel estimates the use of the railroad produced a social saving of $73 million, an amount which represents only six-tenths of one per cent of 1890 gross national product. Intraregionally, wagons and water were a substitute for rail and water in the shipment of farm goods. Here, the economic saving of the railroad, as calculated by Fogel, is greater — $141 million, or 1.2 per cent of 1890 GNP. No detailed measurement of the social saving involved in the rail shipment of nonagricultural goods was attempted by Fogel. He suggests, however, that such a measurement would show the social saving of railroads for all commodities to be under five per cent of gross national product. Fogel's observation that water transportation was in many instances an alternative to the railroad is supported by water traffic statistics. Water freight traffic continued to grow on the Mississippi until 1880, and on the Erie Canal until 1889. Great Lakes traffic continued to expand throughout the 1865 to 1915 period. Indeed, between 1890 and 1915 it increased fivefold, owing largely to shipments of iron ore and coal. However, throughout the period water transportation declined relative to the railroads. To Fogel, the most important implication of his study is that economic growth is "the consequence not of one or a few lucky discoveries but of a broad supply of opportunity created by the body of knowledge accumulated over all preceding centuries." In the reading at the end of this chapter, Leland Jenks expounds the traditional view attacked by Fogel. Although the article was written in 1944, it serves to counter many of the criticisms raised by Fogel.

SOURCES OF RAILROAD CAPITAL

The capital for railroad construction came from three sources: government at all levels, private investors in the U.S., and European investors. Local government aid was in the form of stock investments and cash gifts. At the state level, aid took the form of cash gifts, land grants, loan guarantees, and stock investments. At the Federal level, land grants were the most munificent form of aid, over 130 million acres being given away. Loans were also made in substantial amounts, the Federal Government generally taking a second mortgage on the roads. Total public aid to the railroads has been estimated at $1.25 million, an amount equal to the entire capital investment in railroads in 1860. In return for land grants, the Federal Government was granted the right to ship mail, troops, and government poverty at reduced rates. By the 1870's growing public opposition to Federal land grants resulted in their discontinuance. However, by this time, the railroads had acquired one quarter of the land area of Minnesota and Washington, and one-fifth of the states of Wisconsin, Iowa, Kansas, North Dakota and Montana.

Despite such massive public aid, most of the capital needs of the nation's railroads came from private investors at home and abroad. The Federal Government's success in selling bonds to the public during the Civil War, and the growth of security exchanges in the 1870's and 1880's spurred domestic investment in railroad securities. As for European investors, by 1915 they owned twenty per cent of American railroad securities.

RAILROAD ABUSES

U.S. railroad investment was characterized by speculative financial excess. Financial abuses in road construction were numerous. The reaping of substantial profits was very often the paramount and, indeed, the only goal of railroad construction. Construction companies were a favorite vehicle for the garnering of such profits. Such companies, generally owned by the railroad promoters, charged grossly excessive construction fees. These fees were paid in railroad stock which was immediately sold to the public by the construction companies. As a result, the true value of the roads fell far short of the value of the outstanding stock. For example, let us assume that a given amount of construction cost $500,000. A separate company, organized by the railroad promoters, would be created to perform the work, and would submit a bill for $1,000,000. This bill would be paid in railroad stock, which the construction company would sell to the public. The difference between construction costs and stock revenues would be pocketed by the promoters. Then, too, roads were often constructed as flimsily as possible, and were soon in need of major repair.

Adding to the railroads' financial woes was the construction of competing roads, each of which could not possibly hope for sufficient growth in freight and passenger revenues to remain financially solvent. Railroad entrepreneurs engaged in competitive rate reductions to lure customers away from rival lines. In the process, rates were established which covered operating costs and only a part of fixed costs. Thus, depreciation reserves fell short of capital replacement needs. To recoup uncovered costs discriminatory rates were charged along rights of way where noncompetitive conditions existed. The significant decline in railroad traffic which accompanied economic downturns accentuated the industry's financial plight and forced many major firms into receivership. In the latter decades of the nineteenth century, for example, a number of major railroads, including the Erie, Northern Pacific, Kansas Pacific, Union Pacific, the Santa Fe, the Burlington, and the Norfolk and Western were forced into bankruptcy.

The chaotic financial conditions wrought by periodic price wars led many railroads to seek the financial haven offered by collusive rate-making agreements. In 1897, in the *Trans-Missouri Freight Association* case, such rate-making agreements were held in violation of the Sherman Antitrust Act. Railroads responded by seeking consolidation with their rivals. Financial capitalists like J.P. Morgan often were the driving force behind such mergers. A holding company, for example, was established to control the Great Northern and Northern Pacific railroads, and eliminate competition in the Northwest. In 1904, in the *Northern Securities* case, this action was also held in violation of the Sherman Act. Despite government attempts to avoid concentration, the railroad network of the United States in the early twentieth century was effectively dominated by seven economic interests, those of Cornelius Vanderbilt, J.P. Morgan, Jay Gould, James J. Hill, E.H. Harriman, the Pennsylvania Railroad, and the Rock Island Railroad. Despite this concentration of economic power, the financial problems of railroads intensified. They continued to experience receivership, and by World War I the bulk of railroad equipment was in a state of disrepair.

RAILROAD REGULATION

Railroad rate-making abuses evoked a demand for regulation. Farmers who found themselves the victims of excessive and discriminatory charges pressed for public control over railroad rates and service in Illinois, Minnesota, Wisconsin, and Iowa. From 1871 to 1874 these states passed legislation forbidding railroads from charging higher rates for short-haul traffic than for long-distance traffic. Regulatory commissions were empowered to fix maximum rates, and the consolidation of competing roads was forbidden. However, in 1886 the Supreme Court decision in *Wabash, St. Louis and Pacific Railway Co. v. Illinois* restricted these commissions' jurisdiction solely to intrastate commerce. The case involved a railroad which transported goods from Illinois to New York. Shippers from points geographically closer to New York were being charged higher rates than those located at more distant points. The Illinois regulatory commission's prohibition of this practice was overruled by the Supreme Court, which stated that the Illinois commission had no power to determine the rates on goods being shipped outside the state.

The need for Federal action was obvious. It was forthcoming in 1887 with the passage of the Interstate Commerce Act. The Act required that interstate railroad rates be "just and reasonable." Discriminatory rates, including charging customers more for short hauls than for long hauls, were forbidden. Furthermore, railroads were required to publish a schedule of rates, and were forbidden from pooling revenues. The Interstate Commerce Commission, the first Federal regulatory agency, was established to administer the Act.

Supreme Court decisions and experience with the Act led to further legislation. The Elkins Act of 1903 tightened regulations on rebates by holding the receivers of rebates as well as railroads liable to prosecution if discrimination was practiced. Furthermore, any departure from published rates was held to be prima facie evidence of guilt. The Hepburn Act of 1906 substantially augmented the Interstate Commerce Commission's power by authorizing it to fix maximum rates. The Commission's orders were held binding prior to judicial review. The Act also prohibited railroads from shipping goods of a business which they owned, with one exception, lumber. This prohibition was aimed at railroads who owned their own coal mines. It was the practice of such roads to charge independent coal companies higher transportation charges than those levied against subsidiary coal companies. The effect was to raise the costs of competing coal companies, thus hampering their ability to compete. The Mann-Elkins Act of 1910 tightened the law on long- and short-haul discrimination. Under previous law railroads were forbidden to charge more for short than long hauls where "substantially similar circumstances and conditions" existed. However, in the *Alabama Midland* case of 1897 the Supreme Court held that railroads were to be the judge of what in fact were "substantially similar circumstances and conditions." The Mann-Elkins Act authorized the Interstate Commerce Commission to make such determinations.

THE GROWTH OF INDUSTRY

ECONOMIES AND DISECONOMIES OF SCALE

Urban growth accompanied the development of a national transportation network. These two developments generated both external and internal economies of scale. The former reduced production costs by enabling firms to acquire raw materials, labor, transportation, banking and other needed services at reduced prices. To illustrate, industrial firms situated themselves along major transportation routes and close to the economic resources necessary for the production process. This in turn attracted labor, banks, and other business firms who were either customers or suppliers of those firms. Thus, an urban area with a ready-made market was created. The growth of this market set into motion a self-generating process of additional external economies. Expanding markets encouraged larger firm size which produced internal economies of scale. In the larger firms which resulted, decreased unit production costs were realized due to division of labor, the use of more complex, efficient equipment, a more balanced production process and better utilization of by-products. A portion of the cost savings resulting from external and internal economies of scale were passed on to consumers in the form of lower prices and better quality goods. A part was retained by the companies themselves. These profits provided a ready source of savings for capital accumulation, which when plowed back into the company was an important source of economic growth. Until the late 1800's, firm growth was internally generated by re-investment of earnings. By the end of the century, mergers and consolidations were becoming the dominant vehicle for firm growth. Economies of scale associated with growing firm size were not limitless. Beyond a certain point, diseconomies of scale occurred in some firms. As the latter grew bigger, they became too bureaucratic and unwieldly for entrepreneurs to run efficiently. The result was increasing costs.

Operating efficiency was not the only reason for growing firm size in the late nineteenth and early twentieth centuries. Attempts to acquire monopoly control, growth for its own sake, and the immediate financial rewards from arranging mergers and consolidations were other causes of growing size. Whatever the causes, growing firm size was the general rule of the period. By 1904 more than 5,200 separate establishments had been merged into a little more than 300 companies, accounting for approximately forty per cent of the nation's manufacturing capital.

THE MAJOR INDUSTRIES

By World War I a developed industrial complex had evolved in the United States. The ten leading industries of 1914 ranked according to value added were iron and steel, textiles, food and kindred products, paper and printing, lumber, chemical and allied products, liquors and beverages, land transportation vehicles, metal and metal products, and stone, clay, and glass products. (See Table 12.1.) In comparison to 1860, a smaller number of the leading industries were involved in satisfying basic human needs. In addition, the leading manufacturing sector of 1914 was a capital goods industry, whereas in 1860 it was a consumer nondurable goods industry (cotton textiles). The leading industry of 1914 was responsible for adding more than twenty-five times as much value as the leading industry of 1860. Even the tenth largest industry of 1914 added more than six times as much to product value as did the leader of 1860. By 1914 the total value of manufactured goods stood at twenty-four billion dollars, a twelvefold increase over the $2 billion which existed on the eve of the Civil War. Within the country the regional pattern of manufacturing shifted west and south. By World War I, while

TABLE 12.1. *The Ten Leading Manufacturing Industries of 1914*

Industry	Employment (thousands)	Value of Product (millions of $)	Value Added (millions of $)
Iron and Steel	1,601.1	$3,223.1	$1,460.8
Textiles	1,498.7	3,414.6	1,421.6
Food and Kindred Products	496.2	4,816.7	988.2
Paper and Printing	452.9	1,456.0	875.3
Lumber	833.5	1,599.7	837.4
Chemicals and Allied Products	299.6	2,001.6	712.3
Liquors and Beverages	88.2	772.4	529.9
Land Transportation Vehicles	263.1	1,034.5	447.8
Metals and Metal Products	262.2	1,417.0	393.7
Stone, Clay and Glass Products	334.7	614.2	375.4

SOURCE: U.S. Department of Commerce. *Statistical Abstract of the United States, 1917.* Washington, D.C.: U.S. Government Printing Office, 1918, p. 184.

the Middle Atlantic states continued to be the dominant manufacturing section of the economy, accounting for approximately a third of total value added in manufacturing, the Midwest (East North Central states) had replaced New England as the second leading manufacturing area of the nation. (See Table 12.2.) It accounted for more than a fourth of value added, while New England accounted for less than a seventh. Southern value added (South Atlantic and South Central states) equaled that of New England.

In 1865 the value of manufacturing output was only about two-thirds that of agriculture. Agriculture continued to be dominant as late as 1880. By 1890, however, manufacturing value exceeded that of agriculture, and by 1900 it was double the latter in value. As the twentieth century opened the United States was the leading manufacturing nation of the world. Its manufacturing output by 1910 was almost twice the output of the world's second largest manufacturer, Germany. By World War I the United States was responsible for producing more than a third of the world's manufacturing output.

TABLE 12.2. *The Geographic Location of Manufacturing in 1914*

Region	Number of Firms	Capital Investment (millions of $)	Employment (thousands)	Value Added (millions of $)
Middle Atlantic[1]	85,466	$7,836.1	2,780.7	$3,372.7
East North Central[2]	59,896	5,913.7	2,008.9	2,747.2
New England[3]	25,193	2,948.0	1,268.2	1,269.0
South Atlantic[4]	28,925	1,644.5	776.5	679.9
West North Central[5]	27,199	1,424.2	484.6	634.4
Pacific[6]	16,206	1,153.3	290.4	420.5
East South Central[7]	14,410	713.4	307.7	313.7
West South Central[8]	12,417	687.8	250.3	275.6
Mountain[9]	6,079	470.0	98.2	165.4

SOURCE: U.S. Department of Commerce, *Statistical Abstract of the United States 1919*. Washington, D.C.: U.S. Government Printing Office, p. 209.

[1] Includes New York, New Jersey and Pennsylvania

[2] Includes Illinois, Indiana, Ohio, Michigan and Wisconsin

[3] Includes Connecticut, Maine, Massachusetts, New Hampshire, Rhode Island and Vermont

[4] Includes Delaware, Florida, Georgia, Maryland, North Carolina, South Carolina, Virginia and West Virginia

[5] Includes Iowa, Kansas, Minnesota, Missouri, Nebraska, North Dakota, South Dakota

[6] Includes California, Oregon, Washington

[7] Includes Alabama, Kentucky, Mississippi, and Tennessee

[8] Includes Arkansas, Louisiana, Oklahoma, and Texas

[9] Includes Arizona, Colorado, Idaho, Montana, Nevada, New Mexico, Utah and Wyoming

IRON AND STEEL

As cotton textiles dominated pre-Civil War manufacturing in the United States, so iron and steel dominated manufacturing growth from the Civil War to World War I. Between 1860 and 1914 the growth of this industry was phenomenal. On the eve of the Civil War Great Britain produced 3.9 million tons of pig iron annually compared to 0.8 million tons in the United States. By 1914 the United States was the world's largest producer of pig iron, producing 23.3 million tons annually. Its steel capacity (31 million tons) exceeded the combined total of Germany (17 million tons), Great Britain (7 million tons), and France (5 million tons).

Several technological breakthroughs stimulated the growth of output. These included increases in the size of blast furnaces, the Bessemer process, the open-hearth process, and integration of the production process. In 1850 an average size blast furnace could handle an output of ten tons a day. By 1875 capacity had grown to 100 tons a day, and by 1900 it had soared to 500 tons. The Bessemer process of steel manufacture commenced commercially in 1866. Prior to this development steel was manufactured from wrought iron by heating the iron with charcoal in steel furnaces. The resulting product, called blister steel, was of uneven quality. It was made into a high quality product, called crucible steel, by breaking it up and melting it in small clay crucibles using charcoal as a fuel. The cost of this operation was high, three tons of charcoal being used to produce one of steel. Moreover, the process took ten days. The Bessemer process, discovered independently by William Kelly in the United States and Henry Bessemer in England, directed a blast of air on molten pig iron to oxidize 99 per cent of the carbon content. Unfortunately the process did not control the quantity of carbon or oxygen removed from the ore. Robert Mushet corrected this deficiency through the use of spiegeleisen, a compound containing iron, carbon, and manganese. The manganese in the compound removed all oxygen from the molten iron, while the carbon remained to create steel. In the 1860's the open-hearth process was developed by the Siemens brothers in England and the Martin brothers in France. It involved the ability to generate higher temperatures in the puddling process, thereby dispensing with the need for manipulation of the iron by puddlers. In addition, it utilized low-priced scrap and produced a superior product of more uniform quality. By 1908 it surpassed Bessemer steel in importance. (See Table 12.3.) A further step in increasing steel productivity was the integration of all steps in the production of steel, thereby reducing fuel needs. Coke ovens, blast furnaces, steel furnaces, and rolling mills were placed in proximity to one another to minimize the need for reheating the output at each stage of the production process. It should be noted that by the mid-1870's bituminous coal had replaced anthracite as the principal fuel for steel manufacture. (See Table 12.4.) The combined impact of these innovations enabled steel prices in 1898 to reach an historic minimum. At that time steel rails sold for $12 a ton, compared with crucible steel production costs of $75 a ton during the Civil War.

The transportation sector provided iron and steel with its first major markets. Before the Civil War steamboat machinery and railroad steam engines consumed large quantities of iron. The westward movement of the railroads in the 1860's and 1870's and continued construction in the East created a vast demand for iron and steel rails. During the railroad boom of the early 1880's, rails accounted for over ninety per cent of rolled steel products. Other sectors of the economy were also important users of iron

TABLE 12.3. *Steel Ingot and Castings Production by Process 1870–1910*

Year	Thousands of Gross Tons	
	Bessemer	*Open-Hearth*
1870	38	1
1880	1,074	101
1890	3,689	513
1900	6,685	3,398
1910	9,413	16,505

SOURCE: Peter Temin. *Iron and Steel in Nineteenth Century America.* Cambridge: M.I.T. Press, 1964, p. 270.

and steel. The increasing use of machinery in manufacturing and agriculture, and the introduction of structural shapes in construction spurred the growth of the industry. As the industry grew in size, its demand for iron ore outstripped the limited capacity of widely scattered local mines. The search for new sources of supply led to the development of Lake Superior iron sites, the most notable of which is the Mesabi range. During the 1870's the Lake region supplied one-fourth of all iron ore and by 1900, two-thirds.

As pointed out in an earlier chapter, the iron industry prior to the Civil War was ubiquitous. By the 1800's, however, Pennsylvania had become the nation's leading steel state, with Ohio following at some distance

TABLE 12.4. *Fuel Use in the Iron and Steel Industry 1854–1910**

	Bituminous	Anthracite	Charcoal
1854	7%	46%	47%
1860	13	57	30
1870	31	50	20
1880	45	42	13
1890	69	24	7
1900	85	12	3
1910	96	2	1

SOURCE: Peter Temin. *Iron and Steel in Nineteenth Century America.* Cambridge: M.I.T. Press, 1964, p. 268.

*Figures may not add to 100% due to rounding.

in second place. Western Pennsylvania's and eastern Ohio's accessibility to Lake Superior by both water and rail, supplies of coking coal and labor, and proximity to major markets minimized production and distribution costs. Competing for third place were Illinois and Alabama. The former's accessibility to Lake Superior ore and its importance as a market for both the agricultural west and the railroad industry assured it a place of importance. The latter state owed its prominence to major discoveries of iron ore and coal in the 1870's.

Concurrent with the geographic concentration of the iron and steel industry there occurred a significant growth in firm size and a diminution in the number of firms. The growth in the operating capacity of individual units is epitomized by the Edgar Thomson Steel Works, which produced 6,000 tons of metal in 1875, 100,000 tons in 1880, and almost 750,000 tons in 1903. The objective of increasing operating efficiency through the acquisition of raw material suppliers and iron and steel fabricators, coupled with the desire to reduce competitive pressures, encouraged the consolidation of competing firms. Inducements to consolidation were heightened by the failure of earlier efforts to curb price competition within the industry through price fixing. Between 1869 and 1899 the number of blast furnace establishments decreased from 386 to 223, and major iron and steel empires were created. Andrew Carnegie, who entered the industry around the Civil War, had by 1879 amassed a complex capitalized at $5 million which extended over the Edgar Thomson Steel Company, Lucy Furnaces, Union Mills of Pittsburgh, and coal and ore land in Pennsylvania. In 1881 the Homestead Plant near Pittsburgh was begun, and by 1891 the company, reorganized with a capital of $75 million, had acquired the Duquesne Steel Works, Beaver Falls Mills, and Keystone Bridge Co., as well as additional coal mines, coke ovens, and iron mines.

Rivaling the Carnegie empire was the Illinois Steel Co. of Chicago, founded in 1889 with a capitalization of $25 million. It resulted from the merger of the Union Iron and Steel, Joliet Steel, and North Chicago Rolling Mill companies. With ten thousand employees, Illinois Steel boasted of five plants with fourteen blast furnaces, four Bessemer plants, 1,150 coke ovens, and numerous coal fields, railroads, and rolling mills. In 1891 its capitalization was increased to $50 million, and one year later its steel output was greater than that of either Russia, Sweden, or Belgium. In 1899 the Illinois Steel Co. was merged with the Minnesota Iron Co., the Lorain Steel Co., and the Chicago Outer Belt Line Railway, to form the Federal Steel Company, capitalized through J.P. Morgan at $200 million, and under the direction of Elbert H. Gary. In the process of formation the company also acquired additional ore lands, railways, coke ovens, mineral lands, docks, and ships.

Meanwhile, the Carnegie Empire was also growing. In 1899 it acquired the Lake Superior Iron Co., a feat that made it the largest shipper of ore from Lake Superior. At this time the Carnegie enterprises produced seventeen per cent of the pig iron and twenty-two per cent of all Bessemer steel made in the United States. In addition to owning the companies already listed, it owned or controlled the Lorimer Coke Works, Carey Blast Furnace, Allegheny Coke Works, Pittsburgh, Bessemer, and Lake Erie Railroad Company, H.C. Frick Coke Co., and Oliver Mining Co., as well as various natural gas, dock, and limestone companies. It was in this year that Andrew Carnegie expressed a desire to retire from active management of his concern. In 1901 Carnegie and his partners sold their interests to J.P. Morgan and his associates for $492 million, the highest price ever paid for a company up to that time. Almost immediately a merger between Federal Steel and Carnegie Steel was consummated. The resulting corporation, U.S. Steel, had a capitalization of $1.4 billion, and the capacity to turn out 7.4 million tons of pig iron and 9.4 million tons of steel ingot. It also owned the largest fleet of ships sailing under the U.S. flag, and a thousand miles of railroad track. This giant enterprise, which was formed to eliminate what Morgan considered to be competitive excesses, was destined historically to grow absolutely, but decline relatively. Thus, during the first ten years of its existence, while its output grew forty-one per cent, that of the industry grew sixty-eight per cent. The growth of other steel companies during the period was epitomized by Bethlehem Steel, and Youngstown Sheet and Tube Company. The former's capitalization grew by 3,800 per cent from 1901 to 1911, while the latter's grew by 4,900 per cent from 1902 to 1913.

U.S. TECHNOLOGY

Post-Civil War innovations were not confined to the iron and steel industry. Major innovations occurred in the power and machine tool industries. The major changes in the power industry were the replacement of water power by steam, and steam by electricity as the major sources of energy for American industry. The increased efficiency of steam engines, the scarcity of adequate water sites, and the abundance of coal to use as a fuel for steam production accounted for the dominance of steam following the Civil War. In turn, the ability to produce electric power at a lower cost, and its capability of being transported longer distances, led to the displacement of steam by electricity. As early as 1820 Michael Faraday had devised a crude electric motor, but little additional progress was made until Z.T. Gramme perfected an efficient generator in 1870. In 1880 Thomas Edison developed the carbon filament electric light bulb. Shortly thereafter, he commenced the sale of electricity to businesses and households from a power station located in lower Manhattan. At about the same time George

Westinghouse's transformer permitted the transmission of electricity over long distances at reasonable cost. By 1900 electricity and steam each supplied about the same proportion of power to industry, but thereafter electricity dominated. Innovations in the machine tool industry were in response to the demand for more complex and varied producer and consumer goods. These goods required hundreds of different interchangeable parts, and each part, in turn, required a special machine to manufacture it. Moreover, the increasing number of interchangeable parts needed for the production of a good required increased planning in factory layouts and production scheduling. This, in turn, spurred the development of scientific management. It is no coincidence that Frederick W. Taylor, who invented high speed machine tools in the 1890's, pioneered in the application of scientific management principles in the United States. The growth of the armament, aircraft and auto industries in World War I provided particular stimulus to the industry.

Other innovations occurred in food processing, aluminum and copper production, and the textile, clothing, and shoe industries. In food processing, the application of refrigeration to railroad cars proved to be a major technological innovation. Developed in the 1870's by meat packing firms which were already using refrigerated rooms in their slaughterhouses, these cars permitted the shipment of meat to national markets, thereby encouraging large-scale meatpacking operations. In turn, this made feasible the commercial utilization of by-products for the production of soap, leather, and other items. Concomitant with these developments, important strides were made in food canning. By 1915 all steps in canning, including the preparation of food, had been fully mechanized. At the same time commercially produced bread, biscuits and cake were made available. Low-cost aluminum production was made possible in 1886 by development of the electrolytic process of aluminum production by Charles Martin Hall and Paul Heroult. Aluminum prior to this date had prohibitive production costs, and was comparable in value to precious metals. Industry growth proceeded at a slow pace, however, and prior to World War I was largely confined to the manufacture of pots, pans, and other kitchen utensils. A major technological breakthrough in the copper industry occurred in 1914 with the introduction of the Froth Flotation Process, which permitted the use of low-grade ore that hitherto could not be economically processed. Copper was particularly important owing to its role in the transmission of electricity.

In the textile, clothing, and shoe industries innovations were numerous. First, in the 1870's the application of mechanical combing in the woolen industry permitted the separation of short woolen fibers from long worsted fibers, and fostered the growth of the fine woolen industry. Second, in cotton textiles, the Northrop Automatic Loom of 1895 represented a significant technological breakthrough. This loom automatically inserted fresh bobbins of yarn when needed and stopped operations whenever any thread broke. Hitherto, constant supervision of looms had been required to guard against thread breakage and to insert new bobbins periodically. Third, experiments were being conducted with artificial fibers. Rayon was first produced in France in the 1880's, and in 1911 commercial production was begun in the United States. Not until after World War I, however, did artificial fibers make inroads into natural fiber markets. Fourth, in the 1870's rotary cutting machines were introduced that permitted the cutting of several garments simultaneously. Fifth, in the 1890's power driven sewing machines were widely adopted, and early in the twentieth century the factory production of women's clothes commenced. Sixth, in the last quarter of the nineteenth century a number of processes were introduced for the machine assemblage of shoes. One of the most important was the Goodyear Welt Process for attaching soles to the upper part of shoes. By 1915 the industry was highly mechanized with most shoe machinery being controlled through patents held by the United Shoe Machinery Company, still the dominant firm in the industry.

PUBLIC REGULATION OF INDUSTRY

The growth of the size and power of business firms led to public agitation for government control of monopoly power. This agitation was fueled by the "muckrakers," writers of the day who exposed the predatory practices of many captains of industry. As was noted earlier, regulation first occurred in the railroad industry, with passage of the Interstate Commerce Act in 1887. Three years later, a more general law, the Sherman Antitrust Act, was passed. This 1890 Act stated in part:

> Every contract, combination in the form of trust or otherwise, or conspiracy, in restraint of trade or commerce among the several States, or with foreign nations, is hereby declared to be illegal.

> Every person who shall monopolize, or attempt to monopolize, or combine or conspire with any other person or persons, to monopolize any part of the trade or commerce among the several states, or with foreign nations, shall be deemed guilty of a misdemeanor, and, on conviction thereof, shall be punished by fine not exceeding five thousand dollars, or by imprisonment not exceeding one year, or by both said punishments, in the discretion of the court.

Under the Act the Federal Government brought suit against the Standard Oil and American Tobacco monopolies, seeking their legal dissolution. Both companies were found guilty, and ordered to divest themselves of a portion of their holdings. Suits were also instituted against U.S. Steel,

American Can, and International Harvester, each of which dominated their respective industries. However, these companies were found not guilty. In the above cases the Supreme Court formulated what became known as the Rule of Reason. That rule held that only companies who misused monopoly power in a predatory or unreasonable manner fell under the ban of the Sherman Act. U.S. Steel, American Can, and International Harvester, though possessing monopoly power, were found not to have made unreasonable use of their power.

Executive and legislative attempts to strengthen the law led in 1914 to passage of two major pieces of legislation. The Clayton Act forbade a number of activities where the effect was substantially to lessen competition or tend to create a monopoly. These included price discrimination in the sale of commodities of like grade, quality, and quantity, tying and exclusive dealing contracts, interlocking directorates, and corporate stock acquisitions in competing firms. The Federal Trade Commission Act forbade unfair methods of competition. It also established the Federal Trade Commission, with broad investigatory powers, to share enforcement of the Clayton Act with the Department of Justice. Despite the specific prohibitions of these laws, subsequent court decisions demonstrated the existence of many weaknesses in them. Price discrimination, for example, continued through the sale of varying quantities of a good, and competing companies continued to be acquired, if not through purchase of stock, then through purchase of assets.

In the post-Civil War period the question arose as to the right of a state to regulate a business within its sovereignty. In Illinois a law was passed fixing the maximum rate which grain elevators could charge for storage. This law was challenged in the Supreme Court in the 1877 case, *Munn v. Illinois*. A grain elevator company charged that its business was private in nature and that state regulation violated the Fourteenth Amendment of the Constitution, which forbids states from depriving citizens of their property without due process of law. The Supreme Court, noting that "it had been customary in England from time immemorial and in this country from its first colonization to regulate ferries, common carriers, bakers, millers, wharfingers, innkeepers, and so forth," ruled the grain elevator business to be "affected with a public interest," and a proper object of state regulation. This was the first of several landmark cases which helped to define the boundaries of public utility regulation. In the *German Alliance Insurance Company* case of 1914, the Supreme Court held that fire insurance was a proper subject for government regulation. The Court ruled that "a business, by circumstances and its nature, may rise from private to be of public concern and be subject, in consequence, to governmental regulation."

Of co-equal importance with the issue of what businesses could be regulated was the question of what profits should be allowed them. Here, the landmark case was *Smyth v. Ames*, decided in 1898. The Supreme Court ruled:

> We hold . . . that the basis of all calculations as to the reasonableness of rates to be charged . . . must be the fair value of the property being used . . . for the convenience of the public. And in order to ascertain that value, the original cost of construction, and the amount and market value of its bonds and stock, the present as compared with the original cost of construction, the probable earning capacity of the property under particular rates prescribed by statute, and the sum required to meet operating expenses, are all matters for consideration, and are to be given such weight as may be just and right in each case. We do not say that there may not be other matters to be regarded in estimating the value of the property. What the company is entitled to ask is a fair return upon the value of that which it employs for public convenience.

The effect of this decision was to create two alternative methods of determining the value of a firm's capital investment, original cost, and reproduction cost. In times of inflation, utilities favored valuations based on reproduction costs, while rate commissions favored original cost. In times of deflation, the reverse was true. The Supreme Court from *Smyth v. Ames* through the mid-1920's, a period dominated by inflation, tended to favor reproduction cost as the measure of valuation, and overturned any commission-fixed rate which did not take adequate account of it.

Concomitant with judicial clarification of state regulatory powers was the development of more effective regulatory commissions. The state commissions which existed in the Northeast prior to the Civil War lacked effective enforcement powers. Their principal weapons were disclosure and the force of public opinion. In the 1870's western states, more sensitive to the abuses of monopoly power such as that exercised by the railroads, pioneered in the establishment of more effective commissions. These commissions were given power to enforce their regulations through court orders and penalties. Commencing in 1907 eastern regulatory commissions were given similar authority. By 1915 about half of all states had such agencies. Two of the most influential figures in strengthening state regulatory agencies in the early twentieth century were Governor Charles Evans Hughes of New York and Governor Robert L. La Follette of Wisconsin. The former was elected largely on the basis of his 1905 exposé of insurance industry malpractices. In 1907, under his leadership, the New York Public Service Commission was created. Shortly thereafter, principally on the urging of Governor Robert L. La Follette, the Wisconsin legislature strengthened its existing commission to include jurisdiction over railroads, street railways, telephone, telegraph, light, heat, power, water, and gas companies. These two commissions served as prototypes for the development of similar commissions in other states.

NOTES

1. Robert W. Fogel. *Railroads and Economic Growth*. Baltimore: Johns Hopkins Press, 1964.

SELECTED REFERENCES

1. Arthur R. Burns. *The Decline of Competition, A Study in the Evolution of American Industry*. New York: McGraw-Hill, 1936.
2. Victor S. Clark. *History of Manufactures in the United States, 1607-1914*, Vols. II-III. New York: McGraw-Hill, 1929.
3. Robert W. Fogel. *Railroads and American Economic Growth*. Baltimore: Johns Hopkins Press, 1964.
4. Malcolm MacLaren. *The Rise of the Electric Industry During the Nineteenth Century*. Princeton: Princeton University Press, 1943.
5. John Moody. *The Truth about Trusts; Description and Analyses of the American Trust Movement*. New York: Moody, 1904.
6. L. T. C. Rolt. *A Short History of Machine Tools*. Cambridge: M.I.T. Press, 1965.
7. George R. Taylor and Irene Neu. *The American Railroad Network, 1861-1890*. Cambridge: Harvard University Press, 1956.
8. Peter Temin. *Iron and Steel in Nineteenth Century America*. Cambridge: M.I.T. Press, 1964.

reading

what role did railroads play in spurring u.s. economic development?

leland h. jenks

        Any attempt to discuss the way in which railroads have promoted the rise of the American economy must assume some theory of economic evolution.[1] The following analysis is based upon Schumpeter's theory of innovations.[2] Briefly this theory holds that economic evolution in capitalistic society is started by innovation in some production function, that is, by new combinations of the factors in the economic process. These innovations may center in new commodities or new services, new types of machinery, new forms of organization, new firms, new resources, or new areas. As Schumpeter makes clear, this is not a general theory of economic, much less of social, change. Innovation is an internal factor operating within a given economic system while the system is also affected by external factors (many of them sociological) and by growth (which means, substantially, changes in population and in the sum total of savings made by individuals and firms). These sets of factors interact in economic change. "The changes in the economic process brought about by innovation, together with all their effects, and the response to them by the economic system" constitute economic evolution for Schumpeter.[3]

        Railroad development has had three phases or moments which have involved innovation in distinctive ways. I shall consider (1) the railroad as an idea, (2) the railroad as a construction enterprise, and (3) the railroad as a producer of transportation services.[4]

Reprinted with permission from "The Railroads as an Economic Force in American Development" by Leland H. Jenks, in *Journal of Economic History,* IV (May 1944), pp. 1-20.

By the railroad as an idea is not meant the original design of steam locomotion on rails. It pertains to the inception in particular areas of particular projects, conceived as likely to be appropriate opportunities for business enterprise. In this sense the idea of any major innovation, such as the railroad, is a potent economic force. For once railway projects have been conceived and plans for their execution elaborated, it becomes easier for other innovating ideas to be entertained.[5] On the one hand, the sociopsychological deterrents against entering upon new ways are lowered. On the other, the characteristics of the prospective future are altered; they assume an aspect more favorable to men and firms with new plans than to men and firms whose position is established. Thus early railway projects were attended by a retinue of satellite innovations.

The first railway projects emerged in the United States in the thirties in a situation in which the psychological risks had already been appreciably lowered by the general passion for internal improvements displayed in a plethora of projects for canals, turnpikes, plank roads, bridges, banks, and other enterprises.[6] The earliest railways paralleled, supplemented, or improved transport systems that were already in being.[7] The real railway revolution dates from the forties, prior to the California gold discoveries, in projects to cross the Appalachians, to link the seaboard with the interior, the Ohio Valley with the Great Lakes, and, breaking away from the contours of water transport, to unite distant points by more direct routes.[8] It was the determination to build railroads in advance of traffic that gave the "railroad idea" prolonged force in American economic life. The conviction that the railroad would run anywhere at a profit put fresh spurs to American ingenuity and opened closed paddocks of potential enterprise.

Innovations are the work of enterprisers. For the railroad as idea, the role of entrepreneurship was pretty much identical with promotion; and the promoter was rarely limited in outlook to the railroad itself. In action, he was omnicompetent and omnipresent. His imagination leaped readily from the concrete problem of securing authority for a right of way to visions of a countryside filled with nodding grain, settlements of industrious families, and other evidences of progress and civilization. Each railway project involved the sanguine judgment of enterprising individuals and groups in particular, local situations that a certain line would be of direct or indirect pecuniary advantage to themselves. It was linked to specific plans for town promotion and real-estate speculation, to combinations for contracting services and supplies or for exploitation of resources, in anticipation of the actual movement of traffic by rail. But as projects multiplied they collectively acquired a symbolic function, dramatizing broader purposes. The railway projector became an exemplification of the power of steam, of the advantages of the corporate form of business organization, of the ability of man to master his environment. The early railway

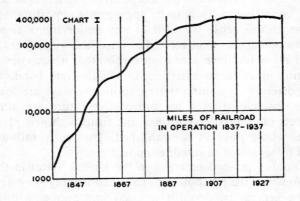

CHART I

400,000

100,000

10,000

MILES OF RAILROAD
IN OPERATION 1837-1937

1000

1847   1867   1887   1907   1927

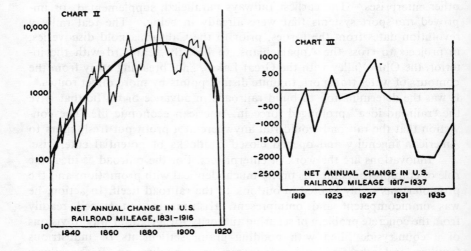

CHART II

10,000

1000

100

10

NET ANNUAL CHANGE IN U.S.
RAILROAD MILEAGE, 1831-1916

1840   1860   1880   1900   1920

CHART III

1000
500
0
-500
-1000
-1500
-2000
-2500

NET ANNUAL CHANGE IN U.S.
RAILROAD MILEAGE 1917-1937

1919   1923   1927   1931   1935

promoter was not only a potential economic agent; he embodied the dream of developing communities, regions, the continent.

Thus, as the barriers to new projects were periodically lowered by the inception of new railway systems, the first moment of the railroad as an economic force was manifested in a wavelike profusion of new enterprises of many sorts. Moreover, its effects in the United States were not exhausted in a decade or so, as they were in England. The railroad idea was periodically renewed for region after region and route after route, as national development, at least facilitated by the earlier railroads, widened the horizons of enterprise.

The second moment of the railroad as an economic force came with the actual construction of new lines. The statistics of net mileage added in each year from 1837 to 1937 give a quantitative measure of this contribution of the railroad to development, as appears on the accompanying charts. Two general statements are strikingly supported by these data.[9] In the first place, railway building proceeded in an undulating pattern, paralleling closely the general contours of major business cycles until the First World War. From 1850 to the nineties, omitting the years of the Civil War, the rise and fall in new construction in fact led by a perceptible interval most other indices of business conditions.[1J] In the second place, there was a long-run trend in new railway construction, which was predominantly upward in absolute figures from the late 1840's to about 1890. The rate of this upward trend tended to slacken with the aggregate movement approximating graphically a logistic curve, but, for the whole period, expansion of railway plant averaged about 10 per cent a year. The trend since 1890 has been irregularly downward, bearing the aspect of a reversed logistic curve. The early persistent succession of fresh waves of railway construction, arising largely in the development of new areas in the American West and South, must be regarded as one of the basic phenomena in the total economic growth of the United States, while the logistic curve of total experience presents in outline a picture of an industry passing from youth through adolescence to maturity.

But how did railway construction as such act as an economic force? How could it be a pace setter? The answer is broadly that it operated directly to create a demand for various factors of production. In response to this demand there were rises in prices or increases in supply or both. Increase of supply could come only from some sort of further innovations, such as the drawing of fresh increments of land, labor, or capital into economic uses or the transfer of such factors to more effective combinations. This process meant the periodic dislocation of the economic structure as well as the disruption of the activities of individuals and communities. At the same time it enhanced the opportunities for enterprisers having a high degree of flexibility, pioneering individuals and groups, the agents of innumerable innovating firms and procedures.

The land for railroad construction was largely new land, previously not of economic use. It cost virtually nothing to the railway companies, and not very much to anyone else.[11] Socially the land devoted to railroad purposes more than paid for itself by the increment in productivity of adjacent land. This was so obvious to everyone connected with railway building that periodic land booms came to communities even before the rails were laid. The speculative activity thus diffused in anticipation of railroad construction may have brought many creative innovations in its wake. But, by distracting labor and enterprise from productive to parasitic activities, it frequently delayed the realization of the plausible hopes upon which railroad projects were primarily based.

The demand for labor initiated a chapter in the history of immigration and colonization.[12] It also disciplined migratory and local labor power to co-operative industrial effort. But it had wider repercussions. Laborers were paid wages and the wages were spent for goods. They went to market to buy the produce of American farms and mills. Thus the demand for labor stimulated the spread of market economy and the more extensive production of goods and services for distant markets, and thereby contributed to the spread of economic specialization.

The demand for capital functioned in parallel to the demand for labor. I am speaking of real capital, of goods, of the picks and shovels, sleepers and steel rails, engines and rolling stock and bridgework and culverts and ordinary building material, which make up the physical plant of a railroad. The construction moment of railway history brought an initial demand for these durable goods.[13] Hence there was a chance for the innovator in the lumbering industry, in quarries, in iron mills and carriage works. Indeed these industries were hard put to keep pace with railway construction. Until the later eighties, every boom period found American factories unable to meet the demand for rails, and there were heavy importations from England and Wales. As late as the nineties, over one fifth of the total output of pig iron in the United States was being rolled into railroad bars.[14]

Much of this demand for durable goods turned eventually into a demand for labor in mine and quarry and mill, into wage payments to labor. And these wages too were spent for consumers' goods and meant widening markets, increased specialization, and, presumably, greater productivity.

Thus the initial impetus of investment in railway construction led in widening arcs to increments of economic activity over the entire American domain, far exceeding in their total volume the original inputs of investment capital. To this feature of modern capitalism, John Maynard Keynes and others have applied the term "multiplier."[15] It is believed that for present-day England the efficiency of the multiplier may suffice to double the impact of a new investment in construction. For nineteenth-century United States, its efficiency seems to have been considerably greater than that.

I have spoken of inputs and investment. In our economy the demand for land and labor and capital has meant another demand, a demand not for an independent factor of production, but for something equally essential, a demand for money capital.[16] In fact, without a supply of money capital there could have been no effective demand for any of the real factors, no railways, and no stimulus from them for economic development. Hence it is convenient to think of the building of railroads as an investment of money capital. To this investment there corresponded in the long run the accumulation of savings. That saving came first and investment in the railroads afterwards is a proposition for which there is little historical evidence, at least in the United States. It is true that the practice of thrift as an individual and family responsibility was built into our social system by the Puritans. But the savings thus made in the middle of the nineteenth century went largely into land, into improvements on the farm, into the mill, the private business, and, in relatively small amounts, into public securities. Few railroads were originally financed by direct subscription of the shareholders at par in ready cash.[14]

In final analysis, the funds for railway construction came from the extension of credit by American banks and from foreign exchange supplied by European investors. This was accomplished by many devices which called into play the charitable cupidity of contractors and iron manufacturers on both sides of the Atlantic, and the lively anticipations of property owners in the area which the railroad was to develop.[18] Some of the shares were sold at a heavy discount to local residents, but more were given outright for land, for legal and legislative services, for banking accommodation, or as a bonus to promote the sale of bonds. Frequently there was a construction company, analogous to the Credit Mobilier, which took all the securities in payment for the road and operated it pending the completion of construction. Since the books of these organizations have been conveniently mislaid, it will always be impossible to ascertain what our railroads really cost originally in money capital. The construction companies turned over whole blocks of securities to manufacturers and contractors in payment for goods and services. These enterprisers usually seem to have pledged the securities with banks for working capital in the process of supplying the goods. In New York and elsewhere, speculators and specialists in railway finance, operating also on bank loans, facilitated this inflationary process by their dealings in stocks and bonds and daily risked the credit of the railway companies in their furious contests of bulls and bears.

The American banking mechanism did not have to bear this periodic strain alone. Every burst of new railway construction, in the thirties, in the fifties, at the close of the Civil War, through the eighties, and again from 1904 to 1907, meant new investments from abroad by British, Dutch, and German capitalists.[19] Schumpeter states that the boom from 1866 to 1873, which doubled our railway mileage, was entirely financed by an estimated two billion dollars of capital imported during those years.[20]   It is incorrect to suppose, as he apparently does, that any such amount of foreign money was at that time invested directly in the railways. British, Dutch, and German investors were then buying nearly half of the Civil War debt, chiefly in 5-20's and 10-40's, to the amount of more than a billion dollars par. The railroads obtained directly only about half a billion. The purchase of government bonds by foreigners, however, released savings and bank resources for railway, industrial, and commercial promotion in the United States. In no subsequent period was the impact of foreign capital as momentous; but it is easy to exaggerate its importance. Although something like one fifth of the nominal value of American railroads was foreign-owned in 1873, the whole volume of foreign claims amounted to only 6 or 7 per cent of national wealth.[21] While in the course of subsequent fluctuations foreign ownership of railroad securities may have reached the proportions of one third in 1890 and nearly as much just before 1914, yet at these later dates it constituted a smaller proportion of the total national wealth than it had in 1873. According to the estimates, foreign investments did not keep pace with the growth of national wealth.

It would be desirable to measure more precisely the investment of money capital at successive periods. Available figures of railway capitalization are entirely unsatisfactory for historical purposes. Apart from the obscurities of early railroad finance already mentioned, tabulations and estimates do not carefully and regularly include net floating debt or exclude intercorporate securities. The pathology of early stock watering has no necessary connection with the "overcapitalization" from which most railroad systems have suffered in recent years. This overcapitalization is entirely compatible with real historical investment as large as the nominal capitalization. But the available statistics give no adequate clue, before the last few decades, when such amounts actually were invested.

Whatever the source or timing of the application of money capital, the financing of railroad construction encouraged innovations in financial enterprise: the development of stock exchanges and their techniques; the specialization of firms, old and new, in investment banking and in security brokerage; the specialization of banking institutions (especially trust companies) as trustees and registration agents for securities, and as agents for distributing capital and interest payments; the rise of legal firms specializing in corporation law and in adjusting construction activities to the intricacies of the American political system.

New financial techniques and innovations in corporate structure were involved when established railway companies became agents in the flow of capital. By the early fifties the Pennsylvania was using its credit to supply funds for the building of western connections which it only informally controlled.[22] With the establishment of the Pennsylvania Company in 1869, the holding company became a permanent feature of the American scene. In many cases initial construction was of the sketchiest sort and by the seventies it was an established practice, of which foreign security holders bitterly complained, for companies to invest their earnings in necessary improvements and extensions. This financing of corporate growth from within may fairly be claimed to be an American innovation in capitalistic technique, which has only recently been diffused to the British Isles.

With financial innovation came a transformation of the role of the enterpriser in connection with particular railway systems. In the initial moments of construction, the typical enterpriser was still pretty much the omnicompetent pioneer, the individual of imagination, daring, and energy. Like General W. J. Palmer of the Denver and Rio Grande, he considered himself an agent of civilization, an embodiment of collective purpose.[23] No aspect of the task of railway building was too technical for his consideration and none too petty. In looking for the enterpriser of particular lines, official titles should not deceive. There was usually one man or a small informal group of unspecialized associates who could get things done, who could deal effectively at the same time with laborers, suppliers, politicians, and the local citizenry, and could command the confidence of sources of credit. At the construction moment, administration of a large formal organization was not necessarily involved. The mechanism of subcontracting provided a pattern for the cooperation of innumerable lesser enterprisers of a similar type.

Such enterprisers were rarely able, however, to cope with recurrent financial involvements. The elaboration of the superstructure of railroad securities sooner or later compelled a more formal division of tasks and responsibilities in the continuance of construction. In some cases this involved a shift of the center of decision from the engineer-promoter to financial and legal experts either within or outside the railroad organization.[24] The financier-enterpriser assumed many guises, now entering upon new construction to win stock-exchange battles, now basing a program of calculated expansion upon a re-ordering of company accounts, now entering belatedly, as did William Rockefeller in Northwestern, the race for competitive bigness.[25] There was inescapably a narrowing of horizon; the financier-enterpriser could decide freely only problems stated in financial terms, and he focused his attention chiefly on relations with potential intermediaries and rivals for the supply of capital.

Thus the second moment of the railroad as an economic force came with a demand for the factors of production in new construction, accompanied by the rise of new techniques and institutions of finance, by the aggregation of capital in mobile forms, and by the gradual displacement of the omnicompetent type of enterpriser.

The third moment to be surveyed is that of the railroad as a going concern, a complex of tracks and engines and cars and managers and employees engaged in the business of carrying passengers and freight. By rendering this transportation service, the railroad in operation has doubtless added directly to the real income of the United States, and indirectly to economic expansion.[26] There appears to be no satisfactory technique for giving a precise measure to the extent of this contribution. It seems that the railways carried irregularly increasing ton-miles of freight until 1929, while the aggregate of passenger-miles expanded until 1920. The quanta involved, said to be from 13 billions of freight in 1870 to 450 billions in 1929, are certainly enormous.[27] But the available figures, at least before 1890, are neither accurate nor complete. There have been important changes in the composition of traffic. As Pigou points out, any attempt to measure differences in real income between situations involving substantial variations in the use of productive factors and in the composition of demand is theoretically at least precarious.[28] For contemporary comparison, Holmstrom has worked out a technique by which "virtual costs" (operating and maintenance charges plus interest on replacement cost of ways and works plus depreciation and profits) are equated with "direct benefits" on the one hand and "consumer costs" plus public subsidies on the other.[29] In view of the defective character of the data and the violence of price fluctuations in the United States, there is little hope of applying these means of measurement to the historical problem.

It is commonly assumed that the great contribution of railroad transportation came from the reduction of shipping costs. As compared with pre-motorized forms of highway transportation, the advantage of the railroad has always been obvious. There is no convincing evidence, however, that railways have ever carried freight at lower costs either to shippers or to society than canals or waterways.[30] The advantages that early railways showed over canals, such as speed, flexibility of service, and special adaptability to short hauls, are analogous to those of modern highway transport over the railroad. It was far more important that the railroad brought transportation to areas that without it could have had scarcely any commercial existence at all. At a later epoch, the motor highway provides means to achieve this result, at least in British colonial areas, at lower initial social cost. But historically, the very existence of most American communities and regions, of particular farms and industrial firms and aggregates, was made possible by the railroad.

Holmstrom's study of the cost characteristics of various forms of transportation brings other considerations to the forefront of analysis. He shows that the traffic potential of the railroad per unit of installation is even now far greater than that of any other form of transportation that he considers. For colonial areas in the early 1930's, for example, he computes that human porters could carry a maximum of 1,450 ton-miles of freight per annum; heavy animals, 3,600; "horsed wagons," 118,800; tractor trains, 1,000,000; and broad-guage railways, 3,613,500.[31] Thus an initial and continuing potential contribution of the railroad has come from the volume of traffic it has been able to carry.

The converse of this proposition is the fact that the railroad constitutes a case of increasing return, with special features that give a decisive bent to its impact upon economic structure. Its social costs per unit of traffic decrease rapidly with traffic density.[32] A familiar manifestation of this condition was the well-known shift from passengers and light traffic as principal sources of revenue in the early railroad days to bulk traffic. Any isolated railroad system would tend to expand along those lines. But as new railroads in the United States became linked to previously existing lines, and as the innovation of freight-car interchange was established after the Civil War, a principle of acceleration was manifested enabling newer lines to begin farther along the cost curve. Between 1890 and 1941 the average actual haul of each ton of freight became 50 per cent longer (increasing especially during the First World War and the 1930's); there was an increase of more than 100 per cent during the same period in the distance traveled by the average passenger. These are revealing data about the long-run function of the railroad in the economic system.[33] Such expansion is, however, not a measure of innovation; the recent increase reflects to no small degree adjustments by railroads to other innovations in the economic system. What is significant about the principle of increasing return in the railroad is that it indicates directions in which railway transportation affects the economic structure.

That the railroad tends to attract factors of production to its right of way needs no comment; this perception lay at the heart of the American railroad innovation. As Holmstrom points out, however, this supply of potential traffic does not distribute itself at random. It is polarized first about line terminals, and secondarily about traffic intersections.[34] There is a further tendency. Irrespective of rate differentials, the service of the railroad is of greatest advantage to large shippers requiring a fairly regular flow of traffic.[35] Thus railroad transportation provides a considerable addition to the external economies that firms can realize from large-scale operations. Such phenomena as the ecological structure of wholesale trade, the localization and concentration of primary processing establishments, and the vertical integration of production units in spite of their geographical separation are thus functionally related to railroad transportation service. In more concrete terms, attention may be directed to the initial localization of the textile industry in New England, the development of the factory system in some other industries at points remote from water power and dependent upon rail supply of coal, the establishment of stockyards in Chicago and other terminals, the rise of assembly plants, and generally the concentration, at terminals convenient to the source of supply, of industries processing and reducing the bulk of raw materials. In all these respects, railway transportation has worked in the same direction as, but in different areas from, water transport. It has functioned differently from the realized and probable tendencies of highway traffic.

The organization of railway enterprise itself early displayed the same tendencies to differentiation that it encouraged in other industries. On the one hand, the railways transferred to other enterprises part of their business. First in individual railway lines, and gradually on a more national scale, came the innovation of express companies, specializing in the rapid transmission of small items of high value. Opportunity arose for Pullman and other specialists in high-cost passenger service. On the other hand, individual railways themselves engaged in other business activities. If their land departments developed in order to implement construction, they proved of more value in augmenting traffic density to remunerative levels. Reading and other companies acquired anthracite fields in the interest of controlling the supply of bulk traffic between terminals. A great deal of change in the internal structure of railway organizations was merely a function of their expansion, involving innovations of a highly derivative and adaptive character; but other changes involved the positive quest of increasing return. The extension of particular systems by purchase, lease, and contract did not invariably contemplate development, but often aimed at controlling for the benefit of original main lines the supply of traffic at terminal points. The consolidation movement and much resistance to it on the part of particular companies may be interpreted from this point of view.

It must be clear that to yield real income and participate in expansion are not the same as to be a force for economic development. On the economic structure, the impact of the railway as a going concern was most decisive in the early years of the expansion of each system and in many respects came from the network as a whole rather than from any particular part. In time many other forces reinforced the polarizing tendency of the railroad. Urban centers tended to generate conditions that made for their own growth into metropolises. The returns to railways from increasing density tended to increase at slackening rates. Change in the railways gradually became more a matter of adjustment to external innovations than a primary source of disturbance to the economic structure.

As early as the eighties, railway systems that had been daring ventures only a decade before found themselves embarking on extensions and improvements, not as acts of innovating faith, but to enable them to handle traffic that had been offered them or to keep somebody else from getting the business.[36] In region after region development initiated by the railroad outran the plans of the projectors. The business of the railroad came increasingly to consist not in starting something but in keeping pace with what others were doing. That the railway would carry freight at known rates and with gradual change in the quality of service came to be part of the normal expectations of every business firm, a stable part of an environment which, of course, might still be disturbed by other innovations.[37] While the real income accruing to society from railway transportation probably continued to grow until 1929, the railroad functioned decreasingly as a pace setter or as an inciting force in the expansion of which it was a part.

By the time of the financial reorganizations of the nineties, many American railways manifested signs of belonging to an industry that has reached maturity.[38] The signs became more widespread in the first decade of the present century with the completion of the last cluster of new systems. For enterprises in general, Oxenfeldt thinks "newness of economic consequence" can be assumed to have worked itself out within a year of establishment.[39] This seems too short a period for the railroad. Although the bulk of improvement in the early years of American railway systems is properly classed as "construction," the leverage of increasing return in this field involves such extensive relocation of productive forces that opportunity for major business decisions may recur for several years after "completion" of the system.[40]

That some innovations have been made by railroads since 1910 must be conceded. Both technological and organizational changes are involved in the recent rapid increase in ton-miles of freight handled per employee and per unit of capital, in the increased capacity of cars, in speed of train units, in locomotive efficiency, etc. The National Resources Planning Board, however, takes the view that potentialities in this direction are thus far more an idea than an actuality.[41]

Consolidation looms as the source of the most important innovations in the near future. In 1933 only 16 per cent of the time of a typical freight car from shipper to consignee was consumed in hauling; 37 per cent of the time was attributable to railroad terminal movement; and a total of 84 per cent was spent in terminals.[42] Co-operation among carriers could improve this condition, but changes of innovational consequence seem to wait upon government action.

But what has been the role of the entrepreneur in the railroad as a going concern? What is the source of innovation in an enterprise almost wholly concerned with rendering transportation service? The rise of a line organization with few staff features was an early aspect of railway operations, and was well established by the eighties. The Pennsylvania Central seems to have led the way in the practice of promotion from within, a practice that developed rapidly into seniority policies at all levels and the establishment of railroading as a career. For a couple of decades after the Civil War, the training thus afforded made the Pennsylvania an important source from which new companies drew top executives who often developed entrepreneurial talents as individuals. Thomas A. Scott, who rose from the ranks to the presidency of Pennsylvania, was of pioneering quality. As horizons of opportunity narrowed, however, selection from within tended to bring competent administrators of a more routine sort to top executive positions, men who had spent so many years mastering the complexities of detailed management along established lines that they had little interest in changing those procedures. This tendency has been marked in many railroad systems, and is associated with the shift to adaptive change as the principal relation of the railroads to economic expansion in recent years.

Nevertheless, some innovation has taken place, and it can occasionally be traced to pioneering leadership. Large organizations as such, however, apart from their degree of maturity, set up certain hazards to innovation. to continue operations they require the delegation of specialized authority and responsibility to a considerable number of individuals. An innovation disturbs their tasks and their relations with each other quite as much as it does economic relations and activities outside the organization. This disturbance to internal equilibrium is not adjusted through market mechanisms and bargaining transactions. It involves planning activity. Decisive importance can scarcely be allowed to attach to individuals who conceive new ideas, even when this duty is delegated to them as a specific task. The locus of decision tends to spread to a group that includes persons in a position to know and deal with prospective internal disturbances which are only partially of an economic character.[43] It is not clear than this development has explicitly gone far in railroad organization. As an innovation in the role of entrepreneurship itself, it is emergent in some newer large-scale industries. The extent to which the management-enterpriser type, as we may call it, has actually functioned in railroads informally and without explicit recognition deserves inquiry.

This general interpretation of the role of the railroad as an economic force suggests what might be undertaken in greater detail to apply the innovation theory to the history of particular companies and of the railroad system as a whole. What was the impact of the railroad upon technological, locational, structural, and organizational alterations in particular firms, industries, and regions? Parallel inquiries could be made regarding the part played by other major innovations, such as the more recent rise of the electromotive industries. It is not a question of applying the facts of economic history to verify an economic theory. It is a question of using a theory as a tool to coherent understanding of the facts. Economic historians seem increasingly willing to make use of conceptual aids for this purpose. It is one of the most prominent symptoms of what may be a wider tendency to employ analytical procedures in historical studies.

For the study of long-run change, the innovation theory stresses two important aspects of historical process: (1) the distinction between innovating (disturbing, inciting, evolutionary) change and various types of adjustment (including expansion), and (2) the distinctive role of entrepreneurship. The first of these aspects provides the framework for systematic exploration of the relation between changes in several sectors of the economy, in so far as these can be interpreted in economic terms. The breakdown of the railroad innovation into three "moments" is only a convenience that may be peculiar to transportation. In any case, the distinction between innovating and adaptive change is a device that should become more serviceable to the historian as it is sharpened by application to a number of particular situations. It does not necessarily require the economic historian to take into account other than economic events and processes. Indeed, its logical adequacy can only gain from rigorous limitation to the items that are considered to be a part of an economic system.

The emphasis upon entrepreneurship as the crucial factor in capitalistic evolution involves both theorist and historian in considerations that go far beyond the limits of economics. Schumpeter is explicitly aware of this fact, and insists that in his conception the economy is not isolated but functions in a larger universe which requires in the first instance sociological analysis for its interpretation. The theory of innovations is neither a "great man" nor a "better mousetrap" theory of history. The innovator is a person whose traits are in some part a function of his sociocultural environment. His innovation is a new combination of factors and elements already accessible. It relates in every phase to previously developed business and monetary habits, technological skills, and variable tastes, none of which can be regarded as functions of economic activity alone. Thus Schumpeter's theory involves the question of the sociological factors favorable to the emergence of entrepreneurship. In a recent work he has presented a partial analysis of such factors.[44] Further analysis seems to be called for, at least so far as American capitalism is concerned, analysis that will come to closer grips with the special features of American social structure and the various influences which made for a strong entrepreneurial bias in the "social character" of the nineteenth-century American.

Despite his sociological sophistication, however, Schumpeter tends to think of his entrepreneur pretty much as a deviant person—a particular individual or at most a family. This approach tends to make highly problematical the existence of any entrepreneurship in a bureaucratic enterprise such as the railway, whether under private or public ownership. It must be recognized that innovations in a socialist economy would work themselves out by mechanisms other than under capitalism. But not all of such differences would be peculiar to socialism. Practically, large-scale organization offers a new type of social resistance to innovation. At the same time, as Schumpeter himself vigorously argues, the large organization offers real support to technological change, at least, by mobilizing resources for its systematic planning.[45]

It is possible that there is a real social lag in conceptions of the entrepreneurial function. The question deserves to be considered whether policy formation by group action is an obstacle to innovation, not inherently, but only because of certain peculiarities in our culture. Is the entrepreneurial role in large organizations increasingly the function of a co-operating group? Is it true that this tendency is not absolutely new but can be discerned in earlier phases of modern industry; that it is less important in entrepreneurial studies to single out the contributions of one individual than to ascertain the personal composition of the group with which he usually interacted and the way in which the members compensated for their respective shortcomings and were adjusted to each other? In so far as there is validity in affirmative answers to these questions, a practical problem of much importance falls upon the large organizations of the present day, that of cultivating social techniques for facilitating innovations. But there would be a broader social problem, that of developing personalities whose practical imagination and responsibility for decision will be stimulated rather than frustrated by membership in policy-determining groups. This would be a task for the family and other educational institutions and for socializing processes in the wider society.

NOTES

1. This article is an elaboration and extension of a paper delivered at the meeting of the Mississippi Valley Historical Association, Washington, D.C., December 28-31, 1938.
2. Joseph A Schumpeter, *Business Cycles* (New York and London: McGraw-Hill Book Company, 1939), Vol. I, esp. chaps. iii and vii; *idem, The Theory of Economic Development* (Cambridge: Harvard University Press, 1934), chaps. ii and vi; *idem,* "The Instability of Capitalism," *The Economic Journal,* XXXVIII (1928), 361-86. Cf. the theory of Allyn A. Young, "Increasing Returns and Economic Progress," *ibid.,* 527-42.
3. *Business Cycles*, I, 86.
4. These distinctions are hinted at but not developed in *Business Cycles,* I, 130-36. They are not to be construed precisely as stages or periods, although each was relatively more conspicuous in certain decades than in others.
5. Three types of obstacles to innovation are distinguished in *Business Cycles,* I, 100: hostility to the new idea, absence of facilitating economic functions, and inhibitions against entering upon a relatively incalculable course. Young in *The Economic Journal,* XXXVIII (1928), 534, stresses the need to remake human material in terms of new skills and habits and in terms of redistribution of population.
6. Carl Russell Fish, *The Rise of the Common Man* (New York: The Macmillan Company, 1927), chaps. iv and v.

7. One thinks of the Boston & Lowell, New York & New Haven, Philadelphia & Columbia, Allegheny Portage, the original Baltimore & Ohio, and the lines connecting Albany with Buffalo.

8. The most dynamic set of American innovations consisted in plans to build railways in anticipation of traffic. Lewis Henry Haney, *A Congressional History of Railways in the United States to 1850* (Madison: University of Wisconsin, 1908), p. 31. Congressional land grants were a factor, as in the case of the Illinois Central, the first large system built through sparsely settled territory. Paul Wallace Gates, *The Illinois Central Railroad and Its Colonization Work* (Cambridge: Harvard University Press, 1934). Canal building had, however, in the old Northwest, anticipated the railroad less successfully in building ahead of population. Frederic L. Paxson, *History of the American Frontier 1763-1893* (Boston and New York: Houghton Mifflin Company, 1924), chap. xxx. For early systems and projects, cf. Caroline E. MacGill *et al.,* Balthasar Henry Meyer, editor, *History of Transportation in the United States Before 1860* (Washington: Carnegie Institution of Washington, 1917); J. L. Ringwalt, *Development of Transportation Systems in the United States* (Philadelphia: The Author, 1888).

9. The data for these charts are derived from the United States Treasury Department, Bureau of Statistics, *Statistical Abstract of the United States, 1900* (Washington: United States Government Printing Office, 1901); *ibid., 1914*, p. 637; and *ibid., 1937*, p. 379. Chart II is adapted from Simon S. Kuznets, *Secular Movements in Production and Prices* (Boston and New York: Houghton Mifflin Company, 1930), pp. 191, 526-27.

10. This correlation was initially based upon inspection of the mileage data in comparison with the chart in Schumpeter, *Business Cycles*, II, 465, and the analyses of business conditions in Willard Long Thorp, *Business Annals* (New York: National Bureau of Economic Research, 1926) and National Bureau of Economic Research, *Recent Economic Changes* (New York: McGraw-Hill Book Company, 1929), II, 892. More decisive support is provided by John E. Partington, *Railroad Purchasing and the Business Cycle* (Washington: The Brookings Institution, 1929). As Partington includes orders for replacements as well as for original basic construction, he finds that orders of railway capital goods led business-cycle changes as late as 1907. Throughout this period, he finds, railway earnings followed, instead of preceded, changes in purchases.

11. Frederick A. Cleveland and Fred Wilbur Powell, *Railroad Promotion and Capitalization in the United States* (New York: Longmans, Green and Company, 1909), pp. 199-200. "In the Southern States, and the Mississippi Valley . . . . all the real estate required for way, and for depots, stations, etc., are generally gratuity to the roads." *American Railroad Journal*, XXV (January 3, 1852), 13. Cf. James Blaine Hedges, *Henry Villard and the Railways of the Northwest* (New Haven: Yale University Press, 1930), *passim*.

12. Gates, *The Illinois Central Rail-road*, pp. 89, 94-8. Despite its crucial importance, the subject of labor supply has been too frequently neglected by railway historians. Adequate data for labor employed in new construction are available only for a few large lines such as the Central Pacific, Union Pacific, and the Illinois Central. On each of these, upwards of 10,000 men were employed at the peak of construction. Probably a thousand men were needed for every hundred miles. Assuming that twice as many miles were in progress as were completed in any given year, the figure of 200,000 men is reached as the maximum employed at any one time in the construction of these railways. This figure was not attained until the eighties, by which the time the census reported 250,000 officials and employees of railroads, presumably engaged directly or indirectly in transportation service.

13. Cf. files of railways periodicals for advertisements of manufacturers and dealers in railway materials and supplies. Ringwalt, *Development of Transportation Systems in the U. S.,* pp. 132-36, 210.

14. For details, cf. *Statistical Abstract of the U. S., 1902,* p. 380, and corresponding tables in earlier volumes.

15. John Maynard Keynes, *The General Theory of Employment, Interest and Money* (London, 1936), chap. xi; R. F. Kahn, "The Relation of Home Investment to Unemployment," *The Economic Journal,* XLI (1931), 173-98.

16. Admittedly "money capital" constitutes merely a vehicle or instrumentality, the means of acquiring command over the several factors of production. More commonly it is spoken of as long-term credit or capital funds. But sometimes an instrument becomes so important that it exerts influences by itself and requires consideration on its separate account.

17. These were chiefly railroads built in the thirties and forties. Cf. Frank Walker Stevens, *The Beginnnings of the New York Central Railroad* (New York and London: G. P. Putnam's Sons, 1926). Even in these cases, as we know from accounts of the crises of 1854 and 1857, the subscribers carried their shares on bank loans. Cf. Schumpeter, *Busniess Cycles,* I, 325-30.

18. Cleveland and Powell, *Railroad Promotion and Capitalization,* is still the most adequate account for aspects before 1900. Cf. William Z. Ripley, *Railroads; Finance and Organization* (New York: Longmans, Green and Company, 1915), pp. 10-52; Cleveland and Powell, *Railroad Finance* (New York: D. Appleton and Company, 1912), chaps ii-iv and the very rich bibliography; Charles F. Adams, Jr., "Railroad Inflation," *North American Review,* CVIII (1869), 138-44.

19. This paragraph is based upon original research in London and the United States, made possible by a sabbatical from Wellesley College and a grant from the John Simon Guggenheim Memorial Foundation. An introduction to the subject is available in Cleona Lewis, *America's Stake in International Investments* (Washington: The Brookings Institution, 1938), chap. ii; Ripley, *Railroads; Finance and Organization,* pp. 1-10; and Leland H. Jenks, *The Migration of British Capital to 1875* (New York and London: Alfred A. Knopf, 1927), chap. iii and pp. 169, 255-59 and notes. Before the Civil War the share of foreign investors was smaller than it became later. In only a few cases was it an initiating factor in railroad development.

20. Schumpeter, *Business Cycles,* I, 335.

21. Lewis, *America's Stake in International Investments,* p. 560.

22. Pennsylvania Central R. R. Co., *Annual Reports, passim.*

23. William J. Palmer, *The Westward Current of Population in the United States (London, 1874) and Glenn Chesney Quiett, They Built the West* (New York and London: D. Appleton-Century Company, 1934), chaps. ii-vi, throw light upon the career of this neglected enterpriser.

24. N. S. B. Gras, *Business and Capitalism* (New York: F. S. Crofts and Company, 1939), pp. 246-59, 272-75, indicates the "normal" process by which financial capitalists became involved in industry. He is correct, I believe, in implying that the opportunity and need have not been confined to late phases of the construction moment. From the standpoint of innovation, the emergence of the financial enterpriser in the railroads is not to be identified with the rise of special departments within the organization. The latter, or their heads, may be simply parts of a formally established group functioning as management-enterpriser. See section IV below.

25. Max Lowenthal, *The Investor Pays* (New York: Alfred A. Knopf, 1933).

26. Ringwalt, *Development of Transportation Systems in the U. S.,* pp. 382-85 and Henry V. Poor, *Influence of the Railroads of the U. S. in the Creation of its Commerce and Wealth* (New York, 1869) are representative of early discussions. "Our new railroads increase the value of farms and open markets for their products. They lessen the time and cost of travel. They give a value to commodities otherwise almost worthless. They

concentrate population, stimulate production, and raise wages by making labor more efficient. Our existing railroads are computed to create more wealth every year than is absorbed for the construction of new railroads." *Commerical and Financial Chronicle,* XVI (January 11, 1873), 41.

27. Attempts to use railway data in connection with the study of changes in real income and "productivity" are exemplified by Arthur F. Burns, *Production Trends in the United States since 1870* (New York: National Bureau of Economic Research, 1934) and Spurgeon Bell, *Productivity, Wages, and National Income* (Washington: The Brookings Institution, 1940). A brief factual summary of the role of the railways in the economic system after the First World War is provided by the Bureau of Railway Economics, *The Railways and Economic Progress* (Miscellaneous Series No. 50, Washinton, 1929). The theory there suggested that the "economic contribution" of the railways is measured by the volume of their expenditures of all kinds is, however, at variance with the premises of this paper. Incidentally, this is an unusual place to find a theory popularly associated with New Deal economics. On railroad expenditures, cf. Partington, *Railroad Purchasing and the Business Cycle.*

28. A. C. Pigou, "Comparisons of Real Income," *Economica, New Series, X (May, 1943),* pp. 93-8.

29. J. Edwin Holmstrom, *Railways and Roads in Pioneer Development Overseas* (London: P. S. King and Son, 1934), chap. i. Cf. E. A. J. Johnson, "New Tools for the Economic Historian," *The Tasks of Economic History,* supplemental issue of *The Journal of Economic History,* December, 1941, pp. 30-8.

30. General treatments of the economic significance of improved transportation are also found in D. Philip Locklin, *Economics of Transportation* (Chicago: Business Publications, 1938), chap. i, and Cleveland and Powell, *Railroad Finance,* Chap. i. On comparative costs of service, cf. MacGill, *History of Transportation in the U. S. before 1860,* pp. 574-82; Haney, *Congressional History of Railways in the U. S.,* chap. iii; Charles H. Ambler, *A History of Transportation in the Ohio Valley* (Glendale, California: The Arthur H. Clark Company, 1932), pp. 358 ff.; Harold Kelso, "Waterways versus Railways," *The American Economic Review,* XXXI (1941), 537-44.

31. Holmstrom, *Railways and Roads in Pioneer Development Overseas,* p. 56. Palmer, *The Westward Current of Population in the U. S.,* relates that in 1866 the stage line from the terminus of the Kansas Pacific in Topeka carried six passengers daily to Denver. Two years later, daily trains carried westward one hundred to five hundred passengers daily.

32. Holmstrom, pp. 104-12.

33. United States Interstate Commerce Commission, *Statistics of Railways in the United States, 1941* (Washington: United States Government Printing Office, 1943), pp. 159-60.

34. Holmstrom, pp. 265-66, 273.

35. *Ibid.,* pp. 271-72.

36. For instance, new financing was sought by the Grand Trunk of Canada in the seventies and the Norfolk & Western in the eighties to make it possible to handle traffic already being offered. It was not always an extension that was involved but more often doubletracks, sidings, rolling stock, and improvements in the right of way.

37. Schumpeter, *Business Cycles,* I, Chap. ii,   presents a representative theoretical analysis of this "equilibrium" position to which railway enterprises have been approximating.

38. E. G. Campbell, *The Reorganization of the American Railroad System, 1893-1900* (New York: Columbia University Press, 1938).

39. Alfred R. Oxenfeldt, *New Firms and Free Enterprise* (Washington: American Council on Public Affairs, 1943), p. 75.

40. The degree to which in recent decades public regulation has restricted this opportunity as far as pricing of services is concerned has been the subject of a suggestive inquiry by the National Resources Planning Board. *Transportation and National Policy* (Washington: United States Government Printing Office, 1942), esp. pp. 87-128.

41. *Ibid.*, pp. 60-5.

42. *Ibid.*, p. 41.

43. An introduction to the sociological theory of organization can be found in Chester I. Barnard, *The Functions of the Executive* (Cambridge: Harvard University Press, 1938). Cf. T. N. Whitehead, *Leadership in a Free Society* (Cambridge: Harvard University Press, 1936), chaps. vi and viii. The problem at a lower level of enterprise structure is analyzed in F. J. Roethlisberger and William J. Dickson, *Management and the Worker* (Cambridge: Harvard University Press, 1939), chaps. xxiv and xxv.

44. Joseph A. Schumpeter, *Capitalism, Socialism, and Democracy* (New York: Harper and Brothers, 1942), chaps. xi-xiv.

45. *Ibid.*, pp. 96-8. Schumpeter seems to regard this change as more than adaptational. In so far as it is innovational, however, it functions less to develop capitalist structure than to further its incipient transformation into something else.

chapter **13**

entrepreneurial developments

THE INDUSTRIAL CAPITALIST

Fundamental changes in the structure of the American economy produced a new type of entrepreneur. The merchant capitalist yielded his position of importance to a new breed, the industrial capitalist. The latter was an individualist who built an industrial empire through his own ingenuity, and with little help from bankers or advisors. He was highly competitive, and primarily interested in expanding production, opening new markets, and adopting the latest technological innovations. Unlike the merchant capitalist, the industrial entrepreneur tended to concentrate his energies on one item, such as oil, steel or railroads. Two outstanding examples of this type of entrepreneur are Andrew Carnegie (1835-1919) and John D. Rockefeller (1839-1937).

ANDREW CARNEGIE

Andrew Carnegie emigrated to Pittsburgh from Scotland with his family when he was a young boy. After serving a short time as a telegraph operator he secured a position with the Pennsylvania Railroad.

415

Diligence, good business sense, and an eagerness to assume responsibility earned him the superintendency of the Pittsburgh division of the Pennsylvania Railroad at the age of 30. When the Pennsylvania Railroad began to experiment with iron bridges to replace wooden ones, Carnegie left the company and organized his own bridge-building concern. Before long he shifted his operations to the production of steel, which he regarded as the metal of the future. He was one of the first producers of steel rails in the United States. In producing steel rails, Carnegie disregarded the advice and caution of his partners and was not dismayed that all previous efforts had failed. His success gave him a head start on his competition, a lead which he never relinquished. It is significant that Carnegie began construction of his Edgar Thomson (named after the President of the Pennsylvania Railroad) steel works in 1872, just one year before a panic and major depression. Instead of being discouraged by the turn in economic affairs, Carnegie poured every dollar he could into the new undertaking. He felt that a depression was the appropriate time to expand operations since costs were low and materials and labor readily available. This willingness to act in time of economic stress was one of the most important factors accounting for Carnegie's rise to the top of the steel industry. Another was the fact that he was constantly seeking new ways of cutting costs and modernizing his plant and equipment. Realizing that large size was a fundamental route to low costs, his organization achieved complete integration of all the necessary ingredients that went into the production of steel. Carnegie was a strong advocate of the theory of competition and an ardent follower of Herbert Spencer, the patron saint of industrial capitalists. According to Spencer, social relationships were governed by the same laws of selection as the natural environment. While Carnegie recognized that unbridled competition had some serious disadvantages, he felt that its net gains to society justified its cost. Despite his professed belief in free competition, Carnegie did not hesitate to engage in monopolistic practices, and was one of the first to secure railroad rebates and drawbacks.

During his active business life Carnegie gave all his energy to steel. When he wasn't in Pittsburgh running the company's affairs, he was traveling around the country and world trying to sell his products and learn new ways to make steel more cheaply. Even when he became quite wealthy he rarely engaged in other investments, despite suggestions that he do so. Carnegie's often quoted philosophy was to "put all your eggs in one basket and then watch the basket." He went on:

> ...I believe the true road to preeminent success in any line is to make yourself master in that line. I have no faith in the policy of scattering one's resources, and in my experience I have rarely if ever met a man who achieved preeminence in money-making—certainly

never one in manufacturing—who was interested in many concerns. The men who have succeeded are men who have chosen one line and stuck to it. It is surprising how few men appreciate the enormous dividends derivable from investment in their own business. There is scarcely a manufacturer in the world who has not in his works some machinery that should be thrown out and replaced by improved appliances; or who does not for the want of additional machinery or new methods lose more than sufficient to pay the largest dividend obtainable by investment beyond his own domain. And yet most business men whom I have known invest in bank shares and in far-away enterprises, while the true gold mine lies right in their own factories.

I have tried always to hold fast to this important fact. It has been with me a cardinal doctrine that I could manage my own capital better than any other person, much better than any board of directors. The losses men encounter during a business life which seriously embarrass them are rarely in their own business, but in enterprises of which the investor is not master.[1]

If Carnegie had another interest in life it was philanthropy. At 33 years of age, when he earned $50,000 a year, he expressed the desire to retire early in life to devote himself to spending his wealth for the good of mankind. He believed that the wealthy had a responsibility to employ the same skill and zeal in spending their money as they employed in earning it. Being selected by God to exercise a stewardship over a vast amount of resources, the business leader should not relinquish this responsibility to others by leaving his wealth to heirs or to private charities. Carnegie supported inheritance taxes in order to encourage the rich to dispose of their wealth during their lifetime. During his life he gave away an estimated $325 million, or about ninety per cent of his fortune. The principal benefactor was the world of arts and letters.

JOHN D. ROCKEFELLER

About the same time that Carnegie was entering the iron and steel business, John D. Rockefeller was making his start in the oil refining industry. Upon graduation from high school in 1855 he secured a position as bookkeeper for a Cleveland firm of commission merchants. Within a few years he and another clerk, Maurice Clark, went into the grain commission business, each investing two thousand dollars. From its inception the business was quite successful, but Rockefeller saw in oil refining even greater opportunities for profit. The sinking of the first successful commercial well in Titusville, Pennsylvania in 1859 promised to revolutionize the illuminating oil industry. In 1862 Rockefeller, Clark, his two older brothers, and Samuel Andrews, began operating a small refinery. The business prospered but there was continual friction between Rockefeller and the Clarks. Rockefeller favored expansion while the Clarks were content with the existing scale of operations. After purchasing the Clarks' interest in the business, Rockefeller turned his efforts to achieving the most efficient operation in the industry. Just as quickly as he could acquire capital he built new facilities to expand and modernize operations. Like Carnegie, it was by turning out a better quality product at lower prices that Rockefeller became the leading oil refiner in the United States.

In the 1860's oil refining was a fairly simple process, and anyone with $10,000 could start a small refinery. As a result, in the 1860's in Cleveland alone there existed some fifty companies. In 1870 Rockefeller and his associates formed the Standard Oil Corporation of Ohio, and proceeded to acquire all the property of its major rivals in Cleveland. Taking advantage of the depression years 1873-1877, the company next bought up facilities in New York and Pennsylvania. By the 1880's Standard did about 90 per cent of the country's refining business. As the number and size of the company's holdings grew it became increasingly difficult to manage the business, particularly since at this time a corporation could only manufacture and own property in the state where it was chartered. Standard Oil of Ohio had no legal right to have assets outside of the state or to operate an interstate business. This problem was solved in 1882 by adopting the ancient legal device of the trust to Standard's needs. A corporation was created in each state where Standard had important products or affiliates. The stockholders of these companies turned over their shares to a single board of trustees, giving the latter control over Standard's vast empire. The device was quite effective and in time spread to several other industries. When Ohio in 1892 altered Standard's charter to prohibit the establishment of a trust, the company was rechartered as a holding company under New Jersey law. In 1893 New Jersey had amended its incorporation laws to permit one corporation to acquire the stock of other corporations for the purpose of control.

Rockefeller preferred to acquire rival firms by persuasion rather than by coercion. In the process of absorbing other firms he emphasized negotiation and fair play rather than predatory tactics. Nevertheless, his extensive use of railroad rebates, the strict secrecy of his organization, and above all the growing power of Standard Oil made him very unpopular. As the years passed the number of government investigations, lawsuits, and journalist attacks on Standard Oil and Rockefeller multiplied. Rockefeller became America's number one villain. Throughout the attacks he remained silent, refusing to defend himself. Even his retirement from a corporate role in the business in 1899 was kept a secret. As a result the public continued to hold him personally responsible for the activities of Standard Oil for many years after he was no longer head of the firm.

Both Rockefeller and his wife were deeply religious. From the early 1860's Rockefeller took an active role in his church and was a liberal contributor. As his wealth increased the number of his charities and amount of his giving kept pace. He was like Carnegie in feeling a sense of responsibility for the wealth he accumulated. Ably assisted by his son, John D. Rockefeller, Jr., his total philanthropies amounted to over a half a billion dollars. With the same skill and daring which had characterized his business career, he blazed new trails in the field of philanthropy. The various foundations which he established became models for others all over the world.

THE FINANCE CAPITALIST

THE TRANSITION TO FINANCE CAPITALISM

The industrial entrepreneurs' forte was production. They were specialists in improving, adapting and implementing the production process. With unshakable faith in the future of America they conquered the production frontier. In their bold quest to conquer the world of business, however, industrial capitalists often found themselves vulnerable to the vicissitudes of the business cycle. As long as prosperity reigned industrial capitalists had no trouble paying their debts. But when panic and depression set in they were often forced into bankruptcy. Few industrial entrepreneurs were able to operate their businesses on an even keel through good and bad time as did Carnegie and Rockefeller. Nor were most able to avoid the price wars which flared from time to time and aggravated their plight during periods of economic distress. During such times they were either gobbled up by a stronger competitor or forced to turn to the financial community for assistance. The investment banker, together with brokerage houses, commercial banks and insurance companies often were able to rescue the industrial capitalist. In return, ownership of a substantial block of the stock, a key position on the board of directors, or the creation of voting trusts were often demanded.

Equally important as the capital he provided was the finance entrepreneur's solution to the problem of unrestrained competition. Few industries were able to solve the problem internally as did Rockefeller in oil refining, most having to seek the outside assistance of investment bankers to achieve order and stability. Time and time again railroad entrepreneurs had unsuccessfully tried to control the forces of competition within their industry. It was only when financial entrepreneurs took a hand that a relatively stable community of interest was secured. The same situation was true in the steel industry. It has been recounted that Carnegie dominated the steel industry in the last half of the 1800's, and that by the turn of the century, through a series of combinations, other large steel companies had also emerged. These newer companies specialized in finished steel products such as pipes, tubes, hoops, wires and the like, while Carnegie continued to concentrate on crude steel. The finished steel companies, eager to expand and immunize themselves from dependence on Carnegie, decided to produce crude steel. When Carnegie heard of their intention to cancel orders for his steel and produce it themselves, he immediately set about to build facilities for the production of finished steel. A full-fledged price war was looming and most finished steel producers were alarmed, particularly since they were in a weak financial position and in little doubt that Carnegie could undersell them. The only alternatives were either to back down or to buy out Carnegie. While it was well known that Carnegie had wished to retire for some time, the finished steel producers were in no position to raise the necessary funds. Only the financial community had the resources to meet Carnegie's price. Accordingly, the finished steel producers approached J. Pierpont Morgan and asked him to assist. Morgan agreed and organized a syndicate to form a giant steel combination, U.S. Steel, which purchased the interests of Carnegie and his partners.

Even in periods of prosperity, industrial entrepreneurs were often dependent on financial assistance. The rapid growth of business after the Civil War rendered internal corporate savings insufficient. Many companies were forced to turn to outside sources of capital. As the volume of new security offerings grew it became increasingly difficult to market them. Only if a company allied itself with a major banker could it obtain needed funds. The finance entrepreneurs were specialists in financing. Through alliances with brokerage houses, banks, trust companies, insurance companies, and foreign banking houses, they possessed the ability to raise large amounts of capital in a relatively short period of time.

Finance capitalists believed that nothing short of active participation in the management of companies in which they were financially interested would assure managerial stability. This usually involved representation for them on boards of directors. Since finance capitalists were not experts in production or management, they generally did not meddle in these areas. As long as management seemed to be following a sound course, meeting interest charges, earning a reasonable profit, and declaring suitable dividends, they were content. A distaste for competition and a desire for lucrative reorganization fees led finance capitalists to promote industrial combinations. Finance capitalists were convinced that competition was a destructive economic force. In restraining it they believed they were performing a valuable service for society by creating an ethical and orderly business community. Reason, negotiation, and cooperation were preferred to economic coercion in achieving this goal. However, if the facts warranted it, finance capitalists were not above using their enormous power against any businessman who strayed out of line. The fees of finance capitalists were generally quite high. It has been estimated that one-half of the total capital stock of U.S. Steel was paid directly or indirectly to financial entrepreneurs for promotional services.

J. P. MORGAN

Of the dozen or so major financial entrepreneurs who were active in the late 1800's and early 1900's, J. P. Morgan (1837-1913) unquestionably was the most influential. Morgan's grandfather and father were both successful businessmen. At the time J. P. Morgan was completing his formal schooling, his father Junius Spencer Morgan had gone to London to secure a partnership in the international banking firm of George Peabody and Company. When Peabody retired during the Civil War, the firm became J. S. Morgan and Company. Young Morgan began his career at 20 years of age as a general accountant with a private bank in New York. Four years later he went into business for himself, buying and selling on his own account and acting as the New York representative for his father's firm. In 1869 he had his first real encounter with big business, an experience which was to make a profound impression on the young investment banker. As an associate of President Joseph H. Ramsey of the Albany and Susquehanna Railroad, Morgan became involved in what was called by the newspapers "The Susquehanna War." The Erie Railroad, then in the hands of Jay Gould, had wished to gain control of the A & S. Gould tried to buy A & S shares and to induce corrupt judges to issue injunctions against the present management. Ramsey countered with his own injunctions. For a time industrial warfare flared, with law officers at the Binghamton end of the line making arrests in accordance with the dictates of judges who allied themselves with Gould, and law officers at the Albany end carrying out the decrees of judges who sided with Ramsey. An actual battle was fought for control of a strategic tunnel on the railroad line. Although Ramsey eventually won the war, J. P. Morgan was disgusted by the violence, corruption, and waste which the war involved. How much better, he thought, if people would join forces and cooperate rather than dividing into opposing groups and competing with one another.

After a period of bad health, during which Morgan considered retirement from active business, he was induced to join forces with Drexel and Company of Philadelphia. Drexel was one of the largest investment banking firms in Philadelphia, second only to the great house of Jay Cooke and Company. When Jay Cooke and Company failed during the crisis of 1873, Drexel, Morgan and Company became the dominant firm in the U.S. government bond market. In 1879 J. P. Morgan was asked by William H. Vanderbilt, son and heir of Cornelius Vanderbilt, the great railroad entrepreneur, to dispose of some of his holdings of New York Central Stock. The younger Vanderbilt was smarting under increasing public criticism because of his 87 per cent ownership of one of America's great railroad systems. Morgan disposed of a substantial portion of the shares privately in England before anyone in the financial world knew what was happening, and as a result found himself sitting on the board of directors of the New York Central as the New York representative of his clients. During the 1880's Morgan intervened in several railroad disputes, bringing the combatants together and working out compromises. The 1893-97 depression offered Morgan the opportunity to effect more binding solutions. Within a year after the crisis of 1893 most of the major and minor railroads of the country were in bankruptcy. Since their services were essential to the communities they served, they had to be reorganized. Drexel, Morgan and Company were involved in most large reorganizations. In each Morgan set the rules of the game, which included lowering fixed charges to the expected minimum earnings of the company, assessing present stockholders to provide working capital, issuing new stock, both preferred and common, placing himself on the board of directors, and charging a substantial reorganization fee. As a consequence, in addition to his position on the board of the New York Central, Morgan had a substantial voice on the directoral boards of the New Haven, Erie and Reading, Norfolk and Western, Lehigh Valley, and Southern Reading systems. In addition, in alliance with James J. Hill, he exercised control of the Great Northern, the Northern Pacific, and the Baltimore and Ohio railroads. Moreover, the Pennsylvania, Lackawanna, and Delaware and Hudson railroads were all in hands friendly to Morgan. It was also during this period that Morgan came to the assistance of the United States Government. Faced with a run on Treasury gold stocks, President Cleveland enlisted his aid to sell Government bonds abroad for gold. Without Morgan's assistance the Government would have had no choice but temporarily to suspend convertibility of the currency.

Having achieved a substantial voice in the management of U.S. railroads, Morgan turned greater attention to other sectors, particularly manufacturing. At this point in his business career he was strictly on his own, for both his father and Drexel had died, leaving him in control of their respective companies. Morgan was not new to the manufacturing field, for he was one of the organizers of the General Electric Company in 1892. In 1898 he helped to finance the formation of Federal Steel, which at that time was the second largest producer in the industry. This led to his promotion of the United States Steel Corporation in 1901. Not all Morgan's companies were successful. His effort to create a huge shipping combine, the International Mercantile Marine Company failed, and his insistence that the New Haven railroad acquire virtually all transportation facilities in New England converted a sound and profitable company into an overcapitalized, financially burdened railroad. His influence, however, continued to grow. During the Panic of 1907 Morgan was recognized by the financial community as its spokesman, and during several weeks of crisis personally directed the efforts of Wall Street to mitigate the panic.

Ever since he had risen to national prominence in the early 1890's Morgan had been the target of groups attacking the concentration of economic power. In 1902 the Federal Government, whom Morgan believed he had served unselfishly, joined the opposition with an antitrust suit against the Northern Securities Company, which Edward Harriman and Morgan had established a year earlier to control the Northern Pacific and Great Northern Railroads. Much to Morgan's surprise, the Supreme Court in 1904 upheld the Government's case. Even more disheartening was the U.S. antitrust action against United States Steel in 1911. In 1912-13 there was a public investigation of Morgan's activities by a Committee of Congress. The Pujo Committee, as it was called, examined in detail Morgan's influence, and although Morgan himself denied that he exercised unreasonable power, the Committee revealed that he and his associates together held 341 directorships in 112 corporations, with a total capitalization of over 22 billion dollars.

When Morgan died in 1913 the public was surprised by the relatively modest size of his estate, 68 million dollars, not including his art collections which were estimated at 20 to 50 million dollars. The sum was smaller than that left by associates of considerably less ability and influence. Morgan was not a speculator, and derived his income chiefly from conservative investments and commissions which, although large, were shared with many other firms. He lived on an increasingly magnificent scale, spending and giving freely. His art collection alone, acquired during the last fifteen years or so of his life, cost him about a million dollars a year. He is estimated to have given away a half a billion dollars during his lifetime.

DEVELOPMENTS IN MERCHANT CAPITALISM

RETAILING

While both the industrial capitalist and the finance capitalist tended to overshadow the merchant capitalist in post-Civil War years, the merchant continued to occupy a most important place in the economy, shifting his attention from wholesaling to retailing. It was around the middle of the nineteenth century that major retail stores were founded. For example, Gimbel Brothers of New York was founded in a frontier town of Indiana in 1842. The store was unique in its time and area in that it adhered to a one price policy rather than having individual bargains struck between clerks and customers. And, during the same decade, W. & J. Sloane opened a furnishings enterprise, Mark Cross a leather goods store, and Cartier a jewelry shop.

In this period the leading retail merchant was Alexander Stewart. It was Stewart who pioneered the department store, an enterprise which, unlike speciality shops, carried a full line of merchandise to satisfy most consumer needs. By 1900 John Wanamaker had replaced Stewart as the king of retail merchants. Wanamaker was the first retailer to make extensive use of newspaper advertising in promoting sales. As early as 1865 he had initiated a policy of offering money back guarantees to his customers. The largest department store in the world today, Macy's was founded in New York City in 1858 by Rowland Macy as a dry goods establishment selling ribbons, laces, hosiery, gloves, and artificial flowers. From its inception the store pursued a one price policy. By 1876, the year of Macy's death, it was organized along department lines, and had sales of one and a half million dollars. Among its services were home delivery and a customer lunchroom. In 1874 the Straus family leased and began operating the china, glassware, and silver departments. An odd price policy was initiated—selling a good at $1.98 instead of $2.00—to make customers think they were getting a bargain. Before long these departments became the most prosperous part of the store and the Straus family bought complete control of Macy's. In 1888 sales totaled five million dollars, and by 1902, the year the store moved from 14th street to 34th street, sales of ten million dollars were being recorded. In that year a six per cent cash policy was introduced under which Macy's pledged to charge its cash customers six per cent less than the prevailing price of a good at rival stores where charge accounts were in operation. To check on prices charged by competitors, a comparison shopper department was inaugurated.

In 1862 Montgomery Ward, the nation's first mail-order house, appeared in the United States. In 1886 Richard Sears founded Sears Roebuck, the largest retailer in the world today. Sears was a railroad employee who bought a shipload of undelivered watches and retailed them at a lower markup than jewelry shops. One year later he entered partnership with Alvah Roebuck, whose job it was to repair and assemble watches. Sears watches were guaranteed, and a money back offer awaited any customer dissatisfied with his purchase. Before long jewelry, diamonds, silverware and pistols were added to the line of goods offered for sale. In 1893 a mail-order catalogue was printed for distribution in rural areas. It advertised such items as sewing machines, furniture, dishes, wagons, harnesses, bicycles, shoes, baby carriages, and musical instruments. In 1894, when annual sales equaled four hundred thousand dollars, the company was reorganized and Julius Rosenwald became a major stockholder. By 1900 sales had leaped to eleven million dollars. To promote business customers were induced to give catalogues to their friends, receiving in return premiums applicable to the purchase of Sears merchandise. By 1908, when Sears retired and Rosenwald assumed control, sales exceeded fifty million dollars.

During the same decade that mail-order houses appeared, the 1860's, George Huntington Hartford inaugurated the chain store. His company, the Atlantic and Pacific Tea Company (A & P), was originally founded to sell tea. One of the company's early hallmarks was its give-away promotional stunts, which acted to boost sales. Gradually, other commodities were added to the store's inventory and additional stores added. By 1865 there were five stores, by 1869 eleven stores, and by 1876 sixty-seven stores. In 1912 the company abandoned the then traditional policy in the grocery business of offering charge and delivery service. In return for lower prices, it launched a cash and carry program that proved an immediate success. The number of stores expanded from four hundred in 1912 to one thousand in 1915. What made A & P a great financial success was its philosophy of low markup and high volume. In the words of John Hartford, son of the company founder, "We would rather sell two hundred pounds of butter at a penny a pound profit than one hundred pounds at two cents a pound profit."

The role of the entrepreneur in American economic development has been the subject of considerable controversy. In the readings at the end of this chapter, two points of view are expressed. Matthew Josephson views the great captains of industry as "Robber Barons," while Joseph A. Schumpeter regards them as an indispensable element in the process of economic growth.

NOTES

1. Andrew Carnegie. *Autobiography*. Boston: Houghton Mifflin, 1920.

SELECTED REFERENCES

1. Frederick L. Allen. *The Great Pierpont Morgan*. New York: Harper and Bros., 1949.
2. Louis D. Brandeis. *Other People's Money*. New York: Frederick A. Stokes Co., 1932.
3. B. Emmet and J. E. Jeucks. *Catalogues and Counters*. Chicago: University of Chicago Press, 1950.
4. N. S. B. Gras and H. L. Larsen. *Casebook in American Business History*. New York: Crofts, 1939.
5. Burton J. Hedrick, *The Life of Andrew Carnegie*, Vol. I-II. New York: Doubleday, Doran and Co., 1932.
6. Ralph Hower. *History of Macy's 1858-1919*. Cambridge: Harvard University Press, 1943.
7. Allan Nevins. *Study in Power: John D. Rockefeller*, Vol. I-II. New York: Charles Scribner and Sons, 1953.

readings

what was the contribution of
the entrepreneur
to u.s. economic development?

ONE VIEW: *matthew josephson*

1893: panic! Like the tropical hurricane or the earth
tremor, it breaks always with fearful suddenness for the great masses of
men. Business men who yesterday were affluent tear up the day's newspaper and fall sobbing at the feet of their wives, crying, "We are ruined!"
So the reminiscences and engravings of the time picture the ravages of
these regularly recurring economic storms. Behind the heavy red or green
velours curtained windows of the thousands of middle-class American
parlors, the national melodrama is reenacted in its familiar, classical form.
A warm glow of gas lamps floods the rich interior with its bric-a-brac,
its gilt and burled walnut furniture, its lacy doilies and what-nots. There
is an ornate marble fireplace, and over it the legend: *In God We Trust*.
Here sits the master of the house, with his plump cheeks, his full, curling
mustaches, his fine Prince Albert, facing his wife, long-corseted,
elegantly dressed in her gorgeous velvet robe. On her face there is a
look of composed alarm; upon his one of rending anguish. For ruin has
fallen upon their house. Tomorrow their hopes, all their worldly
possessions, their home with its Oriental bric-a-brac, gas lamps, what-
nots, must disappear all together in the gulf of bankruptcy.

In reality the wreck of the small undertaker, pathetic though it seems,
is of little moment compared with the mass effects of depression upon
the general populace. Chiefly it signifies that transfer of individual

Reprinted with permission from *The Robber Barons* by Matthew
Josephson. New York: Harcourt, Brace, 1934, pp. 375-387.

fortunes, that expropriation of pygmy capitals by giant capitals which is so greatly hastened with each renewed phase of the economic cycle. Sometimes his individual folly or greed leads a man to the graveyard of business; but more often nowadays it is the consequence of a "deliberate mismanagement," skillfully applied under the system of absentee owner-ship. Large railroads and other enterprises, plunged in reckless expan-sions, are now seen by the disillusioned to have "officially overstated" their income, to have paid dividends out of capital, and to have given a semblance of extraordinary value to securities which were in fact worth-less. At the beginning of 1893, the National Cordage Trust declares a 100 per cent stock dividend, in addition to its usual payments at the rate of 10 per cent in cash per annum. The investors who had entrusted their savings to this corporation are filled with joy. But a few weeks later, in May, the insolvency of the company is announced, a receiver is appointed, and the treasury is found to be empty. The mishaps of the Santa Fe and Baltimore & Ohio railroads, to mention only a few of the great enterprises that collapsed with incredible suddenness, showed a mismanagement and waste of capital no less grievous than that of National Cordage. Yet these alarming and cruel "deflations" do not seem to afflict giant fortunes, whose owners, forewarned and forearmed (as may be judged), pass calmly through the crisis to emerge relatively enhanced in strength.

Sore losses are met by the middle class of savers and investors; but for the hosts of workers in cities and mills, or tillers of farms, the excesses of individual heads of overcapitalized enterprises result in more drastic and extensive derangements. As grains and stocks crash, factories and commercial houses to the number of 15,000 shut their doors, and 500 banks are plunged in bankruptcy, the "flight of capital" and the hoarding of gold mounts in pace with stark fear and hysteria. Through the whole economic organism, now more close-knit and interdependent than ever before, the general dislocation and paralysis is quickly transmitted. Uncomprehending the farmer stares at his cotton which is nearly worth-less, his corn which he must use for fuel. And with even less comprehen-sion the laborer feels his thinning pay envelope, or in extreme penury leaves the bitter hovel which he and his family may no longer occupy, to join in those mass uprisings which color the time: the great strikes in the industrial cities or the coal fields, the burning of railroad cars, the combats with soldiers. And before the year is out, while William Bryan thunders against the "Goldbugs in Washington," "General" Jacob Coxey's "Industrial Army," uniformed in rags, but with flags and banners flying, begins its long march across the country to offer the President a "petition in boots."

Disaster now literally seems visited upon the whole nation; but it comes no longer through an Act of God, evil season, war or flood, or through weakening energy and skill of the people. It comes, though the whole continent still cries out for productive enterprise, because those who lead in such enterprise have no further wish to produce or to construct. They, the barons of industry, are now in the grip of the "rich men's panic" (as the panic of 1893 and others were vaguely but truthfully called). No longer captains of industry "enriching others while they enrich themselves," they wish only to see to their pecuniary interest, to vie with each other in converting all their capital investments into ready money or gold—so far as possible. Yesterday, they had been engaged in "over-saving" as J. A. Hobson interprets it. They had been setting aside more and more capital with which to pay for long-term improvements, drains, railroads, ponderous new machinery; they had been preparing themselves ever for the day when they must bring forth still greater quantities of cotton cloth or steel, while making no provision that the buying power of the community increase enough to consume such quantities. The decline of such buying power, the stage when all prices and wages seemed to them "too high" had brought a sudden cessation of such capital investment or "saving," and in its train "glut" and stagnation. Now, as J. A. Hobson interprets it:

> The true excess shows itself in the shape of idle machinery, closed factories, unworked mines, unused ships and railway trucks. It is the auxiliary capital that represents the bulk of over-supply, and whose idleness signifies the enforced unemployment of large masses of labor. It is machinery, made and designed to increase the flow of production of goods, that has multiplied too fast for the growth of consumption.

Evidences of uncontrolled capital investment were the doubling of railroad indebtedness, in many cases, between 1880 and 1890, the tremendous increase in the size and range of industrial combinations of all sorts. But what else could be done under a scheme of distribution which brought to a few men incomes of from ten to twenty millions per annum, while even the skilled among the underlying population enjoyed a purchasing power of no more than $500 a year—and this by no means stable? And even this mass purchasing power would be undermined by the masters. "The workmen now earns the equivalent of a barrel of flour each day," William Vanderbilt had complained to the stockholders of the New York Central Railroad in advocating wage reductions. Yet at the same time preparations of all sorts were made to produce and market more flour, more goods, more railroad services than the people could afford to use.

The intimate statements, the authorized documents of the time show us that the income of the captain of industry is often so great that he literally cannot consume it himself or cause it to be consumed. Thus Murat Halstead tells us that toward 1890, a year before he died, Jay

Gould's income was approximately ten millions of dollars a year. "Mr. Gould cannot begin to use even a small portion for his own personal use—even a small part of the interest which his dividend money alone would yield. He must reinvest it, and he does reinvest it. It is safe to say that he takes this money . . . and buys other securities." In other words, he makes new capital investments.

In the case of the Vanderbilts, we are also told that they applied their immense income from two hundred millions of securities to capital invest-ments in new railroads lines, in opening more coal mines, and in introducing new machinery which diminished hand labor. We see Rockefeller also prompted by the same irresistible impulse—extending new pipe lines, erecting new terminals, building tank ships, acquiring new factories. "The more the business grew," Rockefeller states, "the more capital we put into it, the object being always the same: to extend our business by furnishing the best and cheapest product." Another industrialist states that "the first wedge calls as a rule for the second, and so the great railway I was building made further and further demands upon me. To satisfy these I extended my activities. . . ." And Andrew Carnegie, who said that he hoped that the time would come when he would no longer have to expand his business, remarks that he always found that "to put off expanding would mean retrogression." We find him in 1885 reconstructing and altering his Pittsburgh works radically, so that steel may be produced more swiftly, with fewer hands. We find him later investing more capital in changing from the Bessemer converter to the improved open-hearth furnace—and always he, like Gould and Vanderbilt and others of their rank, seeks to resist the tendency of wages to rise and keep pace with the increasing prosperity and productivity of industry.

"They extended their activities." During the whole period the race between overcapitalized industries continued; railroads in addition to those already existing tried to reach Chicago or the Pacific through undeveloped territory. Industrialists, coming upon new machinery which gave them an advantage, tried to despatch rivals whose methods were obsolete, always adding to the output and the improvement of their plants far beyond the needs of the existing population or its current purchasing power. From beginning to end their whole policy of management, as Hobson has commented, served to spread "underconsumption," to make depressions "deeper and more lasting."

The approach of "hard times" was pretty largely foreseen by the more important captains of business enterprise, not because they possessed supernatural sight, but because they were posted at the very nerve-centers of the industrial system. Not only were they generally able to escape the heaviest blows of adversity and stand "like a rock against the wave," but the end of the storm would see these powerful figures more solidly entrenched, the field swept clear of opposition.

In the Northwest we see Hill accumulating cash in the treasury of his railway, while watching uneasily the federal government's fiscal policies. As fear of suspension of specie payments spread, we find Jim Hill hoarding, "always quietly on the watch." In the notes of Clarence Barron, Samuel Hill, son of the railroad magnate, recalls the time of the Baring failure:

> In May, 1890, James J. Hill told me: "We are going to have a panic next September. It will take five years to get over it." He had advices daily from every capital of Europe. At that time he predicted within four days the exact date of the panic. Then he had nothing in his box. As he said, "Not a pound of meal." He had only cash. He had sold everything in Great Northern and Northern Pacific. Perhaps he had $50,000,000.

These are no doubt boastful statements and should not be swallowed entire; yet they indicate the tactics clearly. Hill, according to letters in Pyle's biography, had also foreseen the failure of the rival Northern Pacific line which he longed to control, saying to his partners, "That company has run its length." The depression, he judged accurately, would be more massive, more prolonged than ever before, because everything was "built-up," we were "no longer a frontier country...."

January 24, 1890, the brilliant Harriman wrote to the directors of his railroad, the Illinois Central, urging severe retrenchments. "It would be unwise at this time to pass any resolution adopting a policy for a large expenditure of money.... Our whole force should be devoted to *making* and *saving* money." Thus while the Erie, the Baltimore & Ohio, Northern Pacific, Union Pacific, Reading, Santa Fe, and a hundred and forty-nine other roads capitalized at $2,500,000,000 collapsed, Harriman's road went through the panic with no lack of resources. Then as the crisis deepened and passed its climax, we note also how Harriman was in position to use the chances it offered. Taking command of the huge but bankrupt Union Pacific, he would, according to the statement of Otto Kahn, levy great sums from his associates for equipment and improvements because "labor and materials were then extremely cheap."

During the crisis those barons who had the largest war material, the heaviest reserves, the strongest positions at the "narrows" of trade, pressed their advantages without stint. The collapse of the ambitious Reading Railroad in the Pennsylvania coal regions would be the occasion for the Morgan-Vanderbilt combination to sweep together into one monopoly the mines and carriers of this field. The loss of gold from the federal Treasury in 1894 would furnish the chance for the pool of money-lenders which Morgan headed to make loans to the government at its own terms. In the year of the panic, finding opponents gathering in force to share his profits, Carnegie would break suddenly from the steel pool and cut prices sharply, saying to his rivals: "I can make steel cheaper than any of you. The market is mine whenever I want to take it." In short, the more powerful the monopoly, such as that of Carnegie in steel, or of Rockefeller in oil, or of Havemeyer in sugar, the more they extended their domain over the industry they exploited, holding their margin of profit firm, while using to the full the demoralization of the raw-materials industries which fed into their own.

Carnegie, for instance, not only expanded the capacity of his mills several times in the five years after 1893, but also made provisions for enormously increased sources of raw iron ore at low prices. The powerful alliances of the Carnegie and Rockefeller interests in the Lake Superior ore business, John Moody holds, "caused a great fall in the price of iron ore and forced many small producers to the wall. Their holdings were thereupon bought in by the Carnegie and Rockefeller combination."

During all this period of economic misery, the great Trusts, as Montague concludes in his painstaking study of their activities "were scarcely inconvenienced." Their steadfast growth, their large-scale economies and their stability, revealed how much they were on the side of destiny.

AN ALTERNATE VIEW:
joseph a. schumpeter

The . . . point consists in the reaction of the social environment against one who wishes to do something new. This reaction may manifest itself first of all in the existence of legal or political impediments. But neglecting this, any deviating conduct by a member of a social group is condemned, though in greatly varying degrees according as the social group is used to such conduct or not. Even a deviation from social custom in such things as dress or manners arouses opposition, and of course all the more so in the graver cases. This opposition is stronger in primitive stages of culture than in others, but it is never absent. Even mere astonishment at the deviation, even merely noticing it, exercises a pressure on the individual. The manifestation of condemnation may at once bring noticeable consequences in its train. It may even come to social ostracism and finally to physical prevention or to direct attack. Neither the fact that progressive differentiation weakens this opposition—especially as the most important cause of the weakening

Reprinted with permission from *The Theory of Economic Development* by Joseph A. Schumpeter. Cambridge: Harvard University Press, 1934, pp. 86-94.

is the very development which we wish to explain—nor the further fact that the social opposition operates under certain circumstances and upon many individuals as a stimulus, changes anything in principle in the significance of it. Surmounting this opposition is always a special kind of task which does not exist in the customary course of life, a task which also requires a special kind of conduct. In matters economic this resistance manifests itself first of all in the groups threatened by the innovation, then in the difficulty in finding the necessary cooperation, finally in winning over consumers. Even though these elements are still effective to-day, despite the fact that a period of turbulent development has accustomed us to the appearance and the carrying out of innovations, they can be best studied in the beginnings of capitalism. But they are so obvious there that it would be time lost for our purposes to dwell upon them.

There is leadership *only* for these reasons—leadership, that is, as a special kind of function and in contrast to a mere difference in rank, which would exist in every social body, in the smallest as in the largest, and in combination with which it generally appears. The facts alluded to create a boundary beyond which the majority of people do not function promptly by themselves and require help from a minority. If social life had in all respects the relative immutability of, for example, the astronomical world, or if mutable this mutability were yet incapable of being influenced by human action, or finally if capable of being so influenced this type of action were yet equally open to everyone, then there would be no special function of leadership as distinguished from routine work.

The specific problem of leadership arises and the leader type appears only where new possibilities present themselves. That is why it is so strongly marked among the Normans at the time of their conquests and so feebly among the Slavs in the centuries of their unchanging and relatively protected life in the marshes of the Pripet. Our three points characterize the nature of the *function* as well as the *conduct* or behavior which constitutes the leader type. It is no part of his function to "find" or to "create" new possibilities. There are always present, abundantly accumulated by all sorts of people. Often they are also generally known and being discussed by scientific or literary writers. In other cases, there is nothing to discover about them, because they are quite obvious. To take an example from political life, it was not at all difficult to see how the social and political conditions of France at the time of Louis XVI could have been improved so as to avoid a breakdown of the *ancien regime*. Plenty of people as a matter of fact did see it. But nobody was in a position to *do* it. Now, it is this "doing the thing," without which possibilities are dead, of which the leader's function consists. This holds good of all kinds of leadership, ephemeral as well as more enduring ones.

The former may serve as an instance. What is to be done in a casual emergency is as a rule quite simple. Most or all people may see it, yet they want someone to speak out, to lead, and to organize. Even leadership which influences merely by example, as artistic or scientific leadership, does not consist simply in finding or creating the new thing but in so impressing the social group with it as to draw it on in its wake. It is, therefore, more by will than by intellect that the leaders fulfil their function, more by "authority," "personal weight," and so forth than by original ideas.

Economic leadership in particular must hence be distinguished from "invention." As long as they are not carried into practice, inventions are economically irrelevant. And to carry any improvement into effect is a task entirely different from the inventing of it, and a task, moreover, requiring entirely different kinds of aptitudes. Although entrepreneurs of course *may* be inventors just as they may be capitalists, they are inventors not by nature of their function but by coincidence and vice versa. Besides, the innovations which it is the function of entrepreneurs to carry out need not necessarily be any inventions at all. It is, therefore, not advisable, and it may be downright misleading, to stress the element of invention as much as many writers do.

The entrepreneurial kind of leadership, as distinguished from other kinds of economic leadership such as we should expect to find in a primitive tribe or a communist society, is of course colored by the conditions peculiar to it. It has none of that glamour which characterizes other kinds of leadership. It consists in fulfilling a very special task which only in rare cases appeals to the imagination of the public. For its success, keenness and vigor are not more essential than a certain narrowness which seizes the immediate chance and *nothing else.* "Personal weight" is, to be sure, not without importance. Yet the personality of the capitalistic entrepreneur need not, and generally does not, answer to the idea most of us have of what a "leader" looks like, so much so that there is some difficulty in realizing that he comes within the sociological category of leader at all. He "leads" the means of production into new channels. But this he does, not by convincing people of the desirability of carrying out his plan or by creating confidence in his leading in the manner of a political leader—the only man he has to convince or to impress is the banker who is to finance him—but by buying them or their services, and then using them as he sees fit. He also leads in the sense that he draws other producers in his branch after him. But as they are his competitors, who first reduce and then annihilate his profit, this is, as it were, leadership against one's own will. Finally, he renders a service, the full appreciation of which takes a specialist's knowledge of the case. It is not so easily understood by the public at large as a politician's successful speech or a general's victory in the field, not to insist on the fact that he seems to act — and often harshly — in his individual interest alone. We shall understand, therefore, that we do not observe, in this case, the emergence of all those affective values which are the glory of all other kinds of social leadership. Add to this the precariousness of the economic position both of the individual entrepreneur and of entrepreneurs as a group, and the fact that when his economic success raises him socially he has no cultural tradition or attitude to fall back upon, but moves about in society as an upstart, whose ways are readily laughed at, and we shall understand why this type has never been popular, and why even scientific critique often makes short work of it.[1]

We shall finally try to round off our picture of the entrepreneur in the same manner in which we always, in science as well as in practical life, try to understand human behavior, viz. by analysing the characteristic motives of his conduct. Any attempt to do this must of course meet with all those objections against the economist's intrusion into "psychology" which have been made familiar by a long series of writers. We cannot here enter into the fundamental question of the relation between psychology and economics. It is enough to state that those who on principle object to *any* psychological considerations in an economic argument may leave out what we are about to say without thereby losing contact with the argument. For none of the results to which our analysis is intended to lead stands or falls with our "psychology of the entrepreneur," or could be vitiated by any errors in it. Nowhere is there, as the reader will easily satisfy himself, any necessity for us to overstep the frontiers of observable behavior. Those who do not object to *all* psychology but only to the *kind* of psychology which we know from the traditional textbook, will see that we do not adopt any part of the time-honored picture of the motivation of the "economic man."

In the theory of the circular flow, the importance of examining motives is very much reduced by the fact that the equations of the system of equilibrium may be so interpreted as not to imply any psychic magnitudes at all, as shown by the analysis of Pareto and of Barone. This is the reason why even very defective psychology interferes much less with results than one would expect. There may be rational *conduct* even in the absence of rational *motive*. But as soon as we really wish to penetrate into motivation, the problem proves by no means simple. Within given social circumstances and habits, most of what people do every day will appear to them primarily from the point of view of duty carrying a social or a superhuman sanction. There is very little of conscious rationality, still less of hedonism and of *individual* egoism about it, and so much of it as may safely be said to exist is of comparatively recent growth. Nevertheless, as long as we confine ourselves to the great outlines of constantly repeated economic action, we may link it up with wants and the desire to satisfy them, on condition that we are careful to recongize that economic motive so defined varies in intensity very much in time; that it is society that shapes the particular desires we observe; that wants must be taken with reference to the group which the individual thinks of when deciding his course of action— the family or any other group, smaller or larger than the family; that action does not promptly follow upon desire but only more or less imperfectly corresponds to it; that the field of individual choice is always, though in very different degrees, fenced in by social habit or conventions and the like: it still remains broadly true that, within the circular flow, everyone adapts himself to his environment so as to satisfy certain *given* wants—of himself or others—as best he can. In *all* cases, the *meaning* of economic action is the satisfaction of wants in the sense that there would be no economic action if there were no wants. In the case of the circular flow, we may also think of satisfaction of wants as the normal *motive*.

The latter is not true for our type. In one sense, he may indeed be called the most rational and the most egotistical of all. For, as we have seen, conscious rationality enters much more into the carrying out of new plans, which themselves have to be worked out before they can be acted upon, than into the mere running of an established business, which is largely a matter of routine. And the typical entrepreneur is more self-centered than other types, because he relies less than they do on tradition and connection and because his characteristic task—theoretically as well as historically—consists precisely in breaking up old, and creating new, tradition. Although this applies primarily to his economic action, it also extends to the moral, cultural, and social consequences of it. It is, of course, no mere coincidence that the period of the rise of the entrepreneur type also gave birth to Utilitarianism.

But his conduct and his motive are "rational" in no other sense. And in *no* sense is his characteristic motivation of the hedonist kind. If we define hedonist motive of action as the wish to satisfy one's wants, we may indeed make "wants" include any impulse whatsoever, just as we may define egoism so as to include all altruistic values too, on the strength of the fact that they also mean something in the way of self-gratification. But this would reduce our definition to tautology. If we wish to give it meaning, we must restrict it to such wants as are capable of being satisfied by the consumption of goods, and to that kind of satisfaction which is expected from it. Then it is no longer true that our type is acting on a wish to satisfy his wants.

For unless we assume that individuals of our type are driven along by an insatiable craving for hedonist satisfaction, the operations of Gossen's law would in the case of business leaders soon put a stop to further effort. Experience teaches, however, that typical entrepreneurs retire from the arena only when and because their strength is spent and they feel no longer equal to their task. This does not seem to verify the picture of the economic man, balancing probable results against disutility of effort and reaching in due course a point of equilibrium beyond which he is not willing to go. Effort, in our case, does not seem to weigh at all in the sense of being felt as a reason to stop. And activity of the entrepreneurial type is obviously an obstacle to hedonist enjoyment of those kinds of commodity which are usually acquired by incomes beyond a certain size, because their "consumption" presupposes leisure. Hedonistically, therefore, the conduct which we usually observed in individuals of our type would be irrational.

This would not, of course, prove the absence of hedonistic motive. Yet it points to another psychology of non-hedonist character, especially if we take into account the indifference to hedonist enjoyment which is often conspicuous in outstanding specimens of the type and which is not difficult to understand.

First of all, there is the dream and the will to found a private kingdom, usually, though not necessarily, also a dynasty. The modern world does not know any such positions, but what may be attained by industrial or commercial success is still the nearest approach to medieval lordship possible to modern man. Its fascination is specifically strong for people who have no other chance of achieving social distinction. The sensation of power and independence loses nothing by the fact that both are largely illusions. Closer analysis would lead to discovering an endless variety within this group of motives, from spiritual ambition down to mere snobbery. But this need not detain us. Let it suffice to point out that motives of this kind, although they stand nearest to consumers' satisfaction, do not coincide with it.

Then there is the will to conquer: the impulse to fight, to prove oneself superior to others, to succeed for the sake, not of the fruits of success, but of success itself. From this aspect, economic action becomes akin to sport—there are financial races, or rather boxing-matches. The financial result is a secondary consideration, or, at all events, mainly valued as an index of success and as a symptom of victory, the displaying of which very often is more important as a motive of large expenditure than the wish for the consumers' goods themselves. Again we should find countless nuances, some of which, like social ambition, shade into the first group of motives. And again we are faced with a motivation characteristically different from that of "satisfaction of wants" in the sense defined above, or from, to put the same thing into other words, "hedonistic adaptation."

Finally, there is the joy of creating, of getting things done, or simply of exercising one's energy and ingenuity. This is akin to a ubiquitous motive, but nowhere else does it stand out as an independent factor of behavior with anything like the clearness with which it obtrudes itself in our case. Our type seeks out difficulties, changes in order to change, delights in ventures. This group of motives is the most distinctly anti-hedonist of the three.

Only with the first groups of motives is private property as the result of entrepreneurial activity an essential factor in making it operative. With the other two it is not. Pecuniary gain is indeed a very accurate expression of success, especially of *relative* success, and from the standpoint of the man who strives for it, it has the additional advantage of being an objective fact and largely independent of the opinion of others. These and other peculiarities incident to the mechanism of "acquisitive" society make it very difficult to replace it as a motor of industrial development, even if we would discard the importance it has for creating a fund ready for investment. Nevertheless it is true that the second and third groups of entrepreneurial motives may in principle be taken care of by other social arrangements not involving private gain from economic innovation. What other stimuli could be provided and how they could be made to work as well as the "capitalistic" ones do, are questions which are beyond our theme. They are taken too lightly by social reformers, and are altogether ignored by fiscal radicalism. But they are not insoluble, and may be answered by detailed observation of the psychology of entrepreneurial activity, at least for given times and places.

NOTES

1. It may, therefore, not be superfluous to point out that our analysis of the role of the entrepreneur does not involve any "glorification" of the type, as some readers, of the first edition of this book seemed to think. We do hold that entrepreneurs *have* an economic function as distinguished from, say, robbers. But we neither style every entrepreneur a genius or a benefactor to humanity, nor do we wish to express any opinion about the comparative merits of the social organization in which he plays his role, or about the question whether what he does could not be effected more cheaply or efficiently in other ways.

chapter 14

land and agriculture

LAND

THE TURNER THESIS

In the period following the Civil War the United States population continued to press westward. Aided by the continuance of a liberal land policy, large portions of the public domain were transferred to the private sector. By 1890 the frontier era in American history had drawn to a close. In that year the U.S. Census reported that there were no longer substantial areas of the continental United States possessing more than two but less than six people per square mile. (See Figure 8.2.) The historian Frederick Jackson Turner regarded the closing of the frontier as a major milestone in American historical development.[1] In so doing he shifted the focus of American historical thinking to the role of the frontier in shaping American life and away from the heritage of western Europe. What Turner stressed most was the geographic context of the settlement process. He believed that each successive territorial conquest differed from the previous one depending on the particular physical environment. He denied the prevailing notion that American institutions were merely outgrowths of European culture. Our old-world heritage, he felt, accounted only for the similarities between European and American society. The differences, hitherto neglected according to Turner, were a result of the United States' unique physical environment. And this uniqueness was due to the frontier. Every successive frontier community had to begin anew and struggle upward to the complexities of modern civilization. During the rebirth something of the old was lost, and something of the new environment was borrowed.

From the economist's viewpoint one of the most important aspects of Turner's thesis was the safety valve doctrine. This doctrine holds that the frontier was a vital force in promoting America's free enterprise spirit, economic equality, and a high level of wages. A worker would not accept subordination within a class-oriented society when "with a slight effort he might reach a land wherein to become a co-worker in the building of free cities and free states on the lines of his own ideals." The concept of free land as labor's safety valve is rooted in the colonial and pre-Civil War period. Turner's restatement brought it once again to the forefront of public attention. Numerous scholars, however, have raised doubt as to the existence of a savety valve. Ray Billington, in the reading at the end of this chapter, critically examines the doctrine.

During the depression of the 1930's a different type of safety valve doctrine evolved. This time the frontier was regarded not as an outlet for surplus eastern labor, but for surplus eastern savings. This thesis, held by an influential group of American economists, regarded the Great Depression as more than a temporary aberration from full employment. It was felt that the nation had reached economic maturity and could expect, barring substantial government intervention, to operate chronically below full employment. The source of this stagnation was the disparity between the levels of savings and investment. No longer did the nation possess sufficient investment outlets to absorb its large volume of savings. The stagnationists regarded the frontier's closing as one of the principal reasons for the narrowing of investment opportunities. According to Hansen, the principal architect of the thesis, the frontier was, together with inventions and population growth, one of the constituent elements of economic progress. In his 1938 presidential address to the American Economic Association, he stated that ". . . the approaching cessation of population growth and the disappearance of new territory for settlement and exploitation may cut off a half or more of the investment outlets which were wont to appear in the past."[2] Again, the significance of the frontier was overstated. There is no questioning that the opening up of western territory provided many investment opportunities, such as the building of transportation lines and other socially necessary facilities. But western areas, because of their underdeveloped economic status, could afford little else in the way of capital formation. Thus, they spent considerably less than eastern regions on residential and commercial buildings and on plant and equipment associated with consumer durable and nondurable industries.

The above analysis should not be interpreted to mean that the western frontier played an unimportant role in U.S. economic growth. Its contributions, real and psychological, were considerable. If Turner and the stagnationists overstated its importance, it was in part because their respective generations welcomed such interpretations. As Turner himself points out:

> It is a familiar doctrine that each age studies its history anew and with interests determined by the spirit of the time. Each age finds it necessary to reconsider at least some portions of the past, from points of view furnished by new conditions which reveal the influence and significance of forces not adequately known by the historians of the previous generation. Unquestionably each investigator and writer is influenced by the time in which he lives and while this fact exposes the historian to a bias, at the same time it affords him new instruments and new insight for dealing with his subject.[3]

LAND DISPOSAL AND CONSERVATION

One thing which the close of the frontier did was to sharpen the realization that U.S. resources were not limitless. This gave birth to a conservation movement in the nation. It is difficult to pinpoint when the shift in public policy to conservation first began. Indeed, the policy of conservation has been practiced side by side with continued land disposal. Although the conservation movement is generally regarded as having commenced in the 1890's, acreage entries under the Homestead Act peaked during the World War I period. (See Figure 14.1.) During the post-Civil War years land speculators and mining interests succeeded in having legislation passed providing for the continued liberal disposal of lands within the public domain. While such legislation was often rationalized as being directed toward the enrichment and more effective use of the nation's natural resources, it also resulted in the enrichment of private special interest groups. Such legislation included the Timber and Stone Act of 1878, which opened valuable timber and stone lands in Nevada, California, Oregon, and Washington for sale at $2.50 an acre; the Timber Cutting Act of 1878, which permitted the residents of certain western areas to cut trees on public lands free of charge, and the Dawes Act of 1887, which opened up a hundred million acres of Indian territory to public sale. These acts served to transfer substantial quantities of the public domain into private hands with little or no regard for the nature or quality of the resources which they contained.

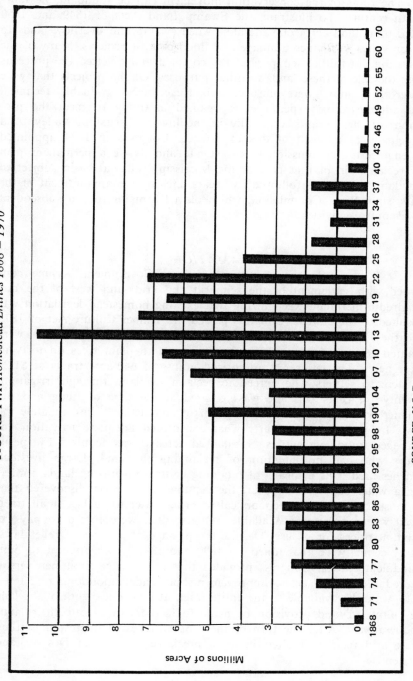

FIGURE 14.1. *Homestead Entries 1868 – 1970*

SOURCE: U.S. Department of Interior

The roots of the conservation movement can be found in the nineteenth century. To illustrate, the Swamp Land Acts of 1849 and 1850 ceded 65 million acres of Federally-owned swamp and overflow lands to fifteen states to finance drainage and flood control projects. Many of the states did not fulfill their part of the compact and diverted the proceeds from the sale of these lands to other purposes. Of the projects that were undertaken, most were unsuccessful. Nevertheless, valuable technical and administrative experience was gained in trying to meet the provisions of these grants, especially in the lower Mississippi Valley. And principally as a result of this experience, Congress in 1874 appointed an engineering commission to investigate and devise a permanent plan for reclamation of that part of the Mississippi alluvial basin subject to inundation. This was followed five years later by the appointment of the Mississippi River Commission, which played a major role in subsequent flood control activities.

LAND RECLAMATION

In the 1870's the Federal Government became concerned with settlement of the semiarid and arid land west of the one hundredth meridian. Recognizing that existing homestead legislation was unsuited to these areas, Congress passed the Timber Culture Act of 1873 and the Desert Land Act of 1877. Under the former, individuals were granted 160 free acres of land if they agreed to plant trees on forty of these acres. The latter Act authorized grants of 640-acre tracts at $1.25 an acre to settlers who agreed to reclaim the land through irrigation. Twenty-five cents per acre was required at the time of filing and the balance within three years upon proof of compliance. Unfortunately the law's failure to define clearly what constituted adequate irrigation encouraged fraudulent entries. Substantial acreage was acquired by speculators who had no intention of reclaiming the land. Large livestock ranches used it as a means of retaining control of grazing lands bordering a water supply. Moreover, the genuine settler soon discovered that in most cases it was uneconomical to bring water to such a small tract. Even where water was available, settlers often were forced to pay exorbitant prices for its use. Despite the passage of a series of relief laws, many claims were abandoned. In 1890 and 1891, in an attempt to limit fraudulent entries, Congress provided that the acreage limit per person be reduced to 320 acres, improvements be made amounting to $3 per acre, water be available to the entire tract, at least one-eighth of the land be cultivated, and provision be made for settlers to irrigate their lands cooperatively. After the turn of the century renewed interest in settling these arid regions resulted in an appreciable increase in Desert Land Act entries.

The Carey Act of 1894 was another means of reclaiming the arid West. It offered certain states arid portions of the public domain, not to exceed one million acres each, if they agreed to promote settlement, irrigation and cultivation of these lands. When the Act's provisions had been satisfied, the Federal Government was to grant patents to the states or to assignees of the states. The states were to hire private construction companies to build irrigation works, which in turn would sell water rights to settlers to reimburse themselves for the cost of construction. Land could only be sold to settlers who agreed to purchase water rights. Unfortunately, this encouraged construction companies to charge high prices for the delivery of water. And since a settler could not obtain title to the land until actual irrigation and cultivation had been achieved, he was placed in a very difficult position. These facts, together with the states' inexperience in the construction and administration of large-scale irrigation projects, prevented the Carey Act from achieving most of its goals. In 1921 the Secretary of the Interior was authorized to restore segregated lands to the public domain unless construction of reclamation works was started within three years after segregation. Land on which irrigation works had been constructed but not used for ten years was also subject to return.

The Reclamation Act of 1902 represented another fundamental effort to bring arid land into cultivation. Unlike the Desert Land and Carey Acts, the Federal Government under this Act took a more direct role in promoting conservation. The Act authorized the Secretary of the Interior to locate and construct irrigation works in the seventeen contiguous western states and Alaska and Hawaii. Originally these projects were financed by a revolving fund known as the Reclamation Fund. The Fund received its initial capital from public land sales in the western states and territories. Each settler, who could receive water for no more than 160 acres of his land, was obligated to pay his proportionate cost of construction in not more than ten annual installments. Experience soon proved that these financial arrangements were inadequate and a number of changes were effected. First, the payment period was extended, in some cases to forty years. Second, repayment obligations were transferred from individual settlers to groups of settlers who formed water user associations under state and local laws, usually with statutory powers of assessment to enforce collection. Third, the Fund's capital was augmented by oil royalties, sales of public power, and specific Congressional appropriations. The Reclamation Act was designed primarily to provide water to arid land; however, it was evident from the beginning that other conservation needs could be met at the same time. Thus, one of the first major projects, on Arizona's Salt River, provided both the water and the electric power which made possible the modern city of Phoenix.

FOREST AND MINERAL RECLAMATION

In 1865 the Reverend Fredrick Staff predicted in a report to the Department of Agriculture that the nation would face a timber famine within thirty years, and recommended an immediate research program to improve forest management. Franklin Bough's address to the American Association for the Advancement of Science in 1873 inspired a recommendation to Congress that a Federal forestry commission be established. The Association's memorial also emphasized the value of timber stands, the importance of forest lands in maintaining favorable water flows, and the need for protecting forests on public lands. In 1876 the American Forestry Association was founded for the "protection of the existing forests of the country from unnecessary waste, and the promotion of the propagation and planting of useful trees." The Association took on added significance in 1882 when it merged with the American Forestry Congress, organized earlier that year. An outstanding leader of the expanded Forestry Congress was Carl Schurz who as Secretary of the Interior from 1877 to 1882 repeatedly urged the reservation of all public domain timber lands. In the Land Revision Act of 1891 the National Forest System was established, and the President of the United States was empowered to reserve public domain lands for the protection of timber and watershed areas. However, opposition to this legislation on the grounds that it restricted settlement and retarded economic growth soon led Congress to repeal the President's authority over forest reserves.

Equally important was the problem of how to administer the national forests. The 1891 Land Revision Act made no provisions for protecting or managing the reserves. Timber thieves and grazers continued to or ate without restrictions, and no steps were taken for fire protection, emoval of dead or damaged trees, and replanting, In 1897, as an amendment to a bill temporarily suspending some hasty forest reservations by President Cleveland, Congress instructed the Secretary of the Interior "to make provision for protection against fire and trespassing; to make rules and regulations for occupancy and use of the reserves and their products; to sell after due examination and appraisal dead and mature timber; and to allow free use of timber by bona fide settlers and others for their domestic needs." Unfortunately, both the technical knowledge and the trained personnel to fulfill this legislative mandate were lacking. In 1898 Gifford Pinchot was appointed Chief of the Division of Forestry of the Agriculture Department, and immediately took steps to build a cadre of professional foresters. Under his leadership a number of colleges and universities established forestry departments, a student training program was initiated in the Department of Forestry, and the Society of American Foresters was founded. In 1909 the Division was renamed the Bureau of Forestry and its activities and authority broadened.

By the end of Theodore Roosevelt's administration the National Forest System was well established. However, it was confined almost exclusively to the rugged forests of the Northwest and Far West. The Weeks Act of 1911 placed the Federal forest program on a national basis by providing for the purchase of forest lands on the headwaters of navigable streams. Congress prescribed that no land could be acquired by the Government unless there was evidence that Federal control would promote navigation, flood control, and timber production. In addition, the states in which the land existed had to give their consent to Federal acquisition.

The conservation of mineral lands in the United States dates back to 1879 when the Geological Survey was established. Actually, geographical surveys had been made since colonial days. The Land Ordinance of 1796, for example, required surveying to describe the land's soil, water, vegetation, and mineral characteristics. Little was done with this information, however, except to reserve certain mineral rights. In 1879 Major John W. Powell, after extensive study of western lands, recommended detailed land classification and the establishment of a scientific survey system. In that same year Congress established the Geological Survey with Powell as its head to collect and present information on the nation's land, water, and mineral resources. By the turn of the century, on the basis of information secured, Federal authorities were convinced that future transfers of mineral wealth to private ownership should be regulated. Beginning in 1900 the Interior Department, pending Congressional action, began to withdraw all land known or thought to contain mineral deposits for the purpose of examination and classification. In a fifteen-year period several million acres of oil, gas, coal, phosphate, potassium, and sodium lands were withdrawn. Lands found to contain no important mineral deposits were returned to entry, whereas others which possessed valuable deposits were made subject to agricultural entry rights only, or sold to private developers.

AGRICULTURE

REGIONAL CROPS

Between the Civil War and World War I the balance of farmable land in the United States came under cultivation and the final pattern of regional agricultural specialization emerged. Corn was the principal crop of the period. (See Table 14.1) In 1860 production centered in Illinois, Ohio, and Missouri. By 1915, while Illinois remained the

TABLE 14.1. *Value of the Corn, Wheat, and Cotton Crops 1866–1915*

| | Millions of Dollars | | | |
	1866	*1880*	*1899*	*1915*
Corn	411.5	679.7	828.2	1,722.7
Wheat	232.1	474.2	369.9	942.3
Cotton	—	242.1	323.8	795.8

SOURCE: U.S. Department of Commerce. *Statistical Abstract of the United States.* Washington, D.C.: U.S. Government Printing Office, Various Issues.

leading state, the center of production shifted westward to encompass Iowa and Nebraska. (See Table 14.2.) A corn belt extended through the entire north central region of the country, stretching from western Ohio into Indiana, Illinois, Iowa, and eastern Nebraska. (See Figures 14.2 and 14.3.) As indicated in an earlier chapter, corn and hogs were intimately linked. The availability of reasonably priced transportation enabled the profit maximizing farmer of the 1870's to allocate his corn output between direct sale and hog production. In that decade it was noted that one bushel of corn would yield ten pounds of hog. This being true, if corn sold for fifty cents a bushel and the price of hogs exceeded five dollars a hundred pounds, corn would go into hog production rather than finding its way into the market. This would depress hog prices and raise corn prices, which would ultimately lead to a drop in hog production and an increase in the supply of corn in the marketplace. This in turn caused a rise in hog prices, a fall in corn prices, and increased hog production once again. A complete hog-corn cycle lasted from four to six years, and explains the price fluctuations evident in these commodities. Chicago, located at the center of the Corn Belt, possessed excellent rail connections with the East. As a consequence it was the leading hog processing center of the nation.

Wheat, the second major crop in terms of value, centered in Illinois, Indiana, and Wisconsin on the eve of the Civil War. By World War I production had shifted westward to North Dakota, Kansas, and Nebraska. Cultivation in the Dakotas concentrated on spring wheat, while winter wheat was grown in Kansas and Nebraska. Cotton, the third major crop of the nation, also moved westward. The major producing states of 1860 were Mississippi, Alabama, and Louisiana. By the end of the century Texas was the leading state, producing more cotton than the entire South had on the eve of the Civil War. In 1915 the three leading producing states were Texas, Georgia, and Mississippi.

TABLE 14.2. *The Leading States in Cotton, Corn and Wheat Production 1860–1915*

1860	1890	1915
	Cotton	
Mississippi	Texas	Texas
Alabama	Georgia	Georgia
Louisiana	Mississippi	Mississippi
	Corn	
Illinois	Illinois	Illinois
Ohio	Iowa	Iowa
Missouri	Kansas	Nebraska
	Wheat	
Illinois	North Dakota	North Dakota
Indiana	Minnesota	Kansas
Wisconsin	Ohio	Nebraska

SOURCE: U.S. Department of Commerce. *Statistical Abstract of the United States.* Washington, D.C.: U.S. Government Printing Office, Various Issues.

*Data are for 1899.

Other important agricultural activities included the growing of fruits and vegetables, dairy cows, and the raising of cattle. The growing of fruits and vegetables prior to the 1880's was restricted to areas adjacent to population centers. Thereafter, the development of refrigerated railway cars enabled production centers to emerge in California and Florida. Dairying, like fruit and vegetable production, prior to the refrigerated railroad cars was concentrated in areas with high population density. On the eve of the Civil War, milk, butter, and cheese production centered in the populous states of New York and Pennsylvania. By World War I, although New York and Pennsylvania continued to be important producers, they were joined by Wisconsin, Iowa, and Minnesota. The ability of cattle to feed on uncultivated range land enabled this industry to move west earlier than the rest of agriculture. On the eve of the Civil War, the two leading producers were Texas and Illinois. While the westward movement of railroads and population moved production out of the Midwest to the more

FIGURE 14.2. *Regions and Geographic Divisions of the United States*

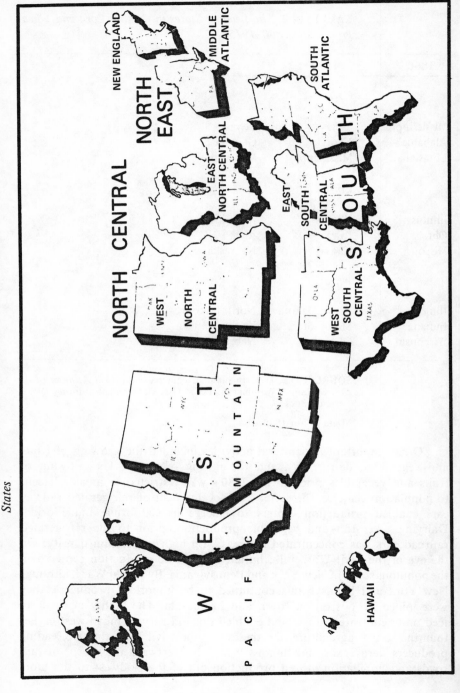

FIGURE 14.3. *Regional Crop Areas of the U.S.*

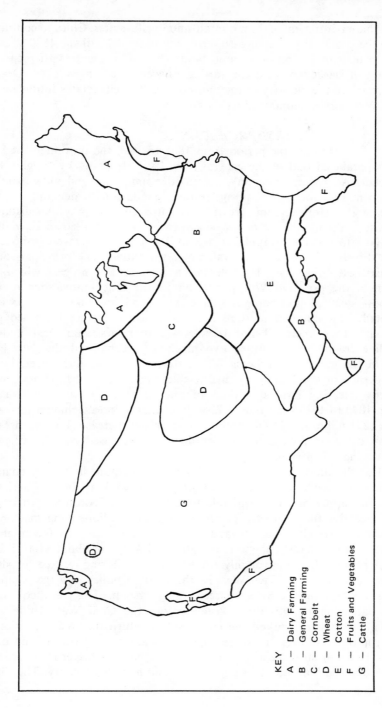

KEY

A — Dairy Farming
B — General Farming
C — Cornbelt
D — Wheat
E — Cotton
F — Fruits and Vegetables
G — Cattle

SOURCE: U.S. Department of Agriculture

favorable environment of the mountain and Pacific states, Chicago continued
to be the principal processing center of the nation. Until the 1880's, cattle
were principally fed on open range land. Thereafter, due to settlement and
the use of barbed wire, cattle raising was confined to ranches. Despite
the growth of the industry in the mountain and Pacific states following the
Civil War, Texas maintained its dominance.

FARM PROBLEMS

In the period from 1865 to 1896 the movement of farm
prices paralleled that of the general price level, declining by roughly fifty
per cent. A growing economy, increased population, and an expanding
foreign market for American agricultural goods caused demand to grow
substantially. However, this growth was outpaced by supply. A substantial
increase in the number of farms—from two million in 1860 to six million
by 1900—together with rapid increases in farm productivity were responsible
for a threefold increase in the value of farm output. The principal source
of increased efficiency was farm mechanization. The process which had
begun in the pre-Civil War period continued. The innovations of that
period—steel plows, reapers (harvesters), and the like—were widely
adopted. New innovations were introduced which further increased productivity. These included binders, harvester-threshers (combines), and the
gasoline tractor. The former two machines mechanized the last basic
step in the harvesting process. The latter, which was introduced in the
first decade of the twentieth century, eliminated the need for horsepower,
thereby releasing large quantities of grazing land for food cultivation.
From 1870 to 1915 the value of farm implements and machinery increased
from $271 million to $1,849 million, a sevenfold increase. Largely because
of this development agricultural productivity increased by over fifty per
cent during this period.

For the most part the South did not participate in this mechanical
revolution. Freedom for the slaves after the Civil War did not seriously
alter the supply of labor available to the South. Accordingly, there was
little incentive for Southern farmers to introduce labor-saving machinery.
Freed men were given neither land nor capital, and relatively few migrated
to the North or West. They were initially paid wages of about $100 to $150
a year plus food, a sum roughly equivalent to the hiring out fee for slaves
at the outbreak of the Civil War. By the 1870's a policy of wage payments
in cash was replaced by a sharecropping system. This resulted in the
same labor immobility that existed before the Civil War. Under this
system the laborer worked the land, and in return received a portion of
the crop output. Often the sharecropper was advanced groceries and other
needs by local storekeepers in return for a lien on his crop, a practice
which plunged him into debt and further tied him to a locality. The share-

cropper's income was tied to the price of cotton. Since cotton prices declined markedly from the end of the Civil War to the late 1890's the lot of Southern agricultural workers remained dismal. Low income limited the ability of the sharecropper to provide his family with adequate food. Poor food caused pellagra, hookworm, and general malnutrition, all of which resulted in low productivity. In terms of farm labor and capital equipment the South by the end of the nineteenth century was decidedly a backward area.

FARM POLITICS

The farmer reacted to falling prices by advocating inflation, antimonopoly legislation, greater public utility regulation, the establishment of farm cooperatives, and higher tariffs. During this period the Greenback and Free Silver movements were the principal proinflation advocates in the economy. Both groups sought to increase the money supply, the former by the issuance of paper money and the latter by the free coinage of silver. As indicated in Chapter 9, greenbacks backed solely by government decree were first issued to help finance the Civil War. In the face of falling prices, it seemed logical to proinflationists to increase prices by increasing the quantity of greenbacks in circulation. Despite limited success at the polls, the Greenback Party was unable to achieve its objectives. Their only achievement was to limit the contraction of greenback circulation. Major silver discoveries in the 1870's and subsequent declines in its price led to the development of the Free Silver movement. Its aim was to increase the money in circulation, specifically through the issuance of silver coins and silver-backed paper currency. The movement achieved limited success with passage of the Bland-Allison Act of 1878 and the Sherman Silver Purchase Act of 1890. These acts required the Federal Government to buy limited quantities of silver and to issue coins and paper money based on these purchases. Unable to stem declining prices, the farmer joined with labor groups to form the Populist Party in 1891. The Party's principal goals included the free and unlimited coinage of silver, government ownership of banks and railroads, stronger antimonopoly laws, the popular election of senators, a graduated income tax, and a shorter workday. After a disappointing showing in the Presidential election of 1892, the agrarian-dominated Populist Party joined forces with the Democratic Party and its standard bearer, William Jennings Bryan, to press for free silver. Once again the inflationists lost the major battle. Even though they persisted into the early twentieth century, they were never able to achieve their goal.

The farmers achieved a greater measure of success in their antimonopoly efforts. As small businessmen in a nation of increasing economic concentration, farmers recognized that they were at a competitive disadvantage. They sought two remedies, legislative relief and the development of cooperatives. Agrarian interests were one of the principal forces fostering state and Federal antitrust and regulatory activities. In particular, they sought to restrict the discriminatory practices of railroads. (See Chapter 12.) Cooperatives were an outgrowth of the activities of major farm organizations such as the Grange and Farmers Alliance, which were formed to further the economic and social interest of the farm population. These organizations established cooperatives to furnish the farmer with equipment at reasonable cost, and to aid in the processing and marketing of his output. Among cooperatives established were creameries, grain elevators, flour mills, insurance companies, general stores, mail-order houses, and farm machinery manufacturing establishments. For the most part, these cooperatives failed owing to poor management and inadequate funding. One of the notable exceptions was Montgomery Ward, which was established to buy consumer goods at wholesale prices for resale to farmers at less than retail prices.

In his pursuit of prosperity the farmer fell prey to protectionist propaganda. He became convinced that tariffs were necessary to protect his domestic markets from foreign incursions. He therefore supported restrictive tariff legislation. Economically, however, farmers injured themselves, for as American imports declined owing to rising tariffs so did the dollar earning of foreign nations and their ability to purchase American farm output.

Beginning in 1896 farmers entered an era of prosperity which lasted until 1920 and is known as the golden age of agriculture. The secular downward trend of the general price level reversed itself due to an accelerated growth in the money supply. While the number of farms continued to grow, they did so at a sharply reduced pace. With most of the best land already in cultivation, the number of farms grew from six million in 1900 to only six and a half million in 1920. The latter year represents the high-water mark in the number of United States farms. Farm population during this period stabilized as the number of farm births were offset by an exit of individuals to urban centers. Rising prices, increasing demand, and a constant farm population meant higher agricultural per capital income. The onset of World War I in 1914 resulted in a major increase in both foreign and domestic demand for American agricultural output. In responding to this increased demand, the farmer increased his acreage in cultivation by roughly twenty per cent. In so doing, he greatly expanded the scope of his operations and the magnitude of his fixed debt.

NOTES

1. Frederick Jackson Turner. *The Frontier in American History*. New York: Holt Publishing Company, 1921.

2. Alvin Hansen. "Economic Progress and Declining Population Growth," *American Economic Review*, XXIX, No. 1, Part 1 (March, 1939), 11.
3. Turner, p. 323.

SELECTED REFERENCES

1. Lewis Atherton, *The Cattle Kings*. Bloomington: Indiana University Press, 1954.
2. E.A. Goldenweiser and L.E. Truesdale, *Farm Tenancy in the United States. Census Monograph No. 4*. Washington: Government Printing Office, 1924.
3. John D. Hicks, *The Populist Revolt*. Minneapolis: University of Minnesota Press, 1911.
4. John Ise, *United States Forest Policy*. New Haven: Yale University Press, 1920.
5. Fred A. Shannon, *The Farmers Last Frontier: Agriculture 1860-1897*. New York: Farrar and Rinehardt, 1945.
6. Leo Rogin, *The Introduction of Farm Machinery in its Relation to the Productivity of Labor in the Agriculture of the United States During the Nineteenth Century*. Berkeley: University of California Press, 1931.
7. F.J. Turner, *The Frontier in American History*. New York: Holt, 1921.

reading

did the frontier serve
as a safety valve for
oppressed eastern labor?

ray a. billington

Economics statisticians have summoned columns of
figures to prove a rather obvious point: pioneers moved westward when
times were good and did not when times were bad. They have established
a direct relationship between land sales in the West and commodity prices
in England and on the Continent; when prices soared settlers or speculators
bought land heavily. Thus between 1815 and 1820 booming demands for
cotton from British textile mills stimulated expansion in the Southwest
where the commodity could be grown, and in the old Northwest where corn
and wheat and hogs could be produced to feed plantation hands. In 1820
cotton prices slumped, and with them the demand for southern lands, but
wheat prices continued high until 1827 and land sales remained brisk in
the Northwest until that time. Prosperity stimulated migration; depressions
halted the westward-flowing stream.

This simple fact contradicts one of the basic assumptions in the folklore of American expansion. From the dawn-days of the Republic, and
even before, the frontier was believed to be a "safety valve" through
which the dispossessed and unfortunate could escape the buffetings of
economic storms. In bad times, so the theory held, the unemployed had
only to pack their bags, move westward where cheap lands could be
purchased, and start farms of their own. This constant exodus drained
excess workers from the Eastern labor market, especially when that
market was most overcrowded, forcing wages up as employers bid for
the services of those remaining, and preventing the growth of a militant
labor class in the United States.

Reprinted with permission from *America's Frontier Heritage* by Ray
A. Billington. New York: Holt, Rinehart & Winston, 1966, pp. 29-38.

Belief in a frontier safety valve originated in the seventeenth century, and persisted until well into the twentieth. As early as 1634 Governor John Winthrop of the Massachusetts Bay colony favored limiting the land holdings of poorer colonists to prevent "the neglect of the trades" by those who found independent farming more satisfactory than artisanship. His views were echoed by Benjamin Franklin, who believed that labor would never be cheap in America where "no Man continues long a Labourer for others, but gets a Plantation of his own," and by George Washington, who viewed the Ohio Valley as a "Land of Promise" where anyone "who is heavy laden and wants land to cultivate" could find new prosperity. Thomas Jefferson and Alexander Hamilton, although at swords' points on most issues, agreed that as long as vacant lands availed class feeling would be minimal in the United States because, in Jefferson's words, "whenever it shall be attempted by the other classes to reduce them to a minimum of subsistence, they will quit their trades and go to labouring the earth."

During the nineteenth century the safety-valve concept was so firmly fastened in the public mind, at home and abroad, that it became a part of the American creed. Englishmen built their colonization schemes on the belief that the poor could always escape to the frontiers; Karl Marx based aspects of his teachings on this seemingly indisputable fact. Thomas Carlyle saw the cheap lands of the United States as "verily the Door of Hope to a distracted Europe; which otherwise I should see crumbling down into the blackness of darkness." His words were echoed in Germany by Wilhelm Friedrich Hegel, who wrote in his famous essay on the philosophy of history that through repeated migrations westward, "the chief source of discontent is removed, and the continuation of the existing social condition is guaranteed." Travelers by the score filled their accounts of life in the United States with hymns of praise for a frontier that stabilized society by equalizing economic opportunity as nowhere else in the world.

Americans subscribed to these sentiments with no less enthusiasm than Europeans. Easterners took pious solace in the belief that the West was, as Edward Everett put it, "the safety-valve of states," and that workers who disliked low wages or miserable factory conditions could escape if they wished. Westerners were just as convinced; "no poor man in the Eastern states," wrote an Illinois editor in 1832, "who has feet and legs, and can use them has any excuse for remaining poor where he is." Horace Greeley voiced his famous "Go West, young man, go forth into the Country" because he believed unquestioningly that the drainage of excess laborers would improve the lot of those left behind. His philosophy underlay the efforts of land reformers who during the 1850s agitated for a homestead act that would grant free plots to all actual settlers. "My point," one advocate of that measure told his Congressional colleagues, "is that his 'homestead bill' will take labor from the manufacturing states to the land states—from the manufactures of the East to the farms of the West—and thereby increase the cost of labor." Post-Civil War industrialization only strengthened faith in the operation of a safety valve, as sharpening class antagonisms heightened fears that the end of the era of free lands would usher in a period of class warfare. By the 1890s this was the universal belief of the American people, often popularly expressed, and never questioned.

Not surprisingly, in view of this climate of opinion, Frederick Jackson Turner incorporated the safety-valve concept into his frontier hypothesis, but with a lack of emphasis that suggested his own doubts of its validity. In early writings he was inclined to follow the traditional interpretation, observing that whenever capital tended to press upon labor or impede political freedom "there was this gate of escape to the free conditions of the frontier," and that "the freedom and abundance of land in the Great Valley opened a refuge to the oppressed of all regions." In his lectures of that era, too, he referred to the West as "always open as a gate of escape to the discontented and unprosperous in the older areas." During his later years he apparently became skeptical of the doctrine's validity, as more extended research convinced him that a safety valve never operated exactly as its proponents claimed. Until the coming of the transcontinental railroads, he wrote in his last book, "the opportunity of direct access to cheap Western lands was not open to the poorer people of the Northeastern states and of Europe. Few scholars of his generation, however, exhibited such restraint. To them, as to Americans in general, the frontier was a safety valve operating successfully to keep the national economy on an even keel, elevate wages, and stifle class discontent.

If we are to judge the validity of their conclusion, we must recognize that no less than four types of "safety valves" have been said to operate in the United States. One was a "direct" safety valve of the sort popularized by Horace Greeley who believed that Eastern workers could escape to the West's cheap lands in time of depression. A second was "indirect"; Eastern farmers dislodged by competition with Western farmers went west themselves, rather than competing with Eastern workers for factory jobs. A third was a "resources" safety valve through which the successive development of the rich reservoir of natural resources kept wages high and prevented the growth of unrest or radical thought among laborers. Finally, a "socio-psychological" safety valve has been recognized; as long as workers *believed* that the frontier offered a haven from economic storms, they were less inclined to develop class consciousness and proletarian philosophy. Did one or all of these safety valves operate during America's frontier era? Economists and historians have weighed this question carefully since the 1930s, and have reached conclusions that Horace Greeley would find bewildering but comforting.

One is that a "direct" safety valve—draining Eastern wage earners directly to frontier farms in periods of depression—never functioned during the nineteenth century. This does *not* mean that workers from seaboard cities never moved west; many migrated from Eastern cities to Western towns and villages where they could find jobs suitable to their training, and at higher wages than they had earned at home. Travelers along the western roads often noted "a company of tinners" or other craftsmen bound for the frontier. It *does* mean that Eastern wage earners almost never moved directly to the cheap lands of the West, for farming was a profession requiring skills, training, and capital largely unavailable to the urban workman; even Horace Greeley admitted that "no man born and reared in the city can remove to a farm at thirty or forty years of age and become immediately an efficient, thrifty, successful farmer." Even those workers with an urge to become pioneer farmers were prohibited from making the transition by the cost of moving and placing land under cultivation. In the middle nineteenth century, transportation westward to the Illinois frontier from New York by coach or canal boat approximated $30 a person, even the cheapest government land sold for $1.25 an acre, and the charges for needed farm equipment, livestock, fencing, and housing were seldom less than $500. The most frugal manager required some $1,500 to bring a 40-acre farm into production, a sum far beyond the reach of Eastern workers whose wages ranged between $1.00 and $2.00 a day. Nor were these high costs unknown to Easterners; they were prominently mentioned in many guidebooks used by immigrants to the West.

Further evidence that workers displaced by the East's industrial storms seldom fled toward the West's cheap lands—either as independent farmers or as hired farm laborers—is provided by migration statistics. These reveal that throughout the nineteenth century the westward-moving population tide swelled during good times and diminished in depression periods when the safety valve should have been operating. This is not surprising; spiraling prices in the boom eras preceding panics usually wiped out such savings as workers had accumulated, depriving them of the resources needed to move. Fragmentary data show that train travel westward in the 1850s declined by one half in depression years, that labor turnover in Eastern factories multiplied in periods of prosperity and declined during hard times, and that Western communities increased their population in almost direct proportion to the nation's well-being. Thus Michigan's settlers doubled in the boom years between 1834 and 1837, but increased only 22 percent in the three years of the panic that followed. No rush of artisans to the West occurred in bad times. Nor did philanthropic societies formed to finance the movement of workers to the frontier during depressions play a significant role; while a number operated during the 1830s and 1850s, they apparently transported only about 500 Easterners to the West each year. Even those who moved did not always remain. A random sample of migration from New England and New York towns shows that seven of every ten who tried the West returned within a few years.

There seems little doubt that very few actual wage earners left Eastern cities to become frontier farmers; the rural frontier was settled largely by experienced farmers or younger sons of farmers, most of them from adjacent or nearby areas. After 1865 their numbers were supplemented by farmer-immigrants who came directly from abroad. In thirty of the thirty-four states, the superintendent of the census noted in 1860, *"native emigrants have chiefly preferred to locate in a State immediately adjacent to that of their birth."* The frontier fattened on itself, rather than on an influx of depression-lashed factory workers from the East. A "direct" safety valve in the sense understood by the nineteenth century never operated.

The answer to the question of whether an "indirect" safety valve operated to drain westward Eastern farmers who might otherwise have entered factories as competitors for jobs is less clear. Before the Civil War many farmers from the Northeastern states did move westward to occupy much of the eastern half of the Mississippi Valley, for expelling forces in the seaboard states sparked a migration not entirely typical of the usual settlement pattern. Responsible was the completion of the Erie Canal in 1825 and the construction of the network of branch waterways that brought the Great Lakes and Ohio River within commercial reach of New York and Philadelphia. Farmers in the Northeast found that the products of their worn soils could not compete in Eastern markets with produce grown on the virgin lands of the Old Northwest. Thousands upon thousands of them abandoned their exhausted fields and joined the exodus westward, leaping across the adjacent occupied areas of New York and Pennsylvania to settle in Ohio, Indiana, Illinois, Michigan, Wisconsin, and eventually Iowa. Had no such outlet existed, many would have sought factory employment in the Northeast, competing for jobs and depressing wages. During this period an "indirect" safety valve did operate.

After the Civil War the question becomes more confused; economists have variously employed statistical evidence to "prove" that the frontier both was and was not an outlet for surplus Eastern laborers. On the one hand some argue that the total immigration from East to West between 1860 and 1900 was insufficient to alter the labor market appreciably. During those years, say the anti-safety-valvers, the nineteen million farmers in the United States should have increased to forty-six million if the normal growth rate had been projected; instead the total farm population numbered only twenty-eight million in 1900. This proves, they maintain, that nearly twenty farmers moved to towns or cities for every one industrial worker who moved to the land; the city served as a safety valve for rural discontent rather than the opposite. Using somewhat different statistics, the pro-safety-valvers insist that if twenty million discontented farmers left the rural areas, then over forty million persons must have taken their place, for the total population of this sector increased from twenty-five million in 1860 to nearly forty-six million in 1900. This number was sufficient to affect the labor market and create an actual safety-valve situation. The frontier even after 1860, they argue, served as an "indirect" safety valve, even though not as a "direct" safety valve.

All of this speculation, figure juggling, and manipulation of fragments of evidence fails to come to grips with the basic problem of who went west and how the national economy was altered as a result. The actual importance of the frontier as a safety valve can be understood only if *all* aspects of the nation's economy are surveyed, not simply this or that segment of the population. If this is done, the concept of the frontier as a "resources" safety valve and a "socio-psychological" safety valve is endowed with new significance.

Preliminary to exploring this theme, certain stipulations must be made. First, what the Eastern wage earner did when he reached the West has nothing to do with proving or disproving the thesis; what is important is that his departure from the East changed the labor market there, whether he continued as a wage earner in a frontier town or became a farmer or farm laborer. We know that mechanics and craftsmen did move, for Western communities were furnished with millers, blacksmiths, carpenters, and dozens of other skilled workmen. We know also that by moving these workers increased their income relative to what it would have been in the East, and that a higher national wage level was the result. Second, the fact that workers were not drained westward during economic depressions does not invalidate the safety-valve thesis; solely important is the fact that they moved, whether in good or bad times, and thus lessened pressure on the Eastern wage scale. Third, that strikes and labor unrest did exist in the East during the 1870s and 1880s is no proof that a safety valve was not operating, for this discontent must be weighed relative to the situation in other countries with no frontier. Labor was not sublimely happy anywhere, but it was less discontented in the United States than in European countries.

Finally, we must recognize that even if in the post-Civil War era more farmers went to the city than city dwellers to farms, and even if immigrants from abroad more than replaced farmers and workers who migrated westward during boom periods from the East, the operations of the safety valve did not cease as they would have if a static economy had existed in both East and West. Instead the agricultural sector was growing in the West and the industrial in the East, so that newcomers entering either labor market were not victims of unemployment. Jobs were continually multiplying, and a key question is: Did they multiply as rapidly in both sectors as the newcomers came in, and if so was this the result — direct or indirect — of the expansion of the economy westward? Simply to look at the supply side of the market is not enough; the elasticity of the *demand* for labor as well as the supply must be evaluated. If both demand and supply showed dynamic upward shifts, and if the frontier accounted for these advances, the market position of the workers was more favorable than it would have been, and the safety valve was operating.

By viewing the frontier's economic impact on workers in this light, two things become apparent. One is that any deflection of laborers to the West — whether wage earners, farmers, farm laborers, tenants, or craftsmen — would relieve pressure in the East and have a buoyant effect on wages. To say that the migration of wage earners alone would have such an impact is to obscure the true issue. All classes, both native-born and foreign, migrated to the frontier during eras of prosperity. Whatever their status in the East's economy, their departure was felt, for any movement from a relatively inelastic labor market — even of a half-dozen people — would have a slight effect on wages. To borrow the complex terminology of wage theory, "any given percentage decrease in the labor supply will exert an upward pressure on wage rates in inverse proportion to the absolute magnitude of the elasticity of the demand for labor." The frontier accentuated that upward pressure by making Westerners out of immigrants who might have become Easterners, Western farmers out of Eastern farmers, and Western wage earners out of Eastern wage earners.

A second, and no less important, conclusion can be drawn from the concept of the frontier as a region whose full economic potential was not developed at once, but over the course of a number of years. We must think of the successive Wests as regions of unexploited natural resources that could be exploited sequentially; "slab" after "slab" was peeled away as the application of technological skills made ever more intensive utilization possible. In the early stages of the development of each new agricultural frontier, farmers and younger sons of farmers from adjacent Easts were lured by the promise of exceptional yields, deflecting them from factory jobs that were opening to them as the primitive industrialization of the region immediately behind the frontier went on. This deflection prevented a depressing effect on the wage level in the successive Easts. This situation can be contrasted with that in many underdeveloped countries of the twentieth century, where the centuries-long mining of the soil has reduced the marginal production of labor in agriculture to near zero, releasing farm workers to industry at subsistence wages. The frontier prohibited such a situation in the United States of the nineteenth century. At times, when industrial labor was producing more efficiently than farm labor, industry would attract workers from the agricultural sector, as it did in the late nineteenth century. But even then it was forced to pay a higher price than would have been the case had not agricultural expansion decreased the elasticity of the labor supply.

While agriculture continued to contract the labor market available to Eastern employers, the subsequent economic development of successive Wests still further restricted the free market in workers. On each new frontier "slabs" of resources — drawn from the soil, vegetation, and subsurface deposits — were successively utilized as the region "grew into" the economy. This process of "sequential growth" had an extremely favorable effect on the increase of employment and per capita income, for the addition of new resources to those being exploited inevitably raises the marginal product of both capital and labor. In a near full-employment economy such as existed in the United States save during depression periods, the result was not only the bidding up of wages but the bidding down of consumer goods, to produce the highest level of real per capita income in the world of that day. The American worker, thanks to the sequential development of "slabs" of frontier resources, came nearer to realizing the standard of living to which he aspired than his fellow workers in Europe. He may have been discontented, but his discontent was less than in less-favored countries. The operation of the "resources" safety valve saw to that.

Discontent was further lessened by the continued operation during the nineteenth century of a "socio-psychological" safety valve. Even those American workers who would never be able to escape to the frontier were willing to endure their plight because they *believed* that one day they would. This belief rested on some foundation, for the sequential development of successive Wests created an opportunity for upward social mobility unparalleled in other nations. Men literally "grew up with the country" as the enterprising became merchants or lawyers with all the status that went with such positions, the less fortunate enjoyed greater affluence as their lands increased in value, and the least fortunate were pushed upward on the social scale by the continued influx of newcomers even less fortunate than themselves. The fluid society of Western America bred an unquenchable hope and a faith in this rags-to-riches formula that permeated all the land. It also convinced even the most oppressed Eastern workers that their turn on the economic escalator would soon come, for in the newer Wests the traditional symbols of wealth and status were more freely distributed than in conventional societies. None among these ranked higher than ownership of private property, and this the frontier brought within the reach of the common folk. To a laborer who believed that he would someday possess land, the social system seemed worth preserving; why attack capitalism when he was destined to become a capitalist himself. Unionism and labor unrest were both retarded by the operation of this "socio-psychological" safety valve.

In three ways, then, the frontier did operate as a safety valve during the nineteenth century, although its effect gradually diminished as distances to the new settlements multiplied and the dream of rags to riches faded for the Eastern laborer. That it was ever during the nineteenth century a "direct" outlet for displaced wage earners is untrue, just as it is untrue that depressions drove workers from factories to Western farms. But the frontier did convert Eastern farmers into Western farmers and Eastern city workers into Western town workers, removing both the Eastern job market, decreasing the flexibility of the labor supply, and altering the wage structure upward. The frontier did provide jobs through the sequential development of its natural resources as the marginal product of labor was forced upward and the living standard improved. The frontier did offer solace to the oppressed by conjuring visions of limitless opportunity amidst the virgin wealth of the West, and even though few found the pot of gold, the faith that it could be found persisted. Not every gambler must win to keep the faith of gamblers alive. As an "indirect" safety valve, a "resources" safety valve, and a "socio-psychological" safety valve, the frontier played a role in shaping both the economy and the social order of the United States.

chapter **15**

population, labor,

and the rise of the

labor federation

POPULATION

DECLINING GROWTH RATES
The declining rates of population growth which commenced prior to the Civil War continued irregularly throughout this
period. However, every U.S. census of the period, with the exception of
1910, showed increases in the absolute growth of population. (See Table
15.1.) From a pre-Civil War average growth rate of thirty-five per cent
per decade, growth from 1860 to 1890 averaged twenty-five per cent per
decade. From 1890 until 1915 it averaged close to twenty per cent. A
decline in birth rates was responsible for the reduced rate of population
growth. It fell from forty-four per thousand in the 1860's to thirty per
thousand of population in the 1910's. The fall in fertility was due primarily
to urbanization and a rising level of living. As birth rates declined, so
did death rates. In 1850 the life expectancy for males was 38 years, and
41 years for females. By 1900 these figures had increased to 46 years
and 49 years respectively. Much of this progress was due to measures to
control the incidence of communicable diseases, especially those which

attacked infants and young children. By 1900 most cities had sanitary refuse removal systems and had begun to protect their water supplies.

TABLE 15.1 *U.S. Population 1865–1920*

| | | Increase Over Preceding Decade | |
Year	Population (millions)	Number (millions)	Percent
1865	35.7		
1870	39.9	7.1	22.6
1875	45.1		
1880	50.3	11.6	30.2
1885	56.7		
1890	63.1	12.8	25.5
1895	69.6		
1900	76.1	13.2	21.0
1905	83.8		
1910	92.4	16.0	21.0
1915	100.5		
1920	106.0	13.8	15.0

SOURCE: U.S. Bureau of the Census. *Historical Statistics of the United States, Colonial Times to 1957.* Washington, D.C.: U.S. Government Printing Office, 1960, p. 7.

IMMIGRATION

Immigration, in relation to total population, moved irregularly over the period. From a rate of six per thousand in the 1860's and 1870's, it rose to nine per thousand in the 1880's, subsequently declined in the 1890's to five per thousand, and then reached an all-time peak of over ten per thousand in the first decade of the twentieth century. (See Table 15.2.) It should be noted, however, that during this period the number of immigrants who returned to their native land increased sharply. While only ten to fifteen per cent of all pre-Civil War aliens subsequently returned to their native countries, the ratio by the 1870's had risen to twenty-four per cent, and to over forty per cent by the early twentieth century. Nevertheless, net immigration accounted for an average of about fifteen per cent of total population increase over the period. Until 1890 the majority of immigrants came from northern and western Europe where economic and cultural relations with Americans were well developed. By the end of the century the tide of immigration was shifting away from the so-called "old immigrants" to the "new immigrants" of southern and eastern Europe. Improved communication and transportation on the European continent, severe population pressures, and persecution of religious and political minority groups combined to create a mass exodus of emigrants from these countries. At the same time, falling birth rates and rising living standards in northern and western Europe reduced the desire of these people to emigrate. Asiatics came to the United States in significant numbers following major gold discoveries in California in the late 1840's. The region's acute labor shortage, particularly for unskilled workers, led to the wholesale importation of Chinese laborers. In 1866 the Pacific Mail Steamship Company established a permanent route between San Francisco and Hong Kong. By this time the Chinese were employed in a variety of tasks, including agriculture, domestic service, and construction of the Central Pacific Railroad.

Most immigrants were males from 14 to 44 years old. Unlike pre-Civil War years, when men outnumbered women by three to two, the

TABLE 15.2. *U.S. Immigration 1865-1915*

Year	Thousands of Immigrants	Rate of Immigration*
1865	248.1	6.4†
1870	387.2	
1875	227.5	6.2
1880	457.3	
1885	395.4	9.2
1890	455.3	
1895	258.5	5.3
1900	448.6	
1905	1,026.5	10.4
1910	1,041.6	
1914	1,218.5	
1915	326.7	5.7

SOURCE: U.S. Bureau of the Census. *Historical Statistics of the United States.* Washington, D.C.: U.S. Government Printing Office, 1960, pp. 56-7; *Statistical Abstract of the United States: 1970.* Washington, D.C.: U.S. Government Printing Office, 1970, p. 91.

*Annual rate per 1,000 population. 10 year rate computed by dividing sum of annual U.S. population totals by sum of annual immigrant totals for same 10 years.

†The rate of immigration is for the following periods: 1861-70, 1871-80, 1881-90, 1891-1900, 1901-10, 1911-20.

ratio of males to females fell somewhat from 1865 to 1890. This was due to the greater safety of ocean travel and the efforts of western railroads to attract families to settle land along their rights of way. However, after 1890 it rose again under the impetus of the "new immigration," reaching two to one in the first decade of the 1900's. Most post-Civil War immigrants, like their predecessors, were unskilled. Many were youths with little or no employment experience. Among the "new immigrants" even those who had some prior skills were often unable to utilize them due to language, customs and technological differences. Accordingly, the immigrants continued to fill jobs mostly at the lower rungs of the occupational ladder. Most found employment in the industrial centers of the Northeast, and few ventured further inland. Acquiring and cultivating land involved additional expenses which the immigrants could not afford; nor was the European agriculture with which most immigrants were familiar practiced in the United States. Also, many immigrants had been attracted to America because of their inability to make a decent living working the land, and were seeking employment in nonagricultural pursuits. Finally, it was in mining, construction, manufacturing and service industries, not agriculture, that the unskilled immigrant was in greatest demand. The German and Scandinavian immigrants who went West to farm were distinctly in the minority. Even smaller numbers settled in the South, where black labor and scanty manufacturing offered them few opportunities.

In 1920, at the end of the era of "free immigration," three-quarters of the foreign born lived in urban areas in contrast to an average of about half of the white population. New York City, the principal port of entry for European immigrants, had more first- and second-generation Italians and Irish than Rome and Dublin respectively, and New York State contained the largest number of foreign born, followed by Pennsylvania, Illinois and Massachusetts. The smallest number of foreign born were in South Carolina, North Carolina, and Mississippi. On a relative basis the foreign born constituted more than twenty per cent of the white population of Rhode Island, Massachusetts, Connecticut and New York, while at the other end of the scale foreign born were less than one per cent of the white population of North Carolina, Tennessee, Georgia, and Mississippi.

Immigration both in quantitative and qualitative aspects had a profound positive effect on United States economic growth. First, for more than a century it provided a continuous flow of cheap labor to feed the fires of industrial expansion. Without this importation of workers, the development of the factory system, specialization, and the industrialization process itself would have been considerably slowed. Canal and railroad construction, mining, meat packing, iron and steel, textiles, garment manufacturing, and many other industries drew the bulk of their work force from immigrant ranks. They were cheap not only in the sense that they worked for relatively low wages, but also because they provided ready-made additions to the labor force. In contrast to a native worker who was a burden to the economy during his childhood, the immigrant's rearing costs were borne by his country of birth. Most immigrants arriving in their adult years immediately entered the labor force. Second, although most immigrants were unskilled, those that were trained made important contributions to the development of the American economy. This was particularly true in the earlier period of immigration when the United States drew heavily on European industrial experience. There was perhaps no major or minor industry in the United States in the 1800's in which immigrants did not make important contributions. Third, immigration contributed to the dynamic character of the American economy. Each wave of immigrants took for themselves the most arduous and lowest paying jobs thereby pushing all those above them up the economic ladder. Natives as well as older immigrants were able to move up to the more skilled and higher paying occupations, and in turn, each new group of foreigners would look forward to the time when it would be able to move ahead. Fourth, the immigrant was a source of savings for capital formation. Despite his low position on the income scale, he rarely consumed up to his new earning power, particularly since he was strongly motivated to save in order to help his relatives and friends come to the United States.

On the negative side, the immigrants did create a number of problems, both economic and social. By settling principally in the large cities, they contributed to crowding, unsanitary health conditions, delinquency, and crime. Although this is the inevitable effect of moving large numbers of people unfamiliar with local customs and law into a limited space, some of the responsibility must be borne by the community for not taking adequate steps to assist the immigrants in adjusting to his new surroundings. Secondly, immigrants by accepting low wages and poor working conditions did depress wages, at least in the short run. This negative influence on the working class, however, was more than offset by the immigrant's positive impact on occupational mobility and economic growth.

POPULATION AGE STRUCTURE

Changes in birth, mortality and immigration rates necessarily affect a population's age structure. For example, a nation whose population is concentrated in the lower and higher age groups will have a significant portion of its members economically inactive. During the 1800's high fertility and mortality rates produced a very young population. In 1800 the white population's median age was only 16 years. By 1860 the median age had risen to 19 years. However, the so-called productive age group, 16 to 64 years, accounted for only fifty-six per cent of the total population. Thereafter, continued declines in fertility and an increasing number of immigrants arriving in their early adult years increased the percentage of the population in the productive age group. By 1920, the median age of the population had risen to over 25.

THE LABOR FORCE AND THE
RISE OF THE LABOR FEDERATION

America's population growth provided the basis for a growing labor supply. The percentage of the population engaged in the labor force between the Civil War and 1915 increased slightly, from about thirty-five per cent to forty per cent. Whereas fifty-nine per cent of the labor force was engaged in agricultural pursuits in 1860, only twenty-seven per cent was by 1920. The percentage of the labor force that was self-employed also showed a decline, evidencing the trend towards large-size business. Almost half of the nonfarm labor force was self-employed in 1850. By 1900 this figure had dropped to twenty-two per cent. The hours of work in nonfarm jobs slowly declined from about 10.8 hours a day in 1860 to 10 hours by 1890, and 9 hours by 1915. Around the time of World War I, a half day of work was replacing a full day on Saturday. Between the Civil War and 1890 daily real wages in manufacturing rose by fifty per cent, while between 1890 and 1915 the increase was somewhat less, thirty-seven per cent. These increases were the result of productivity gains which stemmed largely from labor being better educated and supplied with more and improved capital equipment, the increasing scale of business enterprise, and improved transportation and distribution facilities.

THE KNIGHTS OF LABOR

War-induced prosperity and labor shortages significantly strengthened the United States trade union movement during the 1860's. This new vitality expressed itself in the formation of many new local and international unions. In addition, three labor federations were established, the National Labor Union of 1866, the Knights of St. Crispin in 1867, and the Knights of Labor in 1869. The first was a loose association of national, city central, and local unions which initially devoted its attention to the establishment of the eight-hour day. It soon became involved, however, in a national movement to promote an "easy money" policy, and like earlier political efforts of organized labor it met with little success. In 1872 it was disbanded. The latter two federations were manifestations of the increasing need of workers to band together for both psychological and economic reasons. The Knights of St. Crispin was organized to protect journeymen shoemakers against the competition of "greenhorns" and apprentices in its industry. Although at one time it boasted a membership of some 50,000 its failure to protect its members against the competition of cheap labor and the introduction of new machinery in the shoe industry led to its demise in 1878.

The Noble Order of the Knights of Labor made a more lasting impression on the American trade union movement, although it, too, eventually fell by the wayside. The most romantic of all American labor unions, it was founded by a group of Philadelphia tailors under the leadership of a Baptist preacher, Uriah Stephens. To protect its membership from blacklists, the organization was made highly secretive. Its ultimate goal was the creation of a new society comprised of workers' cooperatives whose profits would be distributed equally. The 'millenium," it was felt, could be achieved by uplifting the educational level of the workers, forming producers' cooperatives, and appropriate legislative reforms. Some of the Knights' more immediate legislative goals included compulsory education, free textbooks for the labouring class, income and inheritance taxes, compulsory arbitration, government ownership of the railroad and telegraph system, abolition of convict labor, equal pay for both sexes, the establishment of a bureau of labor statistics, and the eight-hour day. Since the wage system was eventually to be abolished, strikes and boycotts to secure higher wages or shorter hours were thought unnecessary, and to be avoided. Membership was open to almost the entire labor force, including the unskilled, farmers, professionals and small businessmen. The only groups specifically barred were lawyers, doctors, bankers, stock brokers, liquor dealers, and professional gamblers.

Ideally, workers in all occupations in a given area would band together in a mixed assembly, but in order to attact the existing international craft unions, skilled workers were allowed to form craft assemblies. This enabled the craft unions to join the Knights without changing their structure or weakening their hold over their own locals. Local assemblies were then combined into district assemblies of the mixed or trade type, which in turn were knit together by the general assembly. Unlike other labor federations up to this time, the general assembly headed by the grand master workman, was endowed by the consitution with "full and final jurisdiction in all matters pertaining to local and district assemblies." In practice, however, local and district assemblies disregarded the decisions of the general assembly.

The rise and fall of the Knights was meteoric. During the 1870's a serious depression, coupled with suspicion over the Knights secretive nature, restricted its membership. In the early 1880's the revival in business activity, improved leadership with the election of Terence Powderly as Grand Master Workman, and the abandonment of secrecy enabled the Knights to increase their membership to about 100,000 by

1885. And then phenomenally, in a twelve-month period from the summer of 1885 to the summer of 1886, the Knights grew to over 700,000. The Knights, despite the reluctance of the General Assembly, had been involved in a number of strikes in the early 1880's with mixed success. In the winter of 1885 the nationally known Jay Gould, to meet competition, had reduced wages by ten per cent on three of his southwestern railroads. A general strike ensued which engulfed the entire Gould system and the reductions were withdrawn. Shortly thereafter Gould retaliated by discharging a number of workers on his Wabash Railroad who were members of the Knights and active in the strike. The General Assembly in turn retaliated by ordering its members not to handle Wabash rolling stock. Gould, who at this time could not afford a prolonged strike, agreed to negotiate the matter. At a series of meetings Gould and the Knights' leadership reached an agreement whereby the strike and boycott were terminated and Gould agreed to cease discriminating against members of the Knights. The unheard-of success of a labor union over the powerful Jay Gould hurled the Knights into the national spotlight. Labor at last found a union that could stand up against a powerful employer and win. Hundreds of thousands of workers, especially the unskilled, who heretofore had no forum to express their discontent, flocked to join. The press acknowledged the Knights as the nation's leading labor union, and politicians sought to curry its favor. But the Knights' success was short-lived. Subsequent strikes against Gould and others were unsuccessful.

The most crushing blow was adverse public reaction to the Haymarket riots in Chicago in May, 1886. For many years organized labor had been seeking the establishment of the eight-hour day. Under the auspices of international craft unions, some of which were affiliated with the Knights, a general strike was called for May 1, 1886 to enforce this demand. The Knights' leadership officially frowned on the eight-hour movement and opposed the strike, but many of its district and local assemblies, together with the rank and file, joined the movement. The protest on May 1st for the most part passed peacefully, and actually fell far short of its leaders' expectations. On May 3rd, however, violence erupted when a group of workers attacked strikebreakers as they left the McCormick Harvester Company plant in Chicago. Police were called and in the resulting melee a number of workers were killed and injured. The following day a mass meeting was called in Haymarket Square in Chicago to protest police brutality. After several hours of oratory the group was about to disperse peacefully when squads of policemen began forceably to break up the proceedings. In the riot that followed, a bomb was thrown which killed one policeman and injured several others. Hysteria gripped the country, and the labor movement was pictured as being controlled by radical groups which sought the overthrow of the government. Large numbers of

TABLE 15.3. *Union Membership, Selected Dates 1869-1920*

Year	Total (in thousands)
1869	170
1872	300
1878	50
1883	200
1886	1,000
1890	400
1897	440
1900	791
1904	2,061
1910	2,116
1914	2,647
1920	5,034

SOURCE: W. S. Woytinsky. *Employment and Wages in the United States.* New York: The Twentieth Century Fund 1953, p. 233; U.S. Bureau of the Census. *Historical Statistics of U.S. Colonial Times to 1957.* Washington, D.C.: U.S. Government Printing Office, 1960, p. 97.

workers, reacting to the public criticism, left labor unions in general and the Knights of Labor in particular. Many local assemblies dissolved and others, who were impatient with the Knights' unwillingness or inability to undertake strikes successfully, joined the newly formed American Federation of Labor. Within a few years the Knight's membership fell to under 200,000 and by the 1890's, except for some local remnants, it was out of business. (See Table 15.3.)

Even in the absence of the Haymarket Riot, the Knights were doomed to failure. The organization's basic weakness lay in its attempt to organize almost the entire working force into a single cohesive unit. Such a heterogeneous labor organization at this stage in the nation's economic growth could be no more than a debating society. The priority given to the mixed assembly made it impossible for the Knights to adapt itself to the problems of specific industries or trades. It might engage with some success in political or governmental reform, but not in collective bagaining. Moreover, the grandiose long-term objectives of the Knights did not harmonize with the average worker's desire for immediate economic improvement. The craft unions remained affiliated only as long as the Knights aggressively pressed for higher wages, shorter hours and better working conditions. The continued pressure of the membership, both skilled and unskilled, for short-term gains forced the Knights to become involved in strikes for which they were not prepared and which consequently had little chance of success. Finally, much of the Knights' resources were directed toward unsuccessful producers' cooperatives.

THE AMERICAN FEDERATION OF LABOR

The basic discontent of skilled workers with the philosophy of the Knights of Labor resulted in 1881 in the formation of a competing labor federation, the Federation of Organized Trade and Labor Unions. Comprised exclusively of craft workers, it made little headway until 1886, when it was reorganized to form the American Federation of Labor (AFL). At that time a number of craft unions which had failed to gain autonomy in the Knights joined the new federation. In the years that followed, all major trade unions with the exception of the railroad brotherhoods became AFL affiliates. The AFL was dominated by Samuel Gompers of the cigarmakers union, who was its president until his death in 1924. In Gompers' own words:

> The ground-work principle of America's labor movement has been to recognize that first things must come first. The primary essential in our mission has been the protection of the wage-worker, now; to increase his wages, to cut hours off the long work-day, which was killing him; to improve the safety and the sanitary conditions of the work-shop; to free him from the tyrannies, petty or otherwise, which served to make his existence a slavery. These in the nature of things, I repeat, were and are the primary objects of trade unionism.
>
> Our great Federation has uniformly refused to surrender this conviction and to rush to the support of any one of the numerous society-saving or society-destroying schemes which decade by decade have been sprung upon this country. A score of such schemes, having a national scope, and being for the passing day subject to popular discussion, have gone down behind the horizon and are now but ancient history. But while our Federation has thus been conservative, it has ever had its face turned toward whatever reforms, in politics or economics, that could be of direct and obvious benefit to the working classes. It has never given up its birthright for a mess of pottage. It has pursued its avowed policy with the conviction that if the lesser and immediate demands of labor could not be obtained now from society as it is, it would be mere dreaming to preach and pursue that will-o'-the-wisp, a new society constructed from rainbow materials—a system of society on which even the dreamers themselves have never agreed.[1]

Gompers believed that this "down-to-earth" unionism could succeed if:

1. All of the union's resources are concentrated on controlling the job and the worker on the job. Capitalism, he believed, is not an ideal

system but it is here to stay. Emphasis must be placed on providing the worker with a means to control his work situation.

2. Membership is restricted to craft workers who have investment in their skill and can be expected to remain loyal to the union in good and bad times. History has proved that unions of unskilled and semi-skilled workers were likely to collapse under employer or economic pressures.

3. Each international union has exclusive jurisdiction over the workers in its craft. Dual unionism, i.e. two unions seeking to organize the same group of workers, fundamentally weakens the trade union movement. The problems of industrial unionism, i.e. workers with skills employed in the same industry, can be solved by the voluntary merger of craft unions or the establishment of trade or industry departments such as the building trades department.

4. The ultimate power of the federation resides in the international unions. Local unions are intrinsically irresponsible and may undermine standards and squander strike funds if they are not supervised by the international. The role of the federation through its president and executive council is to advise, coordinate activities, and mediate disputes between the international unions.

5. The federation remains aloof from political affairs. Labor should support its friends in government and punish its enemies, but not become associated with any particular party. Government intervention in economic affairs is to be distrusted, any real gains for labor have to be won at the collective bargaining table, not in the halls of Congress.

Able leadership and sound philosophy enabled the AFL to make steady, if modest, gains during the 1880's and 1890's. For the first time organized labor weathered a major depression, that from 1893 to 1897, even increasing its membership slightly during the period. On the negative side, the trade union movement lost two major strikes, the Homestead Strike in 1892, and the Pullman Strike in 1894. Both involved considerable violence and resulted in permanent damage to the unions involved, the Amalgamated Iron and Steel Workers and the American Railway Union. The years 1897 to 1904 were ones of substantial gain, with trade union membership increasing almost fourfold. The period was marked by a lull in the conflict between management and labor, as progressive business-men sought to solve their labor problems by negotiations rather than strikes. For a time, under the auspices of the National Civic Federation, Gompers and other labor leaders joined with wealthy eastern capitalists, corporate officers, editors, and professional men to promote industrial peace. But the honeymoon did not last very long, and employers, reacting to the spread of unionism, soon sponsored an open-shop drive. More militant employer opposition, sparked by the National Association of

Manufacturers and some unfavorable court decisions, significantly slowed union progress.

In addition, the AFL suffered from the competition of the radical Industrial Workers of the World (IWW). Formed in 1905, with the aggressive Western Federation of Miners as its nucleus, it offered the growing number of unskilled and semiskilled workers a means to express their discontent. Ignored and shunned by the AFL, these workers welcomed any union which would accept them as members. A heterogeneous grouping of radicals and idealists, it was essentially a syndicalist organization which hoped eventually to do away with the wage system and the existing forms of government control. Although it conducted a number of successful strikes it was never able to consolidate its gains. Irreconcilable differences between the radical groups which comprised it, together with its opposition to United States participation in World War I, led to its dissolution. However, not all unions of unskilled workers suffered the plight of the IWW. John R. Commons in the reading at the end of this chapter discusses the successes of the Teamsters of Chicago. The article also depicts the characteristics of a typical union of the period.

LABOR AND THE LAW

Labor union growth in the United States from the Civil War to 1915 was made difficult by the attitude of the courts. It has been pointed out that in 1842, in *Commonwealth v. Hunt,* a classic ruling was issued that an association of workers was not to be considered a conspiracy in restraint of trade unless it used its power to infringe on what were considered the lawful property rights of employers. What constituted an unlawful use of union power and an infringement of an employer's rights was very broadly interpreted by the courts. In most labor disputes employers found a ready ally in the judiciary and an effective weapon against union power in the injunction. An injunction is a court order prohibiting or requiring the continuance of a specific course of action. If the order is violated, the party named in the action is in contempt of court and subject to civil or criminal penalties or both. The first labor injunction in the United States was issued in the 1880's when workers on a railroad being operated by a court-appointed receiver threatened to strike. The receiver obtained an injunction on the grounds that the workers were striking against the court, and the strike was over in a few hours. The speed and ease with which the strike had been thwarted impressed employers, and by the 1890's the labor injunction was a popular anti-union device. Most companies threatened by a strike or boycott were able to secure a temporary restraining order on the ground that the action would cause irreparable damage to their property. Judges frequently issued this order without a union representative being present. Often, by the time a court considered whether to vacate an order or make it permanent, a strike had been effectively broken either by compliance or because the union leaders were in jail. Many judges went so far as to allow the counsel for a plaintiff to draw up an injunction.

About the same time that the injunction became a popular anti-union device, a new legal barrier to union activity was being erected in the form of antitrust laws. It has already been observed that in 1890 Congress, reacting to an alarming degree of economic concentration among business firms, enacted the Sherman Antitrust Act, which proscribed "every contract, combination in the form of trust or otherwise, or conspiracy in restraint of trade or commerce among the several states or with foreign nations." The Act further provided for the issuance of injunctions, the recovery of treble damages by injured private parties, and the filing of criminal charges against those accused of violating its provisions. Although there is some doubt whether Congress intended the Act to apply to labor as well as business combinations, the Federal Courts held that union activities which substantially interfered with interstate commerce were subject to its jurisdiction. This position was affirmed by the Supreme Court in 1908 in the *Danbury Hatters* case. A nationwide campaign by a hatters' union to establish a closed shop in the industry led to a strike and national boycott against Loewe and Company of Danbury, Connecticut. The Supreme Court, in finding the union guilty of restraining interstate commerce, ruled that the Sherman Act applied equally to businessmen and labor, even though the latter were not themselves engaged in interstate commerce.

In the Clayton Act of 1914 Congress attempted to exempt labor union activities from antitrust jurisdiction and to limit the power of the judiciary in the issuance of injunctions. Section 6 of the Act states that the "labor of a human being is not a commodity or article of commerce. Nothing contained in the antitrust laws shall be construed to forbid the existence and operation of labor ... organizations ... or to forbid or restrain individual members ... from lawfully carrying out the legitimate objects thereof; nor shall such organizations, or the members thereof, be held or construed to be illegal combinations or conspiracies in restraint of trade, under the antitrust laws." Section 20 of the Act barred courts from issuing injunctions "in any case between an employer and employees ... involving or growing out of a dispute concerning terms or conditions of employment."

Labor leaders immediately hailed the passage of the Act, Samuel Gompers calling it "Labor's Magna Carta." Jubilation proved premature, however, for the judiciary was soon to hand down a number of decisions holding such activities as mass picketing, sympathy strikes, and secondary boycotts not to be "legitimate" or "lawful" actions. It was ruled that Section 20 of the Clayton Act applied only to disputes between employers and employees where the union was engaged in "lawful" activities. In the *Duplex Printing Company* case of 1921, for example, a court ruled that a machinist union's efforts to have members of other unions refuse to haul or install Duplex equipment was illegal and thus enjoinable. Not until the 1930's were the courts to be effectively restrained in their use of the labor injunction.

NOTES

1. Samuel Gompers. *Labor and the Common Welfare*, ed. by Hayes Robbins. New York: E.P. Dutton and Co., 1919, p. 20.

SELECTED REFERENCES

1. Selig Perlman. *A History of Trade Unionism in the United States.* New York: Macmillan, 1922.
2. Albert Rees. *Real Wages in Manufacturing, 1890-1914.* Princeton: Princeton University Press, 1961.
3. G. M. Stephenson. *History of American Immigration, 1820-1924.* Boston: Ginn and Co., 1926.
4. Philip Taft. *The AF of L in the Time of Gompers.* New York: Harper, 1957.
5. Conrad Tauber and Irene Tauber. *The Changing Population of the United States.* New York: Social Science Research Council, 1958.
6. Brinley Thomas. *Migration and Economic Growth.* Cambridge: Cambridge University Press, 1954.
7. Leo Wolman. *Growth of American Trade Unions, 1880-1923.* New York: National Bureau of Economic Research, 1924.

reading

a typical union of the period:
the teamsters of chicago

john r. commons

Only since the year 1902 have the teamsters of Chicago discovered their power. They have always been classed as unskilled labor, and the old-line trade unionist ridiculed and discouraged the organizers who ventured to create a teamsters' union. The skilled unions saw the strategic position of the teamster, and the brewery workers made some of the brewery drivers a part of their "industrial" union. But the driver felt that they wanted him, not to help him, but to help them. Only when he broke away and organized his own teamsters' union did he get enthusiasm for union principles.

Again, the teamster had never been clearly distinguished from the team owner. The oldest so-called union was that of the hack drivers, organized in 1867. But that was a union of hack owners as much as hack drivers, since the majority owned the rigs they drove. Consequently their interest lay rather in holding up the fares charged to the public than the wages earned by the driver. Their organization was never influential and often comatose. Not until 1902 did they take in the livery drivers employed by the great companies and thereby become a labor union as well as a guild. Their history since then is similar to that of other teamsters and drivers.

[1]John R. Commons, "The Teamsters of Chicago," *Quarterly Journal of Economics* XIX (1905) 400-433.

477

The laws of the former International Team Drivers' Union, chartered by the American Federation of Labor in 1899, admitted to membership a team owner if he operated not more than five teams. This threw the unions, the conventions, and the laws into the hands of the owners, and prices were more prominent than wages. Such a union was inherently weak. While the larger team owners were formally excluded, yet their teamsters were not attracted to a union whose views respecting wages were those of small team owners. The first object necessary to form an effective union was community of interest, and this required separation from employers. The Chicago teamsters, in defiance of their international organization, refused to admit owners; and finally, in 1902, they seceded, and formed a new national union, including only teamsters and helpers. They admitted the driver who owned the team he operated, but excluded him if he owned a team driven by some one else.

Even this differentiation was not enough. Teamsters are employed in every industry. No craft is so necessary and universal. But teaming in one industry is distinct from teaming in another. The laundry driver has little in common with the coal teamster, except horses and streets. His problems of unionism, such as methods of payment, hours, and discipline, are different. In 1894 coal teamsters, truck drivers, and others were in a general union, just as they are to-day in smaller towns. But that union quickly disappeared. In 1886 something similar had occurred under the Knights of Labor. But in 1902 each industry was organized separately in its own "local." Though each is called a local union, it is more than local in the geographical sense. Each local is a distinct craft, with jurisdiction over the entire city for all workmen of its craft, and the principle recognized for all is the same as that explicitly stated by the Ice Wagon Drivers: "Our Local Union has the powers of self-government, known as Local Autonomy, and, if deemed advisable, to make such by-laws that will be beneficent to the local organization, such as admitting persons who own and operate one team, regulating initiation fees or dues, honorable withdrawal cards, trials, fines, suspensions and expulsions in conformity with the general laws." There are, of course, many cases where locals overlap; and, in order to avoid conflict of jurisdiction, each stable is assigned to the local to which 51 per cent or more of its work belongs.

Thus the teamsters of Chicago were the first to establish two principles new to the occupation, —craft autonomy and wage unionism. Starting with these principles, within two years there were organized 47 locals, from the Truck Drivers with over 5000 members to the Dye House Drivers with 46. Afterwards this differentiation was found too fine, and some of the smaller locals were merged into others. Nearly all were organized during the first year. They created a joint executive council of seven delegates from each local, with power over strikes, and in 1903 they amalgamated with the International Team Drivers, which meanwhile had changed its constitution to exclude employers. The organization is now known as the International Brotherhood of Teamsters, with 821 locals in some 300 cities.

Such sudden and precipitate organization was accomplished and recognized with scarcely a half dozen strikes. This was owing partly to the secrecy maintained, but mainly to an early demonstration of power and a sympathetic interest on the part of one class of team owners. This second factor is explained by the peculiar nature of the business.

The two classes of team owners are those who follow teaming for a living and those whose teaming is an adjunct to their general business. The latter include the department stores, the meat packers, grocers and meat markets, the brewers, the largest manufacturers, the milk dealers, lumber dealers, railway express companies, ice companies, some of the wholesale merchants, and others. The former include truck owners, expressmen and van owners, liverymen, the commission team owners, and, to a lesser degree, coal team owners, ice wagon owners, and similar teaming contractors. The significance of this distinction lies in the fact that many of the manufacturers and most of the wholesale merchants and commission houses do their teaming through contractors. With the manufacturers and wholesale merchants the teamsters' wages are but a small part of their total expenses. With the retail merchants the proportion is larger, the largest being that of the milk dealers, — 15 per cent or less. But with the contracting team owners the wages of teamsters and helpers are 50 to 75 per cent of their total expenses. Consequently, while competition of manufacturers and merchants is but slightly affected by the teamsters' wages, competition of team owners is mainly a question of the wages and hours of their competitors. The manufacturer and wholesale merchant are interested in keeping wages low, but the team owner is interested in keeping them equal. The team owner has therefore welcomed and encouraged the organization of the teamsters, notwithstanding an extraordinary increase in the rates of wages, because the union equalized competition. In taking this attitude his position has not been the same as that of the merchant or manufacturer, whose cost of trucking was increased whether done directly or by contract. One consequence is that the team owners— by which will be meant those with whom teaming is their business and not an adjunct—have organized associations, not only as employers to negotiate with the unions, but also as contractors to regulate rates of cartage and livery. The principal associations of this kind are the Chicago Team Owners, dealing with the truck drivers; the Furniture Movers and Expressmen's Association, dealing with the van teamsters and helpers and the baggage and parcel delivery drivers and helpers; the Commission Team Owners, dealing with the commission drivers; and four liverymen's associations, dealing with the hack, coupe, and livery drivers. These associations determine by joint agreements the rates of wages and the hours and conditions of labor, and the scales thus determined are the union scales paid also by merchants and manufacturers not members of the association to their teamsters employed directly. Many of the other teamsters' unions have joint agreements with employers' associations; but such associations being composed of merchants or manufacturers are loose and informal, while the associations named above are compact and permanent, some of them with bonds and forfeits binding them not only to the scale of wages but also to the scale of prices.

The Coal Team Owners and their drivers deserve special mention by reason of their early leadership and their peculiar methods. The drivers were organized in the fall of 1900 and secured individual agreements during 1901. They made further demands in the winter of 1901-1902, which, added to those already secured, doubled the cost of teaming. For a two-horse wagon they formerly received 50 cents a load of 4 or 5 tons, and for a three-horse wagon 65 cents a load of 6 or 7 tons, regardless of distance. At these rates the labor cost of cartage was about 10 cents a ton, and the teamster earned $8 to $12 a week of indefinite hours. The scale finally agreed upon substitutes weekly and overtime rates for the former piece rates. The two-horse driver receives $15 and the three-horse driver $18 for a week of 66 hours, and 35 cents and 40 cents an hour overtime, respectively. At these rates the labor cost was raised to about 20 cents a ton.

In order to pay these higher wages the coal dealers contended that they must get higher prices for cartage. The antitrust law of Illinois, as amended in 1897, made an exception in favor of any article "the cost of which is mainly made up of wages."[1] To avail themselves of this exception the coal dealers separated their *cartage* from their *coal* and organized, not a dealers' association, but a Coal Team Owners' Association, since the cost of cartage, but not the cost of coal, is "mainly made up of wages," and since a team owner does not have title in the property he delivers and is therefore not responsible for its price to the public. There is also a considerable amount of coal hauled by contract, and contracting team owners who are not dealers are also members of the association. The rates charged for cartage had formerly been 22 to 27 cents a ton. The association adopted and issued a schedule setting the rates at 50 cents a ton for manufacturing and steam use and 60 cents a ton for domestic use within two and one half miles from the point of loading; for each additional mile or fraction thereof 10 cents a ton. Thus the rates for cartage were doubled when the teamsters' wages were doubled. But since they started on different bases it is also true that the absolute increase in cartage was twice as great as the increase in wages, namely 20 to 25 cents a ton when wages were increased 10 cents a ton. There are, of course, other expenses besides wages, mainly, feed and care of horses; and these are offered as a justification for the disproportionate advance, though the occasion thereof was the advance in wages. At the same time, since the dealers mainly own their teams and their prices for coal include delivery, their ability to maintain the rate of cartage really depends on their ability to maintain the price of coal. This they have not been able to do on bituminous coal on account of the many sources of supply, while they have thoroughly succeeded on anthracite coal on account of the centralized control of supply.

However this may be, the coal dealers at first relied upon the teamsters to control the market and even to create one. They made a provisional agreement in January, 1902, to take effect the following May and to continue for five years, if the teamsters meanwhile could demonstrate their power. The agreement provided that none but members of the union should be employed and that the teamsters should work for none but members of the association. With this understanding the agent of the teamsters stopped the delivery of coal to the great firm of Marshall Field & Co. for a few hours in winter until that firm signed a two-year contract with the union to use coal instead of natural gas during the summer. This spectacular demonstration had two results. The managers of other stores and office buildings, who also had made the mistake of building sky scrapers without coal bunkers, signed a similar contract when requested; and nearly all of the teamsters in Chicago joined the union. The astute agent of the coal team owners, John C. Driscoll by name, who had engineered this *coup*, proceeded on his part to organize the team owners in other branches, and eventually became secretary of five such associations. In each case agreements similar to the original one were made with the new teamsters' locals. These and other locals were organized without general strikes, except those of the packing house and department store teamsters in June. Yet, while they had but few strikes on their own account, the teamsters in the first flush of enthusiasm stopped work in sympathy with strikers on the inside; and this in the case of the freight handlers in July was the most destructive since 1894. That disaster sobered the teamster, but it showed him his power.

Springing from these sympathetic strikes came the most remarkable board of arbitration known to industrial disputes. Seven of the largest employers of teamsters and seven agents of the teamsters' unions constituted themselves for one year the industrial umpires of Chicago. Practically all the strikes of new unions during that period came before this board. The older unions, such as the building trades, disdained this upstart jurisprudence and refused to submit their disputes. But it happened that most of the strikes of that period were those of new unions. The board's powers were quasi compulsory, since the employer who would not submit to arbitration could not get teamsters, and the strikers who would not submit could not get the help of the teamsters. Many of the strikes were handled by Driscoll, the agent of the teaming employers, without bringing them before the board of arbitration, and had it not been for his unscrupulous use of money in bribing the leaders of the unions, the board might have continued. But his corruption was finally exposed, the teamsters withdrew their representatives, and eventually deposed the officers who had been on friendly terms with him. The board of arbitration was dissolved. Employers, also, who were willing that Driscoll should use their money to "buy off" the leaders of troublesome strikes, became distrustful when they learned that he secretly fomented strikes to be bought off. He lost his position in all but the Coal Team Owners' Association, and the others substituted men of a different type. Since this reform movement of 1903 the teaming industry can be studied as an economic rather than as a criminal phenomenon.

HOURS AND WAGES

The change most impressive brought about by the unions is that from indefinite hours and wages to definite wages and pay for overtime. The teamsters' occupation is peculiar in that it has carried over and retained in industry the practices of agriculture. The teamster has always been expected to "care for his stock" as well as to drive his wagon. Even where a teaming contractor's business had grown so large as to require the services of stablemen, the teamster was expected to be at the stable before working time and to remain at the stable after working time long enough to feed and curry his horses, clean their stalls, grease and repair his wagon, hitch up and unhitch, and keep his harness clean and the brass polished. This required also several hours on Sunday. For such work he was not supposed to be paid, — it was the necessary preparation for work, not the real productive effort that brought him wages. This continues to hold good under the union agreements, so that, while the teamster says that he now has a ten-hour working day, the day lasts nearly always from six o'clock in the morning to six or half past six in the evening, with one hour for dinner. Consequently, the actual working time for which his stipulated day's wages is paid is 11 or 11½ hours. This enables the truck driver to back his wagon up to the platform for his first load at seven o'clock, the time when the inside workers begin, and to get his last load in time to return to the stable and leave for home at about six in the evening. Formerly he might not get his last load till the inside workers quit, and this might keep him at the barn till eight or nine o'clock and even later. In some lines of teaming not depending on factories and warehouses, such as furniture moving, groceries, markets, and commission driving, he was called out much earlier in the morning or kept later at night according to the amount of work the team owner could find for him to do. The van teamster who took out a sleighing party was not paid for it, because that was night work. Often he and others reported at the stable at three, four, or five o'clock in the morning and left the stable at eight, nine, or ten at night. On this account it is impossible to know the number of hours most of the teamsters formerly worked. As they were not paid for overtime, their former earnings give no indication of the hours employed. In general, they ranged from 70 to 100 hours a week, according to seasons and kinds of teaming.

These hours have been reduced in two ways: first, by cutting out Sunday work, or stipulating that it shall be paid at one and one half or double rates; and second, by stipulating a rate per hour for overtime before six A.M. and after six P.M. Under these conditions the larger team owners employ stablemen to do much of the work formerly done by the teamsters, and in order to avoid the higher rates for overtime, they try to arrange their work to bring it within the regular time. The wholesale merchant who kept his truck driver hauling to the railways during the day and then gave him a city load late in the afternoon now concentrates his schedule of trips. Nevertheless, in some lines the teamster continues to make a large amount of overtime. It is not unusual for the coal teamster, at $18 a week and 40 cents overtime, to earn $20 or $24 a week. In other branches overtime varies greatly according to the business. Consequently, in this industry the policy of reducing the hours of labor is necessarily often a policy of merely getting pay for overtime and so greatly increasing the earnings. The driver must finish his trip and return his team to the stable; and while overtime cannot always be abolished, it can be paid for.

Again, there are some lines in which very little change in the hours, except Sunday relief, has occurred. The railway express drivers never had the care of their horses, and their reduction in hours has been but three or four a week. The laundry and bakery drivers have about the same hours as formerly. The routes of the keg beer drivers had always been equalized, so that they could finish their work in the morning; but they were kept around the barn indefinitely for extra jobs and errands. These extras have been cut off.

The action of the milk wagon drivers deserves special mention. They directed their efforts at first not to the rates of wages, but to the hours of work. Formerly they started out in the summer at from one to four o'clock in the morning, made a delivery of milk in the forenoon and a second delivery in the afternoon, returned at four or five o'clock, spent one or two hours in balancing their books, and got away at six or seven in the evening, making 12 to 18 hours a day. Then they worked 10 hours on

Sunday, delivering milk and caring for their horses and wagons, altogether 100 hours a week for $10 or $12. In the winter they began at six A.M., making 80 hours a week.

Their first step after organizing in January, 1903, was to cut out the second delivery, to fix their hours in winter from 8 to 5, and to decide that in summer no delivery should be made in the afternoon and "all wagons must be off the street by one P.M." This brought the hours to about 52 a week, including 4 hours on Sunday,—a reduction of nearly 50 hours in summer and 30 hours in winter. Within the past three years their wages have advanced to $45 and $60 a month, so that the rate of pay per hour has more than doubled. These are minimum rates. There are also "route men," whose commissions on sales bring their total earnings to $70 or $80 a month.

Public amazement and invective followed the "one-daily-delivery" system. The rule was adopted in January and did not attract attention until warm weather. Then the newspapers, with several columns daily, attacked the union. Early in June the commissioner of health stated in his weekly bulletin: "The 'one-daily-delivery' of milk has begun to reap its harvest. Even in well-to-do families this thirty-six to sixty hours' old milk cannot be kept from souring from one delivery to the next. Herod was more merciful in the method he used in his slaughter of the innocents."

Now that two summers have passed a somewhat cooler estimate can be made of the drivers' action.[2] In fact, the change to the "one-daily-delivery" of milk could have but little direct effect on the death rate of children. The milk formerly delivered in the afternoon was from exactly the same milking as that delivered in the forenoon, the only difference being that the driver carried a part or all of it around in his wagon all day instead of leaving it at the house in the morning. The morning deliveries are always, with the unimportant exception noted below, at least twenty-four and thirty-six hours old, having been drawn the morning of the day before and the evening of the second day before. Furthermore, in the poorer sections of the city, where home refrigerators are scarce, a large part of the milk has always been bought at groceries or depots conveniently located in nearly every block. In 1904 there were issued 2424 milk licenses for such stores against 2516 for wagons. Both drivers and dealers state that almost their only afternoon customers were in the wealthier sections of the city, and the amount taken was small, being only what the mistress wished for an unexpected guest or an extra function. On the whole, it appears that the afternoon delivery was a needless waste, imposed by the thoughtlessness of housewives. The fifty hours saved each week to the drivers have not laid any hardship on the public.

While not directly affecting the death rate, the revolt of the drivers indirectly reduced it by awakening public conscience and bringing about reforms in the municipal health department. The Children's Hospital Society created a Milk Commission, including physicians, bacteriologists, and representatives of the Women's Club, established a laboratory, and by special arrangement sent out in bottles milk fourteen hours old to sick children of the congested districts and the hospitals. The Civic Federation employed the biological department of the University of Chicago to test some three hundred samples of milk from various sources. Their report reflected unfavorably upon the inspection of the Municipal Department of Health, and finally led in 1904 to the appointment of an additional force of milk inspectors, including four country inspectors to visit farms; and all inspectors were instructed to pay special attention to the sanitary condition of dairies and utensils. In this year for the first time the department's bacteriologist made a systematic examination of the city's market milk. Considerable amounts of milk were condemned, nineteen milk peddlers' premises were abolished, several hundred dealers were notified to place and keep their depots in sanitary condition. An ordinance was adopted requiring metal seals to cans, by means of which responsibility can be fixed on the shipper, the railway employee, or the dealer. This has reduced milk watering 50 per cent. The railroads were induced to furnish better facilities for handling.[3] Coupled with a cool summer in 1904 and the completion of sewer systems and the drainage canal, the death rate of all ages declined somewhat, and the death rate of children declined still more, as stated above. On the whole, the stand taken by the milk wagon drivers diverted attention from a false security on two deliveries of milk a day to the real source of danger, — an inadequate milk inspection.

EARNINGS

The wages formerly earned were as indefinite as the hours. While the books of the team owners, if examined, would throw no light on the former rates of pay per hour, they would show the earnings by the week or month. In lieu of such an examination the testimony of employers and men has been found to agree remarkably in some lines and fairly well in others. Apparent disagreements are explained by the existence of exceptionally high or exceptionally low wages. The policy of the unions has been to establish a minimum rate of pay, and then to stipulate that no employee receiving more than the scale shall suffer a reduction. Consequently, exceptional men, especially in those lines where commissions are paid, have not gained an increase in weekly earnings, though the reduction in hours has increased their hourly rates; while the lowest paid positions have been substantially increased by the week and amazingly increased by the hour. Looking at the position of the average teamster without special abilities or disabilities, it may be said that for 70 to 100 hours' work his earnings before organization were $8 to $12 a week. Some grocery drivers, garbage collectors, beer wagon helpers, and many boys got as little as $4.50 and $6, while men on commission got as much as $25 or $30; but the prevailing testimony sets the bulk of the earnings at $9. Since organization the minimum rates per week have been raised, so that they range from $10 for retail grocery drivers to $18 for a three-horse coal team driver; the standard towards which all are aiming being $15 a week of six days, and the rate that the largest number have reached being somewhat less. The advances made for helpers are relatively greater than those for drivers, bringing the two closer together, and both to a higher level.

While these increases are large, they nearly always exaggerate the increased labor cost of the employers. Often the highest paid men were not affected, and the better paid men were already close to the new minimum. In some lines, like department stores and railway express, only one company was paying the extremely low rates, and that usually to boys. In other lines this proportion was larger. The boys have been discharged and men have taken their places; and their greater efficiency somewhat offsets the apparent increase in pay. Furthermore, from the teamster's standpoint the reduction in hours, which has so enormously increased his hourly rate, has often been in the hours uselessly spent in waiting or doing uneconomical work in order to be on hand when wanted. Such wasted hours the employer did not count, and their reduction does not increase proportionately his hourly cost, because now he keeps the teamster busy every minute while on duty. Consequently, the team owner's increased labor cost is not to be measured by the teamster's extraordinary gain by the hour, as would naturally be supposed, but rather by his more moderate gain by the week.

COMMISSIONS

In several lines the teamster is more than a driver: he is a solicitor or order clerk, and can build up or break down his employer's business. In some cases the companies have regular solicitors who are not drivers, but even then the driver must be relied upon to "hold his trade." This takes an extreme form in the laundry business, where in a union of 700 members there are 200 drivers, known as "commission men," who own each a horse and wagon and "control their trade." Some of these men have agencies at hotels, news stands, and so on, where orders may be left. They can transfer their business from one laundry to another, and their commission is 40 per cent. At such rates the most successful driver makes as much as $100 a week. Naturally, the laundrymen objected to this power of transferring business, and they began to require contracts preventing a man on leaving their employment from going into the laundry business for two years thereafter. The courts refused to sustain such contracts, but afterwards, when they were modified so as to limit their operation to a designated territory, they were sustained. The union met the policy of the laundrymen by a clause in their agreements stipulating that drivers owning their own wagon and known as "commission men" should receive not less than 40 per cent of the gross amount of work, and that "no driver shall be requested to sign any contract conflicting with this agreement." Evidently, a union of solicitors owning their places of business, protecting their commissions, and maintaining their power to throw business from one employer to another partakes more of the nature of a merchants' guild than a labor union. In the case of laundry drivers not owning their wagons the union agreement provides a minimum salary of $15 a week, which is an advance of something like 50 per cent on their former wages. In addition, many of them get a commission on business beyond a certain amount. The rule of a minimum salary holds for drivers in all other lines where commissions are paid, the laundrymen owning their wagons being the only class paid solely by commissions without a minimum guaranty.

In the case of the bakery drivers the guaranty is $14 a week, which would be useful only in the out districts where business is light, but where the union does not yet control. The valuable advances are in the rates of commission, and these apply to the large bakeries supply the down-town district. Here the minimum of $14 is significant, not as a true minimum, but as a basis on which to compute the commissions. For example, the best paying company in the city, which formerly paid $14 a week and 6 per cent on sales above $250 now pays $14 a week and 1½ per cent on business up to $150, 3 per cent on the excess to $250, and 7 per cent on the excess above $250. Consequently, a driver who formerly received $17 on a week's business of $300 now gets $22.75. The larger his business, the larger has been the rate of increase in his earnings, a few getting as much as $40 a week and none less than $16.

The commission scheme of the beer drivers is suggestive. The bottle beer driver, more than the keg beer driver, is expected to "hold his trade." In both cases the commission is paid, not on the sales, but on the "empties" returned; and in both cases the commission has always been looked upon as spending-money. The bottle beer driver joins many lodges to which bartenders belong. He seldom sees the saloon proprietor, for his visits are made early in the morning. His persuasiveness is exerted on the bartender. To prevent him from transferring his trade from one brewery to another, the brewers have a strong association and an agreement not to take another brewer's driver. The agreement is enforced by a clearing house, organized as follows. The driver does not get all of the "empties." Many of them are thrown in the alleys and back yards, and come into the hands of junk dealers. These sell them to the clearing house of the brewers' association. The brewer who does not abide by the rules of the association cannot get back his junk bottles through the clearing house until his fine is paid. This is one of the means that hold the brewers together in fixing prices and resisting organized labor. Lacking such a clearing house, the laundrymen have not been able as effectively to resist the "commission men."

The keg beer driver gets his salary of $80 a month and 4 cents additional on empty kegs returned. Before organization his salary was $60 to $80 and his commission was 8 cents, but out of this he paid his helper $20 to $35 a month. Now the helper gets $55 a month paid by the brewer, and the driver tries to keep his commission through a clause in the agreement providing that "peddlers, helpers, and extra drivers shall not be required to spend any money with customers on their routes, and their not spending any money shall not be cause for any complaint or discharge." Under this arrangement the majority "take home" more than their salary, and the best men with the best routes are said to earn, net, as much as $30 or $35 a week.

The milk wagon driver's commission is computed on the basis of "1 cent to the point," a point being the unit of each article sold, as a quart of milk, a half pint of cream, or a pound of butter. This figures out about 14 per cent on sales; but he is usually paid a minimum of $60 a month, if his sales do not yield so much, and one half cent a point on sales above the amount necessary to compute the minimum at 1 cent. The best man earns $100, and the majority in the service of the "big firms" earn $65. The commission is optional, and very few of the small dealers pay it. The union demands for 1905 would make it compulsory, would raise it to 1 1/5 cent, and would for the first time establish a minimum wage of $17.50 per week instead of the fluctuating minima ranging from $45 paid by the small dealer to $60 paid by the large dealer.

The commission system fades into the graded salary system in the case of the yeast wagon drivers (belonging to the bakery drivers' local). The union has changed the grading and promotions from the basis of individual bargaining to the basis of seniority, the driver beginning at $15 and advancing $1 at the end of the first year, and then $1 at two-year intervals, until at the end of the seventh year he reaches $19. Since the starting point was formerly $12 and seniority was counted back for those in the service at the time when the change was made, some of the best men received no advance, while others long in the service but not hitherto preferred by employers were advanced at once from $12 a week to $18 and $19.

In the case of the grocery and market drivers the range of wages was formerly extreme, since experienced men were rare and unsuitable men abundant. The best commanded $25 or $30 a week, and the poorest $5 a week. The union did not attempt to grade all the men according to seniority, but contented itself with grading the order clerks, or "those controlling their own trade," in three classes of $12, $13, and $14 for the first three six-month periods and leaving further promotions to the employer. For other classes of drivers they simply raised the minimum from, say, $11 a week for those in the wholesale trade to $15, and from $5 a week for retail drivers to $10.

The same distinction appears among the railway express drivers. The union grades the "conductor" on a double wagon, since he is a solicitor and the responsible man under bonds, at $62.50 the first three months, $67.50 after three months, and $70 after six months, but fixes a flat rate for the driver. Apart from these three grades, promotions to higher pay are at the discretion of the six companies, among whom competition is keen and the best solicitors eagerly sought.

In these cases we can see the transition to the ordinary teamster, who does not "control his trade." This is the situation with the great bulk of teaming, such as that of the truck driver, coal teamster, building-material driver, and so on. In general, wherever the commission or premium system on sales is possible the union prefers it, and even requires it; but where the commission cannot be definitely measured because the traffic is miscellaneous, the union tries to substitute grading according to seniority. And, finally, where the teamster is only a driver and not a solicitor the union establishes simply a flat minimum. There is one exception to the last statement. This is in the loading, unloading, and hauling of common brick from the cars, employing about 200 men in a union of 700. The price was formerly 36 cents per 1000, raised by agreement with the union to 40 cents, at which the driver earns $3 to $4 a day as against a day rate of $2.25 in the same local union. With this exception the ordinary driver in the different locals is paid by the week or month.

Besides wages and hours the unions have secured relief from exactions which the members consider important. The department store drivers and the livery drivers no longer purchase their uniforms at company prices. The expense of securing bonds, formerly amounting to $5 a year, required of many classes of teamsters, is now borne by the employer. The grocery and market wagon drivers are no longer responsible for goods stolen off their wagons or spoiled by kerosene; and they, as well as the department store and other classes of retail-delivery drivers, are protected against losses for which they are not responsible on C.O.D. packages and on goods returned. The agreements in all cases contain an arbitration clause whereby an umpire decides if employer and employee cannot agree.

STRIKES

The experience of the unions has led to a decided change in the matter of strikes. Sympathetic strikes seem to have been eliminated during the past two years, except where a sister local of teamsters was involved. As far as other industries are concerned, the teamsters have endeavored to adopt the let-alone policy of the railway brotherhoods, although within the past few weeks they have listened to the appeals of the garment workers and violated this policy as well as their agreements.[4] All of their agreements require work to be continued pending arbitration.[5] A vote to strike must be taken on paper ballots, and must have a two-thirds majority of the local. It must then go to the joint executive council. If approved, it is referred to the general executive board of the international organization. That body is prohibited from approving "unless there is sufficient funds on hand in the International Union to pay strike benefits" of $5 a week. If it decides to sustain the local, it sends a representative to take charge of the negotiations and, if he deems it advisable, to order a strike. A local striking without such approval receives no support.

The controlling influence of the International is strengthened by the system of finance. Out of the local dues of 50 cents a month, 15 cents are paid to the International treasury, whose funds are said to be large (no figures are published). The locals have moderate treasuries, mainly for insurance benefits, and the International is expected after the first week to support the strikes it approves. Nearly all of the locals pay death benefits of $100, adding $10 for flowers. The coal teamsters tried sick benefits for a while, but stopped the experiment because "too many got sick."

The initiation fees of several locals are $5.25; but the coal, truck, ice, van, railway express, and a few other locals have advanced the fee to $15. For a time the truck drivers placed theirs at $25, but they reduced it to $15, which seems to be the figure towards which all are tending. Usually the fee is paid in installments extending over five or six weeks after the novitiate has gone to work. Certain ice companies "check off" the fee from wages and pay it over to the union treasury, but this practice is an exception.

THE "CLOSED AND OPEN STABLE"

There is a wide diversity among the agreements respecting the employment of union members. Some of them, like those of the railway express drivers and department store drivers, simply say, "There shall be no discrimination against union drivers." The majority are similar to the truck drivers' agreement, which reads, "Party of the first part agrees to employ members of the Truck Drivers' Union, Local

705, when in their power to do so." The furniture drivers' agreement formerly read as follows: "Party of the first part agrees to employ members of the Furniture Drivers' and Helpers' Local No. 722, or those who will make application within twelve hours after receiving employment and become a member at the next regular meeting of the organization. In hiring men, the union men to have the preference." This is also a form of several other agreements, such as that of the grocery and market wagon drivers. It amounted to an open-shop agreement, and, because advantage had been taken of it to weaken the union, the Furniture Drivers' Local went on strike at its termination in October, 1904, to secure a closed-shop agreement. A compromise was finally made, and this clause was changed to read: "There shall be no discrimination against union drivers or helpers. In hiring men, party of the first part agrees to give preference to members of Local 722." In practice this new agreement makes the union headquarters the employment office of the wholesale furniture dealers.

The commission team owners agree likewise "to employ none but member of Commission Drivers' Union, Local No. 3, in good standing and carrying the regular working card of the organization, if such drivers can be supplied by the business agent of Local No. 3, or competent men who are willing to become members of said Local No. 3." Besides that of the coal teamsters, already cited, the van teamsters' agreement is strictly closed shop, as follows: "Party of the first part agrees to employ none but members of the Van Teamsters and Helpers Union, Local 711, I. B. of T., in good standing and carrying the regular working card of the organization."

Whatever the form of these agreements they operate to give members of the unions steady employment as against the introduction of outsiders. Yet, except in the two or three strictly closed-shop agreements, the team owners say that they can employ any man they see fit, whether union member or not, provided they pay the scale and he joins the union. They discharge him, however, if the union brings charges against him and does not admit him. The high scale of wages makes it to their interest to employ experienced men who know the depots and routes. Hence in the case of the team owners' associations the open-shop question has never come up. In others it causes friction and sometimes strikes. This is especially true of the laundry business, where the only prolonged strike (which has lasted since June, 1904) turns on the clause of the former agreement conceding to the laundrymen the right to hire nonmembers. In some cases the union cannot furnish members when called upon, notably the ice wagon drivers and helpers, more than one half of whose members leave the city during the winter. On this account they take in some 300 new members each season in a total membership of 1800. Their agreement reads: "We concede the employer the right to hire all Ice Wagon Drivers and Helpers, providing he notifies the officials of the Ice Wagon Drivers and Helpers Local Union No. 2 within twelve hours after employing said Drivers and Helpers; and, if there are any charges against said Driver or Helper, the employer on his part agrees to discharge said Driver or Helper within twelve hours after receiving due notice from the officials of the Ice Wagon Drivers and Helpers Local Union No. 2. In hiring men, the Union men to have preference." The above twelve-hour clause is found in most of the open-shop agreements.

In these and all other cases more reliance is placed on the daily attitude of the employers and their representatives than on the wording of the agreements. The unions stand ready to strike on evidence of persistent discrimination, but which is sometimes meant the employment of nonmembers when members are unemployed. The employers on their side, with the exceptions mentioned, practice conciliation, and realize that if they kept nonunion men in their employment they could destroy the unions. Furthermore, the teamster's occupation is more exposed than that of any other craftsman. Each driver is an establishment in himself. In the crowded streets, with 30,000 teamsters organized, there is not much room for the unorganized. Actual or expected violence is looked upon by employers and teamsters as a matter of course. Blockades and obstruction, as well as violence, are effective, and all union drivers are expected to do what the truck drivers explicitly command in their by-laws: "All members of this local shall at all times while on duty wear his union button in plain sight, so it can be seen by any one. Any member failing to do so shall be subject to a fine of not less than $1 for each offense."

It will thus be seen that the agreements, whether "closed-shop" or "open-shop" in form, are "union-shop" in practice. On the other hand, the reciprocal feature of the coal teamsters' provisional agreement, which forbade union drivers to work for employers not members of the team owners' association, has been eliminated. In its place the following was substituted: "The organization agrees on its part to do all in its power to further the interests of said Association." The commission drivers made the same agreement with the Commission Team Owners' Association. The van teamsters and truck drivers agree not to further the interests of the associations of team owners, but simply to "further the interests of their employer." These peculiar clauses do not mean that the drivers will work only for members of those associations, since there are drivers working for nonmembers. They simply mean that the drivers will not work for nonmembers on terms more favorable than those granted to members. The object is not that of an exclusive agreement, but to equalize competitive conditions. One result undoubtedly is to strengthen the team owner's associations, and to enable them better to maintain their official scales of cartage. Prior to the organization of the unions the owners' associations were weak and ineffective. Their official scales were cut by destructive competition. Now they include nearly all the team owners, who seek the cover of the association for protection against the union. The prices for cartage have in most cases been raised, but it is impossible to know how much. The official cartage scales have been advanced 20 to 40 per cent, but this is not decisive, for they were not enforced, whereas the present scales are fairly well enforced. The double wagon, which the truck owners' scale formerly set at $24 a week with driver and which was actually hired by the merchant at $22 to $26, is now hired at a minimum of $31. The single wagon has advanced from a nominal rate of $18 and an actual one of $15 or $20 to an official $22 a week. The carriage to a cemetery, for which $5 was formerly charged, now costs $7. The official scale of the commission team owners was always charged like a uniform freight rate by the commission dealer to the shipper, even when less than that scale was paid by the dealer to the team owner. In this case the new scale was made by agreement between the team owners and the dealers, and cartage charges were raised 10 to 100 per cent, the average on the bulk of the business being about 30 per cent.

This scale and all others are placed at such figures that the team owner, whether member or nonmember, who pays the union scale of wages cannot make a profit if he cuts the scale of cartage. The scale cannot be exorbitant compared with the wages, since merchants and manufacturers have the option of hiring their teamsters directly for the same wages and hours and running their own stables; many of them do so, while others prefer to sell their horses and wagons and let out their teaming to contractors at the official scale. It must be remembered that a teaming contractor assumes the liabilities of a common carrier, and a single accident to his cargo or to a pedestrian may wipe off the profits of a year, or even his entire capital. In the former period of reckless competition no margin was allowed for insurance against such catastrophes, and the wholesale merchant, who now pays the increased cartage to a teaming contractor, pays for the assumption of a risk that formerly cost him nothing, and is usually overlooked, when he does his own trucking, until the accident occurs.

In the case of fares and charges where the general public is concerned, such as those for cabs and express and furniture moving, the maximum scale is usually fixed by municipal ordinance; the changed conditions simply mean that the legal prices are charged, whereas formerly they were undercut. In the case of the charge of Parmelee (the railway baggage express) of 50 cents on trunks from stations, there has been no increase, since that was fixed by agreement with the railway companies. Other expressmen have advanced their 25-cent charges to 35 cents and their

35-cent charges to 50 cents. The municipal ordinance which formerly fixed the hire of cabs at 25 cents per passenger per mile now fixes it at 50 cents per trip per mile, whether one passenger or two.

The economic basis which supports these official scales of cartage in competitive lines may be illustrated by the case of the furniture movers. The van teamsters reported at the barn not later than half past four in the morning, and went home at night when their work was finished. The employer, not paying them for overtime, and being at liberty to keep them as late at night as he pleased without extra cost, often figured on doing a cheap job if the customer would delay the beginning until late in the afternoon, finishing late at night. The labor cost for such a job was practically nothing, and hence there was no bottom to prices. One team owner could not tell how low his competitors would be willing to go, nor could he tell how low he himself could afford to go. Even his horses, skeletonized by overtime, did not set a certain minimum. On two or three occasions the owners had attempted to form an association and to agree on a minimum scale of charges, but their agreements were always broken by the temptation so easily offered to get the teamster's work for nothing, and to give the customer the benefit of the exploitation. When the teamsters organized and reduced their indefinite hours of 90 or more a week to a definite 60, with 25 cents an hour for overtime, then the employer could see a solid foundation on which to maintain the prices agreed upon. The result has been that the unscrupulous team owner who beat his competitors by cheating and overworking his teamsters has not been able to continue in the business; and the other class of owners, who regretted, but could not remedy what some of them now describe as the "actual slavery" of the teamster, are more prosperous than ever before. Their horses and equipment are better cared for, and their services to the public better performed. True, the "public" pay higher charges for cartage than before, but the complaint from that source has partly subsided. In view of the facts their grievance is like that of the Roman populace when the gladiatorial combats were stopped.

The one-team owner who drives his wagon has a peculiar and dubious place in this business. He is the connecting link, as it were, between the ancient guild and the modern organizations of employers and workmen on class lines. He is eligible either to the teamsters' union or the team owners' association. As a member of the owners' association he is expected to observe the scale of cartage, and as a member of the union the owners ask that he be made to observe it. The policy of the unions on this point is to have less and less to do with regulating prices, and therefore to leave the one-team owner free to do as he pleases, unless he employs a helper. Of course, he needs a button or a card in order to travel uninterrupted, and this fact induces him to join one of the associations. If

he joins the truck owners, he gets an association button which the teamsters recognize. If he is an ice wagon driver, he requires a helper, and so
is not eligible to the union; but he is given a card certifying that he
employs a union helper and is "entitled to all courtesies and respect of
members of the I. B. of T." One of the locals, the express drivers, is
composed solely of these one-team owners. Their charges are regulated
by municipal ordinance on work done by the trip. A wagon and driver are
hired by the week at $24. They can work as many hours a day as they
please, since each is his own "employer."

The interests of these small proprietors lead them into a field foreign
to that of the ordinary labor union, as may be seen in the legal activities
of the hack, coupé, and cab drivers. Since 1896 this local has expended
$7000 in securing certain rights of common carriers. Formerly abutting
property owners, including the railway companies, leased the right to
stand on the street in front of their property; and the revenues of hotels
from this seizure of the public highway amounted to $50 or $60, and in
one case $200 a month. The cab drivers won a suit in the criminal court[6]
and another in the Supreme Court of Illinois[7]; and now any driver can
stand on the streets at any place designated by police authorities. Next
they contested the right to solicit passengers inside the depots and to
stand on the line designated by the railroad authorities for Parmelee's
drivers. A railroad company secured an injunction in the United States
Circuit Court, and the union carried it to the Circuit Court of Appeals and
then to the United States Supreme Court, losing each time.[8]

An interesting outcome of the change from indefinite to definite hours
and wages, as well as of the separation of classes, has been the breakdown of the "fatherly feeling" which some of the team owners say they
formerly had for some of their teamsters. They learned to feel an interest
in the men who had been in their service for many years and to share
their sorrows and joys. Though such a man was unfitted for other branches
of work, he was satisfactory in his old position, if he would accept a
lower rate of pay and make himself generally useful. Or the owner
employed a boy at $1 a day out of regard for his widowed mother. Now the
union comes between the owner and his teamster. It compels the owner
to advance his pay by $3 or $6 a week to a minimum rate. It requires a
higher rate for that overtime in which the teamster had shown his general
usefulness. The teamster takes his orders from the union and becomes
a party to the coercion. Estrangement follows. The owner cannot afford
to keep the man or boy at the higher rates of pay. He must have vigorous
young men. He has discharged the boys. A large manufacturer has cut
off the two weeks' vacation on full pay which he formerly gave to his
teamsters. The bargain has lost its indefinite, easy, fatherly relation of
"give-and-take," and has become a close calculation.

A similar estrangement occurs between the team owner and his customers, "the public." The merchant or manufacturer was formerly willing to let the truck owner send an old man or a boy with the team, which he got for a dollar or two less a week on that account. The small team owner, with inferior equipment, formerly secured trade by making concessions in price. Now he must have just as good a team, just as large a wagon, or just as attractive a van as his wealthy competitor in order to get the trade. The public has lost its desire to help out the poor team owner. Its friendly feeling, like the fatherly feeling of the team owner, disappears when no longer paid for. Thus has the cash *nexus* of unionism uncovered and dislodged a certain amount of unconscious hypocrisy.

Naturally, at first, the team owners were at sea in dealing with the new situation. Having lost the personal control of their teamsters, it seemed to them that they must control the organization that had come between them. But these organizations in turn seemed to be simply the union leaders and officers. Consequently, an era of corruption was ushered in, the employers turning over their funds to Driscoll, a "labor expert," but not a team owner, who knew how to handle the leaders. This continued, as described above, until the unions had time to learn self-government and depose the leaders who assumed to sell and deliver them. They also took from the business agents their votes, though not their seats, in the joint teamsters' council. The team owners then, perforce, changed their policy. They deposed Driscoll, and elected plain business men, team owners like themselves. The policy of these men is what they describe as "fair dealing." They try to remedy every grievance, open and aboveboard, on its merits. They realize that the team owner who, by a corrupt bargain with the union agent, is not compelled to remedy the grievance of his teamster has thereby an advantage over his competitors. Equal treatment is as necessary to preserve the team owners' association as it is to preserve the teamsters' union. In this way they cultivate what they call a "friendly feeling" with the teamsters in place of the former paternal feeling.

This new kind of friendly feeling, while severe on individuals here and there, accords with the teamster's view of himself. From what has already been said of his work and wages it follows that he is more than the mere unskilled laborer, as is generally assumed. He is sometimes a traveling salesman and at least a traveling representative. Even the ordinary teamster looks upon his occupation as a craft, and the object of his union is to have it recognized as such. He, like the salesman, is really a man of the world,—comes in contact with many classes of people and learns to deal with men as well as to handle material. His work is a constant adaptation of means to ends in a struggle for business, without the aid of a foreman to do his thinking. He must know the depots, the streets, and the best routes. He is intrusted with his employer's property and with his employer's responsibilities as a common carrier for goods hauled and for pedestrians injured. He often requires special attributes of carefulness and promptness. The van teamster cites with professional pride the expensive furniture moved from a fashionable dwelling without a scratch. The commission team driver feels his responsibility for perishable goods and for prompt and careful handling. The garbage collector calls himself the sanitary teamster. The helpers of the machinery-moving and safe-moving teamsters are millwrights.

Now the efforts of the teamsters to have these qualities recognized as distinguishing a craft and not common to the mere laborer are seen in some of their policies. First, there is the enforcement of weekly salaries, as far as possible, instead of payment by the load or laying a man off when work is interrupted. This policy leads the employer to "bunch" his work better,—to keep a man steadily employed in place of letting him "hang around," waiting for work. Of course, trade in some lines is seasonal, and allowance for this is made by classifying employees as "steady men" and "extra drivers and helpers." The latter in some cases are paid by the hour; the livery "tripper," by 25 per cent of the liveryman's charge. They are considered as serving a kind of apprenticeship, while for the "steady men" in slack times the old employee is to have the preference, being the last laid off and the first taken on. The closed-shop policy, also, is justified as the protection of their craft against the "farmer" or the "hobo," who can drive a wagon but is not a teamster. As long, too, as the minimum wage can be maintained, the team owner is not inclined to employ these inexperienced and less reliable drivers. That the hope of the teamster to make his calling a craft is being realized is borne out by the witness of team owners, who speak sometimes with enthusiasm of the superior character of the men who have come to the front. The "bums" are gradually weeded out by the employers themselves. Men of integrity and self-respect secure the offices in some though not all of the "locals," and the worldly wisdom of the teamster makes him amenable to reason and fair dealing. He harbors no resentment on account of his former treatment, for he acknowledges that the team owners were themselves victims of destructive competition.

NOTES

1. This exception was afterwards declared unconstitutional, as being an unlawful discrimination. See *People* v. *Butler Street Foundry Co.*, 201 Ill. 236.
2. At the close of the first season the health commissioner's statistics showed that the number of deaths of children under five years of age during the three summer months (July, August, and September) was ten less than that of the preceding year, and at the

close of the second season (1904) his figures for the same months showed a still further decrease of 388 deaths. The death rate of children under five for the twelve months remained stationary the first year and fell from 39.39 per 1000 living to 32.64 the second year, and the number of deaths in the three summer months, which had been 30.4 per cent of the year's total in 1902, fell to 26.6 per cent of the smaller year's total in 1904.

3. Report of Bacteriologist and Director of the Municipal Laboratory, 1904 (MS.).

4. The strike of 1905, which resulted disastrously to the teamsters, has had a serious effect on the organization. The membership of the locals which were involved in the strike has fallen off at least one third, due in large measure to the condition imposed by the employers that union buttons must not be worn in conspicuous places by the drivers. The union button worn on the cap or coat lapel was an effective organizing factor among the teamsters.

Another result of the strike is the division in the ranks of the team drivers. The strike was ordered in violation of written contracts, the teamsters having no grievances of their own. They were called out in support of the garment workers. This policy did not meet with favor in a number of local unions and they held the international president responsible. When the annual convention of the International Brotherhood of Teamsters was held in Chicago in August, 1906, it resulted in a split, a number of delegates holding a rival convention and forming what is known as the United Teamsters of America. This latter organization has headquarters in Aurora, Illinois, and its president claims that it has approximately eighty local unions affiliated and a membership of over 20,000. Ten of the Chicago locals have gone over to the seceding faction, among them being the ice-wagon drivers, commission-wagon drivers, and the van teamsters. Nearly all the locals in New York are now affiliated with the seceding faction, as are the St. Louis locals and the unions in a number of smaller cities.

The trial now going on in the Criminal Court for conspiracy has also helped to weaken the organization. It has revealed a series of corrupt receipts of money and betrayals of the unions on the part of certain leaders in ordering the strike and following it up.

While the locals which engaged in the strike have been partially disrupted there has been no general reduction in wages. The unions are not in a position, however, to ask for any new concessions. The locals which kept out of the strike are still in good condition.

5. The truck drivers, like others, issue a card to their stewards, as follows:

ADVICE TO STEWARDS

1. Become acquainted with the laws of the I. B. of T. and of your Local Union.

2. Become acquainted with the agreement of your Local and the Employers'.

3. Examine the Due Books of every member working in the barn in which you are Steward no later than the 10th of each month.

4. When a new man is employed, ask him for his Due Book. If he is not a member of Local 705, or he is three months in arrears (and a member of Local 705 in good standing can be had), object to him going to work.

5. When a member has a complaint, he must report it to the Steward, whose duty it is to take the member to the employer, hear both sides of the case, and, if the employer is right, tell the member so. If he is not satisfied, send him to the officials of the Local. If the employer refuses to comply with the Steward's decision, notify the officials at once.

6. Stewards must not call a strike unless authorized by the Local through its officers.

7. Stewards should use their influence to prevent a strike until the officers have had a chance to adjust the difference.

8. Stewards should attend as many meetings as they possibly can.

6. *City of Chicago* v. *Wilson, Chicago Legal News*, August 16, 1902.
7. *Pennsylvania R. R.* v. *City of Chicago*, 181 Ill. 289.
8. *Donovan et al.* v. *The Pennsylvania Co.*, 116 Fed. 907, 120 Fed. 215 (1903), 199 U. S. 279 (1905).

chapter 16

capital, banking, and
international trade

CAPITAL FORMATION TRENDS

GROWTH

Capital formation increased substantially during the period. In real terms, it rose from an annual rate of $3.5 billion in the 1870's and 1880's, to $8.7 billion in the 1890's and 1900's, and $15.5 billion in the 1910's and 1920's. (See Table 16.1.) Net capital formation, the difference between gross capital formation and capital consumption (depreciation), averaged $2 billion annually in the 70's and 80's, $4.7 billion in the 90's and 1900's, and $7.1 billion in the 1910's and 1920's. Net capital formation's decennial rate of growth was 52 per cent for the 1870's and 1880's to the 1890's and 1900's. Owing to a decline in the growth rate of gross capital formation commencing with the panic of 1907, the decennial rate of growth of net capital formation from that period until the late 1920's declined to 23.8 per cent. The trend of capital formation as a percentage of national output paralleled changes in the rates of growth of gross and net capital formation. Gross capital formation, as a percentage of gross national product, grew from 19.8 per cent in the 1870's and 1880's,

TABLE 16.1. *Average Annual Capital Formation (Billions of Dollars) 1869–1928*

Period	Gross Capital Formation	Capital Consumption	Net Capital Formation	Percentage Rate of Growth of Net Capital Formation per Decade
1869–1888	3.5	1.5	2.0	51.8*
1889–1908	8.7	4.0	4.7	23.8†
1909–1928	15.5	8.4	7.1	

SOURCE: Simon Kuznets. *Capital in The American Economy.* New York: National Bureau of Economic Research, 1961, p. 56.

*Period 1869–1888 to 1889–1908.

†Period 1889–1908 to 1909–1928.

TABLE 16.2. *Capital Formation as a Percentage of National Output 1869–1918*

Period	Gross Capital Formation as a Percentage of Gross National Product		Net Capital Formation as a Percentage of Net National Product	
	Current Prices	*Constant 1929 Prices*	*Current Prices*	*Constant 1929 Prices*
1869–1878	19.8%	22.9%	12.9%	15.1%
1879–1888	19.8	22.2	12.4	14.0
1889–1898	22.0	25.1	13.2	15.2
1899–1908	21.4	23.0	12.9	13.8
1909–1918	20.5	22.1	11.0	11.9

SOURCE: Simon Kuznets. *Capital in the American Economy.* New York: National Bureau of Economic Research, 1961, pp. 93, 96.

to 22.0 per cent in the 1890's and 1900's, and then fell back to 20.5 per cent in the 1910's and 1920's. (See Table 16.2.) The capital-output ratio, with the exception of the depressed 1870's, rose during the period. Measured in gross terms, it increased from 5.3 in the 1870's to 5.9 in the 1910's, and in net terms from 3.5 to 3.6 in the same time span. (See Table 16.3.) The capital-output ratio measures the amount of capital stock necessary to produce a dollar of output. Thus a national capital-output ratio of

TABLE 16.3. *Ratio of Capital Stock to National Output per Decade, 1929 Prices, 1869–1918*

Period	Ratio of Gross Capital Stock to Gross National Product	Ratio of Net Capital Stock to Net National Product
1869–1878	5.3	3.5
1879–1888	4.5	2.9
1889–1898	5.2	3.4
1899–1908	5.3	3.4
1909–1918	5.9	3.6

SOURCE: Simon Kuznets. *Capital in the American Economy.* New York: National Bureau of Economic Research, 1961, pp. 80–81.

3.0 means that $3 of capital stock is required to produce $1 of national output. The ratio's increase for most of the period reflects the basic pattern of industrial growth. At every stage in a nation's development there are forces that tend to push the capital-output ratio up and forces that tend to push it down. In the formative period the ratio-raising forces dominate. Before an industry can begin to produce for mass markets it must substantially enlarge its basic capital stock, especially the construction components. A good deal of these additions are indivisible, such as railroad tracks, terminal facilities, electric transmission lines, complex machinery, and the like, and must be built beyond current needs. There is also a tendency to be optimistic about the future and to increase one's productive potential well beyond present demand. This is encouraged by the rewards of economies of scale. It is often cheaper in the long run to build a larger, more efficient plant even if it is under-utilized for a time than to build a smaller, less efficient one and use it to capacity. Accordingly, the above statistics indicate that the industries developing during the period were capital intensive in nature, requiring heavy investments in plant, equipment, and machinery. This deepening of capital was accompanied by an increase in the net capital stock per worker, which more than doubled between 1869 and 1919, growing from $2,000 to $5,500.

SOURCES AND USES OF CAPITAL

The major source of capital funds after the Civil War, as before, was individual savings. Despite a per capita income growth of 17 per cent per decade, savings remained at a fairly constant percentage of disposable personal income over the period, ranging between 10 and 12 per cent. Simon Kuznets suggests that 5 per cent of the population probably supplied fully one-half of all savings, and that their propensity to save equalled 25 per cent of their income.[1] The rest of the population had a propensity to save of about 6 per cent, a figure that characterizes the U.S. economy today. Foreign investment, which had been important to U.S. economic growth in pre-Civil War days, declined in importance after the Civil War. (See Table 16.4.) The scarcity of European savings in relation to the many investment possibilities both within Europe and throughout the world and the growth of U.S. domestic capital formation reduced its importance.

TABLE 16.4. *Net Changes in Foreign Claims Against the United States as a Percentage of Capital Formation 1869-1918*

Period	Gross Capital Formation	Net Capital Formation
1868-1878	6.9	10.7
1879-1888	1.8	3.1
1889-1898	-0.6	-1.1
1899-1908	-4.3	-8.0
1909-1918	-11.1	-23.1

SOURCE: Simon Kuznets. *Capital in The American Economy.* New York: National Bureau of Economic Research, 1961, pp. 132-33.

During the period important changes occurred in the types and usage of capital. Producers' durables (plant and equipment) increased in importance as the industrialization process intensified, while construction and net changes in inventory declined. As discussed above, the foreign flow of capital to the United States (net changes in claims against foreigners) was reversed. (See Table 16.5.) In terms of the use of capital, the major change was the increasing importance of government. The rising density of population in urban centers and substantial investments in social overhead capital requiring government support caused the government's share to rise from under five per cent to over eleven per cent during the period. (See Table 16.6.) The industrial distribution of domestic business formation reveals an increase in agriculture's share. Due to farm mechanization, it rose from 12 per cent in 1880-1900 to 17 per cent in 1900-1922. The share of mining and manufacturing also rose, from 38 per cent to 47 per cent. In contrast, public utilities experienced a decline from 50 per cent to 36 per cent.

The capital-output ratios for manufacturing and mining combined, agriculture, and public utilities in 1880 were 0.9, 1.7, and 23.6, respectively. Thus, a dollar of capital invested in manufacturing and mining

TABLE 16.5. *Gross Capital Formation by Type of Investment (1929 Prices) 1869-1928*

Period	Construction	Producer's Durables	Net Changes in Inventories	Net Changes in Claims Against Foreigners
1869-1898	70.5%	20.8%	9.9%	-1.2%
1879-1908	68.2	22.9	7.1	1.8
1889-1918	62.6	25.2	6.2	6.0
1899-1928	57.4	28.6	6.6	7.4

SOURCE: Simon Kuznets. *Capital in The American Economy*. New York: National Bureau of Economic Research, 1961, pp. 146-47.

produced more income than a dollar invested in agriculture, and much more income than a dollar invested in public utilities. The magnitude of the capital-output ratio in public utilities is explained by the formidable capital spending necessary during this period to establish intercontinental railroad, electric light and power, and telephone transmission systems. By the early 1920's the ratios for manufacturing and agriculture had risen to 1.8 and 2.3, while the ratio for utilities had fallen to 5.6. The substantial decline for public utilities is explained by the diminishing importance to public utilities of initial construction outlays intended for long-term use.

MONEY AND BANKING

MONEY

After the Civil War, debtor groups, principally farmers and laborers, who had supported unregulated state banking as a means of inflating the money supply in the pre-Civil War period, rallied their forces behind United States Notes (greenbacks) and the free silver issue. In their minds, prosperity depended on a rising price level and this could be best achieved with a sizeable increase in the money supply. Since prices had more than doubled during the Civil War owing to substantial increases in the money supply, 1860 debts paid off in 1865 were halved in real value. It had been the original intention of the Republican-controlled government to retire all greenbacks from circulation after the Civil War. However, by that time U.S. Notes had become an integral part of the money supply and it was recognized that their removal would bring on substantial deflation. The issue aroused such widespread interest that a major third party, the National Greenback Party, was formed in 1875 to fight for retention and increases in greenback circulation. After extensive debate

TABLE 16.6. *Gross Capital Formation by Type of User (1929 Prices) 1869–1928*

Periods	Households	Business	Government
1869–1898	27.9%	67.4%	4.7%
1879–1908	25.0	69.5	5.5
1889–1918	21.0	69.9	9.1
1899–1928	20.5	68.2	11.3

SOURCE: Simon Kuznets. *Capital in The American Economy.* New York: National Bureau of Economic Research, 1961, p. 178.

their circulation was fixed permanently in 1878 at $347 million versus their peak circulation of $449 million in 1864. In time the value of greenback dollars rose from their 1864 low of less than half the value of a gold dollar to full equality by 1879. This was due primarily to three reasons. First, the Supreme Court in 1871 ruled in *Knox v. Lee* that greenbacks could be legally used to settle debts contracted before Congress authorized their creation. Second, there was a substantial contraction of greenback circulation from 1864 to 1868. Third, and most significantly, the output of goods and services increased substantially, more than doubling from the end of the Civil War to 1879. In the same years the money supply showed only a slight increase. Consequently, the pre-Civil War ratio of money to goods and services was restored by 1879, and prices (including that of gold) had resumed prewar levels. This meant that individuals who had incurred debts in 1864 and whose obligations were still outstanding in 1879 found that their real burden had doubled.

Unhappy with this situation, pro-inflationists while continuing to support greenbacks found a new cause to champion, free silver. The mint ratio of 16 to 1 established in 1834 obligated the United States Mint to buy silver at $1.29 an ounce. But little silver was sold to the Mint because a higher price could be procured on the open market. The Coinage Act of 1873, in an attempt to modernize the coinage system, relieved the government of its obligation to buy silver. Shortly thereafter the open market price fell below $1.29 an ounce. New discoveries in the United States, an increase in the productivity of the silver mining industry, and the discontinuance of silver as a monetary unit by a number of nations all contributed to the price decline. Much to the surprise and chagrin of silver miners, their offer to sell silver to the Mint was refused. Believing they had been tricked by "hard" money advocates, inflationists dubbed the Coinage Act of 1873 the "Crime of 1873." Marshalling their forces under the banner of "free silver" they petitioned Congress to resume the unlimited coinage of silver at the old ratio of 16 to 1. Congress refused, but did authorize limited purchases at the going market price in the Bland-Allison (1878) and Sherman Silver Purchase (1890) Acts. Under the terms of the Bland-Allison Act the Treasury was obligated to buy between $2 million and $4 million worth of silver each month at the prevailing market price. Under the terms of the Sherman Silver Purchase Act, which was passed by a "hard" money Republican-controlled Congress to secure the support of silver interests for the McKinley tariff bill of the same year, the Treasury was directed to purchase a flat 4.5 million ounces of silver each month. In dollar amounts, this caused an approximate doubling of silver purchases. Under the terms of both silver acts, the Treasury added about half a billion dollars worth of silver to the nation's money supply. Because of the weight of silver dollars most Americans, with the exception of Westerners, preferred paper currency. To accommodate, the Treasury kept silver in its vaults and issued silver certificates instead. This currency was interchangeable with gold coins and gold certificates in ordinary business transactions.

It was gold, rather than silver, which was responsible for the greatest growth in the supply of currency from 1875 to 1915. In the 1880's the stock of gold doubled and between 1890 and 1915 it trebled, primarily because of the increased output of U.S. mines. Despite such growth, however, there was a severe short-term shortage in U.S. Government gold stocks in 1893. The American people never fully accepted silver-backed currency. A growing supply of silver certificates convertible into gold led in the early 1890's to an increased demand for Treasury gold by both banks and individuals. Simultaneously, a financial crisis in England caused a substantial liquidation of British investments in the United States, resulting in a major gold outflow. Rumors that Federal gold stocks would soon be depleted precipitated a run for gold and the monetary panic of 1893. Faced with this crisis, President Cleveland forced repeal of the Sherman Silver Purchase Act to stop further additions to the supply of silver money convertible into gold. He then sought to increase the Government's gold stock by the sale of U.S. obligations for gold, both in the United States and abroad. Difficulties encountered in bond sales forced Cleveland to turn to J.P. Morgan for aid in marketing these obligations. With Morgan's assistance the Federal Government was able to maintain convertibility of paper currency into gold. These actions, together with the deflation which accompanied the onset of depression in 1893, united debtor groups behind the issue of free silver once again. The "hard" money forces of Cleveland were ejected from the Democratic Party and William Jennings Bryan became its standard bearer. Despite support from the West and South, Bryan was defeated in the election of 1896 by William McKinley. In the Gold Standard Act of 1900, the dollar was defined in terms of 25.8 grains of gold, and the Treasury was required to maintain gold stocks of $150 million to provide for the convertibility of greenbacks, silver, and silver certificates into gold. Thereafter, as a result of substantial increases in the world output of gold, the price level began to increase and the pressure for free silver slowly abated.

While most controversy during this period centered on gold and silver, important developments were occurring in the two other major parts of the money supply, bank notes and demand deposits. State bank notes, which were the major paper currency before the Civil War, were driven out of circulation by a prohibitive tax of ten per cent. This levy, which took effect in 1866, was imposed by the Congress to force state chartered banks to join the National Banking System. It was observed in an earlier chapter that the National Banking System was created during the Civil War to provide the nation with a uniform currency and aid in the sale of Government securities. National bank note circulation grew until 1873 when it reached 340 million dollars. After that date it declined owing to substantial Federal surpluses which permitted the retirement of a substantial portion of United States debt. By 1891, national bank note circulation totaled only $168 million. Thereafter, deficit financing associated with the Spanish-American War and a major revision in the National Banking Act which encouraged increased national bank note issue, expanded circulation to $715 million by 1913, the year in which the Federal Reserve Act was passed.

Improved communication and transportation facilities after the Civil War caused demand deposits (checking accounts) to become the principal form of money supply. Of a total money supply of $579 million in 1860, demand deposits accounted for $250 million, or roughly forty-five per cent of the total. By 1900 demand deposits were $4,942 million, or almost eighty per cent of the total money supply of $6,332 million.

The pro-inflationist view that economic growth can only flourish during a period of rising prices is held by many economists. The reading at the end of this chapter by Milton Friedman and Anna Schwartz refutes this generalization.

THE NATIONAL BANKING SYSTEM

The prohibitive tax levied against state bank notes caused many state banks to seek charters as national institutions. However, state banks soon realized that they could do an equally profitable business using demand deposits rather than bank notes. Moreover, National Banking System regulations were stricter than most state regulations. As a result, the number of state banks grew side by side with national banks, and by the late 1880's exceeded them in number. (See Table 16.7.) In 1913, on the eve of the passage of the Federal Reserve Act, the number of state banks was more than double the number of national banks, and they held fifty per cent more deposits. However, their total assets were only slightly more than a third of all national banks, indicating that state banks were smaller.

TABLE 16.7. *Growth of State and National Banks 1865–1915*

Year	State Banks*	National Banks
1865	349	1,294
1870	325	1,612
1875	1,260	2,076
1880	1,279	2,076
1885	1,661	2,689
1890	4,717	3,484
1895	6,103	3,715
1900	9,322	3,731
1905	13,103	5,664
1910	18,013	7,138
1915	20,420	7,597

SOURCE: U.S. Bureau of the Census. *Historical Statistics of the United States, Colonial Times to 1957.* Washington, D.C.: U.S. Government Printing Office, 1960, pp. 626–28.

*Include commercial banks, mutual and stock savings banks, private banks, and loan and trust companies.

It is therefore not surprising that state banks with their less stringent regulations experienced greater bankruptcies. Between 1900 and 1913 state bank suspensions totaled 972 versus 148 for national banks, almost seven times greater. The ability of the state banking system to flourish alongside the National Banking System institutionalized dual banking in the United States.

In addition to its inability to embrace all banks, the national banking system exhibited many weaknesses. First, it was unstable, tending to break down during periods of economic contraction. Second, national bank notes did not expand and contract with the needs of business. Indeed, they often exhibited a perverse elasticity. Note issues were limited to 90 per cent, later 100 per cent, of the par or current market value of a bank's holding of United States bonds, whichever was lower. Therefore, note issue was most attractive when government securities sold below par and least attractive when they sold at a premium. Typically, during periods of prosperity when more money was required to finance expansion, Treasury surpluses would flow into the money market and bid up the price of bonds, thereby making note issue unprofitable. Third, the system encouraged the pyramiding of reserves in major money markets. For purposes of establishing reserve requirements member banks were divided into country, reserve city, and central reserve city categories. Country banks were permitted to hold sixty per cent of their legally required reserves with a corresponding bank in a reserve city, and in turn, reserve city banks were permitted to hold one-half of their reserves with a central reserve city correspondent, usually located in New York City. These reserves, as well as excess bank funds, flowed into New York during the winter and summer when business activity in farm areas slowed, and flowed out during the spring and the fall. The funds were usually invested by New York banks in twenty-four hour stock market call loans. When outlying banks withdrew their funds, call loans were not renewed, causing tight money conditions that sometimes deteriorated into a major panic. Fourth, no central bank existed to establish policy or serve as a lender of last resort. Aside from some examination responsibilities, the national government exerted little influence on member banks. They were individual private banks, with only a Federal charter in common. Thus, if the country was experiencing a period of potentially dangerous inflation or deflation, there was no central authority to articulate the danger and to seek the banking system's cooperation in taking appropriate remedial action. Moreover, if the system found itself in an illiquid position, unable to convert demand deposits and currency into specie, banks had no choice but to cease operations temporarily. Finally, the National Banking Act fostered a unit banking system. Branch banking, which was widespread before the Civil War, was discouraged because of the fear that money monopolies similar to the Second United States Bank would result and because of the opposition of small banks. Instead, a large number of small, independent banks were created, many with inadequate resources and incompetent management.

Aggravating these problems was the existence of an independent Treasury System which exerted a deflationary influence on the economy. During periods of prosperity the Federal Government ran budget surpluses. This had the effect of draining specie out of the economy for storage in Federal vaults at times when it was most needed to finance continuing economic expansion. Often this acted to aggravate the business cycle and hamper economic growth. It also created a seasonal problem, tending to curtail the normal expansion of money during those periods of the year when business activity accelerated. The Treasury recognized this fact as early as 1902 when it informally began to place federal funds in the nation's banking system in those seasons when the shortage of currency was greatest.

The panic of 1907, and a subsequent short but sharp depression, almost wholly monetary in origin, convinced the nation that fundamental banking reforms were in order. In 1907 the declining price of copper stocks embarrassed an influential group of businessmen who were large holders of copper securities which served as collateral for substantial bank loans. An unsuccessful attempt by them to bolster the price of copper shares shook the confidence of the business community. This uneasiness spread to the banking system since a major figure in these dealings was the president of a prominent national bank. Depositors, fearing that bank assets were heavily tied up in this unprofitable venture, began to withdraw their accounts. Banks, which had their depositors' funds tied up in loans and bonds, could not honor massive requests for withdrawals without selling their assets at well below their true worth. Initially they borrowed funds from other banks, but soon this became impossible as the contagion of the run spread throughout the entire banking system. The United States Treasury sought to stem the panic by transferring funds from Subtreasuries to national banks and by easing the regulations for the issuance of national bank notes. But it was to no avail, and the banking system was forced to suspend operations.

THE FEDERAL RESERVE SYSTEM

Congress responded in 1908 by passing the Aldrich-Vreeland Act. The Act permitted ten or more banks to band together in temporary National Currency Associations to issue emergency paper currency backed by the assets of the member banks. At the same time a National Monetary Commission, composed of eighteen Senators and Representatives, was established to investigate the nation's banking structure and propose long-term solutions to its problems. The commission, headed by Senator Nelson Aldrich of Rhode Island, issued a report in 1912. In 1913 Congress, on the basis of the report, created the Federal Reserve System.

The historic fear of a central bank led Congress to establish twelve separate Federal Reserve District Banks headed by a Board of Governors of limited powers. Each Federal Reserve Bank was to be owned by the participating banks of its region. The latter were to contribute an amount equal to three per cent of the value of their capital and surplus for the purchase of Federal Reserve stock. On this investment they received a six per cent annual dividend. Each Federal Reserve Bank was headed by nine directors, chosen to represent the banking community, the public, and manufacturing, agriculture and commerce. Member banks were to elect six of these directors, with the Board of Governors designating the three public representatives. The Board of Governors was to consist of seven individuals appointed by the President of the United States.

The Federal Reserve System was designed to remedy the weaknesses of the National Banking System. It provided lending (discount) facilities for member banks, particularly in times of crisis, created an elastic currency, acted as fiscal agent for the U.S. Treasury, and cleared and collected all checks for member banks. Federal Reserve Notes, issued by the twelve district banks, were backed by commercial paper and gold. The former collateral, it was reasoned, would result in an elastic note issue since the quantity of commercial paper outstanding would increase during periods of economic expansion and decline during periods of contraction. To prevent

TABLE 16.8. *The Share of Major Financial Intermediaries, 1860–1912 (Assets of all financial intermediaries = 100)*

	1860	1890	1912
Commercial banks*	65	58	64
Mutual savings banks	20	18	12
Savings and loan associations	—	6	3
Life and property insurance companies	10	12	16
Other financial intermediaries	5	6	5

SOURCE: Security and Exchange Commission. *Institutional Investor Study Report*, Vol. 1. House Committee on Interstate and Foreign Commerce. Washington, D.C.: U.S. Government Printing Office, 1971, p. 44.

*Does not include trust departments.

the pyramiding of reserves, each member bank was required to keep its reserves in the Federal Reserve District Bank exercising jurisdiction in its region. The Federal Reserve remained committed to the unit banking system and encouraged branch banking only when it was necessary to make member banks competitive with nonmember state banks. Membership in the Federal Reserve System was compulsory only for National Banks. State banks were invited to join, but most refused.

OTHER FINANCIAL INTERMEDIARIES

Commercial banks dominated financial intermediaries from 1865 to 1915. During the period, however, they were joined by other intermediaries which arose to provide specialized services for both savers and investors. (See Table 16.8.) In addition to banks the only other financial intermediaries in operation before 1800 were life and property insurance companies, and they were not of any significance until mid-century. In colonial America, most insurance centered about shipping and the merchant trade, and was conducted by English insurance companies. The first American marine insurance company was founded in Philadelphia in 1721. In 1752 Ben Franklin was instrumental in establishing the first fire insurance company. It, too, was located in Philadelphia, as was the first life insurance company, established in 1759 for "the Relief of Poor and Distressed Widows and Children of Presbyterian Ministers." In 1792, the Insurance Company of North America, the first company of significant size, was created. It possessed a capital structure of six hundred thousand dollars and engaged in the business of insuring against marine and fire losses. In 1835 and 1842 the first large life insurance companies, the New England Life Insurance Company and the Mutual Life Insurance Company, were founded. Both enterprises continue to the present day. In the last half of the nineteenth century life insurance companies became a significant source of capital funds. Originally quite provincial in their investment activities because of restrictive state laws, they were gradually allowed to place their funds in all areas of the nation. The bulk of their resources was invested in long-term securities — mortgages, corporate bonds, and government bonds. On the eve of World War I, life and property insurance companies accounted for sixteen per cent of the assets of all financial intermediaries.

Modern regulation of insurance by state governments dates from 1905 when New York undertook an investigation of the life insurance industry. Out of that investigation there emerged a New York Insurance Code covering investment, expense, and dividend policies. This code served as a model for other states. In 1910 New York extended its investigation to non-life insurance firms. As a result of that investigation new legislation was enacted which required insurance firms to be licensed, permitted the fixing of rates in concert, forbade rebates, and established a building code to minimize threats to property and life. Once again, other states followed the lead of New York in adopting similar regulations.

Mutual savings banks and personal trust departments emerged shortly after 1800. The former institution was originally founded by philanthropically minded businessmen who wished to provide a depository for the savings of the poor. As their assets grew in size much of their charitable characteristics disappeared and they became important lenders in the capital market. Like insurance companies they were first restricted in their investment activities to local lending and only later were allowed to make investments outside the state in which they were chartered. Their investments primarily were in long-term obligations. Their share of the assets of financial intermediaries declined from twenty per cent in 1860 to twelve per cent on the eve of World War I. This decline was primarily attributable to the restriction of mutual savings bank activities to a few eastern states. Personal trust departments were formed as units of commercial banks and trust companies to provide for the financial needs of certain customers. The first trust company was the Massachusetts Hospital Life Insurance Company which in 1823 received sanction from the state legislature to conduct a trust business. The company wrote life insurance and annuity contracts, and acted as trustees for the investment funds of a large number of individuals. The trust concept had great appeal among the wealthier members of the population and by the end of the century trust companies were a major financial intermediary. Their investment portfolios varied with opportunities for financing. In the early period they accrued considerable amounts of state and local issues. Savings and Loan Associations began in the late 1830's to serve the specialized need of financing construction. The earlier associations were organized a number of ways, including cooperative banks, homestead associations, and building and loan associations. As expected, almost all their funds were invested in residential mortgages. Their share of the total assets of financial intermediaries was one-fourth that of mutual savings banks on the eve of World War I.

The only other significant financial intermediary to develop before 1915 was investment banks. Investment banking activities were conducted by a wide variety of groups and institutions. As early as the colonial period merchants performed a number of investment and financial services for their customers. Private banks, some of which began by conducting lotteries in the early 1800's, became active in the field after the War of 1812. The industry began its modern development with the flotation of railroad issues in the 1830's. At that time the selling of corporate securities was largely a personal affair, with few institutions acting as the intermediary between the seller and the buyer. The success of Jay Cooke and Company during the Civil War in selling United States Government securities to the public helped to broaden the securities market. Thereafter, the investment banker could appeal to a wider population. It was about this time that many houses began to specialize in the securities of a particular industry, with some investment bankers only handling the initiation of an issue, leaving distribution and sale to other specialists. A particularly influential group of houses concentrated on developing international connections, which enabled them to sell American securities abroad. Toward the end of the century the larger investment banking houses took an active role in sponsoring and financing mergers and consolidations of American industry. Despite such developments, however, security ownership before 1915 was not widespread in the U.S. economy. On the eve of World War I it was limited to but two per cent of the population.

INTERNATIONAL TRADE

TRADE TRENDS

In the period from 1865 to 1915 the U.S. was transformed from an agricultural nation to the leading industrial economy of the world. The composition and direction of international trade reflected this structural change. The U.S. increasingly exported manufactured goods, imported raw materials, and directed a larger share of its trade to non-European countries. Manufacturing's share of total exports averaged 20 per cent from 1866 to 1895; thereafter it rose steadily, reaching a level of

46 per cent in the 1911-15 period. (See Table 16.9.) At the same time, raw material exports declined from 58 per cent to 31 per cent. Foodstuffs, reflecting growing markets abroad and increased agricultural productivity, increased from 23 per cent in the late 1860's to 48 per cent in the late 1870's. Thereafter they declined, dropping to 23 per cent of exports in 1911-1915. The composition of imports exhibited an opposite trend. Raw material's share of total imports rose from 12 per cent in the late 1860's to 35 per cent by the early 1900's, while manufactures' fell from 55 per cent to approximately 40 per cent in the same period. (See Table 16.10.) Foodstuffs increased from 33 per cent in 1866-70 to 40 per cent in 1876-80, and fell thereafter, reaching 25 per cent of imports in 1911-15. The principal reason for these changes is explained by the United States achieving a comparative advantage in manufactures.

As in the pre-Civil War period, England was the United States' principal trading partner. However, both imports from and exports to England declined in relative importance. Thus, imports from England as a percentage of total imports dropped from 34 per cent in 1870 to 15 per cent in 1915, while England's share of exports dropped from 53 per cent to 32 per cent in the same period. After 1900 Canada rivaled both Germany and France as a major customer and supplier of the U.S. market. Its share of U.S. exports and imports by 1915 stood at 10 per cent. Cuba also became a major supplier; its share of the U.S. import market was approximately 11 per cent in 1915. U.S. foreign economic policy contributed to changing trade flows. In 1867 Alaska was acquired from Russia, while in 1898 the Hawaiian Islands, Puerto Rico, and the Philippines were acquired from Spain. Within the next five years Wake Island in the Pacific was acquired, an open-door policy was imposed on China, and the Panama Canal Zone was purchased. Such acquisitions led to increased international trade and investment by U.S. businessmen in non-European markets. As a consequence, Europe's share of both U.S. imports and exports declined steadily from the early 1870's to the eve of World War I. (See Tables 16.11 and 16.12.)

Between 1866 and 1915 merchandise exports increased eightfold, from $446 million to $3.7 billion. Merchandise import growth was not as spectacular. It increased fourfold, from $459 million to $1.8 billion. As a result, the United States moved from a nation of adverse trade balances to one of favorable balances. (See Table 16.13.) This shift occurred in the 1870's, and was triggered by the onset of depression in 1873. The latter, by reducing income and prices, had the effect of discouraging imports and stimulating exports. The shift from an adverse to a favorable trade position was accompanied by a shift of equal importance in capital flows. Beginning in the 1870's and continuing to World War I, U.S. interest and dividend payments for past borrowings from Europe plus U.S. capital investments abroad exceeded foreign investment flows to the United States. The

TABLE 16.9. *Percentage Distribution of U.S. Merchandise Exports By Type 1866–1915*

Years	Raw Materials	Foodstuffs*	Manufactures†
1866–70	58%	23%	19%
1871–75	45	35	20
1876–80	32	48	20
1881–85	34	46	20
1886–90	38	40	22
1891–95	34	44	22
1896–1900	26	43	31
1901–05	30	35	35
1906–10	32	27	41
1911–15	31	23	46

SOURCE: U.S. Department of Commerce. *1941 Statistical Abstract of the United States.* Washington, D.C.: U.S. Government Printing Office, 1942, p. 533.

*Includes crude and manufactured items.

†Includes semi- and finished manufactures.

TABLE 16.10. *Percentage Distribution of U.S. Merchandise Imports by Type 1866–1915*

Years	Raw Materials	Foodstuffs*	Manufactures†
1866–70	12%	33%	55%
1871–75	16	34	50
1876–80	19	40	41
1881–85	20	34	46
1886–90	23	32	45
1891–95	24	37	39
1896–1900	29	31	40
1901–05	33	25	42
1906–10	35	23	42
1911–15	35	25	39

SOURCE: U.S. Department of Commerce. *1941 Statistical Abstract of the United States.* Washington, D.C.: U.S. Government Printing Office, 1942, pp. 530–531.

*Includes raw and manufactured items.

†Includes semi- and finished manufactures.

TABLE 16.11. *Percentage Distribution of U.S. Exports by Area 1871–1915*

Years	Europe	North and South America	Other
1871–75	80%	18%	2%
1876–80	83	14	3
1881–85	81	15	4
1886–90	80	15	5
1891–95	80	16	4
1896–1900	77	16	7
1901–05	72	19	9
1906–10	68	24	8
1911–15	64	27	9

SOURCE: U.S. Department of Commerce. *1941 Statistical Abstract of the United States.* Washington, D.C.: U.S. Government Printing Office, 1942, p. 542.

TABLE 16.12. *Percentage Distribution of U.S. Imports by Area 1871–1915*

Years	Europe	North and South America	Other
1871–75	56%	34%	10%
1876–80	50	37	13
1881–85	55	32	13
1886–90	56	32	12
1891–95	51	36	13
1896–1900	53	29	18
1900–05	51	32	17
1906–10	51	31	18
1911–15	47	35	18

SOURCE: U.S. Department of Commerce. *1941 Statistical Abstract of the United States.* Washington, D.C.: U.S. Government Printing Office, 1942, p. 542.

nation had moved from the position of a young debtor to that of a mature debtor. Between 1869 and 1914 long-term foreign investment in the United States increased slightly less than fivefold, from $1.4 billion to $6.7 billion, whereas U.S. long-term investment abroad increased 35-fold, from $100 million to $3.5 billion.

TABLE 16.13. *U.S. Balance of Merchandise Trade, Average Annual Rates 1866-1915 (Millions of Dollars)*

Years	Exports	Imports	Net Exports
1866-70	321	408	-87
1871-75	502	578	-76
1876-80	677	493	184
1881-85	792	667	125
1886-90	738	717	21
1891-95	892	785	107
1896-1900	1,157	742	416
1901-05	1,454	972	482
1906-10	1,779	1,345	434
1911-15	2,371	1,721	658

SOURCE: U.S. Department of Commerce. *1941 Statistical Abstract of the United States.* Washington, D.C.: U.S. Government Printing Office, 1942, p. 523.

TARIFFS AND THE MERCHANT MARINE

The Southern congressional opposition which had kept pre-Civil War tariff rates from rising to the level desired by Northern manufacturing interests was brought to an end by secession and military defeat. As a result high tariff walls were constructed during the Civil War and continued to the eve of World War I. (See Figure 11.2.) The Morrill Act of 1861 and subsequent war tariffs raised the average level of duties to 47 per cent by the close of the Civil War. The 1890 McKinley Tariff increased duties to an average level of 50 per cent, and the 1897 Dingley Tariff made them slightly higher. Not until the Democratic administration of Woodrow Wilson was a serious downward revision of the tariff walls undertaken. In 1913 the Underwood-Simmons Act lowered the average level of duties to about 25 per cent, a level roughly equal to that prevailing in pre-Civil War days.

The U.S. Merchant Marine continued its secular decline between 1865 and 1915. By the early 1900's it carried only 8 per cent of the nation's imports and exports. Lower wage rates for English shipyard workers enabled England to build ships for fifty per cent of the cost of construction in the United States. Moreover, the lower wage rates paid to English sailors made the labor costs of running English ships twenty-five per cent less. Congress attempted to stimulate the American merchant fleet as early as 1864 by a system of mail subsidies. The latter, which continued throughout the period, proved ineffective in eliminating the nation's comparative disadvantage in the production and operation of a merchant fleet.

NOTES

1. Simon Kuznets, *Capital in the American Economy* (Princeton: Princeton University Press, 1961.)

SELECTED REFERENCES

1. Milton Friedman and Anna Schwartz. *A Monetary History of the United States, 1867 1960.* Princeton: Princeton University Press, 1963.
2. Emory R. Johnson, *et al. History of Domestic and Foreign Commerce of the United States.* Washington, D.C.: Carnegie Institution, 1915.
3. Simon Kuznets. *Capital and the American Economy.* New York: National Bureau of Economic Research, 1961.
4. J. L. Laughlin. *History of Bimetallism in the United States.* New York: Appleton, 1900
5. Marquis James. *The Metropolitan Life: A Study in Business Growth.* New York: Viking Press, 1947.
6. Wesley Mitchell. *Business Cycles and their Causes.* Berkeley: University of California Press, 1959.
7. _____. *A History of Greenbacks.* Chicago: University of Chicago Press, 1903.
8. O.M.W. Sprague. *History of Crises Under the National Banking System.* Washington, D.C.: U.S. Government Printing Office, 1910.

reading

can economic growth occur during a period of declining prices?

milton friedman and anna schwartz

The period from 1879 to 1914, in turn, breaks into two nearly equal parts that differ in important economic characteristics, both international and domestic. A combination of events, including a slowing of the rate of increase of the world's stock of gold, the adoption of the gold standard by a widening circle of countries, and a rapid increase in aggregate economic output, produced a secular decline from the 1860's almost to the end of the century in the world price level measured in gold, despite the rapid extension of commercial banking and of other devices for erecting an ever larger stock of money on a given gold base. That trend was reversed in the 1890's by fresh discoveries of gold in South Africa, Alaska, and Colorado combined with the development of improved methods of mining and refining, especially the introduction of the cyanide process. These occurred during a period when there were few further important extensions of the gold standard yet a continued development of devices for "economizing" gold. In consequence, the prior declining trend in world prices was replaced by a rising trend despite a continued rapid increase in physical output.

The decline and subsequent rise in world prices in terms of gold were naturally reflected in U.S. prices, and the different price trends in turn were reflected in domestic monetary politics. The preceding chapter recorded the beginning of the political agitation for an expansion of the money stock. That agitation continued from 1879 to the end of the cen-

Reprinted with permission from *A Monetary History of the United States* by Milton Friedman and Anna Schwartz. New York: National Bureau of Economic Research, 1963, pp. 90-95.

tury. The only difference was that silver instead of greenbacks became the popular means for expansion. The ebb and flow of political agitation during those two decades were an important source of short-term monetary uncertainty which affected the links between external and internal prices. After 1897, "cheap" gold achieved the objectives that had been sought by the silver advocates. The economic basis for the silver movement was thereby eliminated. The gold standard became securely enshrined. Uncertainty about its maintenance did not again play a significant role in our monetary experience until the 1930's.

According to our estimates, the stock of money grew both from 1879 to 1897 and from 1897 to 1914. But the rate of growth during the earlier period, though large by present-day standards and much larger than during the greenback period, was decidedly smaller than during the later period. It averaged about 6 per cent per year from 1879 to 1897, about 7½ per cent from 1897 to 1914. The different rates of monetary growth were associated with a corresponding difference in the behavior of prices. Prices fell at the rate of over 1 per cent a year from 1879 to 1897 and rose at the rate of over 2 per cent a year from 1897 to 1914.[1] The rate of growth of the money stock was not only lower but also decidedly more uneven during the earlier period; it was extraordinarily high from 1879 to 1881 — over 19 per cent per year — and essentially zero from 1892 to 1897. The greater unevenness of monetary growth in the earlier period was associated with a more uneven pace of economic activity. The business cycle contraction from 1882 to 1885 was unusually long and fairly severe; and two relatively severe contractions succeeded one another in the 1890's separated by only an unusually brief expansion. By contrast, the period from 1897 to 1914 was interrupted by only one sharp contraction, in 1907, and that relatively brief.[2] The qualitative evidence assembled by economic historians and other students of the period is perhaps even more striking than these statistical indicators. The decades of the 1880's and the 1890's were notable for political unrest, protest movements, and unsettled conditions; the early part of the twentieth century, for relative political stability and widespread confidence in the rapid economic progress of the country.

These monetary differences, though strikingly reflected in the political climate, leave surprisingly little impress on records of physical performance. Both the earlier and the later periods were characterized by rapid economic growth. The two final decades of the nineteenth century saw a growth of population of over 2 per cent per year, rapid extension of the railway network, essential completion of continental settlement, and an extraordinary increase both in the acreage of land in farms and the output of farm products. The number of farms rose by nearly 50 per cent, and the total value of farm lands and buildings, by over 60 per cent — despite the price decline.[3] Yet at the same time, manufacturing industries were growing even more rapidly, and the Census of 1890 was the first in which the net value added by manufacturing exceeded the value of agricultural output. A feverish boom in western land swept the country during the eighties. "The highest decadal rate [of growth of real reproducible tangible wealth per head from 1805 to 1950] for periods of about ten years was apparently reached in the eighties with approximately 3.8 per cent."[4]

During the first decade of the twentieth century, population, the number of farms, and agricultural output all grew at a somewhat slower rate than in the preceding two decades. Manufacturing output, however, maintained its earlier high rate of expansion, as the country continued to shift from agriculture to industry.

Was economic growth more rapid during the earlier period of declining prices or during the later period of rising prices? Unfortunately, the readily available figures do not yield a simple, clear-cut answer. Kuznets' aggregate net national product in constant prices rises at the rate of 3.7 per cent per year from 1879 to 1897, and at the rate of 3.2 per cent from 1897 to 1914. This implies a rise in per capita net national product of 1.5 per cent a year for the earlier period, of 1.4 per cent for the later. However, the results of such a calculation are extraordinarily sensitive to the choice of dates: the use of 1880, 1896, and 1913, instead of 1879, 1897, and 1914, gives a rise in aggregate net national product of 2.6 per cent per year from 1880 to 1896 and of 4.4 per cent from 1896 to 1913. Inspection of the graph of net national product (see Chart 1, below) suggests little significant change in the rate of growth over the period as a whole, but rather a sharp retardation from something like 1892 to 1896 and then a sharp acceleration from 1896 to 1901, which just about made up for lost time. If this be right, generally declining or generally rising prices had little impact on the rate of growth, but the period of great monetary uncertainty in the early nineties produced sharp deviations from the longer-term trend. This evidence reinforces the tentative conclusion reached [earlier] that the forces making for economic growth over the course of several business cycles are largely independent of the secular trend in prices.

---

1. Fels, following Rostow, whom he cites on this point, believes that the secular decline of interest rates during the period 1879-97 demonstrates that a higher rate of growth of the money stock would not have eliminated the secular price decline (Fels, *American Business Cycles*, pp. 68-70, 81). D. Coppock similarly asserts that "The behaviour of interest rates is the crucial argument against the monetary theory of the price decline" ("The Causes of the Great Depression 1873-96," *Manchester School of Economic and Social Studies*, Sept. 1961, p. 209).

   We do not accept this conclusion. On the contrary, even on the most extreme and naive liquidity preference theory of the interest rate, the fact that interest rates did decline meant that the liquidity preference was not absolute, i.e., that the liquidity preference schedule was not infinitely elastic at the going interest rate. Hence, a more rapid

CHART 1 *Money Stock, Income, Prices, and Velocity, in Reference Cycle Expansions and Contractions, 1879 – 1914*

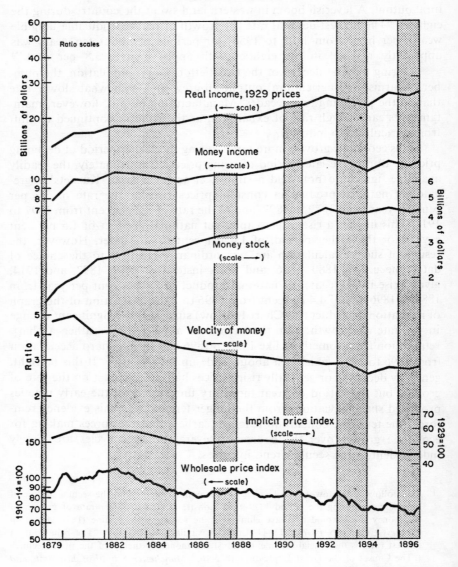

NOTE: Shaded areas represent business contractions; unshaded areas, business expansions.
SOURCE: Wholesale prices, George F. Warren and Frank A. Pearson, *Prices,* New York, Wiley, 1933, p. 13. Other data, same as for Chart 62.

CHART 1 *(Concluded)*

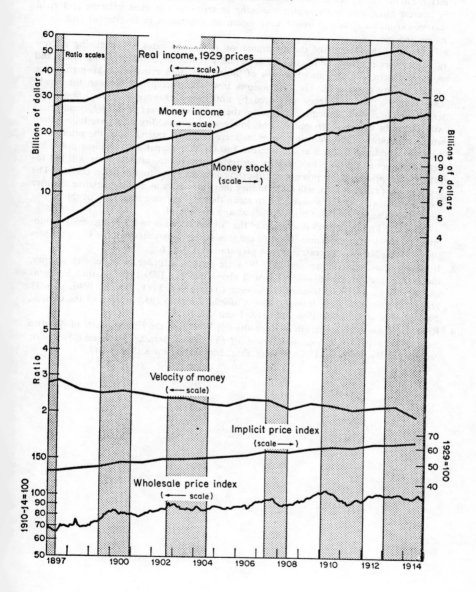

increase in the money stock, even on that theory, would have meant a more rapid decrease in interest rates, and hence, again reasoning in terms of the most extreme and rigid income-expenditure theory, would have meant an expansion in investment and so in money income.

On any other theory of the determination of interest rates, the declining interest rates may very plausibly be interpreted as in part a reflection of the declining prices and as in turn increasing the rate of growth of the money stock required to keep the price decline at any given level. The first follows from the discrepancy between the "real" and "money" rates of interest produced by anticipated changes in prices. Insofar as lenders and borrowers anticipate changes in the purchasing power of money, bond prices will tend to be higher and nominal yields lower when commodity prices are falling than when commodity prices are rising, since the increase in the real value of the principal is a return in addition to the nominal interest. Insofar as anticipations of falling prices lag behind the actual fall in prices, as they generally seem to do, interest rates will fall together with prices in the process of adjusting interest rates to the price decline. The lower interest rates, in turn, will make money more attractive as an asset relative to other fixed nominal value assets and so tend to mean that a larger rate of growth of the money stock is required to keep the price decline at any given level.

See also Phillip Cagan's discussion of the Gibson Paradox in his forthcoming monograph on the determinants and effects of changes in the money stock in the United States since 1875, a National Bureau study, in preparation, Chap. 6.

2. If all business-cycle contractions 1882-1914 are ranked in order of increasing severity, the average for the period 1882-97 is well above that for 1899-1914. (Arthur F. Burns and Wesley C. Mitchell, *Measuring Business Cycles,* New York, NBER, 1946, p. 403).

3. *Historical Statistics of the United States, Colonial Times to 1957,* Bureau of the Census, 1960 (*Historical Statistics,* 1960), Series K-1 and K-4, p. 278.

4. R. W. Goldsmith, "The Growth of Reproducible Wealth of the United States of America from 1805 to 1950," *Income and Wealth of the United States, Trends and Structure, Income and Wealth,* Series II, Cambridge, Eng., Bowes and Bowes,1952, p. 247.

part **V**

from world war I to the 1970's

the service

economy

ECONOMIC GROWTH AND THE SERVICE SECTOR

STAGES OF GROWTH

The service sector generally is viewed as comprising five main areas: wholesale and retail trade; professional, personal, business and repair services; government; finance, insurance and real estate; and public utilities including transportation. In the process of economic growth, all economies pass through three overlapping stages of development. Initially, resources are concentrated on agriculture and other primary activities, and services. Resources then move into manufacturing and construction, and then flow increasingly into services. Such a shift has characterized the United States. Stanley Lebergott estimates that in 1800 almost 75 per cent of the labor force was employed in primary activities.[1] (See Table 17.1.) By 1840 the proportion in primary activities had declined to 64 per cent, while services stood at 22 per cent, and manufacturing and construction had increased to approximately 14 per cent of the labor force. By 1870 manufacturing and construction's share had risen to 25 per cent at the

527

TABLE 17.1. *Industrial Distribution of the Labor Force 1800–1960* (Per Cent)*

Year	Primary (Agriculture, Mining, and Fisheries)		Secondary (Construction, Manufacturing)		Service (Trade, Transport, Finance, Government, etc.)
1800	73.7%	0.8%	n.a.[†]	n.a.	n.a.
1810	80.9	0.7	n.a.	2.8	n.a.
1820	78.8	0.8	n.a.	n.a.	n.a.
1830	68.8	0.9	n.a.	n.a.	n.a.
1840	63.1	1.0	5.1	8.8	22.0
1850	54.8	1.6	5.0	14.5	24.1
1860	52.9	2.0	4.7	13.8	26.6
1870	52.5	1.6	6.0	19.1	20.8
1880	51.3	1.8	5.2	18.9	22.8
1890	42.7	2.1	6.5	18.8	29.9
1900	40.2	2.4	5.7	20.3	31.4
1910	31.4	3.0	5.2	22.2	38.2
1920	25.9	3.0	3.0	26.9	41.2
1930	21.6	2.2	4.1	20.2	51.9
1940	17.0	1.8	3.3	20.1	57.8
1950	12.0	1.5	4.6	23.9	58.0
1960	8.1	1.0	4.9	23.2	62.8

SOURCE: Stanley Lebergott. "Labor Force and Employment 1800–1960," *Output, Employment and Productivity in the United States after 1800.* New York: National Bureau of Economic Research, 1966, pp. 118–19.

*Persons employed (employees, self-employed and unpaid family workers) age ten and over.
[†]Not available.

expense of primary activities, whose share declined to roughly 53 per cent, with the service sector again remaining relatively constant. By 1920 manufacturing and construction peaked at roughly 30 per cent of the labor force and services increased its share to 41 per cent, both at the expense of primary industries, which declined to 26 per cent.

By 1960 manufacturing and construction remained relatively unchanged, while services rose dramatically to almost 63 per cent, and agriculture declined to 8 per cent. A more detailed view of the growth of the service sector is provided by examining changes in the percentage distribution of nonagricultural employment since 1920. On this basis, service's share rose from under 54 per cent of total employment to 67 per cent. During the same period the secondary sector (construction and manufacturing) declined from about 42 per cent to 33 per cent. The greatest growth in the service sector occurred in wholesale and retail trade, government, and health and other services (see Table 17.2). The same forces which produced

TABLE 17.2. *Percentage Distribution of Nonagricultural Employment by Industry Division 1920-1970*

Year	Mining	Construction	Manufacturing	Transportation & Public Utilities	Wholesale & Retail Trade	Finance, Insurance & Real Estate	Government	Health & Other Services
1920	4.4	2.9	38.7	14.6	16.4	4.4	9.5	9.0
1930	3.4	4.7	32.6	12.6	19.7	5.1	10.4	11.5
1940	2.8	4.0	33.9	9.3	20.8	4.9	12.9	11.4
1950	2.0	5.2	33.7	8.9	20.8	4.2	13.3	11.9
1960	1.3	5.3	31.0	7.4	21.0	4.9	15.4	13.7
1970	.9	4.7	27.5	6.4	21.2	5.2	17.8	16.4

SOURCE: U.S. Department of Labor. *1971 Manpower Report of the President.* Washington, D.C.: U.S. Government Printing Office, 1921, p. 256.
1969 Handbook of Labor Statistics. Washington, D.C.: U.S. Government Printing Office, 1969, p. 78.

a shift of resources from agriculture into manufacturing caused the growth of services. Strides in agricultural and manufacturing productivity permitted farm and factory workers to feed more people and produce more goods, thereby releasing resources for service production. Thus far, increases in service worker productivity have lagged behind those in agriculture and manufacturing. Between 1947 and 1970 the average annual percentage rate of increase in output per manhour outside agriculture and manufacturing (principally services) was 2.5 in comparison to 5.7 for agriculture and 3.0 for manufacturing. This difference is attributable to the greater growth in capital per worker in manufacturing and agriculture and the larger scale of operations in manufacturing which have permitted greater economics of scale.

IMPLICATIONS FOR THE ECONOMY

The growth of the service sector has affected the economy in several ways. First, its slower rate of increases in productivity may have dampened the nation's growth rate. Second, it provided greater employment opportunities for women and older workers. The less arduous character of service employment, its more attractive physical conditions, and the greater opportunities for part-time work made the service sector well suited to female and senior workers. This helps to explain the sharply increasing participation of women in the labor force in recent decades. In 1870 women constituted less than 15 per cent of the labor force, whereas in 1970 more than one out of every three workers was a woman. Third, it caused a renaissance in the growth of small business. The modest capital requirements to enter service production makes possible a large number of small firms. The service sector is the major area of the economy where individuals can still exercise the option of self-employment. The typical service firm of the 1970's is relatively small, and takes the form of either a sole proprietership or partnership. In wholesaling and retailing, for example, half of all employees are in firms having less than twenty workers. Fourth, it encouraged workers to achieve a higher level of formal education. In 1970 the median years of school completed for the principal service occupations (clericals and sales workers, and professional and managerial workers) ranged between 12.6 and 14.9 years versus 11.6 years for the principal production worker occupations (craftsmen, operatives and laborers). Fifth, it slowed down the rate of union growth. The service worker's psychological association with management and the small size unit in which he works blunted the appeals of unionization. In the late 1960's less than ten per cent of workers in service industries were unionized, compared with over forty-five per cent in manufacturing. Sixth, it tended to lessen fluctuations in economic activity. In services there can be no inventory build-up requiring corrective production cut-backs as demand falls. And, service consumption, unlike durable goods, is fairly stable over the business cycle. A greater proportion of service workers are either self-employed or salaried, and thus continue working during economic downturns when hourly workers are being laid off.

THE MAJOR PRIVATE AND PUBLIC SERVICE INDUSTRIES

RETAILING

Of all private service industries retail trade is the most important. In the 1920's as well as in the 1960's, this industry accounted for the greatest share of private service workers. In 1970 it employed almost 16 per cent of all nonagricultural workers. Holding first and second position among retailers were Sears Roebuck and A & P, respectively. Until the post-World War I period Sears was primarily a mail-order house. During the 1920's it began establishing retail stores to take advantage of the mobility of farmers made possible by the automobile. In 1931 it entered the automobile insurance business under the brandname, Allstate. In the 1940's it expanded into Latin America, and in the 1950's into Canada. By 1970 it had eight hundred stores, eleven catalogue order plants, and thirteen hundred catalogue sales offices. For its merchandise the store relies on small and medium size manufacturers, to whom it submits detailed specifications for the type of goods which it desires. While Sears annually distributes sixty million catalogues, only twenty-five per cent of its sales, of over eight billion dollars, are derived from this original sales vehicle. A & P also experienced significant growth in the 1920's, and by 1930 its sales passed the billion dollar mark. One year later the number of stores reached a peak of over fifteen thousand. Thereafter, while sales volume increased substantially, the number of stores was cut by three-fourths. By 1970 the company had sales of approximately six billion dollars and employed a staff of over one hundred thousand employees. The company not only sells at retail, but it also manufactures much of what it stocks on its shelves. For example, it owns and operates bakery, cheese, coffee, milk, and cannery plants.

In recent decades the most important development in retailing has been the rise of the discount store. This phenomenon is exemplified by the growth of Korvette's. From an initial investment of four thousand dollars in 1949, Korvette sales totaled two million dollars two years later, and passed one billion dollars by 1967. Essentially, Korvette's and other discount houses succeeded by circumventing "Fair Trade" laws (see Chapter 18) which dictate the minimum prices which large department stores can charge for their products. Relatively unknown discount houses, operating as Korvette's did from a second floor loft, were able to engage in price cutting activities that large established stores found almost impossible. The founder of Korvette's, Eugene Ferkauf, after working in his father's luggage stores, opened his own outlet to sell luggage at discount. Operating on the theory that profits would be greater with a low markup and high turnover, Ferkauf added appliances to attract customers. These appliances were sold at cost. Before long he found his appliances to be the mainstay of consumer interest, and added a small markup. Thereafter, sales rose at a steady pace. In 1965 the Company acquired Hills Supermarkets, a grocery chain doing an annual business of one hundred thirty million dollars. One year later it merged with Spartans Industries, a discount chain and manufacturer of apparel. At that time it was one of the top merchandising firms of the nation. The rapid growth of discount sales has encouraged old-line retail establishments either to meet the prices of the discount chains (Macy's) or enter the field themselves (Kresge's and Woolworth's).

GOVERNMENT

The fastest growing area in the service sector since 1915 has been government. Comprising only 5 per cent of total employment in 1900, it accounted for 18 per cent in 1970. (See Table 17.2.) With the exception of the 1930's and 1940's the greatest growth has occurred in state and local government. Since 1950, in fact, the Federal Government's share of total employment has declined. In 1970 state and local governments employed 80 per cent of all government workers, compared with 67 per cent in 1950. Total government expenditures as a percentage of Gross National

TABLE 17.3. *Federal, State, and Local Purchases of Goods and Services 1929-1970 (Billions of Dollars)*

| Year | Total | Federal* | | | State and Local |
		Total	National Defense	Other	
1929	8.5	1.3	–	–	7.2
1935	10.0	2.9	–	–	7.1
1940	14.0	6.0	2.2	3.8	8.0
1945	82.3	74.2	73.5	0.7	8.1
1950	37.9	18.4	14.1	4.3	19.5
1955	74.2	44.1	38.6	5.5	30.1
1960	99.6	53.5	44.9	8.6	46.1
1965	136.4	66.8	50.1	16.7	69.1
1970	220.5	99.7	76.6	23.1	120.8

SOURCE: *1971 Economic Report of the President.* Washington, D.C.: U.S. Government Printing Office, 1971.

*Excludes Trust Fund expenditures

Product grew from 2 per cent in 1800 to slightly less than 10 per cent by 1900, and to over 20 per cent by 1970.

Government's growth may be traced to war, the changing international role of the United States, population growth, urbanization, automobile usage and the demand for more health, education, and welfare services. On the federal level war was the initial reason for greater federal participation in the economy, and continues to the present day as a dominant reason for most federal activity. (See Table 17.3.) America's involvement in a series of wars from the Revolution to the "Cold War" and Vietnam caused military expenditures periodically to dominate federal spending. In the inter-war years before the 1930's, interest on wartime borrowing and veterans' pensions were the principal items of federal spending. This pattern was broken in the 1930's when relief, public works, and aid to agriculture surpassed war-related expenditures in importance. The emergence of the United States during World War II as the dominant power of the free world thrust upon it a new responsibility. Pitted against the USSR and its Communist supporters, the U.S. has been required to spend the major share of its budget for defense purposes. For the first time in the nation's history, military expenditures have dominated spending in peace years. (See Table 17.4.)

Population growth, its continental dispersion and urban concentration and automobile usage all required increased government spending. The growth of the U.S. population from 4 million in 1790 to over 200 million in 1970, even if per capita government spending remained the same, would

TABLE 17.4. *Major Federal Expenditures 1789-1970*

	Percentage of Total		
	---	---	---
	Armed Forces	*Interest*	*Veterans Benefits*
1789-91	15%	55%	4%
1800	56	31	1
1820	38	28	18
1840	54	1	11
1860	44	5	2
1880	19	36	21
1900	37	8	27
1920	37	16	3
1940	20	12	5
1960	50	9	6
1970	40	9	4

SOURCE: U.S. Bureau of the Census. *Historical Statistics of the U.S., Colonial Times to 1957.* Washington, D.C.: U.S. Government Printing Office, 1960, p. 718-19; U.S. Bureau of the Census. *1970 Statistical Abstract of the U.S.* Washington, D.C.: U.S. Government Printing Office, 1970, p. 377.

have necessitated a fiftyfold increase in the level of spending. The expanding geographical frontiers of the United States and the subsequent movement of the population from East to West increased the number of state and local governments, each of which is required to provide certain services for its citizens. The increased concentration of Americans in urban areas, from 5 per cent in 1790 to almost 70 per cent in 1970, has shifted the responsibility for providing numerous services, such as garbage disposal, water supply, and police and fire protection from the individual to government. The popularity of motor vehicles for business and pleasure has imposed upon government huge expenditures for highways, streets, and roads. More than any other material possession, the automobile has become the status symbol of American society. Automobiles and highways are complementary goods, and as the demand for automobiles increases so does the need for highway expenditures.

In recent decades government has been increasingly concerned with measures to promote the health, education, and welfare of the population. These items have always been a major portion of state and local budgets. (See Tables 17.5 and 17.6.) Major federal expenditures in the health and welfare area commenced in the 1930's. The Social Security Act of 1935 committed the Federal Government to a major role in assisting a large

segment of older, younger, and unemployed Americans. In the 1960'
this responsibility was enlarged to include disadvantaged workers and al
groups in the population whose income fell below a designated poverty
level. The Manpower Training and Development Act of 1962 provided basi
education and jobs for workers who lacked the necessary skills to fit int
modern technology (the structurally unemployed). The Economic Oppor
tunity Act of 1964 provided a variety of educational, community, health
and rehabilitative services to economically disadvantaged groups.

TABLE 17.5. *Major State Expenditures 1902-1968*

	Percentage of Total			
	Education	*Highway*	*Welfare*	*Health & Hospitals*
1902	13	3	8	24
1913	19	9	5	18
1927	16	37	3	12
1934	11	37	18	10
1954	17	32	15	13
1968	40	19	14	7

SOURCE: U.S. Bureau of the Census. *Historical Statistics of the U.*
From Colonial Times to 1957. Washington, D.C.: U.S. Governmen
Printing Office, 1960, p. 728; U.S. Bureau of the Census. *1970 Statis*
cal Abstract of the U.S. Washington, D.C.: U.S. Government Printi
Office, 1970, p. 417.

TABLE 17.6. *Major Local Expenditures 1902-1967*

	Percentage of Total						
	Education	*Highway*	*Welfare*	*Health & Hospitals*	*Police*	*Fire*	*Sanitati*
1902	27	20	3	3	6	5	6
1913	30	22	2	3	5	4	6
1927	35	22	2	3	5	4	5
1934	31	15	10	4	5	4	3
1954	43	11	7	6	5	3	5
1967	49	8	7	6	4	3	3

SOURCE: U.S. Bureau of the Census. *Historical Statistics of the U.*
From Colonial Times to 1957. Washington, D.C.: U.S. Governme
Printing Office, 1957, p. 730; U.S. Bureau of the Census. *1970 Statis*
cal Abstract of the U.S. Washington, D.C.: U.S. Government Printi
Office, 1970, p. 422.

TABLE 17.7. *Source of Federal Receipts 1789–1970*

| | Percentage of Total | | |
	Customs	Excise and Income Taxes	Other*
1789–91	99.5%	—	.5%
1800	83	8	9
1820	84	1	15
1840	70	—	30
1860	95	—	5
1880	53	37	10
1900	41	52	7
1920	5	80	15
1940	6	90	4
1960	3	80	17
1970	3	72	25

SOURCE: U.S. Bureau of the Census. *Historical Statistics of the U.S. Colonial Times to 1957.* Washington, D.C.: U.S. Government Printing Office, 1960, p. 712; U.S. Bureau of the Census. *1970 Statistical Abstract of the U.S.* Washington, D.C.: U.S. Government Printing Office, 1970, pp. 389–90.

*Includes Social Insurance after 1940.

For most of the nation's history, with the exception of war periods, local and state units accounted for most public spending. Thus, at the turn of the century local and state units accounted for 66 per cent of public spending and the federal government for 34 per cent. Even in the depression decades of the 1930's local and state spending exceeded that of the federal government (see Table 17.3). In accordance with past patterns, federal expenditures exceeded local and state spending during World War II. The Cold War punctuated by the Korean and Vietnam conflicts accounted for continued federal dominance until the late 1960's; subsequently, an acceleration in the growth of local and state spending, together with a leveling off of defense expenditures caused local and state spending to exceed federal spending by 1970. This pattern is likely to continue throughout the 1970's. Much debate exists as to what proportion of the nation's resources should be directed to the production of public rather than private goods. In the readings at the end of this chapter, John Kenneth Galbraith argues for more attention to public services, while Henry C. Wallach takes a contrary view.

Increases in Government expenditures have been matched by augmented revenues. The Federal Government until World War I relied pri-

TABLE 17.8. *Major State Tax Revenues 1902-1968*

	Percentage of Total					
	Personal Income	*Corporate*	*General Sales*	*Motor Fuel*	*Property*	*Vehicle and Operator License*
1902	–	–	–	–	53	–
1913	–	–	–	–	47	2
1927	4	6	–	16	23	19
1934	4	3	9	29	14	15
1954	9	7	23	20	4	9
1968	17	7	29	16	3	7

SOURCE: U.S. Bureau of the Census. *Historical Statistics of the U.S.: Colonial Times to 1957.* Washington, D.C.: U.S. Government Printing Office, 1960, p. 727. U.S. Bureau of the Census. *1970 Statistical Abstract of the U.S.* Washington, D.C.: U.S. Government Printing Office, 1970, p. 408.

TABLE 17.9. *Major Local Revenues 1902-1968*

	Percentage of Total	
	Sales	*Property*
1902	–	89%
1913	0.2%	91
1927	0.6	97
1934	0.8	97
1954	6	87
1968	6	86

SOURCE: U.S. Bureau of the Census. *Historical Statistics of the U.S. From Colonial Times to 1957.* Washington, D.C.: U.S. Government Printing Office, 1960, p. 729; U.S. Bureau of the Census. *1970 Statistical Abstract of the U.S.* Washington, D.C.: U.S. Government Printing Office, 1970, p. 408.

marily on tariffs, supplemented by land sales (in the pre-Civil War period) and excise taxes. The increased range of Federal responsibilities by World War I forced it to turn to the income tax as the major revenue source. In assuming taxing power over both personal and corporate earnings, the Federal Government gained control of the nation's major source of revenue.

(See Table 17.7.) State governments, like the federal government, were forced to turn to new sources of revenue during the twentieth century. In the nineteenth century they relied almost exclusively on the general property tax. The newer levies include highway user and sales taxes. (See Table 17.8.) Property taxes have always been the principal source of local tax revenues. While most cities have sought to augment their revenues by levying payroll, income, and sales and excise taxes, the property tax continues to dominate. (See Table 17.9.)

Over the 182-year period from 1789 to 1970 federal budgetary surpluses occurred 108 times and deficits 73 times. In only one quarter of the deficit years did the deficit equal or exceed half of total expenditures (1812-1815, 1847, 1918-1919, 1932-1934, 1936, 1942-1945). These were all war years, with the exception of 1932-34 and 1936. Federal debt between World War I and 1970 rose from 25 billion dollars to over 380 billion dollars. As expected, most of this growth occurred during World War II. In 1945 federal debt was 122 per cent of Gross National Product. Since that date, despite the Korean and Vietnam conflicts and the use of federal budgets to stimulate economic activity, the federal debt as a percentage of Gross National Product has steadily declined, reaching a level of 39 per cent in 1970. (See Table 17.10.) Until the post-World War II period it was believed that the federal budget should always be in balance. From time to time national leaders such as Alexander Hamilton, Albert Gallatin, Theodore Roosevelt, and Woodrow Wilson advocated increased government intervention in the economy, but always in the context of government revenues matching or exceeding expenditures. Rather than lean against the wind of economic change to smooth out fluctuations in economic activity, federal spending has tended historically to be adjusted to revenues, and the latter have followed the course of business activity. The effect was to aggravate rather than to mitigate business cycles. There was, of course, a lagged response of spending to revenue changes that produced an initial contracyclical effect in times of growing unemployment. Thus during economic downturns such as that of 1873 expenditures kept rising in the face of falling revenues. Not until 1875 were expenditures cut. They then continued downward until 1879, when economic activity and revenues began to increase. During upswings, when government revenues exceeded expenditures the budget's initial impact on the economy was deflationary. However, when these surpluses were used to retire the national debt, they pumped spending power back into the economy and enhanced the banking system's ability to create credit. When Federal debt was negligible or accumulating surpluses exceeded maturing debt, the budget had a deflationary influence on the economy. In the period 1832 to 1838, for example, the Federal debt was virtually liquidated while Federal surpluses accumulated. Despite pressures from Congress, President Jackson refused to allow expenditures to rise to the level of revenues. A compromise was effected to distribute a portion of the surplus back to the states. However, before it could be fully implemented, a sharp decline in economic activity turned the surpluses into deficits. In the 1880's, while there was substantial Civil War debt outstanding, its long-term maturity, non-callable nature, and premium price prevented its retirement except at prohibitive cost. Thus, accumulating surpluses could not be returned to the economy. The seriousness of the surplus problem was compounded by the Independent Treasury system. The system, created in 1841, removed government funds from the banking system for storage in Treasury vaults. In years of surplus this resulted in a specie drain on the economy at a time when greater liquidity was needed to finance growing output. This situation acted as a drag on growth. Even if the Federal Government had deliberately sought to manipulate its budgets to influence the level of economic activity, the size of its budget relative to Gross National Product prior to World War I was not of sufficient magnitude meaningfully to influence the course of the economy.

Beginning with World War I, and more particularly, since World War II, the federal budget has assumed a more important role in the economy. The first conscious attempt to stimulate economic activity through deficit spending was made in the 1930's. The New Deal, which committed itself to returning the economy to prosperity, initially attempted to do so while balancing the budget. It was only after the sharp recession of 1937-38, which eliminated much of the economic recovery since 1933, that the New Deal deliberately adopted deficit spending. The onset of World War II, with its hugh deficits, restored the economy to full employment. In its aftermath, the concept of the annually balanced budget was replaced by the cyclically balanced budget. This view was replaced in the 1960's by the concept of a planned deficit. During periods of less than full employment it is appropriate deliberately to increase the size of the federal deficit in order to stimulate the nation's rate of economic growth to achieve full employment.

As observed in Chapter 3, government spending, like private consumption and investment spending, is a component of total spending. Taxation affects total spending by controlling the amount of income which consumers and businessmen have available for spending. During times of unemployment and idle plant capacity, the government can stimulate economic activity by deficit financing. In combating unemployment through deficit spending, three choices are open to government. It may decrease taxes, increase its own spending, or utilize a combination of both. Should it elect to increase spending, questions arise as to the appropriate types of expenditures. Of the several alternatives, public works have been used most widely. They provide needed public facilities, may be planned in advance, and stimulate the construction industry, which often is seriously

TABLE 17.10. *Federal Debt as a Percentage of GNP 1919–1970*

| Year | Billions of Dollars | | Per Cent |
	GNP	Debt	
1919	78.9	25.5	32%
1925	91.3	20.5	22
1930	90.4	16.2	18
1935	72.2	27.7	38
1940	99.7	48.5	49
1945	211.9	259.1	122
1950	284.8	257.4	91
1955	398.9	274.4	69
1960	503.7	286.5	57
1965	684.9	317.9	48
1970	976.8	381.7	39

SOURCE: U.S. Bureau of the Census. *Historical Statistics of the United States, Colonial Times to 1957.* Washington, D.C.: U.S. Government Printing Office, 1960, p. 711.
1968 Economic Report of the President. Washington, D.C.: U.S. Government Printing Office, 1969, p. 284.
1970 Economic Report of the President. Washington, D.C.: U.S. Government Printing Office, 1971, p. 251.

affected by economic downturns. Relief spending has the same economic effect as public works expenditures. In addition, it is more flexible, and cheaper to administer. Its one disadvantage is that it does not provide society with public goods. Should government elect to stimulate the economy through reduced taxes, it must decide what taxes to cut. If it provides relief for businessmen and upper income groups, investment is encouraged, whereas if taxes are reduced for middle and lower income levels, consumption is stimulated. Tax cuts, unlike spending increments, permit the exercise of consumer sovereignty. On the other hand, there is no guarantee that the greater disposable income afforded by tax cuts will be fully spent by consumer and businessmen.

Budget manipulation is equally effective in controlling inflationary pressures caused by excessive spending in relation to production capacity. As in the case of unemployment, there are three ways by which government can reduce aggregate demand. It can lower its own expenditures, increase taxes to curb consumer and business spending, or use a combination of both. Should sales taxes or income taxes for lower and middle income groups be raised, consumption is discouraged. Increasing corporate income taxes and personal income taxes for upper income groups, on the other hand, discourages investment. The political problems of planning and executing an anti-inflation budget program are significant. If inflation is present in an election year, politicians usually hesitate to risk the ire of voters by increasing tax rates. Lowering expenditures might be difficult, since local constituencies and government departments and agencies can be expected to resist strenuously any downward revision of their spending.

A problem common to both deficit and surplus financing is timing. Contra-cyclical policies are most effective if they are applied immediately prior to the onset of rising unemployment or prices. Economic forecasting is far from a science, and the ability to predict impending changes in the level of economic activity is most difficult. Compounding the problem is the slowness of Congressional deliberations on taxing and spending matters. One solution is the use of automatic stabilizers. Such stabilizers as the graduated personal income tax, unemployment insurance, and farm parity payments tend automatically to pump more income into the economy when it is lagging, and withdraw more purchasing power when it is rising. Another solution is to authorize the Executive Branch to impose tax and spending changes within prescribed limits without having to seek Congressional authorization. Efforts to obtain such power in the 1960's proved unsuccessful.

NOTES

1. Stanley Lebergott. "Labor Force and Employment, 1860-1960," *Output, Employment and Productivity in the United States after 1800*. New York: National Bureau of Economic Research, 1966.

SELECTED REFERENCES

1. Boris Emmet and John Jeucks. *Catalogs and Counters*. Chicago: University of Chicago Press, 1950.
2. Solomon Fabricant. *The Trend of Government Activity in the United States Since 1900*. New York: National Bureau of Economic Research, 1952.
3. Milton Friedman. *Capitalism and Freedom*. Chicago: University of Chicago Press, 1962.
4. Victor Fuchs. *The Service Economy*. New York: National Bureau of Economic Research, 1968.
5. Walter W. Heller. *New Dimensions of Political Economy*. Cambridge: Harvard University Press, 1966.
6. L. H. Kimmel. *Federal Budget and Fiscal Policies, 1798-1958*. Washington: Brookings Institution, 1959.

readings

is the role of government
in the u.s. economy adequate?

ONE VIEW: *john kenneth galbraith*

The final problem of the productive society is what it produces. This manifests itself in an implacable tendency to provide an opulent supply of some things and a niggardly yield of others. This disparity carries to the point where it is a cause of social discomfort and social unhealth. The line which divides our area of wealth from our area of poverty is roughly that which divides privately produced and marketed goods and services from publicly rendered services. Our wealth in the first is not only in startling contrast with the meagerness of the latter, but our wealth in privately produced goods is, to a marked degree, the cause of crisis in the supply of public services. For we have failed to see the importance, indeed the urgent need, or maintaining a balance between the two.

This disparity between our flow of private and public goods and services is no matter of subjective judgment. On the contrary, it is the source of the most extensive comment which only stops short of the direct contrast being made here. In the years following World War II, the papers of any major city — those of New York were an excellent example — told daily of the shortages and shortcomings in the elementary municipal and metropolitan services. The schools were old and overcrowded. The police force was under strength and underpaid. The parks and playgrounds were insufficient. Streets and empty lots were filthy, and the sanitation staff was underequipped and in need of men. Access to the city by those who work

Reprinted with permission from *The Affluent Society* by John Kenneth Galbraith. Boston: Houghton Mifflin, 1958, pp. 251-269.

541

there was uncertain and painful and becoming more so. Internal transportation was overcrowded, unhealthful, and dirty. So was the air. Parking on the streets had to be prohibited, and there was no space elsewhere. These deficiencies were not in new and novel services but in old and established ones. Cities have long swept their streets, helped their people move around, educated them, kept order, and provided horse rails for vehicles which sought to pause. That their residents should have a nontoxic supply of air suggests no revolutionary dalliance with socialism.

The discussion of this public poverty competed, on the whole successfully, with the stories of ever-increasing opulence in privately produced goods. The Gross National Product was rising. So were retail sales. So was personal income. Labor productivity had also advanced. The automobiles that could not be parked were being produced at an expanded rate. The children, though without schools, subject in the playgrounds to the affectionate interest of adults with odd tastes, and disposed to increasingly imaginative forms of delinquency, were admirably equipped with television sets. We had difficulty finding storage space for the great surpluses of food despite a national disposition to obesity. Food was grown and packaged under private auspices. The care and refreshment of the mind, in contrast with the stomach, was principally in the public domain. Our colleges and universities were severely overcrowded and underprovided, and the same was true of the mental hospitals.

The contrast was and remains evident not alone to those who read. The family which takes its mauve and cerise, air-conditioned, power-steered, and power-braked automobile out for a tour passes through cities that are badly paved, made hideous by litter, blighted buildings, billboards, and posts for wires that should long since have been put underground. They pass on into a countryside that has been rendered largely invisible by commercial art. (The goods which the latter advertise have an absolute priority in our value system. Such aesthetic considerations as a view of the countryside accordingly come second. On such matters we are consistent.) They picnic on exquisitely packaged food from a portable icebox by a polluted stream and go on to spend the night at a park which is a menace to public health and morals. Just before dozing off on an air mattress, beneath a nylon tent, amid the stench of decaying refuse, they may reflect vaguely on the curious unevenness of their blessings. Is this, indeed, the American genius?

In the production of goods within the private economy it has long been recognized that a tolerably close relationship must be maintained between the production of various kinds of products. The output of steel and oil and machine tools is related to the production of automobiles. Investment in transportation must keep abreast of the output of goods to be transported.

The supply of power must be abreast of the growth of industries requiring it. The existence of these relationships — coefficients to the economist — has made possible the construction of the input-output table which shows how changes in the production in one industry will increase or diminish the demands on other industries. To this table, and more especially to its ingenious author, Professor Wassily Leontief, the world is indebted for one of its most important of modern insights into economic relationships. If expansion in one part of the economy were not matched by the requisite expansion in other parts — were the need for balance not respected — then bottlenecks and shortages, speculative hoarding of scarce supplies, and sharply increasing costs would ensue. Fortunately in peacetime the market system operates easily and effectively to maintain this balance, and this together with the existence of stocks and some flexibility in the coefficients as a result of substitution, insures that no serious difficulties will arise. We are remainded of the existence of the problem only by noticing how serious it is for those countries — Poland or, in a somewhat different form, India — which seek to solve the problem by planned measures and with a much smaller supply of resources.

Just as there must be balance in what a community produces, so there must also be balance in what the community consumes. An increase in the use of one product creates, ineluctably, a requirement for others. If we are to consume more automobiles, we must have more gasoline. There must be more insurance as well as more space on which to operate them. Beyond a certain point more and better food appears to mean increased need for medical services. This is the certain result of the increased consumption of tobacco and alcohol. More vacations require more hotels and more fishing rods. And so forth. With rare exceptions — shortages of doctors are an exception which suggests the rule — this balance is also maintained quite effortlessly so far as goods for private sale and consumption are concerned. The price system plus a rounded condition of opulence is again the agency.

However, the relationships we are here discussing are not confined to the private economy. They operate comprehensively over the whole span of private and public services. As surely as an increase in the output of automobiles puts new demands on the steel industry so, also, it places new demands on public services. Similarly, every increase in the consumption of private goods will normally mean some facilitating or protective step by the state. In all cases if these services are not forthcoming, the consequences will be in some degree ill. It will be convenient to have a term which suggests a satisfactory relationship between the supply of privately produced goods and services and those of the state, and we may call it social balance.

The problem of social balance is ubiquitous, and frequently it is obtrusive. As noted, an increase in the consumption of automobiles requires a facilitating supply of streets, highways, traffic control, and parking space. The protective services of the police and the highway patrols must also be available, as must those of the hospitals. Although the need for balance here is extraordinarily clear, our use of privately produced vehicles has, on occasion, got far out of line with the supply of the related public services. The result has been hideous road congestion, an annual massacre of impressive proportions, and chronic colitis in the cities. As on the ground, so also in the air. Planes collide with disquieting consequences for those within when the public provision for air traffic control fails to keep pace with private use of the airways.

But the auto and the airplane, versus the space to use them, are merely an exceptionally visible example of a requirement that is pervasive. The more goods people procure, the more packages they discard and the more trash that must be carried away. If the appropriate sanitation services are not provided, the counterpart of increasing opulence will be deepening filth. The greater the wealth the thicker will be the dirt. This indubitably describes a tendency of our time. As more goods are produced and owned, the greater are the opportunities for fraud and the more property that must be protected. If the provision of public law enforcement services do not keep pace, the counterpart of increased well-being will, we may be certain, be increased crime.

The city of Los Angeles, in modern times, is a near-classic study in the problem of social balance. Magnificently efficient factories and oil refineries, a lavish supply of automobiles, a vast consumption of handsomely packaged products, coupled with the absence of a municipal trash collection service which forced the use of home incinerators, made the air nearly unbreathable for an appreciable part of each year. Air pollution could be controlled only by a complex and highly developed set of public services — by better knowledge stemming from more research, better policing, a municipal trash collection service, and possibly the assertion of the priority of clean air over the production of goods. These were long in coming. The agony of a city without usable air was the result.

The issue of social balance can be identified in many other current problems. Thus an aspect of increasing private production is the appearance of an extraordinary number of things which lay claim to the interest of the young. Motion pictures, television, automobiles, and the vast opportunities which go with the mobility, together with such less enchanting merchandise as narcotics, comic books, and pornographia, are all included in an advancing gross national product. The child of a less opulent as well as a technologically more primitive age had far fewer such diversions. The red schoolhouse is remembered mainly because it had a paramount position in the lives of those who attended it that no modern school can hope to attain.

In a well-run and well-regulated community, with a sound school system, good recreational opportunities, and a good police force — in short a community where public services have kept pace with private production — the diversionary forces operating on the modern juvenile may do no great damage. Television and the violent mores of Hollywood and Madison Avenue must contend with the intellectual discipline of the school. The social, athletic, dramatic, and like attractions of the school also claim the attention of the child. These, together with the other recreational opportunities of the community, minimize the tendency to delinquency. Experiments with violence and immorality are checked by an effective law enforcement system before they become epidemic.

In a community where public services have failed to keep abreast of private consumption things are very different. Here, in an atmosphere of private opulence and public squalor, the private goods have full sway. Schools do not compete with television and the movies. The dubious heroes of the latter, not Miss Jones, become the idols of the young. The hot rod and the wild ride take the place of more sedentary sports for which there are inadequate facilities or provision. Comic books, alcohol, narcotics, and switchblade knives are, as noted, part of the increased flow of goods, and there is nothing to dispute their enjoyment. There is an ample supply of private wealth to be appropriated and not much to be feared from the police. An austere community is free from temptation. It can be austere in its public services. Not so a rich one.

Moreover, in a society which sets large store by production, and which has highly effective machinery for synthesizing private wants, there are strong pressures to have as many wage earners in the family as possible. As always all social behavior is part of a piece. If both parents are engaged in private production, the burden on the public services is further increased. Children, in effect, become the charge of the community for an appreciable part of the time. If the services of the community do not keep pace, this will be another source of disorder.

Residential housing also illustrates the problem of the social balance, although in a somewhat complex form. Few would wish to contend that, in the lower or even the middle income brackets, Americans are munificently supplied with housing. A great many families would like better located or merely more houseroom, and no advertising is necessary to persuade them of their wish. And the provision of housing is in the private demain. At first glance at least, the line we draw between private and public seems not to be preventing a satisfactory allocation of resources to housing.

On closer examination, however, the problem turns out to be not greatly different from that of education. It is improbable that the housing industry is greatly more incompetent or inefficient in the United States than in those countries — Scandinavia, Holland, or (for the most part)

England — where slums have been largely eliminated and where *minimum* standards of cleanliness and comfort are well above our own. As the experience of these countries shows, and as we have also been learning, the housing industry functions well only in combination with a large, complex, and costly array of public services. These include land purchase and clearance for redevelopment; good neighborhood and city planning, and effective and well-enforced zoning; a variety of financing and other aids to the housebuilder and owner; publicly supported research and architectural services for an industry which, by its nature, is equipped to do little on its own; and a considerable amount of direct or assisted public construction for families in the lowest income brackets. The quality of the housing depends not on the industry, which is given, but on what is invested in these supplements and supports.

The case for social balance has, so far, been put negatively. Failure to keep public services in minimal relation to private production and use of goods is a cause of social disorder or impairs economic performance. The matter may now be put affirmatively. By failing to exploit the opportunity to expand public production we are missing opportunities for enjoyment which otherwise we might have had. Presumably a community can be as well rewarded by buying better schools or better parks as by buying bigger automobiles. By concentrating on the latter rather than the former it is failing to maximize its satisfactions. As with schools in the community, so with public services over the country at large. It is scarcely sensible that we should satisfy our wants in private goods with reckless abundance, while in the case of public goods, on the evidence of the eye, we practice extreme self-denial. So, far from systematically exploiting the opportunities to derive use and pleasure from these services, we do not supply what would keep us out of trouble.

The conventional wisdom holds that the community, large or small, makes a decision as to how much it will devote to its public services. This decision is arrived at by democratic process. Subject to the imperfections and uncertainties of democracy, people decide how much of their private income and goods they will surrender in order to have public services of which they are in greater need. Thus there is a balance, however rough, in the enjoyments to be had from private goods and services and those rendered by public authority.

It will be obvious, however, that this view depends on the notion of independently determined consumer wants. In such a world one could with some reason defend the doctrine that the consumer, as a voter, makes an independent choice between public and private goods. But given the dependence effect — given that consumer wants are created by the process by which they are satisfied — the consumer makes no such choice. He is subject to the forces of advertising and emulation by which production creates its own demand. Advertising operates exclusively, and emulation mainly, on behalf of privately produced goods and services.* Since management and emulative effects operate on behalf of private production, public services will have an inherent tendency to lag behind. Automobile demand which is expensively synthesized will inevitably have a much larger claim on income than parks or public health or even roads where no such influence operates. The engines of mass communication, in their highest state of development, assail the eyes and ears of the community on behalf of more beer but not of more schools. Even in the conventional wisdom it will scarcely be contended that this leads to an equal choice between the two.

The competition is especially unequal for new products and services. Every corner of the public psyche is canvassed by some of the nation's most talented citizens to see if the desire for some merchantable product can be cultivated. No similar process operates on behalf of the nonmerchantable services of the state. Indeed, while we take the cultivation of new private wants for granted we would be measurably shocked to see it applied to public services. The scientist or engineer or advertising man who devotes himself to developing a new carburetor, cleanser, or depilatory for which the public recognizes no need and will feel none until an advertising campaign arouses it, is one of the valued members of our society. A politician or a public servant who dreams up a new public service is a wastrel. Few public offenses are more reprehensible.

So much for the influences which operate on the decision between public and private production. The calm decision between public and private consumption pictured by the conventional wisdom is, in fact, a remarkable example of the error which arises from viewing social behavior out of context. The inherent tendency will always be for public services to fall behind private production. We have here the first of the causes of social imbalance.

A feature of the years immediately following World War II was a remarkable attack on the notion of expanding and improving public services. During the depression years such services had been elaborated and improved partly in order to fill some small part of the vacuum left by the shrinkage of private production. During the war years the role of government was vastly expanded. After that came the reaction. Much of it, un-

*Emulation does operate between communities. A new school or a new highway in one community does exert pressure on others to remain abreast. However, as compared with the pervasive effects of emulation in extending the demand for privately produced consumer's goods there will be agreement, I think, that this intercommunity effect is probably small.

questionably, was motivated by a desire to rehabilitate the prestige of private production and therewith of producers. No doubt some who joined the attack hoped, at least tacitly, that it might be possible to sidestep the truce on taxation vis-à-vis equality by having less taxation of all kinds. For a time the notion that our public services had somehow become inflated and excessive was all but axiomatic. Even liberal politicans did not seriously protest. They found it necessary to aver that they were in favor of public economy too.

In this discussion a certain mystique was attributed to the satisfaction of privately supplied wants. A community decision to have a new school means that the individual surrenders the necessary amount, willy-nilly, in his taxes. But if he is left with that income, he is a free man. He can decide between a better car or a television set. This was advanced with some solemnity as an argument for the TV set. The difficulty is that this argument leaves the community with no way of preferring the school. All private wants, where the individual can choose, are inherently superior to all public desires which must be paid for by taxation and with an inevitable component of compulsion.

The cost of public services was also held to be a desolating burden on private production, although this was at a time when the private production was burgeoning. Urgent warnings were issued of the unfavorable effects of taxation on investment — "I don't know of a surer way of killing off the incentive to invest than by imposing taxes which are regarded by people as punitive."[1] This was at a time when the inflationary effect of a very high level of investment was causing concern. The same individuals who were warning about the inimical effects of taxes were strongly advocating a monetary policy designed to reduce investment. However, an understanding of our economic discourse requires an appreciation of one of its basic rules: men of high position are allowed, by a special act of grace, to accommodate their reasoning to the answer they need. Logic is only required in those of lesser rank.

Finally it was argued, with no little vigor, that expanding government posed a grave threat to individual liberties. "Where distinction and rank is achieved almost exclusively by becoming a civil servant of the state . . . it is too much to expect that many will long prefer freedom to security."[2]

With time this attack on public services has somewhat subsided. The disorder associated with social imbalance has become visible even if the need for balance between private and public services is still imperfectly appreciated.

Freedom also seemed to be surviving. Perhaps it was realized that all organized activity requires concessions by the individual to the group. This is true of the policeman who joins the police force, the teacher who gets a job at the high school, and the executive who makes his way up the hierarchy of Du Pont. If there are differences between public and private organization, they are of kind rather than of degree. As this is written the pendulum has in fact swung back. Our liberties are now menaced by the conformity exacted by the large corporation and its impulse to create, for its own purposes, the organization man. This danger we may also survive.

Nonetheless, the postwar onslaught on the public services left a lasting imprint. To suggest that we canvass our public wants to see where happiness can be improved by more and better services has a sharply radical tone. Even public services to avoid disorder must be defended. By contrast the man who devises a nostrum for a nonexistent need and then successfully promotes both remains one of nature's noblemen.

NOTES

1. Arthur F. Burns, Chairman of the President's Council of Economic Advisers, *U. S. News & World Report*, May 6, 1955.
2. F. A. Hayek, *The Road to Serfdom* (London: George Routledge & Sons, 1944), p. 98.

AN ALTERNATE VIEW: *henry c. wallich*

In addition to free advice about growth, the nation has received helpful suggestions of another sort, in a rather opposite vein. It has been argued that we have all the production we need and to spare, but that too much of our growth has gone into private consumption, too little into public. We are said to be wasting our substance on trivia while allowing urgent public needs to go uncared for. This view does not complain of inadequate growth. But it sees us riding in tail-finned, oversized automobiles through cities that are becoming slums, finds our children sitting glued to the latest TV models but lacking schools where they can learn to read properly, and generally charges us with putting private profligacy ahead of public provision.

The general doctrine that in the United States public needs tend to be underfinanced in relation to private I first heard many years ago from my old teacher Alvin Hansen. It has always seemed to me to possess a measure of appeal. Throughout this book, I have been at pains to argue that with rising wealth and industrialized living, the need for public services advances, and probably faster than living standards. In part this reflects simply the familiar fact that the demand for services tends to expand faster than

Reprinted with permission from *The Cost of Freedom* by Henry C. Wallich. New York: Harper and Bros., 1960, pp. 165-172.

the demand for goods. In part, the social conditions of modern life are also accountable for the growing need for government services. Private business is learning to meet many of these new needs — for instance in the field of insurance. It is not inconceivable that some day we shall become rich enough to be able to indulge increasingly a preference for privately supplied services. But at present, and as far ahead as one can see, the trend seems the other way. I would footnote this reference to my earlier passages by observing that to recognize a rising trend in the need for public services and to claim that at present we have too little of them, are two different things. The more than doubling of federal and also of state and local expenditures since 1950 should drive home that distinction.

The thesis that public services are neglected and private consumption inflated with trivia has found its most eloquent interpretation in *The Affluent Society* by John Kenneth Galbraith, to whom we were previously indebted for important insights into the workings of American capitalism. Galbraith argues that this imbalance is nourished by advertising, which creates artificial wants. He sees it further accentuated by an obsession with production, which keeps us from realizing that our problems are not those of want, but of affluence. The imbalance is epitomized by our supposed tendency to limit public expenditures to what is strictly essential, while we apply no such criterion to private expenditures.

One may reasonably argue that Galbraith exaggerates the distorting influence of advertising. That would not alter the basic assumption on which his thesis rests — the assumption that there are better wants and worse wants. Scientific detachment notwithstanding, I find it extraordinarily difficult to disagree with this proposition. To rate an attendance at the opera and a visit to an (inexpensive) nightclub as equivalents, because the market puts a similar price on them, goes against my grain. So does the equation of a dollar's worth of education and a dollar's worth of chromium on an automobile. And a plausible case could probably be made, on the basis of the evolution of the species, that opera and education do represent more advanced forms of consumption.

But what consequences, if any, should be drawn from such judgment? Does it yield a basis for trying to discourage the growth of the less "good" expenditures? In a free society, we obviously want to move with the utmost circumspection. It is worth remembering that even Thorstein Veblen, who went to some extreme in deriding the "leisure class" and its "conspicuous consumption," did not take an altogether negative view of all conspicuous waste. In *The Theory of the Leisure Class* he said, "No class of society, not even the most abjectly poor, foregoes all customary conspicuous consumption. . . . There is no class and no country that has yielded so abjectly before the pressure of physical want as to deny themselves all gratification of this higher or spiritual need.

For a fair appraisal of the case against trivia, we would also want to know the approximate size of the bill that is being incurred for various frills and frivolities. Gadgets in cars and homes have drawn the special ire of the critics. It is interesting to note, therefore, that expenditures for all kinds of durable consumer goods, including automobiles, run about 14 per cent of personal consumption. The greater part of this, presumably, goes for the essential parts of fairly essential equipment. What is left for ornaments and gadgets does not loom impressively large.

Whatever our private feelings about the gadgetry in our life, we probably do well not to stress them too hard. It is only too easy for some members of a community to work themselves into a fit of righteousness and to feel tempted to help the rest regulate their existence. In an extreme form, and not very long ago, this happened in the United States with the introduction of prohibition. Some of us may lean toward special taxation of luxuries, but surely no one wants sumptuary legislation banishing from our show windows and homes the offending contrivances. A new puritanism directed against wasteful consumption, however understandable, would make no great contribution to an economy that requires incentive goods to activate competition and free markets. Neither would it be compatible with the freedom that we value.

It is the positive side of the case — the asserted need for more public services — that must chiefly concern us. One can listen with some sympathy to the case and to the account of the biases in our economy that work against public and for private spending. The pressure of $10 billions worth of advertising is a bias of that sort. The natural reluctance of taxpayers to vote taxes the benefits of which will be shared by others is a second. A third is the somewhat vague nature of many public benefits — education, welfare, and health, for instance. They are of a kind that the taxpayer himself might tend to neglect a little were he to purchase them in the market place. Then there is the peculiar relationship of state and local authorities to the federal government, which restrains public expenditures by leaving most of the socially useful expenditures to the former while giving the more productive tax sources to the latter. And finally, there is the American tradition which in the interests of freedom puts a special premium on private activity over public.

But what we are in some danger of overlooking are the biases on the other side — the pressures that work for greater public spending. If advertising promotes sales to individuals, those who supply the public authorities are not without means of their own to promote their wares. If some taxpayers object to taxes that will benefit others besides themselves, there are others who vote for expenditures expecting that they will benefit where they have not contributed. Politicians in general have not been averse to voting funds for well supported worthy causes. Vocal minorities that know what they want often can outmaneuver inarticulate majorities that don't know how to stand up for their own interests. Finally, our tax system itself has a built-in bias to encourage spending, because it collects relatively small amounts per head from taxpayers in the lower brackets, while those in the upper brackets pay a good deal. If the benefits that individuals in different brackets derive from public services are not too disparate, taxpayers in the lower brackets obviously are getting theirs at a bargain. Since they constitute a majority, they are in a position to increase the number of these bargains.

As between the forces that inhibit and those that advance public expenditures, no one can say for sure where the balance lies. But on the evidence that thirty years ago taxes of all kinds added up to less than 10 per cent of the Gross National Product, whereas today they account for well over 25 per cent, we have no reason to suspect that the expansive forces lack vigor — even allowing one-third of the present load for major national security.

Meanwhile, those who would like to see public services taking a still larger share must bear in mind two facts, one economic, the other political. The economic fact is that the free provision of public services paid for by taxation is a very inefficient way of catering to consumer needs. I am not referring to popular suspicions about the efficiency of public administration, but to the manner in which costs and benefits are adjusted to each other, or fail to be adjusted. In private dealings, the consumer purchases the exact amount of the exact product he wants, and so gets the most for his money. The taxpayer voting for certain public services has no means of securing such nice adjustment. He may find himself getting less, or more, or something other than he wanted. He has no incentive, moreover, to economize in the use of many of the services offered — usually they come to him free of charge. Our methods of making public decisions and apportioning public services leave much to be desired as compared with the neat job done by the free market.

The political problem that confronts advocates of larger public expenditures is of a different order. We return here to the point stressed earlier in this section — the tendency of our society to produce a balance of interests that impedes ready shifts among private and public resources. This applies also, of course, to budgetary expenditures. Barring some outward disturbance that shakes the balance of interests, such as a military emergency, the balance of expenditures in the budget will also tend to remain stable. If there are to be budget cuts, they are likely to cut all around. If the purse strings are to be relaxed, they are likely to be relaxed not just in one direction, but in all. That is the result of a balance which makes all interests share burdens and benefits in accordance with their bargaining strength.

The consequences, when larger expenditures are proposed, tend to be those we have often observed. The proponents of new expenditures rarely demand that all forms of public spending be enlarged. They have some particular purposes in mind. But the prevailing balance of interests works against such favors for any one group, extended to the exclusion of all the rest. If one form of expenditures is expanded, political pressures develop for giving everybody else something he wants.

The "balance of interests" effect need not, of course, be taken in its most literal sense. Obviously the proportions among different public expenditures always are shifting in some degree. Some expenditures are subject to factors that cannot be controlled, such as fluctuating interest rates or crop yields. Some have a built-in momentum, as does Social Security. And as public opinion and political constellations shift, so does the balance among public functions. Marginal improvements in particular public programs are never out of reach. Major increases, however, are not likely to occur unless accompanied by major shifts in the balance of interests. With that balance intact, the politics of the case incline toward, not "first come, first served," but "come one, come all."

This imposes a heavy surcharge upon expenditures that intrinsically may have much to recommend them. It alters the practical attractiveness of such proposals. To spend public money for a good program is one thing. To have to loosen up on half a dozen unrelated programs as a condition of expanding one is quite another.

A political surcharge of this kind can make the implicit cost of desirable programs very high. Some may argue that this cost will have to be faced. Nevertheless, it should give pause even to those who feel strongly about their proposals. In a free country, no group can expect to change the balance of interests save as they succeed in swinging some of its components to their side. Once more we must note that freedom has its price.

* * *

In the appraisal of a need for faster growth, for more public services, freedom usually appears on the side of the scales that weighs against the quickest way of attaining a goal. It has been the contention of this book that we must make our peace with that fact. We do not know what the future may bring. It may well hold urgencies and periods that would make the fact more difficult to live with. But we should also remember that long-run forces work on the side of freedom. In the long run, as wealth grows, some of our wants and needs will gain strength relative to the rest. Freedom is one of these. As our material needs are more fully met, the value of freedom will stand out with ever increasing clarity. We should find ourselves increasingly willing to pay its price.

chapter 18

manufacturing and business enterprise

MANUFACTURING

THE LEADING INDUSTRIES

The ten leading industries of the United States in 1968 in terms of value added, were transportation equipment, nonelectrical machinery, food and kindred products, electrical equipment and supplies, chemicals and allied products, primary metals, fabricated metals, printing and publishing, apparel and other textiles, and paper and allied products. (See Table 18.1.) It should be noted that the leading industry of 1968 was over twenty-two times more important in terms of value added than the leading industry of 1914, iron and steel. Even the tenth largest industry of 1968 added seven times as much value as did the leader of 1914. From World War I to the late 1960's industry continued to move West and South. The leading region in 1967 was the East North Central, which accounted for twenty-nine per cent of manufacturing value added. (See Table 18.2.) The Middle Atlantic States, which had been first in 1914, created twenty-two per cent of value added. The Pacific and South Atlantic regions each accounted for about eleven per cent of the total. In 1914 they accounted

TABLE 18.1. *The Ten Leading Industries of 1968*

Industry	Employment (thousands)	Value of Product (billions of $)	Value Added (billions of $)
1. Transportation Equipment[1]	1,884.6	79.9	33.3
2. Nonelectrical Machinery[2]	1,849.6	50.4	28.7
3. Food and Kindred Products	1,648.4	88.1	28.2
4. Electrical Equipment and Supplies[3]	1,901.8	46.8	26.6
5. Chemicals and Allied Products	865.7	46.4	26.1
6. Primary Metal Industries[4]	1,273.0	49.8	21.0
7. Fabricated Metal Products	1,369.1	37.4	19.5
8. Printing and Publishing	1,037.4	23.4	15.5
9. Apparel and other Textile Products	1,359.6	22.8	11.2
10. Paper and Allied Products	648.3	22.5	10.5

SOURCE: U.S. Department of Commerce. *Annual Survey of Manufacturers – 1968.* Washington, D.C.: U.S. Government Printing Office, 1970.

[1] Includes motor vehicles, aircraft, and ships.

[2] Includes engines and turbines, farm machinery, metal-working machinery, general industrial machinery, and office and computing machines.

[3] Includes electric test and distributing equipment, electrical industrial apparatus, household appliances, electric lighting and wiring equipment, radio and T.V. equipment, communications equipment, and electronic components and accessories.

[4] Includes iron and steel, aluminum, copper, zinc, and lead.

for seven and four per cent, respectively. These shifts in industry continued to be caused by the growing market potential of the West and South, the abundance of raw materials in these regions, and in the case of the South, a substantial supply of nonunion labor.

PRODUCTIVITY

Manufacturing productivity (output per man-hour) from 1899 to 1953 increased at an average annual rate of 2.2 per cent. From 1947 to 1970 the rate of productivity advanced to an average annual gain of 3.0 per cent. Productivity increases were not constant over the 1900's.

TABLE 18.2. *The Geographic Location of Manufacturing, 1967 Percentage Distribution*

Region	Employment	Value Added
East North Central	26.7%	28.6%
Middle Atlantic	22.6	22.0
Pacific	10.8	11.3
South Atlantic	12.9	11.2
New England	8.1	7.3
West North Central	6.2	6.4
West South Central	5.6	6.3
East South Central	5.6	5.2
Mountain	1.6	1.7

SOURCE: U.S. Bureau of the Census. *1970 Statistical Abstract of the United States.* Washington, D.C.: U.S. Government Printing Office, 1970, p. 697.

During periods of business prosperity productivity gains accelerated, whereas in economic downturns, productivity slowed or even declined. Thus, during all business expansions from 1899 to 1953 increases in output per man-hour averaged 3.4 per cent a year for the economy, whereas during contractions over the same period, productivity showed an average decline of 0.1 per cent. Not only have productivity increases varied with business conditions but they have also varied according to industry. Rubber products, for example, experienced the greatest productivity gains from 1899 to 1953, increasing annually by 4.3 per cent, whereas lumber products showed the least gain in efficiency, increasing by only 1.2 per cent a year.

THE AUTOMOBILE INDUSTRY

As noted above, the leading 1968 manufacturing sector in terms of value added was transportation equipment. Within this sector motor vehicles and equipment is the most important. The rise to this position of eminence has been rapid. Insignificant in 1900, by the late 1920's it had emerged as the nation's number one industry. Not only did it experience rapid internal growth, but it contributed importantly to the growth of other industries such as steel, petroleum, rubber, glass, and highway construction. The earliest innovations in the industry were of foreign origin. (See Table 18.3.) These included the internal combustion engine and the development of a gasoline-powered vehicle. American bicycle manufacturing provided the earliest U.S. contributions to automobile design and operation. Such contributions included pneumatic tires, wire wheels, steel tube frames, differential axles, variable speed transmissions, and ball and roller bearings. Entrepreneurial resources were provided by the bicycle and horse-drawn vehicle manufacturing industries. The former was by far the most important, providing such leaders as the Duryea brothers, William Knudsen, George Pierce, Alexander Winton and John Willys. The latter contributed the Studebaker brothers and William Crapo Durant, the founder of General Motors.

TABLE 18.3. *Major Innovations in the Automobile Industry 1860-1922*

Year	Innovators	Inventions
1860	Jean Lenoi (French)	Internal Combustion Machine
1885	Gottfried Daimler and Karl Benz (German)	Gasoline-Powered Vehicle
1891	Emile Lavassor (French)	Basic Design of Modern Gasoline Automobile
1891	William Morrison (American)	Electric Automobile
1893	Charles and Frank Duryea (American)	First American Gasoline Automobile
1896	Francis and Freelan Stanley (American)	Steam Automobile
1897	Harry Knox (American)	Air-Cooled Gasoline Engine
1901	Ransom Olds (American)	Assembly Line Production of Automobiles
1908	Henry Leland (American)	Use of Interchangeable Parts in Auto Manufacture
1909	Clarence Avery, Henry Ford, and Charles Sorenson (American)	Mechanized Assembly in Auto Manufacture
1911	Charles Kettering (American)	Electric Self-Starter
1922	Roy D. Chapin (American)	Closed Car Design

SOURCE: John B. Rae. *American Automobile Manufacturers.* New York: Chilton, 1959.

The first manufacturer of U.S. automobiles was Ransom E. Olds, who began operations in Detroit, Michigan in 1899 with a capitalization of $200,000. Olds made a car designed to sell for $650. The success of the company was immediate, annual production jumping from 600 cars in 1901 to 5,000 in 1904. Within a space of three years dividends of 105 per cent were declared. In 1904 Olds left his company after differences with financial backers who wanted him to build a more expensive car. In that same year William Durant entered the industry through the purchase of a controlling share of the Buick Motor Company, founded by David Buick. During that year the company manufactured a total of sixteen cars. Another illustrious pioneer in the early days of the industry was Henry Ford. In 1901 the Henry Ford Company was established. After disagreement with financial backers over his desire constantly to experiment, Ford left the company. It was taken over by Henry Leland, who renamed it the Cadillac Automobile Company and began producing cars of high quality. In 1903 Ford established the Ford Motor Company with the $25,000 backing of a coal dealer. In order to augment his limited capital and to secure the necessary technological expertise, he brought in John and Horace Dodge as stockholders. The Dodges made the engines, transmissions, and chassis of Ford's early cars. Ford's ultimate goal was to achieve mass production of a $500 car of sturdy quality, and when the initial backer insisted that expensive cars be built, he was bought out by a coalition of Ford and the Dodge brothers. In 1908 Ford achieved his goal of a low-cost car with the appearance of the Model T. In 1909 the mechanized assembly line was introduced, and in 1913, full-scale assembly line production was begun by Ford in his newly constructed Highland Park plant. The car was an immediate success. Ford output jumped from 8,000 in 1907 to 250,000 by 1914. One year earlier, the Dodge brothers had left Ford to establish their own company.

While Henry Ford's objective was the manufacture of one low-priced automobile, William Durant sought the production of many models at various gradations of price. To accomplish this end, Durant pursued a merger route. After an unsuccessful attempt to merge with Ford and Ransom Olds, he organized General Motors in the same year the Model T was born. In two years he acquired the Oldsmobile, Cadillac, Oakland (made by the Pontiac Buggy Company), Carter, Elmore, Ewing, Marquette, Ranier, Reliance, and Welch Auto Manufacturers, the Northway Motor Manufacturing Company, the Champion Ignition Company, and the Weston-Mott Axle Company. With the exception of Cadillac, which was bought for 4.4 million dollars in cash, all of these companies were acquired for G.M. stock. This resulted in an overcapitalized corporate structure of $60 million and an acute shortage of cash and credit. As bankruptcy loomed in 1910, the investment banking houses of Lee, Higginson, and J.W.

Seligman came to the rescue. Supported by Cadillac's head, Henry Leland, they dictated stiff terms. In return for $12.5 million in cash, they demanded Durant's resignation, $6 million in stock, and the repayment of $15 million at six per cent interest. Durant capitulated and the bankers took control. Under their control the General Motors Research Department was organized to centralize product testing. They also hired Charles Nash, who was to become President of G.M., and Walter Chrysler, who took over operations of the Buick division. Meanwhile, Durant was not idle. In 1911, one year after his exit from G.M., he organized the Chevrolet Motor Car Company to produce cars designed by Louis Chevrolet, a French mechanic. In 1915 he succeeded in producing a car which sold for $490, thus providing direct competition to the Model T. At the same time, the capitalization of Chevrolet was increased from $20 million to $80 million, and Durant began exchanging five shares of Chevrolet stock for every one of G.M. In 1916 he had reacquired presidency of General Motors. During the time that Durant was acquiring G.M. stock the Du Pont Company was doing the same thing. This resulted in Pierre Du Pont being appointed Chairman of the G.M. Board. When Durant re-entered G.M., Charles Nash resigned as President and began his own firm, the Nash Motor Company, the forerunner of American Motors. Because of his alliance with those bankers who had earlier rejected Durant, Henry Leland also left G.M. Like Nash, he formed his own firm, the Lincoln Motor Company. In 1918 Alfred Sloan and Charles Kettering joined G.M. when the latter acquired an auto parts company with which Sloan and Kettering were associated.

At this time Ford dominated the low-priced automobile market, followed by Chevrolet. Among medium priced cars, those selling for $1,000-$1,500, Buick and Studebaker were first and second, respectively. The latter's position was due principally to its introduction of installment buying in 1916. The leading luxury car was Packard. By this period most companies had introduced mass production technology into their operations. The effect on output and industry structure was startling. From a total output of 65,000 cars in 1908, production leaped to 1.9 million by 1917. The small-scale and low-cost nature of the early automobile industry enabled over a hundred companies to exist. The birth rate of firms was high. While the mortality rate was also high, a distinct sellers market existed, automobiles being snapped up by purchasers as soon as they appeared. By 1920, however, large-scale production was concentrating the industry in the hands of a few firms. In that year Ford accounted for fifty per cent of all sales, and General Motors for twenty per cent. Geographically, the industry was centered in Detroit. This is explained by the concentration of entrepreneurial resources in that region. The great early pioneers in the business, men like Ransom Olds, William Durant, Henry Ford, and the Dodge brothers, all grew up in the vicinity of Detroit. The area's existing labor and capital resources were augmented by the migration of additional resources as the industry developed. While the economic necessity of establishing large-scale operations was the underlying reason for the disappearance of most of the industry's small firms, the triggering mechanism was business recession, the first of which occurred in 1920-21. During this downturn, for example, the Lincoln Motor Car Company went into receivership, and was acquired by Ford. Another fundamental force was the replacement of a seller's market by one that was oriented to the consumer. Henry Ford failed to recognize this fact, and lost his position of leadership in the industry to General Motors.

William Durant, like Ford, was eminently successful in creating a great business enterprise. Unlike Ford, who expanded his company by internal growth, Durant pursued a policy of growth primarily through merger. In the post-World War I period he added the Fisher Body Company and the General Motors Acceptance Corporation to the existing General Motors corporate structure. Like Ford, however, he erred in the belief that a large corporation could be operated in much the same way as a small business, with one man making all major decisions. Durant's inability to delegate managerial authority to his associates and his personal financial difficulties led to his ouster from General Motors. In return for financial aid from the Du Pont interests, he agreed to resign. After an interim period Alfred Sloan assumed the presidency of General Motors, and as indicated later in this chapter, introduced modern management techniques. In the late 1920's GM became the number one firm of the industry. Walter Chrysler, who had left GM in a managerial dispute with Durant in 1920, reorganized two auto companies heavily hit by the recession of 1920-21. These companies formed the nucleus of the Chrysler Corporation, organized in 1925. The Chrysler Corporation proceeded to engage in an active expansion program which catapulted it into third place in the industry, behind GM and Ford. In 1928 the Dodge Company was acquired for $170 million. In the same year Plymouth was introduced to compete directly with Chevrolet and Ford.

The industry during the 1920's experienced its greatest growth, output climbing from 2.2 million cars in 1920 to 5.3 million in 1929, a figure that was not to be surpassed for twenty years. Due to the industry's size it was responsible for one-fifth of steel output, three-fourths of rubber and glass output, and nine-tenths of gasoline production. In addition it stimulated the construction of roads, repair stations, filling stations, and motels. The economic health of the nation, therefore, was intimately related to the fortunes of the automobile industry. The 1927-28 recession was almost wholly rooted in the automobile industry. Ford's decision to retool completely resulted in a twenty per cent decline in auto production for 1927. Although the industry and the economy recovered rapidly, automobile

Company	1909 Rank	1909 Assets (Millions)	Company	1970 Rank	1970 Assets (Millions)
U.S. Steel	1	$1,804	Standard Oil (N.J.)	1	$19,242
Standard Oil (N.Y.)	2	800	General Motors	2	14,174
American Tobacco	3	286	Texaco	3	9,924
International Mercantile Marine	4	192	Ford Motor Company	4	9,904
Anaconda	5	170	Gulf Oil	5	8,672
International Harvester	6	166	IBM	6	8,539
Central Leather	7	138	Mobil Oil	7	7,921
Pullman	8	131	General Telephone & Electronics	8	7,739
Armour	9	125	International Telephone & Telegraph	9	6,697
American Sugar	10	124	Standard Oil (Calif.)	10	6,594
U.S. Rubber	11	121	U.S. Steel	11	6,311
American Smelting & Refining	12	119	General Electric	12	6,309
Singer Manufacturing	13	113	Standard Oil (Indiana)	13	5,397
Swift	14	113	Chrysler	14	4,815
Pittsburgh Consolidated Coal	15	104	Shell Oil	15	4,609
General Electric	16	102	Atlantic Richfield	16	4,392
A. C. F. Industries	17	101	Tenneco	17	4,344
Colorado Fuel and Iron	18	101	Western Electric	18	3,744
Corn Products	19	97	E. I. Du Pont de Nemours	19	3,567
New England Navigation	20	93	Union Carbide	20	3,564
American Can	21	90	Westinghouse	21	3,358
American Woolen	22	86	Bethlehem Steel	22	3,331
Lackawanna Steel	23	85	Phillips Petroleum	23	3,057
Jones & Laughlin	24	84	Eastman Kodak	24	3,043
Westinghouse Electric	25	84	Continental Oil	25	3,023

SOURCE: A. D. H. Kaplan. *Big Enterprise in a Competitive System.* Washington, D.C.: Brookings Institution, 1964, pp. 140; *Fortune Magazine,* May 1971, p. 172.

sales growth failed to match its earlier pace, a factor which contributed to the onset of the Great Depression. The Great Depression of the early 1930's continued the industrial consolidation initiated by the 1920-21 recession. The largest firms weathered the storm while most small firms failed. The former, which accounted for seventy-five per cent of 1929 output, increased their share to ninety per cent by 1939. Thus, the era of the small, independent producer came to an end. Of the Big Three, Ford was the most heavily hit, owing to its lack of effective management. It was not until World War II that the industry fully recovered.

The decades since World War II have evidenced little change in the degree of industry concentration. General Motors, Ford, and Chrysler continue to dominate the market, with some competition from foreign producers of low-cost, compact cars and American Motors, formed by the merger of the Nash and Hudson Motor Companies.

GOVERNMENT AND BUSINESS

The trend toward economic concentration which characterized pre-World War I years continues to the present. For the period as a whole there have been two major subperiods. The first of these was the 1920's. The distinguishing characteristic of this decade was vertical acquisitions, involving a company acquiring a supplier or a customer or both. This is in contrast to the first major wave at the turn of the century which was dominated by horizontal acquisitions. This involves a company acquiring another making the same product. Another significant characteristic of the 1920's was extensive use of the holding company device. A holding company is established to acquire the stock of operating companies. By this procedure hitherto independent firms are combined under the control of a single management. This device was used to combine public utility companies operating in different regions of the country for technological efficiency and the gain of financial promoters. The second subperiod was the 1950's and 1960's. Although the number of mergers in this subperiod reached new highs—about 1,500 major mergers of manufacturing and mining companies in 1967 as compared with a little over 200 in 1960—most of them involved firms in different industries rather than the same industry. In 1967, eighty-three per cent of the mergers involved firms in unrelated industries whereas less than sixty per cent of the larger mergers between 1948 and 1953 were of this conglomerate type. It also should be noted that there was a significant shift in the composition of the top twenty-five companies between the pre-World War I period and 1970. Only a handful of the leading manufacturers in 1909 appeared on the 1970 list. (See Table 18.4.)

The changing direction of the American merger movement can best be understood in terms of the prevailing judicial interpretation of antitrust laws, the enforcement policies of the Executive branch of government, and Congressional changes in the law. In the 1920's antitrust effectiveness was vitiated by the Supreme Court, which continued to practice the Rule of Reason. This rule permitted the continued existence of monopoly power provided no evidence existed of the predatory use of that power. Thus, as already indicated, U.S. Steel, although it controlled the lion's share of the steel market, was not deemed in violation of antitrust law. Moreover, the attitude of the Federal Government during the decade was decidedly pro-business. The Executive branch deliberately sought to establish an environment which was conducive to business prosperity. As a consequence, antitrust laws were not vigorously enforced and new legislation was not sought. The onset of the Great Depression brought a further relaxation of antimonopoly policy. To many, the excesses of competition were a principal cause of the downturn. Cooperation between business firms in an industry was viewed as a means of hastening economic recovery. Early New Deal policies were based on this premise. The National Recovery Act of 1933 encouraged firms to draw up Codes of Fair Competition which often provided the vehicle for price fixing and market sharing agreements. This approach failed to bring about the desired results. After the National Recovery Act was declared unconstitutional in 1935 the New Deal turned to vigorous enforcement of the antitrust laws. A Temporary National Economic Commission was established in 1938 which extensively studied and publicized the abuses of monopoly power.

In an attempt to improve the competitive position of small business the Robinson-Patman Act of 1936 was passed. It was specifically directed at A & P, whose pricing policies were tending to drive small grocery stores out of business. The Act empowered the Federal Trade Commission (FTC) to deny a firm access to cost savings realized by its suppliers in serving it compared to other firms. To illustrate, assume that it cost a manufacturer four cents less per can to supply A & P with vegetables than to supply small grocery stores. Should the FTC consider this price spread to be too great to permit small groceries to continue in business, it could restrain the manufacturer from passing on the entire four cent saving to A & P. Similarly, even if A & P bought goods from suppliers in wholesale lots, and itself engaged in distribution of these goods to its retail outlets, the Robinson-Patman Act prevented it from being charged the lower prices paid by wholesale brokerage firms. Finally, if A & P engaged in an advertising promotion for a manufacturer's product, it could not receive an advertising allowance unless a proportionate allowance were allowed all retail outlets. The effects of these restrictions were to increase A & P's costs, force consumers to pay higher prices when buying at A & P, and preserve the ability of small grocery stores to continue in business. The continued existence of small grocery stores, however, did not promote competition. While it is undoubtedly true that in the absence of the Robinson-Patman Act small groceries would have been driven from business by the competition of A & P, large firms the size of A & P would have been encouraged to enter the market. As with manufacturing, economies of scale are present in twentieth century retailing. To prevent customers from obtaining the advantages of these economies in the interest of protecting small food retailers is to restrain, rather than promote, the operation of competitive markets.

The desire to protect the small businessman from extinction at the hands of larger and more efficient firms was also responsible for the passage of "Fair Trade" legislation in the 1930's. These state laws, which received exemption from Federal antitrust attack under the Miller-Tydings Act of 1937, were designed to prevent discount houses from underselling small stores selling such items as toiletries and appliances. They empowered manufacturers to fix the retail price of their product and forebade any retail outlet from charging less than that amount. Manufacturers who refused to enter into a contract fixing the retail price of their product were often coerced into submission by the concerted action of numerous retailers operating through trade associations. As with the Robinson-Patman Act, the results of such legislation were to increase costs, force consumers to pay higher prices, and preserve the small retail stores. A survey by the Department of Justice in 1956 found that prices were nineteen to twenty per cent higher on fair traded items in states with resale price maintenance laws than in other states. In the absence of these laws small business would either have been driven from business or forced to expand operations so as to take advantage of economies of scale. Fair Trade laws proved to be notoriously difficult to police. Moreover, an increasing number of state courts in the 1950's declared them to be unconstitutional. As a consequence, by 1970, although still in effect in twenty-two states, their impact was significantly curtailed.

Since the Second World War, the major piece of legislation enacted in the interest of competition was the Celler-Kefauver Act of 1950. The Act amended Section 7 of the Clayton Act. The original Section 7 had prohibited one firm from acquiring the stock of another firm where the effect would be the substantial lessening of competition or creation of monopoly. The Celler-Kefauver Amendment forbids the acquisition of stock or assets where the effect may be the substantial lessening of competition or the tendency to create monopoly in any line of commerce or in any section of the country. The rewording of the law substantially lowered the burden of proof imposed on the Government in proving a violation of antitrust law. One of the effects of the Act was severely to limit horizontal combinations and, thereby, encourage the growth of conglomerates.

Perhaps the most important change in procompetitive policies was effected by the Supreme Court. In 1945 the Rule of Reason was abandoned. Its demise came in a landmark decision against the Aluminum Company of America, which manufactured ninety per cent of primary aluminum in the United States. The ruling stated that the mere existence of monopoly power, whether used or not, was prima facie evidence of an antitrust violation. Another landmark was the Supreme Court's more rigorous approach in defining a line of commerce or market or both. Is shredded wheat, for example, a line of commerce? Or is it part of a larger line of commerce, cold breakfast cereals; or is it part of an even larger line of commerce, breakfast food? The broader the definition of a line of commerce or market (for example, New York, the Middle Atlantic States, the Northeast, the entire nation), the less likely is the chance of discovering monopoly or a substantial lessening of competition, while the more narrow the focus, the greater is the likelihood of finding an antitrust violation. Until the late 1950's the Court had a broad view of the subject. In 1953, for example, in *U.S. v. E.I. Du Pont de Nemours*, the Government charged that Du Pont was monopolizing the production and sale of cellophane. Du Pont did not deny this, but countered that cellophane was not a line of commerce by itself, but instead part of a larger line of commerce, that of flexible wrapping materials. The Supreme Court agreed, and in so doing, found for Du Pont. But four years later, in another case involving Du Pont, the Court changed its approach. At issue was Du Pont's ownership of a substantial block of General Motors stock. Because of this stock ownership Du Pont supplied General Motors with all of the latter's fabric and paint requirements. This, alleged the Government, resulted in a substantial lessening of competition in the sale of automobile fabrics and finishes. Again, Du Pont did not deny this but alleged that the relevant line of commerce was not automobile paints and fabrics, but paints and fabrics in general. With this analysis the Supreme Court did not agree. Du Pont was found guilty, and ordered to divest itself of its stock holdings in General Motors. Nine years later, in 1966, the Supreme Court continued its narrow focus, this time in terms of defining the market. The *Von Grocery Case* involved the third largest supermarket chain in Los Angeles, which had acquired the city's sixth largest supermarket chain, to create a company ranking second among supermarkets in the city. Despite the fact that the new company accounted for only 7.5 per cent of retail grocery sales in the area, the Supreme Court found the merger to be in violation of the law.

Paralleling legislative and judicial developments in recent decades has been a strengthening of executive enforcement of antitrust law. The

Justice Department under both Democratic and Republican administrations has tended to enforce the letter and spirit of the law.

PUBLIC UTILITIES

The changes characterizing antitrust enforcement have been mirrored in public utility regulation. Again, changing judicial interpretation, new legislation, and more rigorous enforcement have brought about fundamental changes in regulation. In the *Wolff Packing Company Case* of 1923, Chief Justice Taft of the Supreme Court defined public utilities in the following terms:

> Business said to be clothed with a public interest justifying some public regulation may be divided into three classes:
>
> (1) Those which are carried on under the authority of a public grant of privileges which either expressly or impliedly imposes the affirmative duty of rendering a public service demanded by a member of the public. Such are the railroads, other common carriers and public utilities.
>
> (2) Certain occupations, regarded as exceptional, the public interest attaching to which, recognized from earliest times, has survived the period of arbitrary laws by Parliament or Colonial legislatures for regulating all trades and callings. Such as those of the keepers of inns, cabs, and gristmills. . . .
>
> (3) Businesses which though not public at their inception may be fairly said to have risen to be such and have become subject in consequence to some government regulation. They have come to hold such a peculiar relation to the public that this is superimposed upon them. In the language of the cases, the owner, by devoting his business to the public use, in effect grants the public an interest in that use, and subjects himself to public regulation to the extent of that interest, although the property continues to belong to its private owner, and to be entitled to protection accordingly. . . .

Item 3 is most intriguing because of its nebulous nature. Interpreted broadly, it could be found to cover most major businesses in the United States today. Interpreted narrowly, it is an ineffectual statement. Initially, courts interpreted item 3 narrowly, holding in the late 20's and early 30's that employment agencies, theatre ticket brokers, and ice companies could not be properly considered public utilities. Beginning in 1934, in the landmark case *Nebbia v. New York*, a broad interpretation was pursued. The State of New York, concerned lest excessively low competitive prices lead to a decline in health standards, decreed the production and distribution of milk to be affected with a public interest, and established a milk control board to fix minimum wholesale and retail prices. In decreeing such activity to be properly within the sphere of government, the Supreme Court ruled:

> It is clear that there is no closed class or category of business affected with a public interest. . . .

The phrase "affected with a public interest" can, in the nature of things, mean no more than that an industry, for adequate reason, is subject to control for the public good. . . .

If the law-making body within its sphere of government concludes that the conditions or practices of an industry make unrestricted competition an inadequate safeguard of the consumer's interest, produce harmful results to the public, threaten ultimately to cut off the supply of a commodity needed by the public, or portend the destruction of the industry itself, appropriate statutes passed in an honest effort to correct the threatened consequences may not be set aside because the regulation adopted fixed prices reasonably deemed by the legislature to be fair to those engaged in the industry and to the consuming public. And this is especially so where, as here, the economic maladjustment is one of price, which threatens harm to the producer at one end of the series and the consumer at the other. The Constitution does not secure to any one liberty to conduct his business in such a fashion as to inflict harm on a substantial group of the people. Price control, like any other form of regulation, is unconstitutional, only if arbitrary, discriminatory, or demonstrably irrelevant to the policy the legislature is free to adopt, and hence an unnecessary and unwarranted interference with individual liberty.

This decision continues to provide the definitional framework for public utilities and their regulation.

Legislatively, the principal developments have been passage of the Securities Act of 1933, the Securities and Exchange Act of 1934, the Public Utility Holding Company Act of 1935, and legislation establishing commissions to regulate projects on navigable rivers, the interstate shipment of electricity and natural gas, radio and television broadcasting, and commercial air transportation. The first two acts provided for full disclosure of information in the public sale of securities and regulation of trading on security exchanges. Responsibility for administering the acts was vested in an independent regulatory agency, the Securities and Exchange Commission. The SEC has jurisdiction over the establishment of commission rates, the types and form of financial information to be provided to the public, investigation of financial abuses and fraud in the selling of securities, and administration of the Public Utility Holding Company Act. This latter Act regulates the activities of gas and electric holding companies. Specifically, it prohibits the pyramiding of holding companies beyond the grandfather level. Thus a company could control another company which in turn controlled gas and electric companies, but the creation of another unit to hold the first company is not allowed. In addition, the units controlled must be geographically contiguous. Accounting practices, security issues, stock acquisitions in other gas and electric companies, and business dealings with other holding companies and utilities are subject to the jurisdiction and control of the SEC.

The first Federal regulatory commission in the public utility area was the Interstate Commerce Commission, which has been discussed previously. It was followed some thirty years later by the Federal Power

Commission (FPC). The FPC grants licenses for hydroelectric power projects on the public domain and navigable U.S. waterways. Commencing in the 1930's it was also empowered to regulate the rates and services of electric and gas utilities whose operations are interstate in scope. In the case of electric utilities, regulation was extended to cover mergers, accounting practices, and the issuance of securities.

In the same year that the SEC was established Congress created the Federal Communications Commission to assume control of telephone, telegraph and cable companies from the Interstate Commerce Commission. The Commission's powers are typical of those of regulatory agencies. Control extends over rates, service, and accounting procedures. Unlike some commissions, however, the Federal Communications Commission has little control over mergers and security issues. In 1938 the Civil Aeronautics Board was established to regulate the nation's airlines. It is empowered to issue certificates of convenience and necessity, fix minimum and maximum rates, and issue safety regulations. In the Federal Aviation Act of 1958, the Federal Aviation Agency was created to oversee the maintenance, planning, and administering of the airway system and to share safety regulation with the CAB.

THE COMPETITIVE STRUCTURE OF INDUSTRY

Owing to government regulation of business the typical U.S. business firm operates in a monopolistically competitive rather than monopolistic market. Monopolistic competition contains elements of both monopoly and competition. Firms in this market produce the same product and compete for the same customers. Elements of monopoly are introduced through brand names, location, or unique services which no competitor can precisely duplicate. Thus, the monopolistically competitive firm has some ability to control the price of the product he sells. The degree of this control depends on his ability to differentiate his product or service in the minds of potential customers. For example, Crest and Colgate are both toothpastes competing for a share of the toothpaste market. But Crest is a unique product which only Proctor and Gamble can produce. The makers of Crest, therefore, might charge two cents more than their rivals and still sell their product to people because of a brand preference on the part of customers. Similarly, A & P and Grand Union compete for a share of the housewife's dollar. A & P has locations more convenient to some housewives than Grand Union, and vice versa. If the former charges two cents more on the same can of peas as the latter, it may continue to sell to housewives who will not trouble themselves to walk six blocks to Grand Union to shop. Yet A & P remains in competition with Grand Union, as does Crest with Colgate, and consequently it cannot get too far out of line with what its competitors are doing. Because it operates in the same general market, the more its sales can be increased at the expense of competitors, the more will its profits be increased. Thus, a monopolistic competitor is in a constant struggle to enlarge his share of the market at the expense of his rivals. Advertising is a tool to accomplish this end. Manufacturers spend large sums of money to tell consumers of the superiority of their product over that of other companies.

Oligopoly is monopolistic competition where a few firms dominate the industry. In this market a few firms control the major share of the industry and are very conscious of their competitors. An individual oligopolist hesitates to capture customers by cutting prices since it fears that its rivals will match its price cuts. This may result in a price war which is debilitating to all members of the industry. It also hesitates unilaterially to raise prices since it expects that its rivals will not follow suit. If this were to occur profits would be reduced. As a consequence oligopolists shy away from price competition and emphasize nonprice competition. There is also a tendency to follow the pricing practices of a leading firm (price leadership) or collusively to fix prices in violation of antitrust law.

BUSINESS ENTERPRISE

THE RISE OF PROFESSIONAL MANAGEMENT

Concurrent with the continued growth of American industry, there has been a shift in entrepreneurial leadership from the financial entrepreneur to the professional manager. The former flourished in an era when firms were finding it difficult to meet their financial needs. The financial entrepreneur was able to tap substantial sources of savings both here and abroad to satisfy capital needs. Lacking training in business management financial entrepreneurs left this area to others. Although management was often appointed by financial entrepreneurs, in time the former became increasingly independent. As the firms they managed grew, the need for new sources of external capital diminished. Substantial earnings generated sufficient internal funds to supply both dividends and capital needs. And even if it were necessary to float securities, a large company's size and prestige permitted it to sell stocks and bonds to the public without major assistance from financial entrepreneurs. Accompanying the decline in demand for the services of financial entrepreneurs was a sharp rise in their numbers. Between 1922 and 1929 the number of member firms of the Investment Banking Association almost tripled, rendering the industry more competitive and less profitable.

Until the 1920's the financial entrepreneur's decline was gradual. The stock market crash of 1929 and the "Great Depression" which followed

changed an orderly retreat into a rout. The public for some time had been
critical of the vast power held by the financial community. But as long as
the nation prospered they were content with only token action. When the
stock market weakened in late October of 1929 all eyes turned to the
financial leaders. Following the death of J.P. Morgan in 1913, his son, J.P.
Morgan, Jr., had taken over the reins of control. Although he never had
the power which his father held, the House of Morgan was still prominent
in the investment banking community. Just as in the Panic of 1907, financial
entrepreneurs accepted their leadership responsibility and set about
restoring calm in the stock market crisis of 1929. In the midst of a growing
wave of selling the leading financial entrepreneurs of the country met at
the office of J.P. Morgan and Company and confidently issued a statement
that the foundation of the stock market was sound and that many high-
quality stocks were selling at bargain prices. In their opinion the brokerage community was sound, and they advised those with cash to take advantage of the situation to buy good-quality securities. The market recovered
on the news of their statement, but it was only a brief lull in a persistent
storm. Further efforts by financiers to assure the public that all was well
had little impact. Congressional investigations of the stock market crash
further weakened confidence in the financial community. It was revealed
that firms had been advised to issue securities with little thought as to
their ability to meet fixed charges, and that commercial banks has used
demand deposits to support speculative investment activities. Evidence
of stock price manipulation and fraud on the part of many investment
bankers was uncovered. Many prominent financial leaders, including the
acting president of the New York Exchange, were indicted for fraud or
income tax evasion.

A torrent of New Deal legislation sought to remedy the abuses un-
earthed in these investigations. In addition to the regulation of security
markets and public utility holding companies, which has already been
discussed, the Banking Acts of 1933 and 1935 strengthened the power of
the Federal Reserve over the private banking system, forced commercial
banks to divest themselves of their underwriting operations, and eliminated
interlocking bank directorates. In addition, revision of the bankruptcy
statutes transferred a good deal of the burden of corporate reorganizations
from the investment banking community to federal agencies such as the
Interstate Commerce Commission and the Reconstruction Finance
Corporation.

As the power of the financial entrepreneur waned, that of the professional manager expanded. The professional manager is a key executive to
his firm. He is the president, vice president, or member of the board of
directors, or a combination of these. Unlike the industrial entrepreneur,
the professional manager is not a major owner. His holdings of a

company's stock are relatively insignificant and usually are not a factor in his appointment as the chief executive. Rather he is chosen primarily on the basis of his ability to lead. As a specialist in law, finance, production, sales, or distribution, he has generally served many years of apprenticeship in lesser managerial positions. Although he possesses extensive knowledge about a particular product or industry, his greatest asset is his ability to manage a complex business enterprise. This management skill is transferable to other lines of business or to public service. He works closely with his fellow directors and officers. Rarely does he initiate or formulate a policy by himself, this being the function of the entire technostructure. Suggestions, recommendations, and studies flow up and down the management ladder. Decisions are jointly made, and committees set up to deal with particular problems such as finance, operations, and sales. Even when members of the executive team make decisions outside the committee structure, important matters are resolved by informal conferences rather than by a single executive.

The professional manager realizes that a logical, progressive organizational structure is the key to efficient management. Inspired by the career and writings of Frederick W. Taylor, the founder of the scientific management movement, he shares Taylor's belief that:

> In the past the prevailing idea has been well expressed in the saying that "Captains of Industry are born, not made;" and the theory has been that if one could get the right man, methods could be safely left to him. In the future it will be appreciated that our leaders must be trained right as well as born right, and that no great man can (with the old system of personal management) hope to compete with a number of ordinary men who have been properly organized so as efficiently to cooperate. In the past the man has been first; in the future the system must be first. This in no sense, however, implies that great men are not needed. On the contrary, the first object of any good system must be that of developing first class men; and under systematic management the best man rises to the top more certainly and more rapidly than ever before.[1]

He is also aware that the management process should be periodically reviewed. Outside specialists are called in to evaluate the present organizational structure and make suggestions for improvement. Refinements are sought in the processing and analysis of data. Advances in technology and communication are applied to help solve management problems.

According to classical economic theory, the entrepreneur's goal is to maximize profits. In the case of the merchant, industrial, and financial entrepreneur this was the primary objective. However, the professional manager's interest in profits is tempered by his desire to assure the stability of the firm. Abnormally high profits in terms of the company's past performance, or in relationship to other firms in the industry, may encourage excessive wage demands by organized labor, entry by new firms, and public criticism. If a company is performing satisfactorily, it is likely that the professional management team will prefer to "play it safe." Few are willing to do anything which might jeopardize their present position in a company. John Kenneth Galbraith in his book *The New Industrial State* argues that the growth and perpetuation of the large corporation is the principal goal of professional managers (the technostructure). In the reading at the end of this chapter, Robert M. Solow summarizes and attacks the Galbraith thesis.

The professional manager has considerably less freedom of action than his predecessor entrepreneurs. Every major area in which he operates is restricted or influenced in some way by federal, state, and local laws. Regulating commissions police business in such critical areas as mergers and consolidations, pricing, financing, accounting procedures, and advertising. Since most companies of any size are unionized, wages, hours of work, conditions of work, hiring, firing, transfer policies, and the like are jointly determined by management and labor. In addition, many professional managers believe that they have responsibilities beyond those imposed by law or a union contract. As managers of wealthy, powerful companies they feel obliged to conduct themselves and their business in such a way as to foster the welfare of all society. Business decisions are seldom made solely in the interest of the stockholders. The impact on employees, consumers, the community, and the economy are also to be assessed. Furthermore, the corporation and its leaders play an active role in politics, education, and other areas of vital concern to a democratic society. To what extent these policies are encouraged by the fear of greater governmental control is difficult to say. Also, it is difficult to know what weight is given to these outside interests. How much should a firm allow the interests of its employees or the community to intrude on the profits of its owners? There are those, like Fredrick Hayek and Milton Friedman, who argue that business has only one social responsibility, that is to earn maximum profits. If corporations assume responsibilities other than making profits, then they may be courting government intervention to oversee or assume what is really a governmental function.

Despite the professional manager's weak ownership position he is in firm control of his company. The size of the modern corporation has resulted in the separation of ownership and control. Most stockholders view their holdings as an investment rather than ownership. They do not wish to participate actively in the running of the business. Even if they wished to they would be in no position to do so. When they are dissatisfied with management they are likely to sell their shares rather than take action to replace company officials. And how does the average stockholder judge the performance of present management? The company may be mismanaged, but because of its established position still be earning moderate profits, at least enough together with accumulated reserves to continue its regular dividend distribution. Even when it is obvious that something is wrong it is quite difficult to unseat those in control. Only a small percentage of stockholders attends the annual meeting where directors are elected. The great majority vote by proxies solicited by the current management. The solicitation of opposing proxies is quite expensive. In effect, any stockholder wishing to unseat an encumbent management finds it necessary to combat the resources of the very firm he owns.

ALFRED P. SLOAN

The professional manager is less colorful than earlier entrepreneurs. He is a member of a management team and his success and failures are collectively shared. For this reason his name is not as familiar as those of industrial and financial entrepreneurs. If a representative group of economic historians was to select the top ten management entrepreneurs, the lists would be somewhat different. However, there would be one name which would appear on all lists, that of Alfred P. Sloan. Armed with a B.S. degree in electrical engineering from the Massachusetts Institute of Technology, Alfred Sloan began his career in 1895 working for a small producer of antifriction bearings, the Hyatt Roller Bearing Company of New Jersey. The business was badly managed and from week to week it was questionable whether it would survive. Sloan became discouraged and left but soon returned at his father's request. Shortly thereafter he and Charles Kettering assumed control of the firm. The two young executives made good although the business continued to struggle for some time. Only when Hyatt began to receive orders from the fast growing automobile industry did the company begin to earn significant profits. In 1916 Hyatt was sold to W.C. Durant. Hyatt was combined with other parts and accessory firms to form United Motors, with Sloan as its president. In 1918, when United Motors was absorbed by GM, Sloan became a GM director and vice president. As discussed earlier, Durant was forced to leave GM during the 1920-21 recession. Pierre S. Du Pont, head of the Du Pont family, agreed to become president until a suitable successor could be found. In 1923 Sloan succeeded Du Pont and remained General Motor's chief executive until 1946; thereafter, until 1956, he was chairman of the Board of Directors.

Sloan, shortly after joining GM, had conducted a study of the company. His recommendations ultimately became the foundation for the modern General Motors organization. The key to the plan was decentralization with coordinated control. Each division was given a strong management team with considerable discretionary power. Central management, supported by an extensive staff, coordinated activities of the several divisions and made broad policy decisions. The plan called for regular consultation between central management, their staff, and the divisions. Central management did not simply give orders to the divisions, it attempted to sell them its ideas. In turn the divisions were encouraged to develop new techniques in engineering, styling, and the like. Any innovations, however, had to be consistent with the company's general policies. All major policy decisions were joint decisions. Ideally, all those affected and concerned shared in the responsibility of decision making. Sloan was careful to make a distinction between policy and administration. A group may make policies, but only individuals can administer policies. He proposed that in this area the president should have the authority. When Sloan assumed the presidency in 1923 GM was firmly in the control of the Du Pont Family and other financial interests, including J.P. Morgan and Company. At that time the Du Pont's owned almost thirty per cent of the common stock. Their control was exercised principally through the finance committee, which not only supervised the financial and accounting departments, but also determined broad company policy. Sloan objected particularly to the finance committee's role in administration. This he felt was clearly the function of the executive committee, and over the years he fought for an elimination of the overlapping jurisdictions. In time his suggestion for combining the finance and executive committee into a single policy committee, and allowing an administrative committee to deal exclusively with the execution of that policy was accepted. Thereafter the financial entrepreneur's influence in GM waned. The Du Pont directors were quite unhappy about this and persistently petitioned Sloan to re-establish the finance committee. Sloan, just as steadfastly, refused.

Alfred Sloan regarded himself as a representative of both management and the shareholder. Individually, he was one of the largest owners of General Motors, although he never owned more than about one per cent of the common stock. As the chief executive of a giant corporation he recognized that his responsibility went beyond the interest of the owners. In his own words:

> Industrial management must expand its horizon of responsibility. It must recognize that it can no longer confine its activities to the mere production of goods and services. It must consider the impact of its operations on the economy as a whole in relation to the social and economic welfare of the entire community. For years I have preached this philosophy. Those charged with great industrial responsibility must become industrial statesmen. Again we see the scientific approach is essential, because industrial progress becomes possible only as the whole community can support it by its own progress. It becomes a partnership relationship in a common cause.[2]

NOTES

1. Frederick W. Taylor. *Principles of Scientific Management.* New York: Harper and Bros., 1913, pp. 6-7.
2. Alfred P. Sloan. *Adventures of a White Collar Man.* New York: Doubleday, Doran and Co., Inc., 1941, pp. 145-5.

SELECTED REFERENCES

1. A. A. Berle, Jr. and Gardner C. Means. *The Modern Corporation and Private Property.* New York: Macmillan, 1932.
2. Thomas C. Cochran. *The American Business System.* Cambridge: Harvard University Press, 1957.
3. Corwin D. Edwards. *Big Business and the Policy of Competition.* New York: McGraw Hill, 1956.
4. John K. Galbraith. *The New Industrial State.* New York: Houghton-Mifflin, 1967.
5. Allan Nevins. *Ford: The Times, the Man, the Company.* New York: Charles Scribner's Sons, 1954.
6. John B. Rae. *American Automobile Manufacturers.* New York: Chilton, 1959.
7. Alfred P. Sloan, Jr. *My Years With General Motors.* New York: Doubleday, 1964.

reading

what is the principal goal
of big business?

robert m. solow

More than once in the course of his new book Professor Galbraith takes the trouble to explain to the reader why its message will not be enthusiastically received by other economists. Sloth, stupidity, and vested interest in ancient ideas all play a part, perhaps also a wish — natural even in tourist-class passengers — not to rock the boat. Professor Galbraith is too modest to mention yet another reason, a sort of jealousy, but I think it is a real factor. Galbraith is, after all something special. His books are not only widely read, but actually enjoyed. He is a public figure of some significance; he shares with William McChesney Martin the power to shake stock prices by simply uttering nonsense. He is known and attended to all over the world. He mingles with the Beautiful People; for all I know, he may actually be a Beautiful Person himself. It is no wonder that the pedestrian economist feels for him an uneasy mixture of envy and disdain.

There is also an outside possibility that the profession will ignore *The New Industrial State* (Houghton, Mifflin) because it finds the ideas more or less unhelpful. The world can be divided into big-thinkers and little-thinkers. The difference is illustrated by the old story of the couple who had achieved an agreeable division of labor. She made the unimportant decisions: what job he should take, where they should live, how to bring up the children. He made the important decisions: what to do about Jerusalem, whether China should be admitted to the United Nations, how to deal with crime in the streets. Economists are determined little-thinkers. They want to know what will happen to the production of houses and auto-

Reprinted with permission from "The New Industrial State or Son of Affluence" by Robert M. Solow, in *The Public Interest*, No. 9 (Fall 1967), pp. 100-108.

mobiles in 1968 if Congress votes a 10 percent surcharge on personal and corporate tax bills, and what will happen if Congress does not. They would like to be able to predict the course of the Wholesale Price Index and its components, and the total of corporate profits by industry. They are not likely to be much helped or hindered in these activities by Professor Galbraith's view of Whither We are Trending.

Professor Galbraith makes an eloquent case for big-thinking, and he has a point. Little-thinking can easily degenerate into mini-thinking or even into hardly thinking at all. Even if it does not, too single-minded a focus on how the parts of the machine work may lead to a careful failure ever to ask whether the machine itself is pointed in the right direction. On the other side, Professor Galbraith gingerly pays tribute to the little-thinkers whose work he has used, but it is evident that he has been exposed only very selectively to the relevant literature. There is no point squabbling over this: big-think and little-think are different styles, and the difference between them explains why this book will have more currency outside the economics profession than in it. It is a book for the dinner table not for the desk.

I shall try to summarize the main steps in Galbraith's argument, and shall then return to discuss them, one by one.

(1) The characteristic form of organization in any modern industrial society is not the petty firm but the giant corporation, usually producing many different things, and dominating the market for most of them. Nor is this mere accident. The complicated nature of modern technology and the accompanying need for the commitment of huge sums of capital practically demand that industry be organized in large firms.

(2) With few exceptions, the giant corporation is in no sense run by its owners, the common stockholders. The important decisions are made — have to be made — by a bureaucracy, organized in a series of overlapping and interlocking committees. The board of directors is only the tip of an iceberg that extends down as far as technicians and department managers. The members of the bureaucracy are all experts in something, possibly in management itself. Galbraith calls them the "technostructure," but that awkward word is probably a loser.

(3) It is the nature of the highly-capitalized bureaucratically controlled corporation to avoid risk. The modern business firm is simply not willing to throw itself on the mercy of the market. Instead, it achieves certainty and continuity in the supply of materials by integrating backward to produce its own, in the supply of capital by financing itself out of retained earnings, in the supply of labor by bringing the unions into the act. It eliminates uncertainty on the selling side by managing the consumer, by inducing him, through advertising and more subtle methods of salesmanship, to buy what the corporation wants to sell at the price it wants to

charge. The major risk of general economic fluctuations is averted by encouraging the government in programs of economic stabilization.

(4) It would be asking much too much of human nature to expect that the bureaucracy should manage the firm simply in the interests of the stockholders. There is, therefore, no presumption that the modern firm seeks the largest possible profit. Nor does it. The firm's overriding goal is its own survival and autonomy; for security it requires a certain minimum of profit and this it will try to achieve. Security thus assured, the firm's next most urgent goal is the fastest possible growth of sales. (Since firms grow by reinvesting their earnings, this goal is not independent of profits; nevertheless, once the minimum target in profits is achieved, the modern firm will expand its sales even at the expense of its profits.) There are two lesser goals: a rising dividend rate, presumably to keep the animals from getting restless, and the exercise of technological virtuosity.

(5) Modern industry produces mainly things, and it wishes to grow. Everyone will be happier if everyone believes that a growing production of things is the main object of the national life. People will be happier because that is what they in fact get, and the bureaucracy will be happier because they can feel that they serve the national purpose. This belief has been widely inculcated, but it takes effort really to believe it, because American society already has more things than it knows what to do with.

(6) The key resource in the modern industrial state is organized intelligence, especially scientific and managerial intelligence. One of the important things the government does to support the system is the extension of education to provide a supply of recruits for the bureaucracy, and the subsidization of scientific and technological research to provide something interesting for them to do. What Galbraith calls the "scientific and educational estate" therefore acquires a certain moral authority and even mundane power in the society. This is an important circumstance, because the scientific and educational estate — at least its youngest members — can see through the cult of the GNP and observe that it slights the claims of leisure, art, culture, architectural design, and even the innocent enjoyment of nature. Here is the most promising source of social change and of a rather more attractive national style of life.

There is a lot more in the book, much of it full of insight and merriment, but the main logic of the argument seems to be roughly as I have stated it.

It may be unjust and pointless to consider the degree of literal truth of each of the assertions that make up this argument. One would hardly discuss *Gulliver's Travels* by debating whether there really are any little people, or criticize the *Grande Jatte* because objects aren't made up of tiny dots. Nevertheless, it may help to judge the truth of Galbraith's big picture if one has some idea about the accuracy of the details. So, at the risk of judging big-think by the standards of little-think, I proceed.

(1) Professor Galbraith is right that modern economics has not really come to terms with the large corporation. Specialists in industrial organization do measure and describe and ponder the operations of the very large firm. Occasionally some of these specialists propound theories of their financial or investment or pricing behavior. It cannot be said that any of these theories has yet been so successful as to command widespread assent. Perhaps for that reason, much economic analysis, when it is not directly concerned with the behavior of the individual firm, proceeds as if the old model of the centralized profit-maximizing firm were a good enough approximation to the truth to serve as a description of behavior in the large. But this is not always done naively or cynically. Professor Galbraith is not the first person to have discovered General Motors. Most close students of industrial investment or pricing do make room in their statistical behavior equations for behavior that is neither perfectly competitive nor simply monopolistic. (The long debate over the incidence of the corporate profits tax hardly suggests universal reliance on any simple model.)

There is, after all, a moderate amount of economic activity that is not carried on by General Motors, or by the 100 largest or 500 largest corporations. In fact, only about 55 percent of the Gross National Product originates in nonfinancial corporations at all. Not nearly all of that is generated by the giant corporations (of course, some financial corporations are among the giants). Nor is it entirely clear which way the wind is blowing. The giant corporation is preeminently a phenomenon of manufacturing industry and public utilities; it plays a much less important role in trade and services. If, as seems to be in the cards, the trade and service sectors grow relative to the total, the scope of the large corporation may be limited. Alternatively, big firms may come to play a larger role in industries that have so far been carried on at small scale.

Enough has been said to suggest that it is unlikely that the economic system can usefully be described either as General Motors writ larger or as the family farm writ everywhere. This offers at least a hint that it will behave like neither extreme. In any case, counting noses or assets and recounting anecdotes are not to the point. What is to the point is a "model" — a simplified description — of the economy that will yield valid predictions about behavior.

(2) The "separation of ownership from control" of the modern corporation is not a brand new idea. It is to be found in Veblen's writings and again, of course, in Berle and Means' *The Modern Corporation and Private Property*. Recent investigation shows that the process has continued; only a handful of the largest American corporations can be said to be managed

by a coherent group with a major ownership interest. (The non-negligible rest of the economy is a different story.) I do not think the simple facts have ever been a matter for dispute. What is in dispute is their implications. It is possible to argue — and many economists probably would argue — that many management-controlled firms are constrained by market forces to behave in much the same way that an owner-controlled firm would behave, and many others acquire owners who like the policy followed by the management. I think it may be a fair complaint that this proposition has not received all the research attention it deserves. It is an error to suppose it has received none at all. Such evidence as there is does not give a very clear-cut answer, but it does not suggest that the orthodox presupposition is terribly wrong. Galbraith does not present any convincing evidence the other way, as I think he is aware. The game of shifting the burden of proof that he plays at the very end of this book is a child's game. Economics is supposed to be a search for verifiable truths, not a high-school debate.

(3) The modern corporation — and not only the modern corporation — is averse to risk. Many economic institutions and practices are understandable only as devices for shifting or spreading risk. But Galbraith's story that the industrial firm has "planned" itself into complete insulation from the vagaries of the market is an exaggeration, so much an exaggeration that it smacks of the put-on.

Galbraith makes the point that the planning of industrial firms need not always be perfect, that a new product or branch plant may occasionally go sour. By itself, therefore, the Edsel is not a sufficient argument against his position. His is a valid defense — but it is not one he can afford to make very often. No doubt the Mets "plan" to win every ballgame.

Consider the supply of capital. There is a lot of internal financing of corporations; it might perhaps be better if companies were forced more often into the capital markets. But external finance is hardly trivial. In 1966 the total flow of funds to nonfarm nonfinancial corporate business was about $96 billion. Internal sources accounted for $59 billion and external sources for the remaining $37 billion. Besides, depreciation allowances amounted to $38 billion of the internal funds generated by business, and much of this sum is not a source of net finance for growth. External sources provided about one half of net new funds. In 1966, bond issues and bank loans alone added up to about two-thirds of undistributed profits. Trade credit is another important source of external funds, but it is complicated because industrial corporations are both lenders and borrowers in this market. I don't know how the proportions of external and internal finance differ between larger and smaller corporations, but the usual complaint is that the large firm has easier access to the capital market. I do not want to make too much of this, because self-finance is, after all, an important aspect of modern industrial life. But there is, I trust, some point in getting the orders of magnitude right. There might also be some point in wondering if the favored tax treatment of capital gains has something to do with the propensity to retain earnings.

Consider the consumer. In the folklore, he (she?) is sovereign; the economic machinery holds its breath while the consumer decides, in view of market prices, how much bread to buy, and how many apples. In Galbraith's counterfable, no top-heavy modern corporation can afford to let success or failure depend on the uninstructed whim of a woman with incipient migraine. So the consumer is managed by Madison Avenue into buying what the system requires him to buy. Now I, too, don't like billboards or toothpaste advertising or lottery tickets of unknown — but probably negligible — actuarial value with my gasoline. (Though I put it to Professor Galbraith that, in his town and mine, the Narragansett beer commercial may be the best thing going on TV.) But that is not the issue; the issue is whether the art of salesmanship has succeeded in freeing the large corporation from the need to meet a market test, giving it "decisive influence over the revenue it receives."

That is not an easy question to answer, at least not if you insist on evidence. Professor Galbraith offers none; perhaps that is why he states his conclusion so confidently and so often. I have no great confidence in my own casual observations either. But I should think a case could be made that much advertising serves only to cancel other advertising, and is therefore merely wasteful.

If Hertz and Avis were each to reduce their advertising expenditures by half, I suppose they would continue to divide the total car rental business in roughly the same proportion that they do now. (Why do they not do so? Presumably because each would then have a motive to get the jump on the other with a surprise advertising campaign.) What would happen to the total car rental business? Galbraith presumably believes it would shrink. People would walk more, sweat more, and spend their money instead on the still-advertised deodorants. But suppose those advertising expenditures were reduced too, suppose that all advertising were reduced near the minimum necessary to inform consumers of the commodities available and their elementary objective properties? Galbraith believes that in absence of persuasion, reduced to their already satiated biological needs for guidance, consumers would be at a loss; total consumer spending would fall and savings would simply pile up by default.

Is there anything to this? I know it is not true of me, and I do not fancy myself any cleverer than the next man in this regard. No research that I know of has detected a wrinkle in aggregate consumer spending behavior that can be traced to the beginning of television. Perhaps no one has tried. Pending some evidence, I am not inclined to take this popular doctrine very seriously. (It is perhaps worth adding that a substantial proportion of all the sales that are made in the economy are made not to consumers but to industrial buyers. These are often experts and presumably not long to be diverted from considerations of price and quality by the provision of animated cartoons or even real girls.)

Consider the attitude of the large corporation to the economic stabilization activities of the Federal Government. It is surely true that big business has an important stake in the maintenance of general prosperity. How, then, to account for the hostility of big business to discretionary fiscal policy, a hostility only lately ended, if indeed traces do not still persist? Here I think Professor Galbraith is carried away by his own virtuosity; he proposes to convince the reader that the hostility has not come from the big business bureaucracy but from the old-style entrepreneurial remnants of small and medium-sized firms. Their fortunes are not so dependent on general prosperity, so they can afford the old-time religion. Professor Galbraith is probably wrong about that last point; large firms are better able than small ones to withstand a recession. He is right that the more Paleolithic among the opponents of stabilization policy have come from smaller and middle-sized business.

But up until very recently, the big corporation has also been in opposition. Even in 1961 there was considerable hostility to the investment tax credit, mainly because it involved the government too directly and obviously in the management of the flow of expenditures in the economy at large. It was only after further acquaintance with the proposal excited their cupidity that representatives of the large corporation came around. More recently still, they have generally opposed the temporary suspension of the credit as a counter-inflationary stabilization device, and welcomed its resumption. (This warm attachment to after-tax profits does not accord well with the Galbraith thesis.) There is a much simpler explanation for the earlier, now dwindling, hostility that would do no harm to the argument of the book: mere obtuseness.

(4) Does the modern industrial corporation maximize profits? Probably not rigorously and singlemindedly, and for much the same reason that Dr. Johnson did not become a philosopher — because cheerfulness keeps breaking in. Most large corporations are free enough from competitive pressure to afford a donation to the Community Chest or a fancy office building without a close calculation of its incremental contribution to profit. But that is not a fundamental objection to the received doctrine, which can survive if businesses merely *almost* maximize profits. The real question is whether there is some other goal that businesses pursue systematically at the expense of profits.

The notion of some minimum required yield on capital is an attractive one. It can be built into nearly any model of the behavior of the corporation. I suppose the most commonly held view among economists goes something like this (I am oversimplifying): for any given amount of invested capital, a corporation will seek the largest possible profits in some appropriately long-run sense, and with due allowance for cheerfulness. If the return on capital thus achieved exceeds the minimum required yield or target rate of return, the corporation will expand by adding to its capital, whether from internal or external sources. If the return on equity actually achieved (after corporation tax) is any guide, the target of return is not trivial. The main influence on profits in manufacturing is obviously the business cycle; for fairly good years one would have to name a figure like 12 percent, slightly higher in the durable-goods industries, slightly lower in nondurables. In recession years like 1954, 1958, 1961, the figure is more like 9 percent.

Alternatives to this view have been proposed. Professor Galbraith mentions William Baumol and Robin Marris as predecessors. Baumol has argued that the corporation seeks to maximize its sales revenue, provided that it earns at least a certain required rate of return on capital. This is rather different from Galbraith's proposal that corporations seek growth rather than size. These are intrinsically difficult theories to test against observation. Some attempts have been made to test the Baumol model; the results are not terribly decisive, but for what they are worth they tend to conclude against it. Marris's theory is very much like Galbraith's, only much more closely reasoned. He does propose that corporate management seeks growth, subject to a minimum requirement for profit. But Marris is more careful, and comes closer to the conventional view, because he is fully aware, as Galbraith apparently is not, of an important discipline in the capital market. The management that too freely sacrifices profit for growth will find that the stock market puts a relatively low valuation on its assets. This may offer an aggressive management elsewhere a tempting opportunity to acquire assets cheap, and the result may be a merger offer or a takeover bid, a definite threat to the autonomy of the management taken over. Naturally, the very largest corporations are not subject to this threat, but quite good-sized ones are.

Professor Galbraith offers the following argument against the conventional hypothesis. A profit-maximizing firm will have no incentive to pass along a wage increase in the form of higher prices, because it has already, so to speak, selected the profit-maximizing price. Since the modern industrial corporation transparently does pass on wage increases, it can not have been maximizing profits in the first place. But this argument is a sophomore error; the ideal textbook firm will indeed pass along a wage increase, to a calculable extent.

There is, on the other hand, a certain amount of positive evidence that supports the hypothesis of rough profit-maximization. It has been found, for instance, that industries which are difficult for outsiders to enter are more profitable than those which are easily entered and therefore, presumably, more competitive. It has been found, also, that there is a detectable tendency for capital to flow where profits are highest. Serious attempts to account for industrial investment and prices find that the profit-supply-demand mechanism provides a substantial part of the explanation, though there is room for less classical factors, and for quite a lot of "noise" besides.

(5) Professor Galbraith does not have a high opinion of the private consumption of goods and services. "What is called a high standard of living consists, in considerable measure, in arrangements for avoiding muscular energy, increasing sensual pleasure and for enhancing caloric intake above any conceivable nutritional requirement.... No society has ever before provided such a high standard of living as ours, hence none is as good. The occasional query, however logically grounded, is unheard." One wonders if that paragraph were written in Gstaad where, we are told, Professor Galbraith occasionally entertains his muse.

It is hard to disagree without appearing boorish. Nevertheless, it is worth remembering that in 1965 the median family income in the United States was just under $7000. One of the more persistent statistical properties of the median income is that half the families must have less. It does not seem like an excessive sum to spend. No doubt one could name an excessive sum, but in any case the reduction of inequality and the alleviation of poverty play negligible roles in Galbraith's system of thought. His attitude toward ordinary consumption reminds one of the Duchess who, upon acquiring a full appreciation of sex, asked the Duke if it were not perhaps too good for the common people.

(6) I have no particular comment on Professor Galbraith's view of the role of the scientific and educational estate as an agent of social and cultural improvement. But this is perhaps a convenient place for me to state what I take to be the role of this book. Professor Galbraith is fundamentally a moralist. His aim is to criticize seriously what he believes to be flaws in American social and economic arrangements, and to make fun of the ideological myths that are erected to veil the flaws. More often than not, in such expeditions, his targets are well chosen and he is on the side of the angels — that is to say, I am on his side. I trust that readers of his work will acquire some resistance to the notion that any interference by the government in a corporation's use of its capital is morally equivalent to interference in the citizen's use of his toothbrush. I share his belief that American society is under-provided with public services and over-provided with hair oil. I agree with him that men ought to be more

free to choose their hours of work, and that this freedom is worth some loss of productivity.

But Professor Galbraith is not content to persuade people that his values ought to be their values. I don't blame him; it's slow work. He would like an elaborate theory to show that his values are, so to speak, objective, and opposition to them merely ideological. He would like to do, in a way, for the scientific and educational estate what Marx and "scientific socialism" tried to do for the proletariat. The ultimate point of the basic argument is that the economy does not efficiently serve consumer preferences — first because industrial corporations evade the discipline of the market by not seeking profit anyway, and second because the preferences are not really the consumer's own.

As theory this simply does not stand up, a few grains of truth and the occasional well-placed needle notwithstanding. There are, however, other powerful arguments against *laissez-faire:* the existence of monopoly power, inadequate information and other imperfections of the market, the presence of wide divergences between private and social benefits and costs, and a morally unattractive distribution of income. These need to be argued and documented from case to case. It is a kind of joke, but if Professor Galbraith would like to see more and better public services, he may just have to get out and sell them.

chapter **19**

conservation,
pollution control,
and agriculture

CONSERVATION

FLOOD CONTROL

Public concern over conservation accelerated in this period. It has taken many forms, including flood control and water power programs, soil, forest and mineral conservation efforts and, more recently, attempts to restore the ecological balance of the environment by the control of water and air pollution. Flood control before 1915 was considered to be a responsibility of local governments. It was not until the floods of 1915-17 and 1927 that a meaningful Federal program began to evolve. Following the 1915-16 floods, Congress appropriated over $100 million for the construction of an effective levee system on the Mississippi and Sacramento Rivers. The River and Harbor Act of 1927 authorized investigation of the feasibility of flood control and other conservation measures in major drainage basins. These studies — the famous Corps of Engineers "308 Reports" — revealed that the cost of flood control would be far less than that of flood damage. The Flood Control Act of 1936 following the major floods of 1935-36 authorized a national flood control program based largely on information in the "308 Reports." The Act is jointly administered by the Army's Corp of Engineers, the Agriculture Department, and the Interior Department, who have jurisdiction in the areas of inland waterway transportation, soil and watershed management, and reclamation, respectively.

Modern hydroelectric power developments have been largely a by-product of flood control. Levees are effective against floods only if their height exceeds the water level, but costs increase geometrically as height rises, and in many cases there are physical limits to height. A reservoir is an effective way of lowering the flood crest by catching peak flows and releasing them later when the river flow may be safely increased. A combined levee and reservoir system provides complete flood protection at the lowest possible cost, and is the basis for hydroelectric power generation. Reservoirs designed to generate hydroelectric power usually require more storage capacity than necessary for flood control alone. However, the economies attending the construction of larger dams, and the revenues derived from the sale of electric power, offset the higher construction costs. Major water power development was not initiated until the late 1920's and 1930's. The Colorado River Hoover Dam project was authorized in 1928, followed by the Tennessee Valley Authority (TVA), Columbia River Bonneville and Grand Coulee Dam projects, and California Central Valley project in the 1930's. In the 1940's the Missouri River Basin project was begun, followed by the Colorado River Storage project in the 1950's. The Tennessee Valley project is unique in that all activities in it are administered by one authority. In all other multipurpose projects two or more Federal agencies share responsibility. Created as an autonomous government corporation, TVA's responsibilities include navigational improvement, flood control, water power development, conservation, reforestation, the manufacture of nitrate fertilizers, and improvement of the economic and social well-being of the people served by the Tennessee River Basin. Although there is some controversy as to whether it should have been initiated or should continue to be owned by the Federal government, the TVA undoubtedly has been a significant stimulus to economic growth in the region.

In addition to building its own facilities, the government has found it necessary to regulate private developers whose power systems could interfere with navigation. The Federal Water Power Act of 1920 prohibited the issuance of licenses when Federal development was more desirable. License preference is given first to state and local governments, and then to private companies, based in part upon which developer's plans appear best adapted to utilize and conserve a region's water resources. Private licensees generally are required to pay annual charges sufficient to reimburse the Federal government for administrative expenses. The Federal Power Commission administers the licensing provisions of the Act and in this connection engages in appropriate investigations of the nation's water power resources. As indicated previously, in 1935 the FPC was given the additional responsibility of regulating the sale of electricity transmitted in interstate commerce.

SOIL CONSERVATION

Although several Federal and state agencies dealt with the problem of soil conservation in the 1800's and early 1900's, a comprehensive program did not evolve until the 1930's. Congress laid the foundation during the 1929-31 period when it established ten soil erosion experiment stations. The success of these stations led in 1933 to the creation of the Soil Erosion Service. The Service, with the assistance of the Civilian Conservation Corps, established several hundred demonstration projects, ranging in size from a few hundred to several hundred acres. In 1935 the Soil Conservation Act recognized that the continued wastage of soil and moisture resources on farms, grazing land, and forest lands was a menace to the national welfare. The Soil Erosion Service was renamed the Soil Conservation Service and it expanded its program by encouraging the states to establish soil conservation districts. These districts, which usually follow county lines, work closely with local farmers to improve their cultivation procedures and the moisture-holding capacity of their land. The Agricultural Acts of 1936 and 1938 authorized incentive payments to farmers who diverted crop land from current production to soil and range-building crops. Also, payments were made to help finance strip cropping, terracing, contour farming, hedgerow planting, pasture seeding, and farm drainage. Current farm legislation continues these programs. In 1970 more than ninety per cent of the nation's farm and range land was encompassed in soil conservation districts.

Range land presents a special problem of soil conservation. When settlers first entered Western grazing regions they found lush stands of grass growth. Although most of the land was part of the public domain, ranchers pastured their stock with impunity. Overstocking and improper seasonal use of range land was common, and native plant cover soon deteriorated and was replaced by inferior bush and shrubs. In many places the soil was laid bare and subjected to almost continuous wind erosion. Cattlemen viewed the range as their sovereign territory. Since there were no government regulations, stockmen established their own means of control, such as sequestering land containing a region's water supply, fencing in range land, and acquiring ownership of crop land necessary for growing winter feed. The extension of sheep-herding and homesteading onto the range upset this regulatory system and evoked a violent reaction from the cattlemen. Beginning with the 1870's commissioners of the General Land Office called for Congressional action to regulate the use of the public domain's pasturage area. Although there was some recognition of the problem by Congress in the Stock Grazing Homestead Act of 1916, no general control system was adopted until the 1930's. The Taylor Grazing Act of 1934 closed to settlement, pending classification, all remaining unreserved and unappropriated public demain. It authorized the Interior

Department to establish grazing districts for the use of the livestock industry. Grazing districts are administered on a cooperative basis with state authorities and local livestock associations. Each district makes its own decisions on applications for grazing licenses, construction of range improvements, and soil and moisture conservation programs. Preference was given applicants who used public lands prior to the establishment of the district. The cost of the program is financed by grazing and range improvement fees. The Act also sought to simplify the complex ownership pattern which intermingled public and private lands. Arrangements were made for mutual exchanges to consolidate holdings and to benefit conservation management. In the 1950's a program of range inventory was pursued to provide research data for a more effective program. By the early 1960's two-thirds of the 162 million acres of Federal range land had been surveyed. This area is the largest single remaining block of public domain outside the state of Alaska.

POLLUTION CONTROL

POLLUTION AND ECONOMIC GROWTH
Until the 1940's the conservation movement concentrated on the nation's rural economy. Agriculture, mining, forestry and other primary industries were the main focus of efforts to ensure the economy of an adequate supply of food, raw materials and recreational resources. However, by the end of World War II, population growth, industrial development and high levels of per capita consumption had created serious natural resource problems in most major metropolitan areas. These problems were of a more fundamental nature. The growth of industrial society had upset the balance between man and his environment. For most of U.S. history, air, water, and open spaces were considered to be free goods. They existed in almost limitless supply relative to the demand for their use. The deposition of waste materials into the environment by industry, municipalities and consumers was not a problem as long as the volume was such that the air and water could cleanse themselves. Indeed, many factories were located along bodies of water to provide a costless method of waste disposal. However, once the volume of discharge exceeded the environment's ability to absorb it, serious pollution resulted.

The market system, which remains the principal means by which the United States economy measures costs, did not adequately reflect these environmental diseconomies. Most air and water resources were regarded as being held in common. In the absence of regulation, there were no limits to the use of these resources by individuals or organizations. Nor was there any incentive to preserve their quality since the costs of pollution were not usually borne by those who polluted. The manufacturer who deposited his harmful waste material in an adjacent river incurred no expense as a result of the deteriorating water quality. It was the producer and consumer downstream who paid to restore the water to a usable state. Similarly the electric power company which spued noxious smoke and gases into the air did not bear the cost of the property damage and ill health which resulted from these pollutants.

THE SOURCES AND COSTS OF POLLUTION

Water and air pollution are the principal manifestations of environmental contamination. The major sources of water pollution are organic waste, plant nutrients (fertilizers), organic and inorganic chemicals such as pesticides, insecticides, detergents, and sludges, land sediment, radioactive substances and water heat from industry and electric power plants. The decomposition of organic waste removes oxygen from the water, thereby limiting its capacity to support fish, wildlife and recreational activities. Chemicals contaminate drinking water, fish, and wildlife, cause water hardness, the growth of algae, and stream odor and discoloration. Land sediment, caused principally by erosion, reduces stream flow and thus limits the water's capacity to cleanse itself. Radiation waste, depending upon the amount and the conditions of exposure to it may result in harmful biological effects, injury, or death to all forms of fish, animal and human life. Heat discharge may markedly affect the quantity and quality of fish which inhabit a given body of water. Up to a certain point an increase in water temperature can cause a rapid development of fish eggs, faster growth of younger fish and larger fish. However, higher temperatures may reduce the size of the hatch and increase mortalities in the development stage. Migration, prematurely triggered by artifically heated water, may place the fish at an environmental disadvantage later in their life cycle. The temperature at which maximum development occurs in each stage of the life cycle varies with the species.

The damage from water pollution is evidenced by the increased cost of treatment facilities to municipalities, industry, and agriculture, the reduced output of fisheries, and lower property values adjacent to polluted waterways. In 1965 it was estimated that the capital cost of additional municipal sewage treatment plants in the next ten years would be $20 billion. The shellfish industry estimated in the mid-1960's that pollution in tideland areas which led to the spread of hepatitis among clam and oyster beds cost the industry $45 million annually. During the same period recreational losses were assumed to be $6 billion annually.

Air pollution is a by-product of energy conversion in transportation, industry, electric power plants, space heating in homes, office buildings and institutions, and refuse incinerators. The five principal contaminants are carbon monoxide, sulfer oxides, nitrogen oxides, hydrocarbons, and particulate matter (dirt and dust). The Federal Power Commission estimated that in the mid-1960's the combustion of fossil fuels (coal and oil) produced 142 million tons of air pollutants. Motor vehicles discharged 60 per cent of the total, industry 17 per cent, electric power plants 14 per cent, space heating 6 per cent and refuse disposal 3 per cent. (See Table 19.1.) The costs of air pollution are reflected in increased health costs, and property damage. Although it is difficult to isolate the extent of environmentally caused illnesses, rising levels of noxious substances in the air have been statistically associated with an increased incidence of cardiovascular diseases, lung cancer, bronchitis and other respiratory diseases. Property damage has been estimated to be more than $11 billion annually in the mid-1960's. Kenneth E. Boulding, in a reading at the end of this chapter, discusses whether present National Income measures adequately reflect pollution costs.

TABLE 19.1. *Sources of Air Pollution (in millions of tons annually [1965])*

	Carbon Monoxide	Sulfur Oxides	Nitrogen Oxides	Hydro-carbons	Particu-late matter	Totals	Percentage of Total
Motor vehicles	66	1	6	12	12	86	60%
Industry	2	9	2	4	6	23	17
Powerplants	1	12	3	1	3	20	14
Space heating	2	3	1	1	1	8	6
Refuse disposal	1	1	1	1	1	5	3
Total	72	26	13	19	12	142	100%

SOURCE: Joint Economic Committee. *The Economy, Energy, and the Environment.* 91st Congress 2nd Session. Washington, D.C.: U.S. Government Printing Office, 1970, p. 102.

POLLUTION ABATEMENT

As in the other areas of conservation, pollution control has historically been viewed as a state and local responsibility. With some exceptions, however, most state and local statutes have lacked the necessary inspection, enforcement and financing provisions to make them effective. They have been particularly sensitive to the political pressures of industries which have threatened to move their facilities to another jurisdiction if pollution abatement laws are vigorously enforced. Moreover, the nation's water and air basins are interstate in character and cannot be effectively regulated by a single local or state authority. Massachusetts, in 1860, was the first to establish a Department of Public Health. The Department as part of its responsibilties conducted studies of water pollution. In 1886, Massachusetts established a laboratory for pollution control on the Merrimack River and enacted a strict water pollution control law. The Merrimack was a source of power as well as water for three major industries in the area — textiles, leather and paper. These industries utilized the River for the deposit of their waste materials. They became alarmed lest the 1886 statute would adversely affect their profits and spearheaded an effort to seek exemption from the law. In 1887 the Massachusetts legislation exempted the Merrimack River from pollution control. This exemption was not removed until 1946. Recognition by the states that water pollution problems required interstate cooperation led to the establishment of several regional control agencies after World War II. Political, jurisdictional and funding problems, however, limited their effectiveness.

Federal efforts to limit pollution date from 1890 with the passage of the Rivers and Harbors Act. This statute prohibited refuse discharges which impeded navigation. The Oil Pollution Act of 1924 banned the dumping of oil into coastal water. Both Acts, however had little impact since they were administered by the Department of the Army which had neither the interest nor the personnel to deal with the problem effectively. It was not until the passage of the Water Pollution Control Act of 1948 that an effective abatement program was launched on the Federal level. For the first time the Government had the authority to require the elimination of waste discharges in interstate waterways. In addition it authorized technical and financial aid to states, municipalities and regional agencies for prevention and control of water pollution. Matching grants were made available to assist in the construction of treatment facilities. At the same time the Act declared that the states retained the primary responsibility for pollution control. Moreover, enforcement procedures required a number of steps before any remedial action could be taken. These included the gathering of evidence that pollution endangered the health or welfare of specific persons, the convening of a conference of control agencies to draw up a schedule of abatement measures, the holding of public hearings and, if necessary, court action to enforce the regulations. A minimum of twelve months was required before there could be any effective remedial steps. Many enforcement procedures required several years before they were completed. Nevertheless, important progress was made. For example, between 1957 and 1965 completed Federal enforcement actions at ten specific locations resulted in the reduction of pollution to an acceptable level. The 1965 Water Quality Act was designed to accelerate and strengthen enforcement procedures. It established a new agency — the Water Pollution Control Administration (WPCA) — to consolidate and expand enforcement activities. States were required to set water quality standards on their portion of interstate waters and to establish abatement procedures by a fixed date. If they failed to do so the WPCA was empowered to establish appropriate standards. Water quality levels below these standards were subject to Federal abatement proceedings without detailed proof of specific damages.

Efforts to control air pollution are of a more recent origin. The first serious action on the state and local level occurred after World War II when a number of jurisdictions enacted clear air ordinances and established pollution control agencies. These agencies are empowered to establish air quality standards and to issue regulations to control harmful emissions. Pittsburg, Los Angeles, and the state of California were among the first to enact such legislation. By the late 1960's most larger cities had taken measures to control the quantity of pollutants deposited in their air. Federal action was initiated by the Clean Air Act of 1963. The Act provided for cooperation between the Federal Government and the States in dealing with air pollution. Enforcement procedures were established similar to those under the 1948 Water Pollution Control Act. Grants were authorized to establish and maintain state, local and regional air pollution control programs. In addition, the Department of Health, Education and Welfare was authorized to recommend and establish standards of air quality if adequate local standards were not adopted. In 1965 the Act was amended to require that national standards be set for automobile exhaust emissions on 1968 model cars. Despite Federal, state and local efforts the quality of the nation's air continued to deteriorate in the 1960's. In 1970 Congress passed a new Clear Air Act. It legislated broader and more stringent air quality standards. The Newly created Environmental Protection Agency (EPA) was empowered to administer the legislation. The Act authorized the establishment of national ambient air quality standards and emission standards for stationary air pollution sources (incinerators, factories and power plants) and motor vehicles. Standards for the former were to be based on the prevailing state of emission control technology. Automobile carbon monoxide and hydrocarbon emission were set for 1975 models at ninety per cent below 1970 model car standards. Nitrogen oxide emission, for which there were no standards in 1970, was set for 1976 models at ninety per cent below those of the 1971 models. The effective date of these standards could be extended one year at the request of automobile manufacturers. In addition, each state was required to submit plans for achieving national air quality levels. The EPA may impose plans on states not submitting acceptable proposals. Stiff penalties are imposed on violators of state implementation plans and abatement orders.

AGRICULTURE

THE LEGACY OF WORLD WAR I

As was indicated in an earlier chapter, the years from 1896 to 1915 were ones of substantial prosperity for American farmers. The significant increase in both foreign and domestic demand for foodstuff associated with World War I contributed to further prosperity. As farm prices moved upward in response to this growth in demand, U.S. farmers were induced to expand their level of operations. They were aided in this effort by the Federal Government, which in 1916 created the Federal Land Bank System to provide farmers with low-cost farm mortgage credit. The return of peace brought a drop in demand and a decline in farm prices. Between 1920 and 1921 farm prices dropped by more than half. Wheat, which had sold for $2.58 a bushel in June of 1920 dropped to $0.93 a bushel by December of 1921. Corn, which had fetched $1.86, dropped in price to $0.41. Despite a partial recovery of farm prices by 1925, the agricultural sector did not participate with the industrial sector in the general prosperity of the 1920's.

In an attempt to improve economic conditions, the agricultural community turned to cooperatives. Most cooperatives concentrated their attention on the processing of farm goods and their distribution to consumers. These activities accounted for more than half of the consumer's food dollar. The Federal Government actively encouraged such organizations, exempting them from antitrust law in the Capper-Volstead Act of 1922. As in the past, experience with cooperatives was mixed. In the specialized fields of dairy and fruit production they were quite successful. In contrast, for staple crops such as wheat and cotton they proved to be unworkable. The large number of farmers growing these crops prevented the development of enforceable price and market sharing agreements. Unable to solve their own problems, farmers turned to the Federal Government for relief.

FEDERAL AID

It is unique for a major sector of the economy to be singled out for such significant government aid as agriculture has received in the last four decades. Numerous reasons have been put forth as to why the farmer should be so selectively treated. First, he is typically a small-scale entrepreneur in a land of bigness. As a result, only with government support can farmers muster sufficient countervailing power to deal on equal terms with the imperfectly competitive industrial sector. Second, farming is a way of life which has made an important contribution to the character of American life. Therefore, it should be preserved. Third, farmers are victims of the vicissitudes of weather, which result in abundant crops in some years and poor ones in others. Government intervention in the market can smooth out price fluctuations through the purchase of crops in years of glut for sale in years of scarcity. Fourth, the farmer controls a valuable piece of national wealth in the form of land which needs to be preserved for the public good. Unless he is aided, he lacks the ability properly to care for the land which he tills. Fifth, it is asserted that general economic prosperity depends importantly on farm prosperity. A depressed agricultural sector could be the catalyst initiating a general economic contraction.

Even before the onset of the Great Depression, farmers were lobbying for direct government intervention to improve their economic status. During the 1920's farmers sought government purchases of farm goods to raise domestic prices, and the dumping of these surpluses abroad at lower prices. Moreover, they supported high tariffs on foreign agricultural imports to bolster domestic prices. On two occasions bills were passed by Congress which provided export subsidization only to be vetoed by the President. The Farm Bloc was successful, however, in effecting direct Federal intervention in the agricultural market in 1929. The Agricultural Marketing Act of that year organized cooperatives for the specific purpose of purchasing surplus farm products. These cooperatives were financed by a newly created Federal Farm Board capitalized at half a billion dollars. In theory, this sum constituted a revolving fund which was to be used to purchase farm products in years of excess production for resale in years of shortage. In practice, years of shortage never occurred and the Federal Farm Board's resources were quickly exhausted.

The New Deal extended Federal assistance by regulating the supply as well as the demand for agricultural goods. The Agricultural Adjustment Act of 1933 instituted acreage controls for basic crops. Farmers received payments in proportion to the acreage taken out of cultivation. A tax levied on the processors of farm goods, a group which the farmer had long felt was reaping most of the profits from farm sales, provided revenue to pay the farmers. When the Supreme Court declared this tax unconstitutional in 1936, payments for acreage restriction were tied to soil conservation. If acreage restriction proved inadequate, the New Deal's Commodity Credit Corporation stood ready to boost demand for farm output by buying up surpluses for storage. This was achieved through the mechanism of non recourse loans. Based on what was held to be a fair value for an expected crop, loans were made with the crop serving as collateral. If the crop could not be sold at this fair value, the Federal Government would take possession of it and the farmer's loan obligation would be cancelled. The determination of a fair price for farm goods was calculated from the ratio of prices paid by and to farmers in the years 1910-1914, a period of rising farm prices and agricultural prosperity. This is known as the concept of parity. Ordinarily, the Government committed itself to supporting farm prices at some percentage of parity. To illustrate, assume the Government agrees to support wheat prices at ninety per cent of parity and that a bushel of wheat sold for a dollar from 1910-1914. Also, assume that a market basket of non farm goods averaged $2 in the same years. If the latter doubled in price by the mid-1930's, the concept of parity decreed that the farmer should be guaranteed $1.80 a bushel (ninety per cent of $2). If this price was not available in the market place the farmer could secure a non payable loan from the Commodity Credit Corporation at the support price. During World War II, when the demand for farm goods rose significantly, the Commodity Credit Corporation was able to sell the surpluses accumulated during the 1930's. Moreover, acreage restrictions were dropped on all crops except tobacco and potatoes.

Agriculture returned to a depressed economic condition following the end of the war despite the fact that the economy at large experienced full employment and renewed economic growth. Thus, the need for Federal support continued. A number of efforts have been made since the war to modify Federal intervention in the agricultural sector. These include efforts to introduce more of the free market in the determination of agricultural prices, redistribute Federal assistance from wealthy to poorer farmers, and ship surpluses to the populations of less developed countries. For example, attempts were made to alter the base period for the determination of parity prices so as to include any recent ten-year period. This was designed to correct a defect of the original parity formula which failed adequately to reflect basic changes in consumer demand during the several decades since its inception. In addition, the policy of rigid price supports at ninety per cent was abandoned in favor of a more flexible formula. If overproduction occurred in a particular crop, price support could be dropped by the Department of Agriculture to as low as seventy-five per cent of parity.

STRUCTURAL CHANGES IN AGRICULTURE

Total farm population, employment, and the number of farms continued to grow through World War I. (See Table 19.2.) Thereafter they declined. Farm population, which stood at 32 million in 1920, steadily declined, except for a brief upsurge during the 1930's as many unemployed urban dwellers returned to the farm homes of their childhood. By 1970 the farm population had declined to 9.7 million, less than a third of its 1920 level. During this period farm population as a percentage of total population fell sharply, from thirty per cent to under five per cent. The changes in farm population were mirrored in farm employment. In 1920 one worker out of four was employed in agriculture. By 1970 less than one in twenty were in agriculture. The number of farms declined by more than fifty per cent, from 6.5 million to 2.9 million. Agriculture, as a percentage of national income, which was relatively stable from the late 1890's to World War I also declined after 1920. (See Figure 19.1.)

The ability of a shrinking farm sector to feed and clothe an expanding U.S. population with a rapidly rising standard of living is due to increases in agricultural productivity. In 1920 one farmer produced enough output to supply eight people. By 1950 the same farmer produced enough to

TABLE 19.2. *Farms, Farm Population, and Land in Cultivation 1915–1970*

Year	Number of Farms (millions)	Farm Population (millions)	Farm Population as a Percentage of Total Population	Acreage Per Farm
1915	6.5	—	—	140
1920	6.5	32.0	30.1%	147
1925	6.4	31.2	27.0	143
1930	6.3	30.4	24.9	151
1935	6.8	32.2	25.3	155
1940	6.1	30.5	23.2	167
1945	5.9	24.4	17.5	191
1950	5.4	23.0	15.3	213
1955	4.7	19.1	11.6	258
1960	4.0	15.6	8.7	297
1965	3.3	12.4	6.4	342
1970	2.9	9.7	4.8	383

SOURCE: U.S. Bureau of the Census. *Historical Statistics of the United States, Colonial Times to 1957.* Washington, D.C.: U.S. Government Printing Office, 1960, pp. 70, 278; U.S. Bureau of the Census. *1970 Statistical Abstract.* Washington, D.C.: U.S. Government Printing Office, 1971, pp. 572–73.

FIGURE 19.1. *Agriculture as a Percentage of National Income*

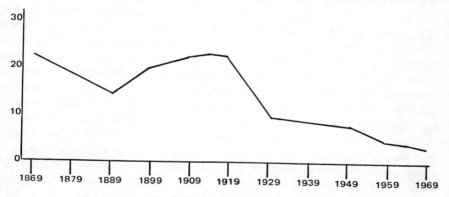

SOURCE: U.S. Bureau of the Census, *Historical Statistics of the United States, Colonial Times to 1957* (Washington: Government Printing Office, 1960); U.S. Bureau of the Census, *1970 Statistical Abstract of the United States* (Washington: Government Printing Office, 1970).

TABLE 19.3. *Persons Supplied by One U.S. Farm Worker 1820-1970*

Year	United States	Foreign	Total
1820	3.8	0.3	4.1
1840	3.7	0.2	3.9
1860	4.1	0.5	4.6
1880	4.5	1.1	5.6
1900	5.2	1.7	6.9
1920	6.8	1.4	8.2
1940	10.3	.4	10.7
1950	13.8	1.7	15.5
1960	22.3	3.5	25.8
1970	39.9	7.2	47.1

SOURCE: U.S. Department of Agriculture. *Agricultural Statistics, 1967 and 1970.* Washington, D.C.: U.S. Government Printing Office, 1967 and 1970, pp. 459, 549.

satisfy the needs of over fifteen people. By 1970 this had risen dramatically to over forty-seven. (See Table 19.3.) Between the two world wars productivity in agriculture increased moderately. Then beginning in 1940, the United States began to experience what has been termed its second agricultural revolution. The extent of the gains in agricultural productivity can be seen by comparing them to the non agricultural sector. In the period from 1947 to 1970 output per man-hour in agriculture rose at an annual rate of 5.7. In contrast, during the same period, productivity in manufacturing grew at an average annual rate of only 3.0 per cent. (See Figure 19.2.) Unlike the first agricultural revolution, which was essentially labor saving, the second revolution was land saving. In the former, increased output per worker was brought about by supplying labor with more capital (for example, harvesters, threshers, and combines) which enabled cultivation of an increased quantity of land — extensive cultivation. In the latter, increased output per worker was brought about by supplying more capital (such as fertilizer, pesticides and improved seed strains) per unit of land — intensive cultivation. This modern revolution has many sources. The twentieth century is an age of scientific farming. Government sponsored research in genetics has taught the farmer how to grow better quality crops and livestock. It has taught the use of chemicals to eradicate plant disease and increase yields per acre. The quantity of commercial fertilizer consumed on the farm, for example, increased by almost sevenfold from 1900 to 1968. Between 1940 and 1968 it increased about fourfold. Equally spectacular has been the application of electricity and the internal combustion engine to farming. These have permitted the

TABLE 19.4. *Farm Machinery and Equipment, 1910 to 1970*

Year	Value of Farm Implements and Machinery (million dollars)
1910	1,265
1920	3,595
1930	3,302
1940	3,060
1950	12,166
1955	18,595
1960	22,344
1965	25,522
1970	34,299

SOURCE: U.S. Bureau of the Census. *Historical Statistics of the United States Colonial Times to 1957.* Washington, D.C.: U.S. Government Printing Office, 1960, pp. 284-85; U.S. Bureau of the Census. *1970 Statistical Abstract of the United States.* Washington, D.C.: U.S. Government Printing Office, 1971, p. 579.

FIGURE 19.2. *Farm and Nonfarm Productivity 1947 – 1969*

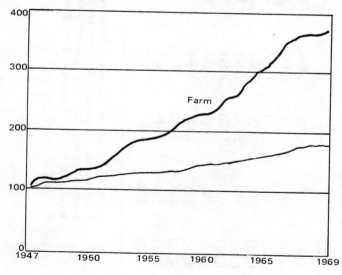

SOURCE: U.S. Department of Labor, *1971 Manpower Report of the President,* (Washington: Government Printing Office, 1971)

TABLE 19.5. *Farms and Land in Farms, by Size of Farm: 1910 to 1969 (in thousands)*

Year	Total	Under Ten Acres	10 to 49 Acres	50 to 90 Acres	100 to 259 Acres	260 to 499 Acres	500 to 999 Acres	1000 and Over
1910	6,362	335	1,919	1,438	2,051	444	125	50
1920	6,448	289	2,011	1,475	1,980	476	150	67
1925	6,372	378	2,039	1,421	1,887	440	144	63
1930	6,289	358	2,000	1,375	1,864	451	160	81
1935	6,812	571	2,123	1,444	1,945	473	167	89
1940	6,097	506	1,780	1,291	1,796	459	164	101
1945	5,859	594	1,655	1,157	1,693	473	174	113
1950	5,382	485	1,478	1,048	1,590	478	182	121
1954	4,782	484	1,212	864	1,417	482	192	131
1959	3,711	244	813	658	1,187	472	200	136
1969	2,730	162	473	460	849	419	216	151

SOURCE: U.S. Bureau of the Census. *Historical Statistics of the United States, Colonial Times to 1957.* Washington, D.C.: U.S. Government Printing Office, 1960, pp. 279–80; U.S. Bureau of the Census. *1970 Statistical Abstract of the United States.* Washington, D.C.: U.S. Government Printing Office, 1970, p. 584. *1972 Statistical Abstract of the United States.* Washington, D.C.: U.S. Government Printing Office, 1972, p. 586.

use of an increased quantity of labor-saving farm machinery and equipment. Between 1940 and 1970 the investment in farm machinery and equipment increased more than tenfold. (See Table 19.4.) Gains in productivity also resulted from an increase in the scale of agricultural operations. This is reflected in the increasing average size of farms and the decline in the number of farms. The average size of a farm, which was about 150 acres at the turn of the century, increased to 167 acres in 1940, to about 300 acres in 1960, and to 383 acres by 1970. (See Table 19.2.) In 1910 there were only fifty thousand farms possessing a thousand or more acres. By the mid-1960's there were one hundred and forty-five thousand. (See Table 19.5.)

The family sized farm which characterized the nation for most of its history has passed. The farmer today operates much like his counterpart in the industrial sector. For example, like the modern corporation he has come to rely more on retained earnings than borrowed bank capital to finance expansion. Thus, from 1910 to 1919, only forty per cent of new capital was financed by the farmer himself. This figure grew to seventy per cent during the 1920's and by the 1950's had climbed to ninety per cent.

SELECTED REFERENCES

1. Murray K. Benedict, *Farm Policies of the United States, 1790-1950.* New York: Twentieth Century Fund, 1955.
2. Marion Clawson, *The Federal Lands.* (Baltimore: Resources for the Future, 1957).
3. Marshall I. Goldman, *Controlling Pollution: The Economics of a Cleaner America.* Englewood Cliffs: Prentice-Hall, 1967.
4. Earl O. Heady et al., *The Roots of the Farm Problem.* (Ames: Iowa State Center for Agricultural and Economic Development, 1965).
5. Henry Jarrett (ed.), *Environmental Quality in a Growing Economy.* (Baltimore: Resources for the Future, 1966).
6. E. J. Mishan, *The Costs of Economic Growth.* (New York: Praeger, 1967).
7. Harvey S. Perloff (ed.), *The Quality of the Urban Environment. (Baltimore: Resources for the Future, 1969).*

reading

does gross national product adequately measure the costs of pollution and resource use?

kenneth e. boulding

We are now in the middle of a long process of transition in the nature of the image which man has of himself and his environment. Primitive men, and to a large extent also men of the early civilizations, imagined themselves to be living on a virtually illimitable plane. There was almost always somewhere beyond the known limits of human habitation, and over a very large part of the time that man has been on earth, there has been something like a frontier. That is, there was always some place else to go when things got too difficult, either by reason of the deterioration of the natural environment or a deterioration of the social structure in places where people happened to live. The image of the frontier is probably one of the oldest images of mankind, and it is not surprising that we find it hard to get rid of.

Gradually, however, man has been accustoming himself to the notion of the spherical earth and a closed sphere of human activity. A few unusual spirits among the ancient Greeks perceived that the earth was a sphere. It was only with the circumnavigations and the geographical explorations of the fifteenth and sixteenth centuries, however, that the fact that the earth was a sphere became at all widely known and accepted. Even in the nineteenth century, the commonest map was Mercator's projection, which visualizes the earth as an illimitable cylinder, essentially a plane wrapped around the globe, and it was not until the Second World War and the development of the air age that the global nature of the planet really entered

Reprinted with permission from "The Economics of the Coming Spaceship Earth" by Kenneth E. Boulding, in Henry Jarrett, *Environmental Quality in a Growing Economy*. Baltimore: Resources for the Future, 1966, pp. 3-13.

the popular imagination. Even now we are very far from having made the moral, political, and psychological adjustments which are implied in this transition from the illimitable plane to the closed sphere.

Economists in particular, for the most part, have failed to come to grips with the ultimate consequences of the transition from the open to the closed earth. One hesitates to use the terms "open" and "closed" in this connection, as they have been used with so many different shades of meaning. Nevertheless, it is hard to find equivalents. The open system, indeed, has some similarities to the open system of von Bertalanffy,[1] in that it implies that some kind of a structure is maintained in the midst of a throughput from inputs to outputs. In a closed system, the outputs of all parts of the system are linked to the inputs of other parts. There are no inputs from outside and no outputs to the outside; indeed, there is no outside at all. Closed systems, in fact, are very rare in human experience, in fact almost by definition unknowable, for if there are genuinely closed systems around us, we have no way of getting information into them or out of them; and hence if they are really closed, we would be quite unaware of their existence. We can only find out about a closed system if we participate in it. Some isolated primitive societies may have approximated to this, but even these had to take inputs from the environment and give outputs to it. All living organisms, including man himself, are open systems. They have to receive inputs in the shape of air, food, water, and give off outputs in the form of effluvia and excrement. Deprivation of input of air, even for a few minutes, is fatal. Deprivation of the ability to obtain any input or to dispose of any output is fatal in a relatively short time. All human societies have likewise been open systems. They receive inputs from the earth, the atmosphere, and the waters, and they give outputs into these reservoirs; they also produce inputs internally in the shape of babies and outputs in the shape of corpses. Given a capacity to draw upon inputs and to get rid of outputs, an open system of this kind can persist indefinitely.

There are some systems — such as the biological phenotype, for instance the human body — which cannot maintain themselves indefinitely by inputs and outputs because of the phenomenon of aging. This process is very little understood. It occurs, evidently, because there are some outputs which cannot be replaced by any known input. There is not the same necessity for aging in organizations and in societies, although an analogous phenomenon may take place. The structure and composition of an organization or society, however, can be maintained by inputs of fresh personnel from birth and education as the existing personnel ages and eventually dies. Here we have an interesting example of a system which seems to maintain itself by the self-generation of inputs, and in this sense is moving towards closure. The input of people (that is, babies) is also an output of people (that is, parents).

Systems may be open or closed in respect to a number of classes of inputs and outputs. Three important classes are matter, energy, and information. The present world economy is open in regard to all three. We can think of the world economy or "econosphere" as a subset of the "world set," which is the set of all objects of possible discourse in the world. We then think of the state of the econosphere at any one moment as being the total capital stock, that is, the set of all objects, people, organizations, and so on, which are interesting from the point of view of the system of exchange. This total stock of capital is clearly an open system in the sense that it has inputs and outputs, inputs being production which adds to the capital stock, outputs being consumption which subtracts from it. From a material point of view, we see objects passing from the noneconomic into the economic set in the process of production, and we similarly see products passing out of the economic set as their value becomes zero. Thus we see the econosphere as a material process involving the discovery and mining of fossil fuels, ores, etc., and at the other end a process by which the effluents of the system are passed out into noneconomic reservoirs — for instance, the atmosphere and the oceans — which are not appropriated and do not enter into the exchange system.

From the point of view of the energy system, the econosphere involves inputs of available energy in the form, say, of water power, fossil fuels, or sunlight, which are necessary in order to create the material throughput and to move matter from the noneconomic set into the economic set or even out of it again; and energy itself is given off by the system in a less available form, mostly in the form of heat. These inputs of available energy must come either from the sun (the energy supplied by other stars being assumed to be negligible) or it may come from the earth itself, either through its internal heat or through its energy of rotation or other motions, which generate, for instance, the energy of the tides. Agriculture, a few solar machines, and water power use the current available energy income. In advanced societies this is supplemented very extensively by the use of fossil fuels, which represent as it were a capital stock of stored-up sunshine. Because of this capital stock of energy, we have been able to maintain an energy input into the system, particularly over the last two centuries, much larger than we would have been able to do with existing techniques if we had had to rely on the current input of available energy from the sun or the earth itself. This supplementary input, however, is by its very nature exhaustible.

The inputs and outputs of information are more subtle and harder to trace, but also represent an open system, related to, but not wholly dependent on, the transformations of matter and energy. By far the larger amount of information and knowledge is self-generated by the human society, though a certain amount of information comes into the sociosphere in the form of light from the universe outside. The information that comes from the universe has certainly affected man's image of himself and of his environment, as we can easily visualize if we suppose that we lived on a planet with a total cloud-cover that kept out all information from the exterior universe. It is only in very recent times, of course, that the information coming in from the universe has been captured and coded into the form of a complex image of what the universe is like outside the earth; but even in primitive times, man's perception of the heavenly bodies has always profoundly affected his image of earth and of himself. It is the information generated within the planet, however, and particularly that generated by man himself, which forms by far the larger part of the information system. We can think of the stock of knowledge, or as Teilhard de Chardin called it, the "noosphere," and consider this as an open system, losing knowledge through aging and death and gaining it through birth and education and the ordinary experience of life.

From the human point of view, knowledge or information is by far the most important of the three systems. Matter only acquires significance and only enters the sociosphere or the econosphere insofar as it becomes an object of human knowledge. We can think of capital, indeed, as frozen knowledge or knowledge imposed on the material world in the form of improbable arrangements. A machine, for instance, originated in the mind of man, and both its construction and its use involve information processes imposed on the material world by man himself. The cumulation of knowledge, that is, the excess of its production over its consumption, is the key to human development of all kinds, especially to economic development. We can see this pre-eminence of knowledge very clearly in the experiences of countries where the material capital has been destroyed by a war, as in Japan and Germany. The knowledge of the people was not destroyed, and it did not take long, therefore, certainly not more than ten years, for most of the material capital to be reestablished again. In a country such as Indonesia, however, where the knowledge did not exist, the material capital did not come into being either. By "knowledge" here I mean, of course, the whole cognitive structure, which includes valuations and motivations as well as images of the factual world.

The concept of entropy, used in a somewhat loose sense, can be applied to all three of these open systems. In the case of material systems, we can distinguish between entropic processes, which take concentrated materials and diffuse them through the oceans or over the earth's surface or into the atmosphere, and anti-entropic processes, which take diffuse materials and concentrate them. Material entropy can be taken as a measure of the uniformity of the distribution of elements and, more uncertainly, compounds and other structures on the earth's surface. There is, fortunately, no law of increasing material entropy, as there is in the corresponding case of energy, as it is quite possible to concentrate diffused materials if energy inputs are allowed. Thus the processes for fixation of nitrogen from the air, processes for the extraction of magnesium or other elements from the sea, and processes for the desalinization of sea water are anti-entropic in the material sense, though the reduction of material entropy has to be paid for by inputs of energy and also inputs of information, or at least a stock of information in the system. In regard to matter, therefore, a closed system is conceivable, that is, a system in which there is neither increase nor decrease in material entropy. In such a system all outputs from consumption would constantly be recycled to become inputs for production, as for instance, nitrogen in the nitrogen cycle of the natural eco-system.

In regard to the energy system there is, unfortunately, no escape from the grim Second Law of Thermodynamics; and if there were no energy inputs into the earth, any evolutionary or developmental process would be impossible. The large energy inputs which we have obtained from fossil fuels are strictly temporary. Even the most optimistic predictions would expect the easily available supply of fossil fuels to be exhausted in a mere matter of centuries at present rates of use. If the rest of the world were to rise to American standards of power consumption, and still more if world population continues to increase, the exhaustion of fossil fuels would be even more rapid. The development of nuclear energy has improved this picture, but has not fundamentally altered it, at least in present technologies, for fissionable material is still relatively scarce. If we should achieve the economic use of energy through fusion, of course, a much larger source of energy materials would be available, which would expand the time horizons of supplementary energy input into an open social system by perhaps tens to hundreds of thousands of years. Failing this, however, the time is not very far distant, historically speaking, when man will once more have to retreat to his current energy input from the sun, even though this could be used much more effectively than in the past with increased knowledge. Up to now, certainly, we have not got very far with the technology of using current solar energy, but the possibility of substantial improvements in the future is certainly high. It may be, indeed, that the biological revolution which is just beginning will produce a solution to this problem, as we develop artificial organisms which are capable of much more efficient transformation of solar energy into easily available forms than any that we now have. As Richard Meier has suggested, we may run our machines in the future with methane-producing algae.[2]

The question of whether there is anything corresponding to entropy in the information system is a puzzling one, though of great interest. There are certainly many examples of social systems and cultures which have lost knowledge, especially in transition from one generation to the next, and in which the culture has therefore degenerated. One only has to look at the folk culture of Appalachian migrants to American cities to see a culture which started out as a fairly rich European folk culture in Elizabethan times and which seems to have lost both skills, adaptability, folk tales, songs, and almost everything that goes up to make richness and complexity in a culture, in the course of about ten generations. The American Indians on reservations provide another example of such degradation of the information and knowledge system. On the other hand, over a great part of human history, the growth of knowledge in the earth as a whole seems to have been almost continuous, even though there have been times of relatively slow growth and times of rapid growth. As it is knowledge of certain kinds that produces the growth of knowledge in general, we have here a very subtle and complicated system, and it is hard to put one's finger on the particular elements in a culture which make knowledge grow more or less rapidly, or even which make it decline. One of the great puzzles in this connection, for instance, is why the take-off into science, which represents an "acceleration," or an increase in the rate of growth of knowledge in European society in the sixteenth century, did not take place in China, which at that time (about 1600) was unquestionably ahead of Europe, and one would think even more ready for the breakthrough. This is perhaps the most crucial question in the theory of social development, yet we must confess that it is very little understood. Perhaps the most significant factor in this connection is the existence of "slack" in the culture, which permits a divergence from established patterns and activity which is not merely devoted to reproducing the existing society but is devoted to changing it. China was perhaps too well-organized and had too little slack in its society to produce the kind of acceleration which we find in the somewhat poorer and less well-organized but more diverse societies of Europe.

The closed earth of the future requires economic principles which are somewhat different from those of the open earth of the past. For the sake of picturesqueness, I am tempted to call the open economy the "cowboy economy," the cowboy being symbolic of the illimitable plains and also associated with reckless, exploitative, romantic, and violent behavior, which is characteristic of open societies. The closed economy of the future might similarly be called the "spaceman" economy, in which the earth has become a single spaceship, without unlimited reservoirs of anything, either for extraction or for pollution, and in which, therefore, man must find his place in a cyclical ecological system which is capable of continuous reproduction of material form even though it cannot escape having inputs of energy. The difference between the two types of economy becomes most apparent in the attitude towards consumption. In the cowboy economy, consumption is regarded as a good thing and production likewise; and the success of the economy is measured by the amount of the throughput from the "factors of production," a part of which, at any rate, is extracted from the reservoirs of raw materials and noneconomic objects, and another part of which is output into the reservoirs of pollution. If there are infinite reservoirs from which material can be obtained and into which effluvia can be deposited, then the throughput is at least a plausible measure of the success of the economy. The gross national product is a rough measure of this total throughput. It should be possible, however, to distinguish that part of the GNP which is derived from exhaustible and that which is derived from reproducible resources, as well as that part of consumption which represents effluvia and that which represents input into the productive system again. Nobody, as far as I know, has ever attempted to break down the GNP in this way, although it would be an interesting and extremely important exercise, which is unfortunately beyond the scope of this paper.

By contrast, in the spaceman economy, throughput is by no means a desideratum, and is indeed to be regarded as something to be minimized rather than maximized. The essential measure of the success of the economy is not production and consumption at all, but the nature, extent, quality, and complexity of the total capital stock, including in this the state of the human bodies and minds included in the system. In the spaceman economy, what we are primarily concerned with is stock maintenance, and any technological change which results in the maintenance of a given total stock with a lessened throughput (that is, less production and consumption) is clearly a gain. This idea that both production and consumption are bad things rather than good things is very strange to economists, who have been obsessed with the income-flow concepts to the exclusion, almost, of capital-stock concepts.

There are actually some very tricky and unsolved problems involved in the questions as to whether human welfare or well-being is to be regarded as a stock or a flow. Something of both these elements seems actually to be involved in it, and as far as I know there have been practically no studies directed towards identifying these two dimensions of human satisfaction. Is it, for instance, eating that is a good thing, or is it being well fed? Does economic welfare involve having nice clothes, fine houses, good equipment, and so. on, or is it to be measured by the depreciation and the wearing out of these things? I am inclined myself to regard the stock concept as most fundamental, that is, to think of being well fed as more important than eating, and to think even of so-called services as essentially involving the restoration of a depleting psychic capital. Thus I have argued that we go to a concert in order to restore a psychic condition which might be called "just having gone to a concert," which, once established, tends to depreciate. When it depreciates beyond a certain point, we go to another concert in order to restore it. If it depreciates rapidly, we go to a lot of concerts; if it depreciates slowly, we go to few. On this view, similarly, we eat primarily to restore bodily homeostasis, that is, to maintain a condition of being well fed, and so on. On this view, there is nothing desirable in consumption at all. The less consumption we can maintain a given state with, the better off we are. If we had clothes that did not wear out, houses that did not depreciate, and even if we could maintain our bodily condition without eating, we would clearly be much better off.

It is this last consideration, perhaps, which makes one pause. Would we, for instance, really want an operation that would enable us to restore all our bodily tissues by intravenous feeding while we slept? Is there not, that is to say, a certain virtue in throughput itself, in activity itself, in production and consumption itself, in raising food and in eating it? It would certainly be rash to exclude this possibility. Further interesting problems are raised by the demand for variety. We certainly do not want a constant state to be maintained; we want fluctuations in the state. Otherwise there would be no demand for variety in food, for variety in scene, as in travel, for variety in social contact, and so on. The demand for variety can, of course, be costly, and sometimes it seems to be too costly to be tolerated or at least legitimated, as in the case of marital partners, where the maintenance of a homeostatic state in the family is usually regarded as much more desirable than the variety and excessive throughput of the libertine. There are problems here which the economics profession has neglected with astonishing singlemindedness. My own attempts to call attention to some of them, for instance, in two articles,[3] as far as I can judge, produced no response whatever; and economists continue to think and act as if production, consumption, throughput, and the GNP were the sufficient and adequate measure of economic success.

It may be said, of course, why worry about all this when the spaceman economy is still a good way off (at least beyond the lifetimes of any now living), so let us eat, drink, spend, extract and pollute, and be as merry as we can, and let posterity worry about the spaceship earth. It is always a little hard to find a convincing answer to the man who says, "What has posterity ever done for me?" and the conservationist has always had to fall back on rather vague ethical principles postulating identity of the individual with some human community or society which extends not only back into the past but forward into the future. Unless the individual identifies with some community of this kind, conservation is obviously "irrational." Why should we not maximize the welfare of this generation at the cost of posterity? *"Apres nous, le deluge"* has been the motto of not insignificant numbers of human societies. The only answer to this, as far as I can see, is to point out that the welfare of the individual depends on the extent to which he can identify himself with others, and that the most satisfactory individual identity is that which identifies not only with a community in space but also with a community extending over time from the past into the future. If this kind of identity is recognized as desirable, then posterity has a voice, even if it does not have a vote; and in a sense, if its voice can influence votes, it has votes too. This whole problem is linked up with the much larger one of the determinants of the morale, legitimacy, and "nerve" of a society, and there is a great deal of historical evidence to suggest that a society which loses its identity with posterity and which loses its positive image of the future loses also its capacity to deal with present problems, and soon falls apart.[4]

Even if we concede that posterity is relevant to our present problems, we still face the question of time-discounting and the closely related question of uncertainty-discounting. It is a well-known phenomenon that individuals discount the future, even in their own lives. The very existence of a positive rate of interest may be taken as at least strong supporting evidence of this hypothesis. If we discount our own future, it is certainly not unreasonable to discount posterity's future even more, even if we do give posterity a vote. If we discount this at 5 per cent per annum, posterity's vote or dollar halves every fourteen years as we look into the future, and after even a mere hundred years it is pretty small — only about 1½ cents on the dollar. If we add another 5 per cent for uncertainty, even the vote of our grandchildren reduces almost to insignificance. We can argue, of course, that the ethical thing to do is not to discount the future at all, that time-discounting is mainly the result of myopia and perspective, and hence is an illusion which the moral man should not tolerate. It is a very popular illusion, however, and one that must certainly be taken into consideration in the formulation of policies. It explains, perhaps, why conservationist policies almost have to be sold under some other excuse which seems more urgent, and why, indeed, necessities which are visualized as urgent, such as defense, always seem to hold priority over those which involve the future.

All these considerations add some credence to the point of view which says that we should not worry about the spaceman economy at all, and that we should just go on increasing the GNP and indeed the gross world product, or GWP, in the expectation that the problems of the future can be left to the future, that when scarcities arise, whether this is of raw materials or of pollutable reservoirs, the needs of the then present will determine the solutions of the then present, and there is no use giving ourselves ulcers by worrying about problems that we really do not have to solve. There is even high ethical authority for this point of view in the New Testament, which advocates that we should take no thought for tomorrow and let the dead bury their dead. There has always been something rather refreshing in the view that we should live like the birds, and perhaps posterity is for the birds in more senses than one; so perhaps we should all call it a day and go out and pollute something cheerfully. As an old taker of thought for the morrow, however, I cannot quite accept this solution; and I would argue, furthermore, that tomorrow is not only very close, but in many respects it is already here. The shadow of the future spaceship, indeed, is already falling over our spendthrift merriment. Oddly enough, it seems to be in pollution rather than in exhaustion that the problem is first becoming salient. Los Angeles has run out of air, Lake Erie has become a cesspool, the oceans are getting full of lead and DDT, and the atmosphere may become man's major problem in another generation, at the rate at which we are filling it up with gunk. It is, of course, true that at least on a microscale, things have been worse at times in the past. The cities of today, with all their foul air and polluted waterways, are probably not as bad as the filthy cities of the pretechnical age. Nevertheless, that fouling of the nest which has been typical of man's activity in the past on a local scale now seems to be extending to the whole world society; and one certainly cannot view with equanimity the present rate of pollution of any of the natural reservoirs, whether the atmosphere, the lakes, or even the oceans.

NOTES

1. Ludwig von Bertalanffy, *Problems of Life* (New York: John Wiley and Sons, 1952).
2. Richard L. Meier, *Science and Economic Development* (New York: John Wiley and Sons, 1956).
3. K. E. Boulding, "The Consumption Concept in Economic Theory," *American Economic Review*, 35:2 (May 1945), pp. 1-14; and "Income or Welfare?," *Review of Economic Studies*, 17 (1949-50), pp. 77-86.
4. Fred L. Polak, *The Image of the Future*, Vols. I and II, translated by Elise Boulding (New York: Sythoff, Leyden and Oceana, 1961).

chapter 20

population, labor and labor unions

POPULATION

Between the Civil War and 1940 the rate of population growth declined significantly. From a decennial rate of 30.2 per cent in the 1870's it fell to 16.2 per cent by the 1920's, and by the 1930's it had plummeted to 7.3 per cent, the lowest rate in the nation's history. At this time many interpreted it to mean that U.S. population growth would soon cease. They regarded the 1930's as the beginning of a period of zero population growth. However, to the surprise of most demographers, population growth in the 1940's and 1950's did not continue to decline, but instead returned to the predepression level of the 1920's. (See Table 20.1.) This represented not only a refutation of the stagnationists, but a reversal of the World War I pattern when all major belligerents experienced declining rates of population increase. It should be kept in mind, however, that the 18.5 per cent rate of the 1950's was but half the rate experienced in the early 1800's, and that in the 1960's the rate dropped sharply to 13.3 per cent, the second smallest in the nation's history. The principal causes of the renewed decline may be attributed to the relatively small number of people born in the 1930's who reached childbearing age in the 1960's, and the fact that women generally were having fewer children.

TABLE 20.1. *U.S. Population 1915–1970*

Year	Population (millions)	Increase Over Preceding Decade		
		Number (millions)	*Per Cent*
1915	100.5		
1920	106.0	13.8	15.0
1925	115.8		
1930	123.2	17.2	16.2
1935	127.3		
1940	132.2	9.0	7.3
1945	140.5		
1950	151.3	19.2	14.5
1955	165.9		
1960	179.3	28.0	18.5
1965	194.6		
1970	204.8	25.5	13.3

SOURCE: U.S. Bureau of the Census. *Historical Statistics of the United States, Colonial Times to 1957.* Washington, D.C.: U.S. Government Printing Office, 1960, p. 7; U.S. Bureau of the Census. *1970 Statistical Abstract of the United States.* Washington, D.C.: U.S. Government Printing Office, 1970, p. 5.

BIRTH AND DEATH RATES

In 1920 the birthrate for the total population had fallen to 27.7 per 1,000 of the population, compared to 43.3 per 1,000 in 1860. By 1940 this figure had declined even more, to below 20 per 1,000 of the population. The reversal of this trend from 1940 to 1957, when it stood at 25 per thousand, ran counter to the predictions of most demographers. Beginning in 1957 the birthrate resumed its decline, reaching a low of 17.5 per thousand in 1968. Planned parenthood, the relatively small number of females of childbearing age, urban living, and the desire for higher standards of living were the major causes of this trend. In 1969 and 1970 a temporary upturn occurred followed by renewed decline in 1971 and 1972.

The mortality rate declined steadily from a rate of 13.0 per thousand of population in 1920 to 9.4 per thousand in 1970. In 1920 the life expectancy for males and females was 53.6 and 54.6, respectively, up from 38.3 and 40.5 in 1850. During the twentieth century the widespread use of immunization, improved medical facilities and care, more healthful working conditions, the discovery and perfection of chemotherapeutics, antibiotics, and insecticides, and a fundamental improvement in nutrition and housing made further gains possible, so that by 1968 the life expectancy for males was extended to 66.6 years, and to 74.0 years for females. By the 1970's the major causes of death, with the exception of accidents, were the degenerative diseases, principally of a cardiovascular or malignant nature. Since females were less susceptible than males to these diseases, they increased their life span differential over males from about a year in 1920 to over 7 years by the late 1960's.

Shifts in birth and death rates have resulted in significant changes in the nation's age structure. High fertility and mortality rates in the early 1800's produced a young population. Subsequent declines in both these rates steadily increased the population age. From 1800 to 1950 the median age of the population rose from 16 to 30. The reversal in birth rates from 1940 to 1957 temporarily reversed the trend. In 1970 the figure stood at 28.3.

IMMIGRATION

Immigration to the United States as a percentage of total population dropped abruptly in this period. This was due initially to World War I, and more fundamentally to the imposition of restrictive immigration laws in the 1920's which continue to the 1970's. (See Table 20.2.) During the 1930's the foreign-born population actually declined by almost 3 million, while the total population rose by almost 9 million. Although there was an increase in net immigration after World War II, its impact on population growth was negligible. Since the 1920's the occupational pattern of immigrants has changed. Modern immigration laws now afford preference to skilled aliens. A United States Department of Labor study of immigrants arriving between 1947 and 1961 reveals that among those who reported occupations, three out of four were in professional, skilled, and semiskilled categories. Professional, technical, and kindred workers constituted 15.7 per cent of the total number of immigrants, as compared with only 9.2 per cent for the entire labor force.

In 1917, based in part on the exhaustive studies of the Immigration Commission from 1907 to 1911, a literacy test was required of all immigrants. All aliens over sixteen years of age who could not pass a test in English or some other recognized language or dialect were to be excluded. This literacy test proved fairly innocuous as a barrier to entry, however, and the volume of immigration after the armistice returned to prewar levels. Shipping companies in the early 1920's were quoted as saying that no less than ten million immigrants were waiting to come to the United States. But popular opinion, strongly insolationist, resentful of being drawn into European wars, and fearful of radical philosophies, demanded outright restrictions. In 1921 Congress passed an emergency measure limiting immigration to three per cent of the foreign born enumer-

TABLE 20.2 *U.S. Immigration 1915–1970*

Year	Thousands of Immigrants	Rate of Immigration*
1915	326.7	5.7†
1920	430.0	
1925	294.3	3.5
1930	241.7	
1935	35.0	0.4
1940	70.8	
1945	38.1	0.7
1950	249.2	
1955	237.8	1.5
1960	265.4	
1965	297.0	1.7
1970	373.0	

SOURCE: U.S. Bureau of the Census. *Historical Statistics of the United States, Colonial Times to 1957.* Washington, D.C.: U.S. Government Printing Office, 1960, pp. 56–7; *1970 Statistical Abstract of the United States.* Washington, D.C.: U.S. Government Printing Office, 1971, p. 89.

*Annual rate per 1,000 population. 10 year rate computed by dividing sum of annual U.S. population totals by sum of annual immigrant totals for same 10 years.

†The rate of immigration is for the following periods: 1911–20, 1921–30, 1931–40, 1941–50, 1951–60, 1961–70.

ated in the 1910 census, excepting nationals of the Americas and children of United States citizens. In 1924 this measure was replaced by a permanent law which set an annual quota of two per cent of the foreign born as of the 1890 census, later changed to the 1920 census, or about 165,000 persons. The alleged purpose of tying the quota to the foreign-born population was to restore immigration to its historical composition. Its effect was to descriminate heavily against the citizens of southern and eastern Europe, and therefore to keep the volume of immigrants below the stated quotas. As a result immigration for the last half of the 1920's was reduced to a level of about 300,000 annually. During the 1930's and World War II it further declined, to about 50,000 per year. At the end of the war special executive and legislative action in response to the plight of millions of refugees increased the volume of immigration to about 250,000 annually. The Immigration and Nationality Act of 1952 (McCarren-Walter Act), while updating the immigration laws, did not change the basic quota formula. The Act's most significant feature was the preferential system it employed in filling quotas. In contrast to the 1924 act which gave first prefer-

FIGURE 20.1. *Immigrants Admitted: 1952 to 1969*

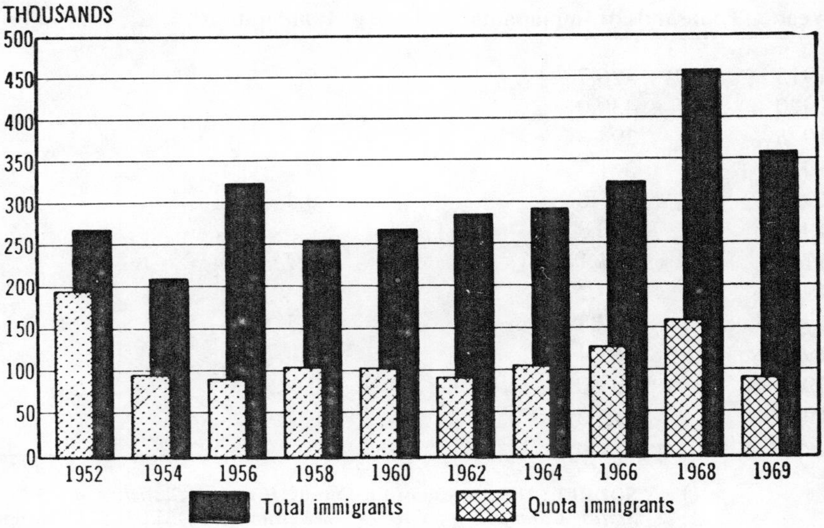

SOURCE: U.S. Bureau of the Census, *Statistical Abstract of the United States: 1970* (Washington: Government Printing Office, 1970), p. 88.

ence to skilled agricultural workers, the 1952 law broadened this to include "qualified quota immigrants whose services are determined by the Attorney General to be needed urgently in the United States because of the high education, technical training, specialized experience, or exceptional ability of such immigrants." This explains the relatively large number of professional and skilled immigrants who entered the United States in the 1950's and 1960's. In 1965 the rigidity of the quota system was eased. At the end of the year the numbers allocated to each country which are not used are transferred to an immigrant pool. In turn, these openings are made available to immigrants who cannot obtain visas because the quota for their country is exhausted. In 1968 a further change was made which limited immigrants from the Eastern Hemisphere to 170,000 with a 20,000 maximum on natives of any one country. For the first time a ceiling of 120,000 was placed on Western Hemisphere natives with no limitation on the natives from any one country. The above changes have had the effect of increasing immigration from southeastern Europe at the expense of northwestern European nationals. It should be noted that actual immigration in the 1950's and 1960's has been more than twice the legal quotas. The present law provides that a so-called "immediate relative" or "special immigrant" is exempted from the numerical ceilings. In the 1950's and 1960's, in most years, so-called "nonquota immigrants" exceeded "quota immigrants." (See Figure 20.1.)

POPULATION DISTRIBUTION

An analysis of population would not be complete without some discussion of regional growth patterns. Although most sections of a country reflect national trends, regional population growth does not proceed uniformly. This is due to differences in birth and death rates and internal migration. The latter is particularly influenced by economic stimuli. Areas which offer the most promising economic opportunities attract population from areas of lesser economic potential. The forces influencing internal migration are comparable to those affecting immigration. However, the former does differ in that there is a considerably greater interchange of population due to the absence of significant cultural, legal and language barriers.

Two principal streams of internal migration have dominated American economic history: the westward movement and the rural-urban movement. In 1970 the population was almost equally divided between the North and the South. From 1800 to 1890 the North Central states (which were not included in the 1790 census) grew more rapidly than either of the older sections, and from 1870 to 1930 this region supported more population than the North or the South. From 1890 to 1970, however, the South's population (except for the 1910-1920 period) grew more rapidly than that of the North Central states, and since 1940 the South has reported a higher population. Despite the rapid growth of Southern population, there has been a major crosscurrent involving both rural whites and blacks moving to the North and West seeking improved living conditions. The bulk of black migration occurred after World War I when immigration quotas curbed the flow of immigration from abroad. The rate of Southern black migration peaked in the 1940's and thereafter, to 1970, has remained fairly stable. During the 1960's the states which received the largest number of black migrants were New York, California, New Jersey, and Michigan. The West, which was first included in the 1850 census, has grown faster than any other region, except in the 1960's. In the latest census period, although California was by far the fastest growing state, the South replaced the West as the region experiencing the largest absolute increase in population. The net effect of these changes is that the nation's center of population for the coterminous forty-eight states has moved from twenty-three miles east of Baltimore, Maryland in 1790 to thirty miles east of St. Louis, Missouri in 1970 a distance 728 miles west and fifty-six miles south. (See Figure 20.2.) It is important to note that despite the population's southward and westward movement, the great majority of the population still resides east of the Mississippi.

This persistent westward push of the population has had the effect of narrowing regional income differentials. In 1880 the real per capita income for the North Central and Western regions, except the Plain States, was above the national average, with the West having the highest level of income. By 1970 the income differential between the West and the rest of

FIGURE 20.2. The Center of U.S. Population 1790 – 1970

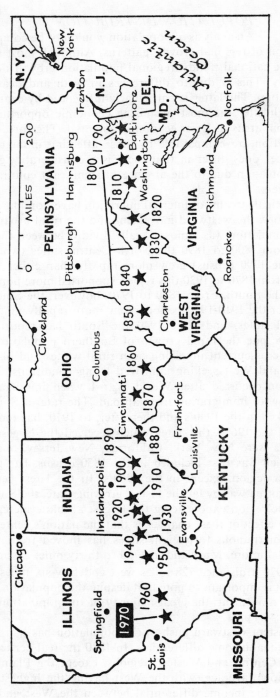

SOURCE: U.S. Bureau of the Census

the nation had narrowed considerably. During this period the South, which had the lowest real per capita income in 1880, had materially improved its relative income position.

Of comparable importance with regional population shifts has been the migration of population from rural to urban areas. Rural communities with generally low levels of living and high fertility rates have continually fed their surplus population to the cities. Since 1920 the urban population has been numerically greater than the rural population. In 1950 it comprised sixty-four per cent of the population and by 1970 its proportion had risen to about three-quarters.

To understand urban growth patterns, one must examine population shifts within so-called metropolitan areas. For statistical reporting purposes, the U.S. Census Bureau defines a Standard Metropolitan Statistical Area (SMSA) as "a county or group of contiguous counties which contain at least one city of 50,000 inhabitants or more, or 'twin cities' with a combined population of at least 50,000. In addition to the county, or counties, containing such a city or cities, contiguous counties are included in SMSA if, according to certain criteria, they are essentially metropolitan in character and are socially and economically integrated with the central city." From 1900 to 1970 SMSA's increased their share of total population from 41 to 67 per cent. Concomitant with the growth of SMSA's there has been a decentralization of population within these areas. This "move to the suburbs" is due to a reduction in the time and cost of transportation, made possible by the automobile, greater flexibility in the location of offices and factories, more leisure time, and improvements in the transmission of electric power, communication, and other vital services to outlying areas. In the 1800's the radial scope of a city rarely exceeded ten miles, whereas in 1970 thirty-five miles or more was common. Until 1920 the central cities were still growing more rapidly than the outlying portions of the SMSA's, but thereafter the faster growth was in the satellite communities. As a result, the central cities' share of SMSA's population declined from sixty eight per cent in 1920 to forty-six per cent in 1970. By the end of the 1960's central cities had replaced nonmetropolitan areas as the slowest growing divisions. Some major cities, such as Buffalo, Cleveland, Louisville, and Rochester actually lost population. Accompanying this phenomenon has been an increase in the black population's share of central city population. By 1970 more than half of the black population lived in central cities. In two large cities, Washington, D.C. and Newark, New Jersey, they accounted for a half or more of the total population, and in Baltimore, New Orleans, Memphis, and Atlanta, they represented forty per cent of the population.

The rural-urban movement has had an effect similar to regional population shifts in narrowing income differentials. In this century, and particu-

TABLE 20.3. *Work Force and Population 1820–1970 (in thousands)*

Year	Work Force	Population	Work Force as a Percentage of Population
Gainful Workers 10 Years and Older			
1820	2,881	9,638	29.9
1830	3,932	12,866	30.6
1840	5,420	17,069	31.8
1850	7,697	23,192	33.2
1860	10,533	31,443	33.5
1870	12,925	38,558	33.5
1880	17,392	50,189	34.7
1890	23,318	62,980	37.0
Labor Force 14 Years and Older			
1890	21,833	62,980	34.7
1900	27,640	76,212	36.3
1910	–	92,228	–
1920	40,282	106,022	38.0
1930	47,404	123,203	38.5
1940	53,299	132,165	40.3
1950	59,671	151,326	39.4
1960[1]	73,226	179,323	40.8
16 Years and Older			
1970*	82,715	204,766	40.4

SOURCE: U.S. Bureau of the Census. *Historical Statistics of the United States, Colonial Times to 1957.* Washington, D.C.: U.S. Government Printing Office, 1960, Series D 36–45, p. 72; *1970 Statistical Abstract of the United States.* Washington, D.C.: U.S. Government Printing Office, 1970, pp. 5, 214.

*Includes Alaska and Hawaii.

larly since World War II, the more rural Southeast, Southwest, and Plains states have significantly narrowed the income advantage of more urbanized New England, Middle Atlantic and Great Lakes areas.

TABLE 20.4. *Labor Force Participation Rate by Sex and Age, 1890-1970**

		MALE				
Year	Total	14-19 yrs.	20-24 yrs.	25-44 yrs.	45-64 yrs.	65 & over
1890	84.3	50.0	90.9	96.0	92.0	68.3
1900	85.7	62.0	90.6	94.7	90.3	63.1
1920	84.6	51.5	89.9	95.6	90.7	55.6
1930	82.1	40.1	88.8	95.8	91.0	54.0
1940	79.7	35.4	88.4	95.6	89.4	42.2
1950	79.0	39.5	81.9	93.3	88.2	41.4
1960†	79.7	46.3	88.9	96.4	91.0	32.2
1970†	80.6	n.a.	86.6	97.8	88.7	26.8
		FEMALE				
1890	18.2	24.5	30.2	15.1	12.1	7.6
1900	20.2	26.8	31.7	17.5	13.6	8.3
1920	22.7	28.4	37.5	21.7	16.5	7.3
1930	23.6	22.8	44.8	24.6	18.0	7.3
1940	25.7	19.0	45.6	30.6	20.0	6.0
1950	29.0	22.6	42.9	33.3	28.8	7.8
1960†	36.1	30.1	46.1	39.4	44.9	10.5
1970†	43.4	n.a.	57.8	48.1	48.7	9.7

SOURCE: U.S. Bureau of the Census. *Historical Statistics of the United States, Colonial Times to 1957*. Washington, D.C.: U.S. Government Printing Office, 1960, p. 71; U.S. Department of Labor. *1971 Manpower Report of the President*. Washington, D.C.: U.S. Government Printing Office, 1971, pp. 204-5.

*As a percentage of total population 14 years and over, except for 1970 which is computed as a percentage of the noninstitutional population 16 years and over.

†Includes Alaska and Hawaii.

LABOR

THE LABOR FORCE PARTICIPATION RATE

The nation's labor force participation rate has increased moderately over its history. As a percentage of total population it increased from approximately thirty per cent in 1820 to forty per cent in 1940. Most of the increase occurred during the 1830-1910 period when there was an appreciable rise in the proportion of the population in the productive age group. Except for a temporary rise during World War II, it remained relatively unchanged through the 1960's. (See Table 20.3.) The proportion of the population in the labor force is heavily influenced by shifts in the labor market activity of age and sex groups. Here the outstanding changes have been the decreasing participation of younger and older males and the increased participation of females. The role of males aged 25 to 65 years has changed very little. It is in the younger and older groups that the shifts have occurred. Since 1890 the 14- to 19-year-old group reduced its participation rate from a high of 62.0 per cent in 1900 to a low of 35.4 per cent in 1940. In the 1940's and 1950's increases occurred which may be attributed to the unusual demand for younger workers during World War II and the postwar period. The rate for 1960 stood at 46.3 per cent. Since 1960, data available for the 16- to 19-year-old group indicates a slight decline in their participation. The 65 years and over male group has, except for a pause during World War II, sharply reduced its activity from 68 per cent in 1890 to 56 per cent in 1970. Concurrently, females, particularly those between 20 and 64 years of age, have dramatically increased their participation in the labor market. Overall, their participation rate has increased from 18 per cent in 1890 to 43 per cent in 1970. The shifts have been most dramatic in the 25 to 64 age range. The participation of this group, particularly married women over 35, has increased from two- to threefold from 1920 to 1970. (See Table 20.4.)

Rising levels of income, child labor laws, the continuing shift of population from rural to urban areas, and the increasing emphasis on education accounted for the reduced participation of the younger age group. The economic activity of older workers also was influenced by rising income levels and the shift away from agriculture. In addition, compulsory retirement was of importance. Female participation rates were affected by the reduction in hours of work, the increased availability of part-time employment, labor-saving devices in the home, the reduction in family size, increased educational opportunities for women, and expansion of employment opportunities in the service industries where women have always been a significant part of the labor force. Some labor economists feel that these basic changes in the labor force mix are related. They believe that the availability of a large pool of suitable female workers is associated with the withdrawal of younger and older males from the labor force. They point out that the data on older males indicates that their participation rate began to decline well before the availability of social security or private pension plans. Furthermore, they indicate that there is a strong correlation between the improved educational level of women and their increasing labor force participation. It is possible, therefore, that older and younger workers to a large extent were displaced by well-trained women available at lower wages. In any case it seems doubtful that employers would have surrendered a significant part of their work force unless there was a suitable alternative.

HOURS OF WORK AND WAGES

A nation's available labor input is dependent not only on population, but also on the number of hours per year that laborers are willing to work. During the twentieth century, particularly between World War I and World War II, the pace of hours reduction quickened. By the 1930's the standard work week was forty-eight hours, and by the end of World War II it was forty hours. In the postwar period, with some exceptions, the eight-hour day, five-day week has remained intact. However, there have been significant reductions in the annual hours of work through increased paid vacations and holidays. From 1940 through the late 1960's the average paid time off has increased by approximately 115 hours annually, or about 2 to 2½ hours per week. Unquestionably the major reduction in hours in the 1800's and early 1900's raised labor productivity, but the benefits were not inexhaustible. Where the dividing line exists is hard to say. Edward Denison approximates that the level of hours prevailing in 1929, 48.6 hours, based on a 52-week year, was the optimum. In 1957, with a 39.8-hour week prevailing, Denison estimated that a one per cent reduction in hours would reduce labor productivity by 0.6 per cent.

As discussed in Chapter 3, advances in productivity are the principal source of increased output and earnings. A comparison of Kendrick's productivity estimates and real hourly earnings reveals almost identical patterns over the long run. In the 1889-1957 period labor productivity measured in terms of physical output per unweighted man-hour and real hourly earnings both rose at an average annual percentage rate of 2.4. In addition, the acceleration of productivity gains after World War I were also reflected in an increased rate of growth in real hourly earnings. From 1919 to 1957 both series advanced at an average annual percentage rate of 2.6. Fabricant's estimates, which update Kendrick's figures through the mid-1960's, indicate that the long-term linkage between real hourly earnings and productivity has been maintained. It should be noted that for individual industries the trends in real hourly earnings and in productivity are only weakly correlated. This is because, as a rule, in industries with high rates of productivity increase, product prices fall in relation to the prices of other goods, while in industries with low rates of productivity, the relative price of products usually increases. In other words, the long-run wage trends in individual industries roughly paralleled the trends in the general average of hourly earnings, regardless of productivity advances in the individual industries.

Changes in labor's share of national income are largely due to the extent of its participation in national productivity gains and to structural changes in the economy which have increased the importance of wages *vis-ā-vis* the other distributive shares of income. Over the long run the constant rate of return on capital has enabled real wages to rise faster than the economy's total productivity, resulting in labor's capture of almost all national productivity gains. Kendrick and Sato estimate that, as a result, between 1919 and 1960 labor's share of national income rose from 72.0 to 77.8 per cent, while capital's share fell from 28.0 to 22.2 per cent. The increased importance of wages, particularly since the 1930's, has resulted from a number of factors. These include the larger role of government in our economy, where all income including that from capital projects such as dams, hydroelectric plants and buildings is treated as compensation of employees, the replacement of individually owned businesses including farms by large corporations where most of the income is received in the form of wages and salaries, the growth in importance of labor intensive service industries, and the long-run decline in rental and interest incomes.

LABOR UNIONS

GROWTH AND DECLINE

On the eve of World War I the U.S. labor movement was in a relatively strong position compared to its past history. Its membership had risen to over 2.6 million, of which the AFL accounted for two million. It had withstood the depression following the Panic of 1907, concerted employer opposition, and unfavorable court decisions. Structurally, the national unions had strengthened their power over their locals and almost universally controlled the right to strike and the use of strike funds. To ensure a maximum production effort during the war, organized labor for the first time was accorded official government recognition. The War Labor Board, one of many agencies on which labor was represented, was guided by the principle that workers had the right to organize and to bargain collectively. In addition, unions benefited from unusually prosperous business conditions and the accompanying shortage of labor. Membership during the war and the immediate postwar period just about doubled, so that by 1920 about one out of five nonagricultural workers were union members.

The 1920's, with the exception of th precipitous 1920-21 downturn, was a decade of general prosperity. Trade unions, based on past history, should have made further gains. The contrary happened, however, as membership fell sharply from over 5 million in 1920 to 3.6 million in 1923 and then stagnated for the balance of the decade. A number of factors were responsible for this phenomenon. First, the business community adopted more sophisticated methods for dealing with their employees. Some observers have termed this period the decade of "welfare capitalism." Direct attacks on collective bargaining were abandoned. Workers were encouraged to form committees or company unions to present their grievances. Profit sharing and incentive pay systems were introduced to encourage and reward increased productivity. Companies took the initiative in improving safety and health conditions, introducing rest periods, and providing recreational facilities. Personnel departments were established to try to bridge the gap between the large impersonal corporation and its employees. More uniform and scientific methods of selection, training, and promotion of employees replaced the haphazard and often prejudiced foreman system. Undoubtedly many workers, particularly the unskilled who had no union representation, gained from these innovations. At the same time few of the employee representation plans introduced in the 1920's developed into genuine unions. Second, trade unions suffered from adverse public opinion. The immediate postwar period witnessed a rash of strikes by unions who were unable to do so during the war. In the minds of many, these strikes were part of an international Communist conspiracy. In 1917 the Bolshevik Revolution in Russia had aroused considerable fear in the United States, and in the suspicious, isolationist environment of the 1920's the public was quick to equate the spread of Communism with militant union activity. It is true that Communist elements were able to infiltrate a number of AFL international union affiliates. However, they were vigorously opposed by the leadership and never constituted a serious

TABLE 20.5. *Union Membership, Selected Dates, 1920–1968*

Year	Total (thousands)	Membership as a Percentage of Nonagricultural Employment
1920	5,034	18.2
1927	3,600	12.1
1930	3,632	11.7
1933	2,857	11.5
1940	8,944	27.2
1945	14,796	35.8
1950	15,000	31.9
1955	17,749	33.6
1960	18,117	31.4
1965	18,519	28.4
1968	20,258	27.9

SOURCE: U.S. Department of Labor. *Handbook of Labor Statistics, 1970.* Washington, D.C.: U.S. Government Printing Office, 1970, p. 339.

threat to legitimate trade union activity. Third, the trade union movement preferred to stand pat rather than vigorously organize the major mass production industries: autos, steel, aluminum, electrical manufacturing, and the like. Despite the fact that the AFL had some industrial unions within its ranks, such as the United Mine Workers, the Amalgamated Clothing Workers, and the International Ladies Garment Workers Union, it still adhered rigidly to the craft method of organization. The AFL craft affiliates refused to surrender their sovereignty over the workers in the mass production industries, and thus no effective organizing campaign could be launched. It was this issue in the 1930's that led to a schism within the AFL and the formation of the Congress of Industrial Organizations (CIO). Finally, the cost of living remained fairly constant throughout the 1920's so that real wages advanced modestly. Typically, during a period of inflation the price level moves ahead faster than money wages, encouraging workers to join unions in order to maintain their standard of living. The net effect of these forces was to reduce labor union membership as a percentage of nonagricultural employment to approximately twelve per cent by 1930. (See Table 20.5.)

DEVELOPMENTS IN THE 1930's

The Great Depression dealt a staggering blow to the labor movement. By 1933, membership had declined to under three million, a level not too far above that of 1914. The 1930's, however, were not destined to be a decade of decline for trade unions. Workers who had been uninterested in unions in the 1920's regarded them in a different light in the 1930's. The harmony hypothesis of the business community had a hollow ring when one out of every four labor force members were unemployed. Public opinion, which had been hostile or at best neutral to unions, now centered its wrath on the giant corporations. The worker needed an organization to protect his interests and to counteract the monopoly power of business. Even the courts took a more tolerant view of union activities. But, by far the most important factors were a changed attitude on the part of the Federal Government, and the more aggressive organizing efforts of the trade movement. Trade unions which in the past had been thwarted innumerable times by government intervention on the side of management, now found the government to be its benefactor.

The Norris-LaGuardia Act removed the courts as an ally of business by declaring the so-called "yellow dog" contract, under which employees contractually agreed not to join or form unions, to be a legally unenforceable document. The Act also required employers seeking injunctive relief in a labor disturbance to show cause why existing police forces were inadequate to maintain law and order. Section 7a of the 1933 National Industry Recovery Act (NIRA) guaranteed the right of employees to form unions and to bargain collectively through representatives of their own choosing. When the NIRA was declared unconstitutional in 1935, Congress replaced Section 7a with the National Labor Relations Act (Wagner Act). The Act reaffirmed the workers' right to organize unions and protected this right by proscribing a number of unfair labor practices by employers. Employers were prohibited from: (1) refusing to bargain in good faith with an authorized bargaining agent of the workers; (2) interfering, restraining or coercing workers in their exercise of union activity; (3) dominating financially or in any other way a labor organization (company union); and (4) discriminating against an employee in hiring, firing or promoting because of union membership, or because he had brought charges or given testimony under the Act. In addition, other legislation in the 1930's established minimum wages and a standard forty-hour week, restricted child labor, and improved physical working conditions.

This fundamental change in social and governmental attitudes did not automatically increase union strength. Ironically, it was dualism, which Gompers regarded as the ultimate form of heresy, which stirred organized labor out of its lethargy. The great potential for union growth lay in the mass production industries. With the passage of favorable legislation many of the workers in these industries formed local unions and applied for admission to the AFL. Temporarily they became directly affiliated by so-called Federal charters, but they hoped shortly to combine with other locals in their respective industries and form separate international unions within the AFL. However, the craft unions which dominated the AFL wished to organize these workers along existing jurisdictional lines. The 1934 AFL convention, after bitter debate, adopted a compromise resolution reaffirming the basic validity of craft unionism but conceding the need for new methods of organization in some segments of industry. It authorized the executive council to issue national charters in the automobile, aluminum, cement and other mass production industries, and agreed to sponsor a major organizing drive in the iron and steel industry. In the year that followed, very little was done to implement this resolution. Actually, the old guard oligarchy that dominated the AFL had no intention of giving up its right to organize workers in the mass production industries, and it still believed that a union comprised largely of semiskilled and unskilled workers could not survive. At the 1935 AFL convention the industrial unions, led by John L. Lewis of the United Mine Workers, were in open revolt. They demanded that unrestricted national charters be issued immediately to the mass production industries. Their proposal was defeated, but the industrial unions were not to be denied. A month after the convention they formed a Committee for Industrial Organization. Originally, the eight industrial unions, with membership of slightly less than a million, hoped to work within the AFL, but immediately they were charged with dualism, and eventually expelled. In 1938 they terminated their temporary status and formed the Congress of Industrial Organizations (CIO).

From its inception in 1935 the CIO vigorously launched organizing campaigns. Workers by the tens of thousands flocked to join CIO unions almost as quickly as organizers could establish headquarters. Unlike the AFL, which would not provide material assistance to a new union until it had demonstrated itself to be a viable organization, the CIO provided generous financial aid and other support in order to help a union get started. Within a few years the CIO unions had achieved considerable success in the automobile, steel, rubber, glass, metal mining, electrical manufacturing, shipbuilding, packing house and textile industries. Only the so-called "Little Steel" companies, Bethlehem, Republic, Inland, Youngstown, and National were able to repulse a major strike effort. By the time of its formal founding in 1938 the CIO had thirty-two international affiliates with a total membership of some four million, or about 400,000 more than the AFL. The AFL could no longer afford to remain quiescent. It, too, began to organize vigorously. Its traditional disdain for the unskilled disintegrated as craft unions entered open competition with CIO unions to sign up all workers regardless of skill. War-induced labor shortages and the need to secure union cooperation to avoid strikes further extended union membership. All of the major holdouts of the 1930's, such as "Little Steel" and major defense industries, signed union contracts. By the war's end unions had increased their percentage of the nonagricultural labor force to thirty-six per cent.

RENEWED DECLINE

The year 1945 proved to be the high-water mark for union strength in the United States. Although numerical growth has continued since 1945 it has not kept pace with labor force increases. Accordingly, the labor union share of nonagricultural employment declined irregularly in the late 1940's and 1950's and significantly in the 1960's. By the end of the 1960's its share had fallen to about twenty-eight per cent. Many of the problems that beset organized labor after World War I reappeared after World War II. Intensive strike activity in the early postwar period, Communist infiltration of some unions, and abuses of union power all aroused public concern. In 1947 the reaction took form in the passage of the Labor Management Relations Act of 1947 (Taft-Hartley Act). The Act placed the government in a more neutral position regarding trade unions. All the safeguards of the Wagner Act were reaffirmed, but in addition workers, management and the public were protected from the abuse of union power. The closed shop was made illegal and procedures for the establishment of a union shop were tightened. The use of a temporary injunction was authorized in strikes which affected the nation's health and welfare. Unions, like employers, were restrained by a list of unfair practices. These included: (1) forcing an employee to join a union except where there existed a fully certified union shop; (2) coercing an employer in the selection of his collective bargaining representatives; (3) forcing an employer to discriminate against an employee; (4) engaging in jurisdictional disputes or secondary boycotts; (5) charging excessive initiation and membership fees; and (6) requiring an employer to pay for services not actually rendered (featherbedding). Subsequent labor legislation has further strengthened the rights of employers and employees *vis-a-vis* union activities. In particular, the Labor-Management Reporting and Disclosure Act (Landrom-Griffin) of 1959 safeguarded the individual rights of union members by granting them specific guarantees (the secret ballot) to participate fully in union meetings and elections. In addition, it strictly regulated the financial activities of union leaders by requiring their bonding and limiting their access to union funds.

Although vigorously opposed by labor unions, these acts do not seem to have been a major factor in restricting union growth. The principal reasons for relative union stagnation appear, instead, to be uninspired union leadership and the inability of trade unions to adjust to the changing occupational and sex composition of the labor force. Practically all union membership gains since World War II have been in manufacturing and transportation industries where they were already established. However, as was discussed earlier, the manufacturing or production workers' share of the labor market is contracting, while the service workers' share is increasing. With some exceptions, unions have not been able to attract the large body of service workers to their ranks. This is particularly true in those cases where women dominate while-collar employment. Women typically have a short-term employment expectation and do not consider themselves as permanent members of the work force. Usually their principal interests are marriage and family, rather than jobs. Also, most white-collar workers tend to associate themselves with management's view of unions. Even those who do not expect any significant job advancement may adopt an indifferent or hostile attitude for prestige purposes. Finally, many of the benefits or unionization such as status, job security, pension plans, paid vacations and the like already exist. However, the factory-like environment of many white-collar jobs, the increased pace of technological change in service occupations, and the more permanent labor force status of women, especially married women over thirty-five years of age, is tending to break down some of these barriers to union membership. But as yet the trade union movement has made no major breakthroughs.

To some extent the failure to attract white-collar and other large non-union segments is attributable to union leadership. The dedicated, idealistic, intellectual leader of the depression era is no longer significantly represented in the labor movement. The missionary zeal of the period has been replaced by a complacent, if not defensive, attitude. Today's union leader concentrates on minding his established domain rather than organizing the unorganized. The AFL-CIO merger in 1955, which was designed to infuse some new life into the labor movement, thus far has fallen far short of its goals. The organization department which was established following the merger has made little headway in its organizing efforts. Unlike the CIO in the 1930's it lacks the prerogatives and the financial means to initiate and sustain organizing campaigns. This basic responsibility rests with the existing international affiliates who pay little more than lip service to major organizing efforts. In several instances conflicting jurisdictional claims have encumbered organizational drives. Moreover, labor's attempts to clean its own house, together with political infighting, have resulted in the two largest international unions, the Teamsters and the United Auto Workers, leaving the AFL-CIO. Unless there is increasing concern with these problems, unions are likely to continue to lose ground.

UNIONS AND ECONOMIC GROWTH

Appraising trade union impact on economic growth is a difficult task. The evidence is complex and primarily qualitative, and any conclusions based upon it are subject to challenge. Moreover, the subject is not one that lends itself to an impartial detached view. Every observer approaches the issue with preconceived ideas which influence his selection and interpretation of the facts. Despite these disabilities, one may begin by noting that American trade unions, with some minor exceptions, have subscribed to the basic values and objectives of capitalism. Their goals have been primarily to exercise some control over the work situation and to receive a larger share of the fruits of progress. In pursuing these objectives unions have had a mixed impact on productivity and, therefore, on the nation's rate of economic growth. On the negative side, work rules imposed to increase the demand for labor, stretch out job time, or indirectly raise wages hampered efficiency. Limiting the number of bricks a man can lay in a given time period, requiring printers to set bogus type, or preventing an employer from reducing the size of his work crew have been common examples of this type of activity. Usually such practices have been most prevalent among craft unions. The well-defined nature of their tasks and the individual character of the work, plus the ability to limit labor supply, have enabled them to impose such restrictions. The industrial unions, rooted in the new technology of the mass production industries, and with less distinct skills, have imposed fewer encumbrances to worker efficiency.

Unions have also reduced labor mobility and thus prevented some workers from moving to positions where they could employ their skills more effectively. A nonunion worker who is unhappy with his employment situation will ordinarily move on if a reasonable alternative presents itself, whereas in a unionized work situation the accepted procedure is to seek remedial action through union channels. This tendency toward immobility is further strengthened by elaborate union-sponsored pension and seniority systems which give preference to employees with extended years of service. Finally, the concentration of union power in the high productivity sectors of the economy has tended to reduce overall national productivity. In the long run, unions have had little impact on the relationship between real wages and productivity or on labor's share of the national income. However, they have been able to raise the money wages of those workers whose income would have been higher in any event due to the superior productivity of their skill and the industry in which they were employed. Generally this resulted in shrinkage of jobs in high productivity sectors causing a disproportionate part of the labor force to find employment in low productivity industries. Albert Rees in the reading at the end of this chapter discusses the impact of unions on wages.

On the positive side, union insistence on safer and more sanitary working conditions has raised the worker's morale and enabled him to function more effectively. In the same vein, the institution of orderly grievance procedures and the elimination of the autocratic and often prejudiced actions of supervisory personnel have given the worker a more positive view of his work situation. The union role in reducing hours of work in the 1800's and early 1900's has also helped to raise productivity. Historical evidence, together with data compiled during World War II, indicates clearly that excessive hours of work seriously impair worker efficiency. Finally, unions by pressing for wage increases have forced some employers to become more efficient.

SELECTED REFERENCES

1. Solomon Barkin. *The Decline of the Labor Movement.* Santa Barbara: Center for the Study of Democratic Institutions, 1961.
2. Charles O. Gregory. *Labor and the Law.* New York: W. W. Norton, 1946.
3. H. G. Lewis. *Unionism and Relative Wages in the United States.* Chicago: University of Chicago Press, 1963.
4. Clarence D. Long. *The Labor Force Under Changing Income and Employment.* New York: National Bureau of Economic Research, 1958.
5. Henry S. Millis and Royal Montgomery. *Organized Labor.* New York: McGraw-Hill, 1945.
6. Conrad and Irene Taueber. *The Changing Population of the United States.* New York: Social Science Research Council, 1958.
7. Brinley Thomas. *Migration and Economic Growth.* Cambridge: Cambridge University Press, 1954.
8. W. S. Woytinsky, *et al. Employment and Wages in the United States.* New York: Twentieth Century Fund, 1953.

reading

have unions
raised wages?

albert rees

        The purpose of this paper is to suggest in highly condensed form the general order of magnitude of the effects of unions and collective bargaining on the allocation of resources.[1] It is widely accepted that unions have the power to raise wages in the establishments where they have bargaining rights. (The term "wages" should be understood to include fringe benefits.) This power comes from their ability to impose costs on management through strikes, slow-downs, or other pressure tactics which, in the short run, are greater than the costs of the wage increases provided through collective bargaining. By changes in relative wages we shall mean changes in wages in establishments covered by collective bargaining relative to wages elsewhere. For the discussion of resource allocation it is not necessary to specify how much of the relative increase arises from an absolute increase in union wages and how much from any possible decrease in nonunion wages. (Such a decrease could occur if labor were displaced from the union sector by rising wages and were therefore in more plentiful supply to the nonunion sector.)

        The existence of a relative wage effect implies the existence of a relative employment effect. If blue-collar labor is made more expensive in the union sector, management will have added incentives to save such labor through closer supervision and through the use of additional labor-saving capital equipment. Such substitution will minimize, but not eliminate, the addition to cost created by union wage gains. The remaining addition to average unit costs will tend to increase the price of final products and

Reprinted with permission from "The Effects of Unions on Resource Allocation" by Albert Rees, in *Journal of Law and Economics*, VI (October 1953), pp. 69-78.

services produced in the union sector and therefore to reduce their consumption. Relative employment in the union sector should therefore decline for two reasons: (*a*) the substitution of other factors of production for union labor and (*b*) the substitution by consumers of cheaper final products and services for the more expensive output of the union sector. Whether these effects are empirically important depends on the size of the relevant elasticities of substitution and of demand.

Empirical estimates of the effect of unions on relative wages and relative employment encounter many difficulties. The basic problem is to correct for factors other than collective bargaining that might have produced differences between the union and nonunion sectors in the movements or levels of wages and employment. The devices used to control for such factors in the estimation of wage effects are discussed in detail in *Unionism and Relative Wages in the United States.*[2]

Lewis' book reviews, criticizes, and amends the previous studies that have estimated union effects on relative wages. In addition, it includes very substantial new work. From all this evidence, Lewis concludes that the effect of unions on relative wages in the late 1950's was about 10-15 per cent (that is, wages of union labor had been raised by unionism 10-15 per cent relative to the wages of nonunion labor). The highest estimate for any part of the period considered is 25 per cent or more at the depth of the Great Depression of the 1930's. In the late 1940's, because of rapid inflation, the union effect is estimated at 5 per cent or less.[3] During rapid inflation, market wages in the nonunion sector tend to rise rapidly, while the rise in union wages is often slowed by rigidities inherent in the bargaining process.

In his paper on *Relative Employment Effects of Unionism,*[4] Lewis estimates that the order of magnitude of the relative employment effect is not significantly different from that of the relative wage effect. In other words, the effect of collective bargaining is to reduce employment in the union sector about 10-15 per cent relative to employment elsewhere. This estimate rests on a less substantial body of work than the estimate of the wage effect.

The effects of unions on resource allocation can be divided into three components: effects via the interindustry wage structure, effects via the intra-industry wage structure, and effects via direct restrictions on output. We shall consider each of these in turn.

Lewis' two works permit us to make a rough estimate of the loss in real output caused by the effects of collective bargaining on the interindustry wage structure. Under certain conventional assumptions, it can be shown that the loss of real output is approximately equal to one-half the product of the wage effect and the employment effect (see Fig. 1). I have used this formula to make a rough estimate for 1957, the last nonrecession year covered in Lewis' estimates. This estimated loss turns out to be approxi-

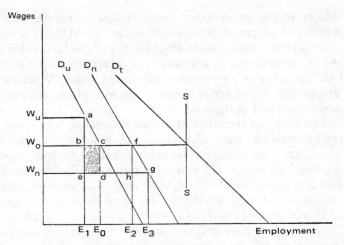

FIGURE 1.–SS *is the supply of labor, and* D_u, D_n, *and* D_t *are the demand for labor in the union sector, the nonunion sector, and both combined. Before the entry of the union, the wage is* W_0. *If the union raises the wage in its sector to* W_u, *employment in the sector declines from* E_0 *to* E_1. *This increases the supply of labor to the nonunion sector, raising employment from* E_2 *to* E_3 *and forcing the wage down to* W_n. *The areas under the demand curves are the real net product of labor. The loss in product in the union sector is* $E_0 c a E_1$, *the gain in product in the nonunion section is* $E_2 fg E_3$. *The difference between these areas is the loss of product shown by the shaded rectangle b c d e. This is equal to the change in employment times one-half the difference in wages. In the more general case, where the demand curves in the two sectors are nonlinear or do not have the same slope, the equality will be only approximate.*

mately 600 million dollars. Since gross national product in 1957 was 443 billion dollars, the loss is approximately 0.14 per cent of national output. This welfare loss is of the same general magnitude as that estimated earlier by Arnold Harberger for enterprise monopoly (0.1 per cent).[5] The method used here is an application of that used by Harberger and derived from Harold Hotelling.[6]

The estimated loss is arrived at as follows. Union membership in the United States in 1957 was approximately 17 million. A relative employment effect of 15 per cent implies a transfer of about 1.7 million workers out of the union sector as a result of bargaining, and a relative wage effect of 15 per cent implies an absolute wage effect of about 700 dollars per worker per year. One-half of 700 dollars times 1.7 million is approximately 600 million dollars.

This calculation assumes that the average compensation of union members is equal to the average compensation of all employees in the highly unionized industry divisions: mining, contract construction, manufacturing, transportation, and communications and public utilities. The last assumption involves offsetting errors. Among production workers, union members in these industry divisions have higher compensation than nonunion workers. However, in manufacturing, which accounts for about 70 per cent of total employment in these divisions, the compensation of nonproduction workers is substantially higher than that of production workers, and nonproduction workers are seldom unionized. Moreover, there are some union members in other industry divisions who will on the average have lower compensation than those in the divisions listed above.

In one very restricted sense, the estimate of 600 million dollars as the interindustry component of welfare loss for 1957 is an upper-limit estimate—it uses the upper limits of the ranges of relative wage effects and relative employment effects estimated by Lewis. Nevertheless, there are other assumptions embodied in the estimate that could lead it to be too low. First, since the estimate of employment effects rests on less evidence than that of wage effects, it is possible that they exceed the upper limit of the estimated range. An alternative method of estimation would be to combine the estimated relative wage effect with an assumed elasticity of demand for labor. This is the method used by Harberger in his study of enterprise monopoly, in which he assumed an average elasticity of demand for products of -1. The assumption of an elasticity of demand for labor of -1 would not change the estimate given above, since this is the elasticity implicit in the estimates used for the wage and employment effects.

The estimate also assumes that the relative wage and employment effects of unions are uniform within the union sector. The more realistic assumption that the size of these effects varies within the sector will not change the estimate provided that there is no correlation across unionized industries between the size of actual employment and actual wage effects. However, if in general large wage effects are associated with small employment effects, the estimate given above is too high; if large wage effects are associated with large employment effects, the estimate is too low.

In general, it seems reasonable to assume that large wage effects are associated with smaller-than-average employment effects — that is, that unions will raise wages most where the elasticity of demand for labor is smallest and the costs in reduced employment are lowest. There is, however, one important case that does not fit this generalization: the bituminous coal industry, where both the wage effect and the employment effect seem to be unusually large.

The estimated loss under discussion also assumes that no unemployment results from the employment effects of unionization. We should not, of course, charge the unions with the losses arising from general deficiencies in aggregate demand. However, the displacement of labor from one industry to another will give rise to frictional unemployment even under conditions of general prosperity, and the costs of this should be added to the interindustry component of welfare loss. These costs will be smaller if unionization is concentrated in expanding industries, since relative employment effects will then take the form of reducing the rate of hiring rather than requiring the dismissal of present employees. In fact, however, much of the strength of unions has been in contracting or stable industries, so that the unemployment costs of unionization are probably significant.

Professor Lewis has reported to me that he has made an unpublished estimate of the welfare cost of the interindustry component of relative wage and employment effects, using a somewhat more sophisticated method of calculation which allows for the dispersion of the relative wage effect within the union sector. The resulting measure of loss is almost the same as that reported above: 0.15 per cent of national product.

Not much is known about the relative wage effects of unions in particular industries. The available industry studies are summarized by Lewis in *Unionism and Relative Wages in the United States,* chapter iii and v, especially Table 49. These studies suggest that the unions of the following groups of workers had larger than average effects (20 per cent or more): skilled building craftsmen, bituminous coal miners, commercial airline pilots, and East Coast seamen. These estimates refer to the 1950's except that for building craftsmen, which is for 1939. The studies also show that one union, the Amalgamated Clothing Workers, had no appreciable relative wage effect in the period 1946-57, though it did in the years from 1919 to 1939. This loss of power was associated with declining demand for the product.

The list of cases with very large estimated wage effects includes three for craft unions and one for an industrial union. Economic theory suggests that craft unions will have larger relative wage effects than industrial unions because their wages constitute a smaller portion of total costs, except in the unusual case where there are very good substitutes for union craftsmen in production and the elasticity of demand for the product is low.[7] But this advantage holds only if the craft unions in an industry bargain individually. If they bargain as a group, or wage patterns are transmitted to all the occupations in the industry, the case becomes similar to that of industrial unionism.

It is possible to put together the available industry studies, the relevant economic theory, and data on wage movements to make informed guesses on which unions not mentioned in the preceding paragraphs have larger-than-average relative wage effects. My leading candidates would be the skilled craft unions in railroads, entertainment, and the printing trades; the teamsters; and the steelworkers. A list of candidates for additional unions with less-than-average relative wage effects would include the unions of ladies' garment workers, textile workers, shoe workers, and white-collar government workers. The first is included because of the similarity of the industry to men's clothing. The next two are examples of unions that have incomplete organization of industries with national product markets. The government unions are included because their political power is probably an inferior substitute for the use of the strike.

The relative wage and employment effects considered so far arise from the impact of collective bargaining on the interindustry wage structure. We turn next to the effects of collective bargaining on the wage structure within industries, which in some cases may be of considerable importance. Geographical wage patterns are one example. In the absence of collective bargaining, manual labor, and particularly unskilled labor, is appreciably cheaper in the South than in other regions. This regional wage differential arises from the more abundant supply of unskilled labor in the South. It tends to be reduced by the migration of labor to the North and of capital to the South, but such movements of resources have not been sufficient to offset the greater rate of natural population increase in the South.

Unions that bargain with multiplant employers or with associations of employers operating both in the South and elsewhere have attempted to eliminate regional wage differentials and frequently have succeeded. The union rate for unskilled labor in the southern operations of these employers is therefore further above the market rate than in their northern and western operations.[8] From this may flow a number of consequences: (1) national employers constructing new facilities both in the South and in the North would normally have an incentive to use somewhat more labor-intensive methods in the South; this incentive is eliminated by the uniform wage; (2) where plant location is oriented toward labor costs rather than access to markets or raw materials, an incentive to locate plants in the South is removed; (3) where plant location has been determined by access to southern markets or raw materials, the national employer may be unable to compete with local nonunion employers able to take advantage of low market rates of wages. Factors of this kind are unlikely to be important in the automobile or steel industries but are of considerable importance in meat packing. The displacement of national by local firms could retard the industrialization of the South to the extent that national firms have access to lower-cost sources of capital, both internal and external.

The elimination of regional wage differentials through collective bargaining benefits the southern workers already employed in the unionized sector. However, it injures those workers, not readily identifiable, who would have been employed in industry had incentives for the expansion of industrial employment in the South not been diminished. Equality is achieved within the union sector at the cost of increased disparity between the union plant in the South and the rest of the southern economy.

Another area in which collective bargaining affects the structure of wages is that of skill differentials. Such effects may be readily apparent to personnel people in industry. However, they have not been much studied by academic economists, and the discussion below is therefore somewhat conjectural. The effects seem from existing literature to be mixed and without a dominant pattern.[9]

In several industries represented by industrial unions, the effect of collective bargaining early in the postwar period appeared to be to compress skill differentials. The compensation of the least skilled workers was raised most by unions, that of the most skilled less or perhaps not at all. Such wage compression could affect resource allocation by reducing incentives to undertake training and could lead to shortages of apprentices for the skilled trades. More recently, such compression has been limited or reversed by the actual or threatened secession of skilled workers to form separate unions of their own and by the operation of percentage wage increases such as annual improvement factors.

An opposite effect on skill differentials can occur under craft unionism if the unions representing the most skilled crafts are stronger than those representing the less skilled. This situation may prevail in portions of the railroad and printing industries. In such cases the effect of unionism is to prevent skill differentials from narrowing as much as would be expected from the general long-run trend; this provides incentives for employers to economize most in the use of skilled labor. However, the ability of employers to substitute other factors for skilled labor may be severely restricted by union rules.

Since union effects on intra-industry wage structures are more difficult to discern than effects on the interindustry structure, the costs of the former are probably less than those of the latter. This would suggest a combined cost of less than 0.3 per cent of gross national product. If this estimate seems low, it is because the social costs of transferring resources to less productive uses are far less than those of wasting resources altogether. This brings us to the third avenue of union effects on resource allocation: direct restrictions of output through control of manning requirements, the work pace, and work practices, often called "featherbedding." In the course of preparing this paper, I have reached the conclusion that losses of this kind — dead-weight losses — probably exceed the social losses from relative wage effects. Indeed, management in a single industry — railroads — claimed in 1959 that obsolete work rules were costing 500 million dollars a year, or over 0.1 per cent of national product. Although this may be an overestimate, particularly through the inclusions of some costs that are in reality higher compensation for necessary work, the comparison between this amount and those mentioned above suggests something about the general magnitudes involved.

The evidence available is not sufficient to permit any numerical estimate of the total costs of union control of manning practices and work rules. The published accounts suggest that a large part of the costs is concentrated in a few industries, especially railroads, printing, longshoring, entertainment, and some aspects of building construction. Costs are especially high in industries with craft union organization where each piece of work, however small, "belongs" to a particular craft, and a member of that craft must be called to do it. On the railroads such practices can result in the payment of a day's pay for a few minutes' work and sometimes in payment to two men for work done by one.[10]

It should be noted, however, that direct union impact on output is not always restrictive. Under some circumstances, unions have made significant contributions to efforts to raise output or productivity, especially where jobs have been threatened by competition from new products or products produced in other locations.

The practices bearing directly on resource use include apprenticeship rules, which can affect the number and quality of people trained, either by their effect on the size and nature of the entering group or by their influence on the percentage of entrants who complete the program. There seems to be general agreement that the number and quality of apprentices in many trades are inadequate to meet probable future needs. Such an effect could arise in any or all of the following ways: (1) the quality of the entering group can be lowered by nepotism or discrimination in the selection of entrants; (2) the number of apprentices can be limited by rules setting the ratio of apprentices to journeymen — this is the best known, but probably not the most important, of the restrictive devices; (3) the numbers of people entering and completing programs will be held down if the programs are unnecessarily long or if the program content is poor; (4) the number entering and completing will be reduced if the apprentice's wage is too low relative to the journeyman's; (5) conversely, the willingness of employers to train apprentices will be reduced if the apprentice's wage rate is too high relative to the journeyman's. All of these observations apply in principle to training programs operated solely by management. However, when management is in sole control of a training program, it has greater freedom to take prompt corrective action if the number or quality of trainees is inadequate.

Union influence on resource allocation that arises from increases in relative wages works unambiguously in the direction of reducing relative employment. Practices that limit output or require unnecessary numbers of men have an unpredictable effect in the long run. In the short run, the effect may be an absolute increase in the employment of the group that institutes the restrictive practices; in the longer run, such practices may encourage types of substitution that the union is powerless to cope with, which will ultimately reduce employment. For example, an effective full-crew law or rule on railroads will increase the number of operating employees per train but may accelerate the substitution of other forms of transportation for rail transportation. In the long run, the number of jobs lost through such accelerated substitution could exceed the number created or preserved by the full-crew rule. The only unambiguous effect is to increase the cost of transportation.

Union restrictions on contracting out work traditionally done in the bargaining unit are less formalized than some other types of restrictions, but may be becoming more widespread. If the work can be done at less cost by the outside contractor, there is an obvious adverse effect on efficiency. In cases where the outside contractor also uses union labor (not necessarily from the same union), any shifts in employment arising from restrictions on contracting out will not be caught by estimates of changes in relative employment in the union sector as a whole.

Throughout the preceding discussion, the implicit comparison has been between the relative wages and distribution of employment existing under unionism and those which would exist under perfectly competitive labor markets. Since the allocation of resources by perfectly competitive markets is known to be optimal, by this standard the impact of the union is necessarily adverse. The standard must be modified to the extent that actual nonunion labor markets are monopsonistic. If nonunion employers, either singly or acting in concert, have the power to hold wages below the levels that would prevail under perfect competition, moderate union effects on relative wages may bring employment closer to an optimal configuration. The scanty available evidence suggests that monopsony power by employers in United States labor markets is small but not nonexistent.[11] However, in some markets where employers have such power (textile-mill towns, for example) there is little unionization, while in others where such power may once have existed (especially coal-mining areas), the union corrective may have gone too far.

If the entire impact of unions on our society could be subsumed under the heading of resource allocation, there would be little difficulty in reading the conclusions that the over-all impact is adverse and that union power is excessive. The difficulties for policy explored in Professor Meltzer's paper[12] arise because this is not the case. Important aspects of collective bargaining, such as grievance procedure, have only tangential implications for resource allocation, but strong effects on equity in work situations and on the meaning and status of manual work. Union representation of workers in political processes is largely noneconomic, yet could be affected by policies designed to deal with problems of resource allocation. The central policy issue is how to design measures that would reduce the adverse effects of collective bargaining on resource allocation while preserving those aspects of bargaining that are socially constructive. There remains much room for debate whether such goals can best be achieved by radical or by cautious measures.

NOTES

1. I am heavily indebted to H. Gregg Lewis for comments on an earlier draft of this paper and for permission to draw freely on two of his works: *Unionism and Relative Wages in the United States* (1963) and "Relative Employment Effects of Unionism," in *Proceedings of Sixteenth Annual Meeting of Industrial Relations Research Association,* 104 (1964). However, he is in no way responsible for the opinions expressed here or for the deficiencies of my estimates.
2. Lewis, *Unionism and Relative Wages in the United States, op. cit. supra* note 1, at 45. A briefer and less technical discussion may be found in Rees, *The Economics of Trade Unions,* 73-75 (1962).
3. These summary figures appear in Lewis, *Relative Employment Effects of Unionism, op. cit. supra* note 1.
4. *Ibid.*
5. Harberger, *Monopoly and Resource Allocation,* American Economic Association Papers and Proceedings, *Am. Econ. Rev.,* May 1954, p. 77.
6. Hotelling, "The General Welfare in Relation to Problems of Taxation and of Railway and Utility Rates," 6 *Econometrica* 242 (1938).
7. See Rees, *op. cit. supra* note 2, at 70-73, and the passages from Marshall and Hicks cited therein.
8. This is especially true in motor freight, where Hoffa has obtained the same mileage rates from southern as from midwestern truckers, removing traditional differentials. Because of superior weather conditions in the South, these bring higher weekly earnings to southern drivers.
9. Reynolds & Taft, *The Evolution of the Wage Structure,* 185-86 (1956).
10. Slichter, Healy & Livernash, *The Impact of Collective Bargaining on Management,* Chap. 11 (1960).
11. Bunting, *Employer Concentration in Local Labor Markets* (1962).
12. See Meltzer, "Labor Unions, Collective Bargaining, and the Antitrust Laws," 6 *J. Law & Econ.* 152 (1963).

chapter **21**

capital and
banking

CAPITAL FORMATION

TRENDS

Capital formation, in constant 1929 dollars, rose from an annual rate of $15.5 billion in the 1910's and 1920's to $33 billion in the ten-year period from 1946 to 1955, an increase of over 100 per cent. Gross private domestic investment in constant 1958 dollars increased almost fifty per cent from 1955-59 to 1970. Owing to an increasing rate of depreciation, net capital formation showed only a modest gain over the same periods. (See Table 21.1.) The rise in capital formation was more than matched by the rise in gross national product. As a consequence, gross capital formation as a percentage of GNP and net capital formation as a percentage of net national product declined in the period between World War I and the first decade following World War II. Thereafter, despite irregular movements, it showed little net change. (See Table 21.2.) The capital-output ratio, measured in terms of the net capital stock, declined following World War I. It stood at 3.6 in the 1910's and at 2.5 in the ten-year period from 1946 to 1955. (See Table 21.3.) This decline

642

TABLE 21.1. *Average Annual Capital Formation 1909–1970**
(Billions of Dollars)

Period	Gross Capital Formation	Capital Consumption Allowances	Net Capital Formation
Kuznets Data (1929 Prices)			
1909–1928	$15.5	$8.4	$7.1
1929–1955	22.7	17.3	5.4
1946–1955	33.0	25.1	7.9
U.S. Department of Commerce Data (1958 Prices)			
1955–1959	70.6	37.6	33.0
1960–1964	78.2	39.4	38.8
1965–1969	105.3	59.2	46.1
1970	103.0	63.4	40.6

SOURCES: Simon Kuznets. *Capital in the American Economy.* New York: National Bureau of Economic Research, 1961, p. 56; *1971 Economic Report of the President.* Washington, D.C.: U.S. Government Printing Office, 1971, pp. 197, 200, 212.

*The Kuznets and U.S. Department of Commerce Data are not strictly comparable. See sources.

was attributable to technological changes which enhanced capital's productivity. Kendrick indicates that the rate of capital productivity gains accelerated after World War I. Net capital stock per member of the labor force grew from $5,500 in 1919 to $6,700 by 1955. In the 1957-68 period the average annual change in the stock of fixed capital per employed person in the private economy grew at a rate of 2.2 per cent.

From World War I through the 1960's construction's share of capital formation declined, while machinery and equipment's share (producers' durables) rose. Inventory's share moved irregularly. (See Table 21.4.) From World War I to 1955, household's share (nonfarm residential construction) of gross capital formation declined while government's share increased. Business' share remained essentially unchanged. (See Table 21.5.) As noted in Chapter 16, the increasing importance of government in the nation's economy accounted for its rising share. Within business investment, agriculture's share dropped from 23 per cent in 1900 to 18 per cent by midcentury, while manufacturing and mining's share increased from 36 per cent to 39 per cent.

TABLE 21.2. *Capital Formation as a Percentage of National Output 1909-1970* (Billions of Dollars)*

Period	Gross Capital Formation as a Percentage of Gross National Product	Net Capital Formation as a Percentage of Net National Product
Kuznets Data (1929 Dollars)		
1909-1918	22.1	10.5
1919-1928	20.6	9.2
1929-1938	13.4	1.6
1939-1948	16.0	4.8
1946-1955	17.3	4.1
U.S. Department of Commerce Data (1958 Dollars)		
1955-1959	15.6	7.9
1960-1964	14.8	6.6
1968-1969	15.6	7.5
1970	14.2	6.1

SOURCES: Simon Kuznets. *Capital in the American Economy.* New York: National Bureau of Economic Research, 1961, p. 93; *1971 Economic Report of the President.* Washington, D.C.: U.S. Government Printing Office, 1971, pp. 198, 202, 212.

*The Kuznets and U.S. Department of Commerce Data are not strictly comparable. See sources.

TABLE 21.3. *Ratio of Capital Stock to National Output Per Decade, 1929 Prices, 1909-1955*

Period	Ratio of Gross Capital Stock to Gross National Product	Ratio of Net Capital Stock to Net National Product
1909-1918	5.9	3.6
1919-1928	6.0	3.5
1929-1938	7.3	3.9
1939-1948	5.4	2.5
1946-1955	5.4	2.5

SOURCE: Simon Kuznets. *Capital in the American Economy.* New York: National Bureau of Economic Research, 1961, pp. 80-81.

TABLE 21.4. *Percentage Distribution of Gross Capital Formation by Type of Investment 1909–1970**

Period	Construction	Producers' Durables	Net Changes in Inventories	Net Changes in Claims Against Foreigners
Kuznets Data (1929 Prices)				
1909–1938	55.0%	33.2%	4.8%	7.0%
1919–1948	45.9	43.7	5.4	5.0
1929–1955	43.1	50.3	5.0	1.6
1946–1955	41.5	49.2	6.8	2.6
U.S. Department of Commerce Data (1958 Prices)				
1955–1959	56.2	39.2	4.6	–
1960–1964	52.7	41.4	5.9	–
1965–1969	43.2	48.3	8.5	–
1970	42.4	54.6	3.0	–

SOURCES: Simon Kuznets. *Capital in the American Economy.* New York: National Bureau of Economic Research, 1961, pp. 146–471; *1971 Economic Report of the President.* Washington, D.C.: U.S. Government Printing Office, 1971, p. 198.

*The Kuznets and U.S. Department of Commerce data are not strictly comparable. See sources.

TABLE 21.5. *Gross Capital Formation by Type of User (1929 Prices) 1909–1955*

Period	Households	Business	Government
1909–1938	18.5%	64.5%	17.0%
1919–1948	14.5	57.8	27.7
1929–1955	12.6	58.2	29.2
1946–1955	14.2	64.6	21.2

SOURCE: Simon Kuznets. *Capital in the American Economy.* New York: National Bureau of Economic Research, 1961, p. 178.

SOURCES

The three major groups in the economy from which savings can be generated are households, including farmers and unincorporated business, corporations, and federal, state and local governments. Capital formation is financed by internal savings or external financing. Corporate capital needs since World War I have been increasingly financed internally while those of households have been increasingly financed externally. The bulk of savings come from household units. Raymond Goldsmith's comprehensive study of saving in the United States from 1897 to 1949 indicates that during normal periods (excluding wars and depressions) personal savings account for about 70 per cent of national savings, corporate savings about 20 per cent, and government savings 10 per cent. The great majority of personal savings occurred in nonfarm households in the highest income brackets. In the post-World War II period the Federal Reserve's *Survey of Consumer Finances* revealed that the 10 per cent of households with the highest income of any one year accounted for over 80 per cent of personal savings in that year. Of the 90 per cent of the households in the lower income groups, a goodly number dissaved. In fact, for all households in any given year approximately one out of every three spent more than its income in that year. However, practically all households saved at one time or another as revealed by the fact that only 10 per cent of the households had no net worth (including consumer durables) by 1950. The ability of corporations to save is limited by a number of factors. Corporate net income is a minor part of national income. Corporate profits before taxes in this century have on the average been less than 10 per cent of national income. Out of this total, taxes and dividends must be paid. The high rate of corporate taxes and the threat of take-over by an insurgent management group if unsatisfactory dividends are not distributed further restricts the volume of corporate savings. The ability of government to save is also limited. Government savings occur when tax receipts exceed expenditures. However, government in our society is not generally supposed to engage in capital formation. If it has a surplus, it is expected to return the surplus to the people in the form of lower taxes. Because of defense and war needs the Federal government in recent decades has been a major dissaver.

THE BANKING SYSTEM

EARLY YEARS OF THE FEDERAL RESERVE

The Federal Reserve System entered World War I as an inexperienced organization and emerged from the war with very little loss of naivety. A lack of coordination and leadership characterized the twelve district banks. This led to the usurpation of control by private bankers over whom the Federal Reserve was empowered to exercise supervisory regulation. One notable exception was the New York Federal Reserve Bank, led by Benjamin Strong, a protege of J. P. Morgan and central banker in the tradition of Nicholas Biddle. Unfortunately, Strong died at the end of 1928, leaving a leadership vacuum in the central banking system on the eve of the Great Depression. With the exception of Strong, Federal Reserve administrators believed the System's major function was to supply the nation with an elastic currency. The backing of Federal Reserve notes was forty per cent gold and sixty per cent commercial paper. Since the supply of the latter expanded and contracted at the same pace as the nation's business, so did the supply of Federal Reserve notes. It was recognized that the Federal Reserve could influence business conditions by actively controlling the quantity of money, curbing its rate of expansion in periods of inflation, and increasing its rate of expansion in periods of recession. However, two factors militated against such a course of action. First, commercial paper contracted during recession, limiting the ability of the Federal Reserve to expand the money supply. Second, the System's leadership could not agree on an appropriate course of action.

On those occasions when the Federal Reserve attempted to influence economic conditions, it had a tendency to overreact. For example, during World War I the Federal Reserve acted to support the Treasury in its flotation of bonds to finance the war. It performed this central bank function by adopting a policy of credit ease to keep interest rates at relatively low levels. In the process, the Federal Reserve became an engine of inflation. Prudent monetary procedure would have required a policy of moderate credit restraint to hold down the growth of total spending to a rate commensurate with the growth of productive capacity and the needs of a war economy, but this was not done. As a result, between 1914 and 1919 consumer prices increased roughly seventy per cent. When the Federal Reserve sought to curb inflation in 1920 it pursued a policy of credit restraint which resulted in the sharpest decline in the rate of growth of the money supply in the nation's history. The brief but severe recession of 1920-21 followed, during which wholesale prices dropped some forty-five per cent.

The Federal Reserve's principal weapon during this period was the discount rate, the price which member banks had to pay to borrow from the Federal Reserve. Bank holdings of commercial paper were the backing for such loans. If the discount rate was increased, this raised bank borrowing costs, which in turn caused banks to increase their interest charges to customers, and discouraged borrowing for investment spending and installment buying. If the discount rate was lowered, interest rates would tend to fall, encouraging borrowing and stimulating total spending in the economy.

CREDIT CREATION

In the early 1920's the Federal Reserve observed that its purchases and sales of government securities influenced credit conditions in the economy. If it bought (sold) securities in the open market, this had the effect of increasing (decreasing) the money supply by some multiple of its purchases. The expansion of the money supply was due to the credit creating power of the banking system. To illustrate, assume that an individual sells a $10,000 U.S. obligation through a broker to the Federal Reserve. He deposits the proceeds from the sale in his checking account in Bank A. Bank A, in business to make money, does so by lending out part of the deposits of its customers. It does not lend out a hundred per cent of all deposits because of legal reserve requirements and the need to honor payment demands. Assuming banks keep twenty per cent of deposits on hand for these reasons, Bank A will keep $2,000 of the $10,000 deposit and lend out the remaining $8,000. The borrower spends this amount by purchasing goods from a businessman with an account in Bank B. The businessman deposits the $8,000 in Bank B. Twenty per cent of this sum is kept, and the remaining $6,400 is lent out, only to find its way into another bank (Bank C) in the accounts of those who sold goods or services to the borrowers from Bank B. Note that the $6,400 deposit in Bank C came from the $8,000 in Bank B, which came from the $10,000 in Bank A. Workint out the implications of this example, one observes that the banking system has an ability to create $50,000 of money based on a $10,000 initial deposit. Of this $50,000, $10,000 represents the initial deposit in the banking system and $40,000 represents credit which has been created. (See Table 21.6.) If the banking system had kept reserves of ten per cent, then a tenfold expansion in the money supply would have been permitted. If it kept reserves of fifty per cent, then a twofold expansion would have been permitted. No creation of money (credit) could occur if reserves of 100 per cent were kept. This ability of the banking system to create money is of great significance. Currency and coins have continually diminished in relative importance as a component of the money supply. Most money, about ninety per cent, is in the form of credit, which resides in the many checking accounts of individuals and business firms within the commercial banking system.

During the 1920's each District Bank determined its own open market policies. In 1923, under the leadership of Benjamin Strong, a committee made up of representatives from each of the District Banks was instituted to coordinate open market operations. Although open market operations were used extensively, their impact was limited by the relatively small quantities of government securities held in the System. Moreover, the law did not permit these securities to be used as backing for Federal Reserve Notes, thus preventing the Federal Reserve from printing currency with which to purchase government securities.

THE COLLAPSE OF THE BANKING SYSTEM

Following the 1920-21 downturn, with the exception of two mild inventory recessions in 1923-24 and 1926-27, the economy experienced

TABLE 21.6. *Credit Creation By the Banking System*

Bank	New Deposits	New Loans and Investments	New Reserves
A	$10,000	$8,000	$2,000
B	8,000	6,400	1,600
C	6,400	5,120	1,280
D	5,120	4,096	1,024
.	.	.	.
.	.	.	.
.	.	.	.
Total for Banking System	$50,000	$40,000	$10,000

prosperity. This prosperity, however, was not mirrored in all sectors of the economy. Construction activity declined after 1925 and the farm sector, as already indicated, was experiencing economic difficulties. The volume of commercial loans declined as business financed a growing share of its capital needs through retained earnings. This encouraged the banking system to lend an increasing percentage of funds for real estate and security purchases, a fact which contributed to buoyant real estate and security markets. In 1928 the Federal Reserve became alarmed at speculative excesses in the stock market. Although it utilized its discount and open market powers to combat these excesses, it never could agree on a decisive course of action. Dissension existed as to whether broker loans were being fed by private funds or Federal Reserve credit. Those who believed that private funds were the source of stock market speculation championed moral suasion as a means of dampening stock market activity. Those who disagreed argued for continued increases in the discount rate. In the course of the debate, neither was used effectively.

The downturn which commenced in August of 1929 was not, like its predecessors, an inventory recession. During it the Federal Reserve failed to take decisive action. To be sure, the discount rate was lowered (eventually to 1.5 per cent) and government securities were purchased in the open market, but it was a case of too little too late. Meanwhile the banking system was undergoing severe contraction, with an attendant sharp decline in the money supply and an acceleration of bank failures. Bank failures were not uncommon in U.S. history. The nation had about 30,000 banks in 1920, three times the number in 1900. During the 1920's roughly 5,500 banks failed. Beginning in 1930 the rate of bank failures increased sharply. From

TABLE 21.7. *Number of Commercial Banks and Bank Failures 1915–1969*

Year	Number of Commercial Banks	Bank Suspensions and Failures*
1915	27,395	152
1920	30,291	168
1925	28,442	618
1930	23,679	1,352
1931	21,654	2,294
1932	18,734	1,456
1933	14,207	4,004
1934	15,348	62
1935	15,488	32
1940	14,534	48
1945	14,126	1
1950	14,146	5
1955	13,780	5
1960	13,484	2
1965	13,818	7
1969	13,681	4

SOURCE: U.S. Department of Commerce. *Historical Statistics of the United States, Colonial Times to 1957.* Washington, D.C.: U.S. Government Printing Office, 1960, pp. 631, 636, 637; U.S. Bureau of the Census. *Statistical Abstract of the United States: 1970.* Washington, D.C.: U.S. Government Printing Office, 1970, pp. 442, 445.

*Includes all banks.

this date through 1933 almost 9,000 went into liquidation. By 1934, only about three-fifths of the banks in existence in 1929 remained in business. (See Table 21.7.) Federal Reserve inaction to stem these failures is difficult to understand. The most likely reasons were an underestimation of the seriousness of the situation, a feeling that bank failures were a problem of bank management and not the responsibility of the monetary authorities, and a lack of effective leadership. Ironically, it is quite likely that if the Federal Reserve System were not in existence at the time, the banking system could have done a better job of coping with its problems. If early in the depression, 1930 or even 1931, they had suspended payments until sufficient liquidity was achieved, as they did in 1907 and other panic periods, the economy would have avoided the wholesale failures and deflation which occurred. But since the Federal Reserve was designed to prevent just such catastrophies, the banking system saw no need to use these pragmatic policies of the past.

BANKING REFORMS

As a consequence of the banking system's collapse, major legislative reforms were undertaken. The Glass-Steagall Act of 1932 authorized the use of government securities as backing for Federal Reserve notes, ending a major restraint on Federal Reserve open market operations. The newly created Reconstruction Finance Corporation made massive loans to the banking community to combat further bankruptcies. The Emergency Banking Act of March 1933 empowered the President to regulate the money supply, including the withdrawal of gold from circulation. In the Thomas Amendment to the Agricultural Adjustment Act of May 1933 the President was empowered to increase the money supply by several means. First, in the Greenback tradition, the Government was authorized to issue up to three billion dollars in U.S. notes. Second, the Federal Reserve could be forced to purchase up to $3 billion of government securities directly from the Treasury, thereby augmenting the money supply by a multiple of this amount. Third, the dollar was subject to devaluation up to fifty per cent. Fourth, in the Populist tradition, the President was authorized to coin silver without limit. In the following month the use of gold in payment of private and public debts was forbidden. In January 1934, after all gold outstanding was ordered turned in to the Treasury in return for paper currency, the U.S. dollar was officially devalued. Devaluation involved decreasing the gold content of the dollar, thereby increasing the price of gold. Its price was raised from $20.67 an ounce to $35 an ounce. Since the value of all currencies was expressed in terms of their gold worth, devaluation not only increased the price of gold, but also the price of foreign currencies in terms of the U.S. dollar. This encouraged foreigners to buy more goods in the United States since a unit of their currency would now secure more dollars. It also discouraged Americans from buying abroad, since now a dollar purchased less foreign currency than it had in the past. The effect produced by devaluation, therefore, was to boost U.S. net exports, a fact which stimulated spending and production at home. However, to a considerable extent this was offset by comparable devaluations by other major nations. Devaluation also importantly affected the money supply. First, since it involved increasing the price of gold, the gold stock of the United States was automatically increased in value. This in turn permitted an increase in the volume of paper currency since Federal Reserve notes were backed forty per cent by gold. Second, it ended the direct relationship between the U.S. money supply and gold flows between the United States and the rest of the world. This in the opinion of Milton Friedman is one of two major reasons why another Great Depression cannot occur in the United States. A fundamental collapse of the European banking community commencing in 1931 resulted in an international drive for liquidity. In the process, significant quantities of gold were withdrawn from the banking systems of all major countries including the United States. This intensified the contraction of the U.S.

money supply and induced the Federal Reserve in 1931 to take the anomalous action of sharply increasing the discount rate from 1.5 to 3.5 per cent during a major contraction in order to stem the gold flow. Although this action was reversed a few months later, it revealed that the fate of the domestic economy was intimately linked to the vicissitudes of international finance. The second reason why a major depression is not likely to occur is the creation of the Federal Deposit Insurance Corporation in 1933. The FDIC insures deposit up to a specified limit thereby assuring public confidence in the banking system.

The Banking Acts of 1933 and 1935 wrought substantial reforms in the structures of the Federal Reserve and the commercial banking system. The power of the Federal Reserve was centralized in a Board of Governors in Washington. This Board was given five major powers. First, it was authorized to review and change discount rates established by the twelve district banks. Second, it was empowered to declare any bank asset eligible backing for Federal Reserve Notes, giving it almost limitless power to lend to any bank in need. Third, it was empowered to determine margin requirements, that is, the percentage of a stock's market price that had to be paid in cash by the purchaser. With this authority it could control speculative activity on the nation's stock exchanges. Fourth, the Board of Governors was accorded a majority voting position on the newly created Open Market Committee which determined the System's purchase and sale of Government securities. Finally, it was granted the power to alter legal reserve requirements for demand deposits between minimum and maximum levels established by Congress. In 1970 the legal reserve requirement range for country banks was seven to fourteen per cent and for city banks between ten and twenty-two percent. As indicated earlier, the size of a reserve requirement determines the extent to which the banking system may create money. The major reform in the nation's commercial banking system involved the separation of commercial and investment banking activities. Henceforth, banks could engage in only one of these phases of activity. In addition, the activities of investment banks were brought under Federal regulation. And as noted previously, the Securities Act of 1933 and the Securities and Exchange Act of 1934 provided for regulation over the sale of securities.

Despite the new power given the Federal Reserve and the centralization of authority in the Board of Governors, the nation's central bank's performance in the latter half of the 1930's showed little improvement. The position of credit ease which the System had pursued since 1932 ended abruptly in 1936 despite the presence of considerable unemployment and excess capacity. The Federal Reserve acted in response to a noticeable increase in prices in 1936 and early 1937. It also feared that the huge volume of excess reserves held by the banking system could be a potential source of inflation. In August of 1936 it raised reserve requirements by fifty per cent. Between March and May of 1937 it increased requirements another thirty-three per cent. The economy immediately turned down. Between September of 1937 and May 1938 output dropped some thirty per cent. In response, the Board of Governors lowered reserve requirements in April of 1938. A recovery followed one month later.

In World War II, as in World War I, the Federal Reserve became an engine of inflation. Once the war economy had reached full employment inflationary forces were unleashed because total spending was growing at a faster rate than productive capacity. The Federal Reserve should have slowed spending by restraining the growth of the money supply. Instead, it pursured a policy of credit ease to keep interest rates low and aid the Treasury in its wartime borrowing. Instead of selling government bonds to sop up excess purchasing power, the Federal Reserve bought government securities to support their price at a pegged rate of interest whenever market conditions showed a temporary inability to absorb a large-scale offering. So significant were Federal Reserve purchases that in 1945 Congress was obliged to lower the gold backing of Federal Reserve notes from forty to twenty-five per cent so as to give the Federal Reserve greater freedom in its pegging operations. These Federal Reserve actions contributed to a forty per cent increase in consumer prices between 1940 and 1946 despite comprehensive price and wage controls.

POST-WORLD WAR II POLICIES

Following the return of peace the Federal Reserve continued to support the U.S. bond market to aid the Treasury in its refinancing of maturing debt. Inflation continued unchecked. Between the summer of 1945 and the summer of 1948 consumer prices increased some thirty-five per cent. As inflation persisted, the Federal Reserve became increasingly uneasy with its policy of credit ease, and publicly expressed its concern to the Treasury. By late 1950 the disagreement between the Federal Reserve and the Treasury was openly debated. Finally, in 1951 an "Accord" was reached with the Treasury. Under its terms the Treasury and the Board of Governors reached "full accord with respect to debt management and monetary policies to be pursued in furthering their common purpose to assure the successful financing of the Government's requirements and ... to minimize monetarization of the public debt." As a result, the Federal Reserve gradually ceased the major share of its activities in support of the government bond market. Freed from this obligation, the Board of Governors turned to a policy of moderate restraint for the economy, a strategy that was not reversed until June of 1953, one month before the onset of the 1953-54 recession. A policy of credit ease was pursued throughout the thirteen months of contraction. Once business turned up in August of 1954 the Federal Reserve moved once again to a position of moderate restraint.

From the beginning of the Accord through 1955 relative price stability existed in the economy. In 1956 and 1957 significant inflation took hold. The Federal Reserve responded by further tightening credit. In July of 1957 the economy reached a business cycle peak and began to turn down. However, the Federal Reserve continued to pursue its policy of restraint until November of that year. With the commencement of recovery in April 1958 the Federal Reserve again adopted a tack of restraint, a policy which was excessive in amount, in the opinion of some economists and contributed to the 1960-61 recession.

Federal Reserve policy decisions during the late 1950's and early 1960's were complicated by a serious balance of payments problem. It has been observed that the U.S. money supply was no longer directly dependent upon international gold flows. When gold outflows in the late 1950's and 1960's reduced the U.S. gold stock to a level near the legal minimum backing imposed by existing legislation, Congress removed the remaining legal linkage between the U.S. money supply and gold. In 1965 the gold backing behind member bank reserves held by the System was eliminated, and in 1968 the corresponding gold reserve against Federal Reserve notes was abandoned. Nevertheless, to safeguard the international position of the dollar, the Federal Reserve maintained an upward pressure on interest rates in order to stem the flight of short-term capital seeking higher interest abroad. At the same time the efforts of the Kennedy Administration to stimulate the rate of growth through an expansive fiscal policy called for an accommodating policy of monetary ease. Other measures by the government to stem the outflow of gold enabled the Federal Reserve to pursue a policy of credit neutrality for the first half of the 1960's. The attainment of a full employment economy and the acceleration of the Vietnam War in the latter half of the decade created severe inflationary pressures. The failure of the Federal government to apply appropriate fiscal restraint in 1966 placed the burden of combating inflation solely on monetary policy. Beginning in late 1965 the Federal Reserve, for the first time in the decade, pursued a policy of credit restraint to curb aggregate demand. By late 1966 this resulted in a "credit crunch" which caused a pause in economic expansion. In response to the slowing down of economic activity, and in anticipation of a tax increase to absorb excessive purchasing power, the Federal Reserve resumed a policy of credit ease in late 1966 which lasted until late 1968. During this period a prolonged debate ensued as to the appropriate tax measure to be passed. In the interim, the pace of inflation quickened. The tax increase enacted in June 1968 proved inadequate to stem advancing prices. The Federal Reserve exercised restraint in 1969, causing interest rates to reach their highest level in over a century. In late 1969 the longest period of economic expansion in U.S. history came to an end. A short and mild recession followed during which the Federal Reserve pursued a policy of credit ease.

TABLE 21.8. *The Share of Major Financial Intermediaries 1912–1968 (Assets of financial intermediaries = 100)*

	1912	1929	1939	1952	1960	1968
Federal Reserve banks	—	4	11	13	8	6
Commercial banks*	64	50	40	42	34	34
Mutual Savings banks	12	7	7	6	6	6
Savings and loan associations	3	6	3	6	11	12
Life Insurance companies	13	13	13	18	18	14
Pension funds†	—	2	4	4	9	11
Other financial intermediaries	8	18	22	11	14	17

SOURCE: Security and Exchange Commission. *Institutional Investor Study Report,* Vol. 1. House Committee on Interstate and Foreign Commerce. Washington, D.C.: U.S. Government Printing Office, 1971, p. 44.

*Does not include trust department.

†Private Trusteed and public funds.

Milton Friedman and other members of the "Monetarist School" feel that the Federal Reserve has traditionally acted too late during periods of monetary stress, and that when it has acted it has overreacted. In the reading at the end of this chapter he presents his view as to the appropriate role of monetary policy. Most economists do not share Friedman's viewpoint. Although they recognize that the Federal Reserve has often erred in the past, they believe that its actions have had considerable success in curbing both inflationary and recessionary forces.

OTHER FINANCIAL INTERMEDIARIES

During the period from 1915 to 1970 commercial banks continued to be the nation's most important financial institution. However, as discussed earlier in this chapter, the creation of the Federal Reserve System, increased reliance by business on non-bank financing and the catastrophic collapse of the banking system during the "Great Depression" significantly weakened their position. In 1912 they held sixty-four per cent of the assets of all financial intermediaries; by 1929 their share had dropped to fifty per cent, and by 1939 to forty per cent. (See Table 21.8.) A limited revival in the 1940's was followed by a further decline in the fifties, causing their share to fall to thirty-four per cent by 1960. This decline was due to the greater importance of internal funds as a source of business capital and the higher interest rates paid by competitors of the · commercial banks. In the 1945-1965 period businesses generally financed two-thirds of their capital needs from retained earnings and depreciation reserves. Of the amount externally raised, banks provided only about fifteen per cent. As part of the banking reform legislation in the 1930's, banks were prohibited from paying interest on demand deposits. Moreover, the maximum interest rates payable on Federal Reserve member bank time deposits (Regulation Q) were lower than those paid by mutual savings banks and savings and loan associations. Businesses and households more sophisticated in the ways of finance placed their idle funds with institutions paying higher interest. In the 1960's, however, commercial banks were able to maintain their relative position. In 1957, effective lobbying led to the first of several liberalizations of the maximum interest rate ceiling on time deposits. In addition, aggressive bank management developed new deposit type claims and revived old ones to lure funds from their competitors. The most important of these instruments was the negotiable certificate of deposit. Initiated in the early 1960's, over sixteen billion dollars worth of these certificates were outstanding by 1967.

One type of institution which grew at the expense of commercial banks was the savings and loan association. The desire of monetary authorities and legislators to encourage the flow of funds to the mortgage market to finance housing placed them in a favored tax and interest paying position. Furthermore, their presence in the rapidly growing capital-scarce Far West enabled them to pay premium rates of interest to their depositors. Effective advertising of these high interest rates attracted funds from the entire nation. Consequently, their share of financial intermediary assets grew from three per cent at the end of the 1930's to six per cent in the early 1950's and to eleven per cent by 1960. In the 1960's a narrowing of interest rate differentials between deposit type institutions and a slowing of construction due to tight money conditions sharply reduced their growth rate. In contrast to the growth of savings and loan associations, mutual saving banks continued their relative decline which commenced after the Civil War. Their failure to spread their activities to the rapidly growing areas of the South and West was the principal reason for their declining significance.

Of all financial intermediaries, pension funds grew most rapidly. Virtually nonexistent after World War I, by the 1960's they were a major holder of savings. The principal catalyst for their growth was the introduction of the social security system in the 1930's. It sparked a desire on the part of households at all income levels to build retirement funds. Both business and government units established pension plans to provide their employees with retirement benefits. Improved pension provisions became a major demand of organized labor. Consequently pension funds' share of total financial intermediary assets rose from four per cent in 1939 to nine per cent by 1960 and eleven per cent by 1968. Life insurance companies, on the other hand, experienced little net change in importance. After maintaining their relative position in the 1920's and 1930's, they increased their share from thirteen to eighteen per cent by the early 1950's. Persistent increases in the price level together with the industry's inability to combine its traditional policies with a suitable inflation hedge prevented further relative gains in the 1950's and 1960's. This, coupled with the growth of noninsured pension funds led by 1968 to a decline in life insurance's share from eighteen to fourteen per cent.

SELECTED REFERENCES

1. George L. Bach. *Federal Reserve Policy Making.* New York: Knopf, 1950.
2. Lester Chandler. *Benjamin Strong: Central Banker.* Washington: Brookings Institution, 1958.
3. Milton Friedman and Anna Schwartz. *A Monetary History of the United States, 1867-1960.* Princeton: Princeton University Press, 1963.
4. Raymond W. Goldsmith. *Financial Intermediaries in the American Economy Since 1900.* Princeton: Princeton University Press, 1958.
5. _____. *A Study of Savings in the United States.* Princeton: Princeton University Press, 1955.
6. Simon Kuznets. *Capital in the American Economy, Its Formation and Financing.* Princeton: Princeton University Press, 1961.

reading

what is the proper role of monetary policy in promoting full employment and economic growth?

milton friedman

There is wide agreement about the major goals of economic policy: high employment, stable prices, and rapid growth. There is less agreement that these goals are mutually compatible or, among those who regard them as incompatible, about the terms at which they can and should be substituted for one another. There is least agreement about the role that various instruments of policy can and should play in achieving the several goals.

My topic for tonight is the role of one such instrument — monetary policy.* What can it contribute? And how should it be conducted to contribute the most? Opinion on these questions has fluctuated widely. In the first flush of enthusiasm about the newly created Federal Reserve System, many observers attributed the relative stability of the 1920s to the System's capacity for fine tuning — to apply an apt modern term. It came to be widely believed that a new era had arrived in which business cycles had been rendered obsolete by advances in monetary technology. This opinion

*Presidential address delivered at the Eightieth Annual Meeting of the American Economic Association, Washington, D.C., December 29, 1967. I am indebted for helpful criticisms of earlier drafts to Armen Alchian, Gary Becker, Martin Bronfenbrenner, Arthur F. Burns, Phillip Cagan, David D. Friedman, Lawrence Harris, Harry G. Johnson, Homer Jones, Jerry Jordan, David Meiselman, Allan H. Meltzer, Theodore W. Schultz, Anna J. Schwartz, Herbert Stein, George J. Stigler, and James Tobin.

Reprinted with permission from "The Role of Monetary Policy" by Milton Friedman, in *American Economic Review*, LVIII (March 1968), 1-17.

was shared by economist and layman alike, though, of course, there were some dissonant voices. The Great Contraction destroyed this naive attitude. Opinion swung to the other extreme. Monetary policy was a string. You could pull on it to stop inflation but you could not push on it to halt recession. You could lead a horse to water but you could not make him drink. Such theory by aphorism was soon replaced by Keynes' rigorous and sophisticated analysis.

Keynes offered simultaneously an explanation for the presumed impotence of monetary policy to stem the depression, a nonmonetary interpretation of the depression, and an alternative to monetary policy for meeting the depression and his offering was avidly accepted. If liquidity preference is absolute or nearly so — as Keynes believed likely in times of heavy unemployment — interest rates cannot be lowered by monetary measures. If investment and consumption are little affected by interest rates — as Hansen and many of Keynes' other American disciples came to believe — lower interest rates, even if they could be achieved, would do little good. Monetary policy is twice damned. The contraction, set in train, on this view, by a collapse of investment or by a shortage of investment opportunities or by stubborn thriftiness, could not, it was argued, have been stopped by monetary measures. But there was available an alternative — fiscal policy. Government spending could make up for insufficient private investment. Tax reductions could undermine stubborn thriftiness.

The wide acceptance of these views in the economic profession meant that for some two decades monetary policy was believed by all but a few reactionary souls to have been rendered obsolete by new economic knowledge. Money did not matter. Its only role was the minor one of keeping interest rates low, in order to hold down interest payments in the government budget, contribute to the "euthanasia of the rentier," and maybe, stimulate investment a bit to assist government spending in maintaining a high level of aggregate demand.

These views produced a widespread adoption of cheap money policies after the war. And they received a rude shock when these policies failed in country after country, when central bank after central bank was forced to give up the pretense that it could indefinitely keep "the" rate of interest at a low level. In this country, the public denouement came with the Federal Reserve-Treasury Accord in 1951, although the policy of pegging government bond prices was not formally abandoned until 1953. Inflation, stimulated by cheap money policies, not the widely heralded postwar depression, turned out to be the order of the day. The result was the beginning of a revival of belief in the potency of monetary policy.

This revival was strongly fostered among economists by the theoretical developments initiated by Haberler but named for Pigou that pointed out a channel — namely, changes in wealth — whereby changes in the real quantity of money can affect aggregate demand even if they do not alter interest rates. These theoretical developments did not undermine Keynes' argument against the potency of orthodox monetary measures when liquidity preference is absolute since under such circumstances the usual monetary operations involve simply substituting money for other assets without changing total wealth. But they did show how changes in the quantity of money produced in other ways could affect total spending even under such circumstances. And, more fundamentally, they did undermine Keynes' key theoretical proposition, namely, that even in a world of flexible prices, a position of equilibrium at full employment might not exist. Henceforth, unemployment had again to be explained by rigidities or imperfections, not as the natural outcome of a fully operative market process.

The revival of belief in the potency of monetary policy was fostered also by a re-evaluation of the role money played from 1929 to 1933. Keynes and most other economists of the time believed that the Great Contraction in the United States occurred despite aggressive expansionary policies by the monetary authorities — that they did their best but their best was not good enough.[1] Recent studies have demonstrated that the facts are precisely the reverse: the U.S. monetary authorities followed highly deflationary policy. The quantity of money in the United States fell by one-third in the course of the contraction. And it fell not because there were no willing borrowers — not because the horse would not drink. It fell because the Federal Reserve System forced or permitted a sharp reduction in the monetary base, because it failed to exercise the responsibilities assigned to it in the Federal Reserve Act to provide liquidity to the banking system. The Great Contraction is tragic testimony to the power of monetary policy — not, as Keynes and so many of his contemporaries believed, evidence of its impotence.

In the United States the revival of belief in the potency of monetary policy was strengthened also by increasing disillusionment with fiscal policy, not so much with its potential to affect aggregate demand as with the practical and political feasibility of so using it. Expenditures turned out to respond sluggishly and with long lags to attempts to adjust them to the course of economic activity, so emphasis shifted to taxes. But here political factors entered with a vengeance to prevent prompt adjustment to presumed need, as has been so graphically illustrated in the months since I wrote the first draft of this talk. "Fine tuning" is a marvelously evocative phrase in this electronic age, but it has little resemblance to what is possible in practice — not, I might add, an unmixed evil.

It is hard to realize how radical has been the change in professional opinion on the role of money. Hardly an economist today accepts views that were the common coin some two decades ago. Let me cite a few examples.

In a talk published in 1945, E. A. Goldenweiser, then Director of the Research Division of the Federal Reserve Board, described the primary objective of monetary policy as being to "maintain the value of Government bonds.... This country" he wrote, "will have to adjust to a 2½ per cent interest rate as the return on safe, long-time money, because the time has come when returns on pioneering capital can no longer be unlimited as they were in the past"[4, p. 117].

In a book on *Financing American Prosperity*, edited by Paul Homan and Fritz Machlup and published in 1945, Alvin Hansen devotes nine pages of text to the "savings-investment problem" without finding any need to use the words "interest rate" or any close facsimile thereto [5, pp. 218-27]. In his contribution to this volume, Fritz Machlup wrote, "Questions regarding the rate of interest, in particular regarding its variation or its stability, may not be among the most vital problems of the postwar economy, but they are certainly among the perplexing ones" [5, p. 466]. In his contribution, John H. Williams — not only professor at Harvard but also a long-time adviser to the New York Federal Reserve Bank — wrote, "I can see no prospect of revival of a general monetary control in the postwar period" [5, p. 383].

Another of the volumes dealing with postwar policy that appeared at this time, *Planning and Paying for Full Employment*, was edited by Abba P. Lerner and Frank D. Graham [6] and had contributors of all shades of professional opinion — from Henry Simons and Frank Graham to Abba Lerner and Hans Neisser. Yet Albert Halasi, in his excellent summary of the papers, was able to say, "Our contributors do not discuss the question of money supply.... The contributors make no special mention of credit policy to remedy actual depressions.... Inflation ... might be fought more effectively by raising interest rates.... But ... other anti-inflationary measures ... are preferable" [6, pp. 23-24]. *A Survey of Contemporary Economics*, edited by Howard Ellis and published in 1948, was an "official" attempt to codify the state of economic thought of the time. In his contribution, Arthur Smithies wrote, "In the field of compensatory action, I believe fiscal policy must shoulder most of the load. Its chief rival, monetary policy, seems to be disqualified on institutional grounds. This country appears to be committed to something like the present low level of interest rates on a long-term basis" [1, p. 208].

These quotations suggest the flavor of professional thought some two decades ago. If you wish to go further in this humbling inquiry, I recommend that you compare the sections on money — when you can find them — in the Principles texts of the early postwar years with the lengthy sections in the current crop even, or especially, when the early and recent Principles are different editions of the same work.

The pendulum has swung far since then, if not all the way to the position of the late 1920s, at least much closer to that position than to the position of 1945. There are of course many differences between then and now, less in the potency attributed to monetary policy than in the roles assigned to it and the criteria by which the profession believes monetary policy should be guided. Then, the chief roles assigned monetary policy were to promote price stability and to preserve the gold standard; the chief criteria of monetary policy were the state of the "money market," the extent of "speculation" and the movement of gold. Today, primacy is assigned to the promotion of full employment, with the prevention of inflation a continuing but definitely secondary objective. And there is major disagreement about criteria of policy, varying from emphasis on money market conditions, interest rates, and the quantity of money to the belief that the state of employment itself should be the proximate criterion of policy.

I stress nonetheless the similarity between the views that prevailed in the late 'twenties and those that prevail today because I fear that, now as then, the pendulum may well have swung too far, that, now as then, we are in danger of assigning to monetary policy a larger role than it can perform, in danger of asking it to accomplish tasks that it cannot achieve, and, as a result, in danger of preventing it from making the contribution that it is capable of making.

Unaccustomed as I am to denigrating the importance of money, I therefore shall, as my first task, stress what monetary policy cannot do. I shall then try to outline what it can do and how it can best make its contribution, in the present state of our knowledge — or ignorance.

I. WHAT MONETARY POLICY CANNOT DO

From the infinite world of negation, I have selected two limitations of monetary policy to discuss: (1) It cannot peg interest rates for more than very limited periods; (2) It cannot peg the rate of unemployment for more than very limited periods. I select these because the contrary has been or is widely believed, because they correspond to the two main unattainable tasks that are at all likely to be assigned to monetary policy, and because essentially the same theoretical analysis covers both.

PEGGING OF INTEREST RATES

History has already persuaded many of you about the first limitation. As noted earlier, the failure of cheap money policies was a major source of the reaction against simple-minded Keynesianism. In the United States, this reaction involved widespread recognition that the wartime and postwar pegging of bond prices was a mistake, that the abandonment of this policy was a desirable and inevitable step, and that it had none of the disturbing and disastrous consequences that were so freely predicted at the time.

The limitation derives from a much misunderstood feature of the relation between money and interest rates. Let the Fed set out to keep interest rates down. How will it try to do so? By buying securities. This raises their prices and lowers their yields. In the process, it also increases the quantity of reserves available to banks, hence the amount of bank credit, and, ultimately the total quantity of money. That is why central bankers in particular, and the financial community more broadly, generally believe that an increase in the quantity of money tends to lower interest rates. Academic economists accept the same conclusion, but for different reasons. They see, in their mind's eye, a negatively sloping liquidity preference schedule. How can people be induced to hold a larger quantity of money? Only by bidding down interest rates.

Both are right, up to a point. The *initial* impact of increasing the quantity of money at a faster rate than it has been increasing is to make interest rates lower for a time than they would otherwise have been. But this is only the beginning of the process not the end. The more rapid rate of monetary growth will stimulate spending, both through the impact on investment of lower market interest rates and through the impact on other spending and thereby relative prices of higher cash balances than are desired. But one man's spending is another man's income. Rising income will raise the liquidity preference schedule and the demand for loans; it may also raise prices, which would reduce the real quantity of money. These three effects will reverse the initial downward pressure on interest rates fairly promptly, say, in something less than a year. Together they will tend, after a somewhat longer interval, say, a year or two, to return interest rates to the level they would otherwise have had. Indeed, given the tendency for the economy to overreact, they are highly likely to raise interest rates temporarily beyond that level, setting in motion a cyclical adjustment process.

A forth effect, when and if it becomes operative, will go even farther, and definitely mean that a higher rate of monetary expansion will correspond to a higher, not lower, level of interest rates than would otherwise have prevailed. Let the higher rate of monetary growth produce rising prices, and let the public come to expect that prices will continue to rise. Borrowers will then be willing to pay and lenders will then demand higher interest rates — as Irving Fisher pointed out decades ago. This price expectation effect is slow to develop and also slow to disappear. Fisher estimated that it took several decades for a full adjustment and more recent work is consistent with his estimates.

These subsequent effects explain why every attempt to keep interest rates at a low level has forced the monetary authority to engage in successively larger and larger open market purchases. They explain why, historically, high and rising nominal interest rates have been associated with rapid growth in the quantity of money, as in Brazil or Chile or in the United States in recent years, and why low and falling interest rates have been associated with slow growth in the quantity of money, as in Switzerland now or in the United States from 1929 to 1933. As an empirical matter, low interest rates are a sign that monetary policy *has been* tight — in the sense that the quantity of money has grown slowly; high interest rates are a sign that monetary policy *has been* easy — in the sense that the quantity of money has grown rapidly. The broadest facts of experience run in precisely the opposite direction from that which the financial community and academic economists have all generally taken for granted.

Paradoxically, the monetary authority could assure low nominal rates of interest — but to do so it would have to start out in what seems like the opposite direction, by engaging in a deflationary monetary policy. Similarly, it could assure high nominal interest rates by engaging in an inflationary policy and accepting a temporary movement in interest rates in the opposite direction.

These considerations not only explain why monetary policy cannot peg interest rates; they also explain why interest rates are such a misleading indicator of whether monetary policy is "tight" or "easy." For that, it is far better to look at the rate of change of the quantity of money.[2]

EMPLOYMENT AS A CRITERION OF POLICY

The second limitation I wish to discuss goes more against the grain of current thinking. Monetary growth, it is widely held, will tend to stimulate employment; monetary contraction, to retard employment. Why, then, cannot the monetary authority adopt a target for employment or unemployment — say, 3 per cent unemployment; be tight when unemployment is less than the target; be easy when unemployment is higher than the target; and in this way peg unemployment at, say, 3 per cent? The reason it cannot is precisely the same as for interest rates — the difference between the immediate and the delayed consequences of such a policy.

Thanks to Wicksell, we are all acquainted with the concept of a "natural" rate of interest and the possibility of a discrepancy between the "natural" and the "market" rate. The preceding analysis of interest rates can be translated fairly directly into Wicksellian terms. The monetary authority can make the market rate less than the natural rate only by inflation. It can make the market rate higher than the natural rate only by deflation. We have added only one wrinkle to Wicksell — the Irving

Fisher distinction between the nominal and the real rate of interest. Let the monetary authority keep the nominal market rate for a time below the natural rate by inflation. That in turn will raise the nominal natural rate itself, once anticipations of inflation become widespread, thus requiring still more rapid inflation to hold down the market rate. Similarly, because of the Fisher effect, it will require not merely deflation but more and more rapid deflation to hold the market rate above the initial "natural" rate.

This analysis has its close counterpart in the employment market. At any moment in time, there is some level of unemployment which has the property that it is consistent with equilibrium in the structure of *real* wage rates. At that level of unemployment, real wage rates are tending on the average to rise at a "normal" secular rate, i.e., at a rate that can be indefinitely maintained so long as capital formation, technological improvements, etc., remain on their long-run trends. A lower level of unemployment is an indication that there is an excess demand for labor that will produce upward pressure on real wage rates. A higher level of unemployment is an indication that there is an excess supply of labor that will produce downward pressure on real wage rates. The "natural rate of unemployment," in other words, is the level that would be ground out by the Walrasian system of general equilibrium equations, provided there is imbedded in them the actual structural characteristics of the labor and commodity markets, including market imperfections, stochastic variability in demands and supplies, the cost of gathering information about job vacancies and labor availabilities, the costs of mobility, and so on.[3]

You will recognize the close similarity between this statement and the celebrated Phillips Curve. The similarity is not coincidental. Phillips' analysis and the relation between unemployment and wage change is deservedly celebrated as an important and original contribution. But, unfortunately, it contains a basic defect—the failure to distinguish between *nominal* wages and *real* wages—just as Wicksell's analysis failed to distinguish between *nominal* interest rates and *real* interest rates. Implicity, Phillips wrote his article for a world in which everyone anticipated that nominal prices would be stable and in which that anticipation remained unshaken and immutable whatever happened to actual prices and wages. Suppose, by contrast, that everyone anticipates that prices will rise at a rate of more than 75 per cent a year—as, for example, Brazilians did a few years ago. Then wages must rise at that rate simply to keep real wages unchanged. As excess supply of labor will be reflected in a less rapid rise in nominal wages than in anticipated prices,[4] not in an absolute decline in wages. When Brazil embarked on a policy to bring down the rate of price rise, and succeeded in bringing the price rise down to about 45 per cent a year, there was a sharp initial rise in unemployment because under the influence of earlier anticipations, wages kept rising at a pace that was higher than the new rate of price rise, though lower than earlier. This is the result experienced, and to be expected, of all attempts to reduce the rate of inflation below that widely anticipated.[5]

To avoid misunderstanding, let me emphasize that by using the term "natural" rate of unemployment, I do not mean to suggest that it is immutable and unchangeable. On the contrary, many of the market characteristics that determine its level are man-made and policy-made. In the United States, for example, legal minimum wage rates, the Walsh-Healy and Davis-Bacon Acts, and the strength of labor unions all make the natural rate of unemployment higher than it would otherwise be. Improvements in employment exchanges, in availability of information about job vacancies and labor supply, and so on, would tend to lower the natural rate of unemployment. I use the term "natural" for the same reason Wicksell did — to try to separate the real forces from monetary forces.

Let us assume that the monetary authority tries to peg the "market" rate of unemployment at a level below the "natural" rate. For definiteness, suppose that it takes 3 per cent as the target rate and that the "natural" rate is higher than 3 per cent. Suppose also that we start out at a time when prices have been stable and when unemployment is higher than 3 per cent. Accordingly, the authority increases the rate of monetary growth. This will be expansionary. By making nominal cash balances higher than people desire, it will tend initially to lower interest rates and in this and other ways to stimulate spending. Income and spending will start to rise.

To begin with, much or most of the rise in income will take the form of an increase in output and employment rather than in prices. People have been expecting prices to be stable, and prices and wages have been set for some time in the future on that basis. It takes time for people to adjust to a new state of demand. Producers will tend to react to the initial expansion in aggregate demand by increasing output, employees by working longer hours, and the unemployed, by taking jobs now offered at former nominal wages. This much is pretty standard doctrine.

But it describes only the initial effects. Because selling prices of products typically respond to an unanticipated rise in nominal demand faster than prices of factors of production, real wages received have gone down — though real wages anticipated by employees went up, since employees implicitly evaluated the wages offered at the earlier price level. Indeed, the simultaneous fall *ex post* in real wages to employers and rise *ex ante* in real wages to employees is what enabled employment to increase. But the decline *ex post* in real wages will soon come to affect anticipations. Employees will start to reckon on rising prices of the things they buy and to demand higher nominal wages for the future. "Market" unemployment is below the "natural" level. There is an excess demand for labor so real wages will tend to rise toward their initial level.

Even though the higher rate of monetary growth continues, the rise in real wages will reverse the decline in unemployment, and then lead to a rise, which will tend to return unemployment to its former level. In order to keep unemployment at its target level of 3 per cent, the monetary authority would have to raise monetary growth still more. As in the interest rate case, the "market" rate can be kept below the "natural" rate only by inflation. And, as in the interest rate case, too, only by accelerating inflation. Conversely, let the monetary authority choose a target rate of unemployment that is above the natural rate, and they will be led to produce a deflation, and an accelerating deflation at that.

What if the monetary authority chose the "natural" rate — either of interest or unemployment — as its target? One problem is that it cannot know what the "natural" rate is. Unfortunately, we have as yet devised no method to estimate accurately and readily the natural rate of either interest or unemployment. And the "natural" rate will itself change from time to time. But the basic problem is that even if the monetary authority knew the "natural" rate, and attempted to peg the market rate at that level, it would not be led to a determinate policy. The "market" rate will vary from the natural rate for all sorts of reasons other than monetary policy. If the monetary authority responds to these variations, it will set in train longer term effects that will make any monetary growth path it follows ultimately consistent with the rule of policy. The actual course of monetary growth will be analogous to a random walk, buffeted this way and that by the forces that produce temporary departures of the market rate from the natural rate.

. To state this conclusion differently, there is always a temporary trade-off between inflation and unemployment; there is no permanent trade-off. The temporary trade-off comes not from inflation per se, but from unanticipated inflation, which generally means, from a rising rate of inflation. The widespread belief that there is a permanent trade-off is a sophisticated version of the confusion between "high" and "rising" that we all recognize in simpler forms. A rising rate of inflation may reduce unemployment, a high rate will not.

But how long, you will say, is "temporary"? For interest rates, we have some systematic evidence on how long each of the several effects takes to work itself out. For unemployment, we do not. I can at most venture a personal judgment, based on some examination of the historical evidence, that the initial effects of a higher and unanticipated rate of inflation last for something like two to five years; that this initial effect then begins to be reversed; and that a full adjustment to the new rate of inflation takes about as long for employment as for interest rates, say, a couple of decades. For both interest rates and employment, let me add a qualification. These estimates are for changes in the rate of inflation of the order of magnitude that has been experienced in the United States. For much more sizable changes, such as those experienced in South American countries, the whole adjustment process is greatly speeded up.

To state the general conclusion still differently, the monetary authority controls nominal quantities — directly, the quantity of its own liabilities. In principle, it can use this control to peg a nominal quantity — an exchange rate, the price level, the nominal level of national income, the quantity of money by one or another definition — or to peg the rate of change in a nominal quantity — the rate of inflation or deflation, the rate of growth or decline in nominal national income, the rate of growth of the quantity of money. It cannot use its control over nominal quantities to peg a real quantity — the real rate of interest, the rate of unemployment, the level of real national income, the real quantity of money, the rate of growth of real national income, or the rate of growth of the real quantity of money.

II. WHAT MONETARY POLICY CAN DO

Monetary policy cannot peg these real magnitudes at pre-determined levels. But monetary policy can and does have important effects on these real magnitudes. The one is in no way inconsistent with the other.

My own studies of monetary history have made me extremely sympathetic to the oft-quoted, much reviled, and as widely misunderstood, comment by John Stuart Mill. "There cannot . . . ," he wrote, "be intrinsically a more insignificant thing, in the economy of society, than money; except in the character of a contrivance for sparing time and labour. It is a machine for doing quickly and commodiously, what would be done, though less quickly and commodiously, without it: and like many other kinds of machinery, it only exerts a distinct and independent influence of its own when it gets out of order" [7, p. 488].

True, money is only a machine, but it is an extraordinarily efficient machine. Without it, we could not have begun to attain the astounding growth in output and level of living we have experienced in the past two centuries — any more than we could have done so without those other marvelous machines that dot our countryside and enable us, for the most part, simply to do more efficiently what could be done without them at much greater cost in labor.

But money has one feature that these other machines do not share. Because it is so pervasive, when it gets out of order, it throws a monkey wrench into the operation of all the other machines. The Great Contraction is the most dramatic example but not the only one. Every other major contraction in this country has been either produced by monetary disorder or greatly exacerbated by monetary disorder. Every major inflation has been produced by monetary expansion — mostly to meet the overriding demands of war which have forced the creation of money to supplement explicit taxation.

The first and most important lesson that history teaches about what monetary policy can do — and it is a lesson of the most profound importance — is that monetary policy can prevent money itself from being a major source of economic disturbance. This sounds like a negative proposition: avoid major mistakes. In part it is. The Great Contraction might not have occurred at all, and if it had, it would have been far less severe, if the monetary authority had avoided mistakes, or if the monetary arrangements had been those of an earlier time when there was no central authority with the power to make the kinds of mistakes that the Federal Reserve System made. The past few years, to come closer to home, would have been steadier and more productive of economic wellbeing if the Federal Reserve had avoided drastic and erratic changes of direction, first expanding the money supply at an unduly rapid pace, then, in early 1966, stepping on the brake too hard, then, at the end of 1966, reversing itself and resuming expansion until at least November, 1967, at a more rapid pace than can long be maintained without appreciable inflation.

Even if the proposition that monetary policy can prevent money itself from being a major source of economic disturbance were a wholly negative proposition, it would be none the less important for that. As it happens, however, it is not a wholly negative proposition. The monetary machine has gotten out of order even when there has been no central authority with anything like the power now possessed by the Fed. In the United States, the 1907 episode and earlier banking panics are examples of how the monetary machine can get out of order largely on its own. There is therefore a positive and important task for the monetary authority — to suggest improvements in the machine that will reduce the chances that it will get out of order, and to use its own powers so as to keep the machine in good working order.

A second thing monetary policy can do is provide a stable background for the economy — keep the machine well oiled, to continue Mill's analogy. Accomplishing the first task will contribute to this objective, but there is more to it than that. Our economic system will work best when producers and consumers, employers and employees, can proceed with full confidence that the average level of prices will behave in a known way in the future — preferably that it will be highly stable. Under any conceivable institutional arrangements, and certainly under those that now prevail in the United States, there is only a limited amount of flexibility in prices and wages. We need to conserve this flexibility to achieve changes in relative prices and wages that are required to adjust to dynamic changes in tastes and technology. We should not dissipate it simply to achieve changes in the absolute level of prices that serve no economic function.

In an earlier era, the gold standard was relied on to provide confidence in future monetary stability. In its heyday it served that function reasonably well. It clearly no longer does, since there is scarce a country in the world that is prepared to let the gold standard reign unchecked — and there are persuasive reasons why countries should not do so. The monetary authority could operate as a surrogate for the gold standard, if it pegged exchange rates and did so exclusively by altering the quantity of money in response to balance of payment flows without "sterilizing" surpluses or deficits and without resorting to open or concealed exchange control or to changes in tariffs and quotas. But again, though many central bankers talk this way, few are in fact willing to follow this course — and again there are persuasive reasons why they should not do so. Such a policy would submit each country to the vagaries not of an impersonal and automatic gold standard but of the policies — deliberate or accidental — of other monetary authorities.

In today's world, if monetary policy is to provide a stable background for the economy it must do so by deliberately employing its powers to that end. I shall come later to how it can do so.

Finally, monetary policy can contribute to offsetting major disturbances in the economic system arising from other sources. If there is an independent secular exhilaration — as the postwar expansion was described by the proponents of secular stagnation — monetary policy can in principle help to hold it in check by a slower rate of monetary growth than would otherwise be desirable. If, as now, an explosive federal budget threatens unprecedented deficits, monetary policy can hold any inflationary dangers in check by a slower rate of monetary growth than would otherwise be desirable. This will temporarily mean higher interest rates than would otherwise prevail — to enable the government to borrow the sums needed to finance the deficit — but by preventing the speeding up of inflation, it may well mean both lower prices and lower nominal interest rates for the long pull. If the end of a substantial war offers the country an opportunity to shift resources from wartime to peacetime production, monetary policy can ease the transition by a higher rate of monetary growth than would otherwise be desirable — though experience is not very encouraging that it can do so without going too far.

I have put this point last, and stated it in qualified terms — as referring to major disturbances — because I believe that the potentiality of monetary policy in offsetting other forces making for instability is far more limited than is commonly believed. We simply do not know enough to be able to recognize minor disturbances when they occur or to be able to predict either what their effects will be with any precision or what monetary policy is required to offset their effects. We do not know enough to be able to achieve stated objectives by delicate, or even fairly coarse, changes in the mix of monetary and fiscal policy. In this area particularly the best is likely to be the enemy of the good. Experience suggests that the path of wisdom is to use monetary policy explicitly to offset other disturbances only when they offer a "clear and present danger."

III. HOW SHOULD MONETARY POLICY BE CONDUCTED?

How should monetary policy be conducted to make the contribution to our goals that it is capable of making? This is clearly not the occasion for presenting a detailed "Program for Monetary Stability" — to use the title of a book in which I tried to do so [3]. I shall restrict myself here to two major requirements for monetary policy that follow fairly directly from the preceding discussion.

The first requirement is that the monetary authority should guide itself by magnitudes that it can control, not by ones that it cannot control. If, as the authority has often done, it takes interest rates or the current unemployment percentage as the immediate criterion of policy, it will be like a space vehicle that has taken a fix on the wrong star. No matter how sensitive and sophisticated its guiding apparatus, the space vehicle will go astray. And so will the monetary authority. Of the various alternative magnitudes that it can control, the most appealing guides for policy are exchange rates, the price level as defined by some index, and the quantity of the monetary total — currency plus adjusted demand deposits, or this total plus commercial bank time deposits, or a still broader total.

For the United States in particular, exchange rates are an undesirable guide. It might be worth requiring the bulk of the economy to adjust to the tiny percentage consisting of foreign trade if that would guarantee freedom from monetary irresponsibility — as it might under a real gold standard. But it is hardly worth doing so simply to adapt to the average of whatever policies monetary authorities in the rest of the world adopt. Far better to let the market, through floating exchange rates, adjust to world conditions the 5 per cent or so of our resources devoted to international trade while reserving monetary policy to promote the effective use of 95 per cent.

Of the three guides listed, the price level is clearly the most important in its own right. Other things the same, it would be much the best of the alternatives — as so many distinguished economists have urged in the past. But other things are not the same. The link between the policy actions of the monetary authority and the price level, while unquestionably present, is more indirect than the link between the policy actions of the authority and any of the several monetary totals. Moreover, monetary action takes a longer time to affect the price level than to affect the monetary totals and both the time lag and the magnitude of effect vary with circumstances. As a result, we cannot predict at all accurately just what effect a particular monetary action will have on the price level and, equally important, just when it will have that effect. Attempting to control directly the price level is therefore likely to make monetary policy itself a source of economic disturbance because of false stops and starts. Perhaps, as our understanding of monetary phenomena advances, the situation will change. But at the present stage of our understanding, the long way around seems the surer way to our objective. Accordingly, I believe that a monetary total is the best currently available immediate guide or criterion for monetary policy — and I believe that it matters much less which particular total is chosen than that one be chosen.

A second requirement for monetary policy is that the monetary authority avoid sharp swings in policy. In the past, monetary authorities have on occasion moved in the wrong direction — as in the episode of the Great Contraction that I have stressed. More frequently, they have moved in the right direction, albeit often too late, but have erred by moving too far. Too late and too much has been the general practice. For example, in early 1966, it was the right policy for the Federal Reserve to move in a less expansionary direction — though it should have done so at least a year earlier. But when it moved, it went too far, producing the sharpest change in the rate of monetary growth of the postwar era. Again, having gone too far, it was the right policy for the Fed to reverse course at the end of 1966. But again it went too far, not only restoring but exceeding the earlier excessive rate of monetary growth. And this episode is no exception. Time and again this has been the course followed — as in 1919 and 1920, in 1937 and 1938, in 1953 and 1954, in 1959 and 1960.

The reason for the propensity to overreact seems clear: the failure of monetary authorities to allow for the delay between their actions and the subsequent effects on the economy. They tend to determine their actions by today's conditions — but their actions will affect the economy only six or nine or twelve or fifteen months later. Hence they feel impelled to step on the brake, or the accelerator, as the case may be, too hard.

My own prescription is still that the monetary authority go all the way in avoiding such swings by adopting publicly the policy of achieving a steady rate of growth in a specified monetary total. The precise rate of growth, like the precise monetary total, is less important than the adoption of some stated and known rate. I myself have argued for a rate that would on the average achieve rough stability in the level of prices of final products, which I have estimated would call for something like a 3 to 5 per cent per year rate of growth in currency plus all commercial bank deposits or a slightly lower rate of growth in currency plus demand deposits only.[6] But it would be better to have a fixed rate that would on the average produce moderate inflation or moderate deflation, provided it was steady, than to suffer the wide and erratic perturbations we have experienced.

Short of the adoption of such a publicly stated policy of a steady rate of monetary growth, it would constitute a major improvement if the monetary authority followed the self-denying ordinance of avoiding wide swings. It is a matter of record that periods of relative stability in the rate of monetary growth have also been periods of relative stability in economic activity, both in the United States and other countries. Periods of wide swings in the rate of monetary growth have also been periods of wide swings in economic activity.

By setting itself a steady course and keeping to it, the monetary authority could make a major contribution to promoting economic stability. By making the course one of steady but moderate growth in the quantity of money, it would make a major contribution to avoidance of either inflation or deflation of prices. Other forces would still affect the economy, require change and adjustment, and disturb the even tenor of our ways. But steady monetary growth would provide a monetary climate favorable to the effective operation of those basic forces of enterprise, ingenuity, invention, hard work, and thrift that are the true springs of economic growth. That is the most that we can ask from monetary policy at our present stage of knowledge. But that much — and it is a great deal — is clearly within our reach.

REFERENCES

1. H. S. Ellis, ed., *A Survey of Contemporary Economics.* Philadelphia 1948.
2. Milton Friedman, "The Monetary Theory and Policy of Henry Simons," *Jour. Law and Econ.,* Oct. 1967, *10*, 1-13.
3. _____, *A Program for Monetary Stability.* New York 1959.
4. E. A. Goldenweiser, "Postwar Problems and Policies," *Fed. Res. Bull.,* Feb. 1945, *31*, 112-21.
5. P. T. Homan and Fritz Machlup, ed., *Financing American Prosperity.* New York 1945.
6. A. P. Lerner and F. D. Graham, ed., *Planning and Paying for Full Employment.* Princeton 1946.
7. J. S. Mill, *Principles of Political Economy,* Bk. III, Ashley ed. New York 1929.

NOTES

1. In [2], I have argued that Henry Simons shared this view with Keynes, and that it accounts for the policy changes that he recommended.

2. This is partly an empirical not theoretical judgment. In principle, "tightness" or "ease" depends on the rate of change of the quantity of money supplied compared to the rate of change of the quantity demanded excluding effects on demand from monetary policy itself. However, empirically demand is highly stable, if we exclude the effect of monetary policy, so it is generally sufficient to look at supply alone.

3. It is perhaps worth noting that this "natural" rate need not correspond to equality between the number unemployed and the number of job vacancies. For any given structure of the labor market, there will be some equilibrium relation between these two magnitudes, but there is no reason why it should be one of equality.

4. Strictly speaking, the rise in nominal wages will be less rapid than the rise in anticipated nominal wages to make allowance for any secular changes in real wages.

5. Stated in terms of the rate of change of nominal wages, the Phillips Curve can be expected to be reasonably stable and well defined for any period for which the *average* rate of change of prices, and hence the anticipated rate, has been relatively stable. For such periods, nominal wages and "real" wages move together. Curves computed for different periods or different countries for each of which this condition has been satisfied will differ in level, the level of the curve depending on what the average rate of price change was. The higher the average rate of price change, the higher will tend to be the level of the curve. For periods or countries for which the rate of change of prices varies considerably, the Phillips Curve will not be well defined. My impression is that these statements accord reasonably well with the experience of the economists who have explored empirical Phillips Curves.

   Restate Phillips' analysis in terms of the rate of change of real wages — and even more precisely, anticipated real wages — and it all falls into place. That is why students of empirical Phillips Curves have found that it helps to include the rate of change of the price level as an independent variable.

6. In an as yet unpublished article on "The Optimum Quantity of Money," I conclude that a still lower rate of growth, something like 2 per cent for the broader definition, might be better yet in order to eliminate or reduce the difference between private and total cost of adding to real balances.

chapter 22

transportation and

international trade

TRANSPORTATION

Long before 1915, a transportation network had been established which joined the United States in a common market. Transportation developments since 1915 have involved the emergence of new and more efficient methods of transportation, the extension of government aid and regulation to these new areas, the economic decline of the railroad, and the wartime stimulation and renewed decline of the Merchant Marine.

RAILROADS

During the twentieth century the financial problems of railroads intensified. Faced with severe competition, particularly from motor vehicles, the railroads were transformed from a growth industry to one of stagnation and decline. Railroad freight traffic measured in ton-miles increased three and a half times from 1890 to 1916; and although it doubled between 1940 and the late 1960's, its relative share of total inter-

675

TABLE 22.1. *Intercity Freight Traffic By Type of Transport 1940–1968 Percentage of Total Ton-Miles*

Year	Railroads	Motor Vehicles	Inland Water-ways	Oil Pipe-lines
1940	63%	10%	18%	9%
1945	69	6	13	12
1950	57	16	15	12
1955	50	17	17	16
1960	45	21	17	17
1965	44	22	16	19
1968	42	21	16	21

SOURCE: U.S. Bureau of the Census. *Statistical Abstract of the United States: 1970.* Washington, D.C.: U.S. Government Printing Office, 1970, p. 535.

TABLE 22.2. *Intercity Passenger Traffic By Type of Transport 1950–1968 Percentage of Total Passenger Miles*

Year	Private Automobiles	Airways	Busses	Railroads
1950	86%	2%	5%	7%
1955	89	3	4	4
1960	90	4	3	3
1965	89	6	3	2
1968	87	10	2	1

SOURCE: U.S. Bureau of the Census. *Statistical Abstract of The United States: 1970.* Washington, D.C.: U.S. Government Printing Office, 1970, p. 535.

city freight traffic decreased from sixty-three per cent to forty-two per cent. (See Table 22.1.) Passenger traffic also experienced a decline. Between 1920 and 1940 the number of passengers carried by U.S. railroads declined from 1,270 million to 456 million and by 1970 the number had fallen to 285 million. Measured in railroad passenger miles little change took place between 1916 and 1950. However, after 1950 a significant absolute decline occurred, the number of railroad passenger miles falling from 32.5 million in 1950 to 13.3 million in 1968. In relative terms, during the same period railroad's share of total intercity passenger miles declined from seven per cent to one per cent. (See Table 22.2.) Associated with the decline of freight and passenger business, railroad track mileage declined from a high of 253,000 miles in 1920 to 234,000 miles in 1940, and to 208,000 miles by the late 1960's. (See Table 12.1.)

The physical decline of the railroads was evident by World War I. Pressed into full usage to meet war needs, they were unable to handle the flow of military personnel and supplies. The Federal government was forced to assume temporary control. Government operation of the railroads as a unified system led to operating efficiencies which did not escape the notice of both government officials and the railroad industry. Although some questioned whether the roads could continue to survive on their own, they were returned to their owners under the Transportation Act of 1920. This Act formulated a bold new government policy to deal with rail problems. The historic hostility of government to consolidation was modified. The Interstate Commerce Commission was directed to draw up a national plan of consolidated railroad systems of equal earning power, pairing off strong and weak roads to permit mutual support, and preserving competition wherever desirable. Unfortunately, the railroads did not look with favor upon the Transportation Act of 1920. All roads wanted consolidation, it was true, but strong roads did not want to be saddled with weak roads as marriage partners. They preferred other strong roads. Few mergers, therefore, resulted.

The Great Depression of the 1930's fell heavily on the industry. Burdensome capital structures forced a fifth of the railroads, representing a third of total track mileage, into receivership. The situation would have been considerably worse had it not been for significant financial support from the Federal Government. The Reconstruction Finance Corporation, established in 1932, made loans to railroads which could not obtain funds on reasonable terms from banks or the general public. In 1933 the Emergency Transportation Act established a Federal Coordinator for Transportation responsible for promoting economies through railroad cooperation. To encourage consolidations, the Transportation Act of 1940 held that mergers no longer had to be in conformity with the national plan drawn up by the ICC under the 1920 Transportation Act. The 1940 Act attempted to coordinate all forms of transportation, thereby eliminating the allegedly unfair competitive position of other forms of transportation vis-à-vis the railroad. It stated:

> It is hereby declared to be the national transportation policy of the Congress to provide for fair and impartial regulation of all modes of transportation subject to the provisions of this Act, so administered as to promote safe, adequate, economical and efficient service, and foster sound economic conditions in transportation and among the several

carriers; to encourage conditions in transportation and maintenance of reasonable charges for transportation services, without unjust discrimination, undue preferences or advantages, or unfair or destructive competitive practices; to cooperate with the several states and the duly authorized officials thereof; and to encourage fair wages and equitable working conditions . . . all to the end of developing, coordinating, and preserving a national transportation system by water, highway, and rail, as well as other means, adequate to meet the needs of the commerce of the United States, of the Postal Service, and of the national defense.

In the Transportation Act of 1958 Congress sought to make the railroads more competitive with other forms of transportation by permitting them to adopt a more aggressive pricing policy vis-à-vis other forms of transportation. Furthermore, the ICC became more receptive in permitting the merger of major roads. This was exemplified by the joining of the Pennsylvania and New York Central systems into the nation's largest transportation company in 1968. Unhappily, the newly formed Penn-Central Corporation was forced into bankruptcy in 1970. In the same year, to relieve the railroads of their burdensome passenger revenue deficits and avert a complete collapse in noncommuter railroad passenger service, Congress established a National Railroad Passenger Corporation (Amtrak). In 1971 Amtrack commenced operations with the elimination of about half of all interstate railroad passenger service.

MOTOR CARRIERS

Motor vehicles are more flexible and convenient than railroads, particularly for short hauls. Unlike the railroads, their rights of way were constructed cost free by government. Federal, state and local construction and maintenance of the nation's highways permits anyone who can afford the price of a truck to enter the trucking business. As a result the typical firm in the trucking industry is of small scale. In contrast to the several hundred railroad companies in operation in the 1960's, there were about twenty thousand regulated motor carriers.

It was stated earlier that initial Federal activities in road construction terminated in the 1830's. Road-building thereafter was principally confined to local governments. Beginning in the 1890's state construction assumed significant proportions and efforts were made to transfer control of roads from municipalities to the state level. Massachusetts led the way by creating the first state highway commission in 1893. The growth of motor vehicle registration resulted in renewed Federal activity beginning with the Federal Aid Highway Act of 1916. Thereafter, local and state governments increasingly depended on federal aid to finance road construction. Under post-World War II programs the Federal government financed up to ninety per cent of all construction expenses. Well over half of these costs have been derived from highway user levies such as gasoline taxes, license fees, and tolls, with the balance coming from general revenues. By 1970, almost four million miles of road were in existence, of which three million miles were intercity routes. Although trucking as a business dates from the late 1920's, significant growth did not occur until the second half of the 1930's. After a hiatus during World War II, rapid expansion resumed. The 1950's and 1960's have been characterized by numerous mergers and consolidations which had the effect of creating nationwide trucking firms, capable of serving the entire U.S. market. Trucking has proven a serious competitor of the railroads in the shipment of freight. Its share of intercity freight traffic doubled between 1940 and 1968. (See Table 22.1.)

Except for state safety legislation, the trucking industry was largely unregulated until the 1930's. The onset of the Great Depression and chaotic competitive conditions led the larger and well-established firms in the industry to seek Federal regulation. The Motor Carrier Act of 1935, later incorporated into the Interstate Commerce Act, introduced safety regulations for all truck carriers. Private trucks (which account for slightly less than half of all truck-traffic ton-miles), carriers operating on a purely local basis (school buses, taxis and trolleys), trucks carrying agricultural produce and newspapers, and vehicles operated by the railroads and airlines were all exempted from economic regulation. Common carriers were required to obtain certificates of public convenience and necessity from the ICC. These are issued only if there exists a need for the services of a new trucking company. Freedom of entry is thus controlled. Contract carriers (companies under contract to one or more firms) must also obtain permits to operate. All rates charged must be just, reasonable and nondiscriminatory. The ICC received the power to fix maximum and minimum rates for common carriers, and minimum rates for contract carriers. Rates must be published, and service must be adequate and safe. All consolidations of common carriers operating over twenty vehicles must be approved by the ICC.

Privately operated automobiles have been the railroad's major competitor for intercity passenger business. The growth of suburban communities, increased affluence, and more leisure time have made the automobile the dominant form of passenger transportation. Its share of intercity passenger miles grew from insignificance in 1915 to over eighty per cent in the post World War II period (see Table 22.2).

AIR CARRIERS

Air carriers also have made major inroads into the railroad's passenger business. Four major categories comprise the industry: domestic trunk lines servicing major urban centers, local service carriers, cargo carriers, and local helicopter carriers. Of the twelve domestic carriers in operation in 1970, four (American, Eastern, TWA, and United) accounted for over two thirds of total trunkline business. Passenger traffic is urban oriented as far as airlines are concerned, seventy-five per cent of it originating in fifteen cities. While the first commercial flights took place in the 1920's, it was not until after World War II that the industry grew to significant size. The industry's great advantage is speed. As a result, it has not only diverted passenger traffic from other means of transportation, but it has also created business where it previously did not exist. Thus, businessmen commute frequently from New York to Chicago by plane, whereas they might not by train, and vacationers from Chicago go to the Caribbean more readily than they might by a combination of train and ship. Its share of intercity passenger miles grew from two per cent in 1950 to ten per cent in 1968. Owing to its high cost, the industry's freight business has been restricted to items which bear a high value in relation to weight.

The airline industry, like motor vehicles, has received substantial government support. Aid has taken several forms. Airmail subsidies, which commenced in the mid-1920's, have been a significant source of airline revenues. In the 1960's, most subsidies were directed to weaker feeder lines rather than the major trunk carriers. Construction and maintenance of airways, which also commenced in the 1920's, provided the airlines with air-route traffic control systems, weather reporting facilities, instrument approach systems, radio-signal stations, traffic control towers, beacon lights, and emergency landing fields. Since 1933, the Federal Government has borne the major share of airport construction and maintenance. In 1946, the Federal Airport Act attempted to systematize airport planning and construction. To receive Federal support a project had to be consistent with the National Airport Plan drawn up by the Civil Aeronautics Authority. As discussed in an earlier chapter, the airline industry is regulated by the Civil Aeronautics Board and the Federal Aviation Agency.

PIPELINES

Pipelines, like motor vehicles and airlines, have grown significantly in the twentieth century. They have the ability to transport bulk commodities at low cost. It has been estimated that they are able to transport these commodities at roughly half the cost of railroads. Consequently, they have been a serious competitor to the railroads. Their one great disadvantage is that they are restricted to commodities in a liquid or gaseous condition. They principally carry two products, petroleum and natural gas. Oil pipelines have the oldest history, the first having been constructed in 1865 in the Pennsylvania oil fields. By 1921, these pipelines, owned for the most part by the major oil companies, were 55,000 miles in length. By 1968, they had grown to 169,000 miles in length. Seventy-five per cent of the pipeline system was used for the transmission of crude oil, and the balance for refined products. Between 1940 and 1968 oil pipeline traffic increased its share of intercity freight traffic from nine per cent to twenty-one per cent. Long distance natural gas pipelines date from the early 1930's. By 1945, 75,000 miles of pipeline had been constructed. Since this date the industry has experienced its greatest growth, with roughly a quarter of a million miles of pipeline in existence by the late 1960's. Government regulation of pipelines commenced in 1906 when the Hepburn Act placed them under the jurisdiction of the ICC. In part this was a reaction to the abuses of the Standard Oil monopoly. The Company's control of existing pipelines, its refusal to ship oil for rival companies, and its alliance with the railroads in opposing the construction of new lines were the principal catalytic agents leading to regulation. Under the Act rates had to be published and were required to be just, reasonable, and nondiscriminatory. Federal regulation of natural gas pipelines began in 1938 with passage of the Natural Gas Act. The Federal Power Commission was empowered to issue certificates of public convenience and necessity, and to order the extension of gas lines. Its approval is needed for abandonment. Rates have to be just and reasonable.

THE MERCHANT MARINE

The Merchant Marine on the eve of World War I was in an advanced state of economic decline. In 1910, only nine per cent of the total value of U.S. exports and imports were being carried in U.S. ships. In addition, most of the fleet was old and in a state of disrepair. World War I promoted a temporary recovery. By 1915 its share of U.S. exports and imports had increased to fourteen per cent, and by 1916 to sixteen per cent. In the latter year Congress created the U.S. Shipping Board to ensure the existence of just and reasonable rates and to study means to increase the size of the U.S. merchant fleet. In 1917, four billion dollars was authorized for the construction of ships, and by 1920 forty-three per cent of U.S. exports and imports was being carried in U.S. ships. In the same year the Jones Act provided subsidization for ship construction to be financed with proceeds from the sale of ships built by the Federal Government during the war. The Jones-White Act of 1928 introduced subsidies in the form of tax exemption and payments for mail shipment. It also provided for the sale of federally owned ships to private enterprise at less than cost, and prohibited foreign ships from engaging in U.S. coastal trade. By 1929 the Federal Government had sold practically all of its merchant fleet. Although at that date the United States fleet ranked second only to Great Britain, it was once again experiencing relative decline due to high construction and operating costs. By the early 1930's, it carried only 35 per cent of all U.S. imports and exports. In the Merchant Marine Act of 1936, a Maritime Commission was established to furnish direct subsidies to American fleet owners for both ship construction and operation. Subsidies were to equal the difference between the cost of building and operating ships in the United States and abroad. During World War II the Federal government once again undertook the construction of ships, and following the war, in the Merchant Ship Sales Act of 1946, it adopted the policy of selling these ships below cost to private enterprise. Despite continued subsidization and a temporary resurgence during the Korean and Vietnam Wars, the Merchant Marine steadily declined. Between 1950 and 1970 the percentage of U.S. exports and imports carried in American bottoms declined from about forty per cent to less than fifteen per cent. In 1971 U.S. passenger liner service on the Atlantic was terminated.

INTERNATIONAL TRADE: THE ASSUMPTION OF WORLD LEADERSHIP

EXPORTS AND IMPORTS

The period 1915-1970 evidenced a continuation of the trend toward greater exports of manufactures (including semimanufactures) and reduced sales of raw materials and foodstuffs (includes crude materials, fuels, food, beverages, and tobacco). Manufactures' share of total merchandise exports rose from 51 per cent in the 1911-1920 period to 75 per cent in 1961-1970. (See Table 22.3.) At the same time, manufactures' share of imports, which had been declining steadily since the Civil War, turned upward. These items, which comprised 35 per cent of total merchandise imports in the 1911-1920 period, increased their share to 50 per cent in 1951-1960, and to 71 per cent in 1961-1970. (See Table 22.4.) These changes reflect the increasing industrialization of the United States and the emergence, particularly since 1960, of strong competitors to American dominance of world markets. Japan, Canada, and the Common Market countries, particularly West Germany, Italy and France, made important industrial strides. Reduced trade barriers, combined with expanded consumer purchasing power, resulted in substantial increases in American purchases of foreign nondurable and durable goods. In turn, the economic growth of these nations enabled them to buy larger quantities of United States manufactures. These changes are reflected in the origin of United States exports and imports. Since 1915 Europe's share of U.S. exports declined from 64 per cent to 32 per cent, while Asia's share rose from 7 per cent to 21 per cent, and the Americas' share increased from 26 per cent to 37 per cent. (See Table 22.5.) In 1915, our principal customers and their respective shares of total exports were: Great Britain, 32 per cent; France, 14 per cent; and Canada, 11 per cent. By 1970 Canada had assumed a dominant position, accounting for 24 per cent of total exports,

TABLE 22.3. *Percentage Distribution of U.S. Merchandise Exports By Type 1911-1970*

Years	Raw Materials	Foodstuffs*	Manufactures†
1911-20	22%	27%	51%
1921-30	27	20	53
1931-40	23	12	55
1941-50	10	17	73
1951-60	13	13	74
1961-70	11	14	75

SOURCE: U.S. Bureau of the Census. *Historical Statistics of the United States, Colonial Times to 1957.* Washington, D.C.: U.S. Government Printing Office, 1960, p. 544; U.S. Bureau of the Census. *Statistical Abstract of the United States: 1970.* Washington, D.C.: U.S. Government Printing Office, 1970, p. 779.

*Includes crude and manufactured items.

†Includes semi- and finished manufactures.

TABLE 22.4. *Percentage Distribution of U.S. Merchandise Imports By Type 1911-1970*

Years	Raw Materials	Foodstuffs*	Manufactures†
1911-20	38%	27%	35%
1921-30	35	24	41
1931-40	33	29	38
1941-50	30	30	40
1951-60	24	26	50
1961-70	13	16	71

SOURCE: U.S. Bureau of the Census. *Historical Statistics of the United States, Colonial Times to 1957.* Washington, D.C.: U.S. Government Printing Office, 1960, p. 544; U.S. Bureau of the Census. *Statistical Abstract of the United States: 1970.* Washington, D.C.: U.S. Government Printing Office, 1970, p. 781.

*Includes crude and manufactured items.

†Includes semi- and finished manufactures.

followed by Japan with 10 per cent and Great Britain with 6 per cent. The three major Common Market countries combined — West Germany, France and Italy — purchased 12 per cent of our exports. Imports by major area

TABLE 22.5. *Percentage Distribution of U.S. Exports By Area 1911-1970*

Years	Europe	North and South America	Asia	Other
1911-20	64%	26%	7%	3%
1921-30	52	33	7	8
1931-40	44	33	17	6
1941-50	46	36	12	6
1951-60	26	43	15	16
1961-70	32	37	21	10

SOURCE: U.S. Bureau of the Census. *Historical Statistics of the United States, Colonial Times to 1957.* Washington, D.C.: U.S. Government Printing Office, 1960, p. 550; U.S. Bureau of the Census. *Statistical Abstract of the United States: 1970.* Washington, D.C.: U.S. Government Printing Office, 1970, p. 788.

TABLE 22.6. *Percentage Distribution of U.S. Imports By Area 1911-1970*

Years	Europe	North and South America	Asia	Other
1911-20	33%	41%	21%	5%
1921-30	30	38	28	4
1931-40	27	39	30	4
1941-50	13	63	16	8
1951-60	23	53	16	8
1961-70	30	44	20	6

SOURCE: U.S. Bureau of the Census. *Historical Statistics of the United States, Colonial Times to 1957.* Washington, D.C.: U.S. Government Printing Office, 1960, p. 552; U.S. Bureau of the Census. *Statistical Abstract of the United States: 1970.* Washington, D.C.: U.S. Government Printing Office, 1970, p. 788.

showed little change over the period. (See Table 22.6.) However, changes did occur in terms of the importance of individual nations. Great Britain was the largest source of our imports in 1915, accounting for 15 per cent of the total. Next in importance were Cuba (11 per cent), Canada (10 per cent), Brazil (5 per cent) and Japan (5 per cent). By 1970 Canada had replaced Britain and increased her share to 29 per cent. Japan assumed second place with 13 per cent of the total, followed by Britain with 6 per cent. The three leading Common Market countries combined provided 13 per cent of our imports.

FROM DEBTOR TO CREDITOR

World War I was a landmark in U.S. international relations. By greatly accelerating long-term developments in U.S. international trade, it propelled the United States into the position of a creditor country. American exports of food and manufactured goods to all belligerents increased sharply. Even when the United States entered the war, it continued to be a heavy supplier of goods to its allies. The productive capacity of the United States, unlike that of Europe, was stimulated rather than destroyed by hostilities. By the end of the conflict, the United States and Europe had exchanged roles as creditor and debtor, Before the war, foreign investment in the United States totaled 7.2 billion dollars, while American investments abroad equaled only 3.5 billion. By 1919 the opposite was true, with U.S. capital abroad equaling 7.0 billion and foreign investment in the United States declining to 3.3 billion. (See Table 22.7.) In addition, allied war debts to the United States, after negotiation with England and France, were set at 12.1 billion dollars.

TABLE 22.7. *International Investment Position of the United States, 1914–1968 (Billions of Dollars)*

Year	U.S. Investments Abroad	Foreign Investments in the U.S.
1914	3.5	7.2
1919	7.0	3.3
1927	13.8	6.6
1930	17.2	8.4
1935	13.5	6.4
1940	12.3	13.5
1945	16.8	17.6
1950	30.0	17.6
1955	42.2	27.8
1960	66.4	41.2
1965	104.7	58.7
1968	126.8	81.1

SOURCE: U.S. Bureau of the Census. *Historical Statistics of the United States, Colonial Times to 1957.* Washington, D.C.: U.S. Government Printing Office, 1960, p. 565; U.S. Bureau of the Census. *Statistical Abstract of the United States: 1970.* Washington, D.C.: U.S. Government Printing Office, 1970, p. 765.

TABLE 22.8. *U.S. Balance of Merchandise Trade Average Annual Rates 1911-1970 (Millions of Dollars)*

Years	Exports	Imports	Net Exports
1911-20	4,513	2,612	1,901
1921-30	4,499	3,742	757
1931-40	2,578	2,074	504
1941-50	10,797	5,030	5,764
1951-60	34,225	24,354	9,871
1961-70	29,084	25,233	3,851

SOURCE: U.S. Bureau of the Census. *Historical Statistics of the United States, Colonial Times to 1957.* Washington, D.C.: U.S. Government Printing Office, 1960, pp. 550, 552; *1971 Economic Report of the President.* Washington, D.C.: U.S. Government Printing Office, 1971, p. 298.

The First World War did much to divert American business attention away from domestic activities and toward foreign ventures. New York began to compete with London as the financial capital of the world. U.S. funds flowed freely to Europe. By 1927, private U.S. investments abroad totaled almost fourteen billion dollars. These capital flows masked international stresses that were a legacy of the Versailles Peace Treaty. American investments in Germany were used to pay German reparations to France and England, and in turn were used by France and England to finance both the repayment of war debts and the purchase of goods needed for reconstruction from the United States. U.S. trade policy aggravated the stresses. The Fordney-McCumber Act of 1922 raised tariff walls to about 40 per cent, thus hampering the ability of foreigners to earn dollars. (See Table 11.7.) At the same time, U.S. exports were growing significantly through the aggressive efforts of the Department of Commerce, headed by Herbert Hoover. As a consequence, the U.S. balance of merchandise trade showed an average annual surplus of roughly three-quarters of a billion dollars throughout the decade. (See Table 22.8.)

WORLD DEPRESSION

Beginning in 1928 American capital flows to Europe began to decline, being diverted instead to the soaring stock market. A chain reaction was set into motion. Unable to continue heavy reparation payments through the use of American capital, Germany tried to earn funds through significantly favorable trade balances. To accomplish this, an internal policy of deflation was pursued. Prices and wages were reduced to make German exports attractive in world markets. The result was a rise in unemployment and a consequent rise of the political fortunes of Adolph Hitler.

Unfortunately, the medicine of deflation was too late and too severe to save the patient. To aggravate matters, Americans began in 1930 a net withdrawal of capital from Europe in response to the onset of depression. Defaults resulted which stimulated additional capital liquidations. The major bank of Austria went bankrupt. This initiated a chain reaction which eventually resulted in the collapse of the international financial community. The citizens of country after country lost confidence in their national currency and sought refuge in gold. In turn, the flight from currency to gold forced many European countries, including Great Britain, to abandon the gold standard. Under such a standard, a nation is obligated to convert all paper and credit currency into gold at a fixed rate. If a nation's gold reserves reach a point where the public believes convertibility is no longer possible, a run on gold occurs and the government has no choice but to suspend gold payments. In place of the gold standard, many nations introduced a series of restrictive regulations, including protective tariffs, import quotas, and exchange controls.

In 1931 Germany ceased its reparations payments. England and France, now unable to pay war debts to the United States, were forced in 1932 and 1933 to default. As worldwide depression took hold, most nations attempted to help themselves without too much thought as to the implications of their policies on other nations. A popular device, as noted in the previous chapter, was currency devaluation. By a stroke of the pen, nations declared that a unit of foreign currency could be exchanged for more units of their currency. This would have the effect of boosting exports and choking off imports, thus stimulating income and employment. These tactics proved fruitless, however, as nation after nation, including the United States, engaged in competitive devaluations. The result was the creation of uncertainty in foreign exchange markets, an unhealthy situation since stable exchange rates are a necessary requirement for the expansion of foreign trade. A businessman must know with relative certainty from month to month what a unit of his currency can buy of foreign currencies. If he does not, he is less likely to engage in international commerce. The latter will, therefore, decline. Trade declines were buttressed by the imposition of high tariff walls to shut out imports. The United States, in the Hawley-Smoot Tariff of 1930, raised tariffs to the highest level in its history, 60 per cent. (See Figure 11.2.) With every nation attempting to shut out imports, exports necessarily had to fall. The result was a worldwide collapse of international trade. Between 1929 and 1932 world trade declined 60 per cent.

INTERNATIONAL COOPERATION

The breakdown of international trade demonstrated to major nations the need for international cooperation. In 1934 the United States inaugurated a Reciprocal Trade Agreement program. Congress authorized the President to negotiate mutual tariff reductions up to fifty per cent between the United States and other countries. A key feature of the program was the "most favored nation" clause. It provided that a concession granted to any one country automatically applied to all nations with whom the United States had a most favored nation agreement. Thus, if the United States agreed to reduce tariffs on a certain grade of Italian wine, it would automatically reduce duties on comparable French wines. In 1936 the United States, Great Britain, and France entered a tripartite agreement in which they pledged to take all necessary measures for the restoration of order in international economic relations. Specifically, they sought to relax the prevailing system of quotas and exchange controls. In 1944 the International Monetary Fund (IMF) and the International Bank for Reconstruction and Development (the World Bank) were established with full U.S. support. The former's purposes are to promote stable foreign exchange rates, to eliminate foreign exchange controls, and to provide for the orderly adjustment of foreign exchange rates when necessary. Member nations are permitted to borrow from the IMF to finance temporary imbalances in trade. More fundamental disequilibria may be resolved by a combination of devaluation and monetary and fiscal policies. Devaluations of less than ten per cent may be undertaken by member nations without IMF approval, whereas devaluations over ten per cent must receive IMF approval. The World Bank is designed to encourage the international flow of capital funds, which had virtually ceased in the 1930's. It turned its attention first to European reconstruction, and then to promoting the growth of less developed economies. It provides funds by two means, guaranteeing private investments, and lending directly. In 1947 the United States became a signatory to the General Agreement on Tariffs and Trade, in which it agreed together with all major non-Communist trading nations to work toward the reduction of tariff barriers.

For the United States, World War II completed the process which World War I began. It emerged from the war as the world's greatest creditor. Through the war the United States had once again been the arsenal of democracy, its undestroyed factories supplying goods to war-torn allies. This time, unlike World War I, the United States possessed a sense of international leadership and responsibility. It was recognized that the allies could finance only a part of their war costs; thus, from 1940 to 1945 the United States provided outright gifts of forty-one billion dollars. Peace presented European nations with the massive problem of rebuilding industries and cities destroyed by the war. Agricultural and industrial goods had to be imported from the United States. This required dollars, which Europe neither possessed nor was capable of earning in large enough amounts. An acute dollar shortage resulted which was resolved for the most part by American economic statesmanship. Under the Marshall Plan, almost twelve

TABLE 22.9. *U.S. Balance of Payments: 1930 to 1970 Billions of Dollars (+ equals receipts; − equals payments)*

Year	Merchandise Exports	Merchandise Imports	Military Payments & Receipts	Investment Income, Remittances, & Other Services	U.S. Government Grants & Capital	U.S. Private Capital, Net	Foreign Capital, Net	Errors & Omissions	Balance Liquidity Basis[1]	Balance Official Reserve Transactions Basis[2]
1930	3.93	−3.10	−.05	−.09	.08	−.56	.07	.32	.60	N.A.
1935	2.40	−2.46	−.04	.05	.00	.54	.32	.36	1.17	N.A.
1940	4.12	−2.70	−.06	.14	−.05	.25	−.09	1.28	2.89	N.A.
1945	12.47	−5.25	−2.43	.68	−7.56	−.55	−.10	.00	−2.74	N.A.
1950	10.20	−9.08	−.58	.81	−3.64	−1.27	.18	−.12	−3.49	N.A.
1955	14.42	−11.53	−2.70	1.36	−2.21	−1.26	.30	.37	−1.24	N.A.
1960	19.65	−14.74	−2.75	1.39	−2.77	−3.88	.37	−1.16	−3.90	−3.40
1965	26.45	−21.50	−2.12	3.34	−3.41	−3.79	.27	−.58	−1.34	−1.29
1966	29.39	−25.46	−2.94	3.37	−3.44	−4.31	2.53	−.49	−1.36	.27
1967	30.68	−26.82	−3.14	3.26	−4.22	−5.66	3.36	−1.01	−3.54	−3.42
1968	33.60	−32.97	−3.10	3.83	−3.96	−5.16	8.57	−.64	.17	1.64
1969	36.49	−35.80	−3.38	3.60	−3.87	−5.01	3.88	−2.96	−7.06	2.71
1970	42.00	−39.40	−3.50	3.90	−3.10	−6.50	3.90	−2.00	−4.40[3]	−8.70[3]

SOURCE: U.S. Bureau of the Census. *Statistical Abstract of the United States: 1970.* Washington, D.C.: U.S. Government Printing Office, 1970, p. 764; *1971 Economic Report of the President.* Washington, D.C.: U.S. Government Printing Office, 1971, pp. 298–99.

N.A.: Not Available

[1] Measured by changes in U.S. monetary reserve assets and in U.S. liquid liabilities to all foreigners.

[2] Measured by changes in U.S. monetary reserve assets, in U.S. liquid liabilities to foreign official agencies, and in certain U.S. nonliquid liabilities to foreign official agencies.

[3] Includes allocation of Special Drawing Rights.

billion dollars was given to Europe for relief and reconstruction. The majority of aid went to England, France, Germany and Italy. In addition, from 1946 to 1961, the United States extended forty-eight billion dollars in foreign grants and loans to the nations of the world. Only twelve billion dollars of this amount had to be repaid. This American largesse enabled Western Europe to achieve a rapid economic recovery and to experience high rates of economic growth. These developments had a mixed impact on the U.S. balance of trade. European nations were able to import more U.S. goods and to compete more effectively with the United States for world markets. On net balance, the United States continued to experience a favorable balance of merchandise trade during the 1950's and 1960's. (See Table 22.8.)

As American grants to Europe began to ebb, they were largely replaced by private capital investments. By the mid-fifties, private American capital exports began to reach the magnitude of the 1920's. These foreign investments, coupled with foreign military spending and continued economic aid, led to persistent balance of payments deficits. (See Table 22.9.) As a consequence, the U.S. gold stock, which stood at twenty-one billion dollars in 1958, was almost halved by 1970. In the same period foreign dollar holdings more than doubled, from under 20 billion dollars to over 40 billion dollars. These developments caused the United States to institute a series of measures to curb capital outflows. These included an interest equalization tax on foreign borrowing in U.S. markets, restraints on U.S. investments abroad by business and financial institutions, and the tying of foreign economic aid to American purchases. It should be noted that while U.S. capital exports contribute to a gold and dollar outflow, dividends and interest payments on these investments ultimately cause a reverse flow. The final stage of economic development for any nation involves assumption of the role of a mature international creditor. In this stage, the dividend and interest payments from past capital exports exceed current outflows, and thus cause a net inflow of funds.

The substantial growth of world trade after World War II was not matched by the production of gold. For most of the period dollar and gold outflows from the United States were sufficient to finance the expansion. However, pressures on the dollar and the dwindling U.S. gold stock caused the international community to seek other means of financing trade growth and maintaining international liquidity. Beginning in the late 1950's, the world turned increasingly to the International Monetary Fund for a solution to this problem. In the early 1960's IMF quotas were increased, thereby enabling the Fund to lend larger amounts of foreign exchange to member countries. Later in the decade Special Drawing Rights (paper gold) were created further to augment member nation reserves.

Reduced trade barriers were a major stimulus to expanded international trade in the post-World War II period. In addition to GATT and periodic renewals of the Reciprocal Trade Program, the United States in 1962 enacted the Trade Expansion Act. This legislation was prompted by the successful growth of the European Economic Community (Common Market), founded in 1958. The Common Market, composed of France, West Germany, Italy, Belgium, the Netherlands, and Luxembourg, seeks the economic integration of member countries. One of its first measures was the erection of a common external tariff against the outside world. To meet this challenge, the Trade Expansion Act authorized the President to negotiate with the Common Market for the reduction or elimination of all tariffs on those groups of products when the U.S. and the EEC together accounted for eighty per cent or more of world trade in a representative period. Negotiations under this Act carried into 1967, when agreement was reached to substantially lower existing tariff walls between both trading areas. By 1970 average U.S. tariff rates were at historic lows, averaging less than 10 per cent for the first time since the early 1800's.

THE DOLLAR ERA COMES TO AN END

By the late 1960's a surfeit of dollars was held abroad. Twenty years of spending more dollars overseas than the United States earned had placed huge dollar holdings in the hands of foreigners. The increasing ability of Japan, Canada and Common Market countries to compete with the United States, together with accelerated United States inflation, reduced the annual U.S. trade surplus from five to seven billion dollars in the early 1960's and to between one and two billion by the end of the decade. Indeed, in 1971 the U.S. experienced its first trade deficit since 1893. Large military and aid spending associated principally with the Vietnam War increased spending abroad, while Government efforts to curb dollar and gold outflows failed. Consequently, the U.S. gold stock fell to a low of $11 billion in 1970, and official foreign dollar holdings rose to over $40 billion. The West German Central Bank alone owned more dollars than there was gold in Fort Knox.

By the late 1960's large foreign U.S. dollar holders had become increasingly restless. Speculative attacks on the dollar had become more common. Some international lenders, particularly the French, called for devaluation of the dollar by increasing the official price of gold. Others suggested a fundamental revision of the world monetary system by transforming the International Monetary Fund into a world bank. As the uncertainty grew the pressures on the dollar intensified. In August 1971 President Nixon, in response to this crisis and the inability of domestic monetary and fiscal policies to dampen inflation at home, rescinded the U.S. promise to convert official dollar holdings into gold. *De facto* the

U.S. dollar was devalued and its exchange rate was allowed to float in relation to other foreign currencies. At the same time the U.S. imposed a ten per cent surcharge on all foreign imports and called for her allies to assist the U.S. in fundamentally solving her balance of payment problems. The U.S. requested that foreign nations revalue their currencies in terms of the U.S. dollar and dismantle discriminatory trade barriers. Particular pressure was placed on Japan whose exports of textiles, automobiles and other goods were allegedly unfairly injuring American producers. After considerable negotiations Japan, together with Hong Kong, Nationalist China, and Korea agreed voluntarily to limit the exports of synthetic and woolen fibers to the U.S. In return the U.S. government lifted the 10 per cent surtax on these products. In December, 1971 following several months of negotiations, the U.S. agreed to raise the official price of gold from $35 to $38 an ounce, thereby devaluing the dollar by 8.57 per cent. At the same time the U.S., in recognition of the more favorable foreign exchange rates for American exports as a result of the devaluation indicated her intention to cancel the ten per cent import surcharge.

The pressures on the dollar and its subsequent devaluation intensified the protectionist pressure that had been building up in the United States since the mid-1960's. U.S. disillusionment with the Vietnam conflict and the strategic withdrawal from Southeast Asia soured many Americans on the nation's role as an international "keeper of peace." Simultaneously Americans became more aware of internal problems of poverty, racial conflict, crime and pollution. Organized labor assumed a protectionist stance. It based its position on the growing practice of American manufacturers to produce and assemble products overseas. Many of these items included components and parts made in the U.S. which were reimported in the final product, resulting in an alleged export of jobs. In addition unions argued that the availability of competitive goods from abroad reduced the effectiveness of domestic strikes. Unions were joined by many industrialists who had become disenchanted with the effects of trade liberalization on their particular industries.

J. J. Servan-Schreiber, in the reading at the end of this chapter, presents a European's view of the impact of American investment on continental Europe. Arthur Schlesinger, in a forword to the reading, discusses the significance of the Schreiber thesis.

SELECTED REFERENCES

1. Bela Balassa. *Trade Liberalization Among Industrial Countries.* New York: McGraw Hill, 1967.
2. C. L. Dearing and Wilfred Owen. *National Transportation Policy.* Washington: Brookings Institution, 1949.

3. Don D. Humphrey. *The United States and the Common Market.* New York: Praeger, 1962.
4. Charles Kindleberger. *Foreign Trade and the National Economy.* New Haven: Yale University Press, 1966.
5. John R. Meyer, *et al. The Economics of Competition in the Transportation Industries.* Cambridge: Harvard University Press, 1959.
6. John R. Meyer, *et al. The Urban Transportation Problem.* Cambridge: Harvard University Press, 1966.
7. J. J. Servan-Schreiber. *The American Challenge.* New York: Atheneum, 1968.
8. Charles A. Taft. *Commercial Motor Transportation.* Homewood: Richard D. Irwin, 1969.

readings

what is the significance of u.s. investment involvement in europe?

THE SIGNIFICANCE OF THE AMERICAN CHALLENGE
arthur schlesinger jr.

The *American Challenge* is a book about the crisis of Europe. It has already had an extraordinary impact. In France no book since the war, fiction or non-fiction, sold so many copies in its first three months. Throughout Europe politicians and civil servants, editors and professors, bankers, industrialists and engineers are studying and quoting it. It has had this impact because M. Servan-Schreiber has stated the dilemma of Europe with brilliant clarity, precision and urgency, and because he has had the further audacity to point the way to a solution. If Europeans respond to his appeal by acting on this book as well as by reading it, *The American Challenge* may do for European unity very much what Thomas Paine's *Common Sense* did for American independence.

Europe, M. Servan-Schreiber says, is in decline. No one, he warns, should be deceived by the existence of the European Economic Community. Either the EEC had to become more than a Common Market, or else it would revert to national patterns. Since is has not moved toward integration, it is beginning to move toward disintegration. Only the Americans, moreover, have understood and seized the opportunities created by the Common Market. The result has been the economic invasion of Europe by the United States. If present tendencies continue, the third industrial

Reprinted with permission from *The American Challenge* by J. J. Servan-Schreiber. New York: Atheneum, 1968, pp. vii-9.

power in the world, after America and Russia, could be, not Europe, but American industry in Europe. The present European generation has only a few years to decide between restoring an autonomous European civilization or allowing Europe to become a subsidiary of the United States.

In evoking the American specter, M. Servan-Schreiber may sound for a moment like General de Gaulle. But he differs sharply from the General both in diagnosis and in remedy. General de Gaulle sees the United States as bent on the establishment of world hegemony. He attributes the economic invasion, as he said in his press conference of November 27, 1967, "not so much to the organic superiority of the United States as to the dollar inflation that it is exporting to others under the cover of the gold exchange standard." He advocates defensive measures to seal off Europe from American economic penetration and political influence. M. Servan-Schreiber's analysis is both subtler and more profound. He sees the American challenge as the result of the dynamism of American society. And he advocates not the insulation of Europe from America but its salvation through discriminating Americanization.

Wherein does the secret of American dynamism lie? Not the least fascinating aspect of this book for American readers is the portrait they will find of their own country. The secret does not lie, as De Gaulle (and Lenin) would insist, in the pressure of surplus American capital for investment outlets abroad; M. Servan-Schreiber argues that nine tenths of American investment in Europe is financed out of European resources. Nor does it lie in American plans for political dominion; M. Servan-Schreiber rejects conspiratorial explanations. Nor does it lie in American scientific and technological superiority; he has no difficulty in showing how many basic discoveries were first made in European laboratories.

The disparity lies rather, M. Servan-Schreiber contends, in the "art of organization" — in the mobilization of intelligence and talent to conquer not only invention but development, production and marketing. He thus defines the "gap," to use the hopeless current jargon, as less technological than managerial. American industry spills out across the world primarily because of the energy released by the American system — by the opportunity for individual initiative, by the innovative knack of teams, by the flexibility of business structure and by the decentralization of business decision.

Yes, some Americans will no doubt comfortably reflect at this point, the Frenchman is right; free enterprise is best. But this is not at all what M. Servan-Schreiber means. He sees in the United States not the unfettered workings of competitive capitalism but something very different: a highly organized economic system, based on enormously large units, nourished by an industrial-academic-governmental complex and stimulated, financed and guided by the national government. And he does not stop there. To speak of a "managerial gap" is really too superficial; the real gap is institutional and cultural. In the end M. Servan-Schreiber traces American dynamism to the social mobility, the individual responsibility, the equalitarian thrust of American life and, above all, to the determination to invest in human beings, especially through the promotion of education. "All clichés to the contrary, American society wagers much more on human intelligence than it wastes on gadgets." The real American secret, he concludes, is the discovery that social justice, far from being the enemy of economic growth, is the necessary technical condition for growth in an industrial society. He charitably refrains from suggesting that the United States has not yet pursued this lesson to the end, particularly in the domain of race.

From this perspective, the European problem is not so much economic or scientific as it is cultural and political. Beginning with General de Gaulle's premise about the overshadowing might of the United States, M. Servan-Schreiber reaches the opposite conclusion. The hope for Europe, he believes, lies in genuine democratization and genuine unification on all levels; it lies in the reform of education, the rejection of inherited social and intellectual rigidities, the modernization of organization and the extension of planning. If Europe really wishes to escape American domination, there is only the way of federalism and social justice. All this, in M. Servan-Schreiber's view, implies Great Britain as a part of Europe; for British scientific and technological skill are necessary if Europe is to have any weight in the world of electronic computers, automated information systems, space technology and atomic energy. British entry into the Common Market, in short, is essential to realize De Gaulle's dream of European independence. And a strong and progressive Europe, he rightly contends (only barely mentioning Vietnam), is vital to save the United States from the temptations and illusions of superpowership: Europe holds in her hands more than her own destiny.

The American Challenge is a manifesto to the European generation of which J. J. Servan-Schreiber himself is a remarkable representative. Born in 1924, he escaped from France in 1943, received training as a pilot in the United States and joined the Free French Air Force. After the war he wrote on foreign policy for *Le Monde* and then established his own weekly magazine of opinion *L'Express*. The Algerian War was now the preoccupying issue; and Servan-Schreiber's lucid and caustic editorials helped mobilize sentiment against the French government. Perhaps in retaliation, the French government soon mobilized him and sent him to Algeria. After serving his tour of duty, he wrote a book, *Lieutenant in Algeria*, which led to his indictment on the ground of supposed injury to the morale of the French Army; in due course, he was acquitted. In the last years of the war he lived under constant threat of assassination from the enthusiasts of the OAS.

When France finally pulled out of Algeria, Servan-Schreiber converted *L'Express* into a highly successful newsweekly, rather as if the *New Republic* were to make itself over on the model of *Time*. In addition to these and other publishing ventures, he has been active in politics, working closely in the fifties with Pierre Mendès-France and in the sixties with Gaston Defferre. His wit and objectivity of expression, his commitment to reasoned argument, his political activism and his personal valor — all stamp him as a European of the Kennedy generation and style. It would not be surprising if he himself were to take a prominent role in shaping the European response to the American challenge.

THE AMERICAN CHALLENGE
j. j. servan-schreiber

Fifteen years from now the world's third greatest industrial power, just after the United States and Russia, may not be Europe, but *American industry in Europe*. Already, in the ninth year of the Common Market, this European market is basically American in organization.

The importance of U.S. penetration rests, first of all, on the sheer amount of capital invested — currently about $14 billion ($14,000,000,000). Add to this the massive size of the firms carrying out this conquest. Recent efforts by European firms to centralize and merge are inspired largely by the need to compete with the American giants like International Business Machines (IBM) and General Motors. This is the surface penetration. But there is another aspect of the problem which is considerably more subtle.

Every day an American banker working in Paris gets requests from French firms looking for Frenchmen "with experience in an American corporation." The manager of a German steel mill hires only staff personnel "having been trained with an American firm." The British Marketing Council sends 50 British executives to spend a year at the Harvard Business School — and the British government foots the bill. For European firms, so conservative and jealous of their independence, there is now one common denominator: American methods.

During the past ten years Americans in Europe have made more mistakes than their competitors — but they have tried to correct them. And an American firm can change its methods in almost no time, compared to a European firm. The Americans have been reorganizing their European operations. Everywhere they are setting up European-scale headquarters responsible for the firm's Continental business, with sweeping powers of decision and instructions not to pay any attention to national boundaries.

These U.S. subsidiaries have shown a flexibility and adaptability that have enabled them to adjust to local conditions and be prepared for political decisions taken, or even contemplated, by the Common Market.

Since 1958 American corporations have invested $10 billion in Western Europe — *more than a third* of their total investment abroad. Of the 6,000 new businesses started overseas by Americans during that period, *half* were in Europe.

One by one, American firms are setting up headquarters to coordinate their activities throughout Western Europe. This is true federalism — the only kind that exists in Europe on an industrial level. And it goes a good deal farther than anything Common Market experts ever imagined.

Union Carbide set up its European headquarters in Lausanne in 1965. The Corn Products Company, which now has ten European branches, moved its coordinating office from Zurich to Brussels and transformed it into a central headquarters. IBM now directs all its European activities from Paris. The Celanese Corporation of America has recently set up headquarters in Brussels; and American Express has established its European central offices in London.

Standard Oil of New Jersey has put its European oil (Esso Europe) headquarters in London, and its European chemical (Esso Chemical SA) command in Brussels. Both have been told to "ignore the present division between the Common Market and the free trade zone [Britain, Scandinavia]." For Esso, Europe now represents a market *larger than the United States*, and one growing *three times faster*.

Monsanto has moved its international department from St. Louis to Brussels, where Mr. Throdahl, one of its vice-presidents, directs not only European operations but all business outside the United States. Monsanto is now building factories in France, Italy, Luxembourg, Britain, and Spain, and preparing plants for Scotland and Ireland. Half of its foreign sales now come from Europe.

The greater wealth of American corporations allows them to conduct business in Europe faster and more flexibly than their European competitors. This *flexibility* of the Americans, even more than their wealth, is their major weapon. While Common Market officials are still looking for a law which will permit the creation of European-wide business, American firms, with their own headquarters, already form the framework of a real "Europeanization."

A leading Belgian banker recently stated: "The Common Market won't be able to work out a European corporate law in time, and during the next few years U.S. corporations will enjoy a decisive advantage over their European rivals." The American giants in Europe become bigger and stronger all the time, and are hiring "development" experts whose job is to seek new acquisitions.

While all this has been going on, Europeans have done little to take advantage of the new market. On the industrial level Europe has almost nothing to compare with the dynamic American corporations being set up on her soil. The one interesting exception is Imperial Chemical Industries (Britain), the only European firm to establish a Continental-scale headquarters to administer its 50 subsidiaries.

Efforts of other European corporations are timid by comparison. Among these the best known is the film company Agfa (part of the Bayer group), which two years ago decided to merge with its Belgian rival, Gevaert. But it was not a very romantic marriage. The two companies exchanged directors, put a hyphen between their names (Agfa-Gevaert), and combined their research departments. That's about all. Aside from that, they have announced their intention to form a truly unified firm the day the Common Market gives the go-ahead by passing a still non-existent statute permitting European-wide Corporations. They are still waiting for legislation.

In the meantime, American firms continue to carve up Europe at their pleasure. In the words of a report by McGraw-Hill: "The founders of the Common Market, men like Robert Schuman, Jean Monnet, and Walter Hallstein, can be proud of helping break down the barriers dividing Europe. But it is American business that has understood their idea and is helping Europe understand its own potential by applying, with some variations, the same methods America used to build its own enormous market."

Europeans especially envy the ease with which American firms reorganize themselves to tap the full potential of the new market, and they are very much aware of the advantages this flexibility offers. The question they ask most often, says an American executive working in France, is simply: "How do you do it?"

Hand in hand with this industrial penetration another giant U.S. enterprise is taking shape in Europe — the creation of management consultant groups.

The three American consultant firms with European branches (Booz, Allen and Hamilton, Arthur D. Little, Inc., and McKinsey and Co.) have *doubled* their staffs *every year* for the past five years. The Americans are creating a "market consciousness" in their wake.

According to an American executive in Frankfurt: "If a German manager wants to increase his production, he studies all the factors that go into the manufacture of his product. But if I want to increase my production, I add to these same calculations our research and market predictions so that I will know not only how to produce, but how to produce the desired quantity at the lowest cost. What interests me is my profit margin. What interests my European competitor is a factory that produces. *It isn't the same thing."* This science of marketing is new in Europe. Now there is hardly a major European executive today who does not put it at the top of his list of his concerns.

Thus, much beyond massive U.S. investments, it is American-style management that is, in its own special way, unifying Europe. As the American businessman from Frankfurt, quoted earlier, added: "The Treaty of Rome is the sweetest deal ever to come out of Europe. It's what brought us here. We're happy to be here. We're making money. And we're going to make a lot more. Whether the European negotiations in Brussels move ahead or not, prospects in commerce and industry are better for us here than they are in the United States."

It really is the sweetest deal anyone ever thought of. But why for the Americans and not for us? Why do they succeed better over here than we do ourselves? By trying to find an answer, we come across a whole new world.

index

R

U

V

W